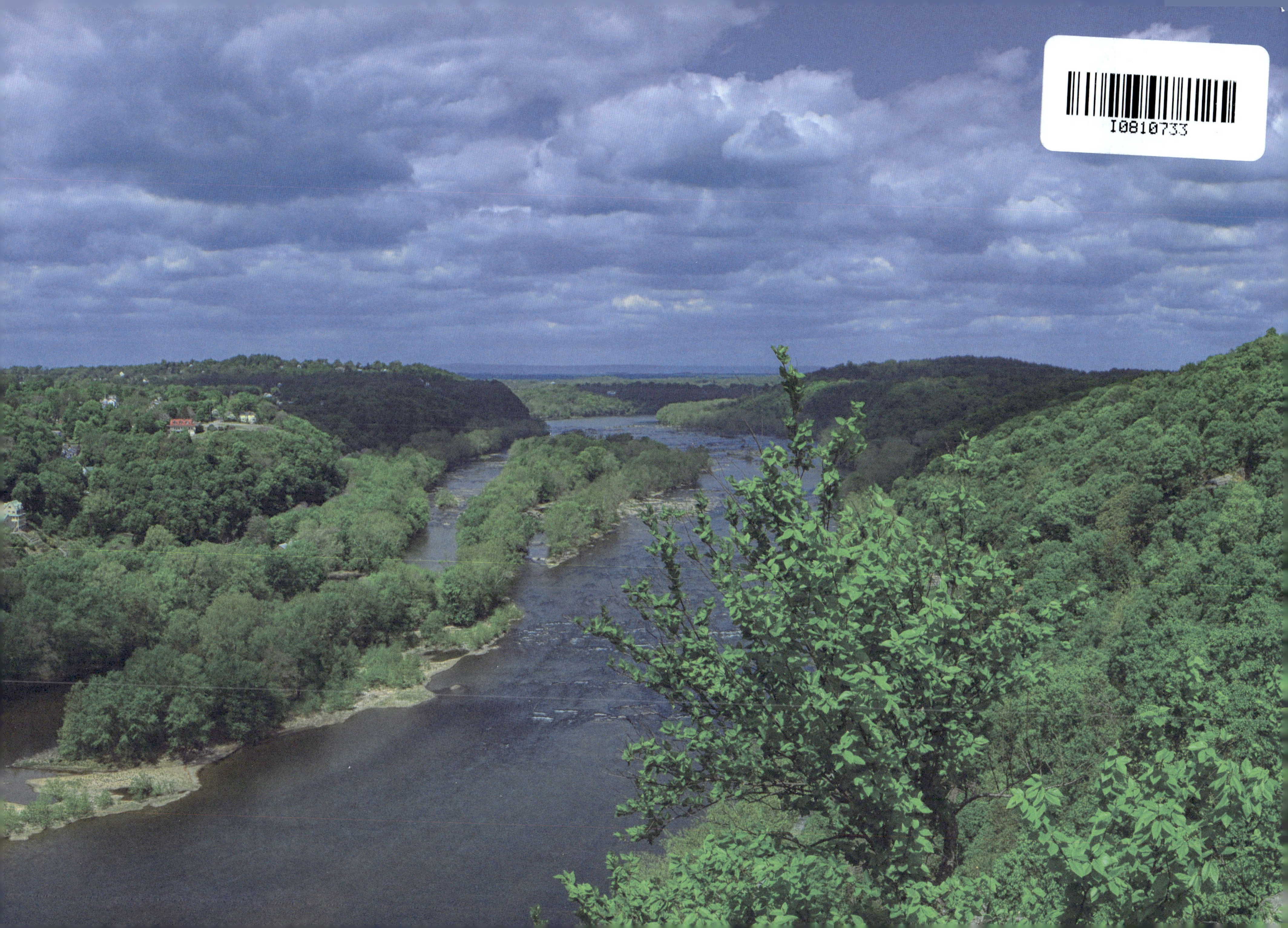

To my parents, who fueled my wanderlust with adventures from an early age—my father, for sharing skiing adventures that inspired the snow scenes, and being the glue that brought this project to life; my mother, for her boundless love and awaiting this book's surprise; my sister, whose early trail days and long training runs I treasure; to my grandparents for being the foundation and inspiring force of my family; my uncle, whose Teton journeys shaped my love for the wild; my late friend, who named me Flash. To my hiking companions, not all still by my side: your echoes linger on the Appalachian Trail. The Schiffer Publishing team, with their dedication and vision, helped me bring the Appalachian Trail to vivid life so all may enjoy it.

CONTENTS

INTRODUCTION

The Appalachian Trail, a 2,197-mile footpath spanning from Springer Mountain, Georgia, to Mount Katahdin, Maine, stands as one of the world's longest continuous hiking trails and a symbol of adventure, conservation, and human perseverance. Frequently referred to as the "AT" by hikers, it attracts millions annually, encompassing both casual day-trippers and resolute thru-hikers who undertake its entirety in a year. This iconic trail traverses the eastern wilderness of North America, providing a profound connection to nature and a testament to collective endeavor. Its historical significance, breathtaking vistas, diverse state crossings, and unique cultural resonance elevate it to the status of a cherished landmark, inviting exploration and contemplation of the natural world's splendor.

The Appalachian Trail emerged from the visionary mind of Benton MacKaye, a forester who in 1921 proposed a wilderness corridor to combat urban sprawl and promote physical and mental well-being. While working on the state of Vermont's Long Trail, MacKaye envisioned a trail connecting community camps for recreation and economic advantages. He published his concept in the *Journal of the American Institute of Architects*. By 1925, the Appalachian Trail Conservancy (ATC), originally the Appalachian Trail Conference, was established to coordinate volunteers and regional clubs. Myron Avery, the ATC's inaugural chairman, played a pivotal role in mapping and constructing the trail, with assistance from the Civilian Conservation Corps during the Great Depression. The inaugural blazed section was the trail connecting Bear and Harriman State Parks. On August 14, 1937, the AT was officially completed, although rerouting has since been undertaken for land preservation. In 1968, the National Trails System Act designated it America's first national scenic trail, ensuring federal protection. Cultural milestones, such as Earl Shaffer's first documented thru-hike in 1948 and Emma "Grandma" Gatewood's pioneering hike at the age of sixty-seven in 1955, cemented its legacy. Currently, the ATC and volunteers continue to maintain the trail against challenges such as climate change and invasive species, preserving its historical significance.

The Appalachian Trail presents a diverse tapestry of America's landscapes, offering hikers vistas that transition from misty southern peaks to rugged New England summits. In Georgia, the trail commences at the summit of Springer Mountain, where rolling hills and oak-hickory forests welcome hikers. It traverses 78 miles through Georgia's dense forests. North Carolina boasts 96 miles of its own trail, encompassing the Smokies, characterized by high-elevation spruce-fir forests and a rich cultural heritage. Additionally, North Carolina's trail shares a significant portion of its mileage with Tennessee (217 miles, and Tennessee has 74 miles of its own). It features the scenic Bald Mountains with grassy summits. The Great Smoky Mountains National Park, spanning both North Carolina and Tennessee, stands tall with Clingmans Dome, the highest point on the Appalachian Trail at 6,643 feet, offering breathtaking 360-degree views of spruce-fir forests and misty ridges. Subsequently, the Appalachian Trail journeys through Virginia for 557 miles. Virginia's Shenandoah National Park presents more-gentle ridges and vibrant wildflower meadows. The state of West Virginia has 2.4 miles of its own and shares about 20 miles with Virginia. It houses the Appalachian Trail's headquarters in Harpers Ferry, West Virginia. Harpers Ferry is also home to National Park Service's Harpers Ferry Historical Park. Maryland's 41 miles offer gentle terrain and scenic views of the Potomac River. Pennsylvania's

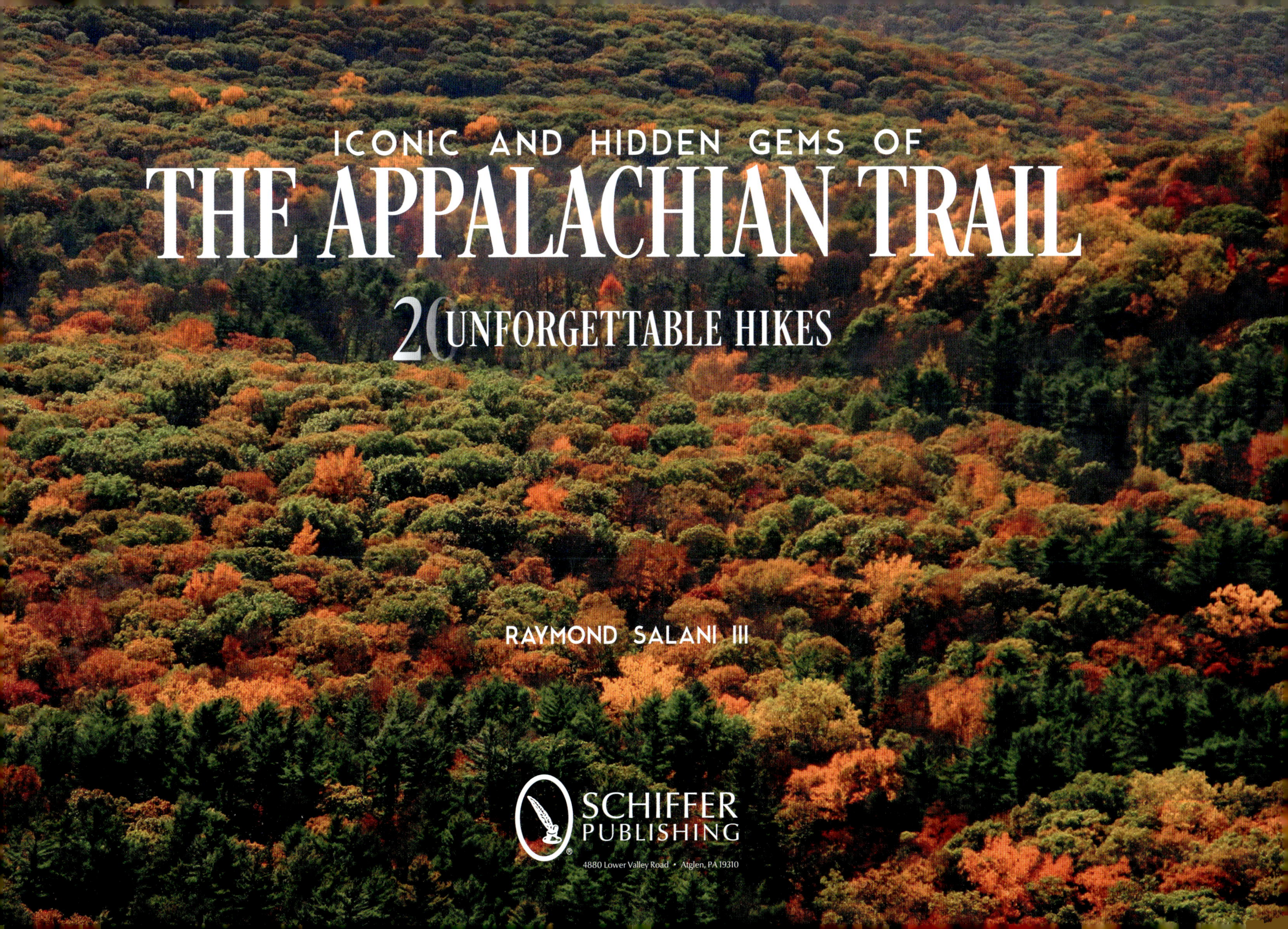

ICONIC AND HIDDEN GEMS OF

THE APPALACHIAN TRAIL

20 UNFORGETTABLE HIKES

RAYMOND SALANI III

SCHIFFER PUBLISHING

4880 Lower Valley Road • Atglen, PA 19310

DISCLAIMER

The information provided in this guidebook is for general informational purposes only. While every effort has been made to ensure the accuracy and reliability of the content, the author and publisher do not guarantee the completeness or applicability of the information contained herein. The use of this guidebook is at the reader's own risk.

The author and publisher are not responsible for any errors or omissions, or for any actions taken on the basis of the information provided. Readers should consult relevant professionals or experts as needed for specific advice or guidance related to their individual circumstances.

The content of this book reflects the author's views and opinions as of the publication date and may not necessarily align with current best practices, regulations, or legal requirements. No part of this book is intended to provide professional, legal, or medical advice.

Library of Congress Control Number: 2025939991

Front end-sheet image shows: View from Maryland Heights Overlook
Back end-sheet image shows: Range vew overlook in Shenandoah at sunset

Edited by Max Bolno
Designed by Alexa Harris
Type set in Desire Pro / Modern Sans / Metropolis

ISBN: 978-0-7643-7106-6
ePub: 978-1-5073-0665-9
Printed in China
10 9 8 7 6 5 4 3 2 1

Published by Schiffer Publishing, Ltd.
4880 Lower Valley Road
Atglen, PA 19310
Phone: (610) 593-1777; Fax: (610) 593-2002
Email: info@schifferbooks.com
Web: www.schifferbooks.com

MIX Paper | Supporting responsible forestry FSC® C104723

230 miles, aptly dubbed "Rocksylvania" due to its rocky terrain, provide vistas such as the Lehigh Gap East and the Delaware Water Gap from Mount Minsi. New Jersey's 72-mile stretch offers a captivating surprise with wetlands, vistas, and glacial lakes. New York boasts an impressive 91-mile segment featuring Bear Mountain and distant glimpses of Manhattan's skyline. Connecticut and Massachusetts, with 52 and 90 miles, respectively, provide charming New England towns and expansive views of Mount Greylock's Berkshires. As the trail travels farther north, Vermont's Green Mountains stretch for 150 miles. It has several views from fire towers, including Glastenbury, Stratton, and Bromley. New Hampshire's section of the trail traverses 161 miles, offering hikers a challenging experience through the White Mountains. Mount Washington's unpredictable weather can pose an obstacle, but the rewards are immense. Maine's Mount Katahdin, the trail's northern terminus, finishes out the 282-mile state after offering very remote hiking. It crowns the journey with awe-inspiring views of pristine wilderness from summit of Baxter State Park's highest peak.

The Appalachian Trail transcends its role as a physical path; it is a cherished historical, scenic, and cultural treasure that beckons exploration across fourteen states. Its enduring legacy lies in its capacity to inspire, unite, and safeguard America's untamed wilderness. Hikers have the opportunity to connect with nature and fellow travelers, whether embarking on a brief day trip, embarking on a months-long adventure, or embarking on a lifelong journey.

Iconic and Hidden Gems of the Appalachian Trail: 20 Unforgettable Hikes is a collection of twenty day hikes or areas to not miss along the Appalachian Trail, with over 250 photographs. Each chapter contains an essay that celebrates the biodiversity, adventure, ecology, and uniqueness of each section of the Appalachian Trail and several fascinating photographs.

The beautiful and scenic Appalachian Mountains of Virginia, West Virginia, Maryland, Pennsylvania, New Jersey, New York, Connecticut, Massachusetts, Vermont, and New Hampshire are depicted in this book.

Award-winning and internationally known photographer Raymond Salani III spent several years collecting photographs of the Appalachian Trail. He also repeated sections in different seasons to capture this collection of over 250 beautiful and captivating photographs chosen for display. Beyond their aesthetics, these photographs facilitate a better understanding of the environmental importance of the area for future generations to come.

Various highlighted trips and photographs in *Iconic and Hidden Gems of the Appalachian Trail: 20 Unforgettable Hikes* include the following:

- Mount Washington, New Hampshire
- Stratton Mountain, Vermont
- Delaware Water Gap National Recreation Area
- Harpers Ferry National Historical Park, West Virginia
- Shenandoah National Park, Virginia

Both well-known and little-known areas are featured. *Iconic and Hidden Gems of the Appalachian Trail: 20 Unforgettable Hikes* is a wild and wonderful journey for all nature and nature photography lovers.

CHAPTER 1
CRABTREE FALLS

AREA MAP

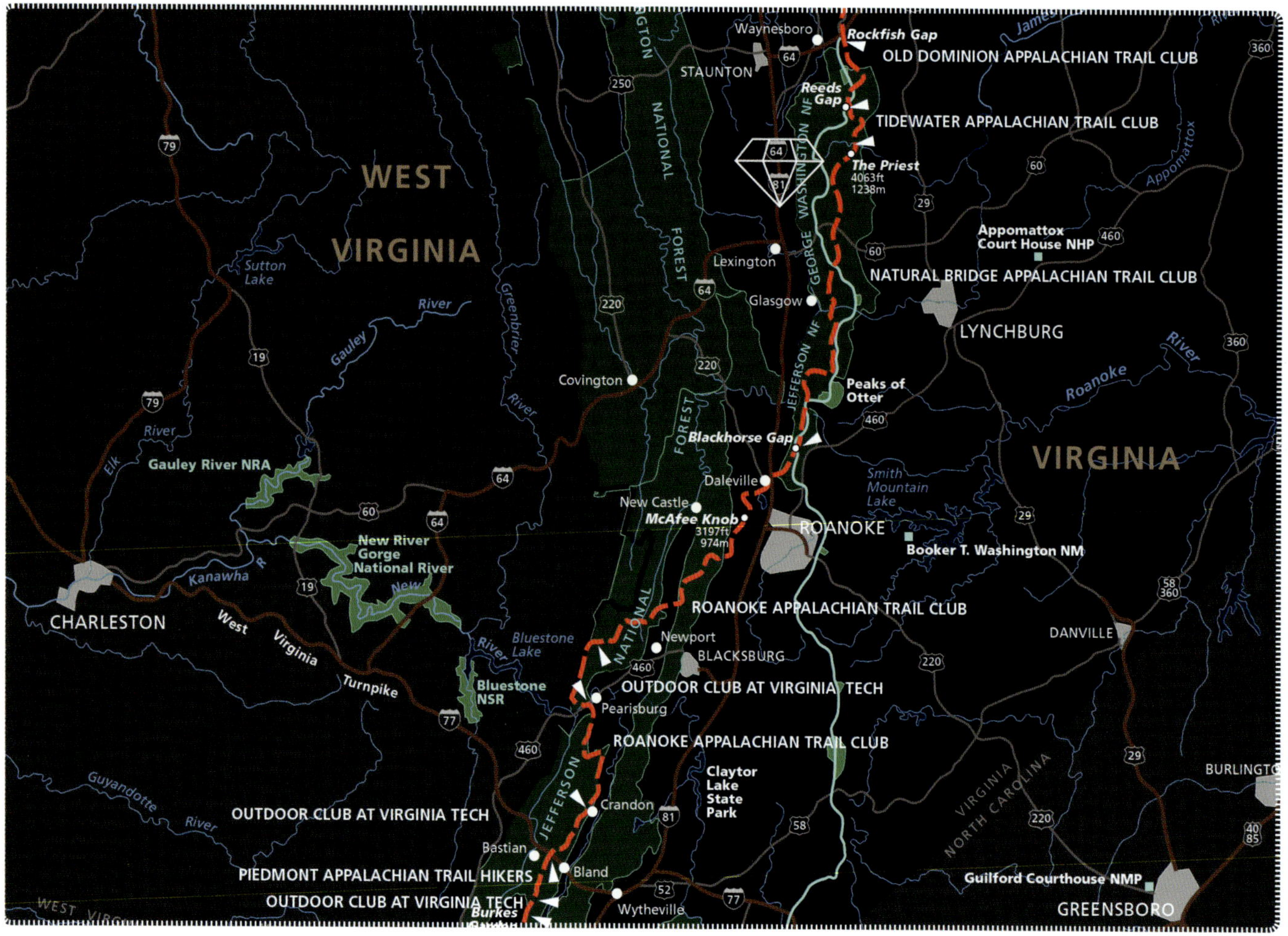

DISTANCE	8.7 miles
ELEVATION GAIN	3,300 feet
ELEVATION LOSS	3,300 feet
LEVEL	Moderate

TYPE: POINT TO POINT

0 10 Kilometers 50

0 10 Miles 50

Appalachian National Scenic Trail

Boundary of **CLUB** management section

North

GEM HIKE

PERSONAL TOUCH

Plan a hike on a day that is going to rain over 9 inches in the hours that you are going hiking. What can possibly go right? I answered everything. When I encountered Crabtree Falls for the first time, that is exactly what happened, and I got amazing photographs as a result. One of my hiking friends and I went hiking in early November. We both found it a perfect temperature, so we didn't cook in our rain gear on the ascent of the Priest. We didn't have a view from the top because we were socked in. As we approached the falls, we were wading in water well over our knees. But when we got to Crabtree Falls, we had the paradise to ourselves, and it was in fact kicking. The sights were amazing, and the sounds of water hitting the rocks with full power were awesome.

BRIEF OVERVIEW

Hiking the Priest and Crabtree Falls in Virginia presents an extraordinary venture to explore the beauty and diversity of the region's natural landscape. With its cascading waterfalls, rich flora and fauna, and breathtaking views, this trail is a must-visit for anyone looking to experience the best of Virginia's wilderness.

DESCRIPTION OF THE GEM HIKE

This gem hike is a blend of the Appalachian Trail and Crabtree Falls Trail. This gem hike starts at Virginia State Route 56 adjacent to the Tye River, climbs the Priest, continues the Appalachian Trail until it reaches the Crabtree Falls Trail, and descends to the Washington-Jefferson National Forest access point at the base of Crabtree Falls.

FLORA, FAUNA, AND VEGETATION

The area surrounding Crabtree Falls and the Priest is rich in biodiversity. Different oak and maple species are the most-popular trees. Mountain laurels are also common. In addition, the forest floor is alive with various plants. In spring, different species of trillium, ferns, and mosses are often seen.

THE PRIEST

The Priest is the highest mountain in Nelson County, Virginia, part of the Blue Ridge Mountains, located about 3.5 miles east of Maintop Mountain in the Priest Wilderness of the George Washington National Forest. It drains into the Tye River. The Appalachian Trail traverses the summit. The summit is accessible from a trailhead along Virginia State Route 56 but requires a 3,000-foot vertical ascent. Crabtree Falls descends the northwest slope of the Priest, with access both to the falls and the trail leading to the summit via the Crabtree Falls Trail and Forest Development Road 826.

CRABTREE FALLS

Crabtree Falls, located in the George Washington National Forest in Nelson County, Virginia, is one of the tallest waterfalls east of the Mississippi River, with a height 1,000 feet according to topographic maps. Crabtree Falls features five major cascades, the highest dropping about 400 feet, making it the tallest vertical drop of any waterfall east of the Mississippi. Crabtree Falls was named after William Crabtree, a settler from 1777. In the late 1960s, L. A. Snead, a former US assistant fuel administrator, led efforts to protect the land from resort development and was successful making it part of the National Forest System in 1968. A maintained trail, known as the Crabtree Falls Trail, provides access to the falls but has been the site of twenty-nine reported deaths of individuals venturing too close to the waterfalls. So please exercise caution.

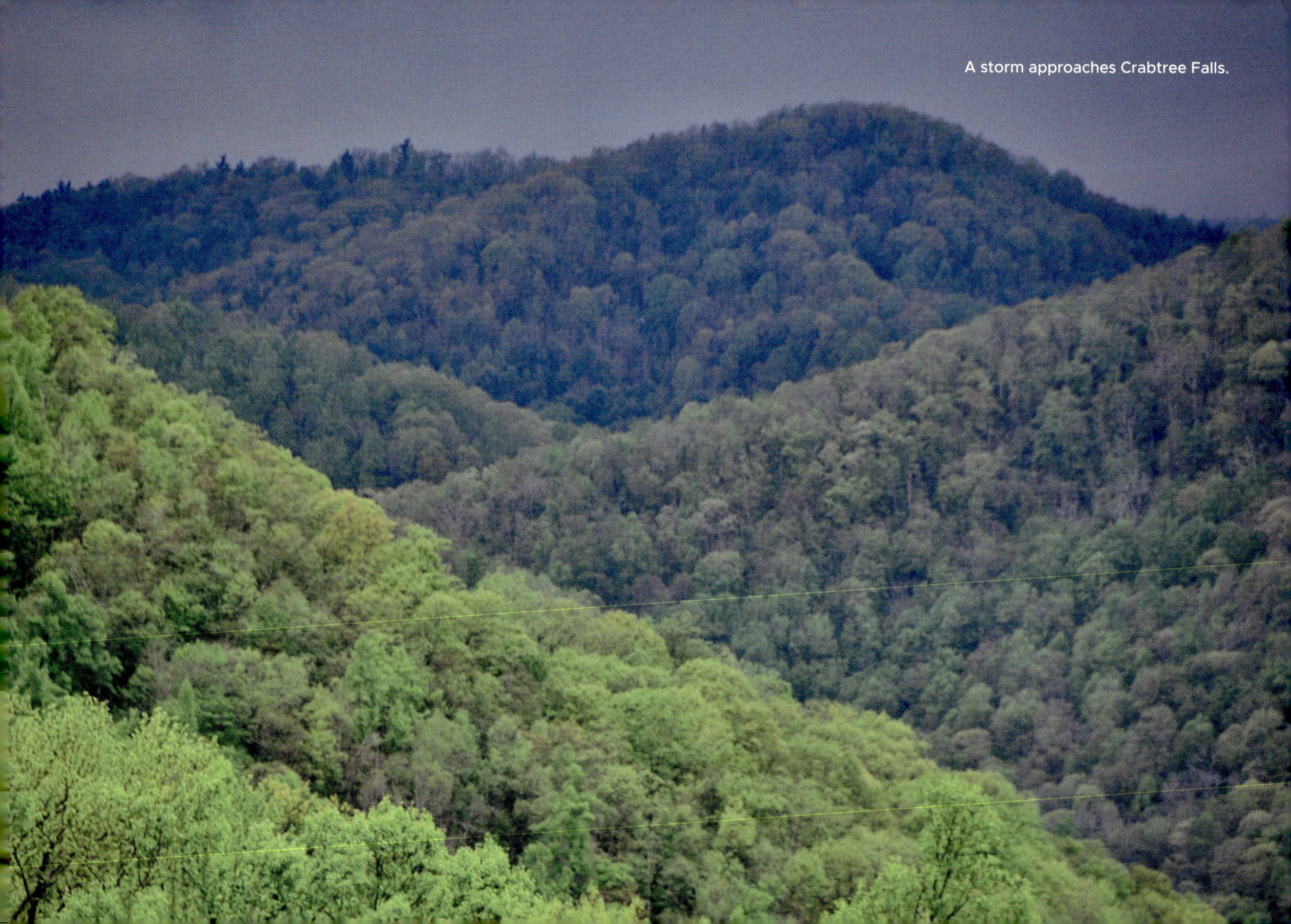

A storm approaches Crabtree Falls.

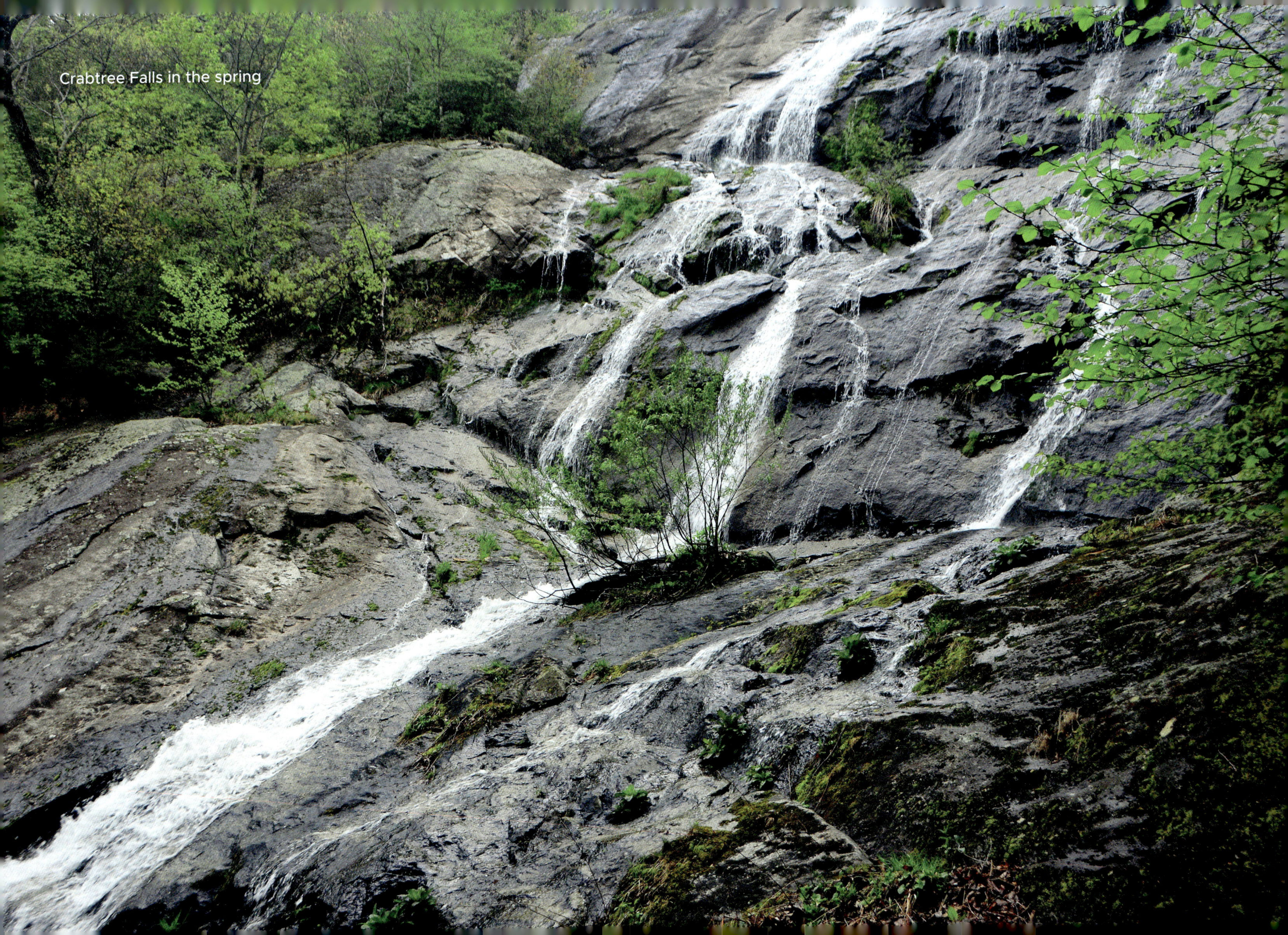

Crabtree Falls in the spring

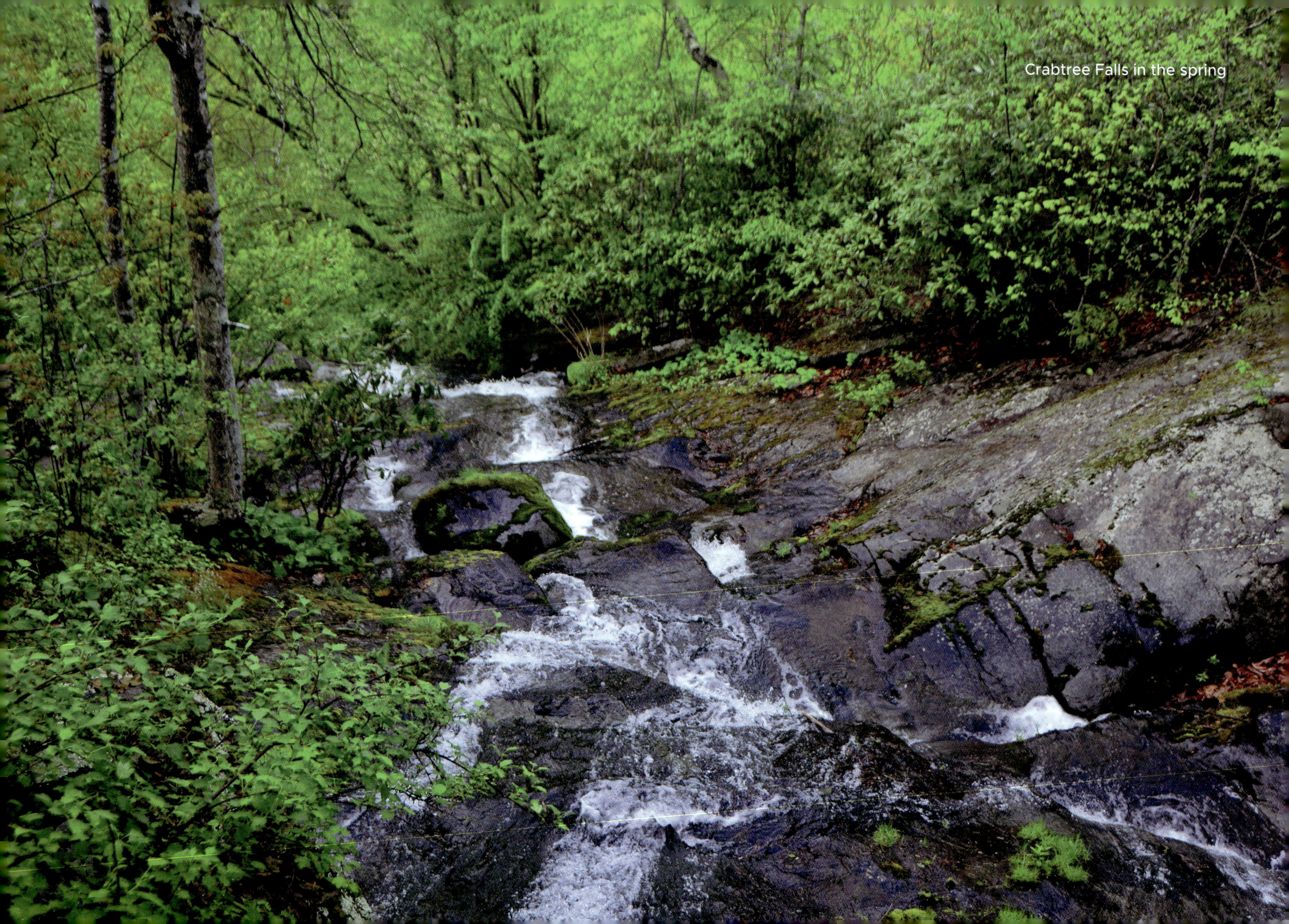

Crabtree Falls in the spring

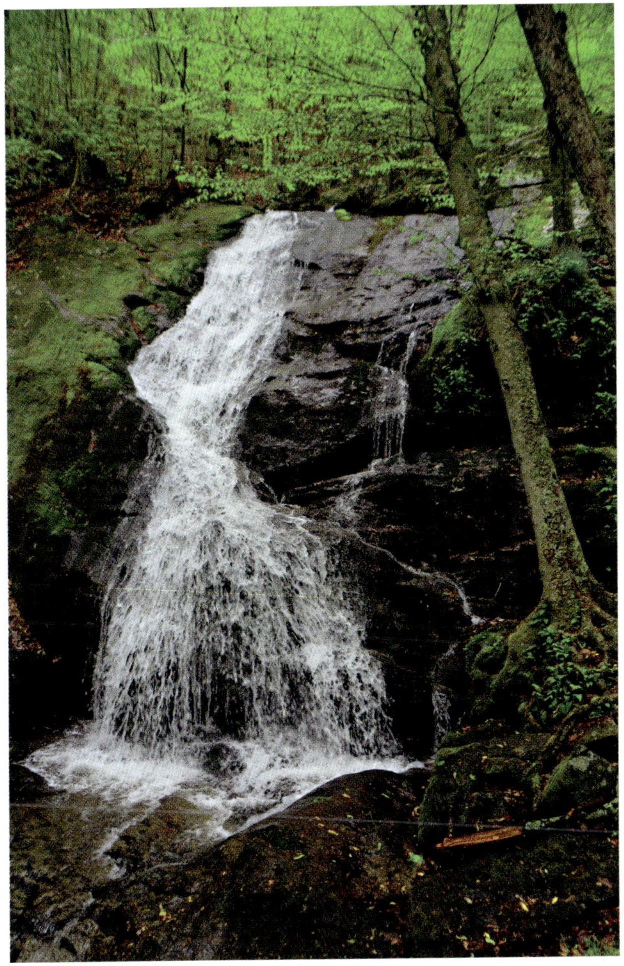

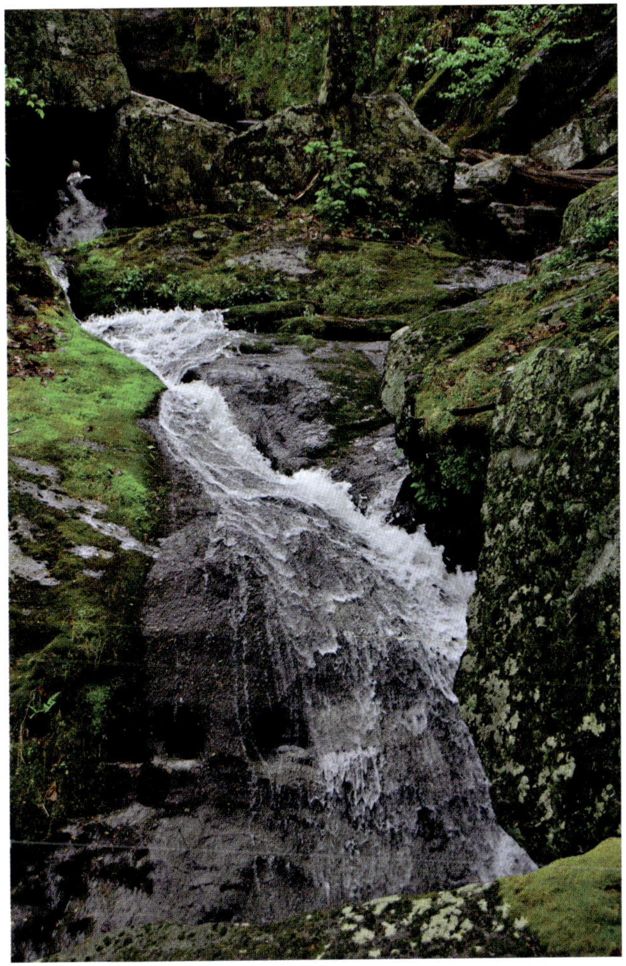

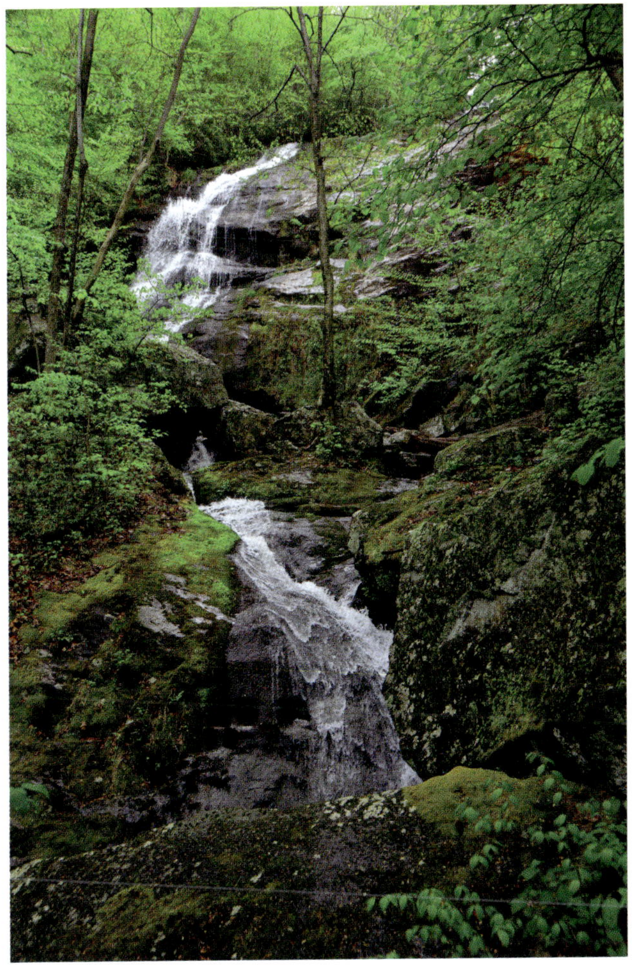

Crabtree Falls in spring

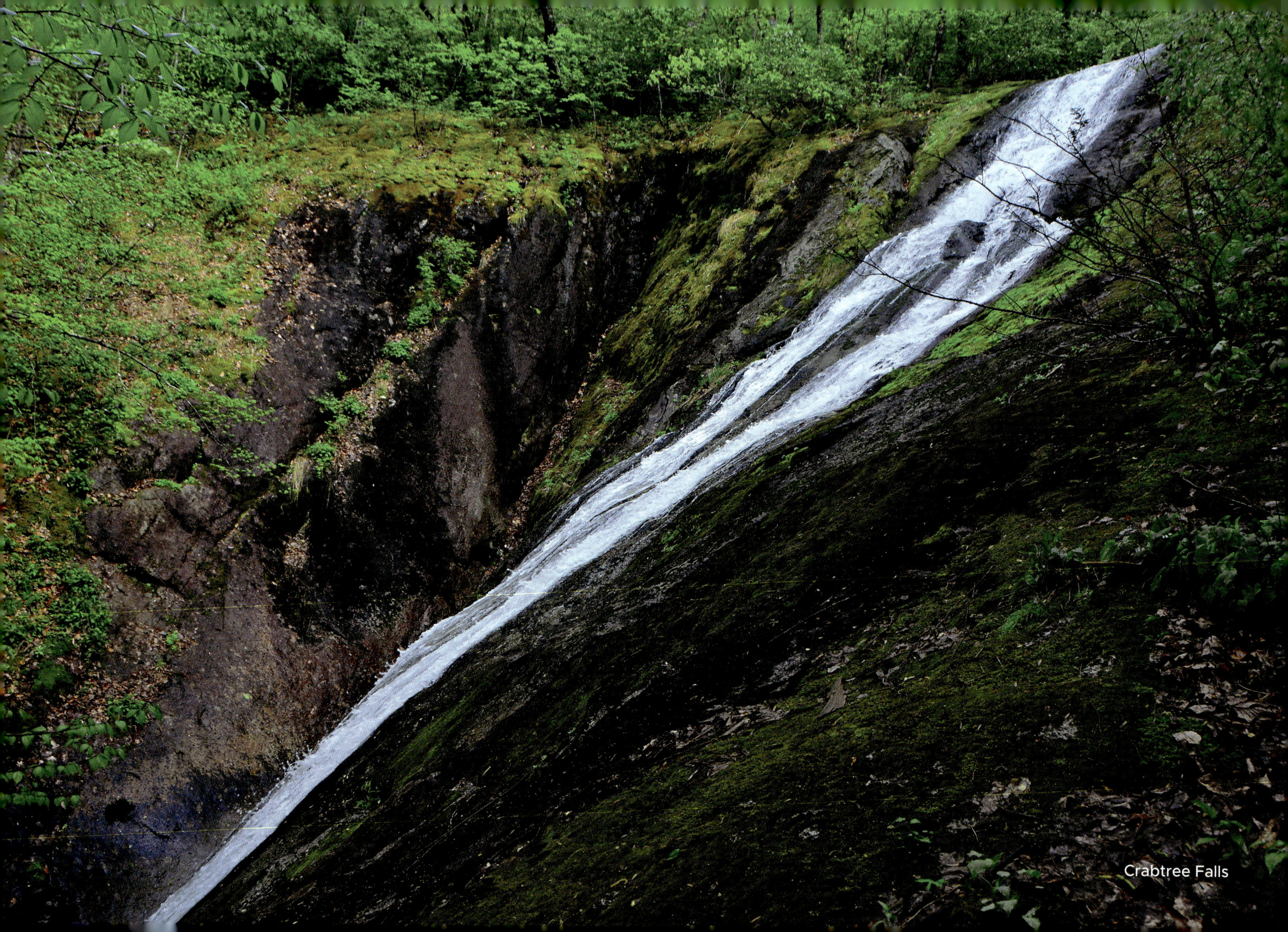
Crabtree Falls

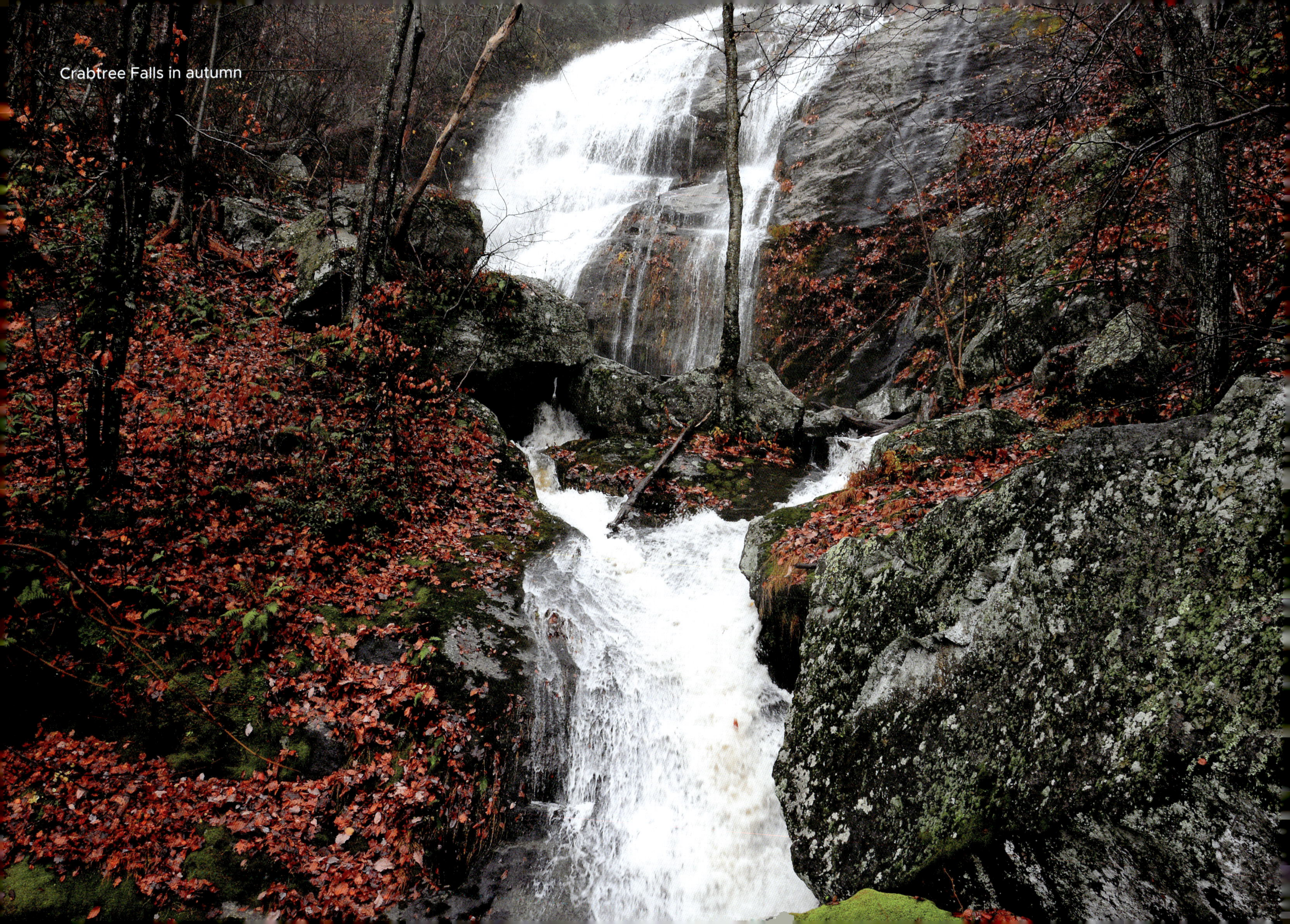

Crabtree Falls in autumn

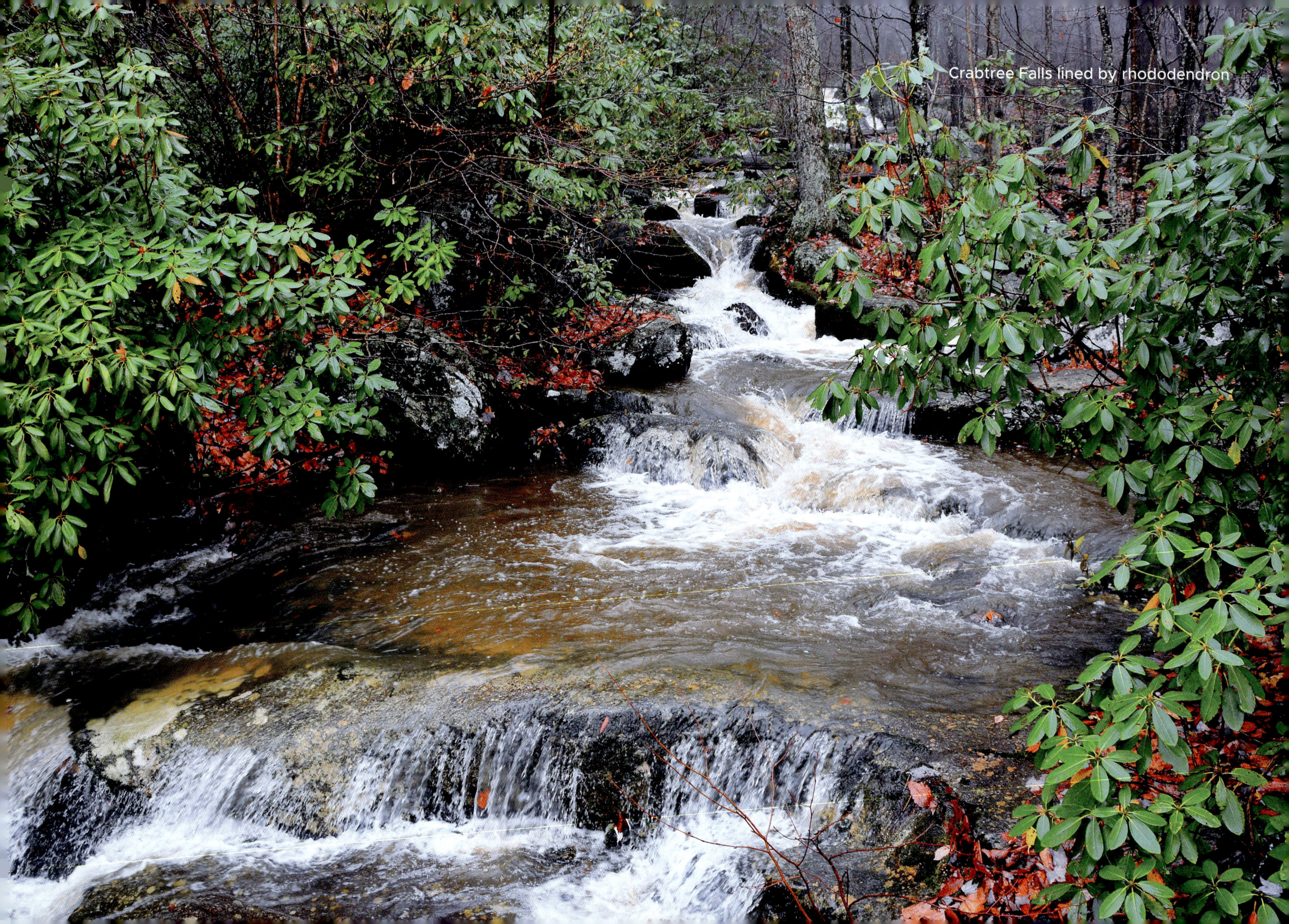

Crabtree Falls lined by rhododendron

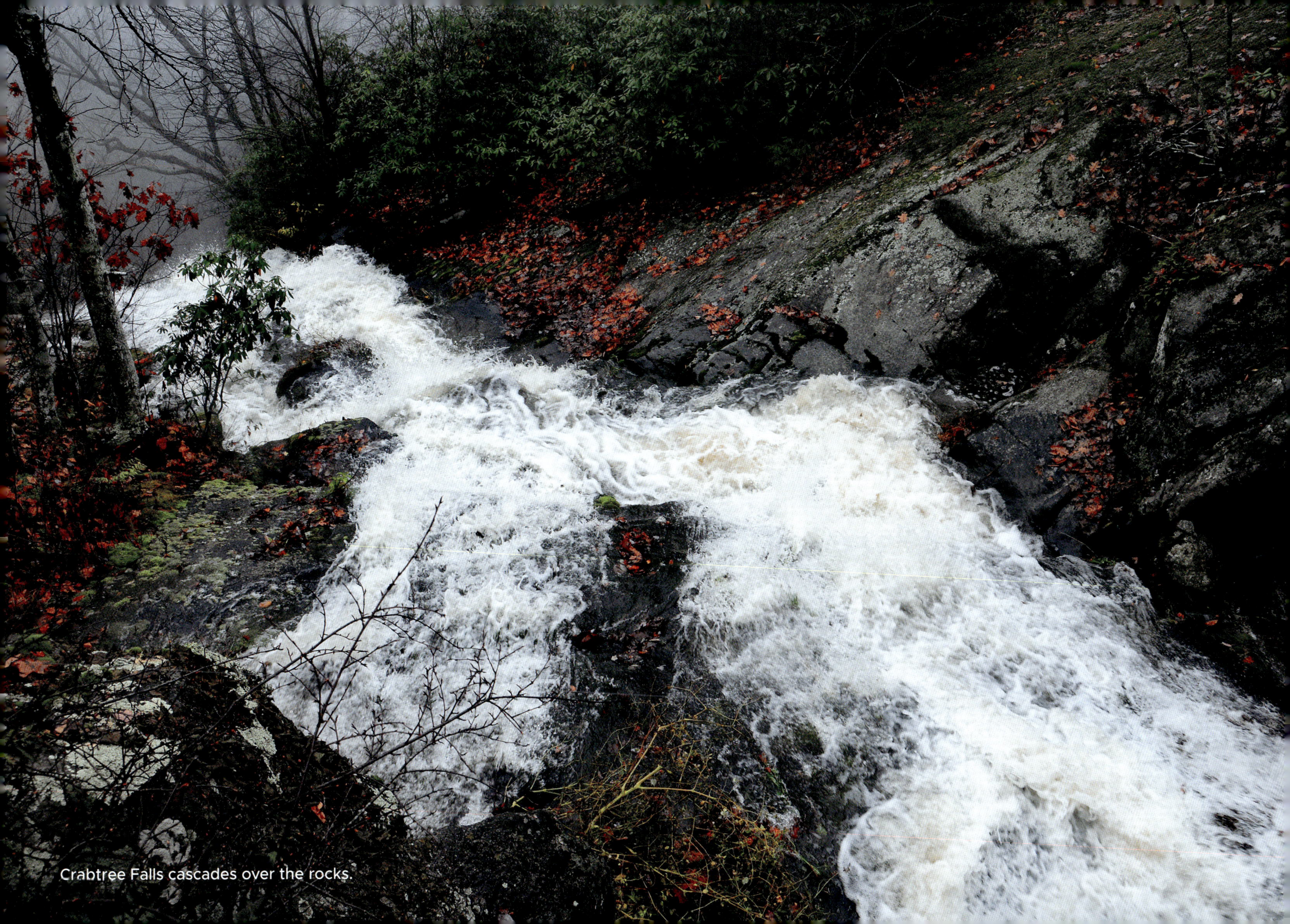

Crabtree Falls cascades over the rocks.

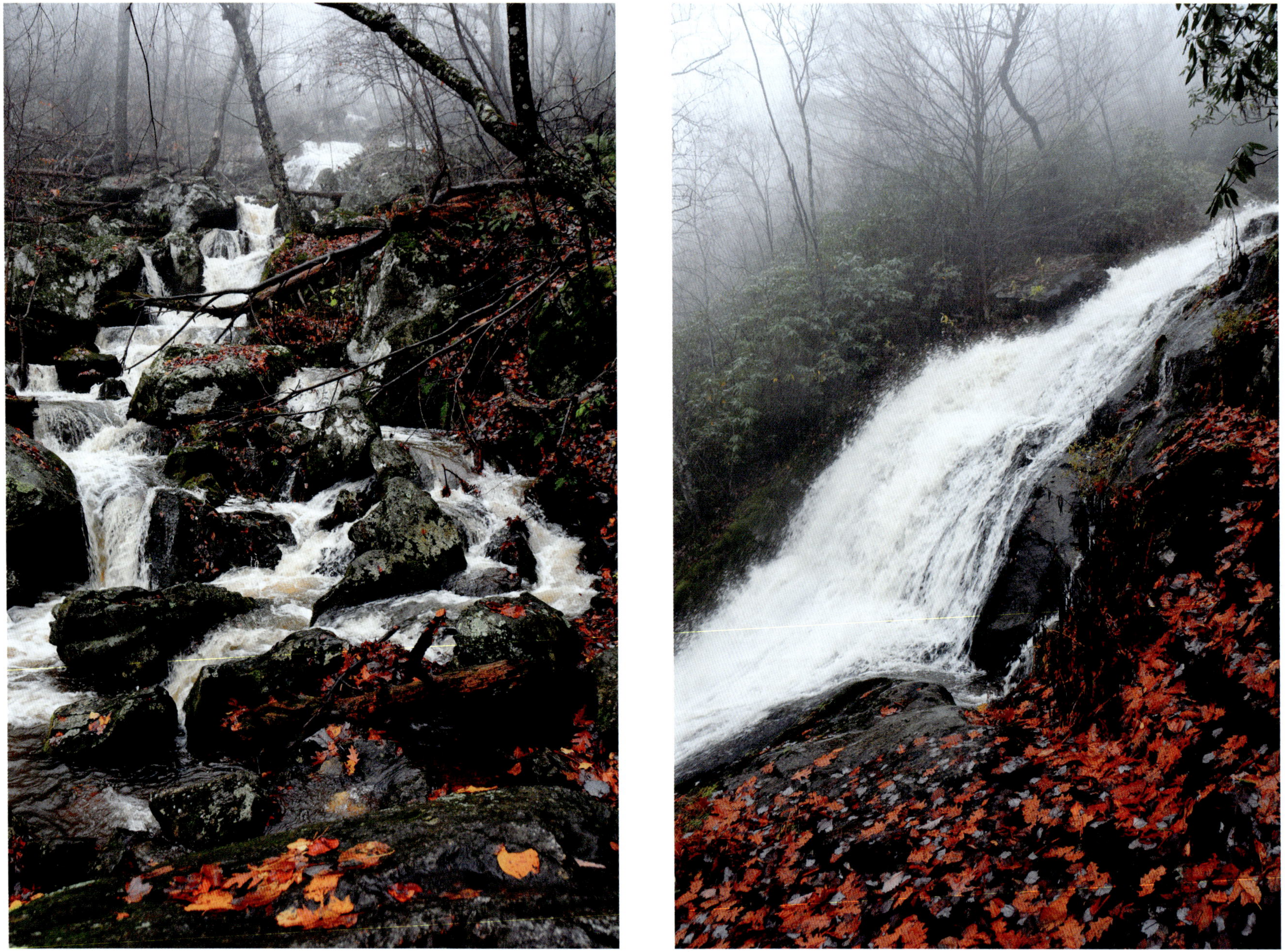

Crabtree Falls in the fall

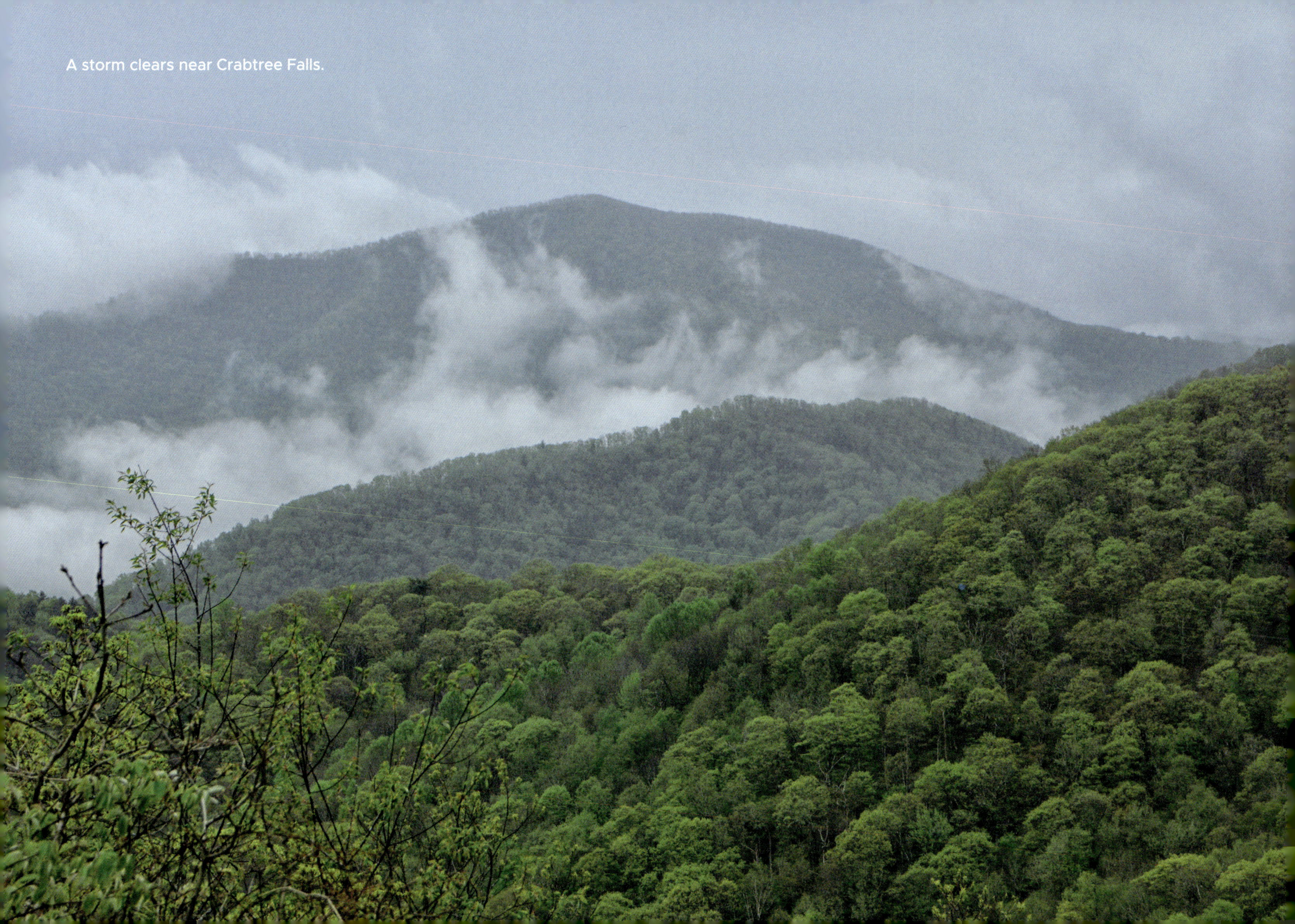

A storm clears near Crabtree Falls.

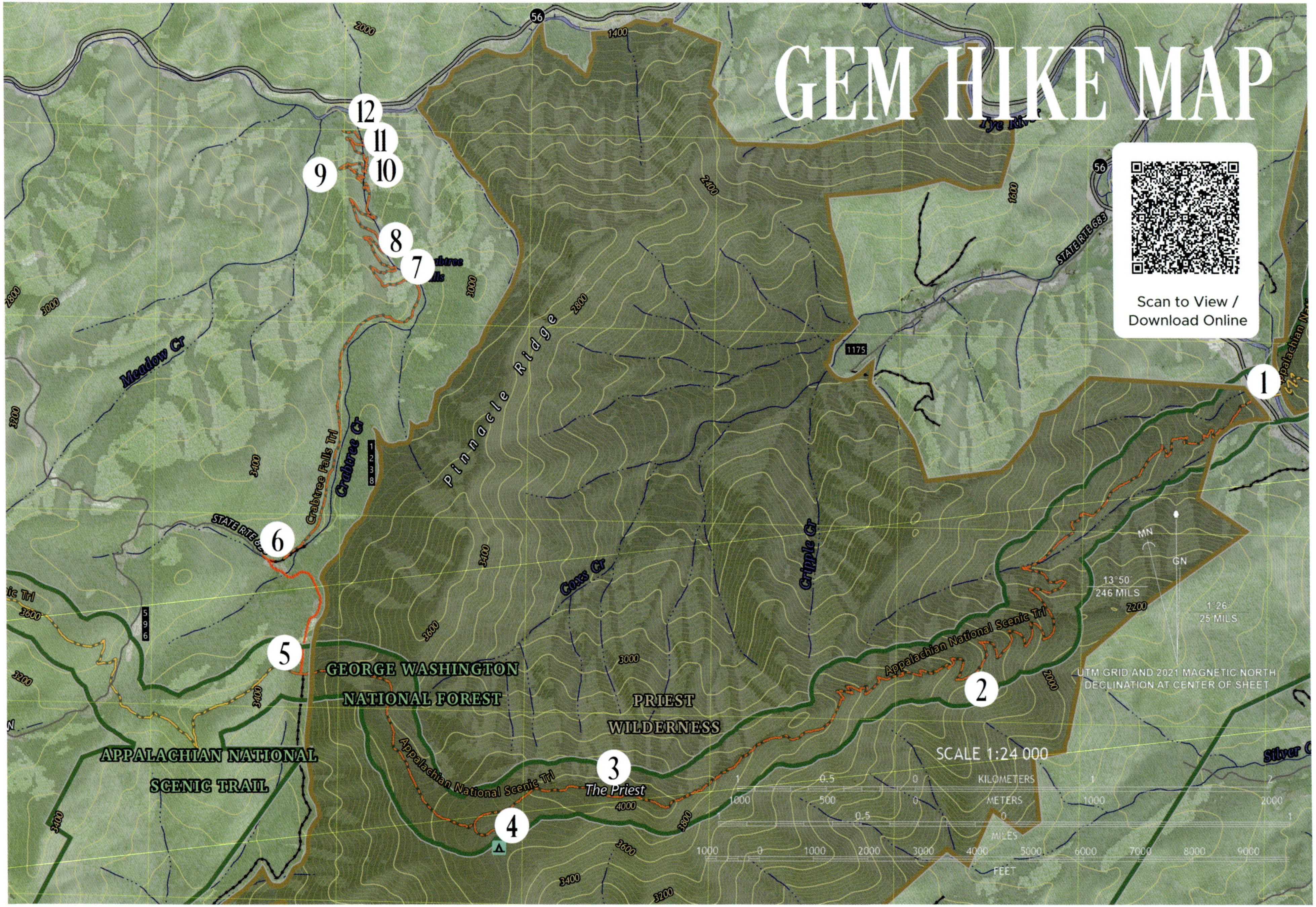
GEM HIKE MAP
Scan to View / Download Online
Pinnacle Ridge
Meadow Cr
Crabtree Falls Trl
Crabtree Cr
Coxs Cr
Cripple Cr
GEORGE WASHINGTON NATIONAL FOREST
PRIEST WILDERNESS
APPALACHIAN NATIONAL SCENIC TRAIL
Appalachian National Scenic Trl
The Priest
SCALE 1:24 000
KILOMETERS
METERS
MILES
FEET
UTM GRID AND 2021 MAGNETIC NORTH DECLINATION AT CENTER OF SHEET
13°50
246 MILS
1.26
25 MILS
MN
GN
1
2
3
4
5
6
7
8
9
10
11
12

DIRECTIONS TO THE TRAILHEAD

East Lexington, Virginia, to George Washington–Thomas Jefferson National Forest's Crabtree Falls
Parking lot (37.850804, −79.0796891) to the Priest Wilderness Parking Area (37.838484, −79.023122)

1. In East Lexington, Virginia, head west on Old Buena Vista Rd. toward US 11 N for 177 feet
2. Turn right onto US 11 N and continue for 15.7 miles
3. Turn right onto VA 56 E and continue for 1.7 miles
4. Turn left to stay on VA 56 E and continue for 10.2 miles
5. Turn right and continue for 0.2 miles, and Crabtree Falls Parking Lot will be on your right (drop a car here)
6. Head northwest toward VA 56 E for 0.2 miles
7. Turn right onto VA 56 E and continue for 4.7 miles
8. Turn right into the Priest Wilderness Parking Area

GEM HIKE DIRECTIONS

1. Leave the Priest Wilderness Parking Area on the Appalachian Trail south and continue for 2.5 miles
2. Reach an overlook, then continue the Appalachian Trail south for 1.4 miles to reach the summit of the Priest
3. Continue 0.5 miles to reach the Priest Shelter
4. Continue 1 mile to reach Crabtree Farm Rd. (VA 826), Crabtree Falls Trail
5. Turn right on Crabtree Farm Rd. (VA 826), Crabtree Falls Trail
6. Continue 1.4 miles to a wood bridge that crosses the top of Crabtree Falls
7. Continue 0.3 miles to reach the base of the upper falls
8. Continue 1 mile to reach to reach the platform at the top of the lower falls
9. Continue 0.2 miles to reach the largest drop of Crabtree Falls
10. Continue 0.5 miles to the base of the Crabtree Falls
11. Continue 0.2 miles to George Washington–Thomas Jefferson National Forest Crabtree Falls Parking Area
12. Reach the George Washington-Thomas Jefferson National Forest Crabtree Falls Parking Area and your dropped car

MORE/LESS AMBITIOUS HIKERS

More-ambitious hikers may wish to add more miles of the Appalachian Trail to the gem hike. Less ambitious hikers may wish to summit the Priest from the Priest and Wilderness Parking Area as an out-and-back or to park at the George Washington–Thomas Jefferson National Forest to ascend Crabtree Falls as an out-and-back as separate day hikes.

CHAPTER 2

SHENANDOAH NATIONAL PARK SECTION OF THE APPALACHIAN TRAIL: MILAM GAP TO SKYLAND RESORT

AREA MAP

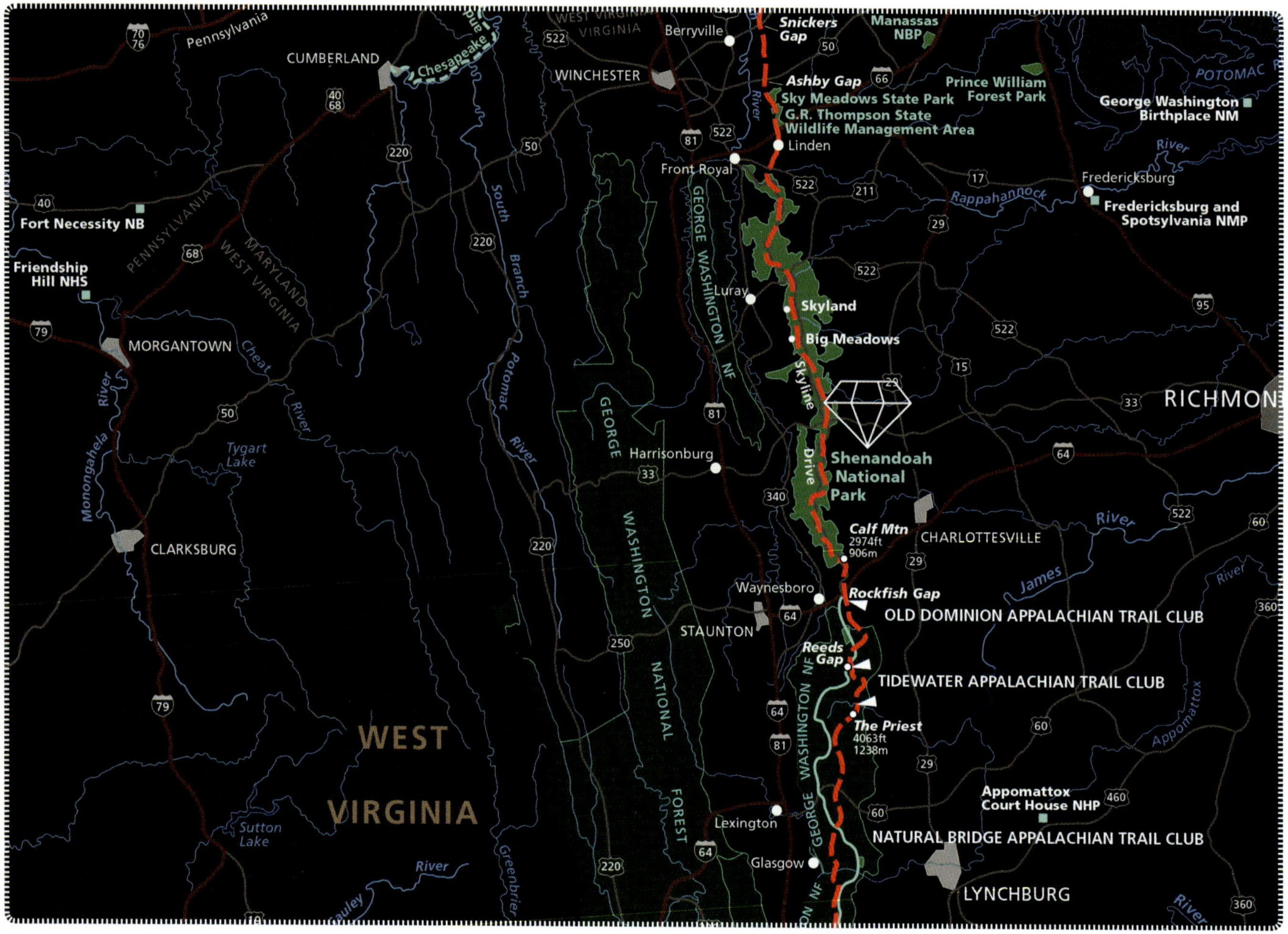

DISTANCE	12 miles
ELEVATION GAIN	1,910 feet
ELEVATION LOSS	1,470 feet
LEVEL	Moderate

TYPE: POINT TO POINT

0 10 Kilometers 50
0 10 Miles 50

Appalachian National Scenic Trail

Boundary of CLUB management section

North

GEM HIKE

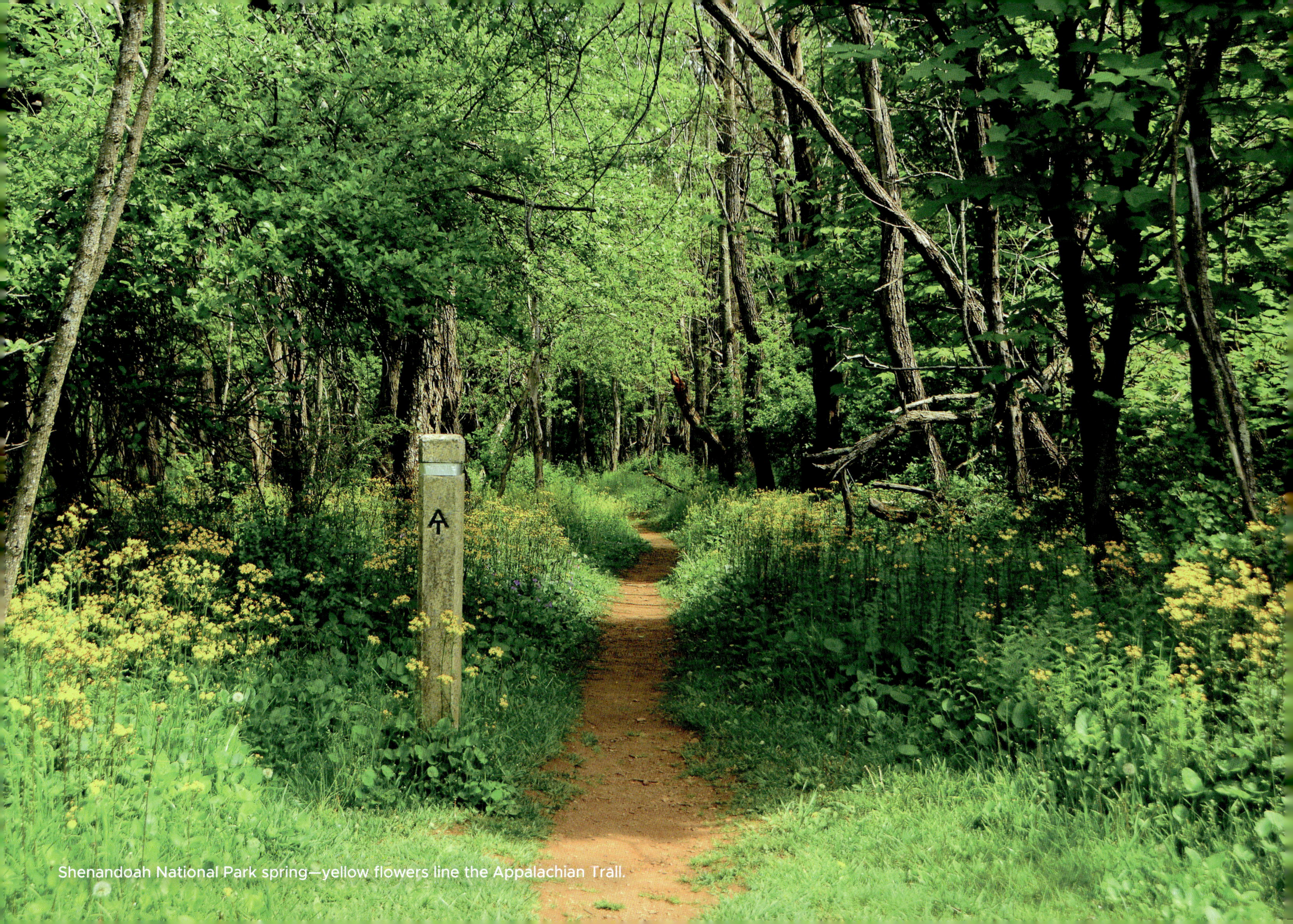

Shenandoah National Park spring—yellow flowers line the Appalachian Trail.

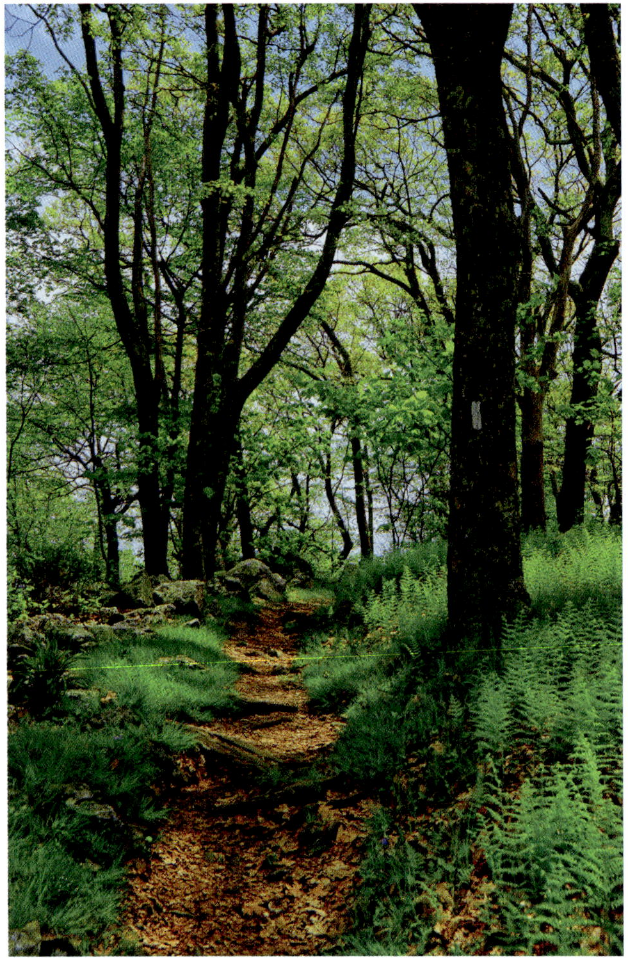

Ferns line the Appalachian Trail.

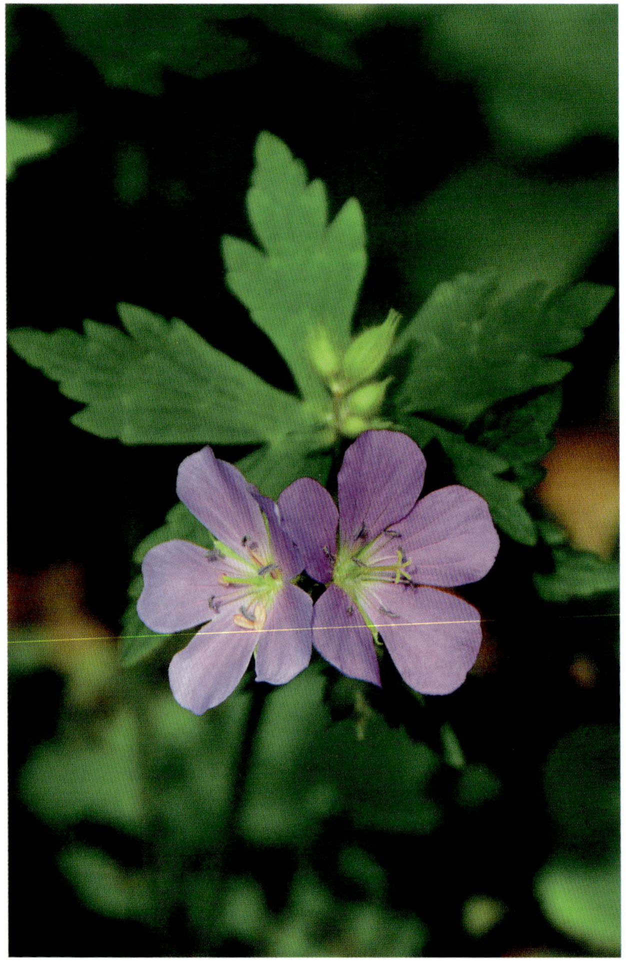

Herb Robert (*Geranium robertianum*)

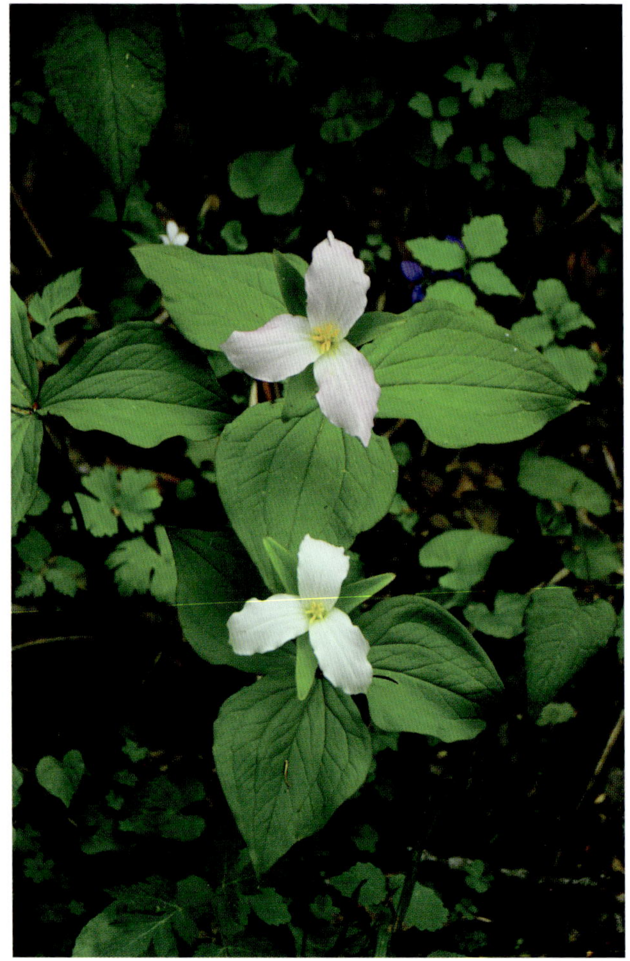

Trillium (*Trillium grandiflorum*)

PERSONAL TOUCH

Lush spring green, late May wildflowers, and the amazing view from Hawksbill Mountain all were fantastic. The spring green was so vibrant that I felt I needed to wear sunglasses. The wildflowers were everywhere. The views from Hawksbill Mountain, in my opinion, were the best of Virginia. From the summit, I towered over the esteemed Old Rag Mountain, and I was able to see for miles and miles. This special Virginia hike has all the treats we seek when we hike. When at the summit of Hawksbill Mountain, I was often confused as to where the sky hit the land, because some clouds started below, and some were slightly above me. I now can say I know where heaven meets the earth: It is on Hawksbill Mountain in Shenandoah National Park, Virginia.

BRIEF OVERVIEW

This section of the Appalachian Trail from Milam Gap to Skyland Resort / Stoney Man Parking Area includes an add-on, Hawksbill Mountain, and is a remarkable part of Shenandoah National Park, encompassing roughly 10.5 miles of varied terrain as a point-to-point hike (12 miles if one adds Hawksbill Mountain via an out-and-back on the Salamander Trail). This section stands out for its meadows, lush green forests, wildflowers, and panoramic vista.

DESCRIPTION OF THE GEM HIKE

Hawksbill Mountain is one of the gems of the Appalachian Trail and is accessible via a blue-blazed side trail from the Appalachian Trail. The Salamander Trail, while not part of the AT itself, leads directly to the summit of Hawksbill Mountain and offers hikers an opportunity to explore the highest point in Shenandoah National Park. The blue blaze trail is well maintained and provides a rewarding add-on to the Appalachian Trail. This add-on is one of the most spectacular viewpoints in the park and Virginia. This hike can offer different wildflowers throughout the spring, summer, and even fall, but it is recommended in late May / early June.

FLORA, FAUNA, AND VEGETATION

The flora in this section varies with elevation and season, but during the growing seasons you will not be disappointed. Wildflowers such as mountain laurel, rhododendron, azaleas, and various orchids can be found, adding vibrant colors to the landscape, particularly in spring and summer.

The region is home to a diverse array of wildlife. Mammals such as black bears and white-tailed deer can be observed, while smaller mammals such as squirrels and raccoons are frequently seen. Birdwatchers are also attracted to Shenandoah National Park. Amphibians and reptiles, including eastern newts, various toad species, and butterflies, can also be seen.

HAWKSBILL MOUNTAIN

Hawksbill Mountain is the highest peak in Shenandoah National Park. It stands at 4,050 feet. Hawksbill Mountain's summit provides hikers with some of the most breathtaking views of Virginia.

SKYLINE DRIVE

Skyline Drive runs the length of Shenandoah National Park, providing a scenic route that offers access to numerous trailheads, including those leading to Hawksbill Mountain. The Appalachian Trail enthusiast would enjoy the drive because it follows the original route, before the National Park Service moved the trail to its current location. The drive is popular for its panoramic views and easy access to the park's natural attractions. It also serves as the gateway for hikers looking to explore the AT and other trails within the park.

SKYLAND RESORT

Skyland Resort, located in the central district of Shenandoah National Park, offers accommodations for visitors exploring the park and the Appalachian Trail. The resort provides a comfortable base for those looking to enjoy the park's beauty while having convenient access to amenities. Its proximity to Skyline Drive makes it an ideal location for hikers and nature enthusiasts alike.

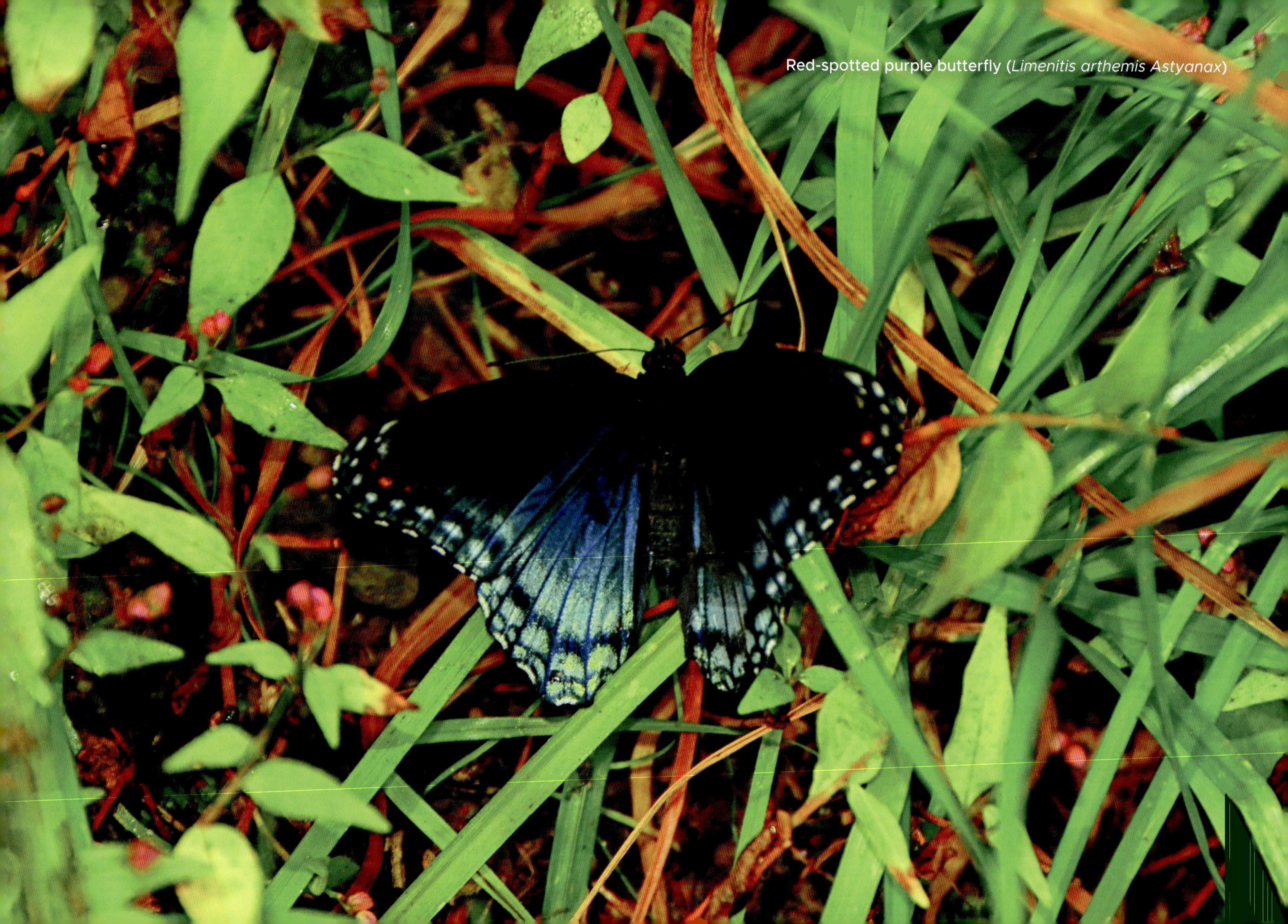

Red-spotted purple butterfly (*Limenitis arthemis Astyanax*)

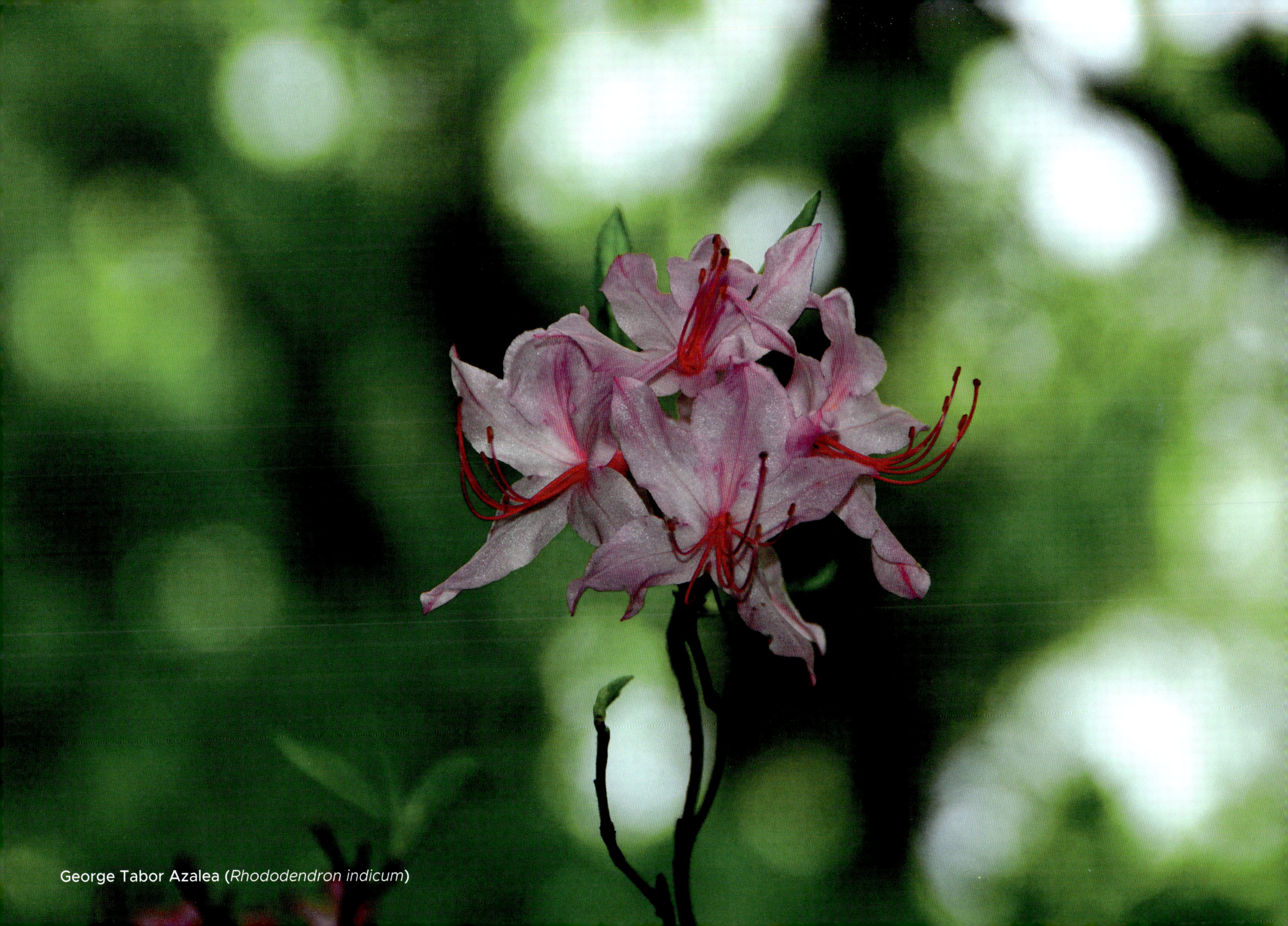

George Tabor Azalea (*Rhododendron indicum*)

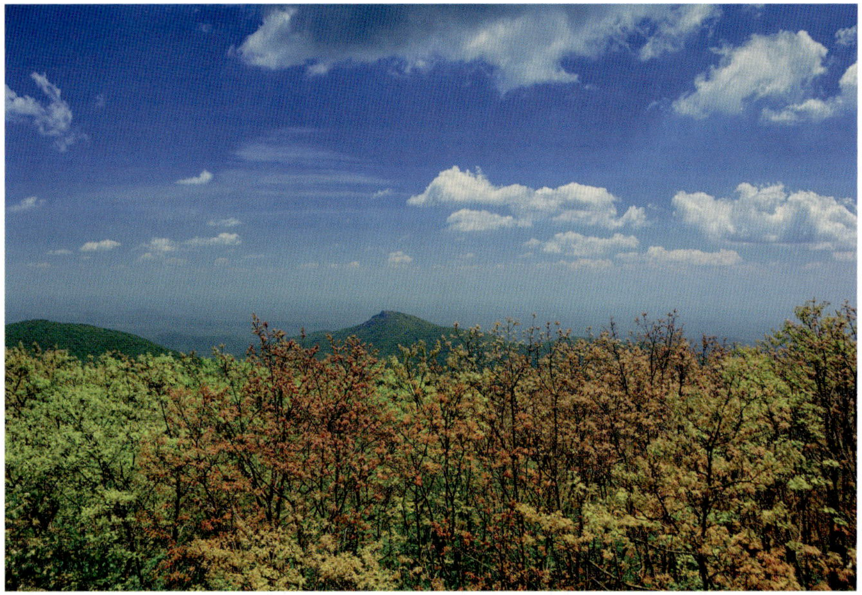

Looking east at Old Rag from the summit of Hawksbill Mountain

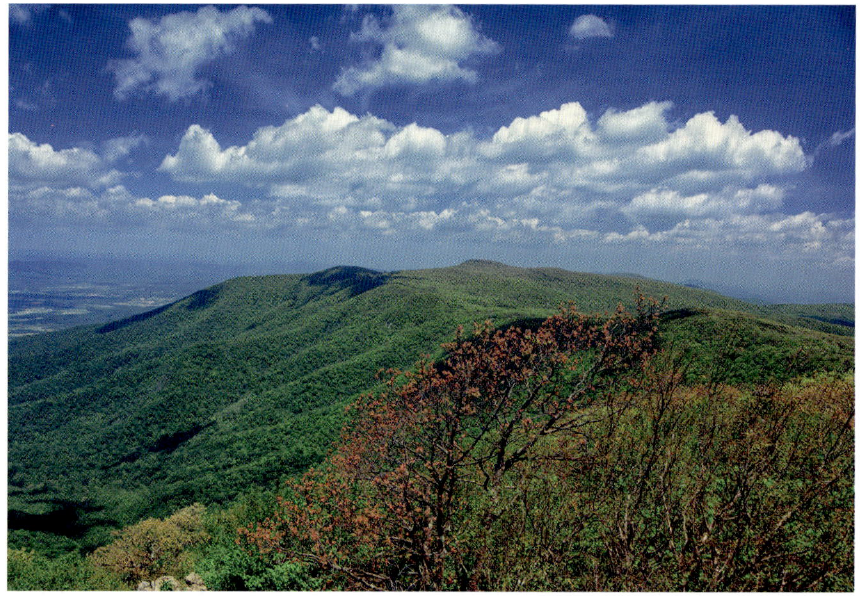

Looking north from the summit of Hawksbill Mountain

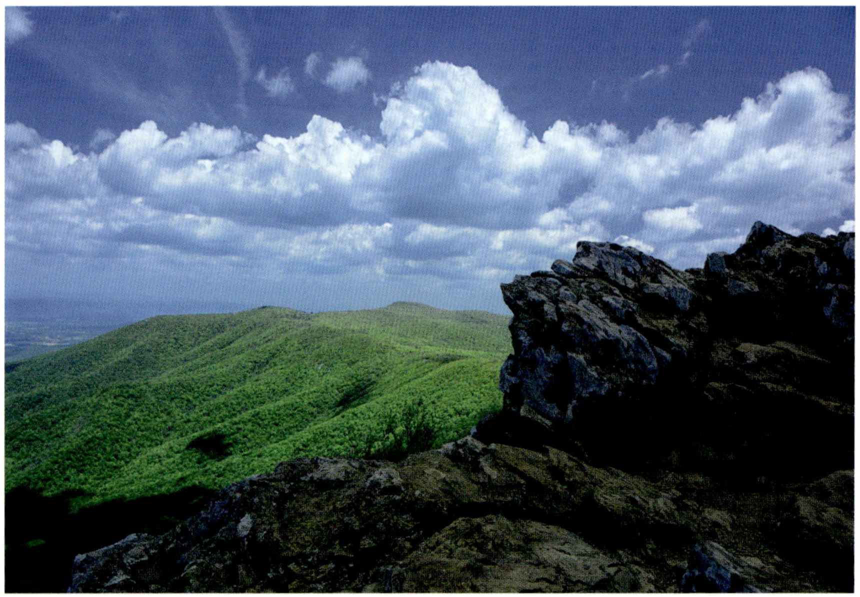

Looking northwest from the summit of Hawksbill Mountain

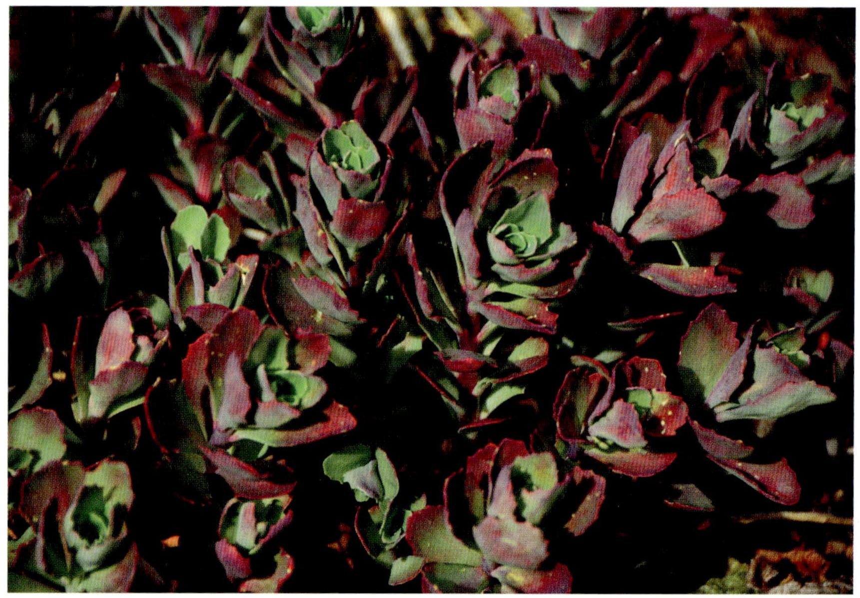

Succulents along the Appalachian Trail in Shenandoah

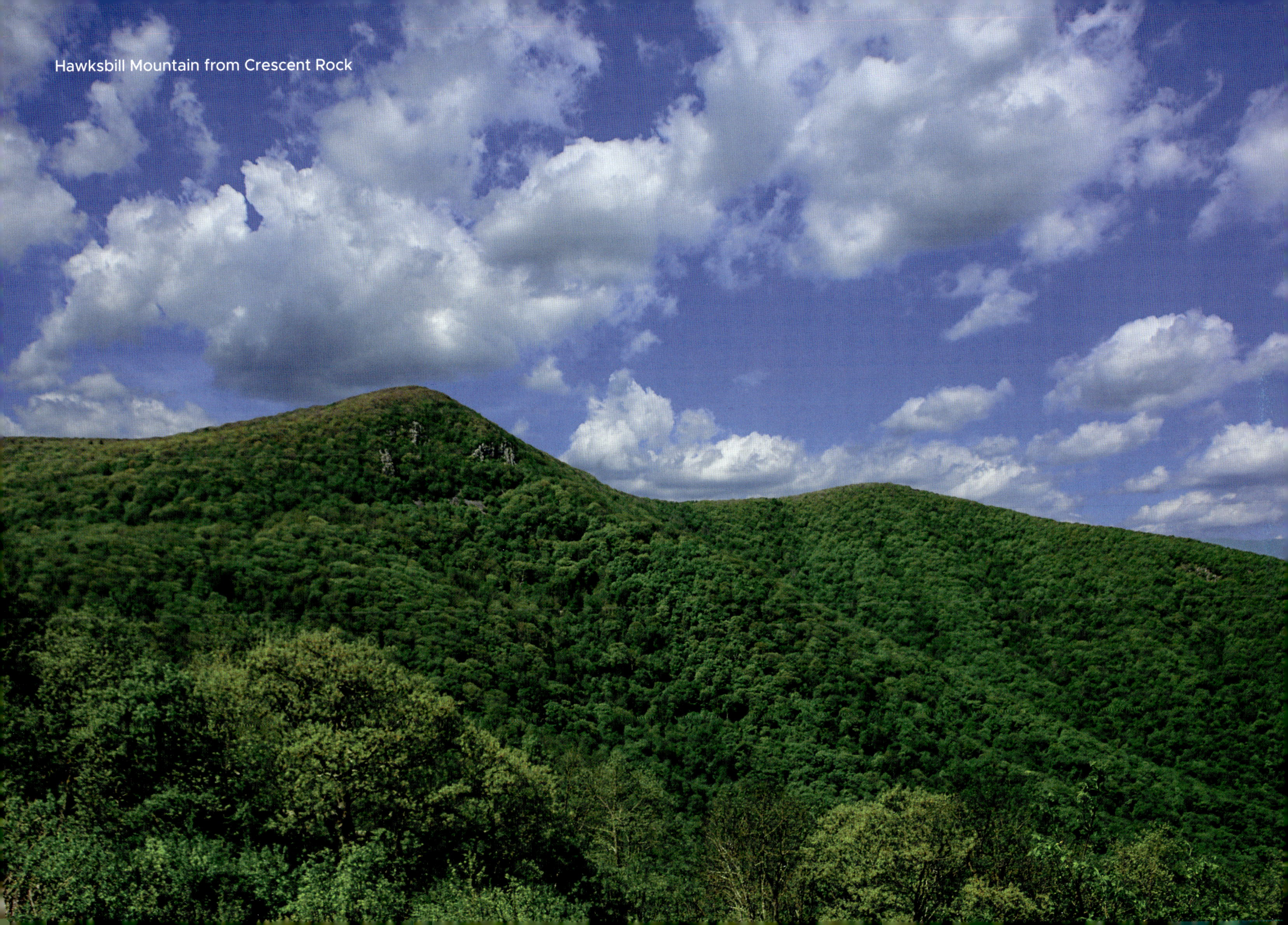

Hawksbill Mountain from Crescent Rock

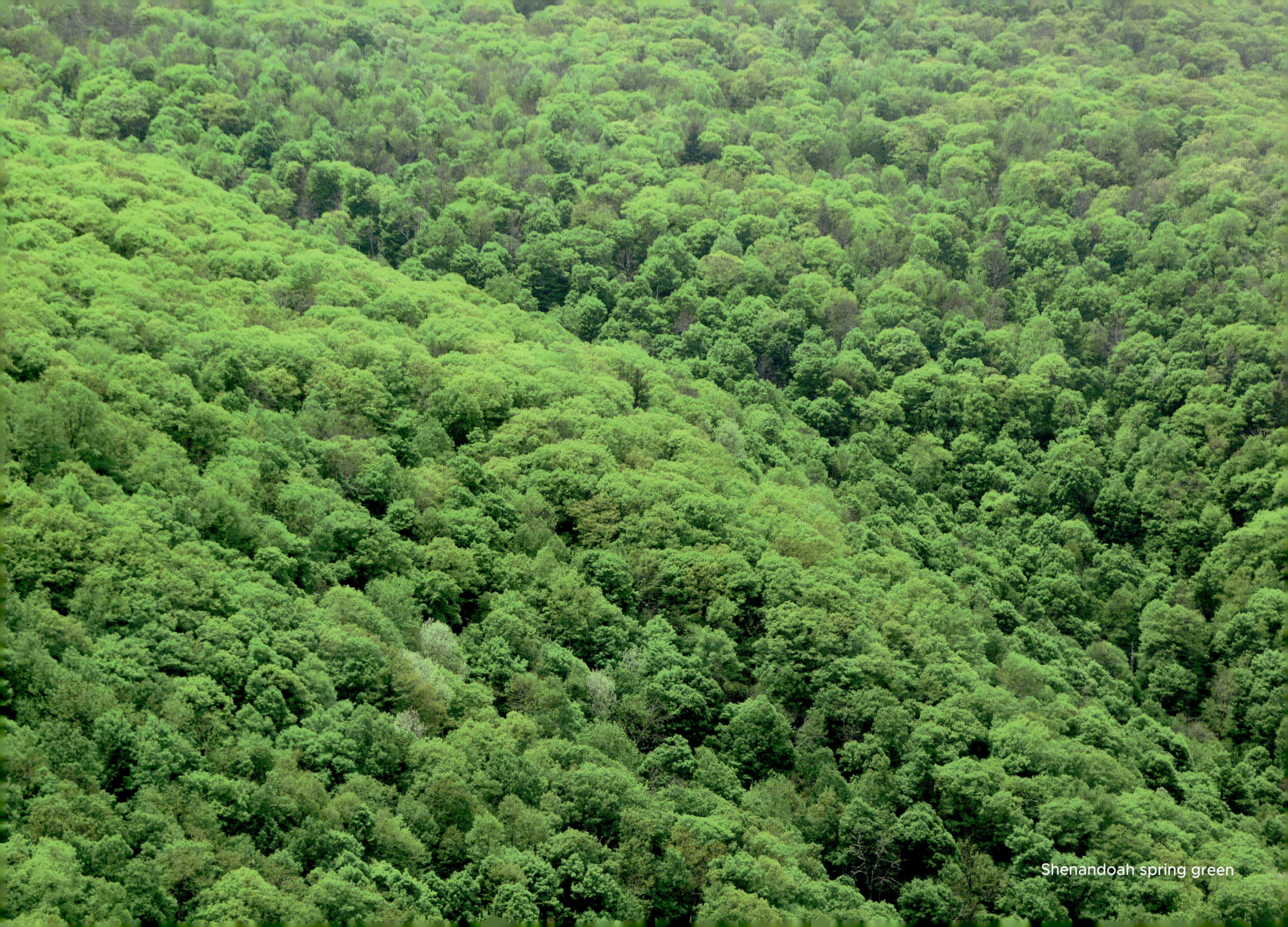

Shenandoah spring green

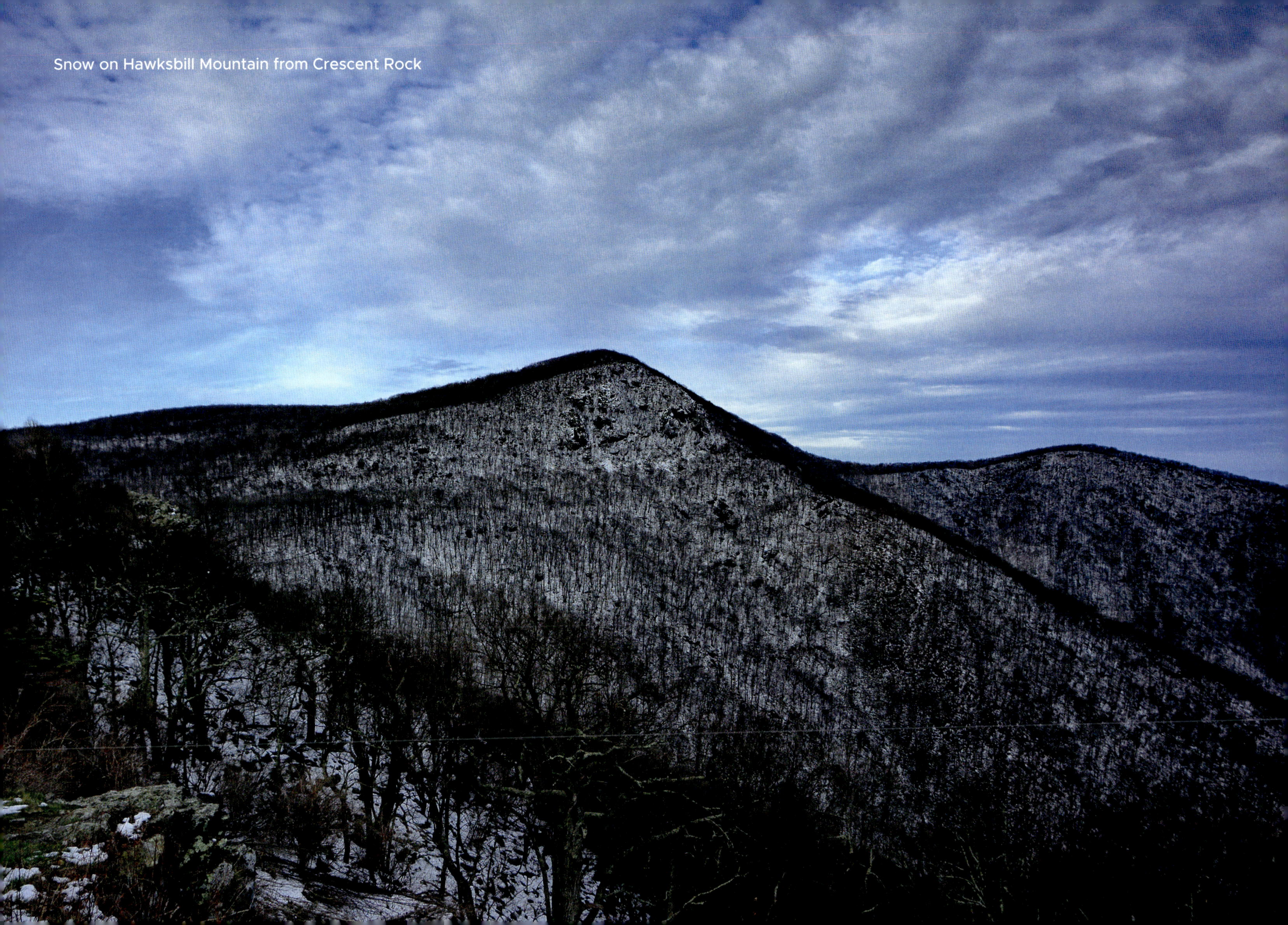

Snow on Hawksbill Mountain from Crescent Rock

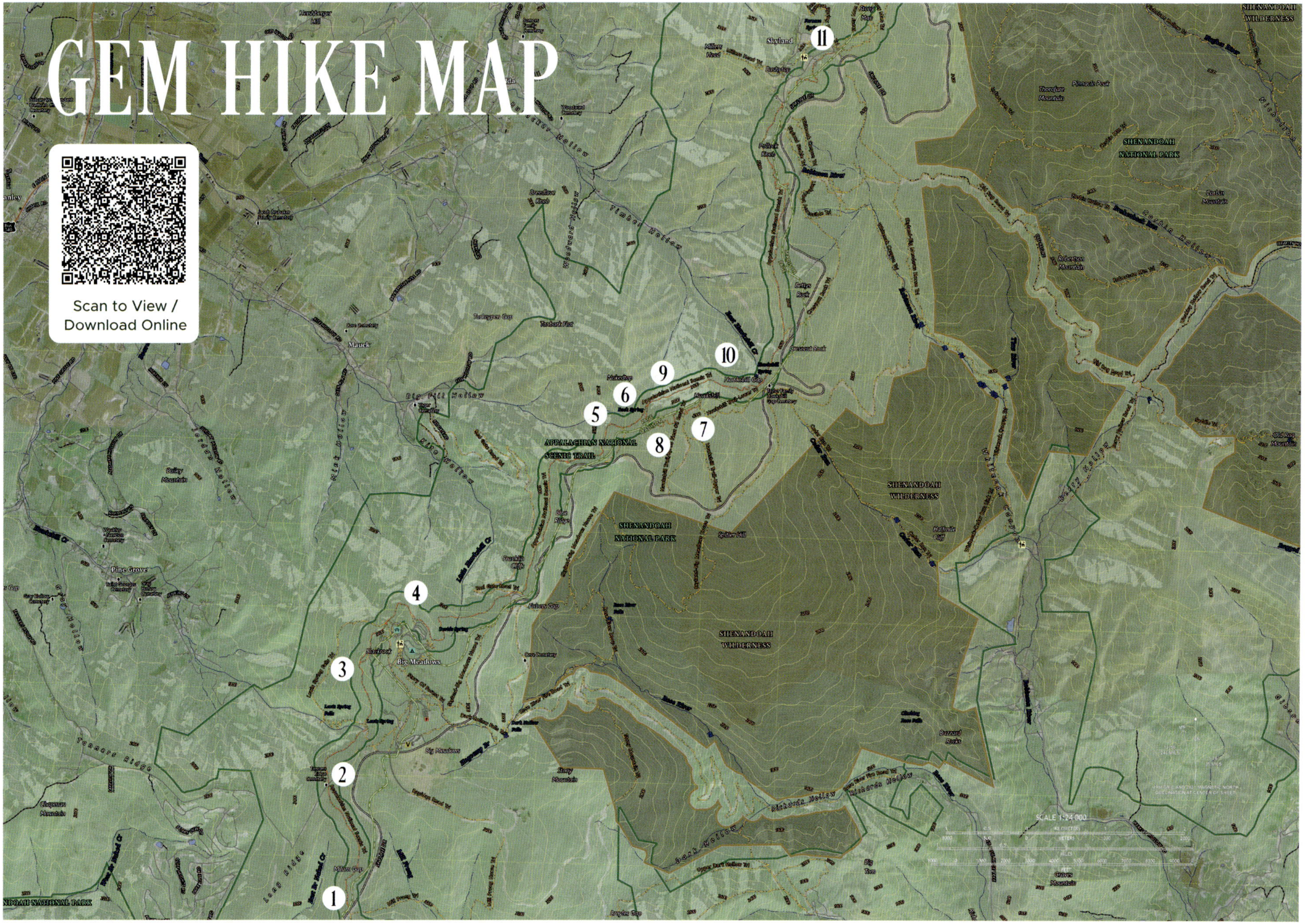
GEM HIKE MAP
Scan to View / Download Online
1
2
3
4
5
6
7
8
9
10
11
Skyland
Big Meadows
APPALACHIAN NATIONAL SCENIC TRAIL
SHENANDOAH NATIONAL PARK
SHENANDOAH WILDERNESS
SHENANDOAH NATIONAL PARK
SHENANDOAH WILDERNESS
SHENANDOAH NATIONAL PARK
SHENANDOAH WILDERNESS
Pine Grove
Mauck

DIRECTIONS TO THE TRAILHEAD

Skyland Resort Conference Center to Stoney Man Trailhead to Milam Gap

The northern trailhead, Stoney Man Trailhead (38.593102, −78.375961), is within Shenandoah National Park's Central District and is at the north end of Skyland Resort. It is in between mileposts 41 and 42 on Skyline Dr.

The southern trailhead is Milam Gap (38.503181, −78.443318). Milam Gap is also in the Central District of Shenandoah National Park. It is in between mileposts 52 and 53 on Skyline Dr.

From Shenandoah National Park's Skyland Resort Conference Hall, directions for this hike are the following:

1. Head northeast on Skyland Lower Loop for 315 feet
2. Turn right to stay on Skyland Lower Loop for 0.3 miles
3. Turn left onto Skyland Upper Loop for 240 feet
4. Turn left; Stoney Man Parking Lot will be on the right, 171 feet (drop a car here at Stony Man Trailhead)
5. Head northwest toward Skyland Upper Loop for 459 feet
6. Turn right toward Skyland Upper Loop for 82 feet
7. Turn left onto Skyland Upper Loop for 69 feet
8. Slight right to stay on Skyland Upper Loop for 213 feet
9. Slight right onto Skyline Dr. and travel 10.6 miles; your destination, Milam Gap, will be on the right

GEM HIKE DIRECTIONS

Hikers approaching from the south can start from the Milam Gap Parking Area within the Shenandoah National Park, Central District, where access to the AT is convenient. This parking lot is between mileposts 52 and 53 on Skyline Dr.

1. Leave Milam Gap on the Appalachian Trail, heading north
2. After 1 mile, cross Tanners Ridge Rd.
3. After 1 mile, cross the trail for Black Rock
4. After 1 mile, pass Big Meadows picnic area
5. At 6 miles, you reach rock spring hut and cabin
6. Shortly after 0.25 miles, you reach the Salamander Trail on the right
7. Take the Salamander Trail for 0.7 miles and reach the summit of Hawksbill Mountain
8. Take the Salamander Trail for 0.7 miles to reach the Appalachian Trail
9. Turn right on the Appalachian Trail north
10. At 8 miles, pass by the trail to get to Lower Hawksbill
11. At 12 miles, you arrive at Skyland North Entrance and Stony Man Trailhead

MORE/LESS AMBITIOUS HIKERS

The summit of Hawksbill also can be accessed by hiking from Skyline Drive on the Lower Hawksbill Trail for 1.8 miles, round trip. Less ambitious hikers can reach the summit of Hawksbill Mountain by hiking from Skyline Drive on the Lower Hawksbill Trail for 1.8 miles, round trip. More-ambitious hikers can extend their hike beyond Skyland to include Stoney Man Overlook.

CHAPTER 3

RANGE VIEW OVERLOOK AS AN ADD-ON TO PANORAMA POINT TO GRAVEL SPRINGS

AREA MAP

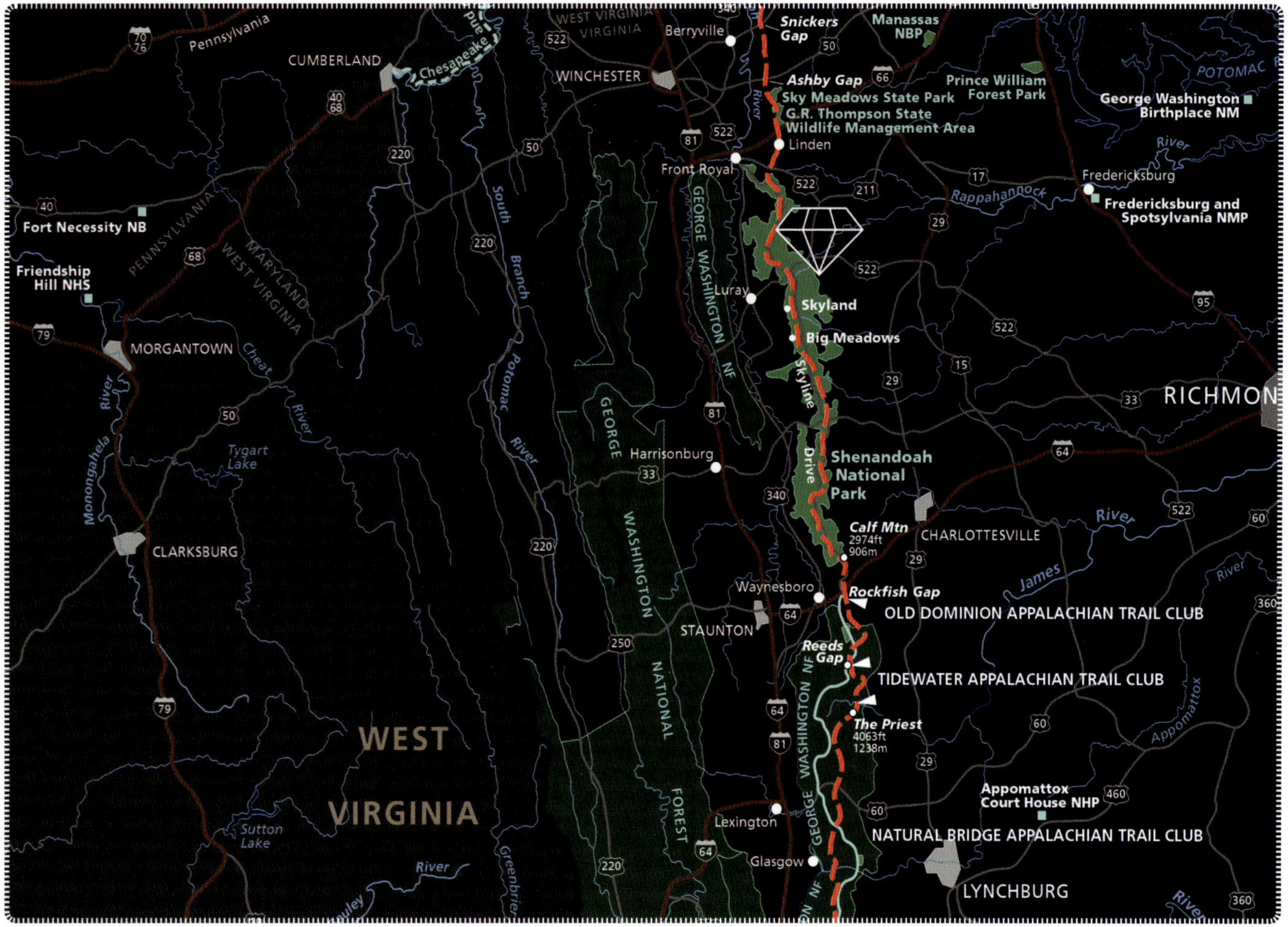

DISTANCE	14.8 miles
ELEVATION GAIN	3,440 feet
ELEVATION LOSS	2,900 feet
LEVEL	Difficult

TYPE: POINT TO POINT

0 10 Kilometers 50
0 10 Miles 50

Appalachian National Scenic Trail

Boundary of CLUB management section

North

GEM HIKE

PERSONAL TOUCH

On this hike I had my favorite hiking moment of all my miles hiked on the Appalachian Trail in Virginia. The sunset at Range View was my favorite moment on the Virginia section of the Appalachian Trail. Range View was a view for the ages. Views consisted of mountains that lasted forever, with no cuts into them. The sky was on fire, and the cool hues of the young foliage of the endless Blue Ridge Mountains were fantastic contrasts for each other.

I felt a deep sense of achievement, having worked relentlessly to become a national parks photographer. I followed a challenging path to earn that title, specifically, the Appalachian Trail, which proved a transformative choice. The evening I caught Range View Overlook in its glory, I also captured a photograph showcasing the Appalachian Trail and Shenandoah National Park that was named Mountain Weather's Photo of the Week, and it held the top spot for several weeks.

BRIEF OVERVIEW

The Appalachian Trail section between Thornton Gap and Gravel Spring Gap in Shenandoah National Park embodies the beauty and biodiversity of the region. Whether you're captivated by the vibrant flora, the majestic trees, or the stunning views from overlooks, this stretch of the AT promises an unforgettable hiking experience. As you traverse the trail, take a moment to appreciate the serenity of the forest and the whispers of the wildlife that call it home.

DESCRIPTION OF THE GEM HIKE:

This hike is a classic Shenandoah National Park hike. It is located in the south end of the North District of Shenandoah National Park. It also uses Skyline Drive to treat hikers to my favorite turnout of Skyline Drive, Range View.

FLORA, FAUNA, AND VEGETATION

As hikers embark on this section of the Appalachian Trail, they are greeted by a diverse array of plant life. The rich understory is often dominated by ferns, wildflowers, and shrubs. There are over 800 species of wildflowers in Shenandoah National Park. Notable species include geranium and trillium. Both wildflowers bloom in spring and can often be seen carpeting the forest floor. Mountain laurel blooms in late spring; this iconic shrub displays beautiful clusters of pink and white blooms. It is often talked about among hikers and nature enthusiasts as being a favorite. The forest canopy consists predominantly of deciduous trees. Key species include oak, eastern, and American chestnuts.

SKYLINE DRIVE

Skyline Drive in Shenandoah runs roughly parallel to the Appalachian Trail and provides an alternative way to experience the park's beauty. With numerous overlooks and pull-offs over the course over 100 miles, visitors can easily access stunning views without the strenuous hike. For those looking to combine driving with hiking, Skyline Drive offers several trailheads and scenic spots to explore. The Appalachian Trail also crosses it several times.

RANGE VIEW OVERLOOK

One of the highlights along Skyline Drive and the Appalachian Trail is the Range View Overlook. This vantage point offers sweeping views of the Blue Ridge Mountains and the Shenandoah Valley. It is particularly stunning at sunrise and sunset. The relationship of light and shadow across the ridges creates a mesmerizing landscape, perfect for photography and reflection.

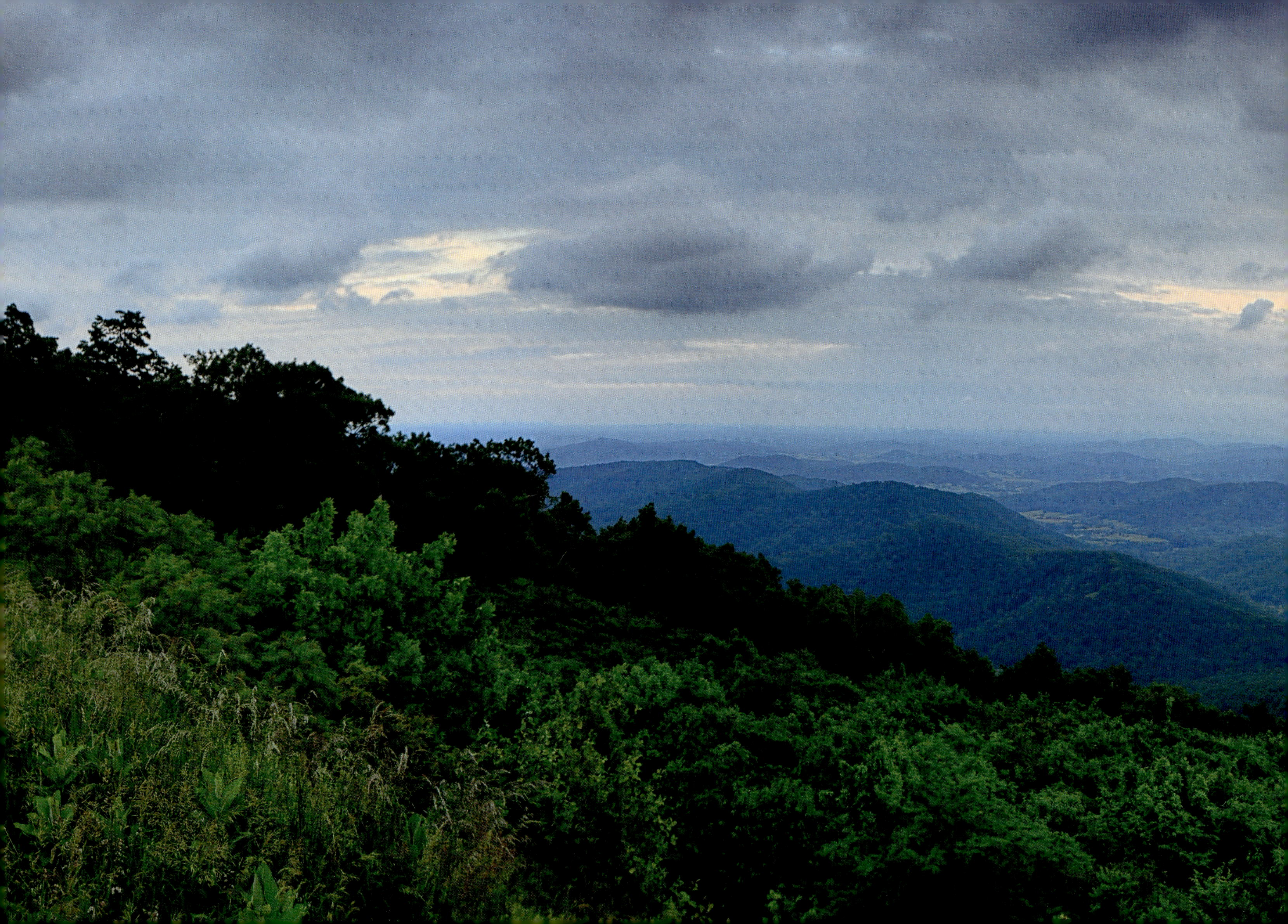

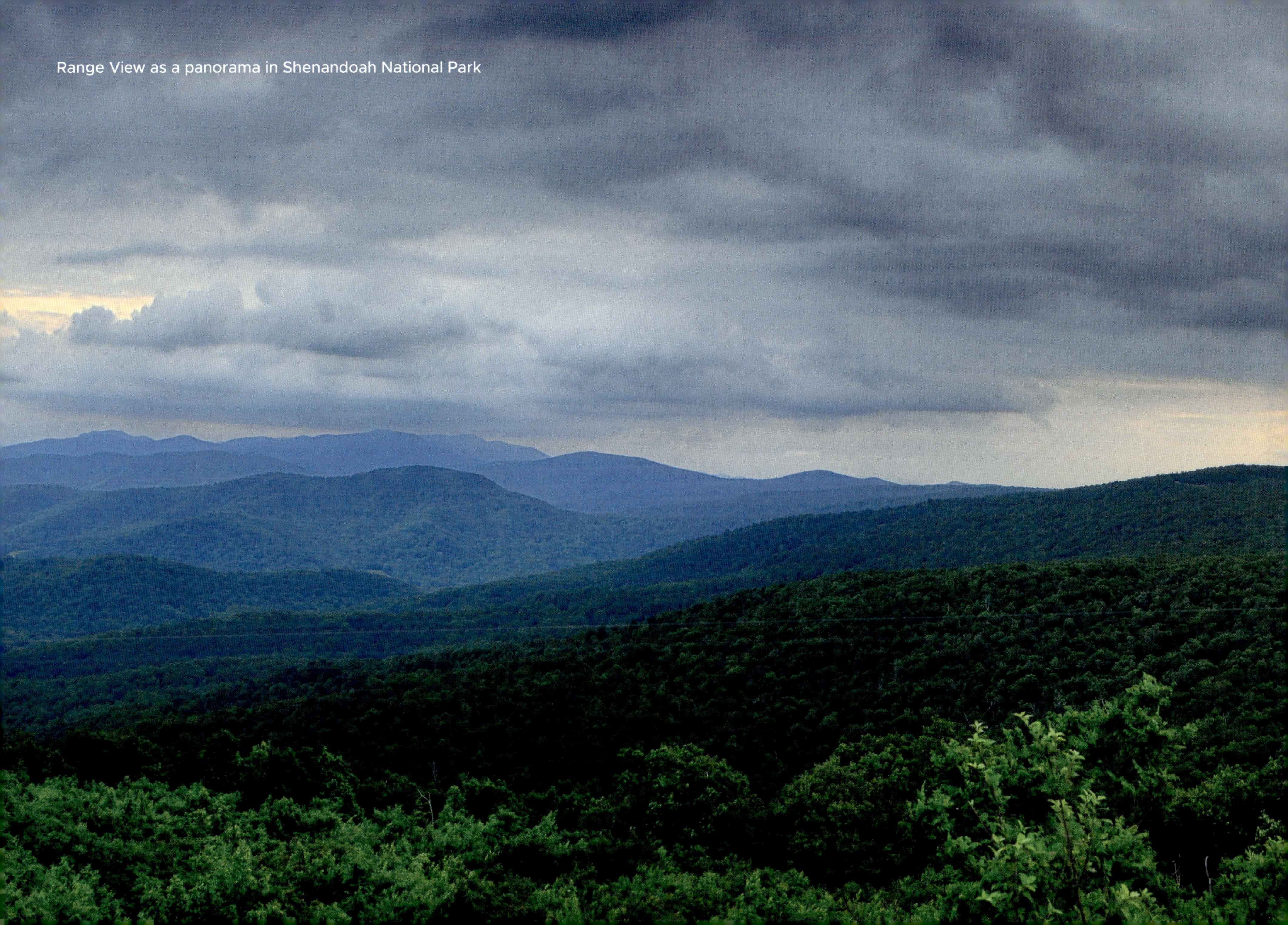

Range View as a panorama in Shenandoah National Park

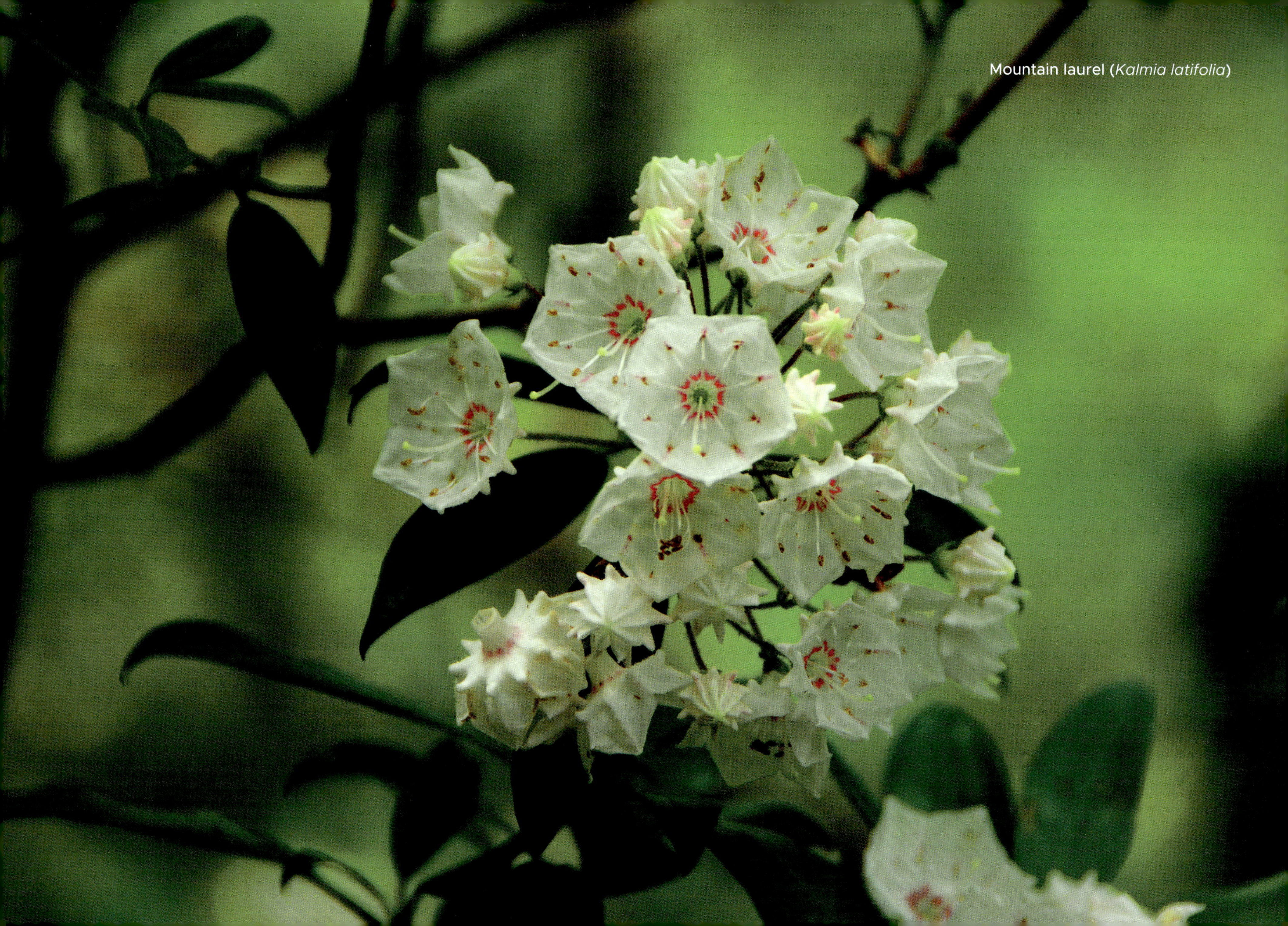

Mountain laurel (*Kalmia latifolia*)

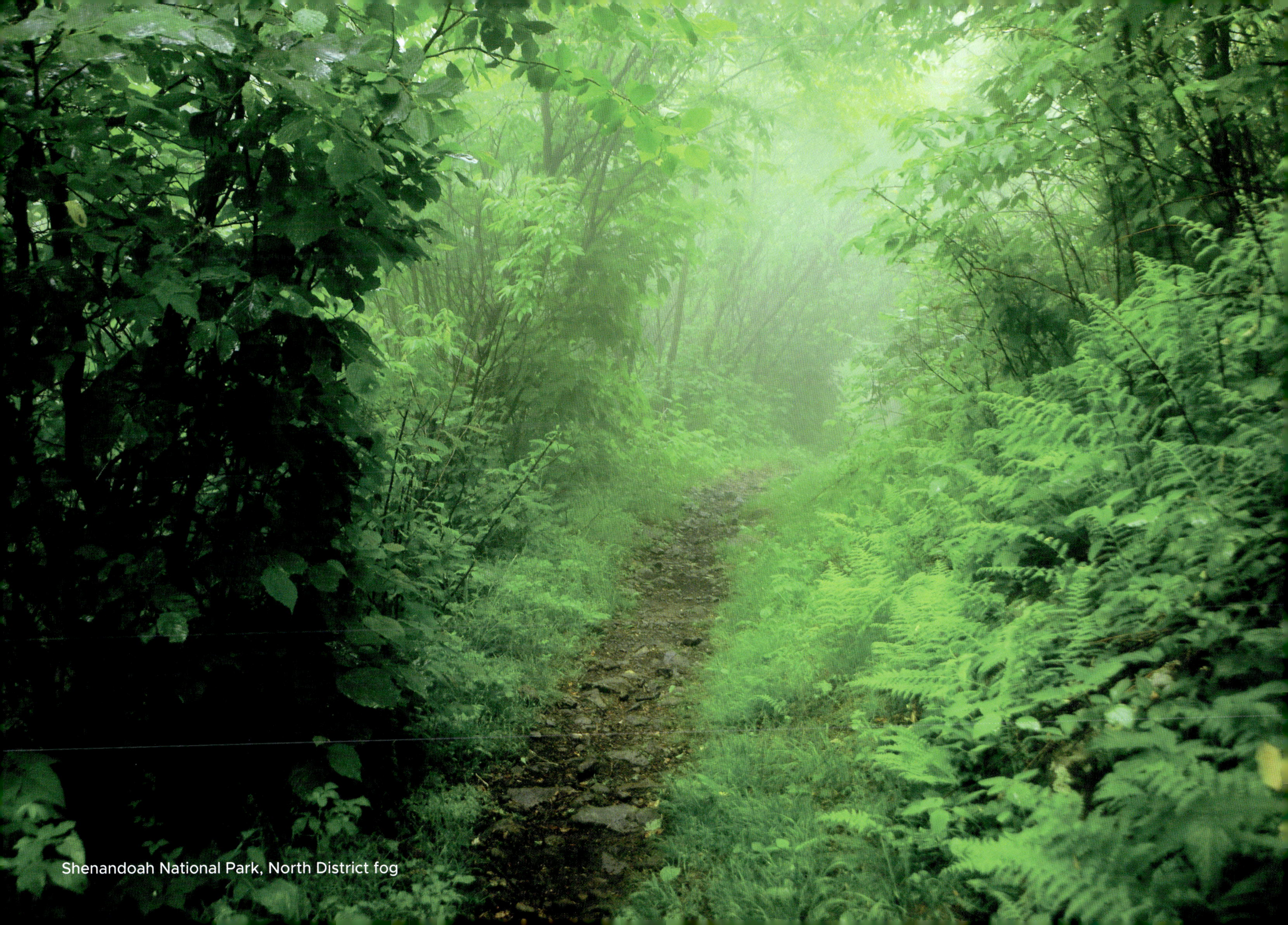

Shenandoah National Park, North District fog

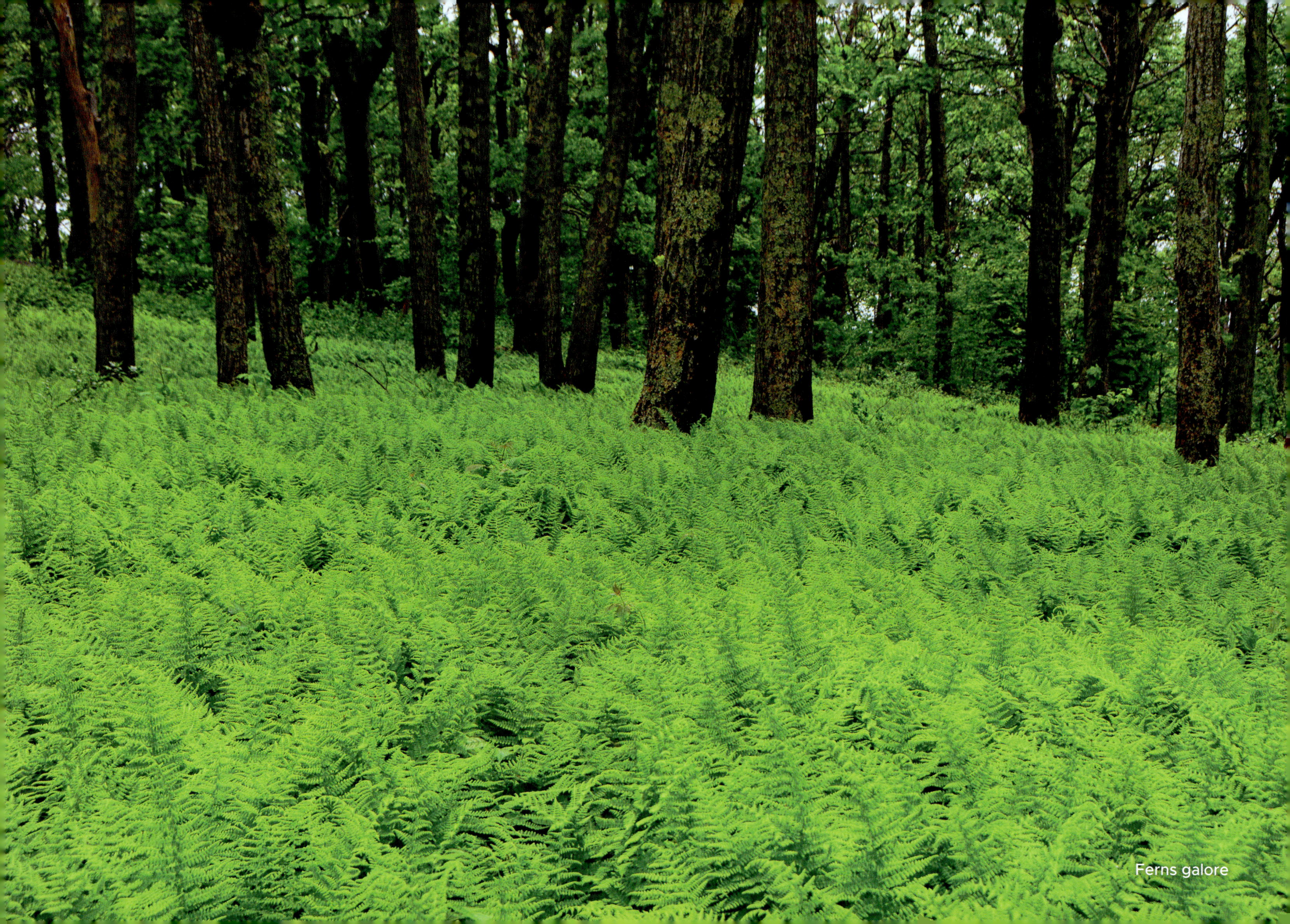

Ferns galore

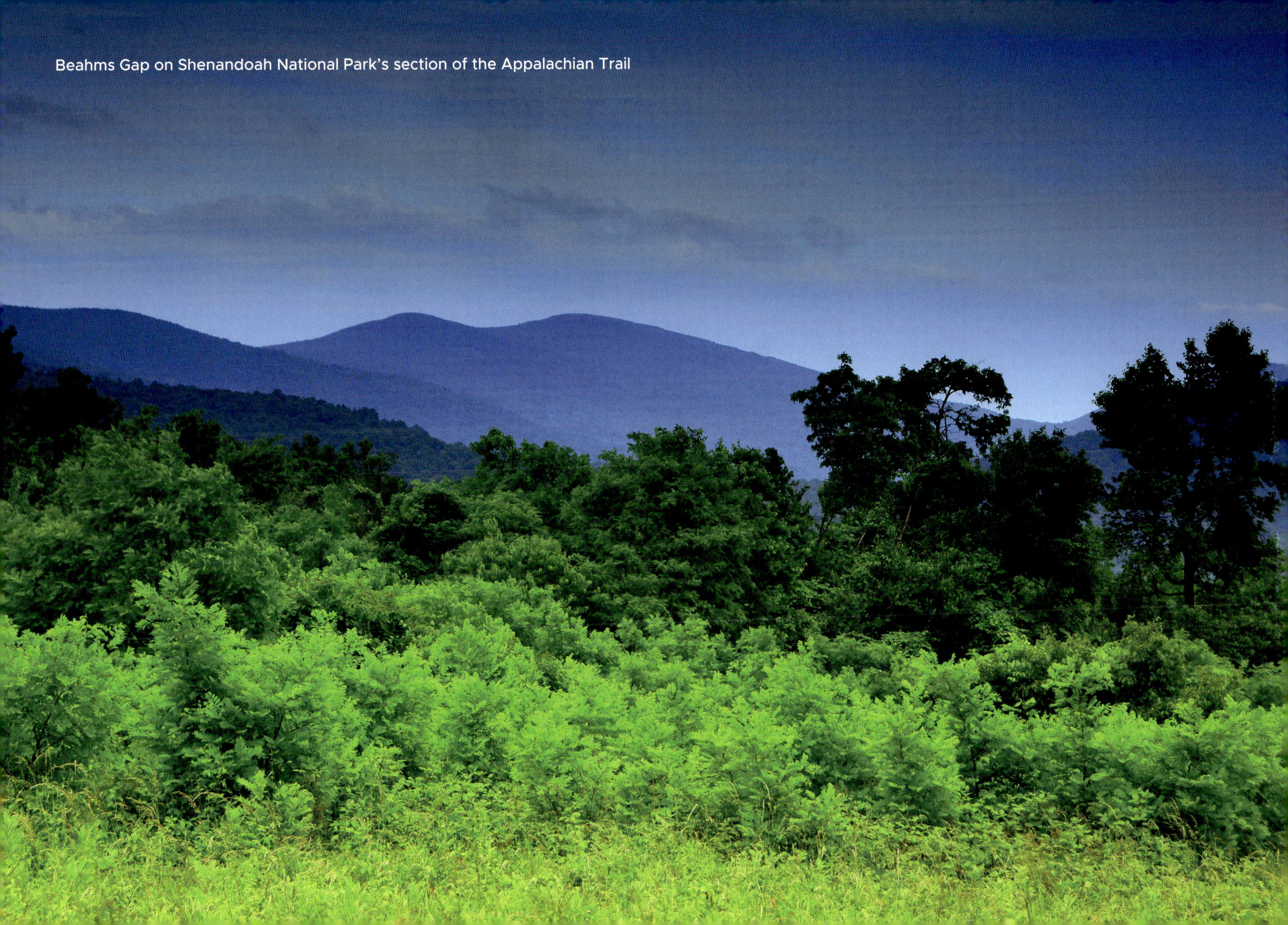

Beahms Gap on Shenandoah National Park's section of the Appalachian Trail

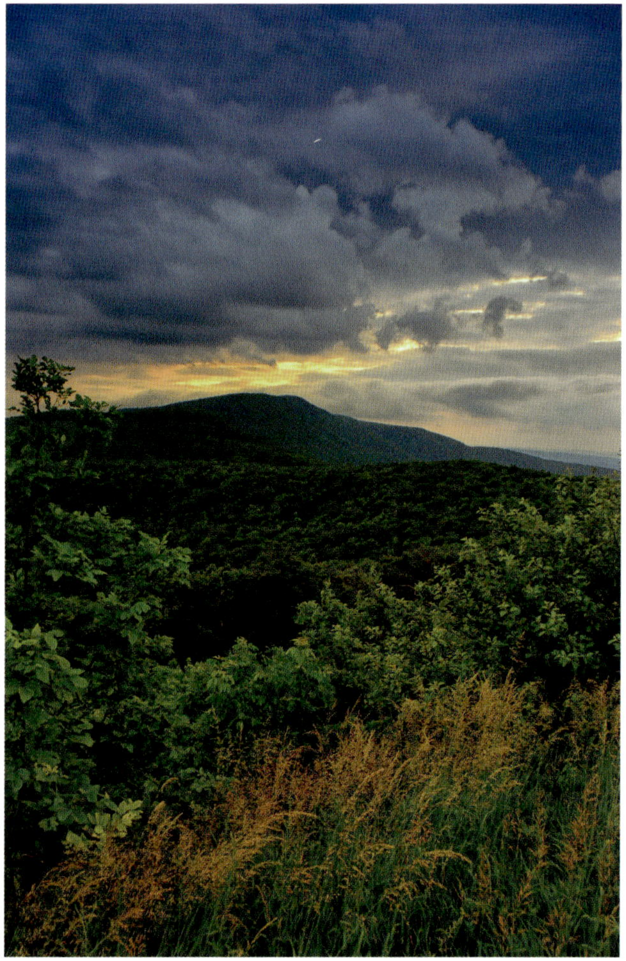

Hogback Mountain from Range View Overlook

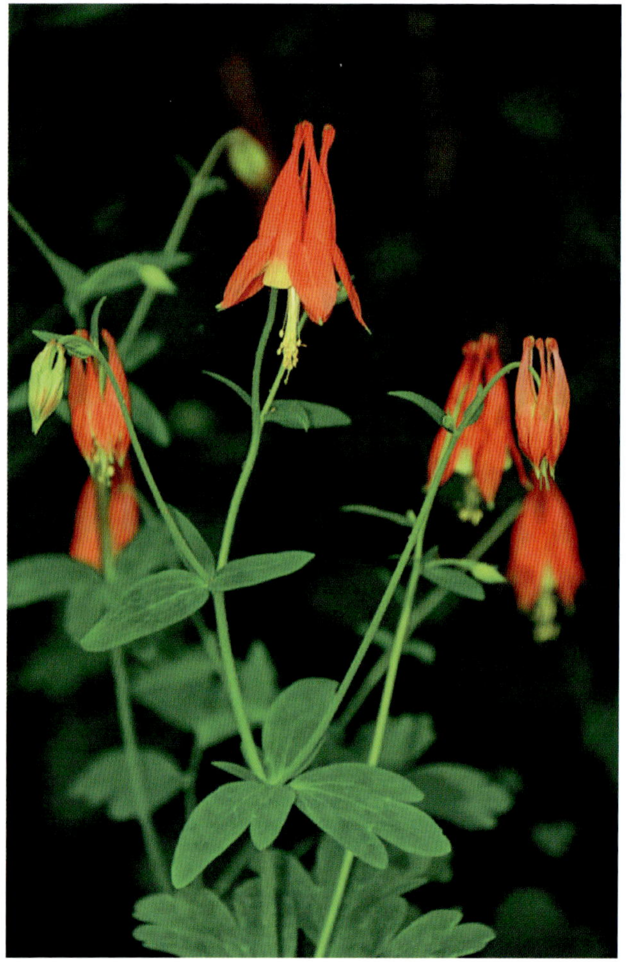

Red columbine (*Aquilegia formosa*)

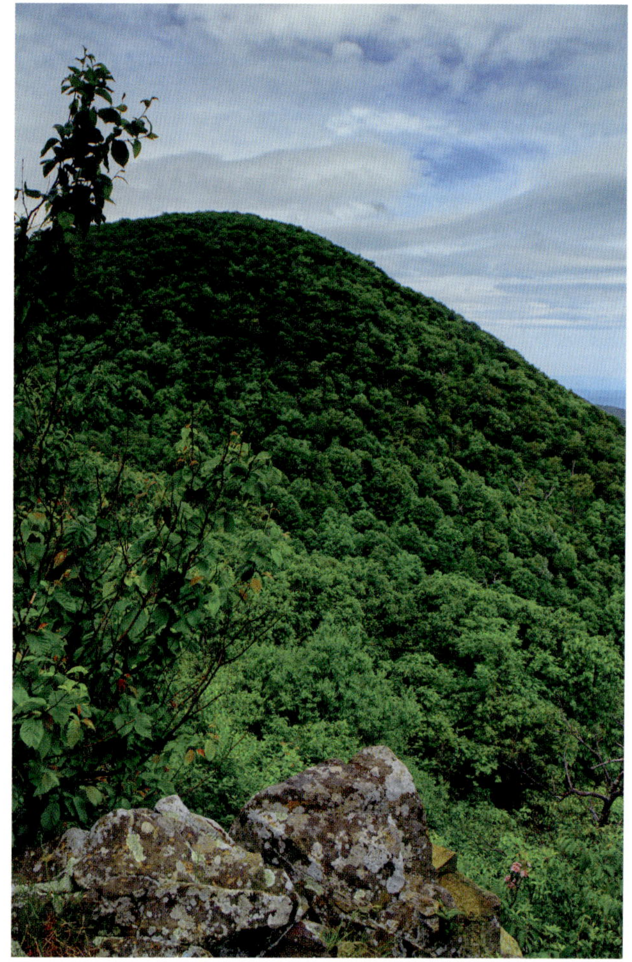

From Little Hogback Mountain, looking at Hogback Mountain

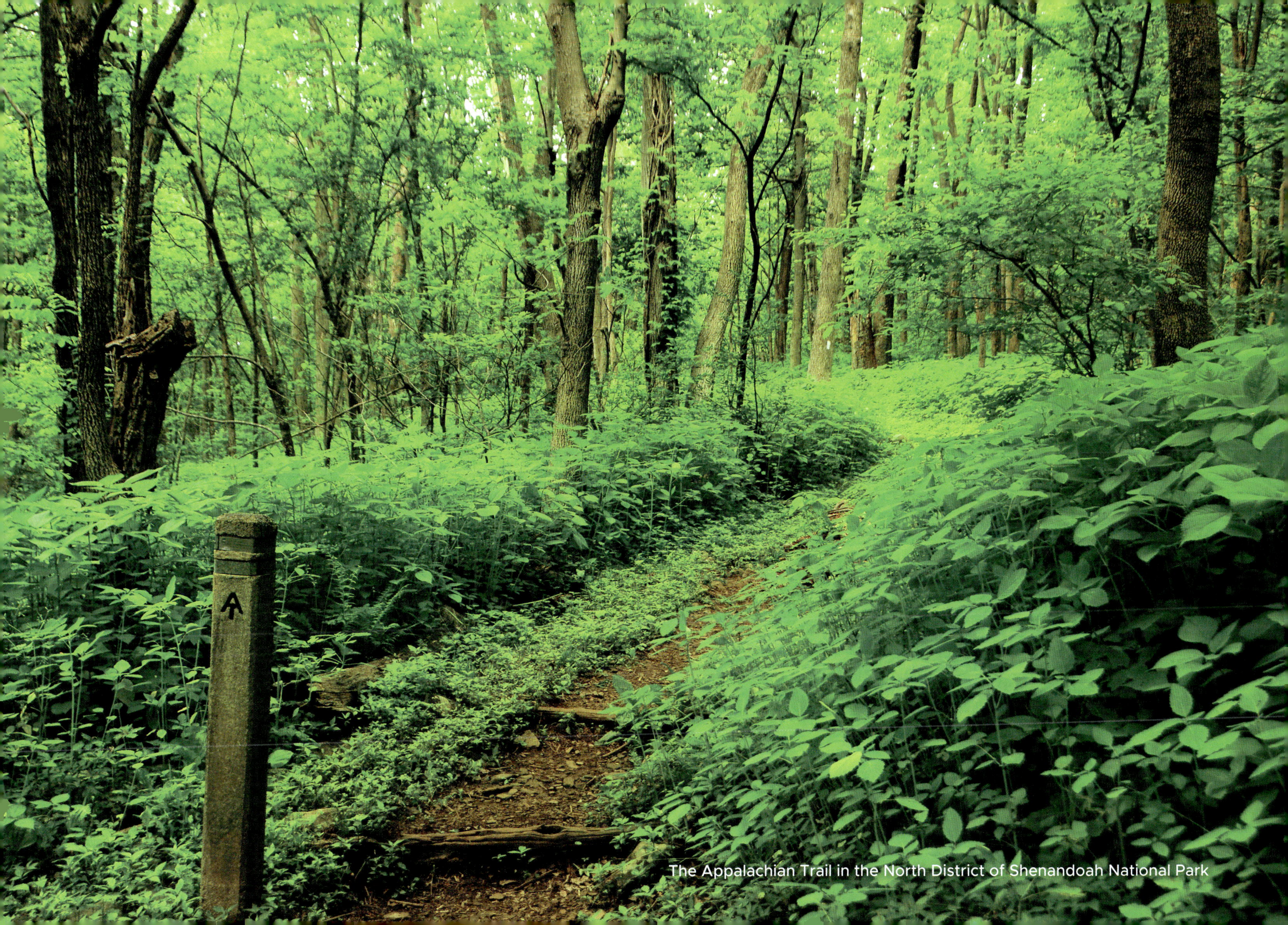

The Appalachian Trail in the North District of Shenandoah National Park

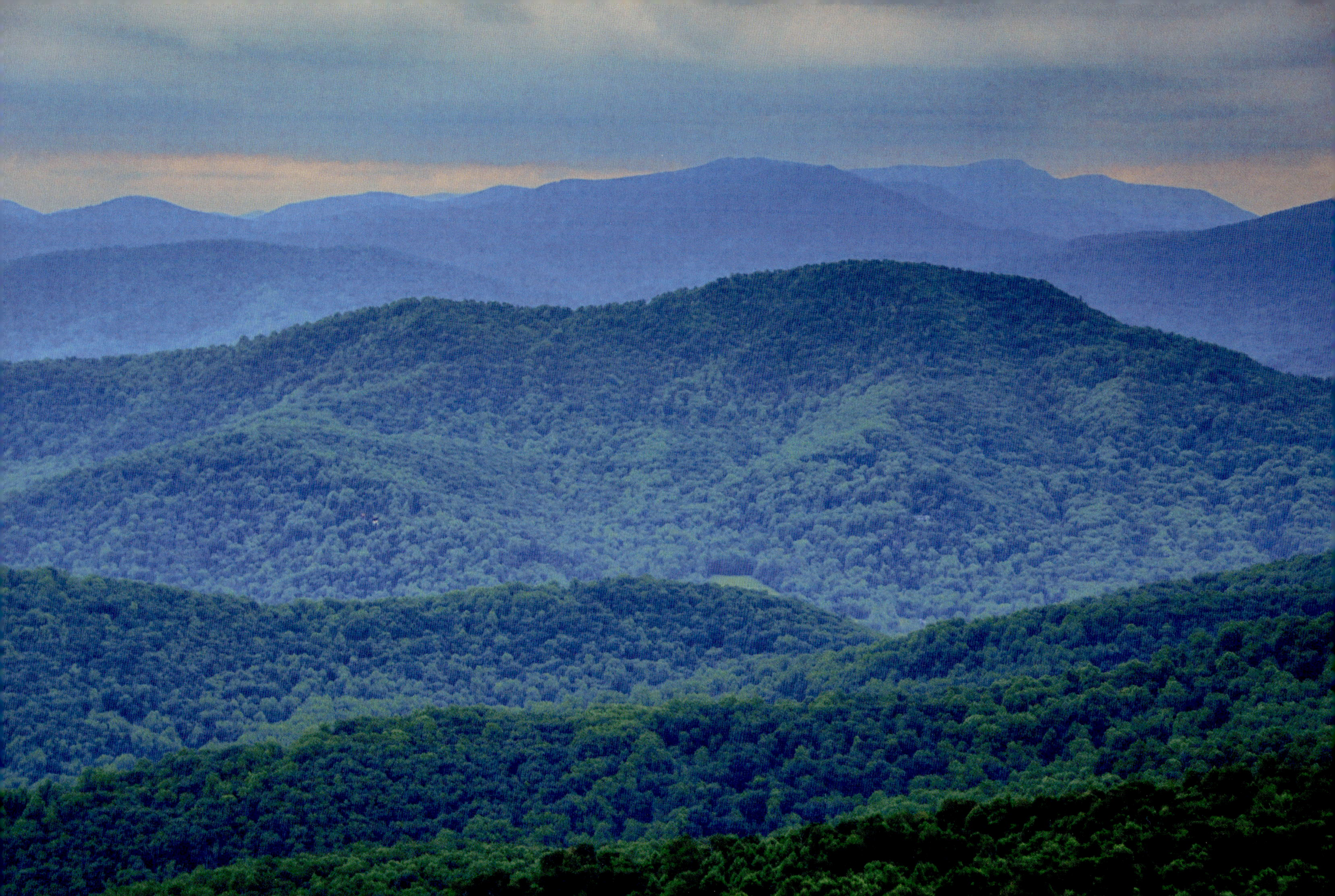

Blue Ridge Mountains from Range View Overlook

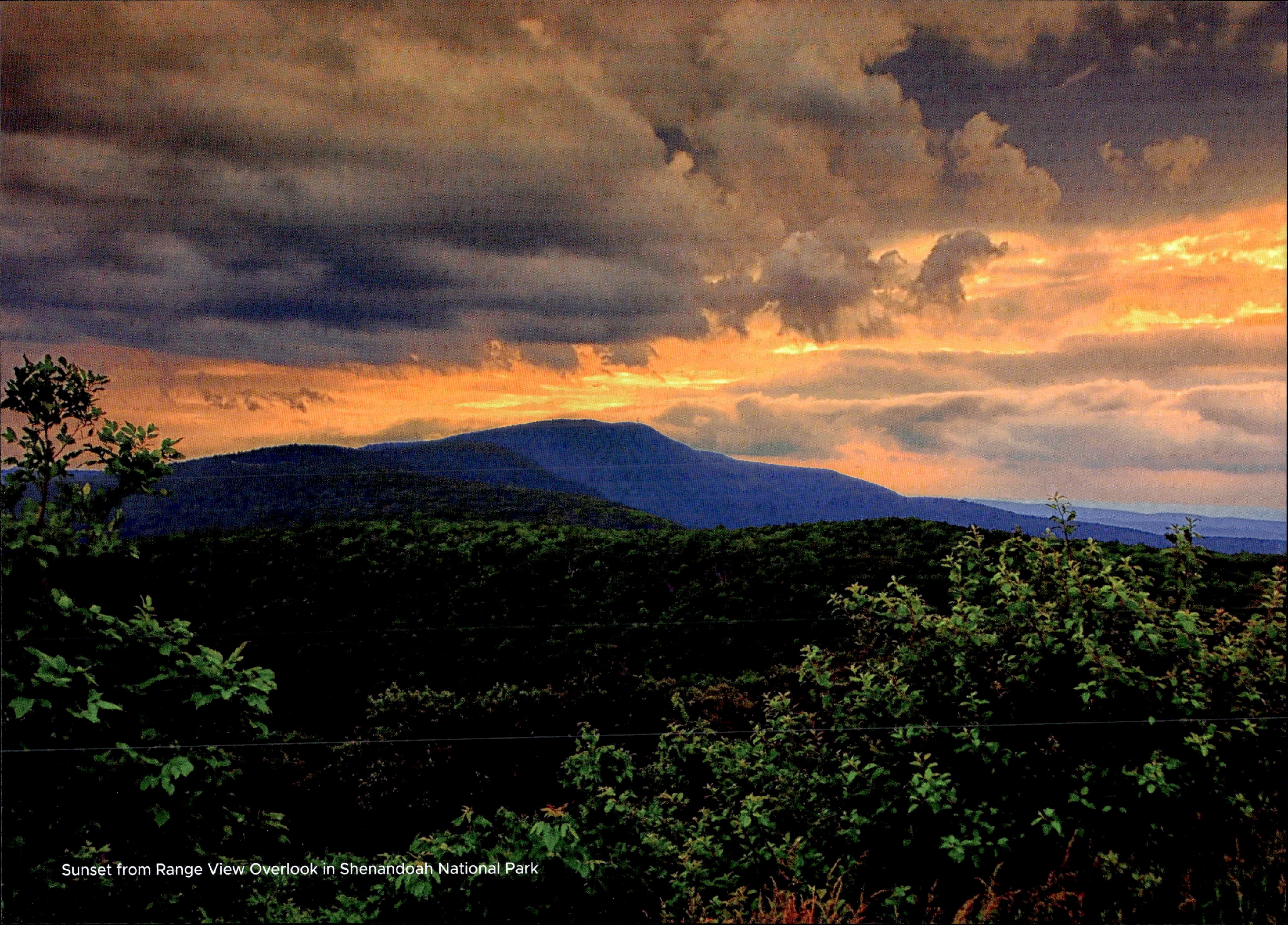

Sunset from Range View Overlook in Shenandoah National Park

GEM HIKE MAP

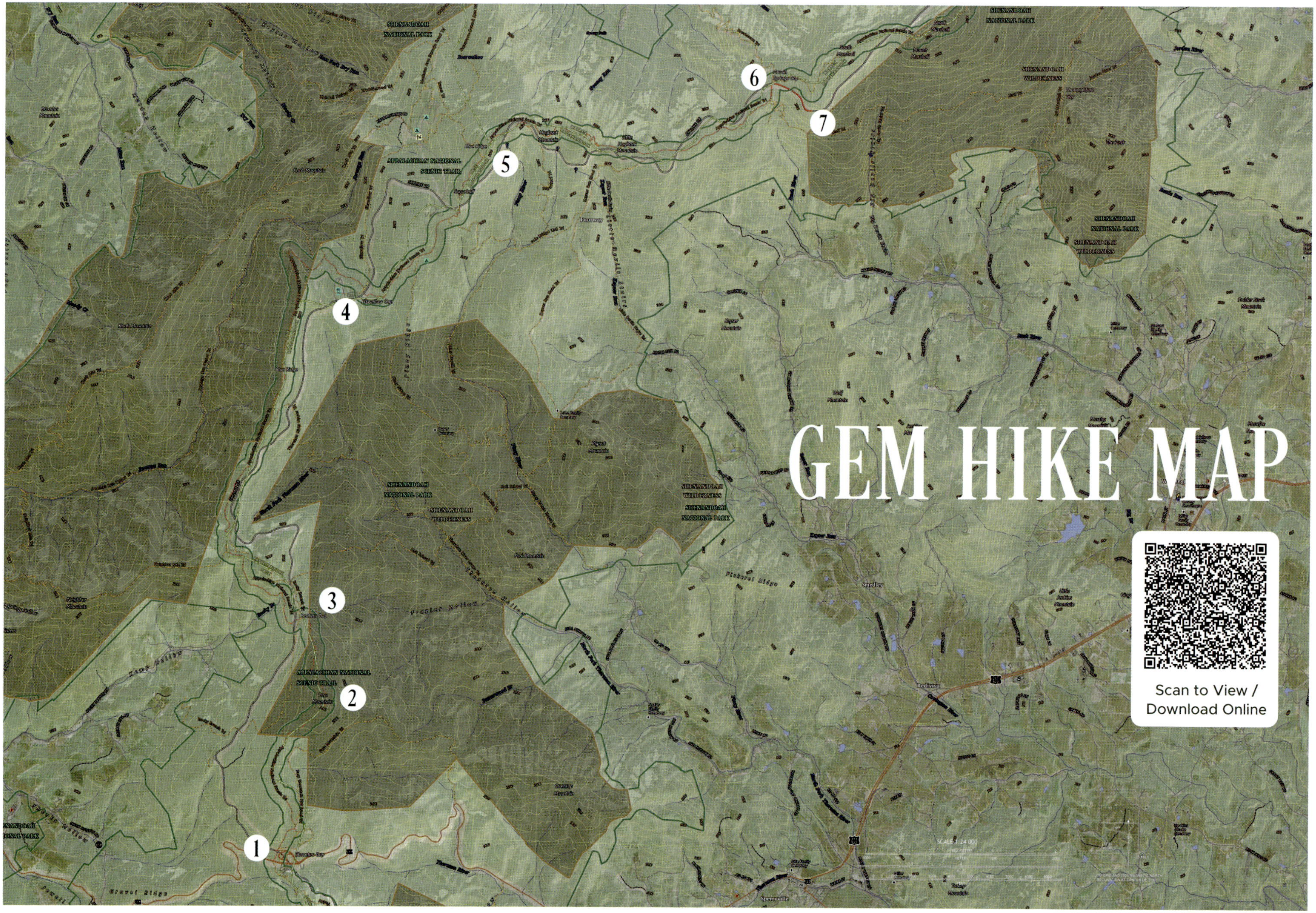

DIRECTIONS TO THE TRAILHEAD

From Luray, Virginia, to Mary's Rock Summit Trailhead: 38.659976, −78.321424
To Gravel Springs: 38.767824, −78.233559
To Range View: 38.764257, −78.227369

1. Head west on E. Main St. toward S Broad St. / Virginia Ave. for 184 feet
2. Turn right and at the first cross street turn onto N. Broad St. / US 340 Business for 0.5 mile
3. Turn right to merge onto US 211 E toward Washington/Shenandoah National Park / Skyline Dr. and continue for 8.6 miles
4. Turn right onto Panorama Lower Parking Road, and Mary's Rock Summit Trailhead will be on your left after 0.1 mile
5. Continue Panorama Lower Parking Road for 0.1 mile and turn onto US 211 E
6. Continue US 211 E for 0.2 mile and turn onto ramp to access N. Skyline Dr.
7. Use the right two lanes to take the ramp for 0.1 mile to Skyline Dr.
8. Continue 13.8 miles on Skyline Dr., and you will reach Gravel Spring Gap Parking Lot
9. Continue 0.4 mile on Skyline Dr., and you will reach Range View Turnout

GEM HIKE DIRECTIONS

For this gem hike, it recommended that you hike northbound on the Appalachian Trail from Mary's Rock Trailhead to Range View Turnout on Skyline Dr.

1. Leave Mary's Rock Trailhead on the Appalachian Trail north for 1.2 miles
2. Pass by Mountain Hut Side Trail and continue the Appalachian Trail for 2.1 miles
3. Reach Beahms Gap and continue on the Appalachian Trail for 5.3 miles
4. Reach Elkwallow Gap (mile 23.9 of Shenandoah National Park)
5. Continue 2.1 miles to Tuscarora Trail Junction
6. Continue 3.7 miles on the Appalachian Trail to Gravel Spring Gap
7. Continue 0.4 mile along Skyline Dr. to Range View Turnout

MORE/LESS AMBITIOUS HIKERS

More-ambitious hikers, please note that over 100 of the Appalachian Trail's roughly 2,200 miles are within the boundary of Shenandoah National Park, so you may opt to make a longer section hike.

Less ambitious hikers should know there are several overlooks along Skyline Drive, and the Appalachian Trail crosses it very frequently, so you may opt for a shorter hike that works for you, but please make sure you enjoy Range View in your travels.

CHAPTER 4

THE APPALACHIAN TRAIL FROM KEYS GAP, WEST VIRGINIA, TO THE POINT IN HARPERS FERRY HISTORICAL PARK

AREA MAP

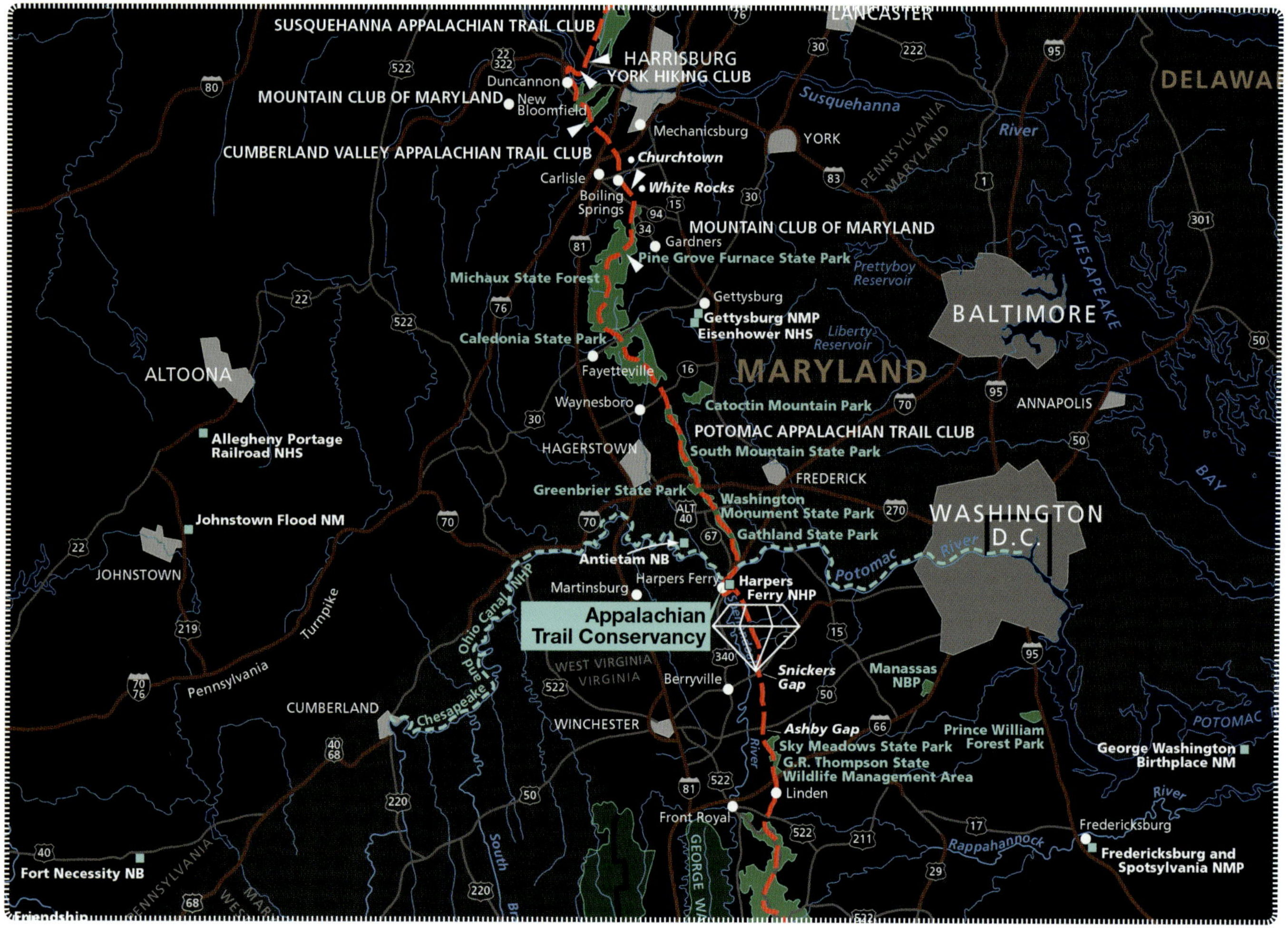

DISTANCE	7 miles
ELEVATION GAIN	800 feet
ELEVATION LOSS	1,440 feet
LEVEL	Easy

TYPE: POINT TO POINT

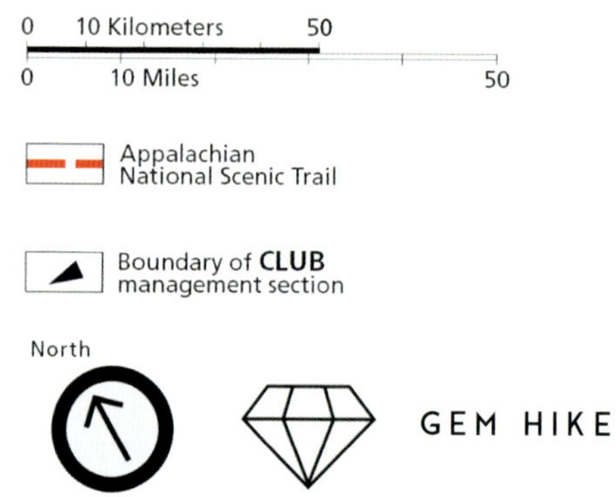

PERSONAL TOUCH

I loved everything about this hike. In fact, I have done this hike five times now. It was special each time. My favorite part was everything coming together perfectly. If I was going to give the award to my favorite after my arm was twisted, I would say the crossing of the Shenandoah River. I enjoyed observing the energy of the battle of the two rivers. It was an all-senses observation. I felt the water particles; I saw the currents battle. As the Potomac won over the Shenandoah, the air tasted moister, with drops of water instead of humidity. I enjoyed feeling the excitement in my stomach and heard the crashes of the currents against each other and the rocks.

BRIEF OVERVIEW

The Appalachian Trail between Keys Gap, West Virginia, and the Point in Harpers Ferry Historical Park offers a dynamic and scenic hiking experience through the Blue Ridge Mountains. This 7-mile section not only is rich in natural beauty but is also loaded with historical importance. This hike can be hiked as an out-and-back from either trailhead. While you're hiking this section of the Appalachian Trail, the historic Harpers Ferry area adds a very special backdrop.

DESCRIPTION OF THE GEM HIKE

The section of the Appalachian Trail from Keys Gap, West Virginia, to the Point in Harpers Ferry Historical Park is a gem hike that comes in at roughly 7 miles if hiked one direction and with a side trip to the Appalachian Trail Conservancy. For this hike it is recommended you hike north along the Appalachian Trail, thus starting at Keys Gap and ending at the Point in Harpers Ferry.

The gem hike starts out on the West Virginia–Virginia state line, so you can claim you have been two places at once. The Appalachian Trail travels through a diverse deciduous forest for a couple of miles. White and pink dogwoods and other flowering trees are gorgeous in the spring. The Appalachian Trail then crosses the Shenandoah River along US 340 and enters the town of Harpers Ferry. From along US 340, the views are amazing. At the top of a hill, you can take an add-on 0.2 mile each way to visit the Appalachian Trail Conservancy's headquarters, and when you are back on the Appalachian Trail, you will head through all the special historical buildings of Harpers Ferry, West Virginia.

FLORA, FAUNA, AND VEGETATION

This section is known to have a very diverse collection of trees, which include oaks, shagbark hickories, maples, beeches, tulips, and dogwoods. Red maples create a special treat in the fall. The dogwoods also produce a lovely springtime flower that is either white or pink depending on species. Dark cherry trees are common along the Shenandoah River. Azaleas are also common along the trail on this section.

APPALACHIAN TRAIL CONSERVANCY

The Appalachian Trail Conservancy (ATC) is a key organization dedicated to preserving, protecting, and managing the Appalachian Trail. It works in partnership with various agencies and organizations to maintain the trail, protect its environment, and provide resources and support for hikers. The ATC's efforts ensure that the trail remains a sustainable and enjoyable experience for all, now and into the future.

HARPERS FERRY TOWN AND HISTORICAL PARK

Harpers Ferry, West Virginia, is located at the confluence of the Potomac and Shenandoah Rivers and is a historic town with significant cultural and historical value. The town is home to the Harpers Ferry National Historical Park, which preserves the area's rich history. The park features preserved nineteenth-century buildings, museums, and exhibits that illustrate the town's historical significance. The town of Harpers Ferry was the site of John Brown's raid in 1859, an event that heightened tensions leading up to the Civil War. During the war, Harpers Ferry changed hands multiple times between Union and Confederate forces due to its strategic location and armory. There are ghost tours held at Saint Peter's Church.

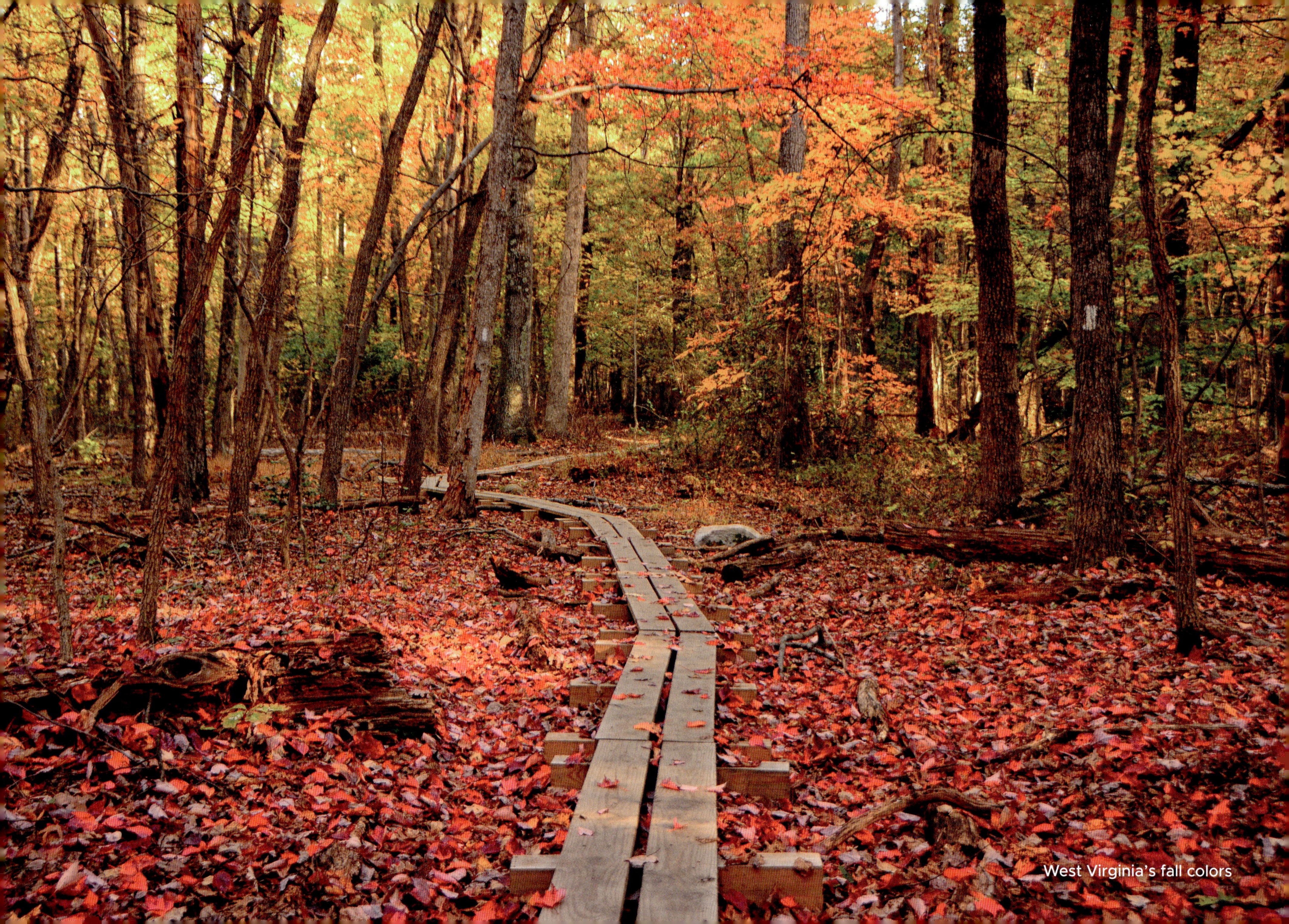

West Virginia's fall colors

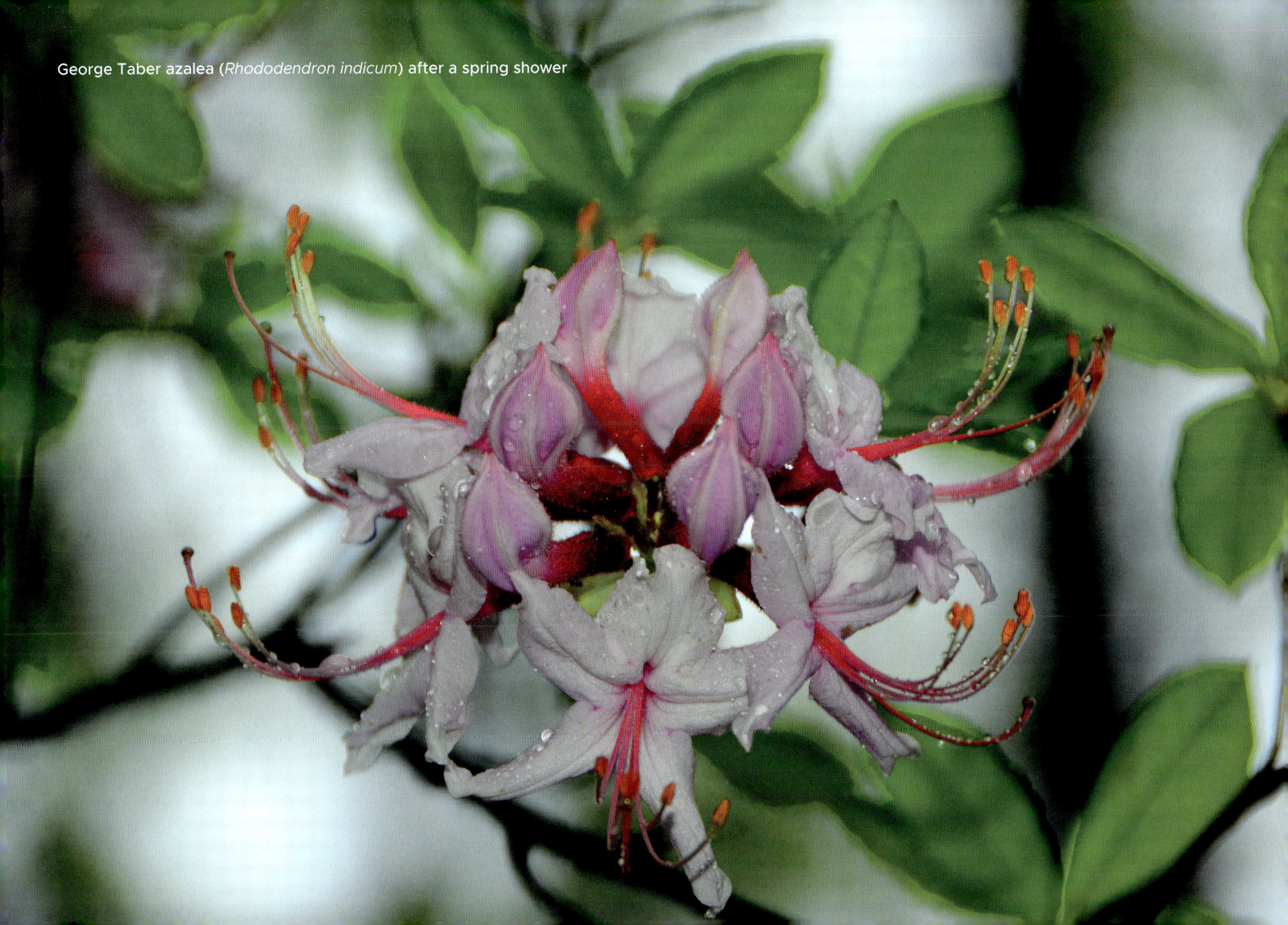

George Taber azalea (*Rhododendron indicum*) after a spring shower

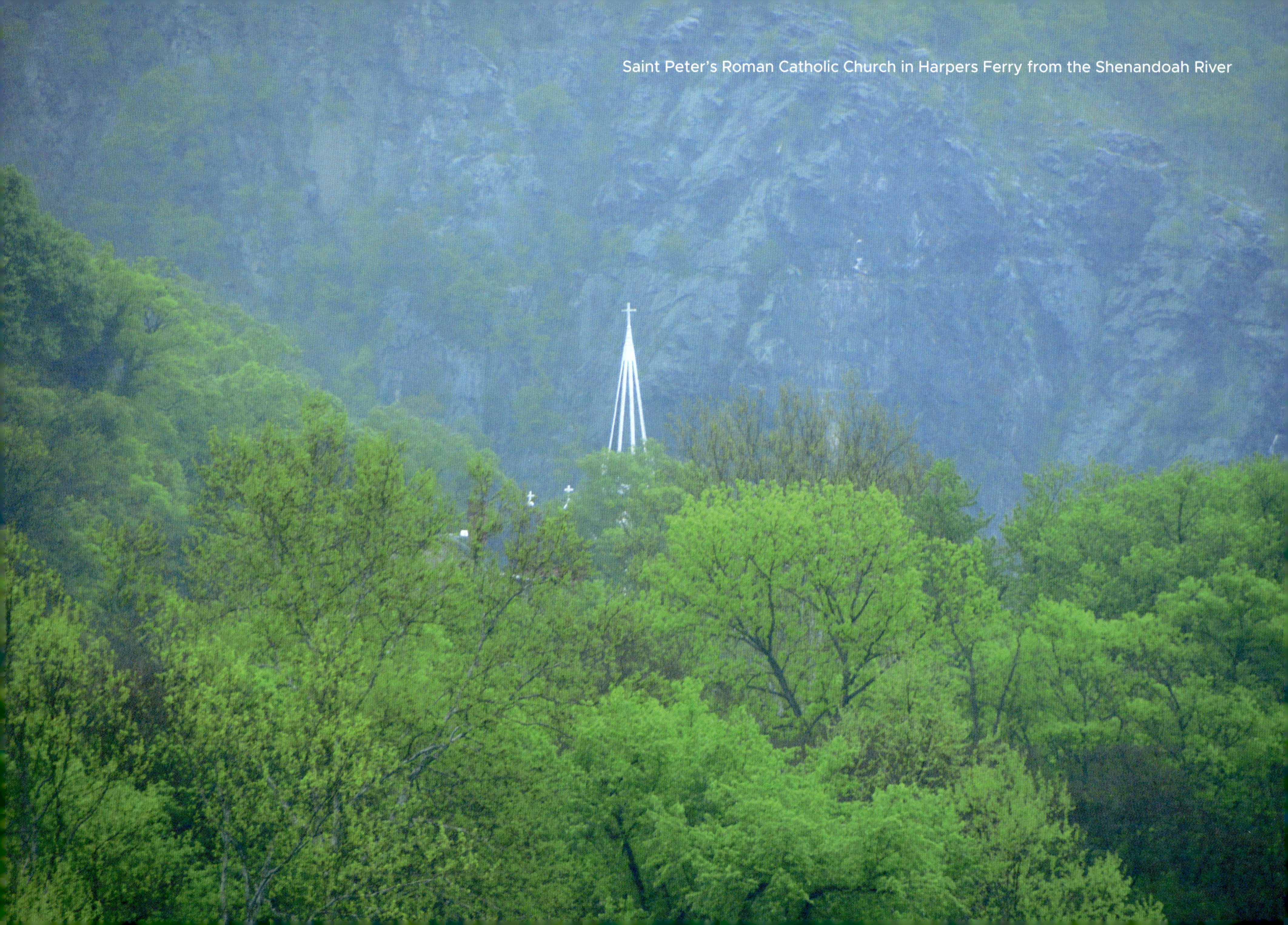

Saint Peter's Roman Catholic Church in Harpers Ferry from the Shenandoah River

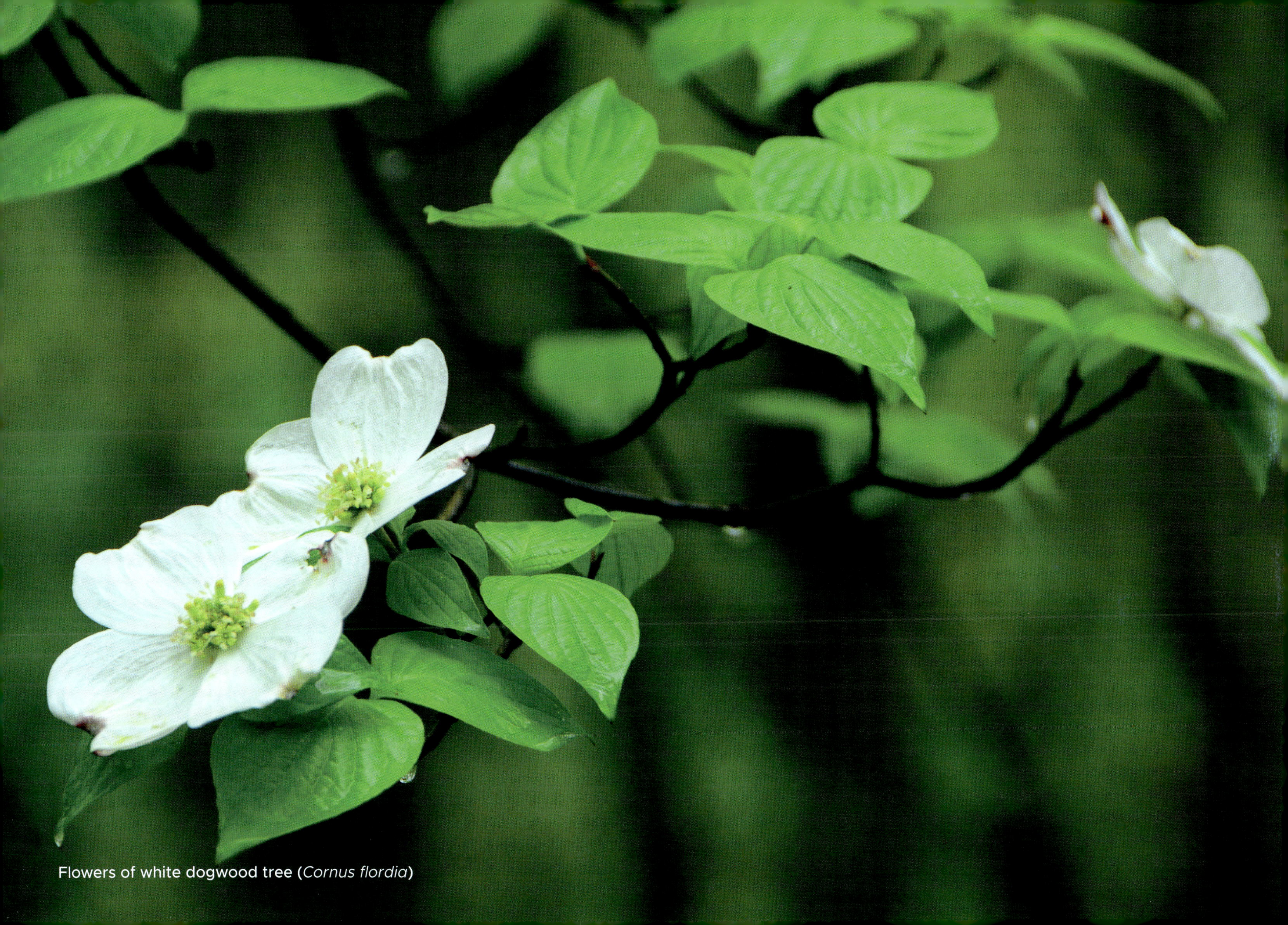

Flowers of white dogwood tree (*Cornus flordia*)

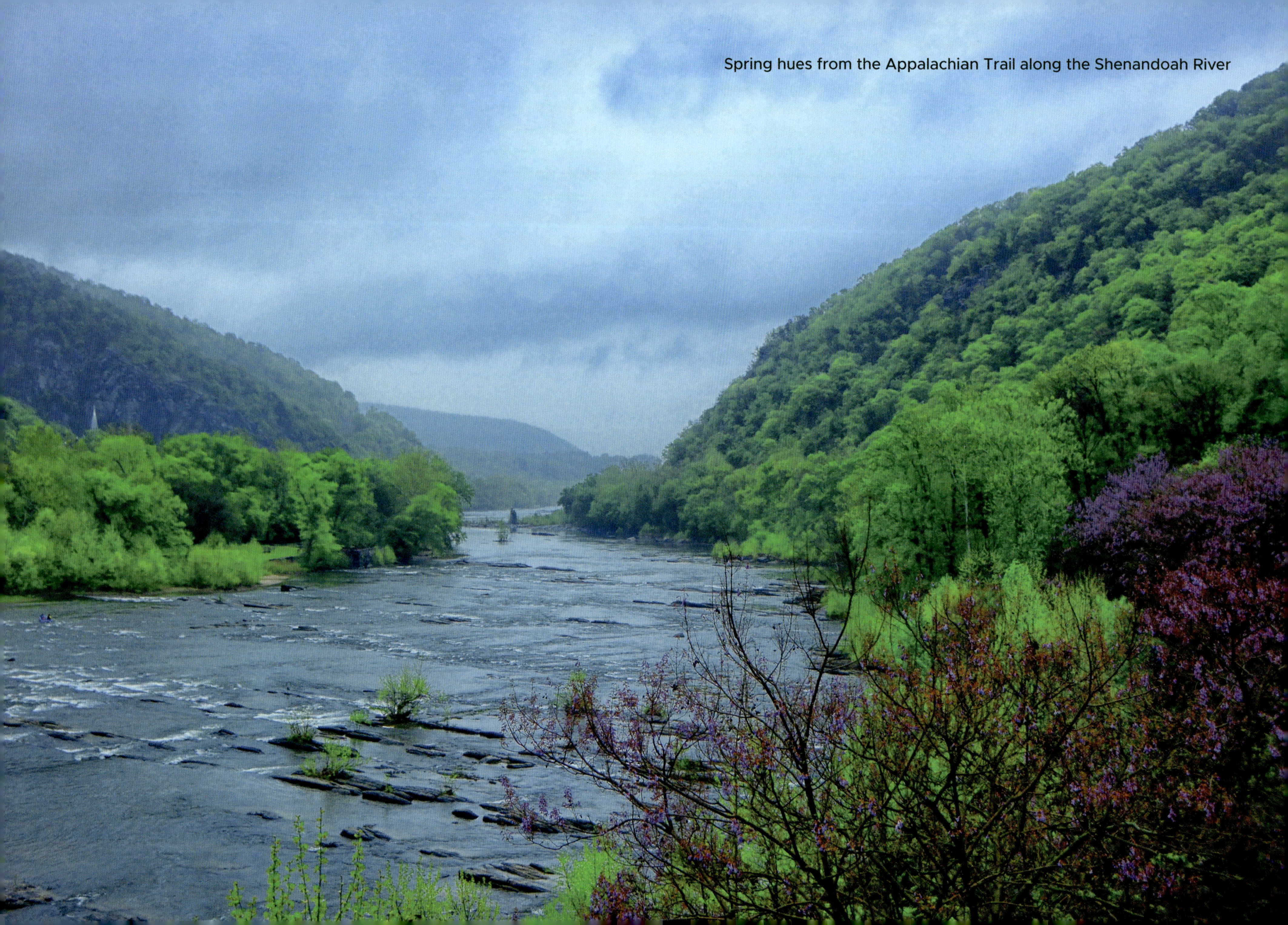
Spring hues from the Appalachian Trail along the Shenandoah River

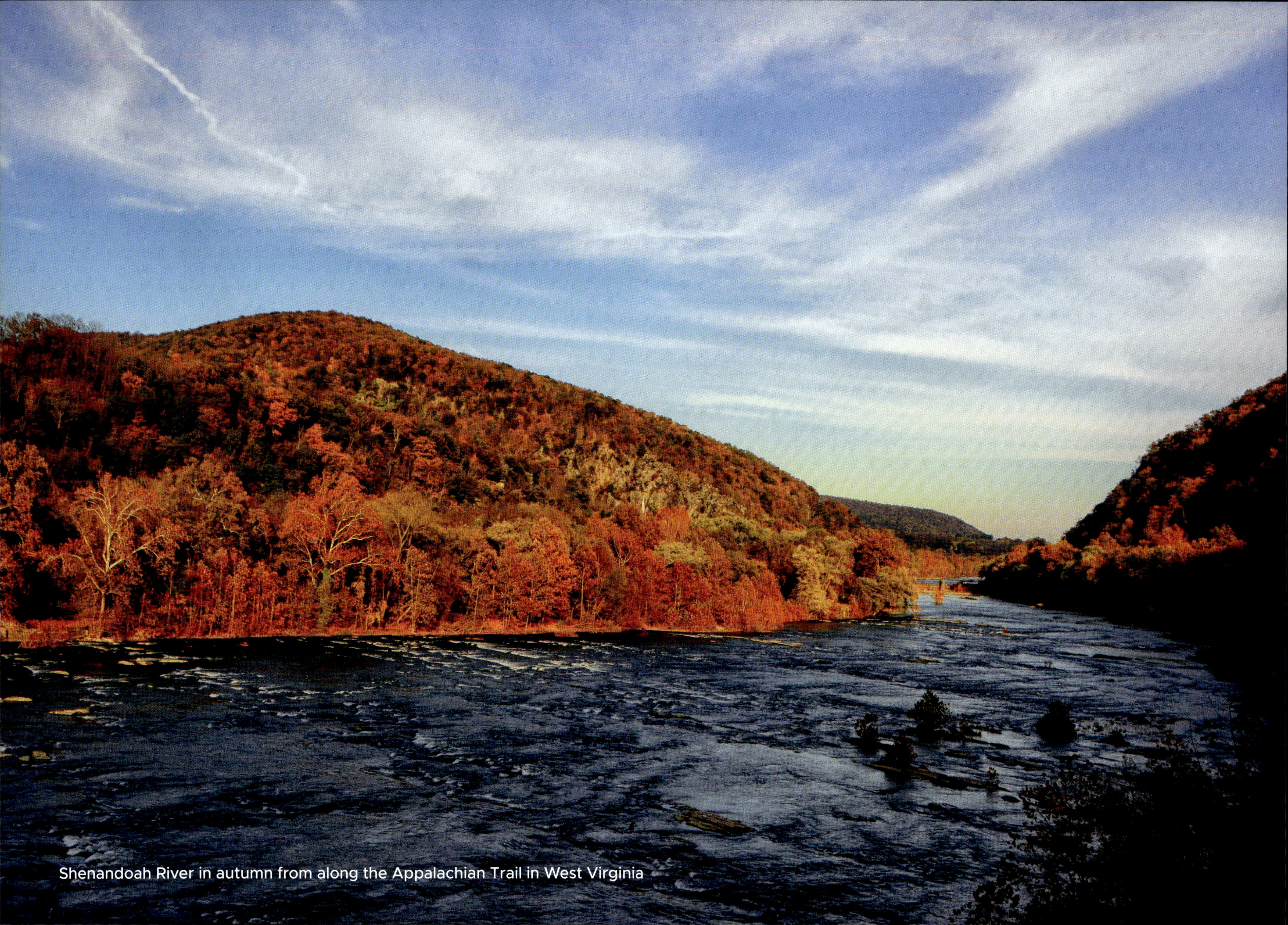

Shenandoah River in autumn from along the Appalachian Trail in West Virginia

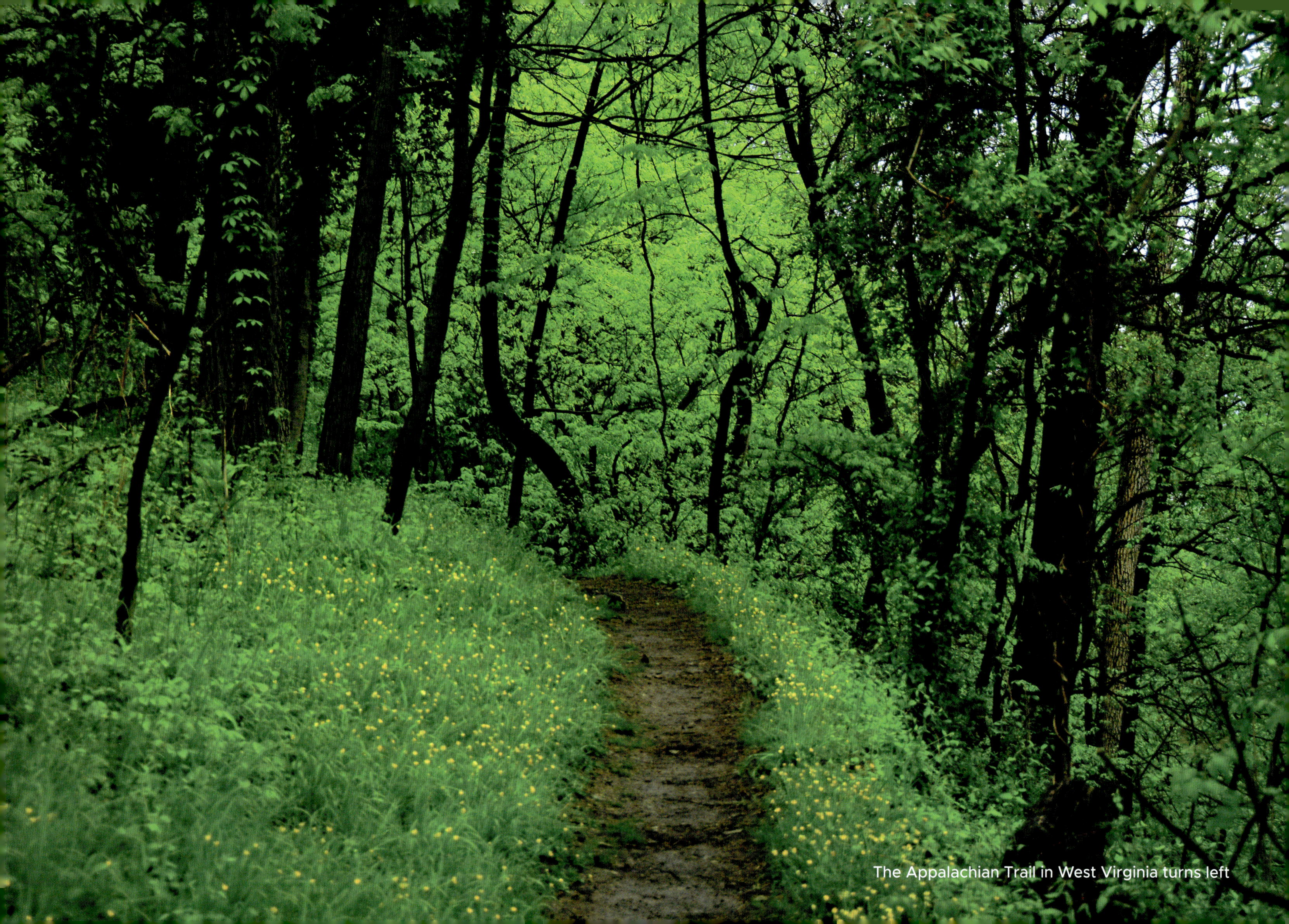

The Appalachian Trail in West Virginia turns left

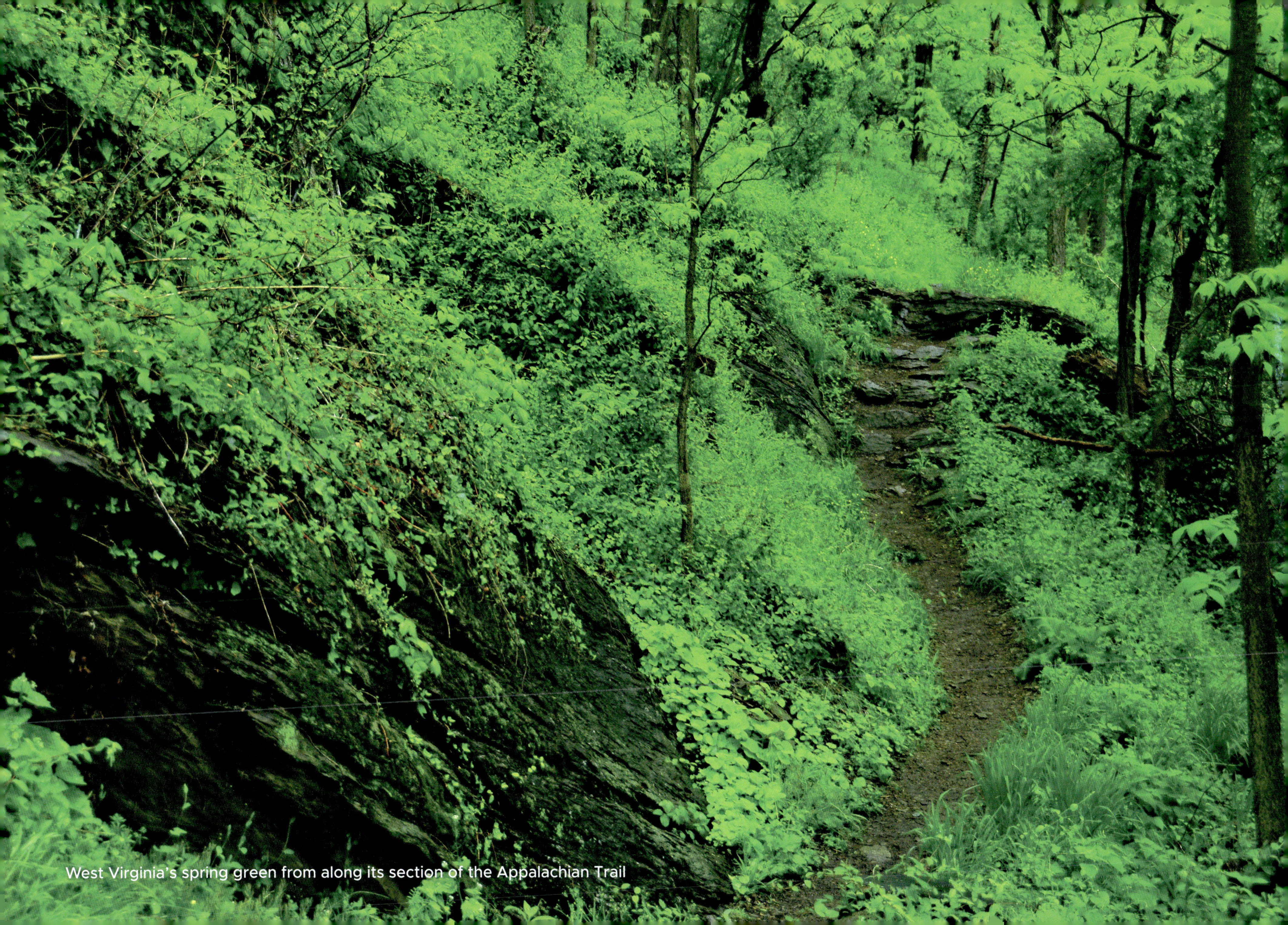

West Virginia's spring green from along its section of the Appalachian Trail

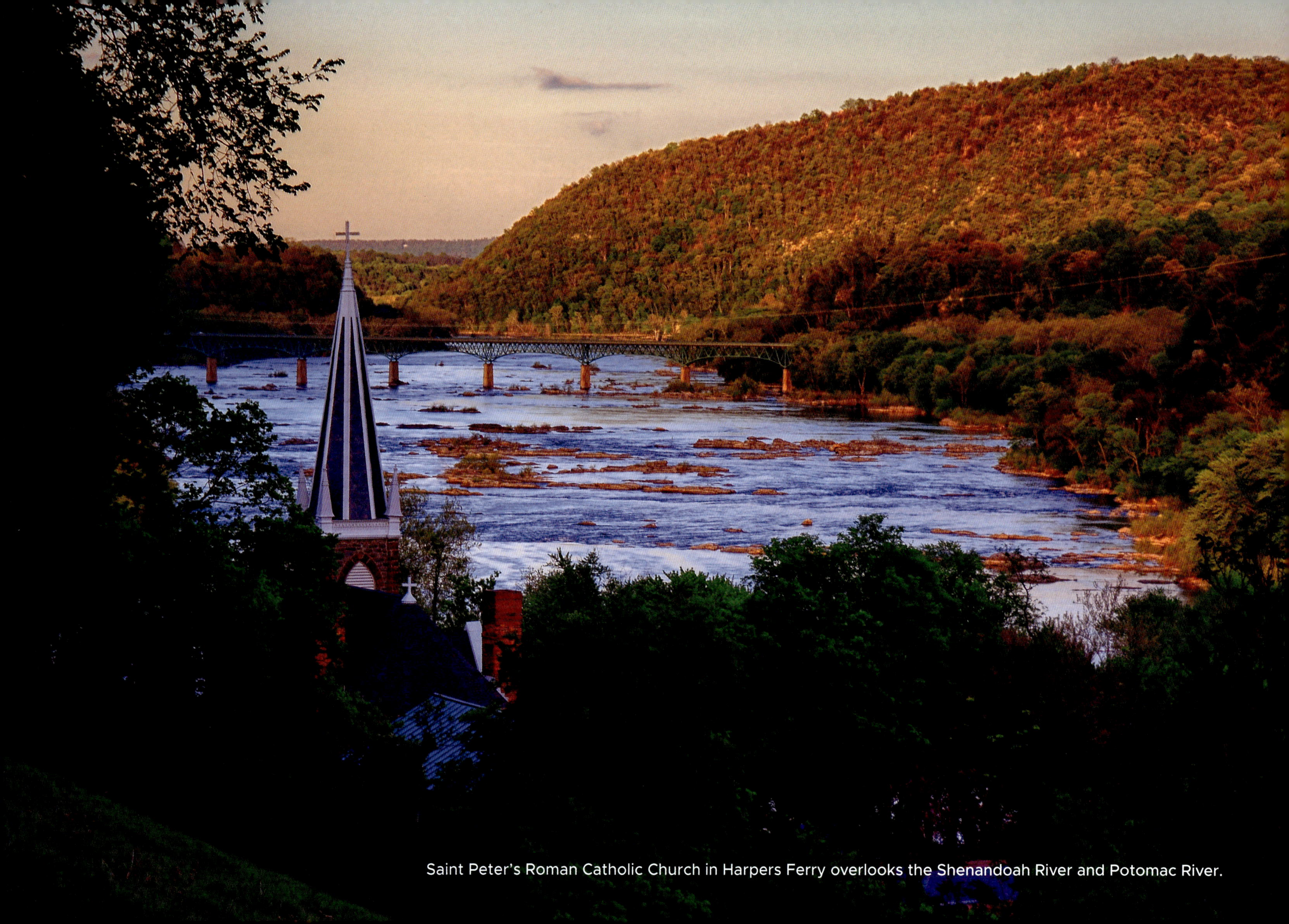

Saint Peter's Roman Catholic Church in Harpers Ferry overlooks the Shenandoah River and Potomac River.

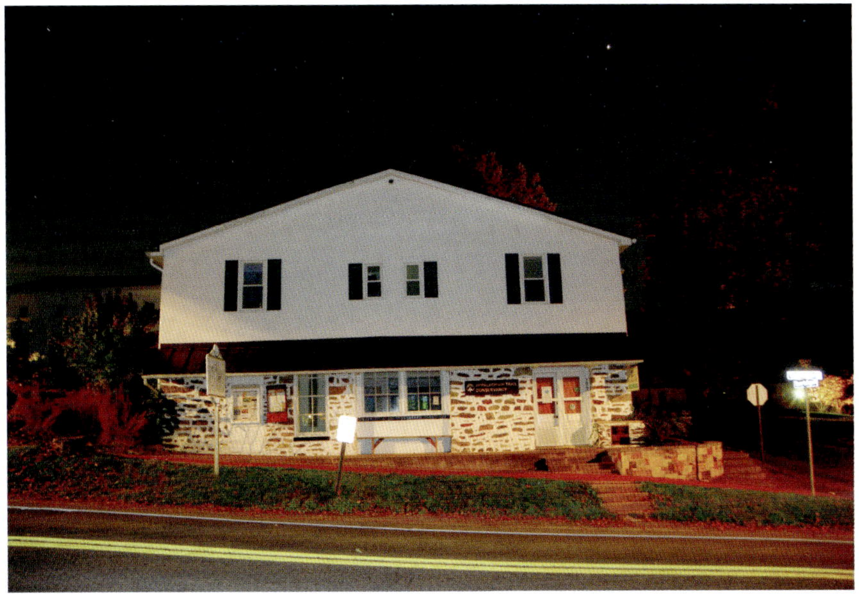

The Appalachian Trail Conservancy under a banner of stars

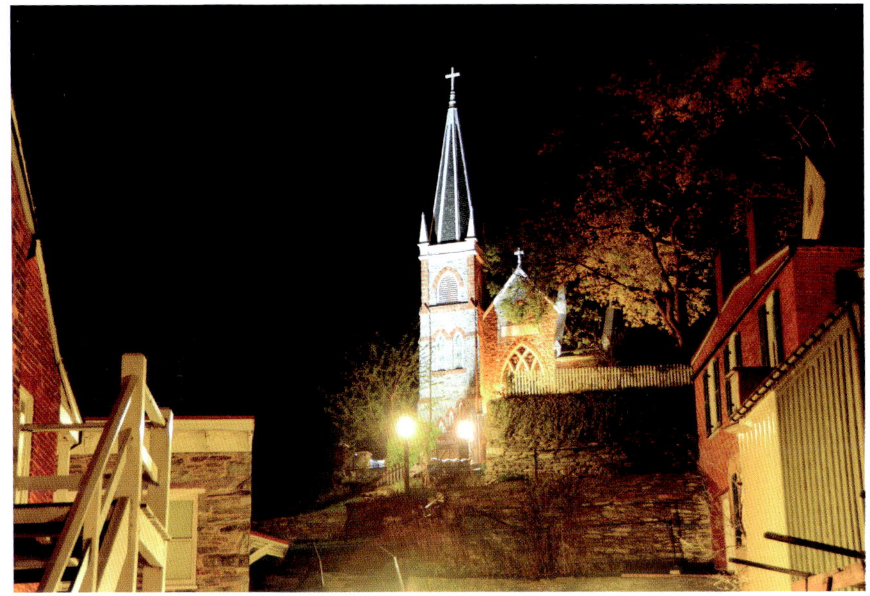

Saint Peter's Church at night from the Appalachian Trail

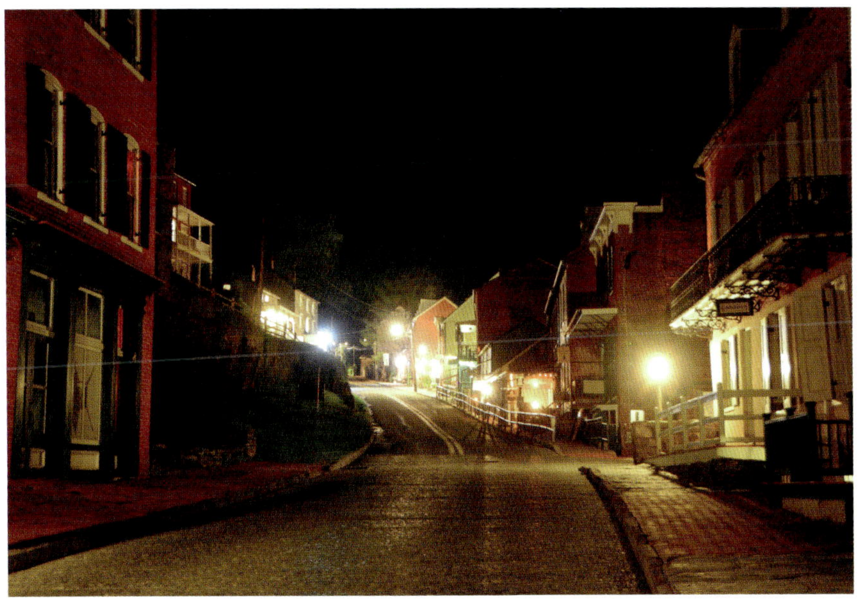

High Street at night from along the Appalachian Trail

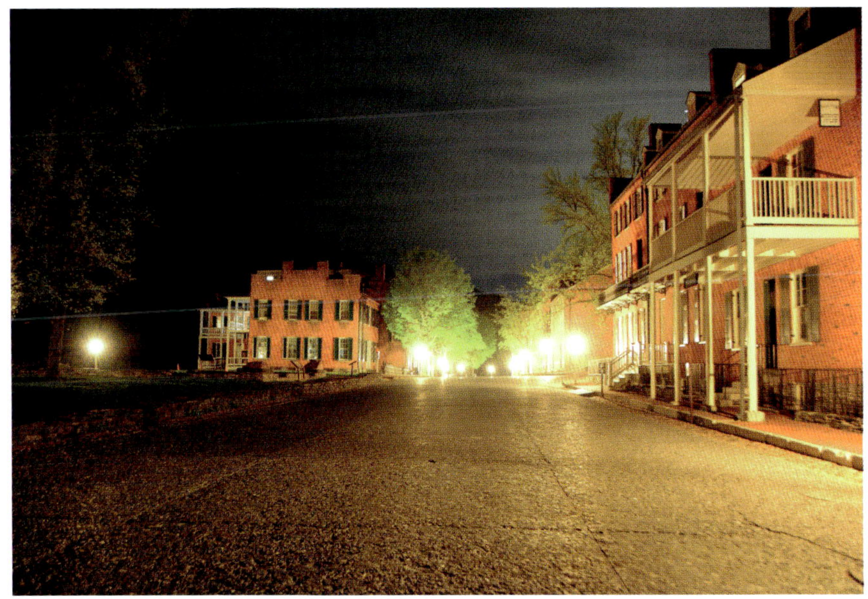

Shenandoah Street at night from the Appalachian Trail

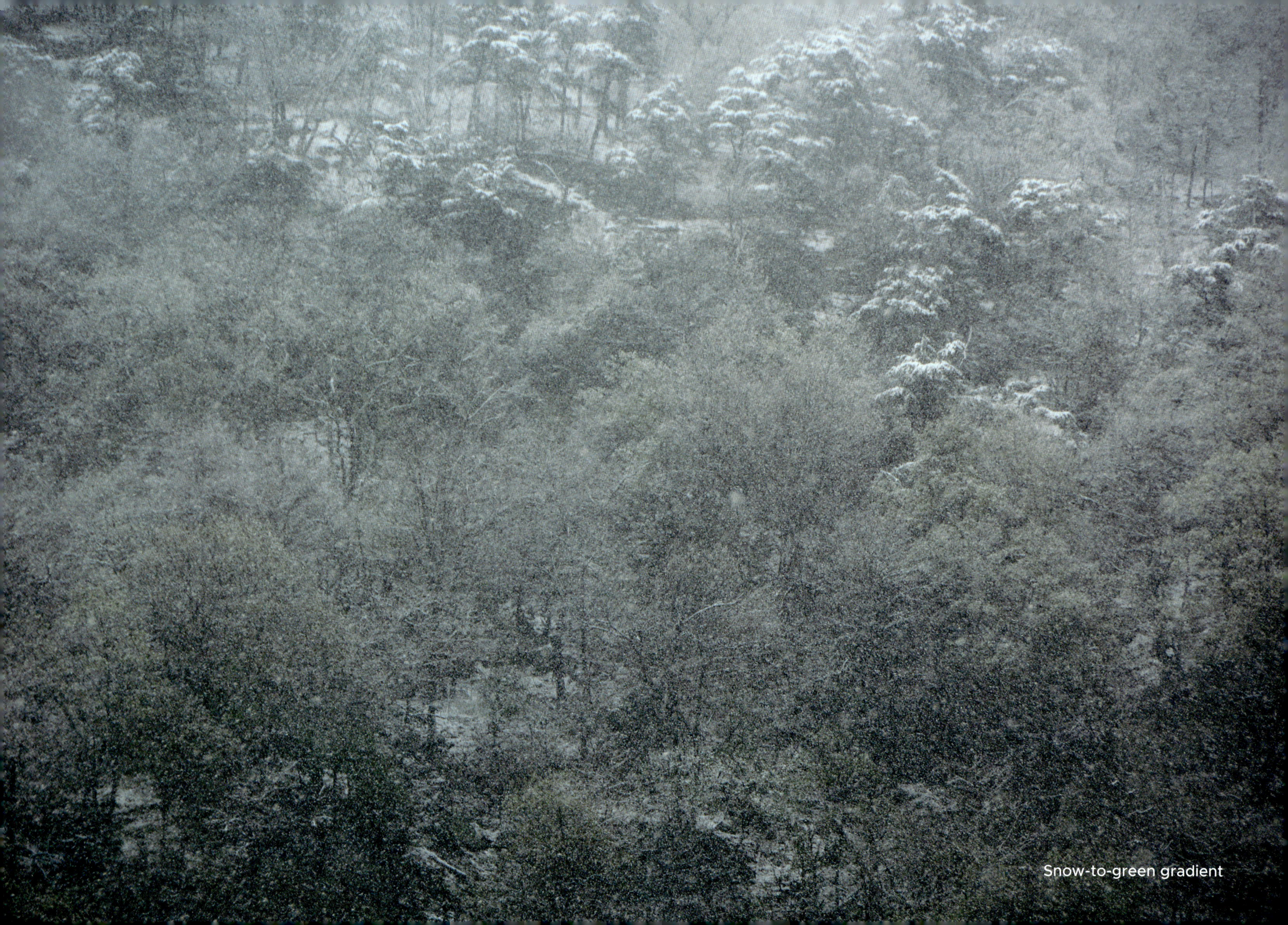

Snow-to-green gradient

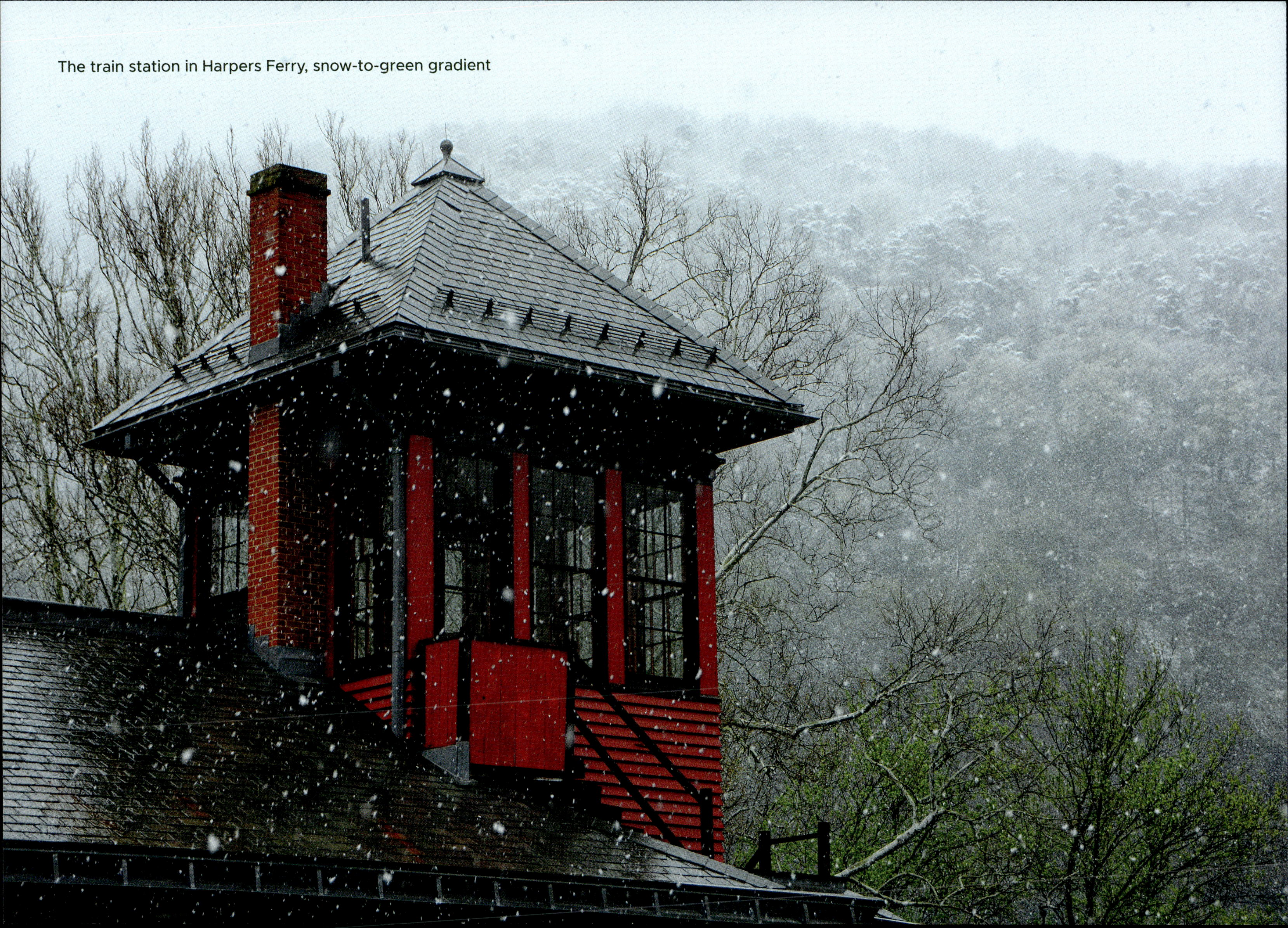

The train station in Harpers Ferry, snow-to-green gradient

GEM HIKE MAP

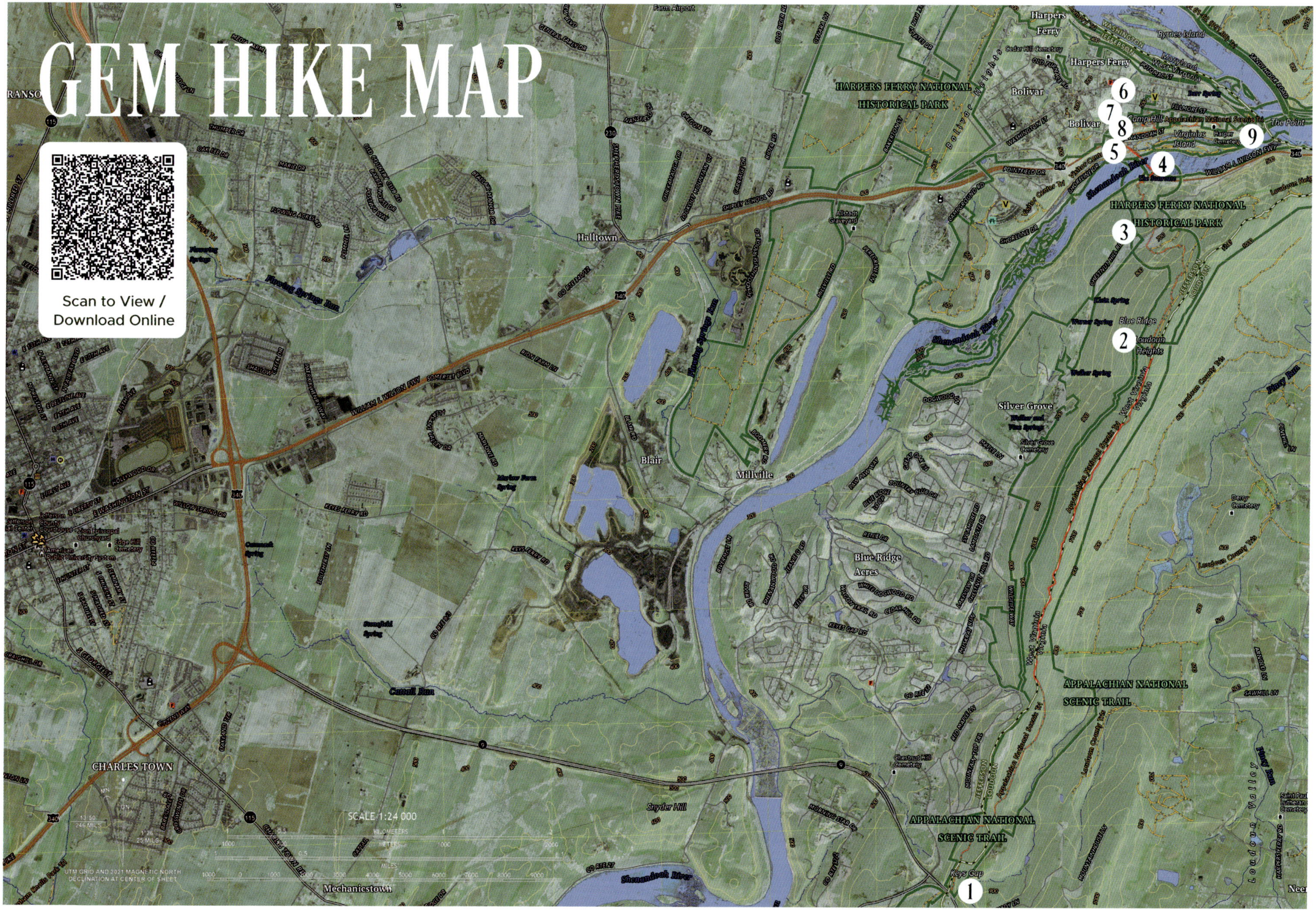
Scan to View / Download Online
Harpers Ferry
Bolivar
HARPERS FERRY NATIONAL HISTORICAL PARK
Halltown
Blair
Millville
Silver Grove
Blue Ridge Acres
Loudoun Heights
APPALACHIAN NATIONAL SCENIC TRAIL
CHARLES TOWN
Mechanicstown
Snyder Hill
Shenandoah River
Flowing Springs Run
Cattail Run
SCALE 1:24 000
1
2
3
4
5
6
7
8
9

DIRECTIONS TO THE TRAILHEAD(S)

Potomac Street Train Station lot: (39.324392, −77.731218)
Keys Gap (39.261350, −77.762557)
The Point (39.323094, −77.728828)
The southernmost trailhead is off West Virginia Route 9. It is called Keys Gap, West Virginia (39.261350, −77.762557). The northernmost point of this hike is the Point in Harpers Ferry Historical Park (39.322938, −77.728551). The Point is the spot where the Shenandoah River converges into the Potomac River. For the trailhead, it is best to park at the train station on Potomac St., but the lot fills up early, and parking must be paid for.
Driving directions for this hike would be the following:
From the Appalachian Trail Conservancy at 799 Washington St., Harpers Ferry, WV 25425

1. Head east on Washington St. toward McDowell St.
2. In 0.4 mile, continue onto High St.
3. In 0.2 mile, turn left onto Hog Alley
4. In 131 feet, turn left onto Potomac St.
5. In 331 feet, turn right for 115 feet
6. The Harpers Ferry Station, at Potomac St. and Shenandoah St., Harpers Ferry, WV 25425, will be on the right (drop a car at this end if you want a point-to-point hike, and continue to step 7 to continue to Keys Gap, West Virginia
7. Head southeast on High St. toward Hog Alley for 0.1 mile
8. High St. turns right and becomes Shenandoah St.
9. In 0.8 mile, turn left onto US 340 N / William L. Wilson Freeway
10. In 0.8 mile, make a sharp right onto Chestnut Hill Rd.
11. Travel 4.3 miles and turn left to stay on Chestnut Hill Rd.
12. In 0.8 mile, turn left onto WV 9 E, and Keys Gap Trailhead, your destination, will be on the left

GEM HIKE DIRECTIONS

1. Leave Keys Gap on the Appalachian Trail, going north on the AT
2. Continue 4 miles and continue past Loudoun Heights Trail
3. At 4.5 miles, cross WV 32
4. At 5.5 miles, reach US 340 and cross the Shenandoah River (via the right side of the roadway)
5. At 6.2 miles, reach the Appalachian Trail Conservancy Headquarters Trail on the left
6. At 6.4 miles, you reach the ATC Headquarters
7. At 6.6 miles, you reach the AT again
8. Turn left to continue the AT north
9. At 7 miles, arrive at the Point in Harpers Ferry Historical Park, West Virginia

MORE/LESS AMBITIOUS HIKERS

Ambitious hikers might wish to start the hike at Snickers Gap, Virginia. This will make for roughly a 20-mile hike. Also, hikers may wish to add chapter 5's hike to Weverton Cliffs.

CHAPTER 5

THE APPALACHIAN TRAIL: THE POINT IN HARPERS FERRY HISTORICAL PARK, WEST VIRGINIA, TO WEVERTON CLIFFS, MARYLAND

AREA MAP

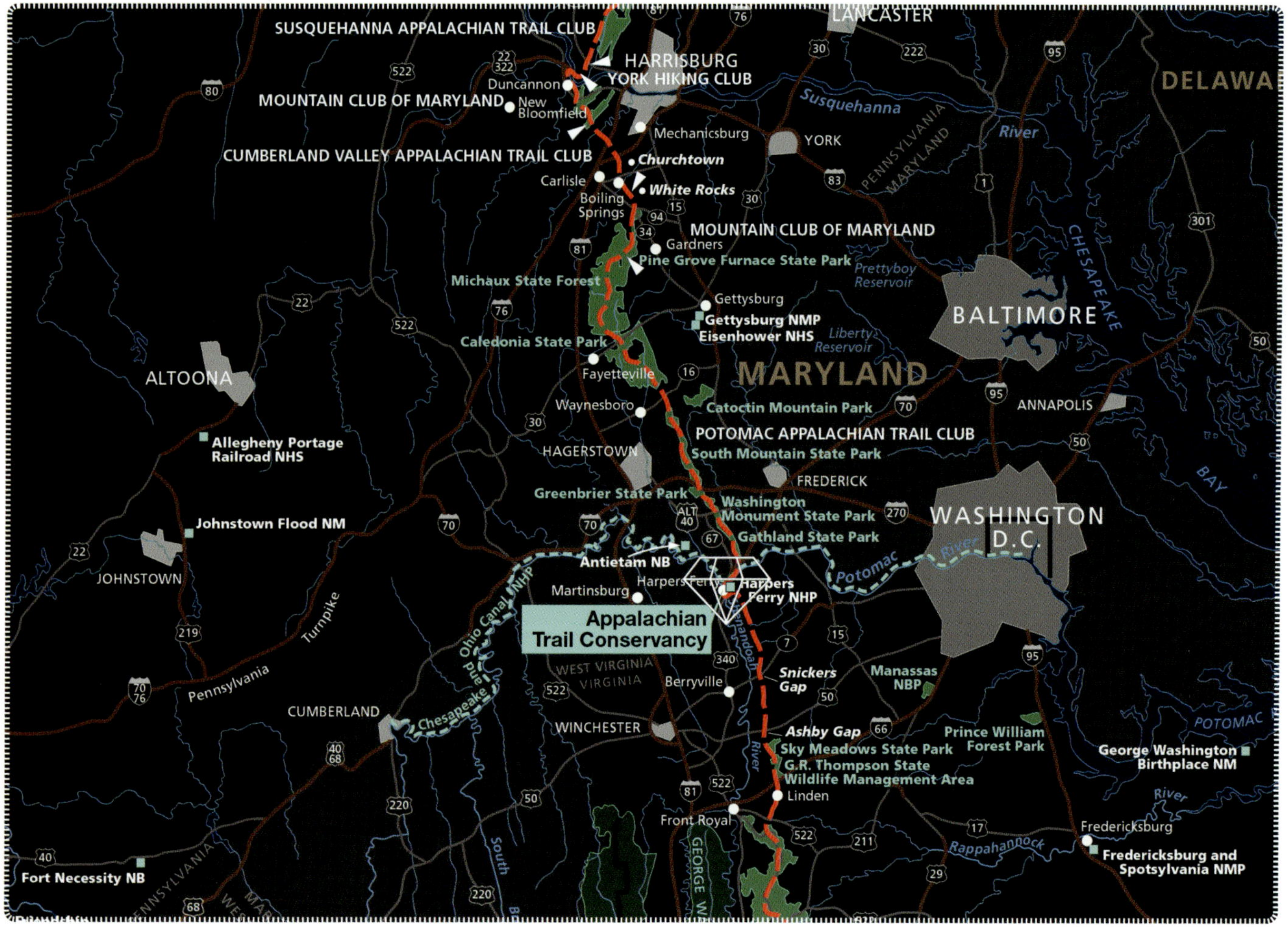

DISTANCE	8.5 miles
ELEVATION GAIN	700 feet
ELEVATION LOSS	700 feet
LEVEL	Easy

TYPE: OUT-AND-BACK

0 10 Kilometers 50

0 10 Miles 50

Appalachian National Scenic Trail

Boundary of CLUB management section

North

GEM HIKE

PERSONAL TOUCH

I remember standing in the darkness on an autumn morning in early November. I was half frozen from getting my camera gear ready in the mist and waiting for sunrise. I was also sweating with excitement. I knew once the sun was ready to wake up that morning, it was going to be something special at the Point. After what seemed like an eternity of waiting, the sun rose. This mist started to line up with the sun exactly where I planned it be. It gave me what I was looking for in less than a minute. I fired a shot, quickly adjusted the camera to the next setting, and got the next round of photographs, including some scenes captured in this chapter. After a couple of minutes, the sun was covered by a passing cloud. Job well done—now time for a trail breakfast and to resume my hike.

The wildlife here will not disappoint you. I always enjoyed the wildlife in this section. The turtles and blue herons were amazing.

BRIEF OVERVIEW

This section of the Appalachian Trail starts at the Point in Harpers Ferry Historical Park, West Virginia, crosses the Potomac River into Maryland, travels along the Potomac River on the same corridor as the Chesapeake and Ohio Canal Towpath until the Appalachian Trail splits off at Lock 31, and heads uphill to Weverton Cliffs, which provide panoramic views of the Potomac River and the surrounding landscape, while the Chesapeake and Ohio Canal continues to Washington, DC.

DESCRIPTION OF THE GEM HIKE

The section of the Appalachian Trail from the Point (39.322938, −77.728550) in Harpers Ferry Historical Park, West Virginia, to Weverton Cliffs, Maryland, is a gem hike that comes in at roughly 4.5 miles if hiked one direction (9 miles total). For this hike, I recommend you start at the Point in Harpers Ferry in West Virginia and head north on the Appalachian Trail until you reach Weverton Cliffs, then returning the same way you came.

FLORA, FAUNA, AND VEGETATION

This section is known to have a very diverse collection of trees. These trees include oaks, shagbark hickories, maples, American beech, tulips, and dogwoods. Red maples and dogwoods create a special treat in the fall. The dogwoods also produce a lovely springtime flower that is either white or pink.

HARPERS FERRY TOWN AND HISTORICAL PARK

Harpers Ferry, West Virginia, located at the confluence of the Potomac and Shenandoah Rivers, is a historic town with significant cultural and historical value. The town is home to the Harpers Ferry National Historical Park, which preserves the area's rich history. The park features preserved nineteenth-century buildings, museums, and exhibits that illustrate the town's historical significance. The town of Harpers Ferry was the site of John Brown's raid in 1859, an event that heightened tensions leading up to the Civil War. During the war, Harpers Ferry changed hands multiple times between Union and Confederate forces due to its strategic location and armory. There are ghost tours held at the Saint Peter's Church.

THE POINT

The Point in Harpers Ferry, West Virginia, is where the Shenandoah River converges with the Potomac River. It is a gorgeous spot to be. It is super special in the fall, when the river is warmer than the air and thus mist is visible above the rivers. An added excellence is to be here at sunrise.

CHESAPEAKE AND OHIO CANAL

The Chesapeake and Ohio Canal, used for transporting goods during the 19th century, offers a scenic and historic route for hikers as well as cyclists. The towpath provides a different style of miles of The Appalachian Trail because it is flat and wide. This area is filled with fantastic water-to-hills views and lots of wildlife. From Lock 31 you have a view looking up Weverton Cliffs.

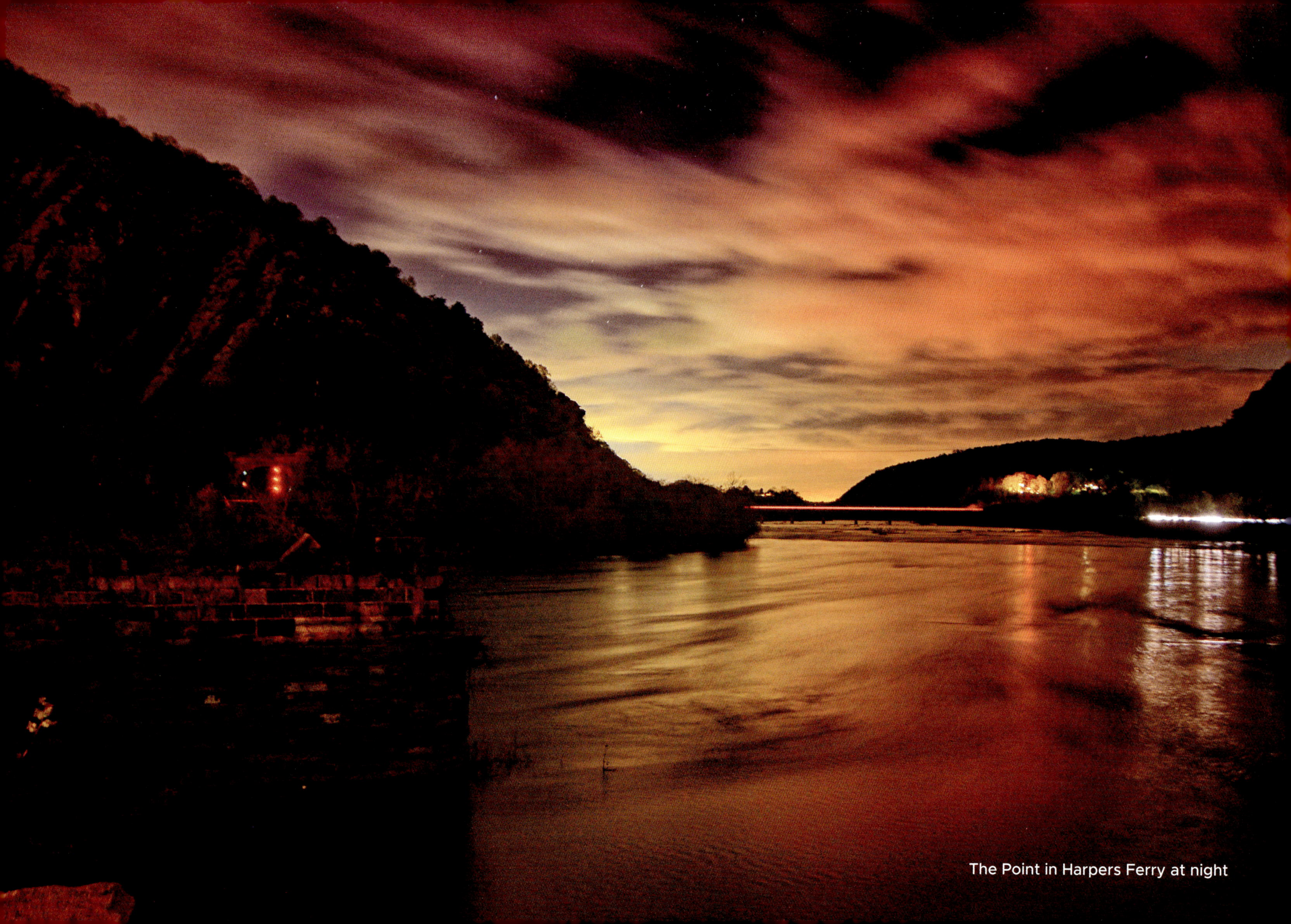

The Point in Harpers Ferry at night

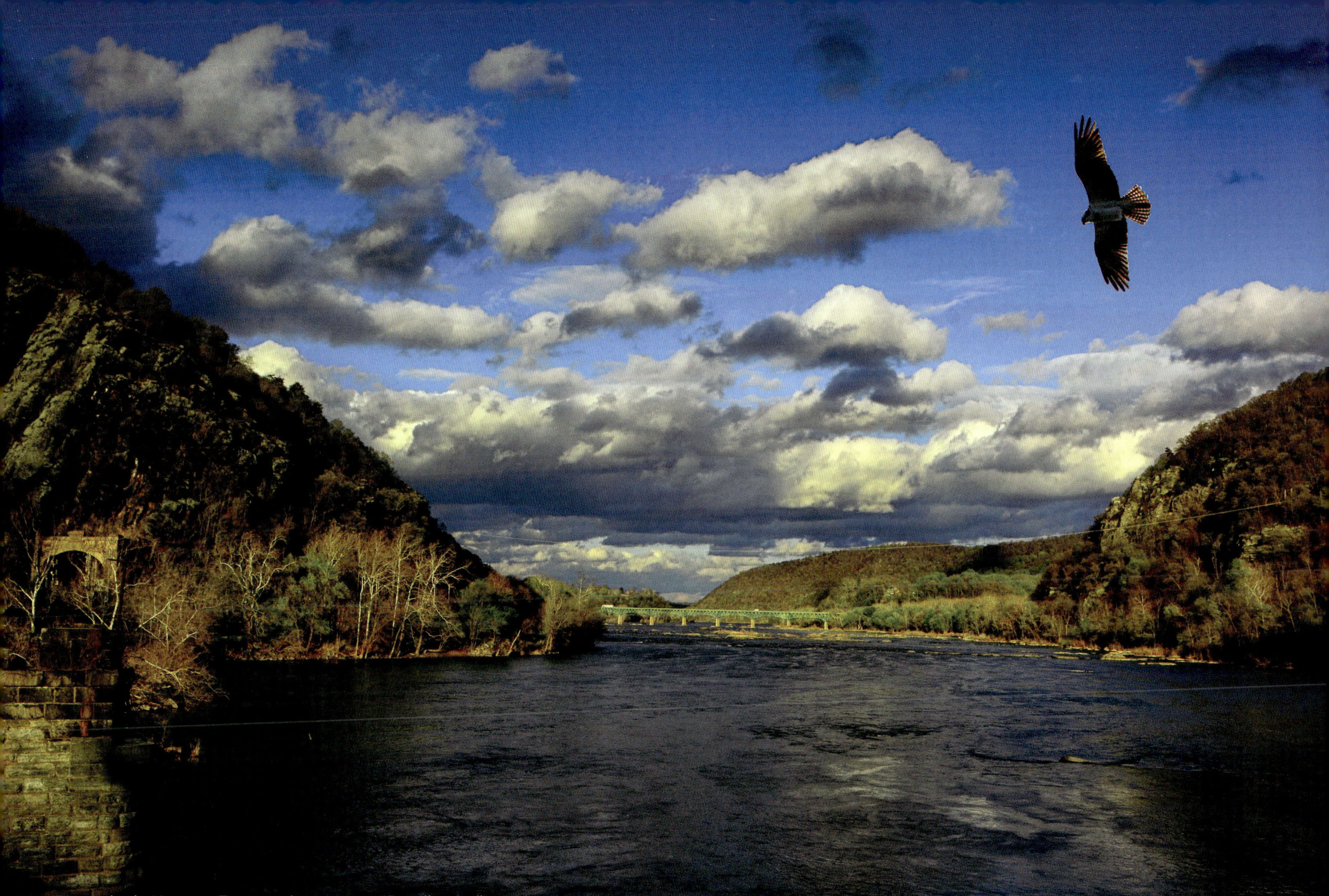

The Point in Harpers Ferry and an osprey (*Pandion haliaetus*).

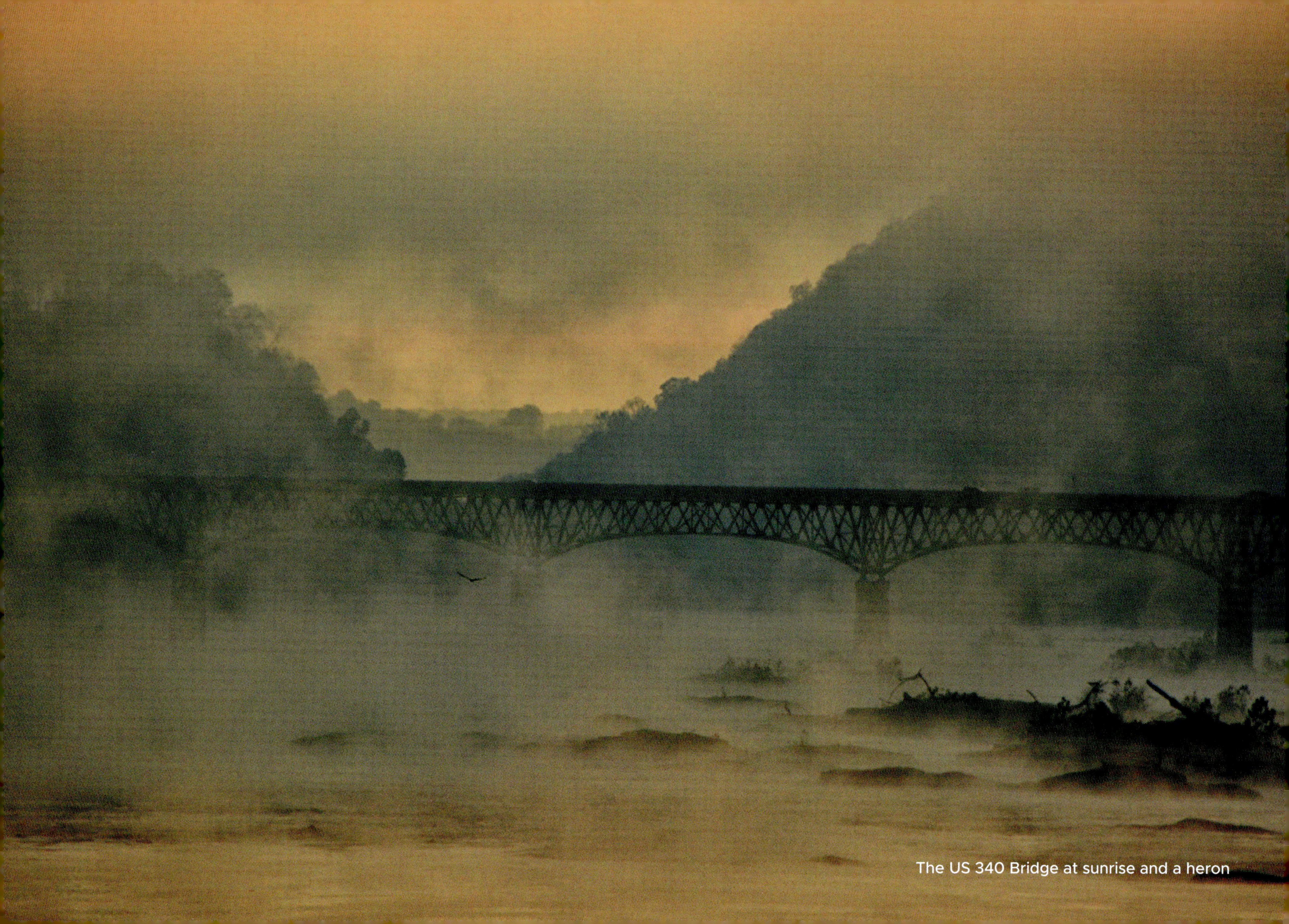

The US 340 Bridge at sunrise and a heron

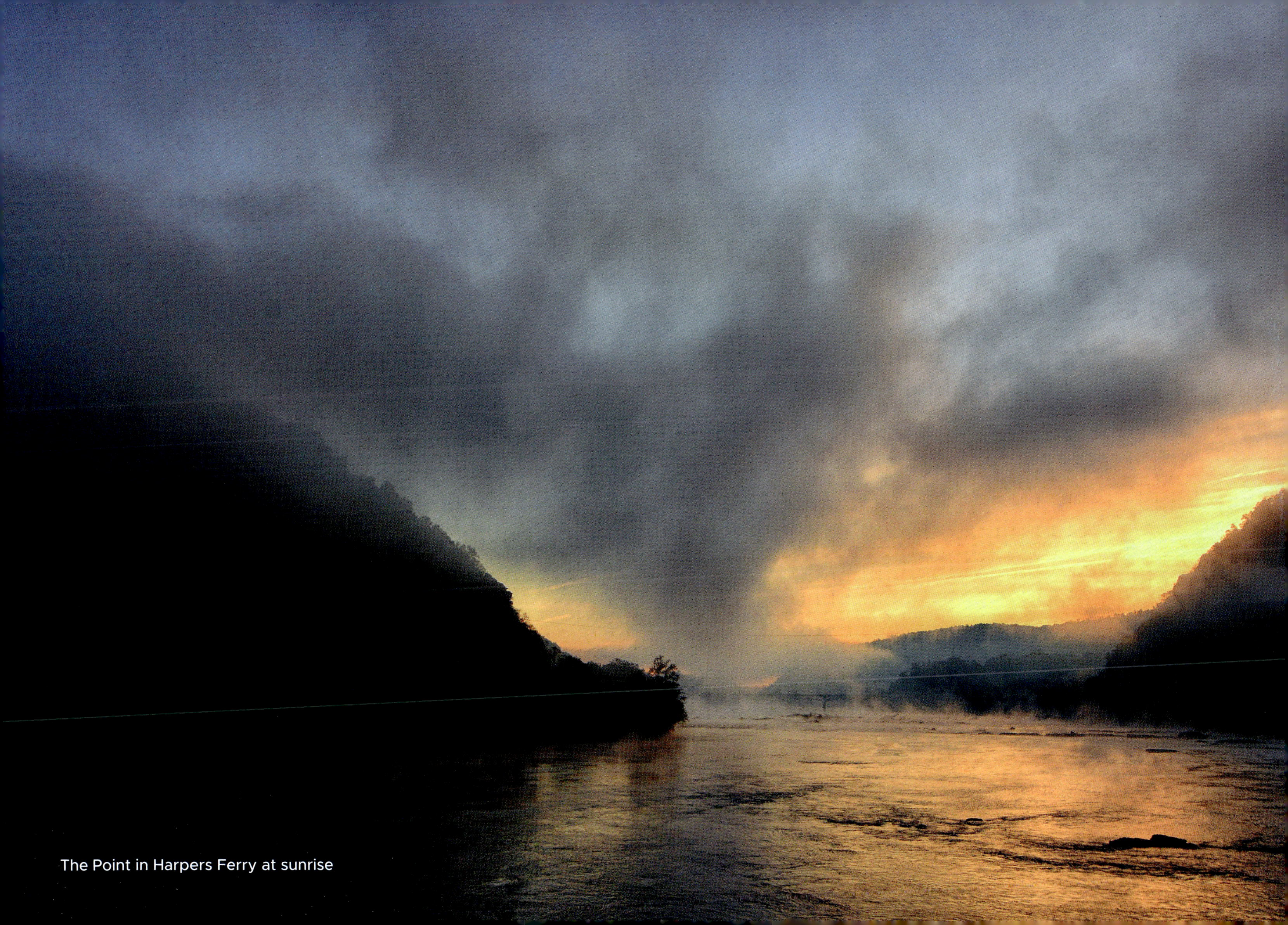

The Point in Harpers Ferry at sunrise

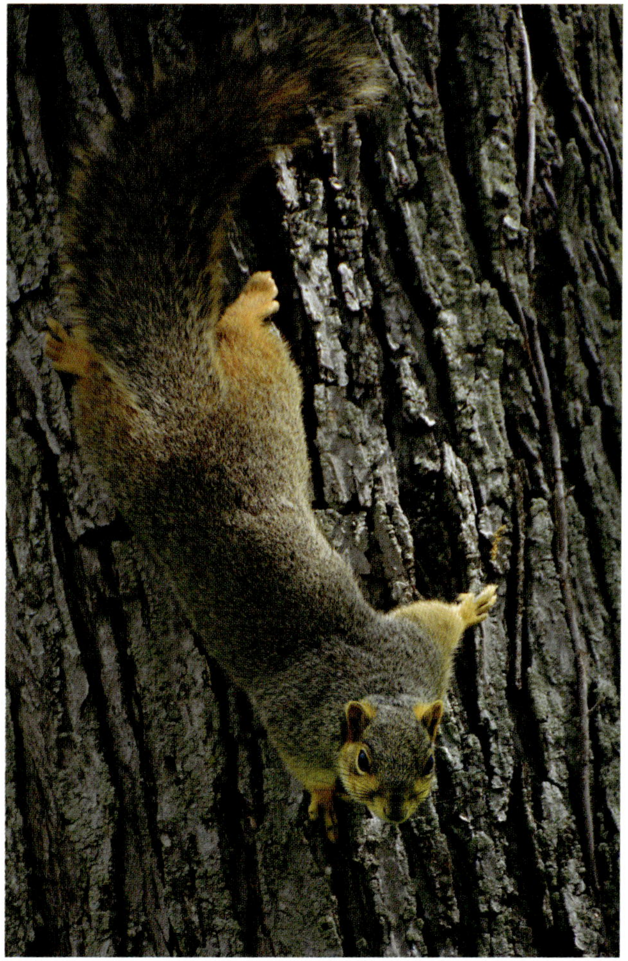

A fox squirrel (*Sciurus niger*)

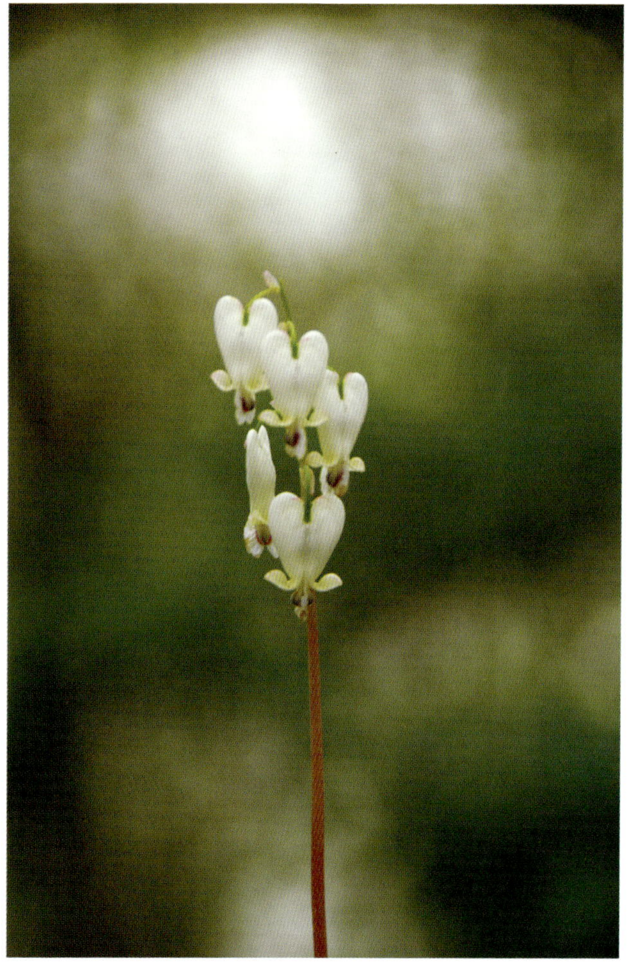

Bleeding hearts (*Lamprocapnos spectabilis*)

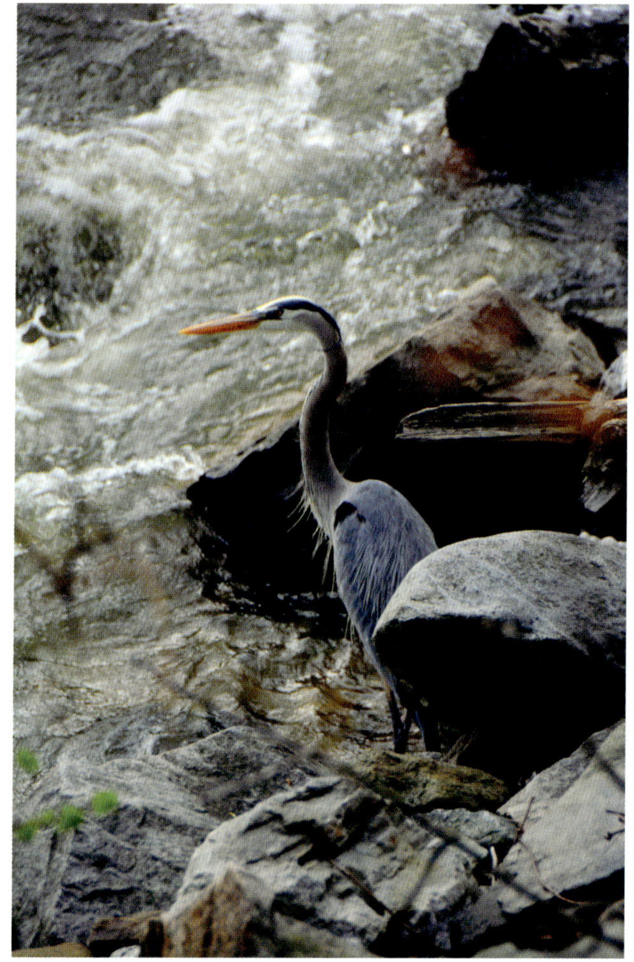

The great blue heron (*Ardea herodias*)

The Canada goose (*Branta canadensis*)

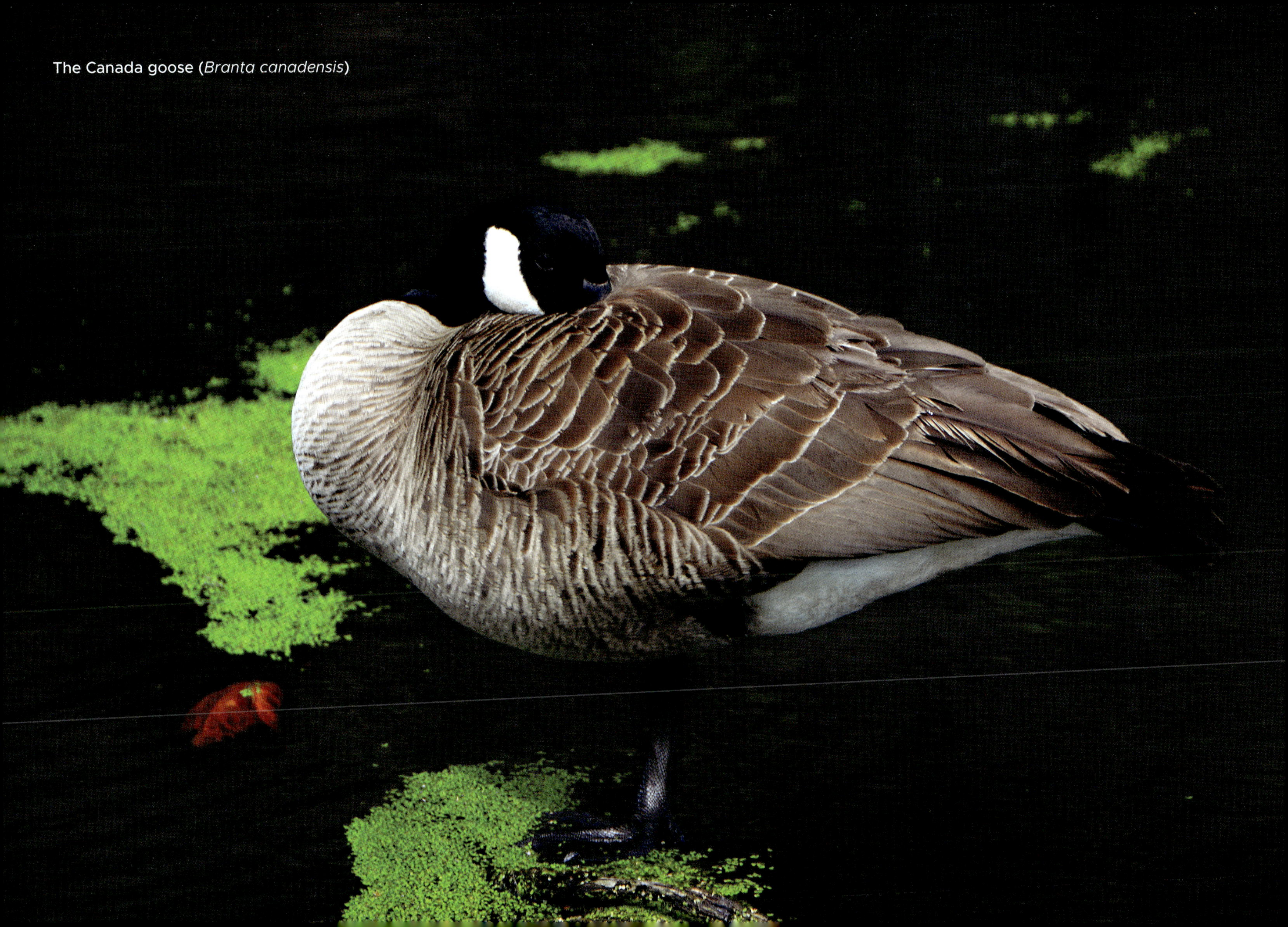

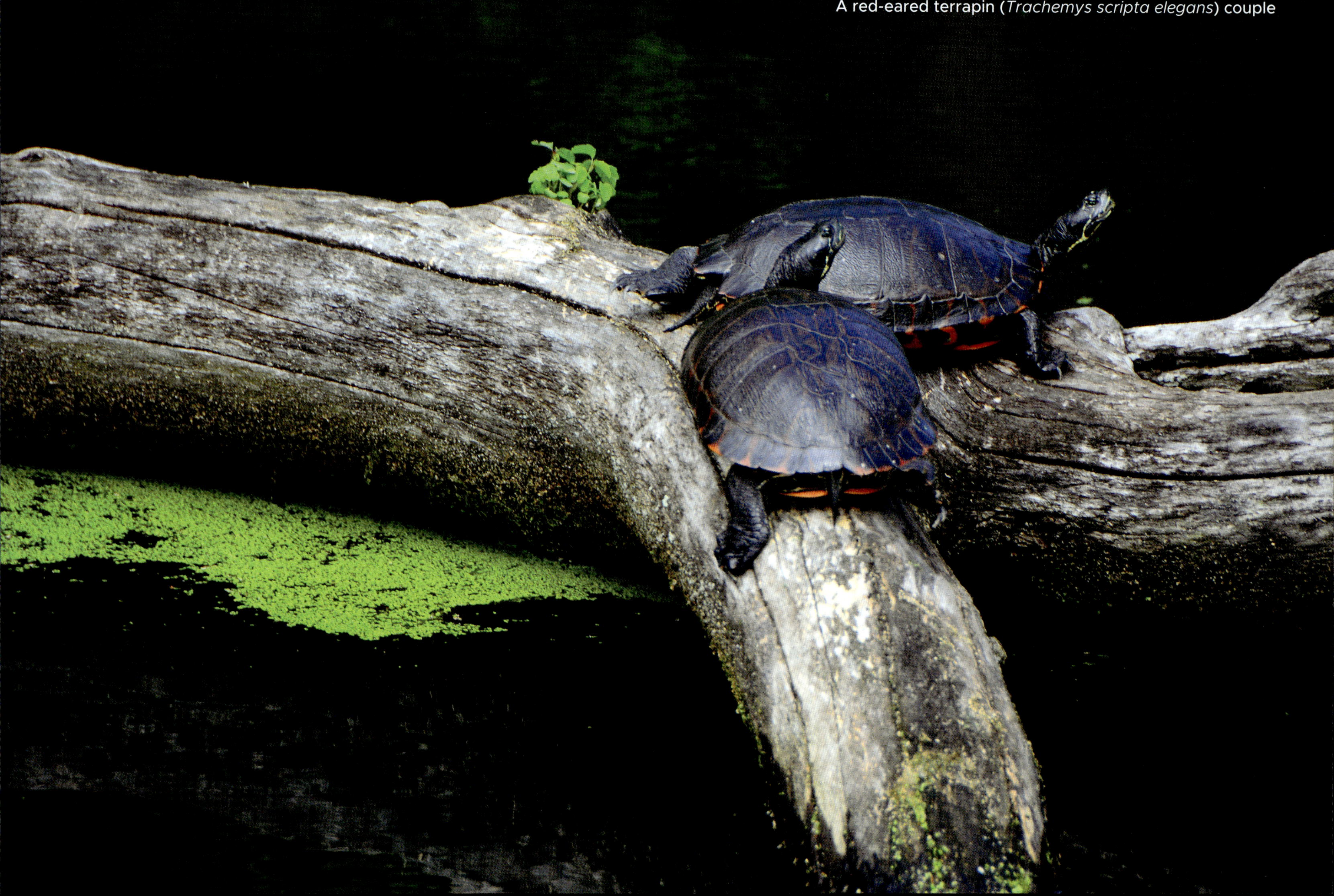

A red-eared terrapin (*Trachemys scripta elegans*) couple

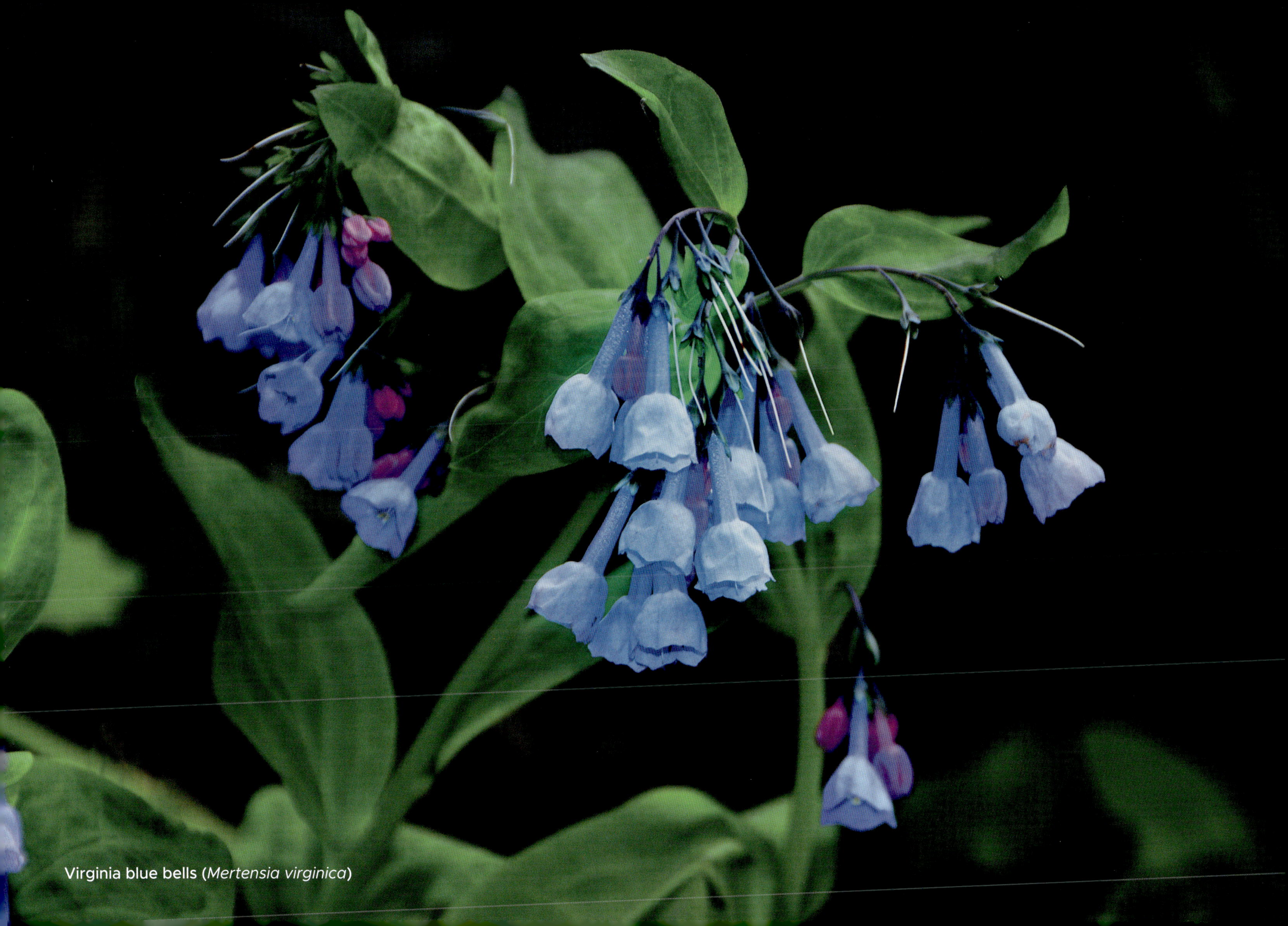

Virginia blue bells (*Mertensia virginica*)

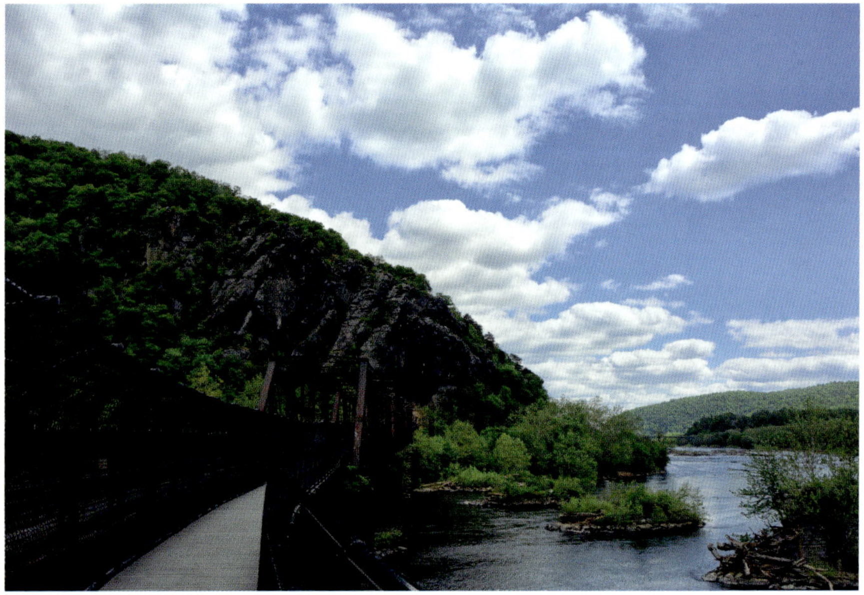

The Appalachian Trail crosses the Potomac River into Maryland.

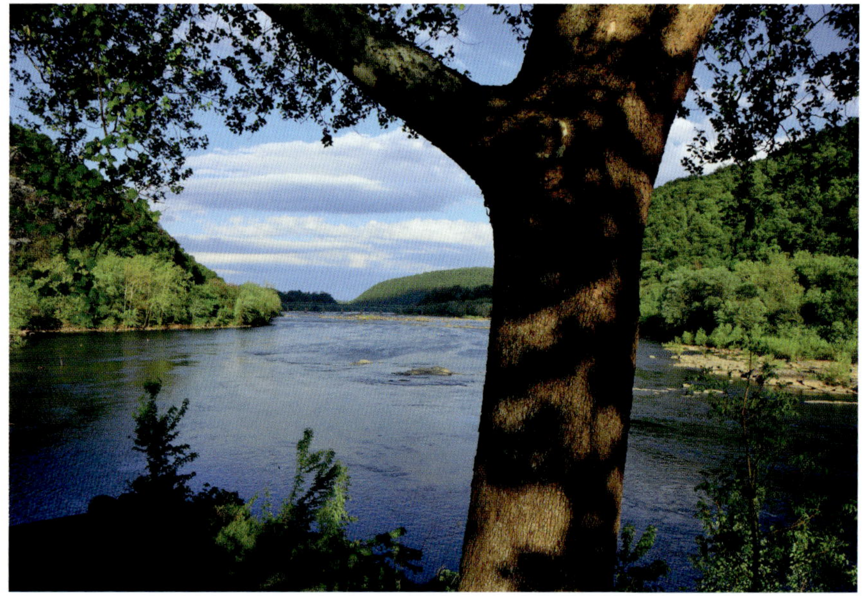

An American sycamore (*Platanus occidentalis*) and the Point

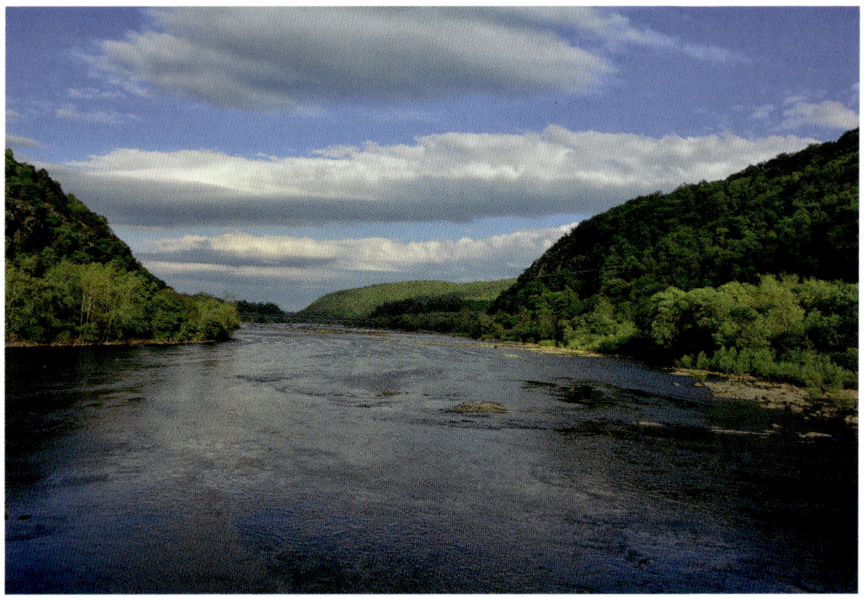

The Potomac River

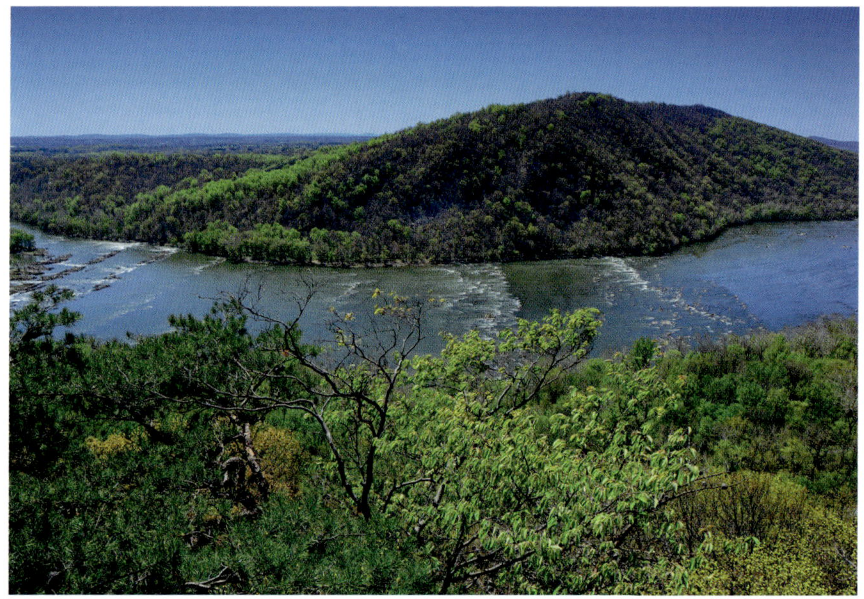

Potomac River from Weverton Cliffs, Maryland, viewpoint

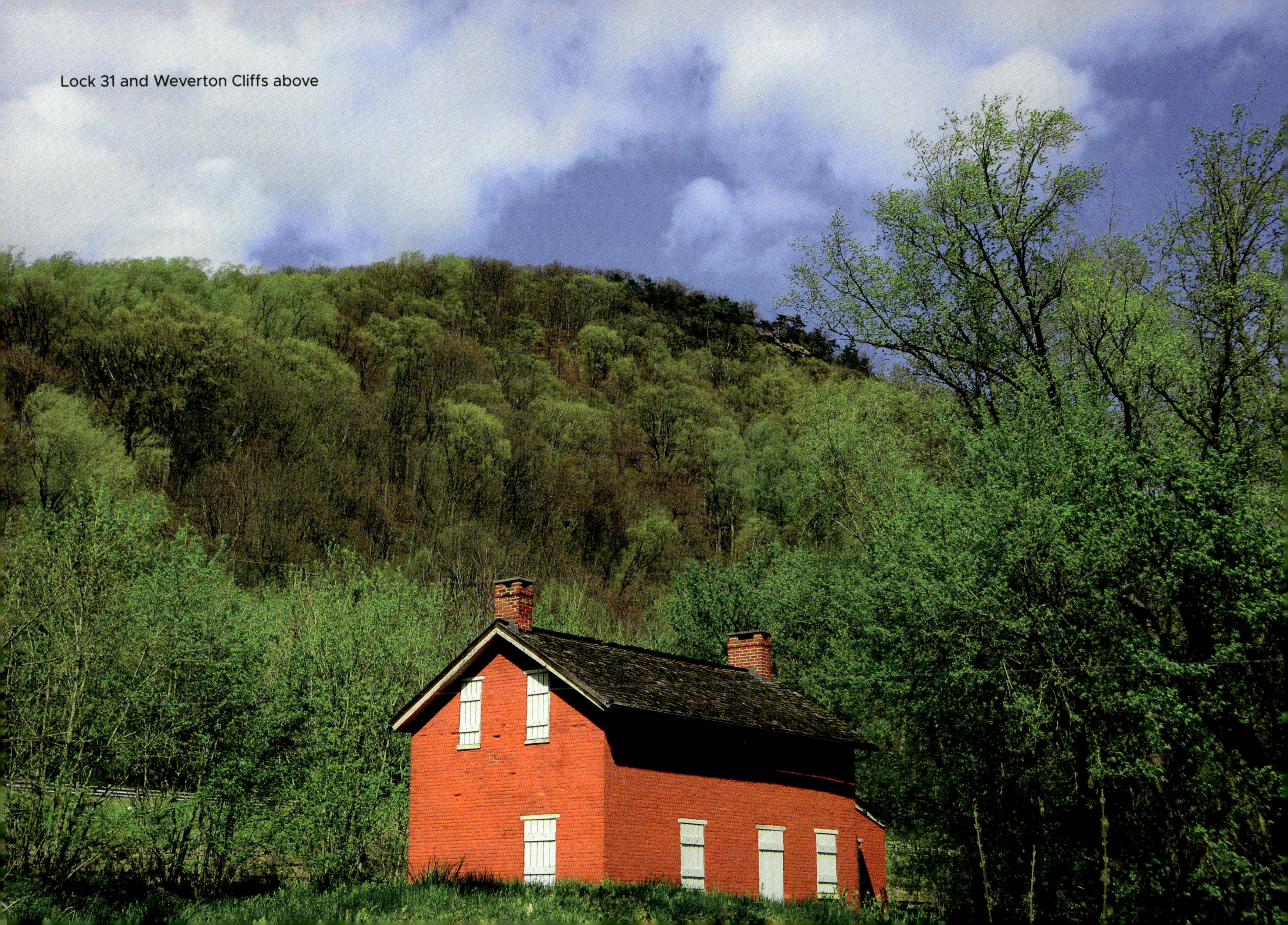

Lock 31 and Weverton Cliffs above

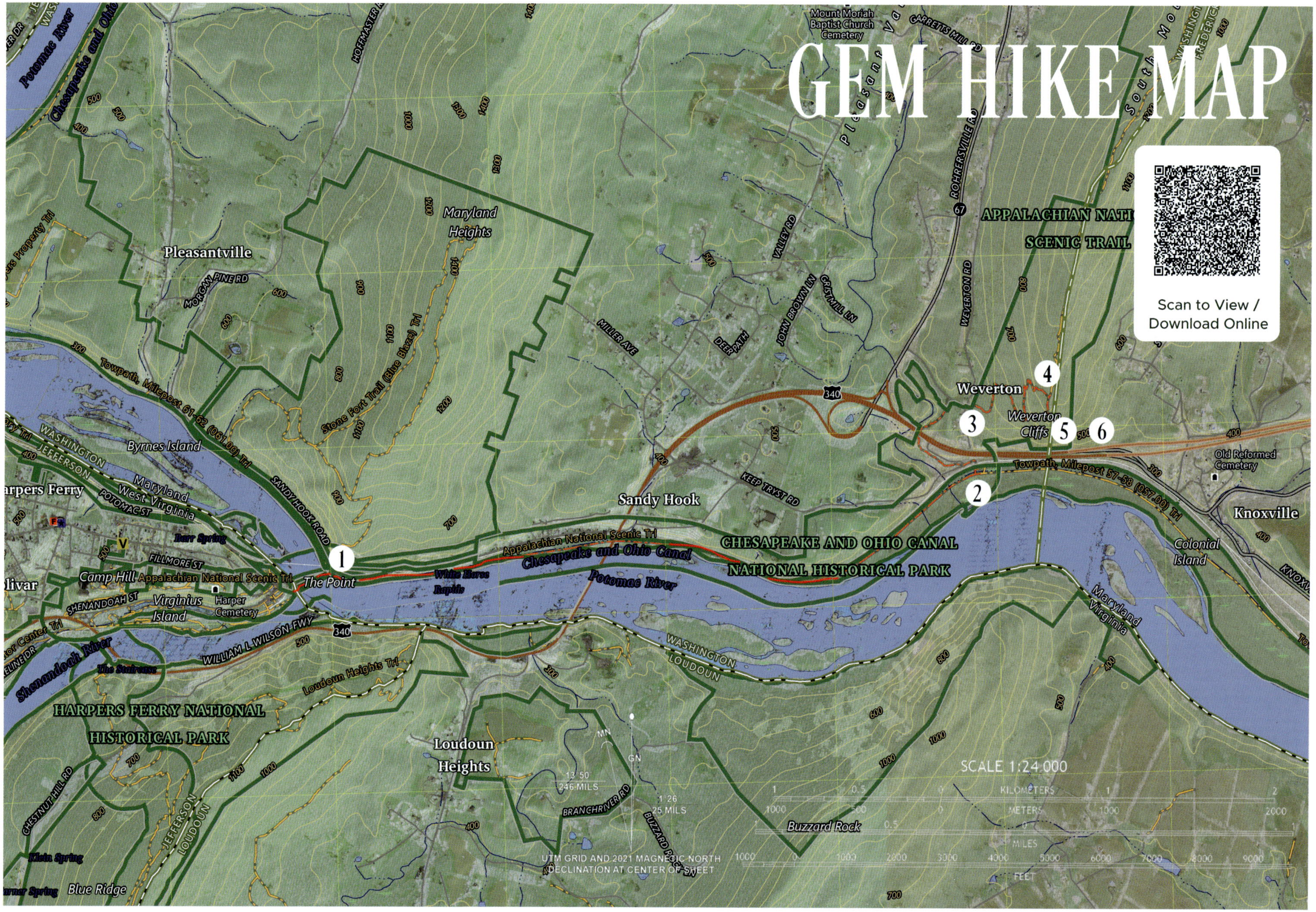
GEM HIKE MAP
Scan to View / Download Online
Pleasantville
Maryland Heights
Stone Fort Trail (Blue Blaze) Trl
Towpath, Milepost 61-62 (061.00) Trl
Byrnes Island
Maryland
West Virginia
Harpers Ferry
Camp Hill
Appalachian National Scenic Trl
The Point
Virginius Island
Harper Cemetery
Shenandoah River
HARPERS FERRY NATIONAL HISTORICAL PARK
Loudoun Heights Trl
Loudoun Heights
Sandy Hook
SANDY HOOK ROAD
Chesapeake and Ohio Canal
Potomac River
CHESAPEAKE AND OHIO CANAL NATIONAL HISTORICAL PARK
Weverton
Weverton Cliffs
Towpath, Milepost 57-58 (057.00) Trl
APPALACHIAN NATIONAL SCENIC TRAIL
Old Reformed Cemetery
Knoxville
Colonial Island
Maryland
Virginia
WASHINGTON
LOUDOUN
Mount Moriah Baptist Church Cemetery
Buzzard Rock
Blue Ridge
SCALE 1:24 000
KILOMETERS
METERS
MILES
FEET
UTM GRID AND 2021 MAGNETIC NORTH DECLINATION AT CENTER OF SHEET
1
2
3
4
5
6

DIRECTIONS TO THE TRAILHEAD(S)

Appalachian Trail Conservancy to Potomac Street Train Station Trailhead
Potomac Street Train Station Lot: (39.324392, –77.731218)
The Point (39.323094, –77.728828)

To reach the trailhead for this section of the Appalachian Trail, it is best to park at the train station on Potomac St. This lot fills up early, and parking must be paid for. When it is full, Harpers Ferry National Historical Park has other parking areas that can be shuttled from to the start of this hike and the rest of the park. Driving directions from the Appalachian Trail Conservancy are the following:

Appalachian Trail Conservancy at 799 Washington St., Harpers Ferry, WV 25425

1. Head east on Washington St., toward McDowell St.
2. In 0.4 mile, continue onto High St.
3. In 0.2 mile, turn left onto Hog Alley
4. In 131 feet, turn left onto Potomac St.
5. Continue 331 feet
6. Turn right and continue 115 feet
7. The Harpers Ferry Station, at Potomac St. and Shenandoah St., Harpers Ferry, WV 25425, will be on the right
8. Once parked, follow these directions on foot: Head southeast on High St. toward Hog Alley
9. In 0.1 mile, turn left onto Shenandoah St., and after 217 feet you will arrive at the Point in West Virginia

GEM HIKE DIRECTIONS

1. At the Point, Harpers Ferry, West Virginia, take the Appalachian Trail north and turn left to cross the Potomac River into Maryland
2. At 2.7 miles, you cross Keep Tryst Rd.
3. At 3.10 miles, pass by Weverton Road Parking Lot (continue the AT north)
4. After another 1.2 miles, you reach the side trail to Weverton Cliffs on the right
5. Travel on the blue blaze 0.1 mile, until you reach Weverton Cliffs in Maryland
6. Return the way you came to the Point, West Virginia

MORE/LESS AMBITIOUS HIKERS

More-ambitious hikers might wish to add a side trip to Maryland Heights before returning across the Potomac River to the Point. The lighting will be better to do this add-on in the morning, unless you are seeking a sunset. More-ambitious hikers might also want to add chapter 4's hike to Keys Gap to their hike.

Less ambitious hikers may wish to do this hike as two out-and-back trips: one from Weverton Cliffs Parking Area to Weverton Cliffs, and one from the Point to Weverton Cliffs Parking Area and back.

CHAPTER 6

LEHIGH GAP EAST, PENNSYLVANIA

AREA MAP

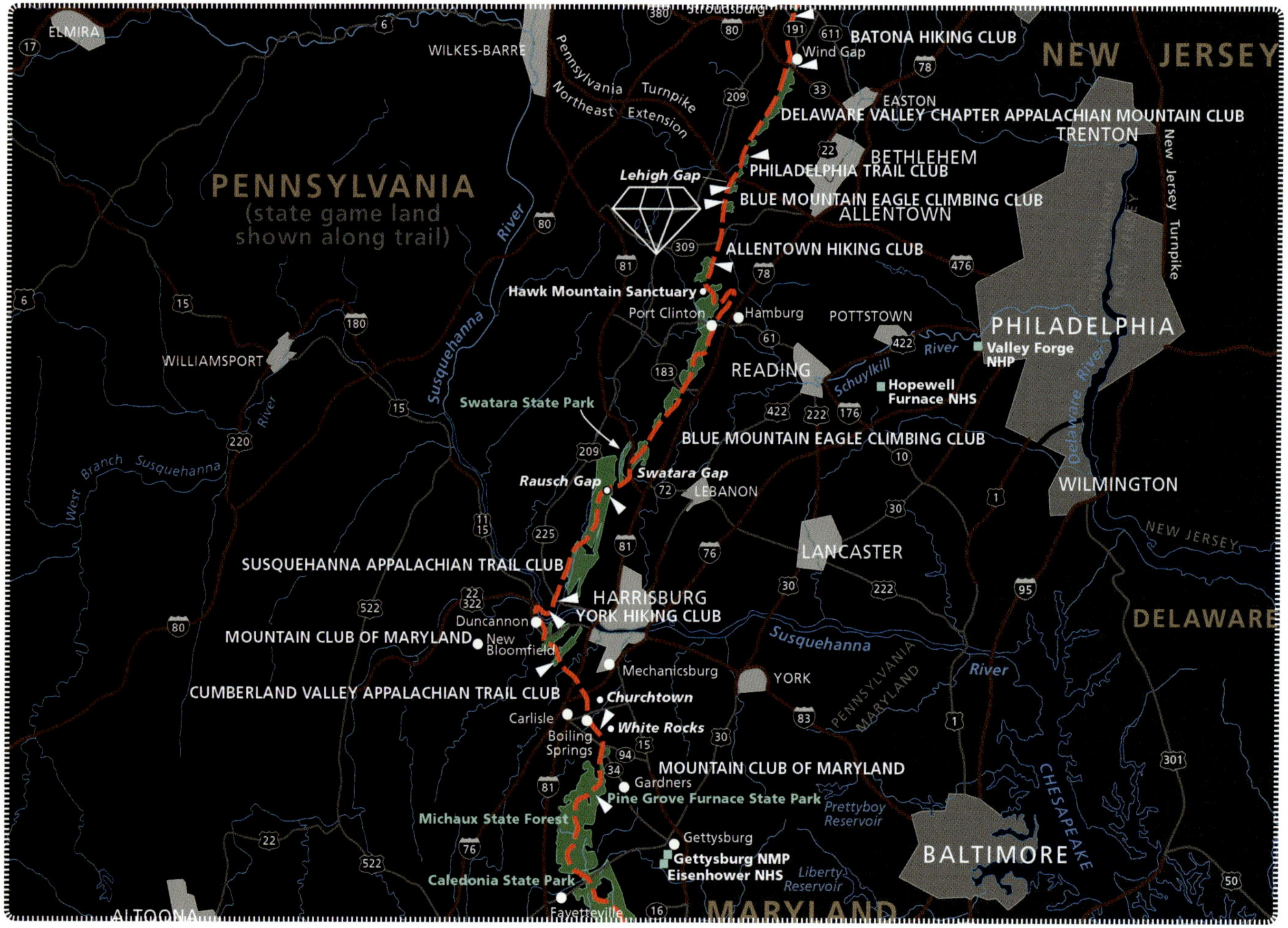

DISTANCE	12 miles
ELEVATION GAIN	2,220 feet
ELEVATION LOSS	2,220 feet
LEVEL	Difficult

TYPE: OUT-AND-BACK

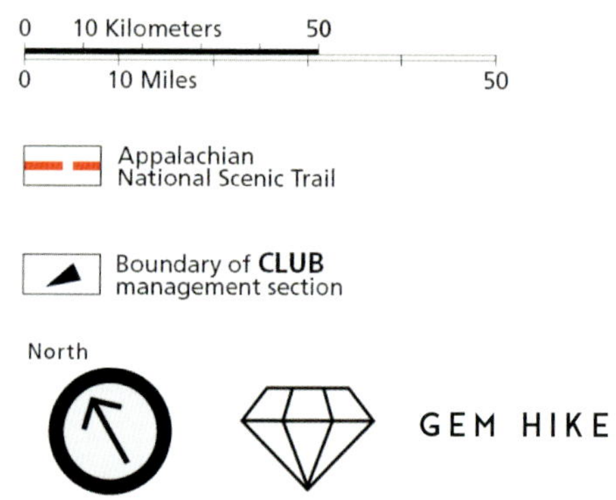

PERSONAL TOUCH

This was not my first section of miles on the Appalachian Trail, but it started my photographic journey along the Appalachian Trail once I had the idea to embark on it. This was also my first section as a hike leader for the Appalachian Mountain Club's Delaware Valley Chapter. In the spring, I attended the Appalachian Mountain Club's leadership training. After a full check and cross-check, I was sent my log-in credentials for their hike-listing website.

The day of my first hike, it was a hot and humid day in early June. I decided not to shorten my preplanned hike for a group of Appalachian Mountain Club hikers. We all consumed at least 5 quarts of water as we hiked the 12 miles. On the surface, you would think we would suffer, but we all enjoyed the hike, and my hike theme was born: section day hikes on the Appalachian Trail. Some of the Appalachian Trail hikes were out-and-backs, some were loops, and others were point-to-point hikes. These hikes gave me a lot of my photographs and hike ideas for this book. I am grateful to Lehigh Gap, Pennsylvania, to have started it all.

BRIEF OVERVIEW

Hiking from Lehigh Gap Nature Center to Little Gap on the Appalachian Trail is an experience rich in natural beauty and ecological diversity. Lehigh Gap is home to a large wildlife sanctuary. You will have a memorable river crossing with the Appalachian Mountains above and a challenging rock climb and descent on your return. After summiting the gap, the trail navigates through the forest and high meadows with fine views of Pennsylvania towns nested in the natural landscape.

DESCRIPTION OF THE GEM HIKE

The Appalachian Trail stretch between Lehigh Gap Nature Center, Pennsylvania, and Little Gap, Pennsylvania, offer hikers a captivating blend of natural beauty, diverse ecosystems, and rich history. Spanning approximately 6 miles, this segment is characterized by its rugged terrain, vibrant flora, and impressive views. Ideal for experienced hikers, the trail meanders through Pennsylvania's stunning landscapes, providing a unique glimpse into the region's ecological diversity. This gem hike of diverse wildlife starts at Lehigh Gap Nature Center.

FLORA, FAUNA, AND VEGETATION

Due to the work of Lehigh Gap Nature Center to restore this area and maintain a wildlife sanctuary, the species of plants and wildlife are especially diverse in this section of the Appalachian Trail. This area has fourteen species of reptiles, fifteen species of amphibians, five species of fish, forty-three species of butterflies, sixteen species of dragonflies, twelve species of damselflies, thirty-two species of bees, six species of wasps, twenty-three species of mammals, and one hundred eighty-one species of birds.

LEHIGH GAP NATURE CENTER

Lehigh Gap Nature Center is perfectly placed within the Appalachian Mountains, along the Lehigh River, Pennsylvania. Lehigh Gap Nature Center is a nonprofit environmental education center and wildlife refuge located near Slatington, Pennsylvania. The wildlife refuge is a 756-acre wildlife refuge featuring hundreds of native species and endless opportunities for learning, ecological research, and outdoor recreation. They have 13 miles of trails neighboring the Appalachian Trail and Delaware & Lehigh trails that enthusiasts can enjoy.

SCENIC VIEWS

The highlights of this hike are undoubtedly the panoramic views that reward your efforts. As you ascend the rocky terrain, lookout points offer sweeping vistas of the Lehigh Valley and the other ridge lines of the Appalachian Mountains. One of the best viewpoints can be found at the top of Lehigh Gap East, where you can catch a glimpse of the Lehigh River winding its way through the valley below.

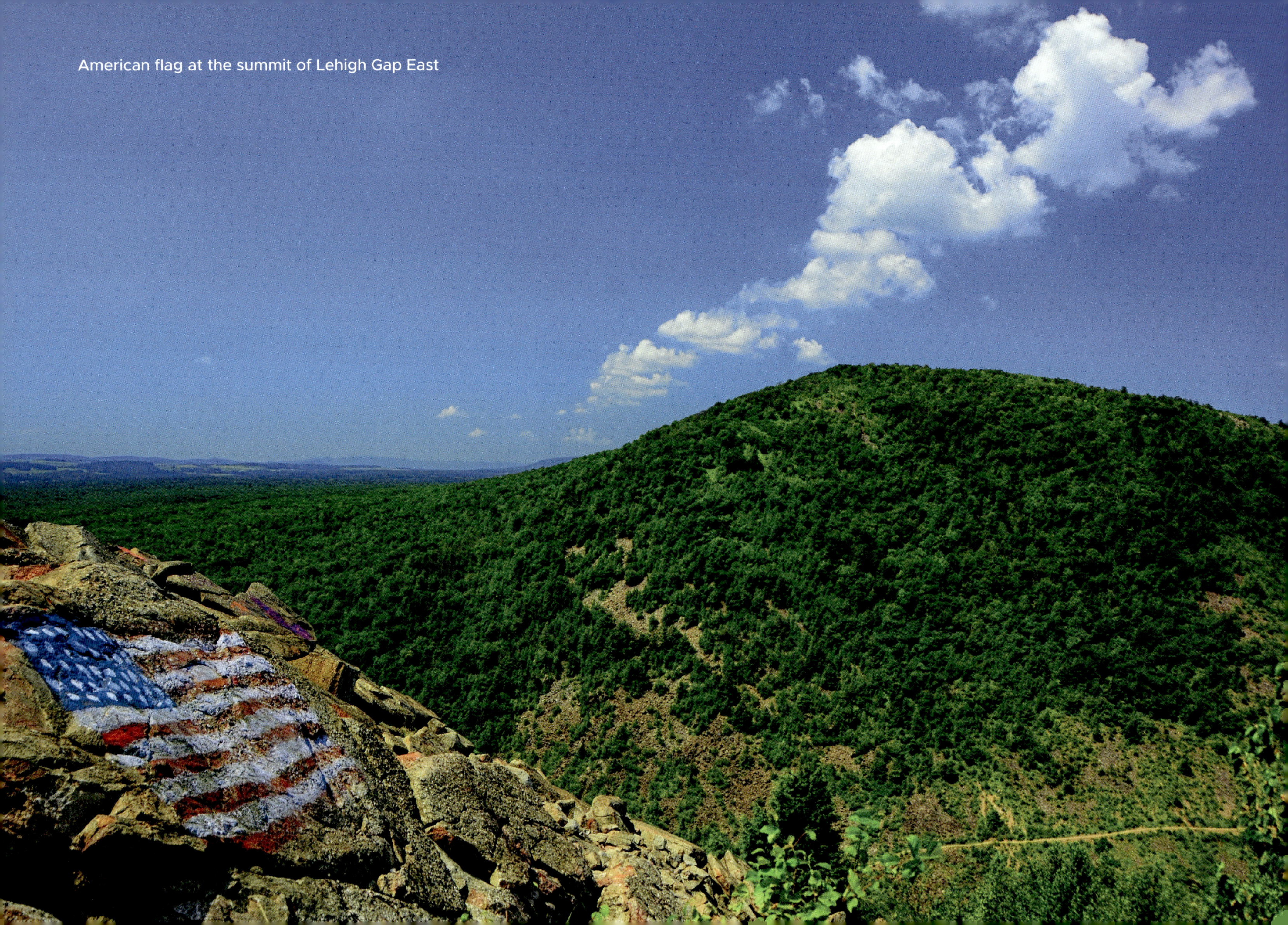

American flag at the summit of Lehigh Gap East

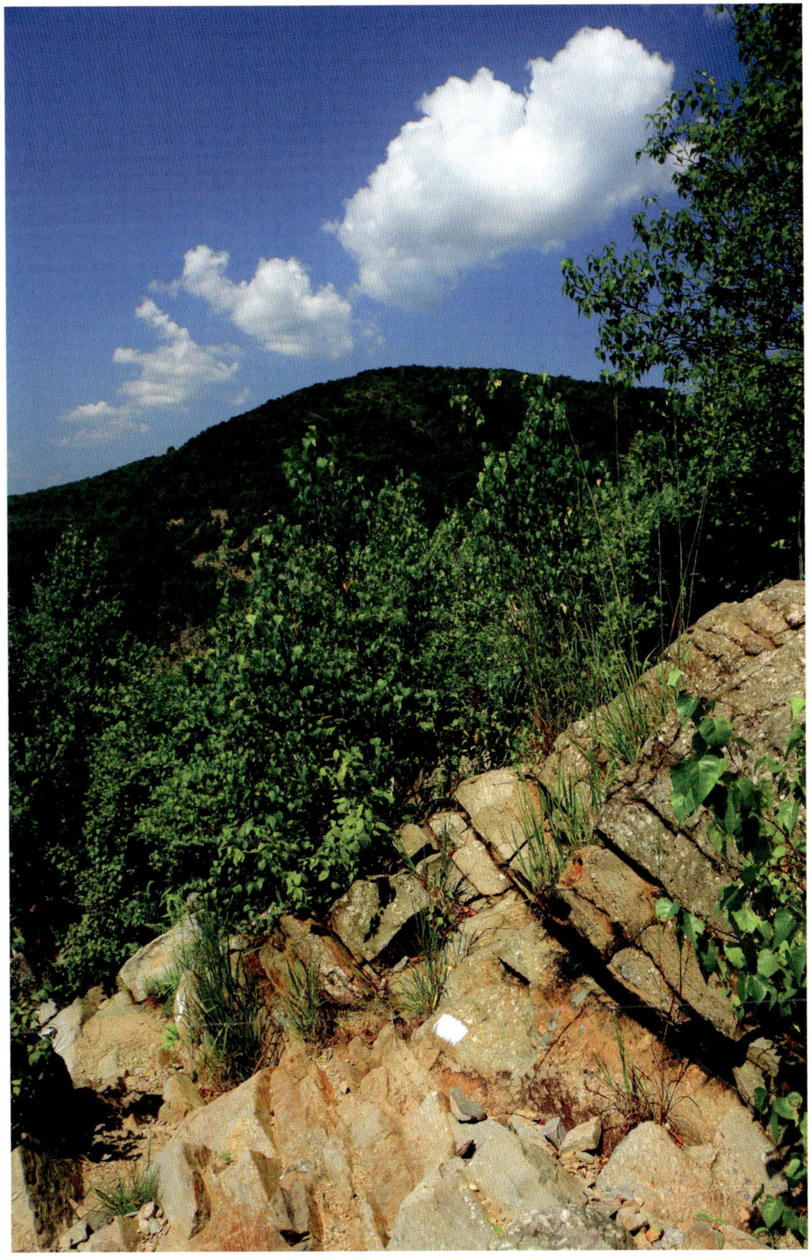

Lehigh Gap West as the Appalachian Trail climbs Lehigh Gap East

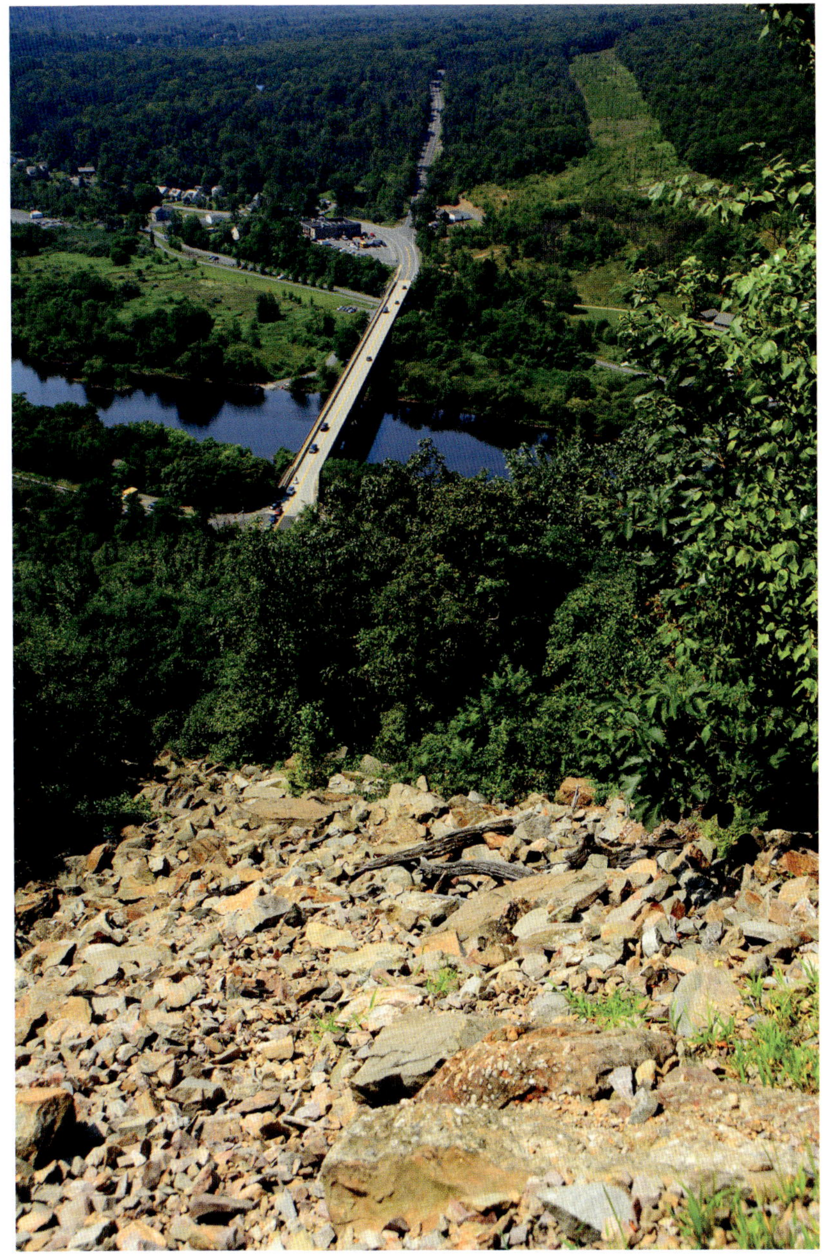

Looking down Lehigh Gap East at the Lehigh River

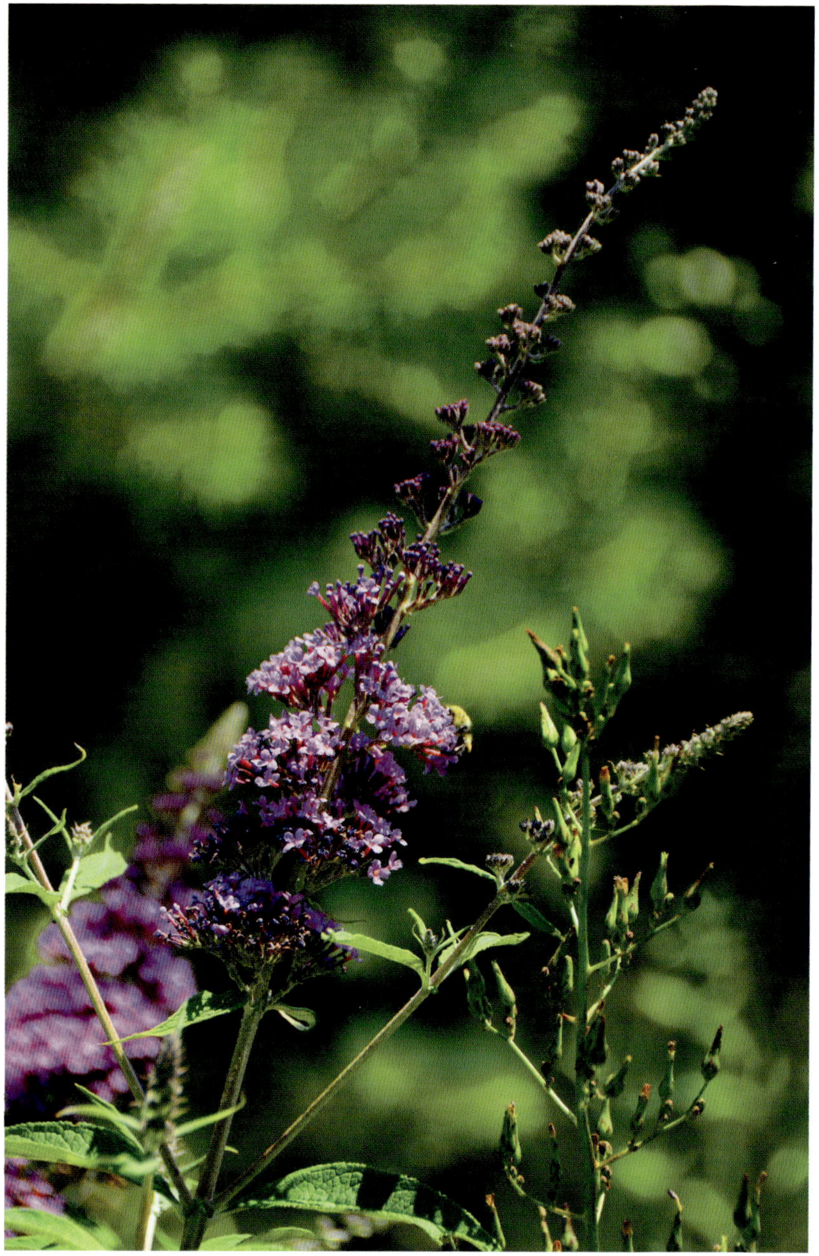

Butterfly bush (*Buddleja davidii*)

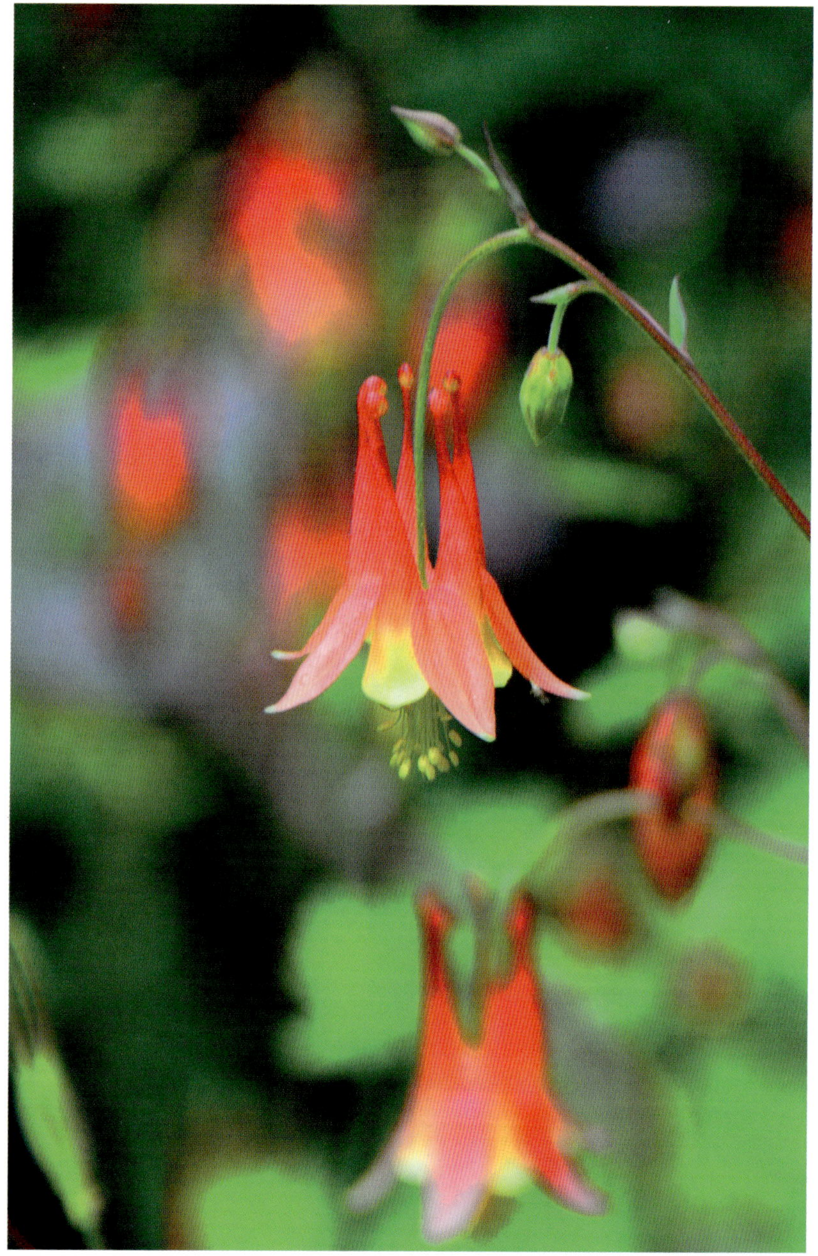

Eastern red columbine (*Aquilegia canadensis*)

Pennsylvania's section of the Appalachian Trail

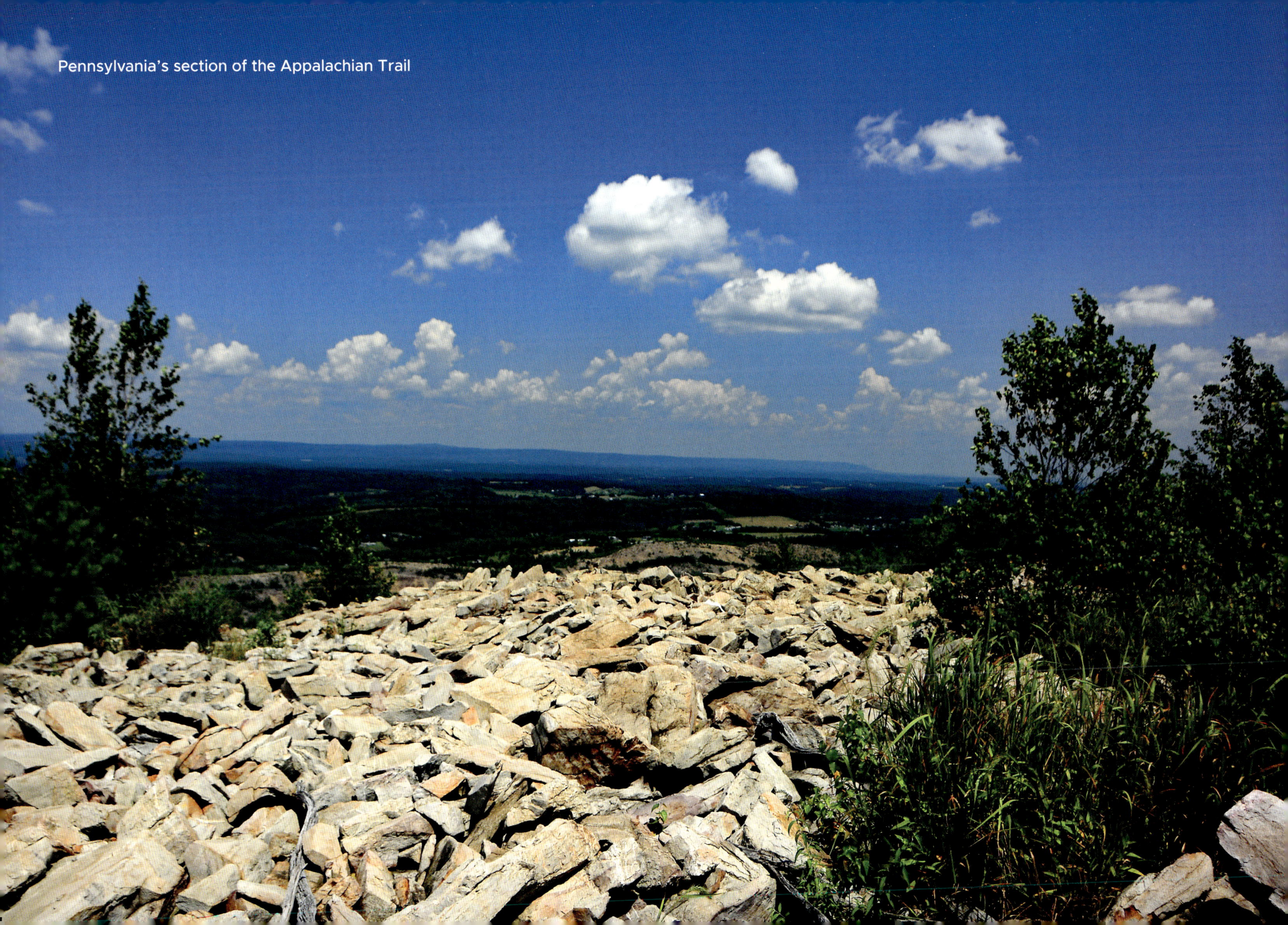

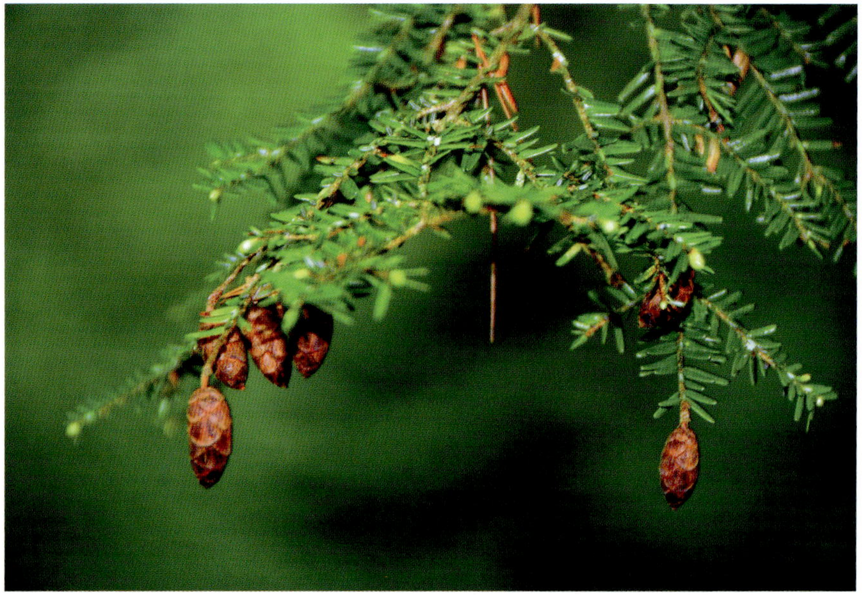

Pine cones of an eastern hemlock (*Tsuga canadensis*)

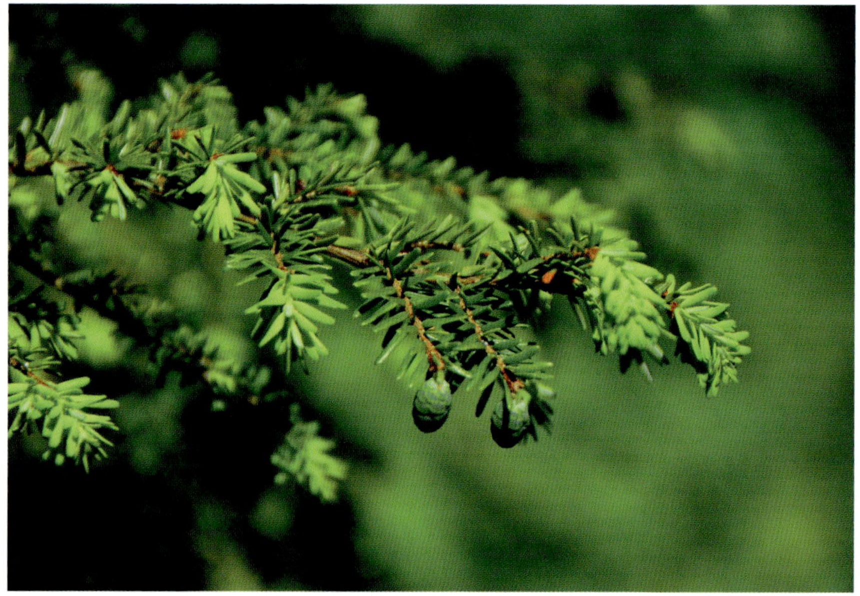

Young pine cones of an eastern hemlock (*Tsuga canadensis*)

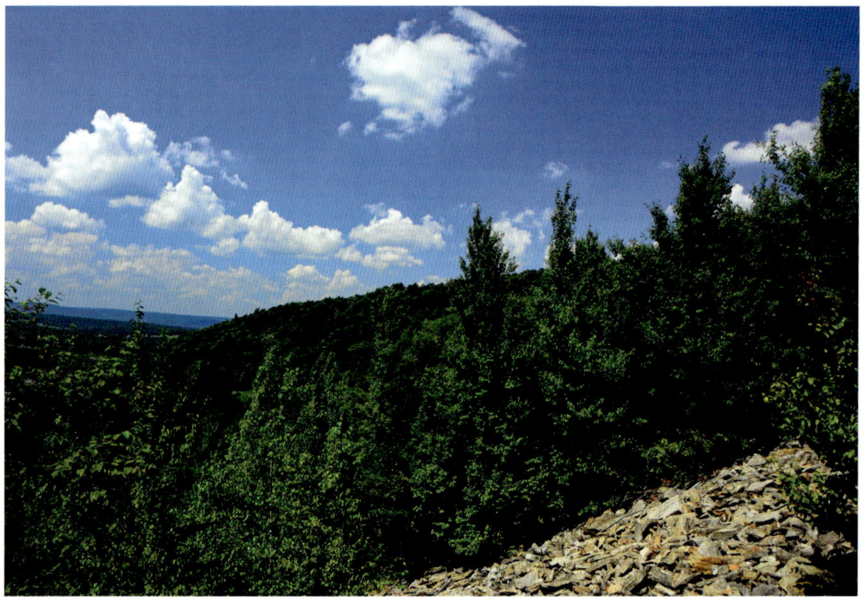

Heading north on Pennsylvania's section of the Appalachian Trail

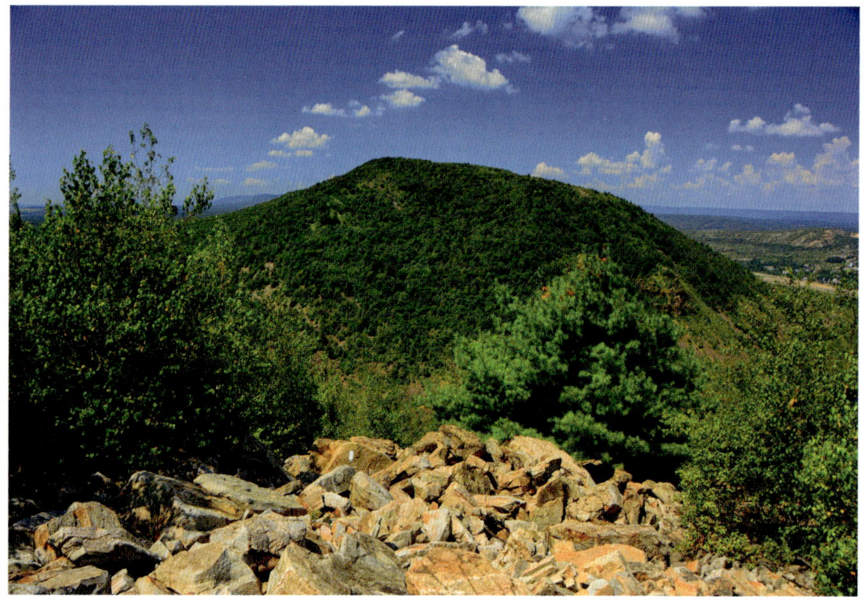

View of Lehigh Gap West

Flowering Queen Anne's lace (*Daucus carota*)

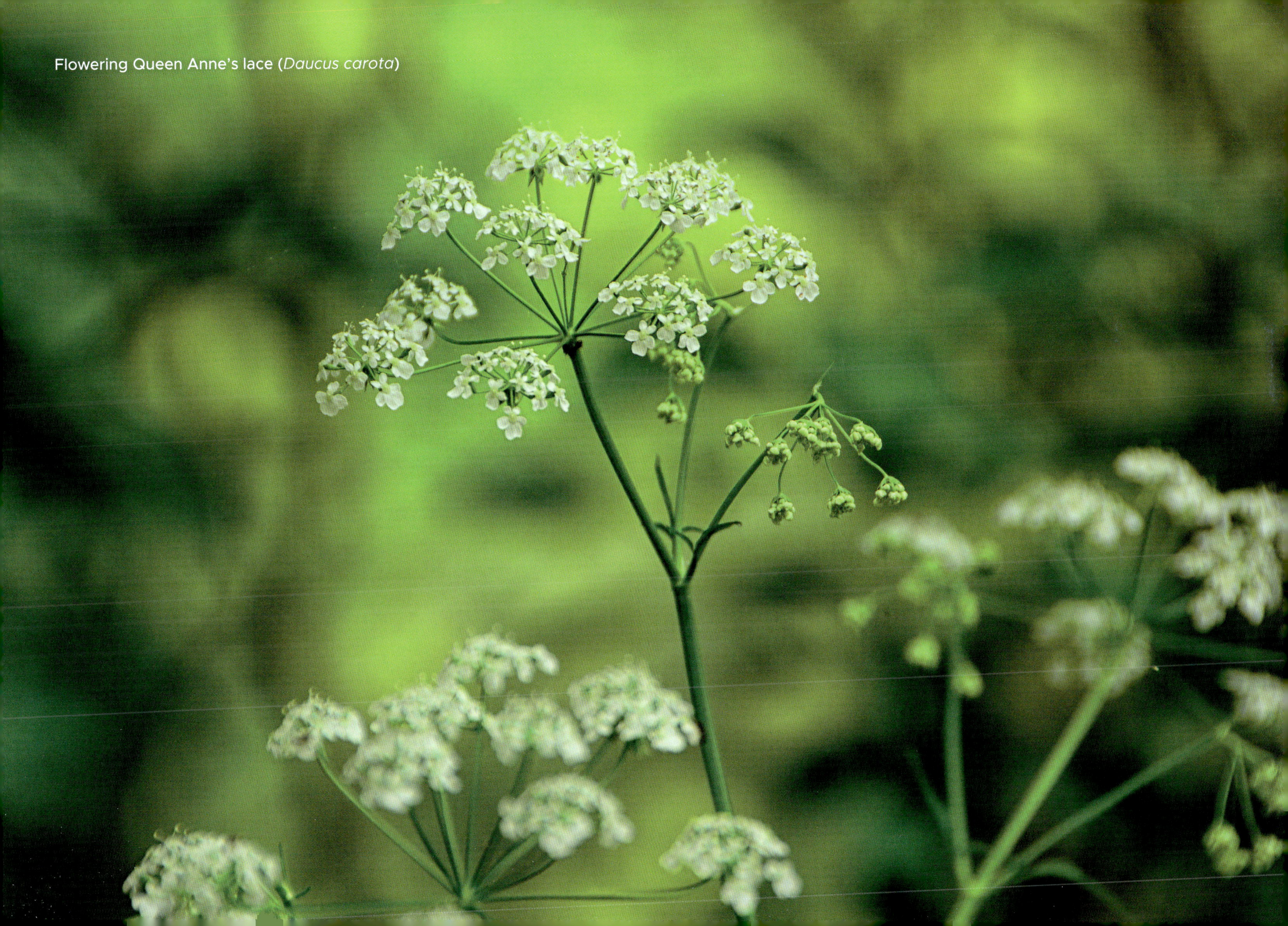

The Appalachian Trail heads north of Lehigh Gap East.

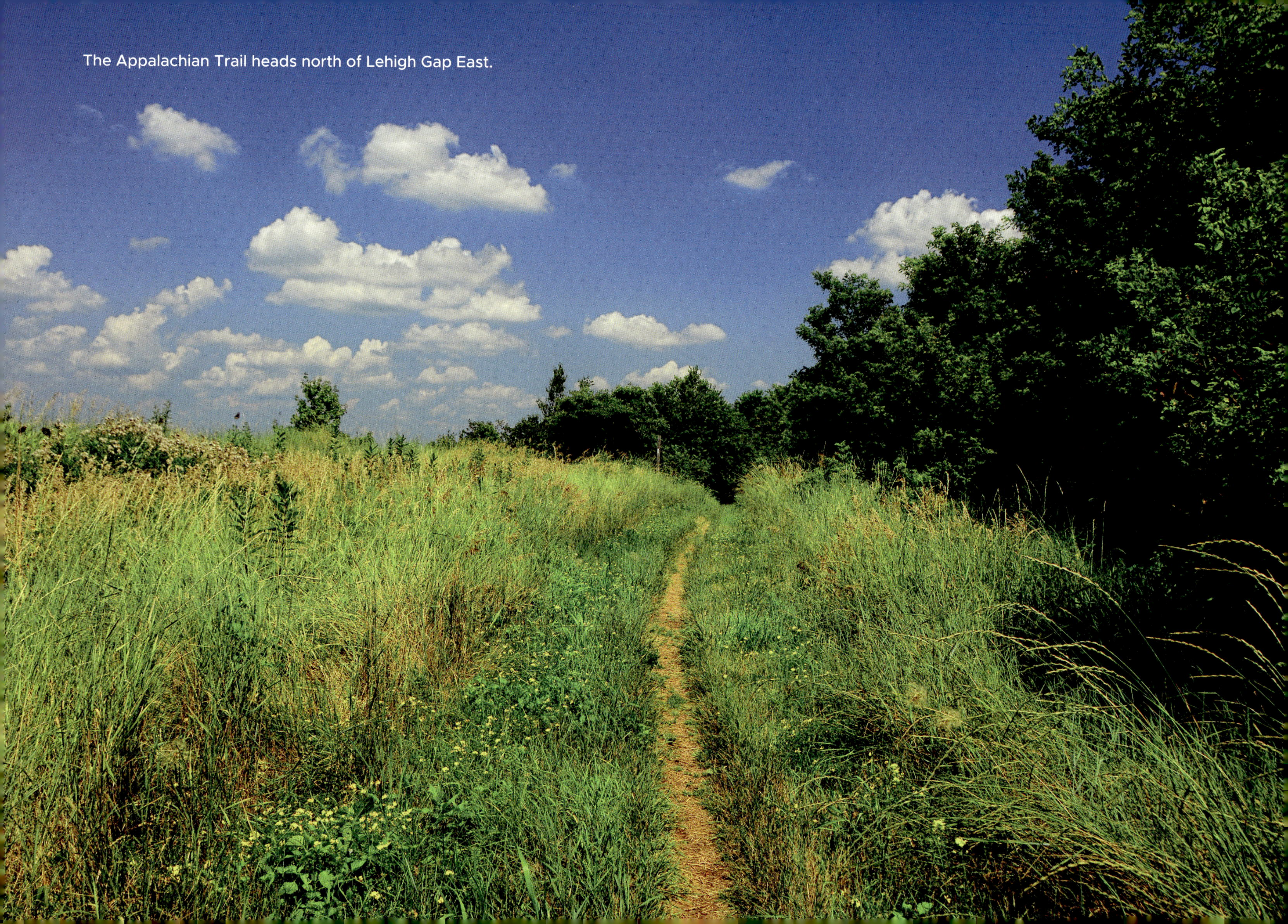

Reeds from along Pennsylvania's section of the Appalachian Trail

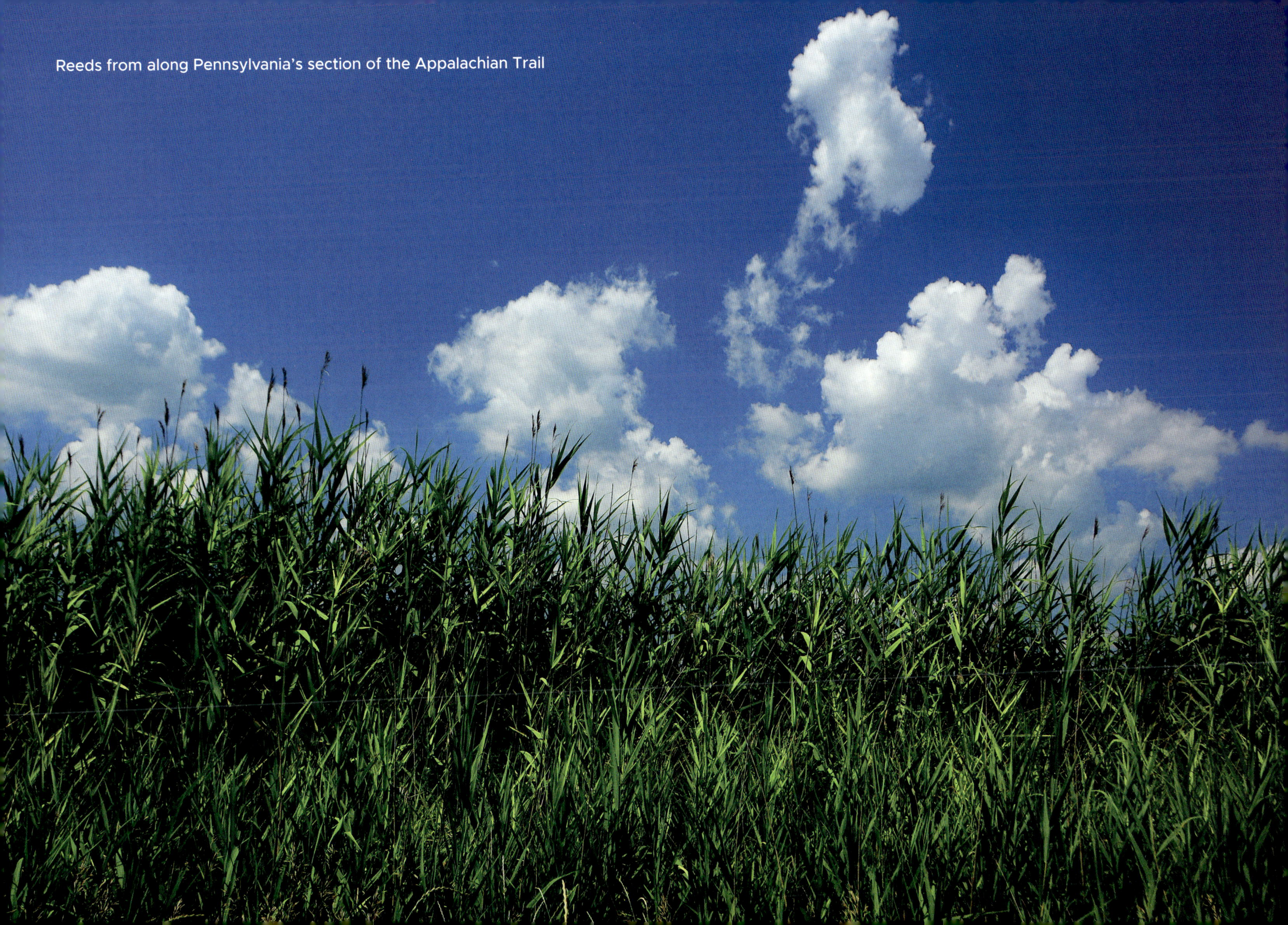

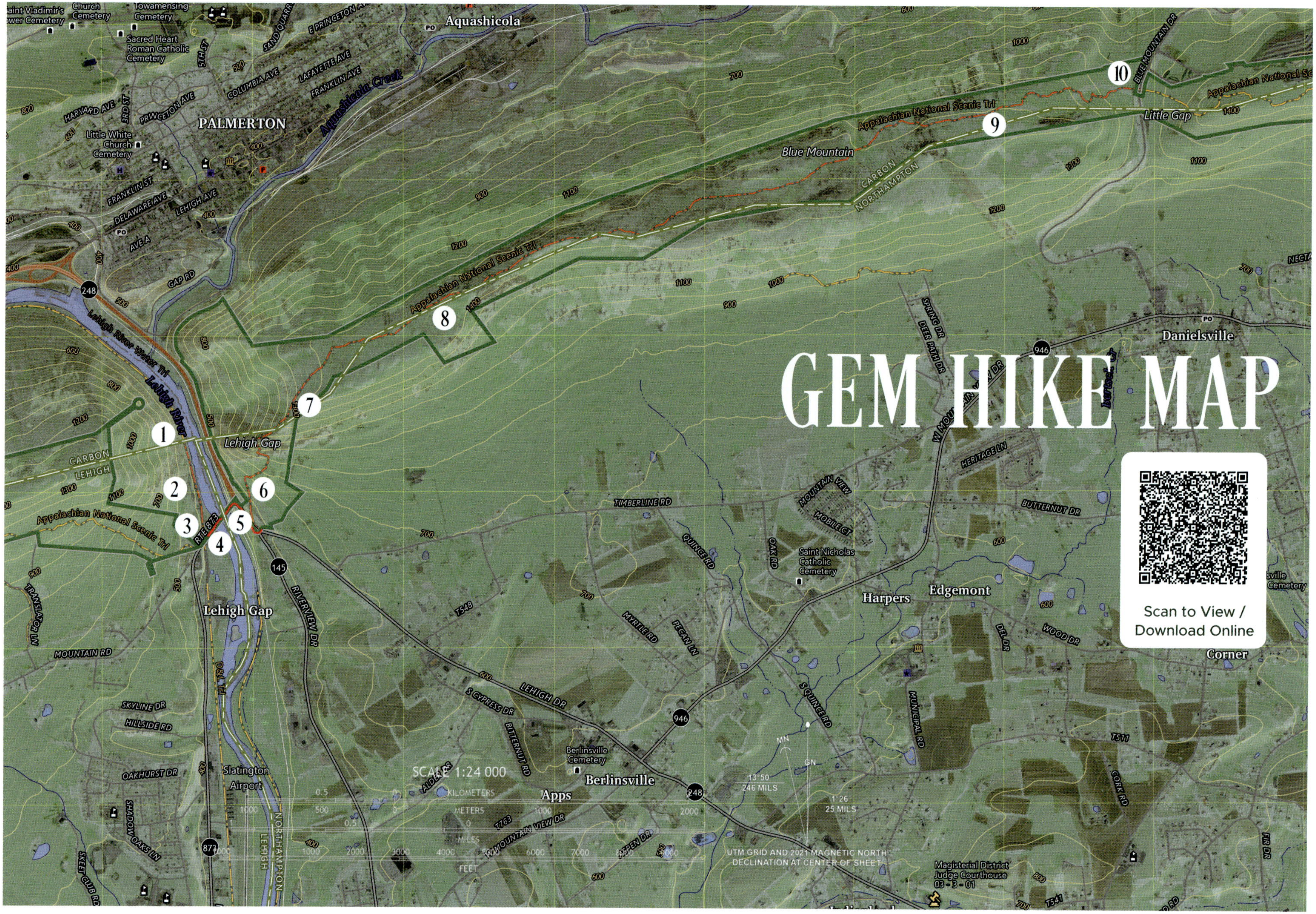
GEM HIKE MAP
Scan to View / Download Online
PALMERTON
Aquashicola
Aquashicola Creek
Blue Mountain
Appalachian National Scenic Trl
Little Gap
Lehigh Gap
Lehigh River
Lehigh River Water Trl
CARBON
LEHIGH
NORTHAMPTON
Danielsville
Harpers
Edgemont
Berlinsville
Apps
Slatington Airport
TIMBERLINE RD
MOUNTAIN RD
RIVERVIEW DR
LEHIGH DR
BUTTERNUT DR
HERITAGE LN
WOOD DR
SKYLINE DR
HILLSIDE RD
OAKHURST DR
Saint Nicholas Catholic Cemetery
Berlinsville Cemetery
Little White Church Cemetery
Sacred Heart Roman Catholic Cemetery
Towamensing Cemetery
Magisterial District Judge Courthouse 03-3-01
SCALE 1:24 000
UTM GRID AND 2021 MAGNETIC NORTH DECLINATION AT CENTER OF SHEET
1
2
3
4
5
6
7
8
9
10

DIRECTIONS TO THE TRAILHEAD(S)

Lehigh Gap Nature Center Trailhead at 8844 Paint Mill Rd., Slatington, PA 18080 (40.784141, –75.609149), from Allentown, Pennsylvania

1. Head east on Hamilton St. toward S. Church St. for 486 feet
2. Follow PA 145 N to PA 873 S in Lehigh Township for 16.9 miles
3. Turn left onto N. 6th St. and continue 0.8 mile
4. Turn left onto Washington St. and continue 0.1 mile
5. Turn right onto N. 7th St. and continue 0.3 mile
6. Continue onto PA 145 N / MacArthur Rd. and continue 0.7 mile
7. Continue to follow PA 145 N
8. Pass by Mattress Firm Whitehall North (on the right) in 1.2 miles
9. Continue 14.8 miles
10. Turn left onto PA 248 W and continue 0.2 mile
11. Follow PA 873 S and Paint Mill Rd. for 1.1 miles
12. Turn left onto PA 873 S and continue for 0.6 mile
13. Turn left onto Paint Mill Rd. and continue 0.5 mile
14. Turn left after 325 feet, and you will arrive at Lehigh Gap Nature Center

GEM HIKE DIRECTIONS

1. Lehigh Gap Nature Center is located at 8844 Paint Mill Rd.
2. Turn right on Paint Mill Rd. and continue 0.3 mile
3. Turn right on PA 873 and continue 970 feet
4. Walk over the bridge on PA 873 and continue 0.2 mile
5. Take a right onto Lehigh Dr. and continue 0.2 mile
6. Take a right off the road to stay on the Appalachian Trail for 0.7 mile
7. In 0.9 mile, you will reach the intersection with Winter Trail
8. Continue the Appalachian Trail for 3.7 miles, until you cross under a power line
9. Continue 1 mile until Little Gap / Blue Mountain Rd.
10. Turn around and retrace your steps back to Lehigh Gap Nature Center

MORE/ LESS AMBITIOUS HIKERS

More-ambitious hikers may wish to add hiking up and down Lehigh Gap West as an add-on to this hike. Less ambitious hikers may opt to descend the Winter Trail on the return to Lehigh Gap, but make sure you are comfortable with this hike.

CHAPTER 7

DELAWARE WATER GAP NATIONAL RECREATION AREA

AREA MAP

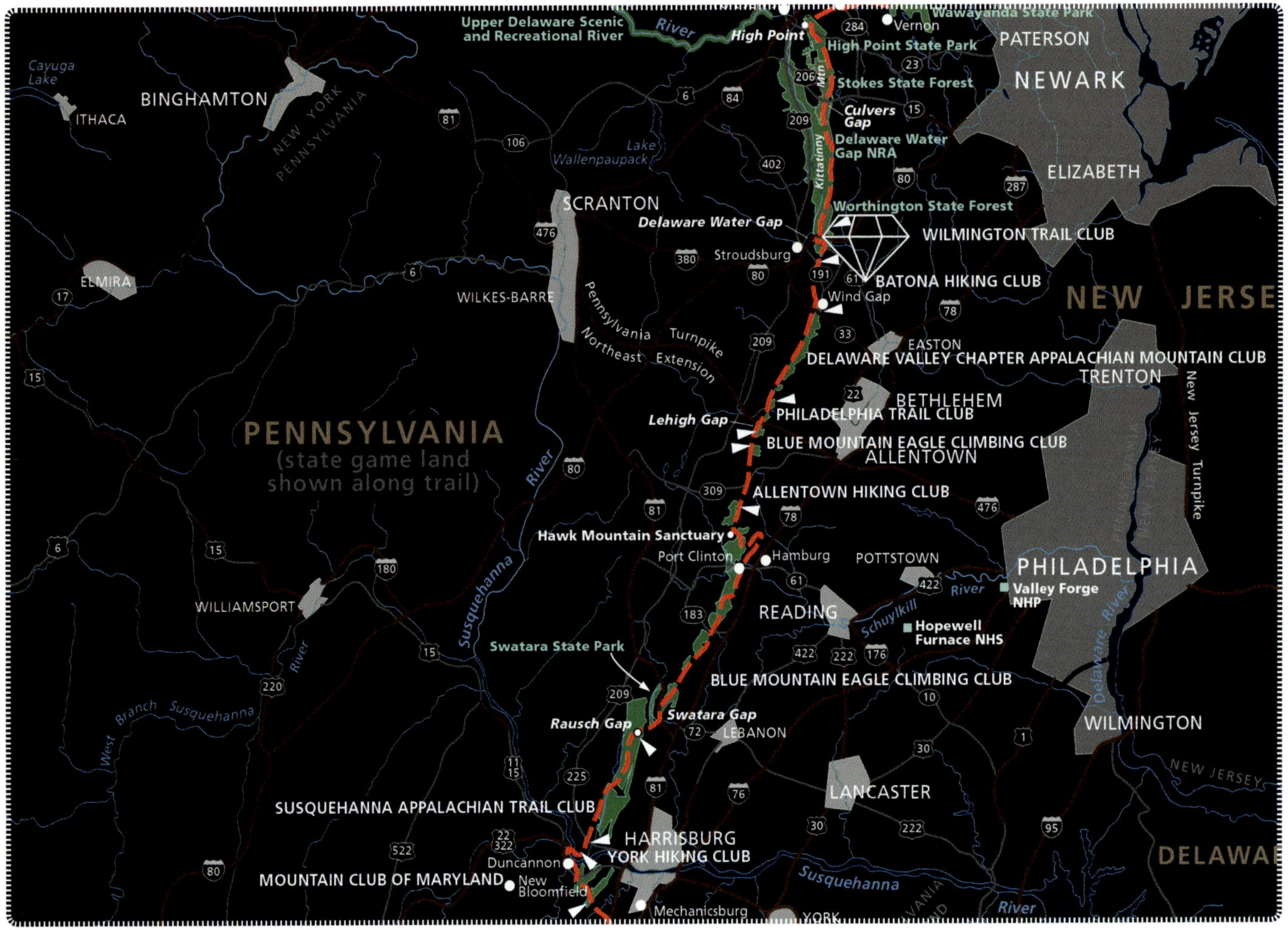

DISTANCE	16.1 miles
ELEVATION GAIN	1,950 feet
ELEVATION LOSS	1,950 feet
LEVEL	Difficult

TYPE: OUT-AND-BACK/LOOP

0 10 Kilometers 50

0 10 Miles 50

Appalachian National Scenic Trail

Boundary of CLUB management section

North

GEM HIKE

PERSONAL TOUCH

One of my favorite places to be in New Jersey is just sitting along the Delaware River looking up at Mount Tammany and the east face of Mount Minsi. I may have to drive over 1.5 hours to get to this location, but it is so worth it. It is truly a gem of New Jersey and the Appalachian Trail.

It may be just off I-80, but for me this area is relaxing, and it recharges my mental batteries. It reminds me how small we are in relation to the rest of the world. Mount Tammany's relationship to the river makes you feel small. We as individuals can make changes more easily because we are nimble, unlike the river, which took millions of years to make its dent on the landscape.

BRIEF OVERVIEW

The stretch of the Appalachian Trail from Fox Gap to the Kittatinny Point Visitor Center in the New Jersey section of the Delaware Water Gap National Recreation Area offers an incredible blend of natural beauty, historical richness, and opportunities for solitude. As hikers traverse the diverse landscapes and encounter the flora and fauna of the region, they also connect with the rich history that defines this area. In addition to the natural world, this hike invites reflection on the enduring relationship between people and the land.

DESCRIPTION OF THE GEM HIKE

This hike will take a hiker to the summit of Mount Minsi, into the town of Delaware Water Gap, Pennsylvania, across the I-80 Bridge, along the Delaware River, to the Delaware Water Gap National Recreation Area's Kittatinny Point Visitor Center and back.

FLORA, FAUNA, AND VEGETATION

The plant life along this section of the Appalachian Trail is diverse because of the varying elevations and microclimates of the region. The Appalachian Trail passes through lush deciduous forests dominated by oak, maple, and some birch. At the higher elevations, coniferous species such as eastern hemlock and white pine become more prominent. The plants under the trees are typically ferns, and, in the late spring, red columbine and other wildflowers are popular.

DELAWARE WATER GAP NATIONAL RECREATION AREA

The Appalachian Trail runs through a portion of the Delaware Water Gap National Recreation Area, which protects the unique geological and ecological features of the area. The Delaware Water Gap National Recreation Area was established in 1965, and it encompasses over 70,000 acres. It preserves critical wildlife and plant life habitats and provides numerous recreational opportunities. The Delaware Water Gap includes the Delaware River, Mount Minsi on the Pennsylvania side of the river, and Mount Tammany on the New Jersey side of the river.

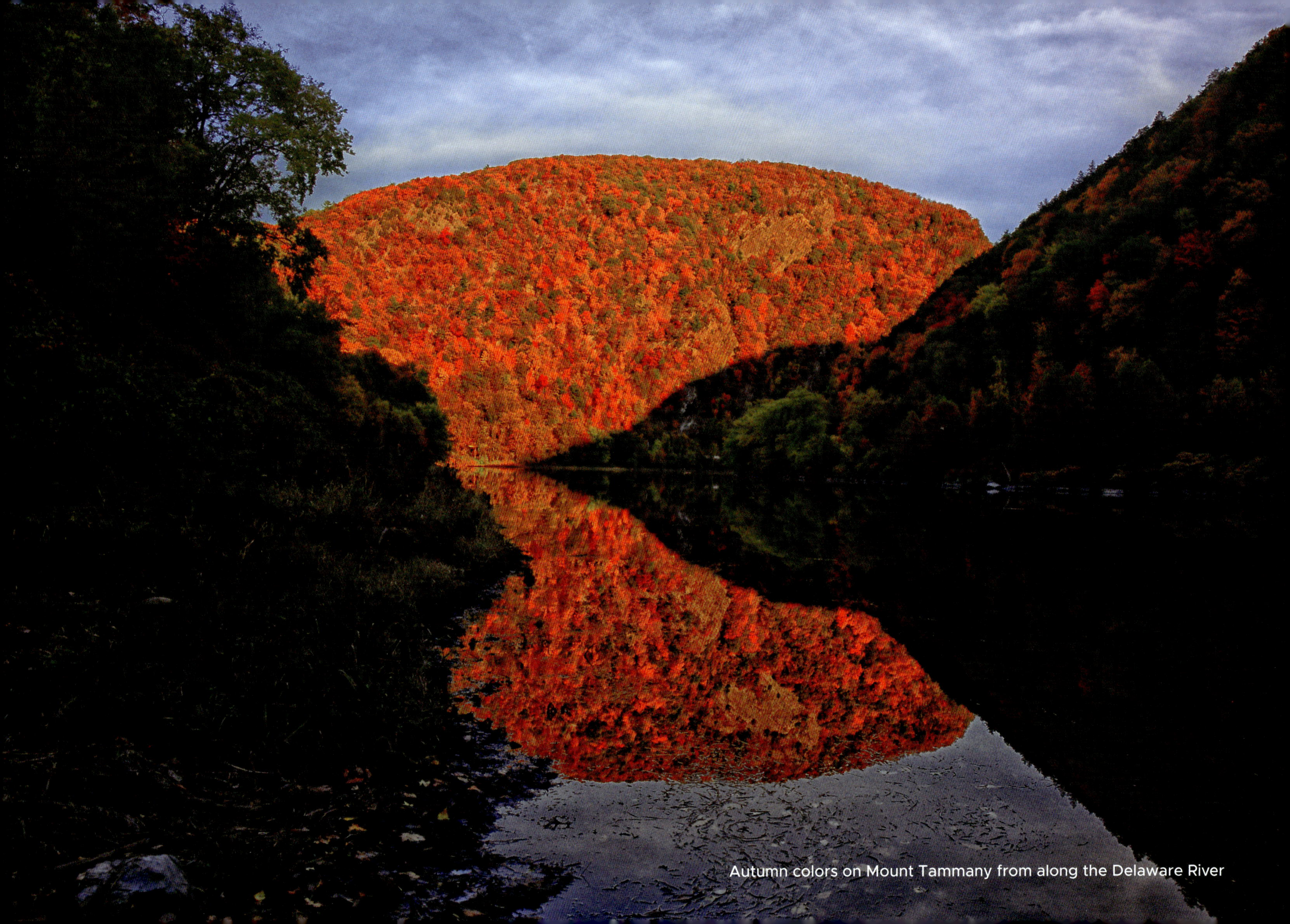

Autumn colors on Mount Tammany from along the Delaware River

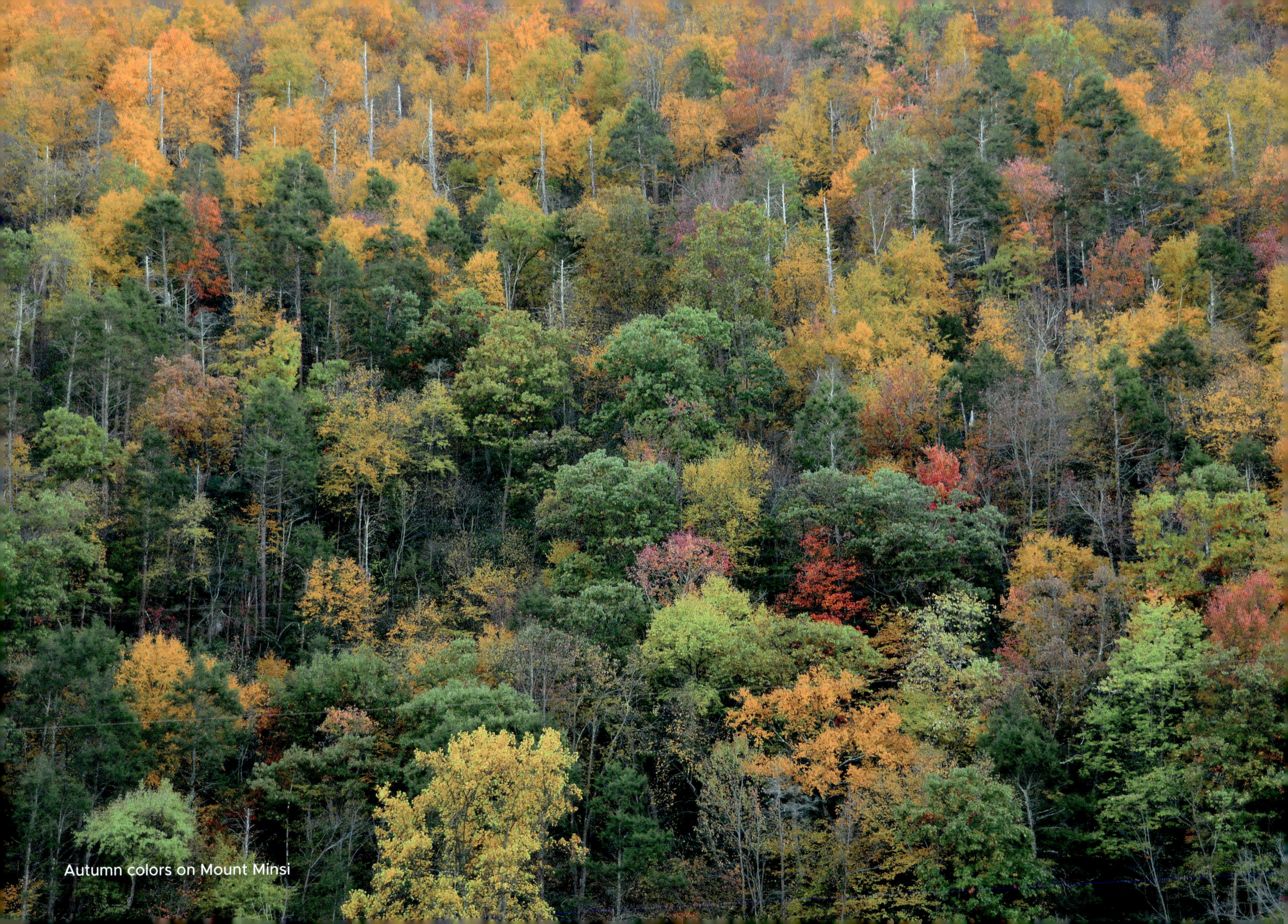
Autumn colors on Mount Minsi

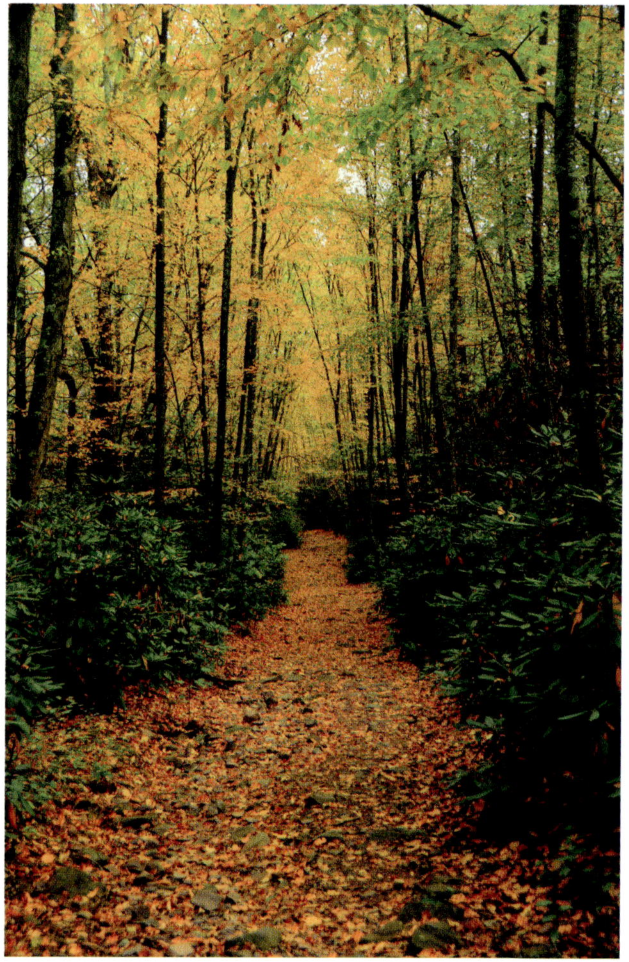

Looking up the Pennsylvania section of the Appalachian Trail

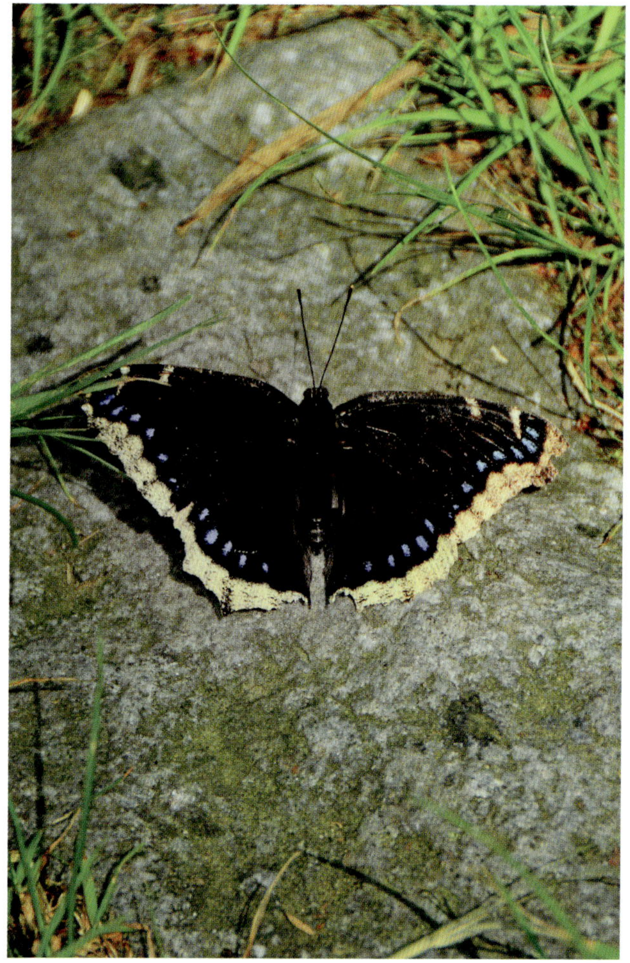

Red admiral butterfly (*Vanessa atalanta*)

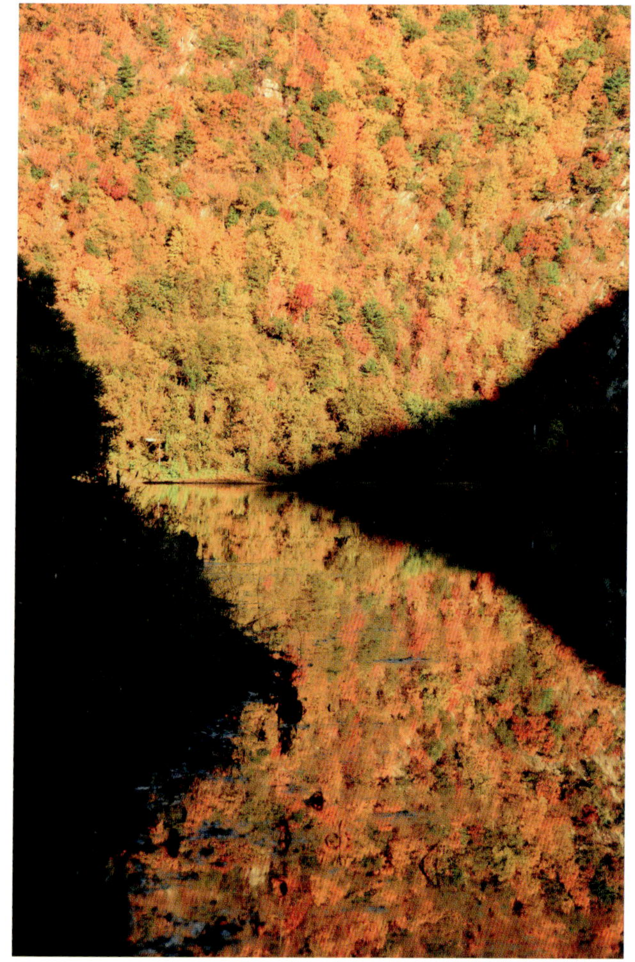

New Jersey autumn colors

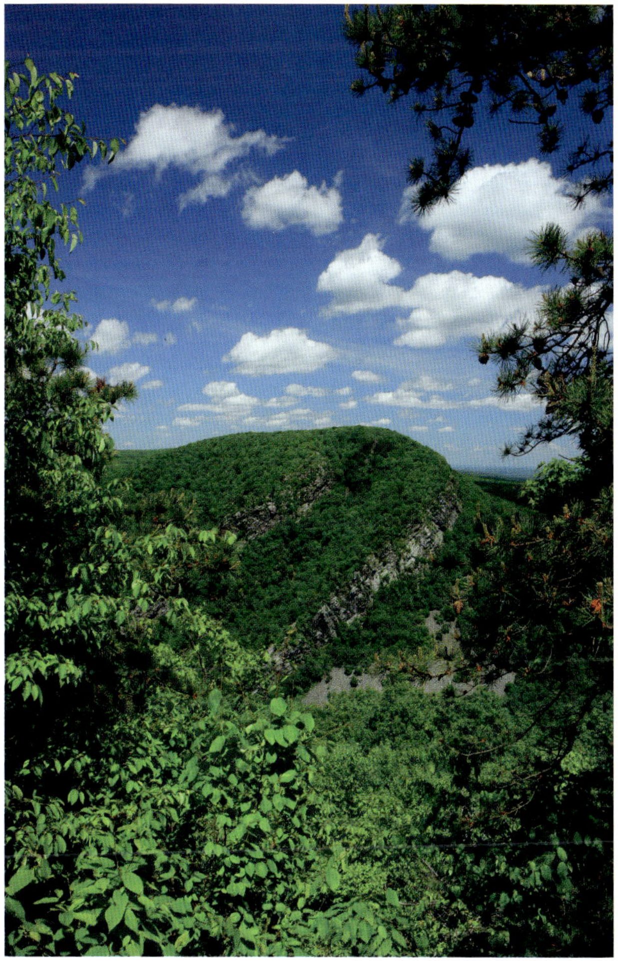

Nature-framed Mount Tammany

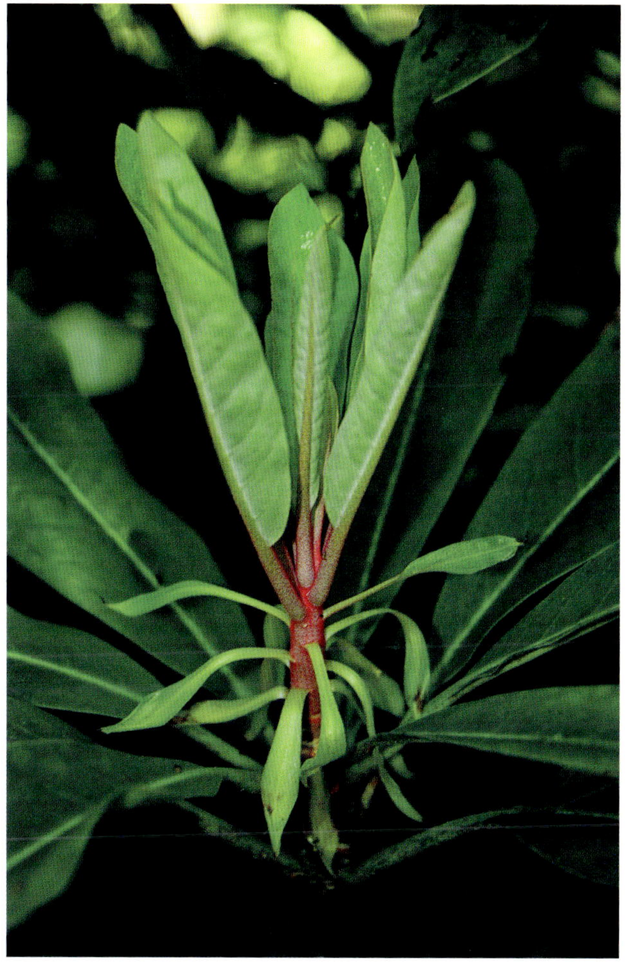

New leaves on a rhododendron

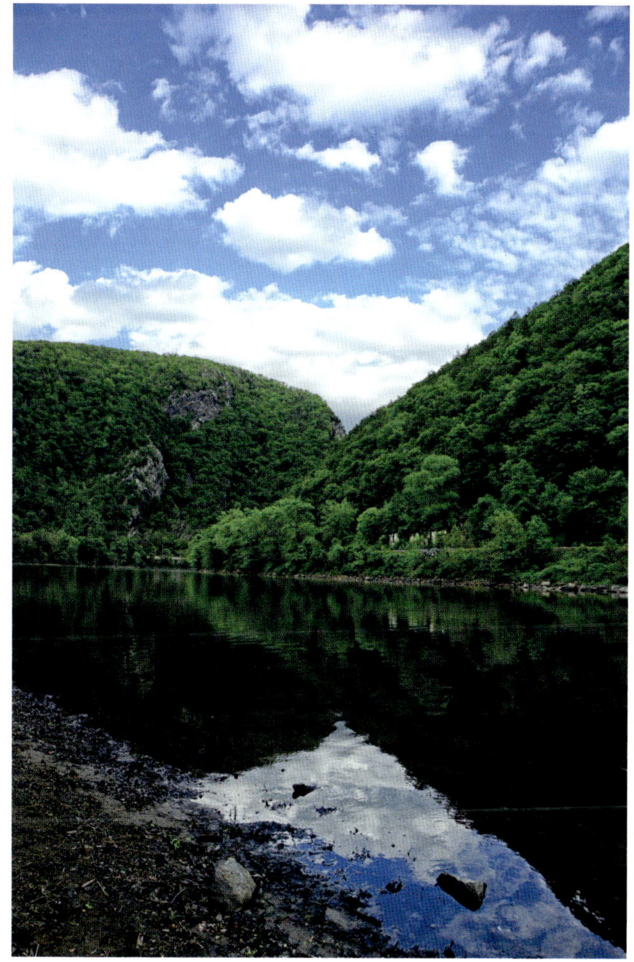

Delaware Water Gap

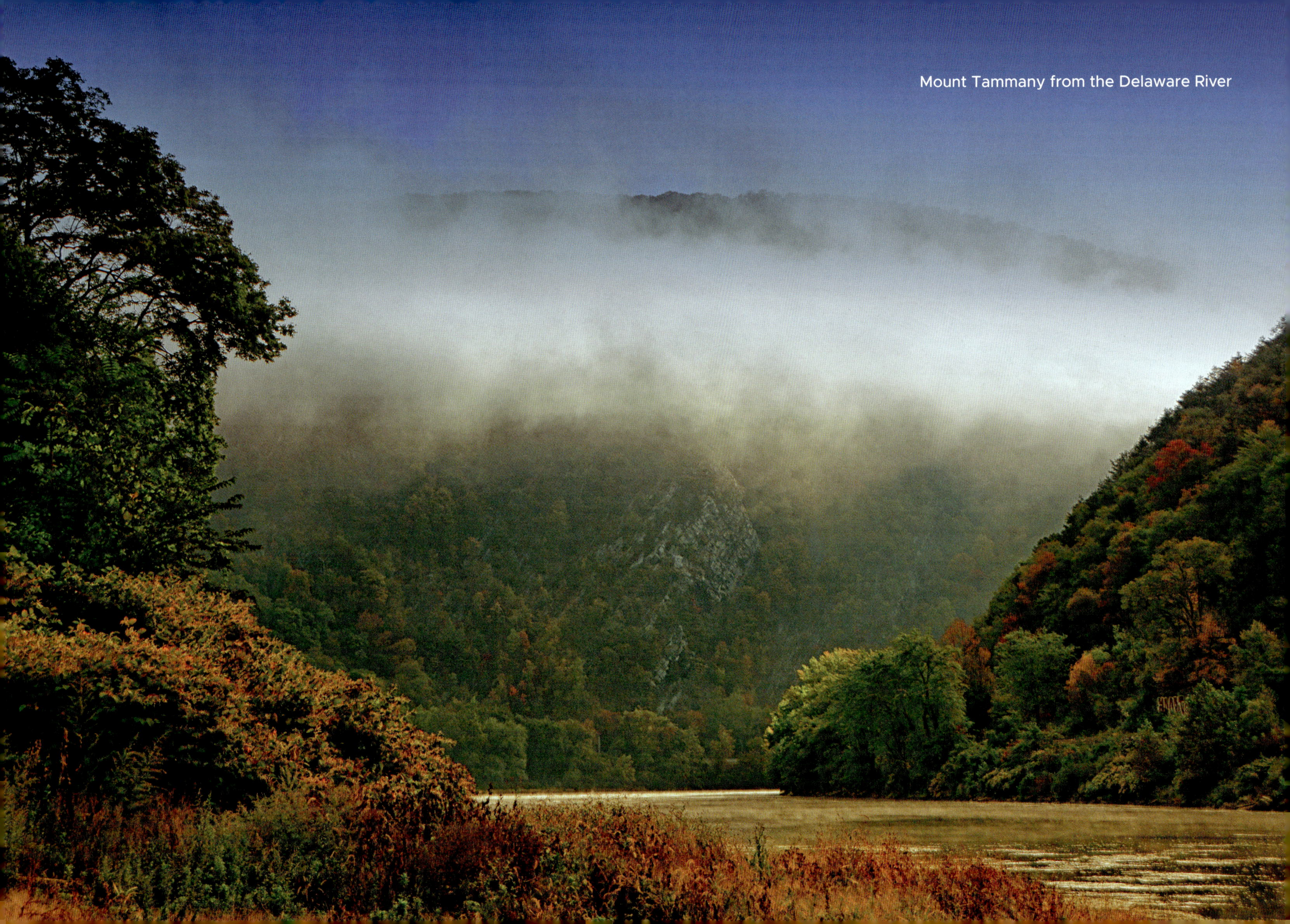

Mount Tammany from the Delaware River

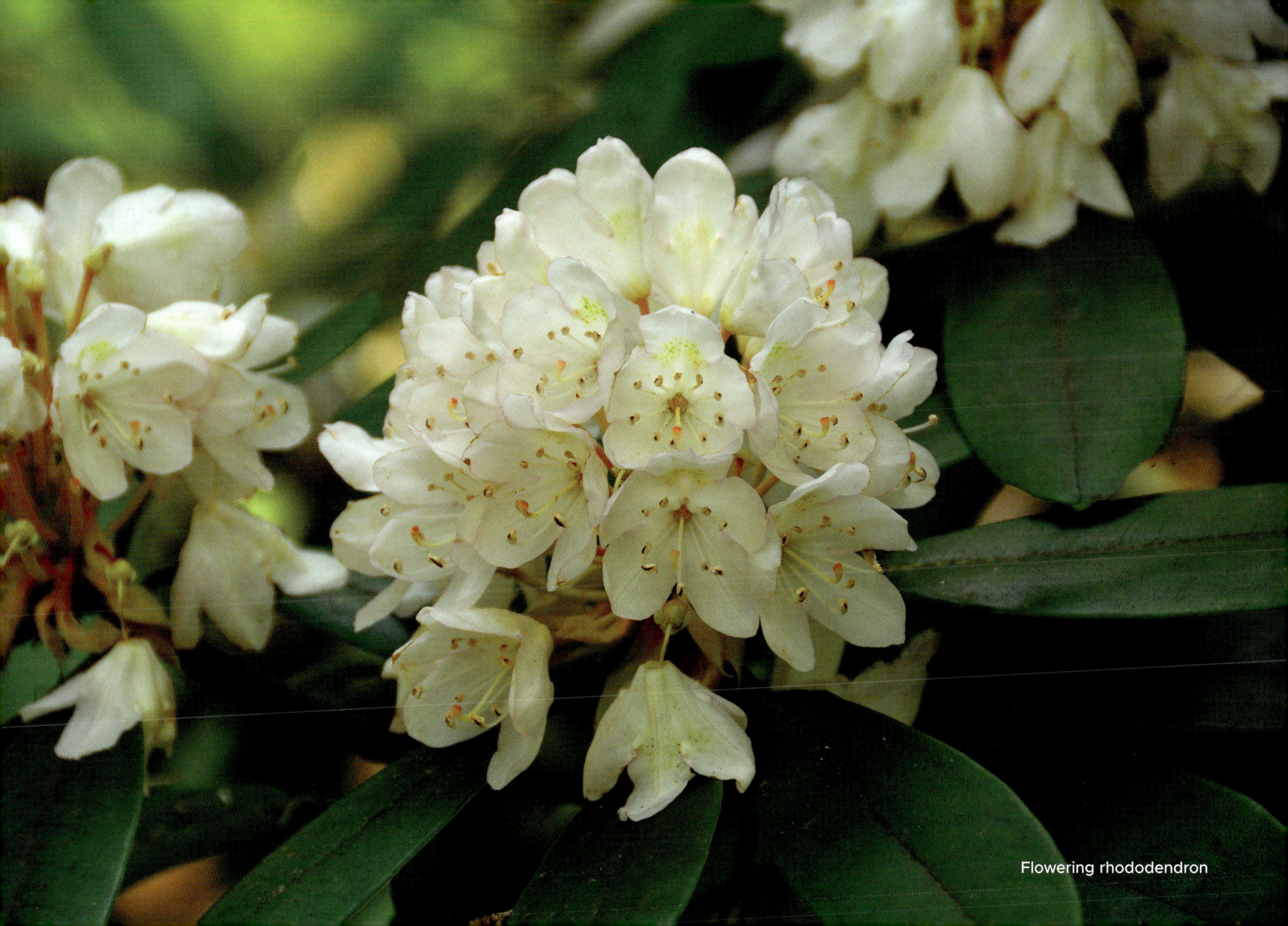

Flowering rhododendron

Delaware Water Gap tele-scape

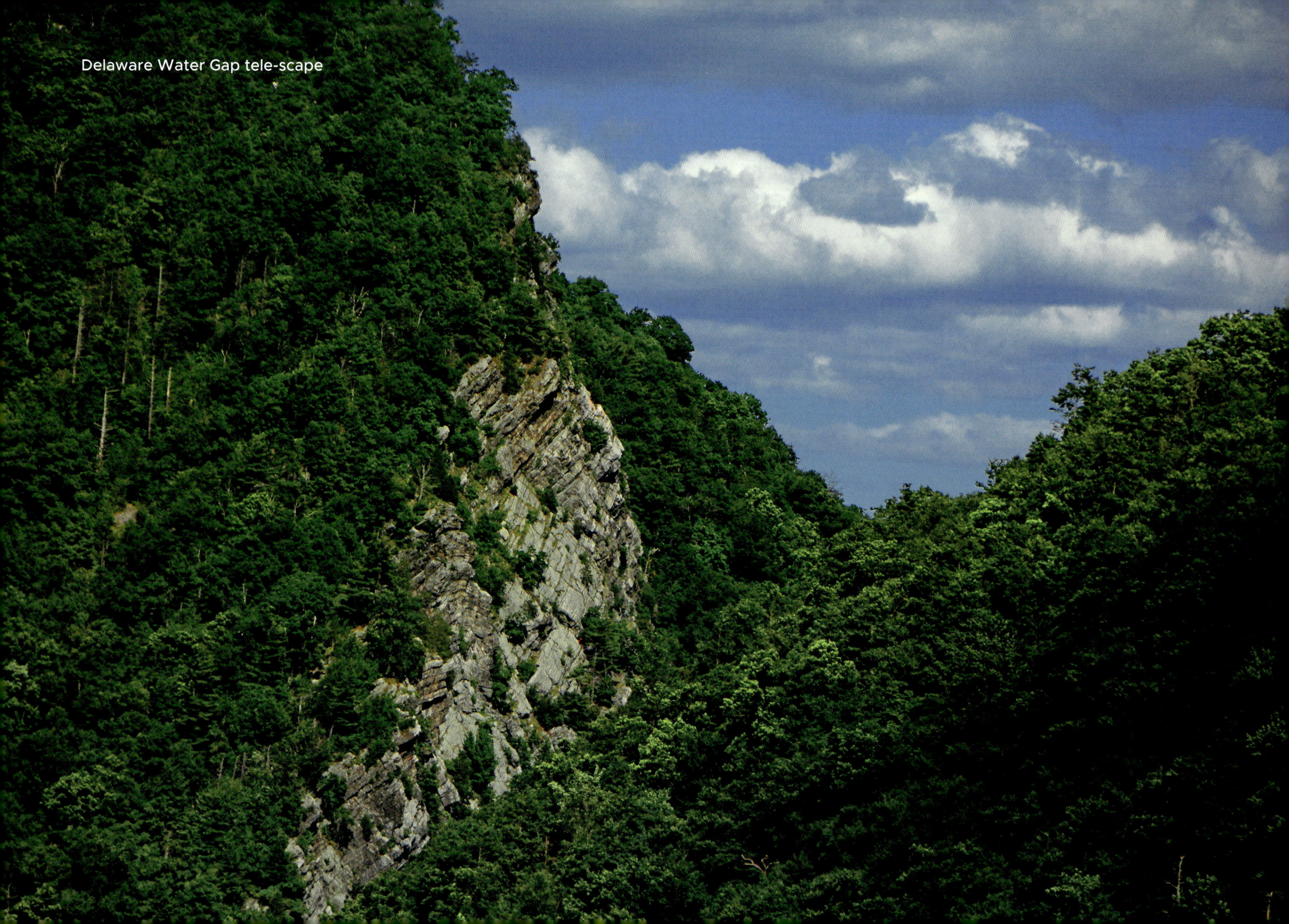

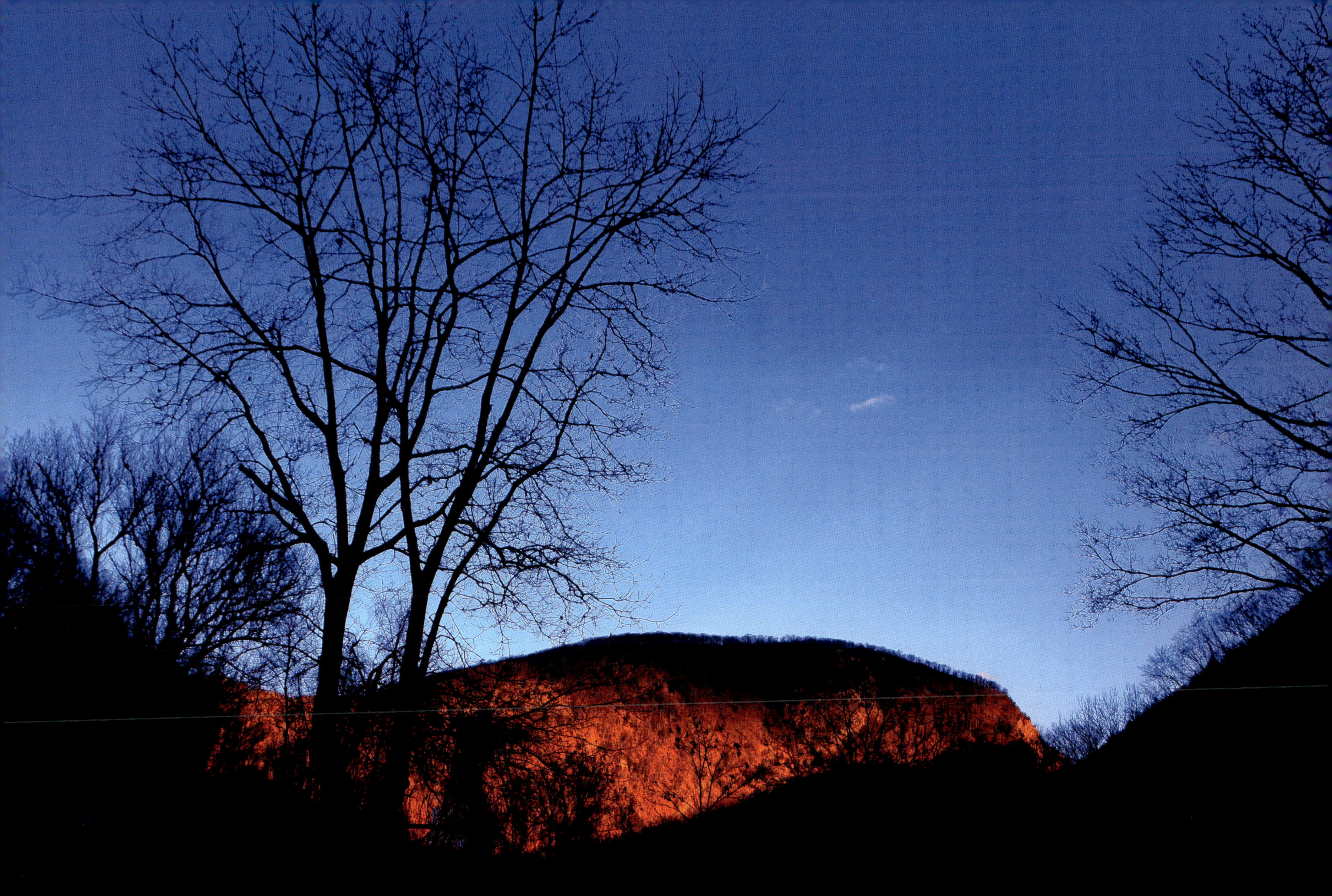

Alpenglow Mount Tammany at sunset

GEM HIKE MAP

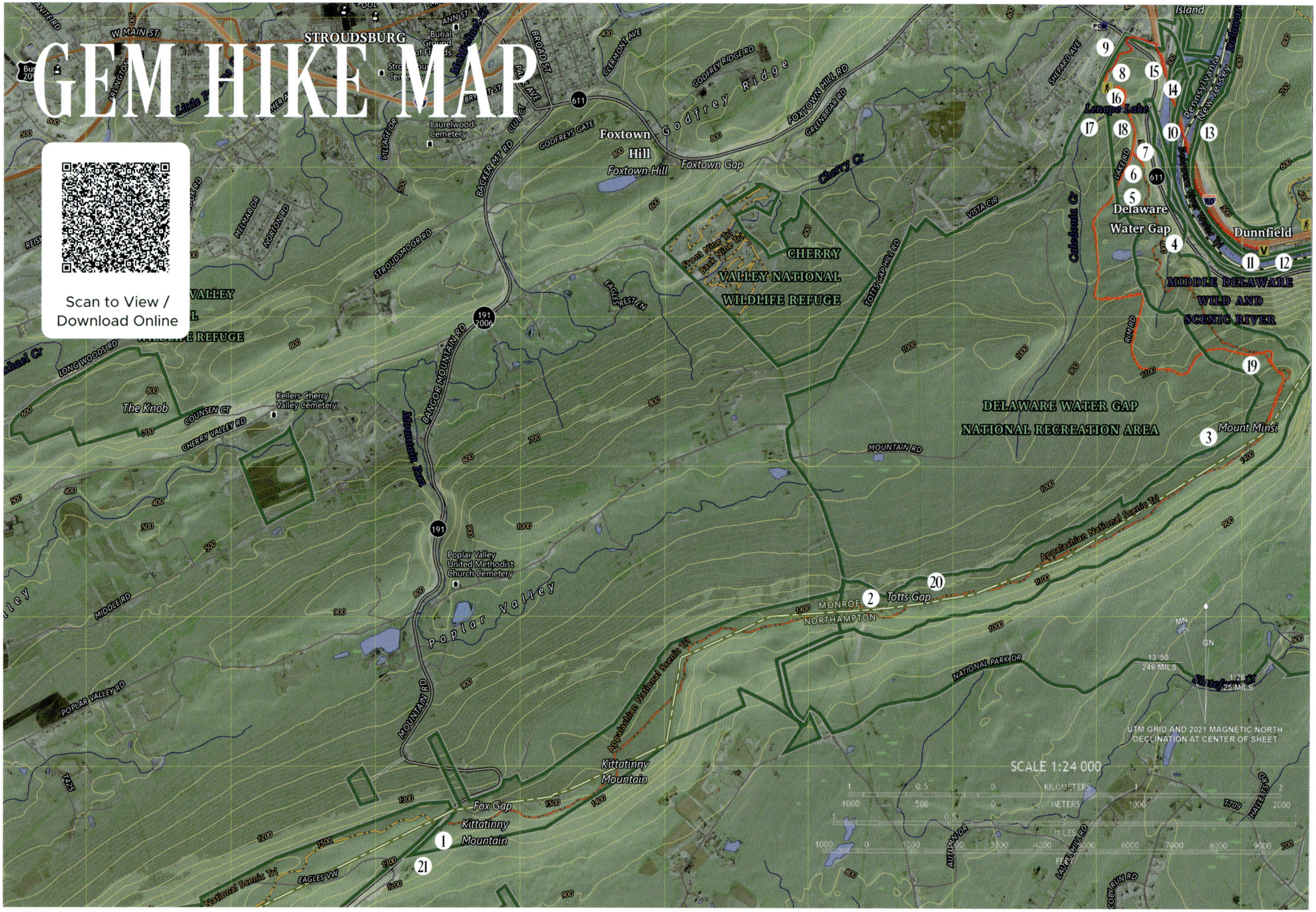

Scan to View / Download Online
STROUDSBURG
W MAIN ST
BROAD ST
Laurelwood Cemetery
Godfrey Ridge
GODFREY RIDGE RD
GODFREYS GATE
Foxtown Hill
Foxtown Gap
FOXTOWN HILL RD
GREENBRIAR RD
Cherry Cr
CHERRY VALLEY NATIONAL WILDLIFE REFUGE
VISTA CIR
TOTTS GAP HILL RD
STROUDSMOOR RD
BACKER MT RD
EAGLES CREST LN
BANGOR MOUNTAIN RD
Mountain Run
LONG WOODS RD
The Knob
Kellers Cherry Valley Cemetery
COUNSEN CT
CHERRY VALLEY RD
Poplar Valley United Methodist Church Cemetery
Poplar Valley
MIDDLE RD
POPLAR VALLEY RD
MOUNTAIN RD
MOUNTAIN RD
MONROE
NORTHAMPTON
Totts Gap
Appalachian National Scenic Trl
NATIONAL PARK DR
Kittatinny Mountain
Fox Gap
Kittatinny Mountain
EAGLES VW
Lenape Lake
Delaware Water Gap
Dunnfield
Pennsylvania
New Jersey
Caledonia Cr
RIM RD
MIDDLE DELAWARE WILD AND SCENIC RIVER
DELAWARE WATER GAP NATIONAL RECREATION AREA
Mount Minsi
SHEPARD AVE
Island
UTM GRID AND 2021 MAGNETIC NORTH DECLINATION AT CENTER OF SHEET
SCALE 1:24 000
KILOMETERS
METERS
MILES
FEET

DIRECTIONS TO THE TRAILHEAD(S)

East Stroudsburg, Pennsylvania, to Fox Gap Trailhead in Delaware Water Gap National Recreation Area

1. From East Stroudsburg, Pennsylvania 18301, head west on E. Broad St. for 30 seconds (417 feet)
2. Turn left onto N. Courtland St. and travel for 0.4 mile
3. N. Courtland St. turns right and becomes Washington St. and travel for 0.5 mile
4. Continue onto McConnell St. and continue for 0.2 mile
5. Keep left to stay on McConnell St.
6. In 0.1 mile, merge onto PA 191 S / N. 5th St.
7. Continue to follow PA 191 S for 1.5 miles
8. Slight right to stay on PA 191 S
9. In 0.2 mile, slight left to stay on PA 191 S and continue for 2.6 miles
10. Turn left onto Kirkridge Rd., and the parking area is the side of PA Route 191

GEM HIKE DIRECTIONS

1. Leave the trailhead on the Appalachian Trail north for 0.6 mile
2. At 1.9 miles, cross Totts Gap (a gravel road)
3. Travel the Appalachian Trail for another 1.4 miles to the summit of Mount Minsi
4. Travel 1 mile and arrive at Look Out Rock Overlook
5. Continue another 0.2 mile and cross a stream
6. After the stream, continue on the Appalachian Trail for 0.6 mile and arrive at Council Rock Overlook
7. After 0.1 mile, turn right (east) on a gravel road
8. After 0.4 mile, you reach a hiker parking lot
9. Continue 0.2 mile in the town of Delaware Water Gap, Pennsylvania
10. In 0.3 mile, you reach the Pennsylvania / New Jersey border on the I-80 bridge
11. Continue the Appalachian Trail another 1 mile, and you will reach the Kittatinny Point Visitor Center
12. Turn around at the Kittatinny Point Visitor Center on the Appalachian Trail south
13. Continue for 1 mile and you will reach the New Jersey / Pennsylvania border
14. In 0.3 mile, you reach the town of Delaware Water Gap, Pennsylvania
15. Continue for 0.2 mile and reach a hiker parking lot
16. Travel 0.1 mile and don't get on the Appalachian Trail
17. After 0.1 mile, turn right on the Table Rock Trail
18. After 0.6 mile, turn right on Mount Minsi Fire Road Trail and continue for 1.5 miles
19. Turn right on the Appalachian Trail south
20. Travel the Appalachian Trail for 2 miles and cross Totts Gap Rd. for the second time
21. After crossing Totts Gap Rd., travel 2.5 miles on the Appalachian Trail and arrive back at the trailhead at Fox Gap, Pennsylvania, Route 191

MORE/LESS AMBITIOUS HIKERS

More-ambitious hikers may wish to continue beyond Kittatinny Point Visitor Center and Worthington State Forest Parking Lot. Less ambitious hikers may wish to start the hike at Totts Gap. Less ambitious hikers may also wish to set up a car shuttle and do this hike in one direction and decide if they would rather hike more uphill or downhill.

CHAPTER 8

THE APPALACHIAN TRAIL: WORTHINGTON STATE FOREST AND SUNFISH POND

AREA MAP

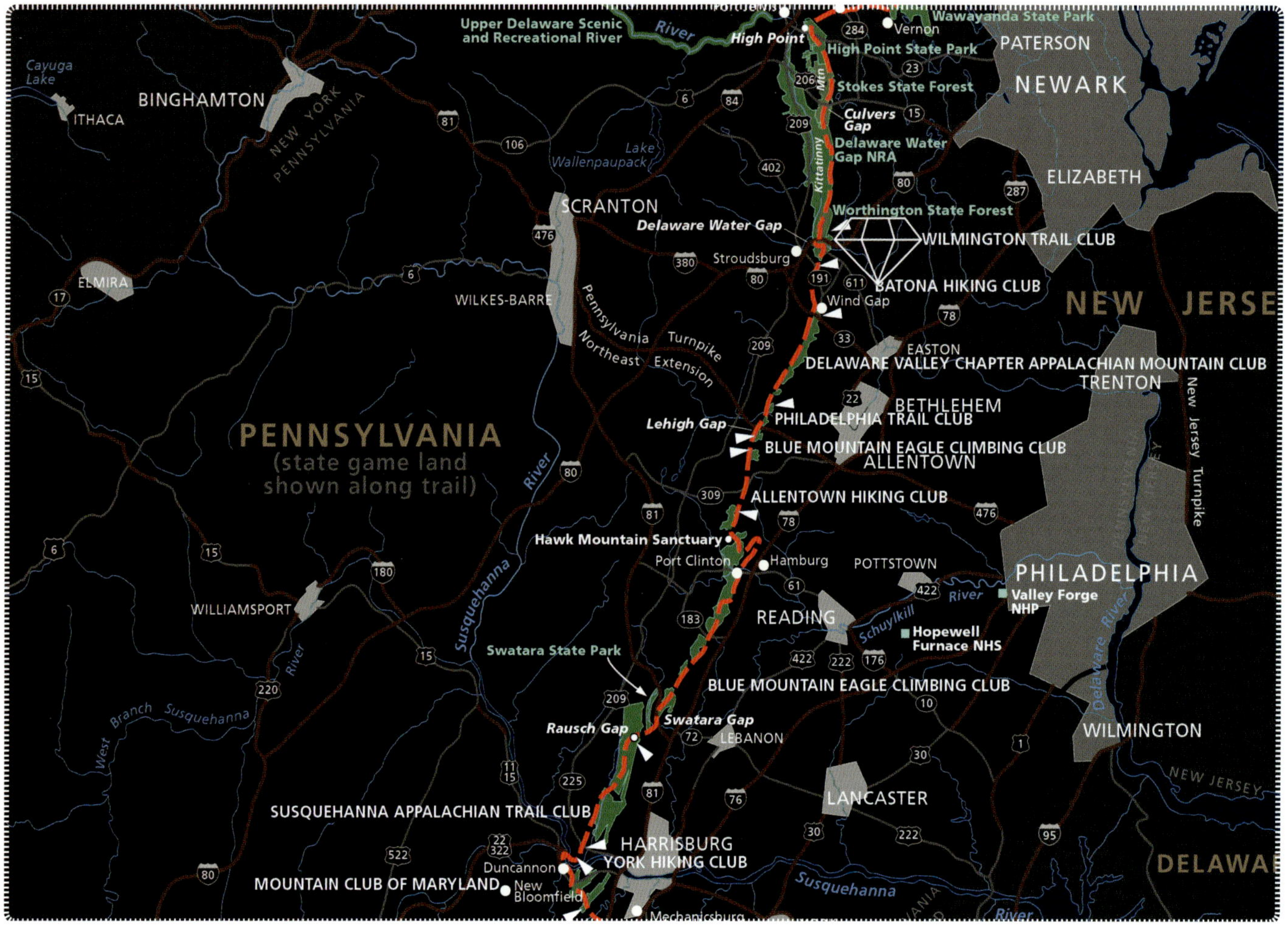

DISTANCE	9.3 miles
ELEVATION GAIN	1,200 feet
ELEVATION LOSS	1,200 feet
LEVEL	Moderate

TYPE: LOOP

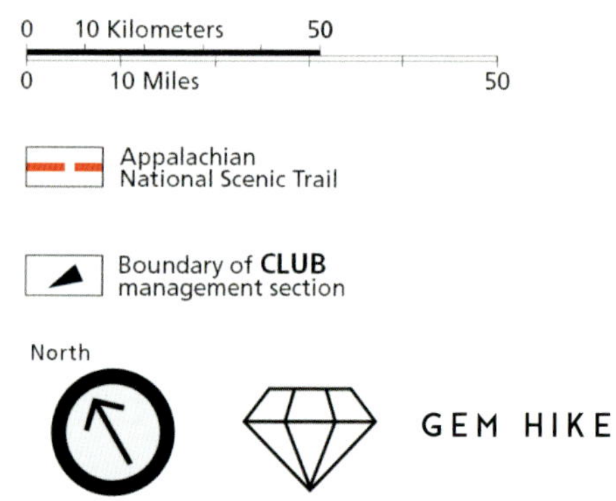

PERSONAL TOUCH

What do Lake Michigan and Sunfish Pond have in common? Well, besides the obvious answer, both being bodies of water, the answer is that they are both glacial lakes from a prior ice age. This might be hard to believe because of their names, but names can be deceptive.

This hike offers water in different forms. Sometimes it rushes when Dunnfield Creek swells after a rainstorm. Other times it has been sitting since the last ice age, at Sunfish Pond. Both types of water work together to create a unique landscape that both the young and old can enjoy now and into the future.

BRIEF OVERVIEW

Accessing the Appalachian Trail from Dunnfield Creek is straightforward, with a well-marked trailhead located near the parking area along I-80. The trail initially follows the course of Dunnfield Creek, where hikers can enjoy the soothing sounds of rushing water. As the trail ascends, it becomes a little more rugged as it approaches Sunfish. When navigating the Appalachian Trail around Sunfish Pond, the trail is extremely rocky.

DESCRIPTION OF THE GEM HIKE

This hike begins in Worthington State Forest's Dunnfield Creek Parking Area, located just off I-80 (40.971691, −75.125689). It travels to and along Sunfish Pond, a glacial lake from the last ice age, and hikers have the option to hike back the way they came or explore the water crossings of Dunnfield Creek Trail.

FLORA, FAUNA, AND VEGETATION

The plant life along this section of the Appalachian Trail is diverse and vibrant. The trail passes through mixed deciduous and coniferous trees. There are also plenty of undergrowth plants. Dominant trees include oak, maple, and hickory, and a rich assortment of wildflowers, ferns, and shrubs.

DUNNFIELD CREEK

Dunnfield Creek acts as the starting point for this section of the trail. It has crystal-clear waters flowing over rocks and pebbles. The creek is an important ecological feature. The sound of the creek's flowing water enhances the tranquil atmosphere of the area.

SUNFISH POND

Sunfish Pond is a breathtaking glacial lake located at the northern end of this trail segment. The pond is also known for its crystal-clear waters and serene surroundings. Sunfish Pond is also a prime spot for birdwatching and photography.

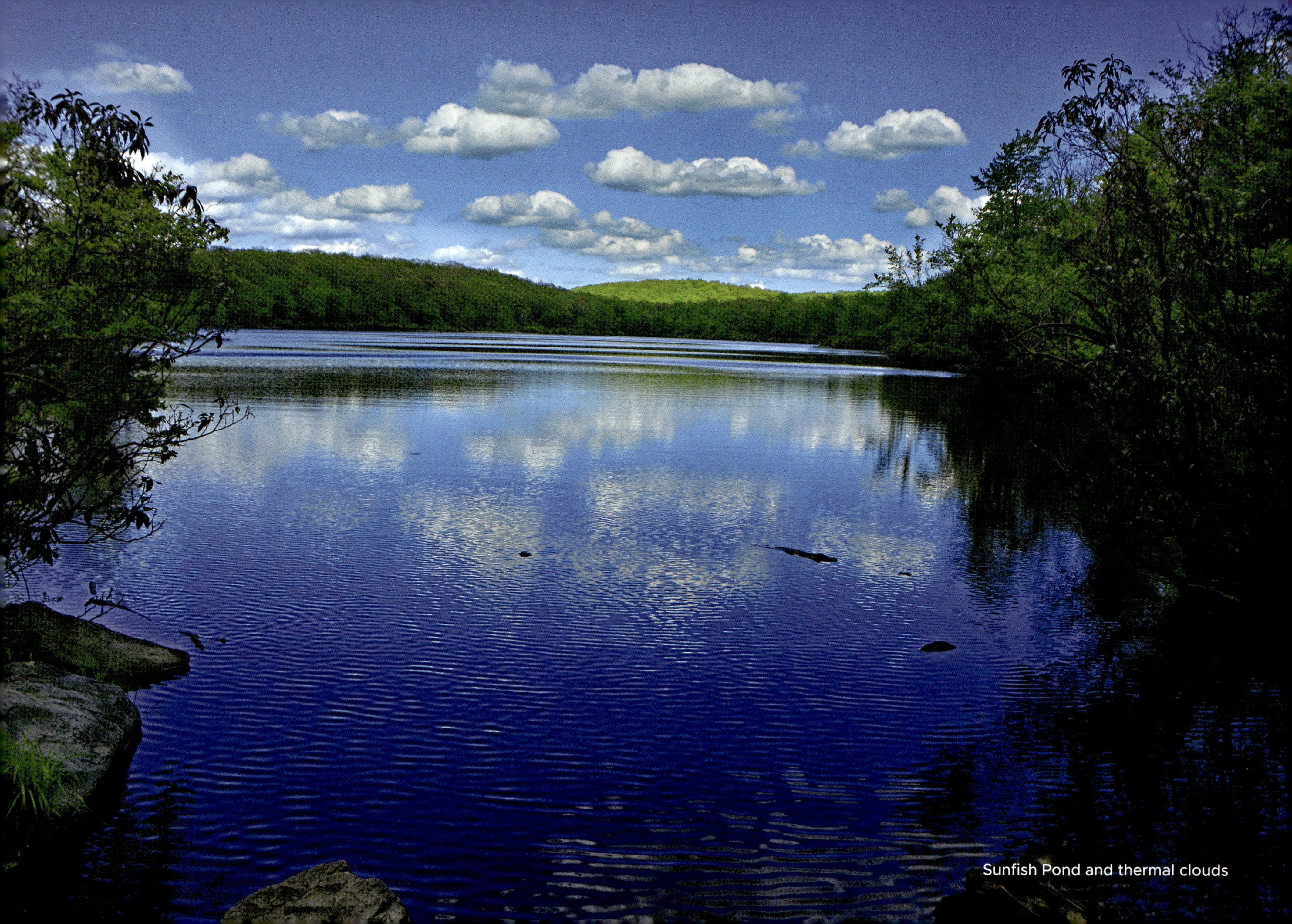

Sunfish Pond and thermal clouds

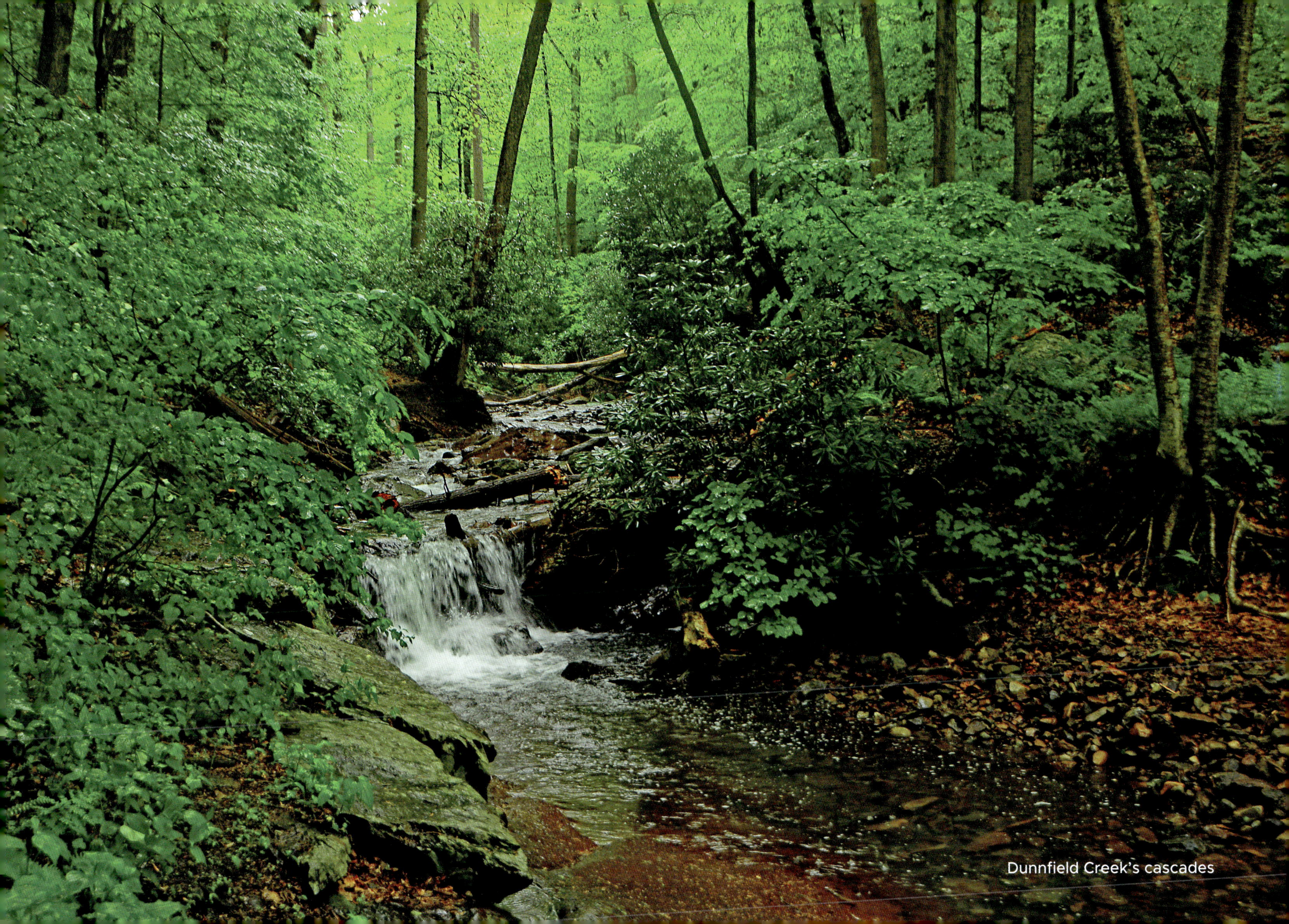

Dunnfield Creek's cascades

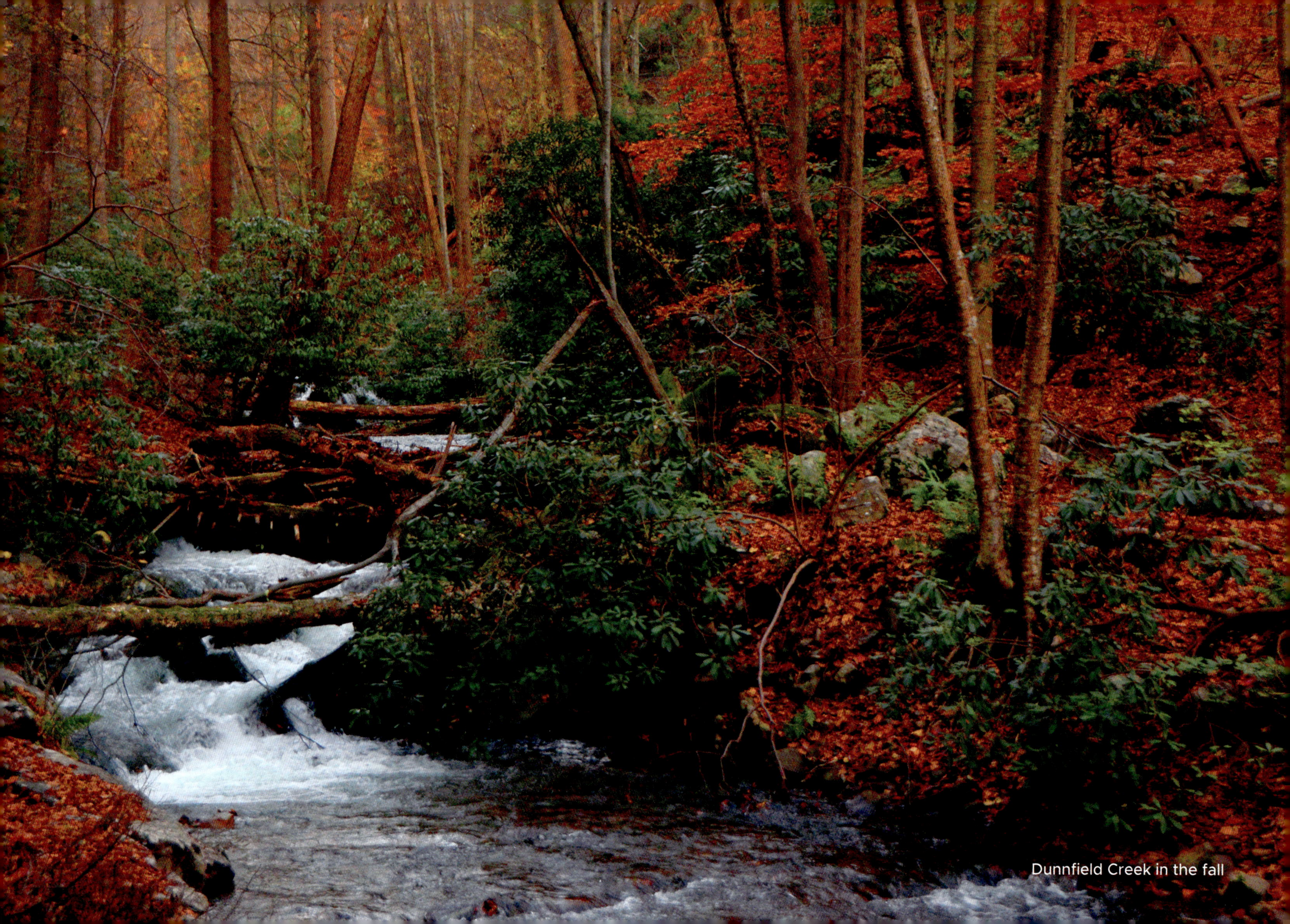

Dunnfield Creek in the fall

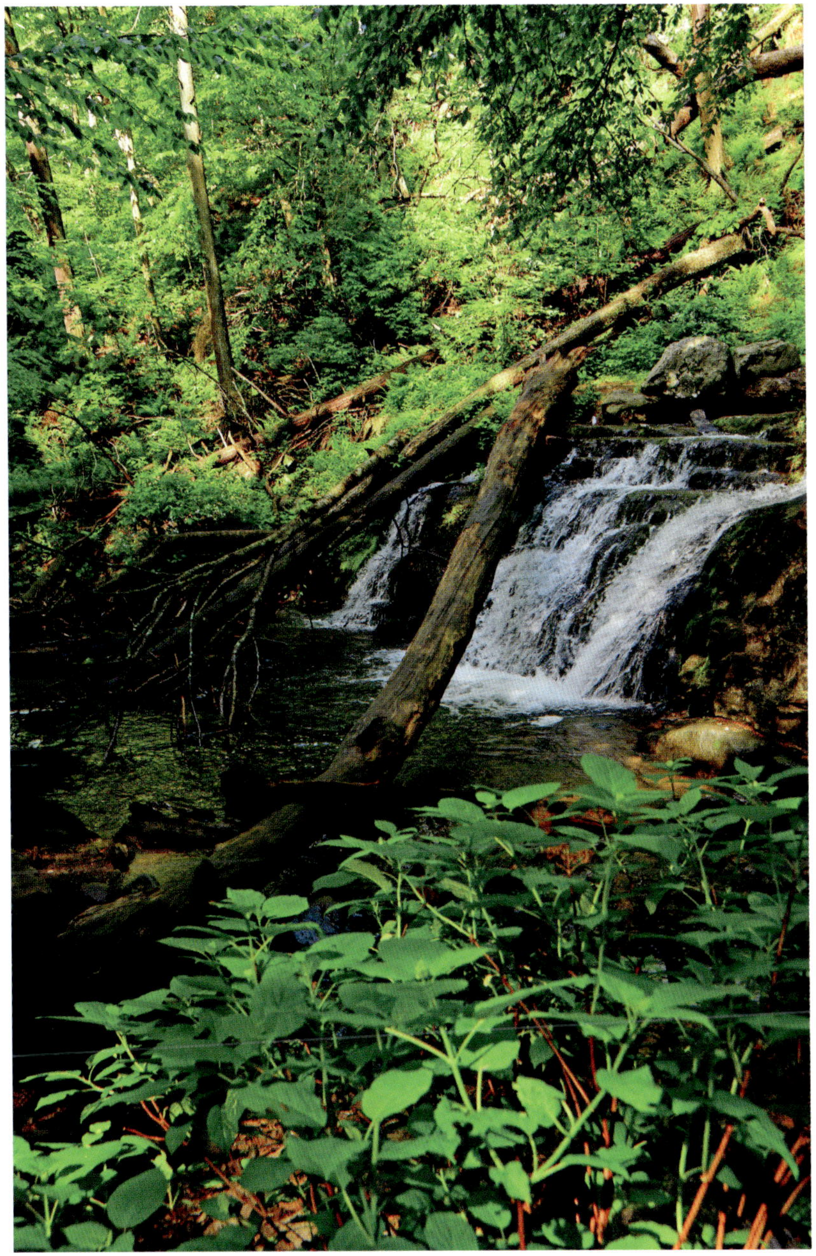

A waterfall in Dunnfield Creek

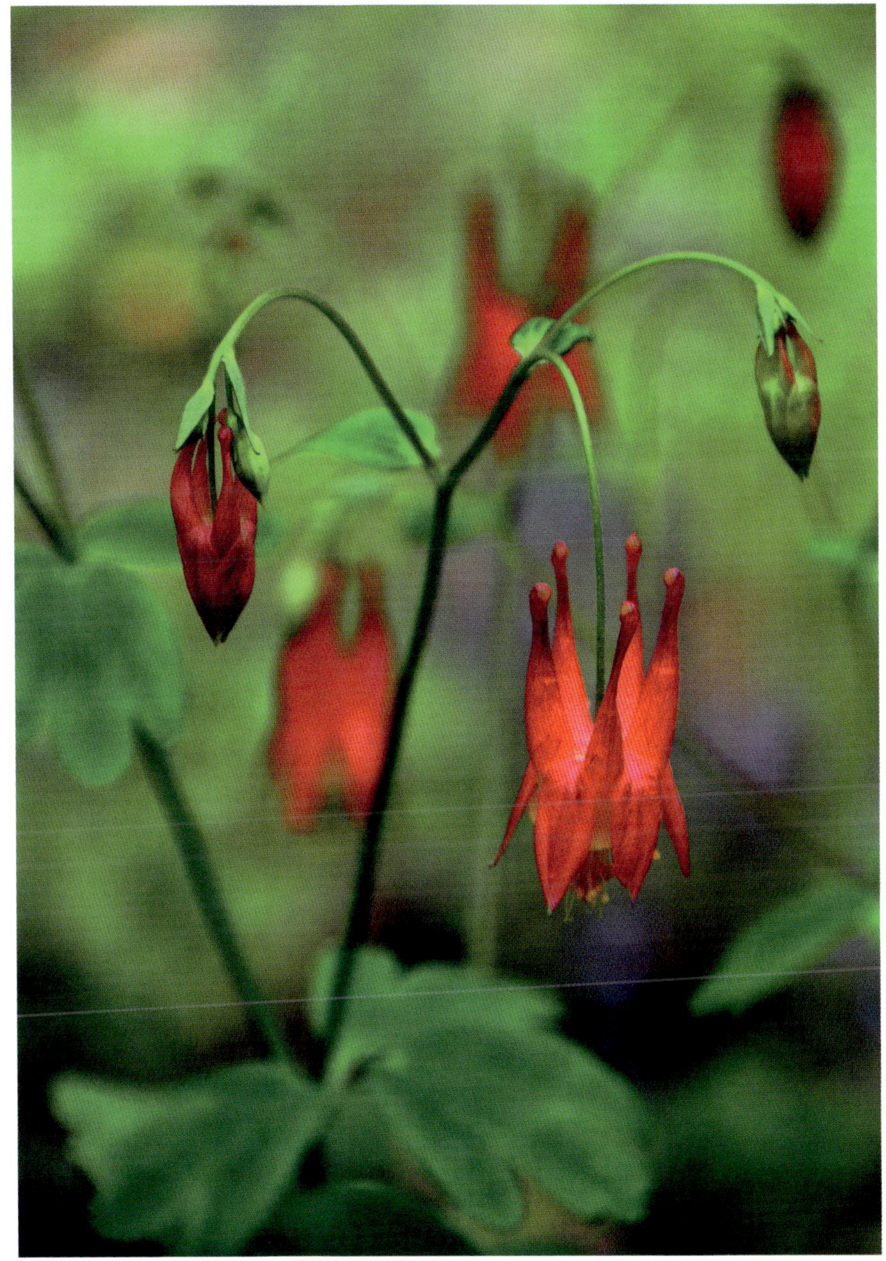

Eastern red columbine (*Aquilegia canadensis*)

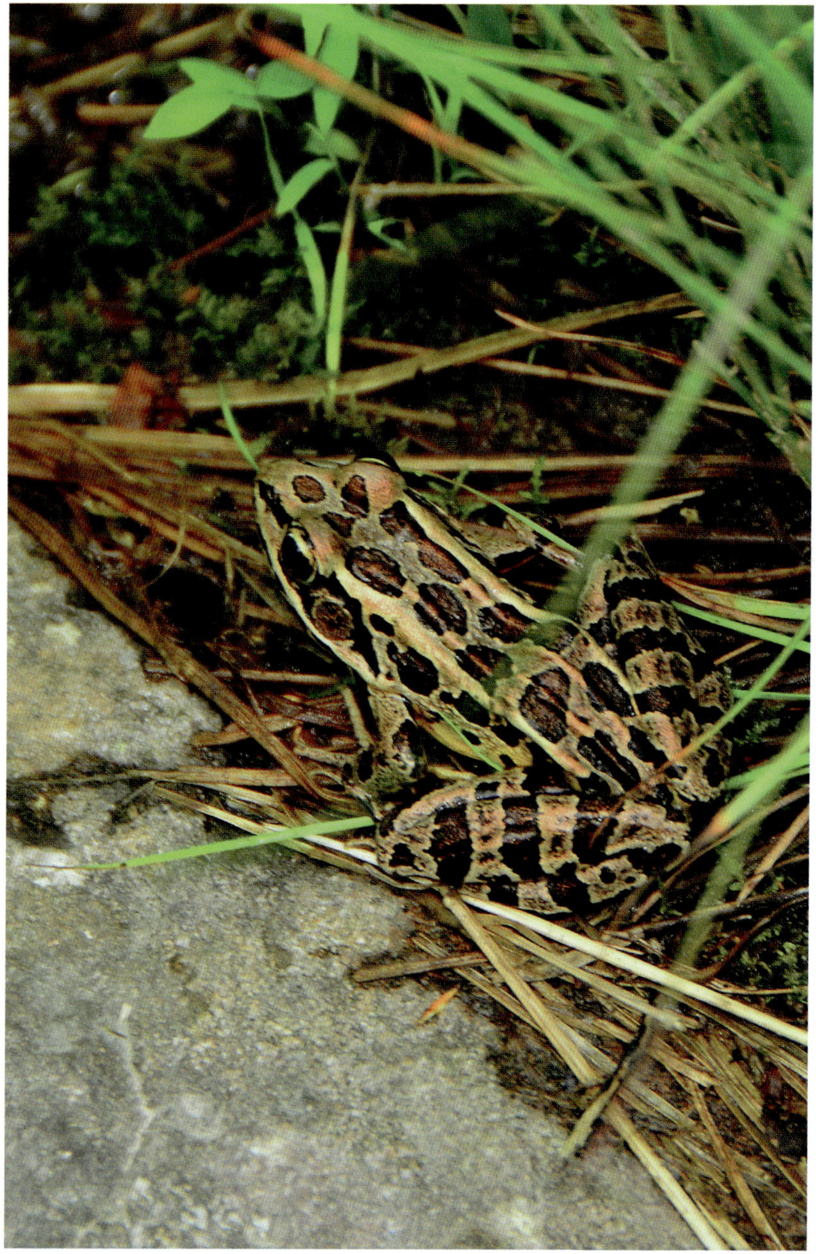

A pickerel frog (*Lithobates palustris*) calls the New Jersey section of the Appalachian Trail home.

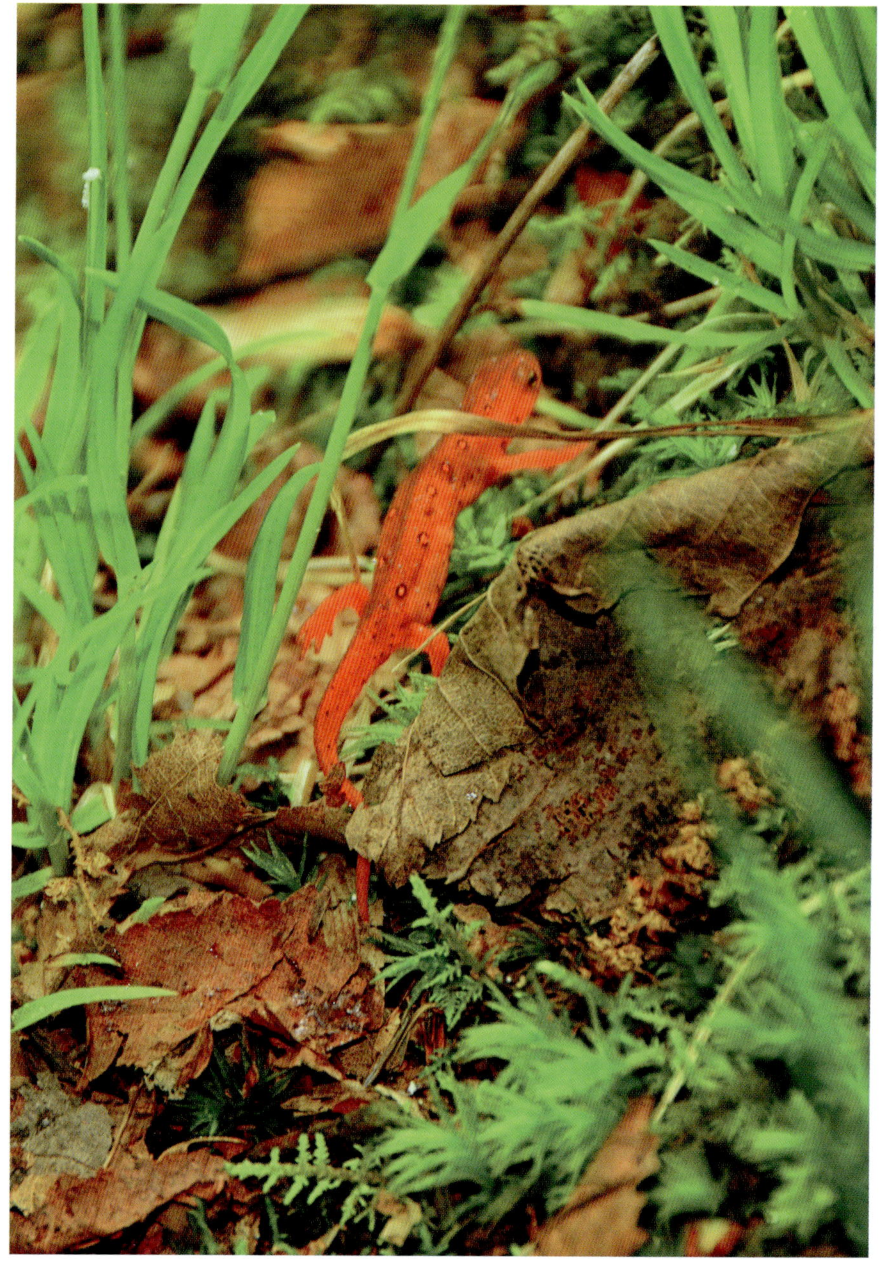

Red eft (*Notophthalmus viridescens*) is your hiking companion.

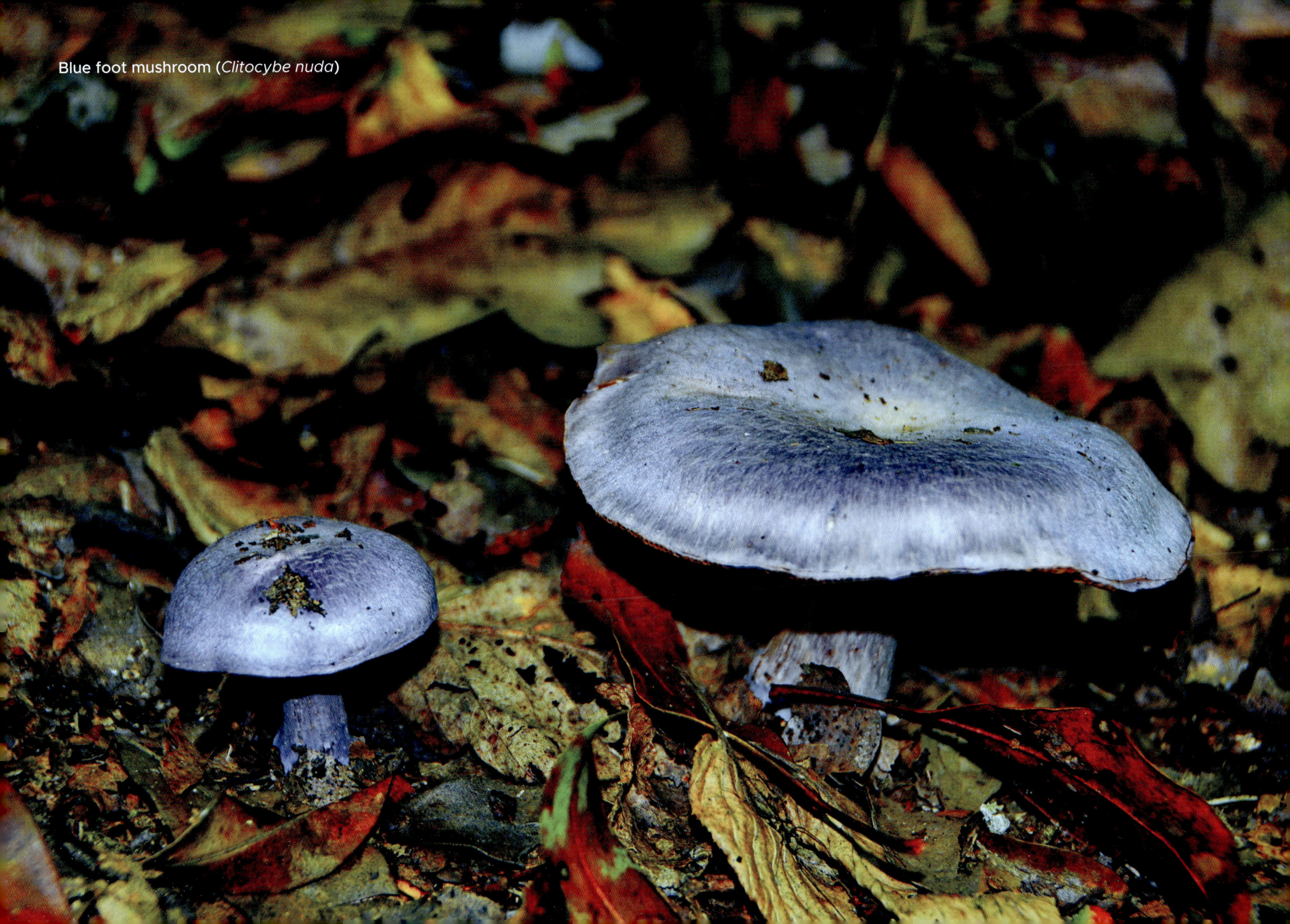

Blue foot mushroom (*Clitocybe nuda*)

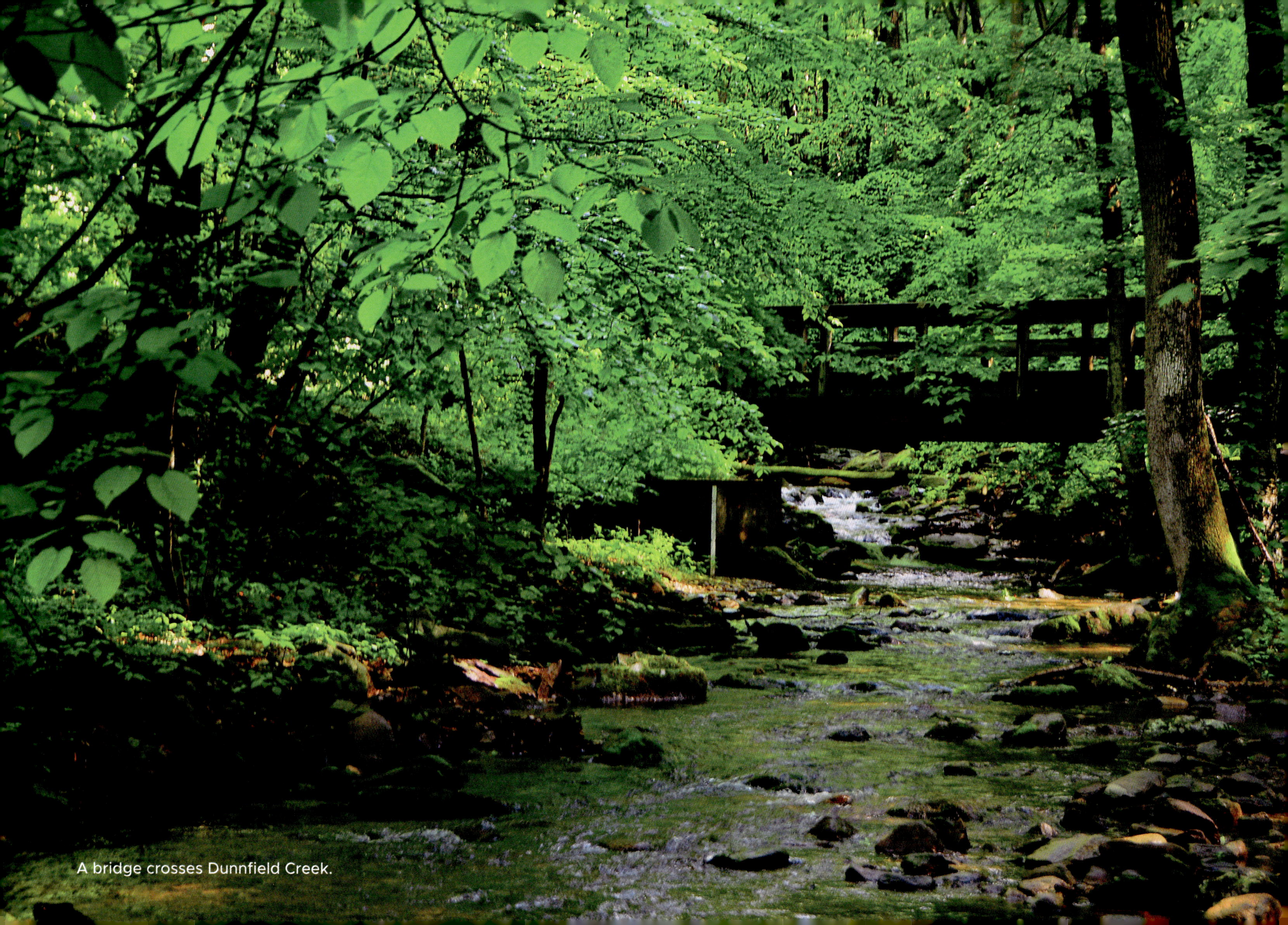

A bridge crosses Dunnfield Creek.

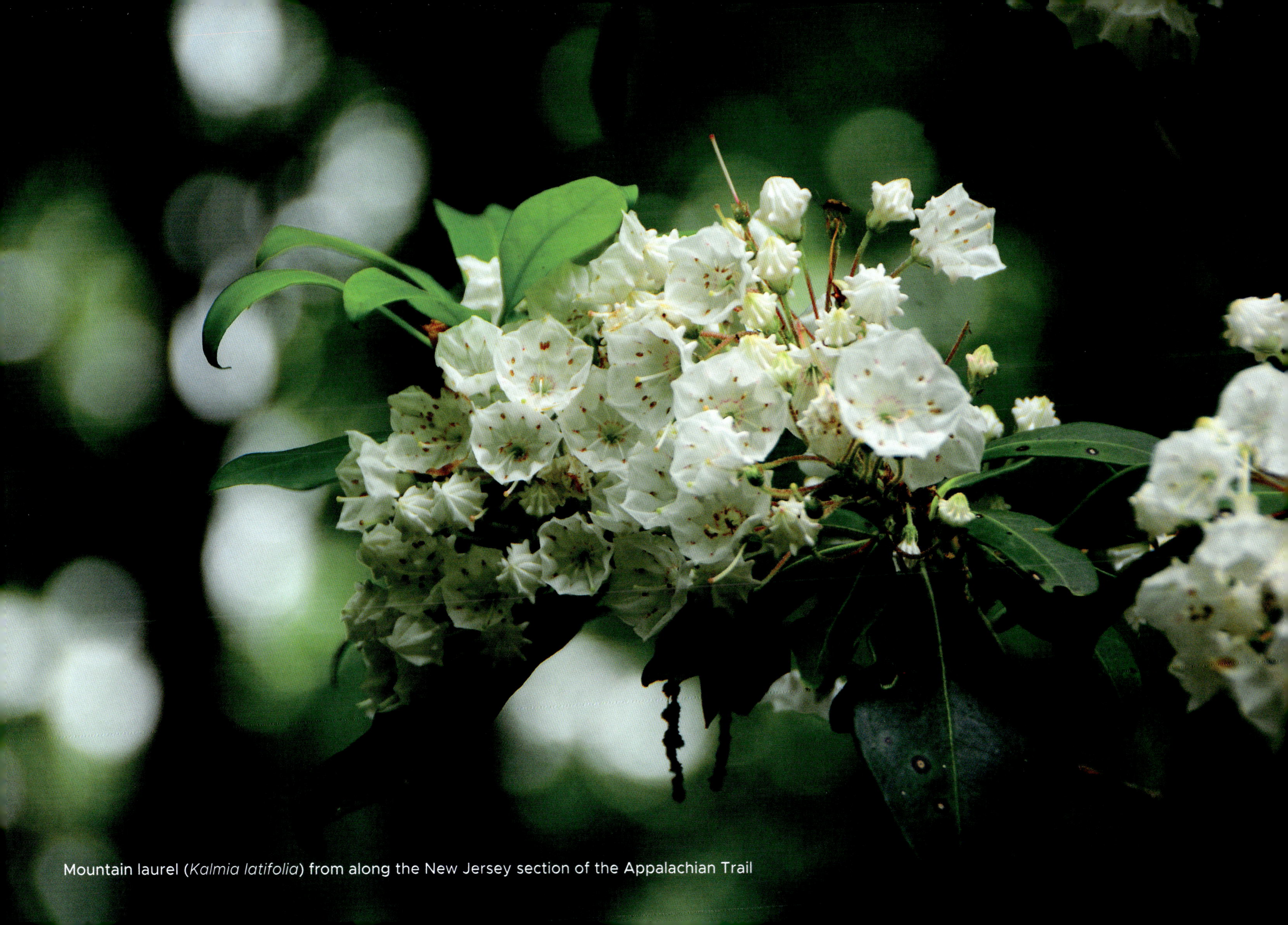

Mountain laurel (*Kalmia latifolia*) from along the New Jersey section of the Appalachian Trail

GEM HIKE MAP

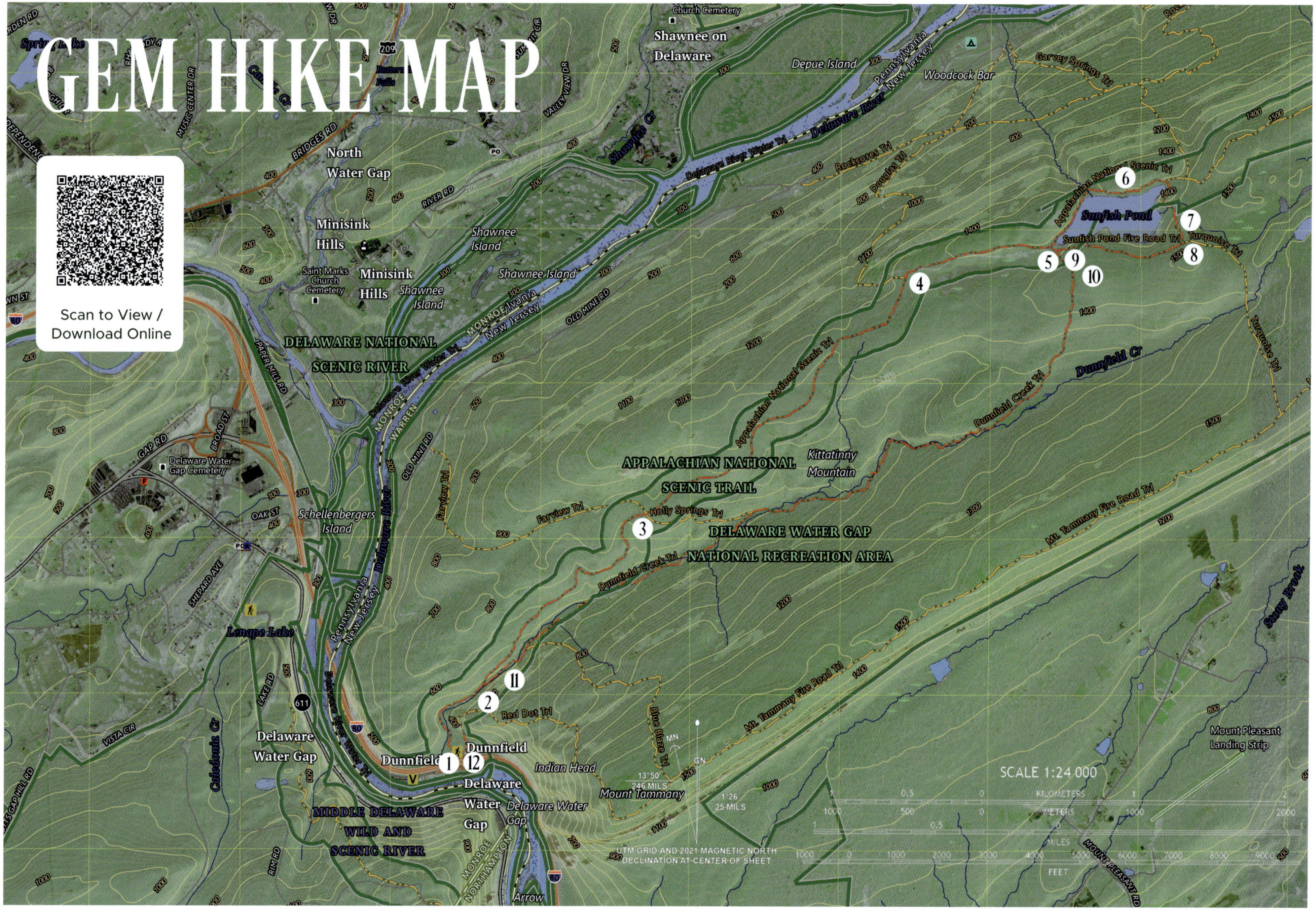

Scan to View / Download Online
North Water Gap
Minisink Hills
Shawnee on Delaware
Depue Island
Woodcock Bar
Shawnee Island
Saint Marks Church Cemetery
DELAWARE NATIONAL SCENIC RIVER
Delaware Water Gap Cemetery
Schellenbergers Island
Lenape Lake
Delaware Water Gap
Dunnfield
Indian Head
Mount Tammany
Delaware Water Gap
MIDDLE DELAWARE WILD AND SCENIC RIVER
APPALACHIAN NATIONAL SCENIC TRAIL
Kittatinny Mountain
DELAWARE WATER GAP NATIONAL RECREATION AREA
Sunfish Pond
Sunfish Pond Fire Road Trl
Dunnfield Creek Trl
Dunnfield Cr
Holly Springs Trl
Fairview Trl
Red Dot Trl
Blue Blaze Trl
Mt. Tammany Fire Road Trl
Turquoise Trl
Garvey Springs Trl
Rockcores Trl
Douglas Trl
Delaware River Water Trl
Stony Brook
Mount Pleasant Landing Strip
SCALE 1:24 000
UTM GRID AND 2021 MAGNETIC NORTH DECLINATION AT CENTER OF SHEET

DIRECTIONS TO THE TRAILHEAD(S)

Orange, New Jersey, to Dunnfield Creek Trailhead in Worthington State Forest

1. Head west toward I-280 W for 0.2 mile
2. Merge onto I-280 W and travel for 9.9 miles
3. Use the left two lanes to merge onto I-80 W
4. Continue of I-80 W for 45.4 miles
5. Take the exit Dunnfield Creek / Appalachian Trail ramp for 0.1 mile
6. Continue straight for 335 feet
7. Slight right; after 187 feet, Appalachian Trail parking in Worthington State Forest

GEM HIKE DIRECTIONS

1. Start at Dunnfield Creek Trailhead in Worthington State Forest on the Appalachian Trail north for 0.3 mile
2. Continue past the blue- and green-dot trails junction
3. After 1.2 miles, continue on the AT, passing Holly Springs Trail (Red Blaze) on the right
4. After another 2.1 miles, you will reach Backpacker Campsite / Douglas Trail (Blue Blaze) junction and continue on the Appalachian Trail
5. After traveling another 0.8 mile, you will reach the south end of Sunfish Pond
6. Continue on the Appalachian Trail for another 0.6 mile, to the north end of Sunfish Pond, to a junction with the Turquoise Trail
7. Turn right on the Turquoise Trail and continue for 0.4 mile
8. Reach Sunfish Pond Fire Rd. and take a right and travel for 0.5 mile
9. Reach Sunfish Pond south bank (for the second time)
10. Take a left on the Dunnfield Creek Trail (Green Blaze) and travel 3.4 miles
11. Meet up with the Appalachian Trail southbound by taking a left
12. Travel 0.3 mile, and you will reach the parking lot that you started from

MORE/LESS AMBITIOUS HIKERS

More-ambitious hikers may want to summit Mount Tammany via the red-dot trail and come down the blue-dot trail. The red-dot trail is the other trail that leaves this trailhead. Less ambitious hikers may wish not to return down through Dunnfield Creek because of the water crossings. They may opt to take the Appalachian Trail as an out-and-back hike from the Dunnfield Creek trailhead.

CHAPTER 9

THE APPALACHIAN TRAIL IN NEW YORK: SECTION 17A TO ELK PEN IN HARRIMAN BEAR STATE PARK

AREA MAP

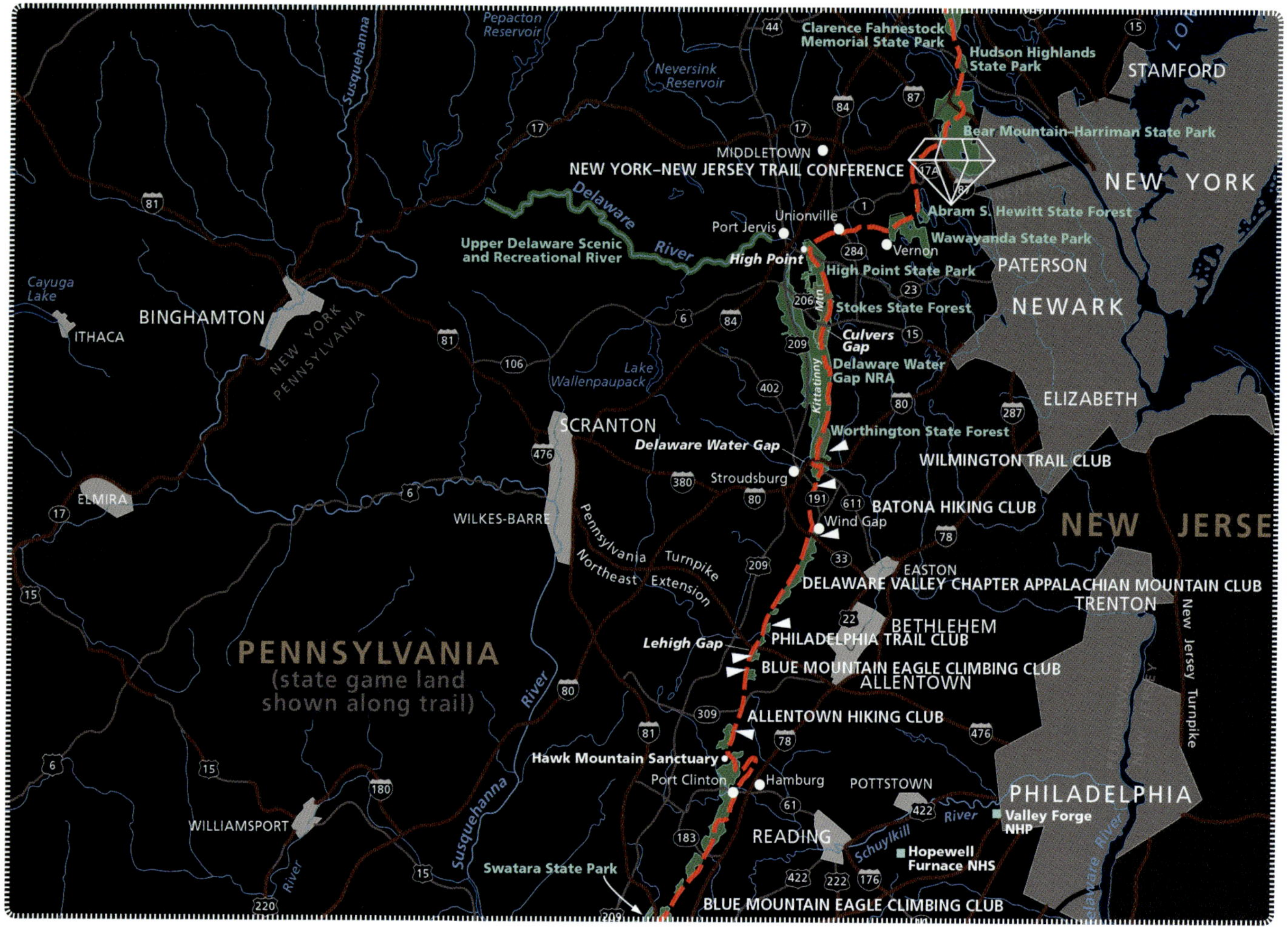

DISTANCE	12.4 miles
ELEVATION GAIN	1,800 feet
ELEVATION LOSS	2,400 feet
LEVEL	Difficult

TYPE: POINT TO POINT

0 10 Kilometers 50

0 10 Miles 50

Appalachian National Scenic Trail

Boundary of **CLUB** management section

North

GEM HIKE

PERSONAL TOUCH

This was a perfect springtime hike. If you can have vistas, wildflowers everywhere, waterfalls, views of tranquil ponds, and perfectly placed trees to make a surreal forest all in the same hike, how do you not feel you won the hike lottery? I felt like I did.

I remember lying on my stomach when a white moth landed on a pink lady's slipper orchid. I did not want to waste time and have it fly away without being part of my photographs. These pink flowers are special to me because most people think orchids are tropical plants that you can purchase at a florist. Well, I like these orchids; I know where to find them on this section hike along the Appalachian Trail, the closest hike to my home.

BRIEF OVERVIEW

This 12-mile stretch of the Appalachian Trail navigates through a varied landscape from the gentle paths in the beginning near Route 17A and rocky scrambles that pose a challenge for hikers in either direction. It has serene, forested areas and scenic vistas. Key features of this section include the challenging Agony Grind, the crossing of Interstate 87 on Arden Road, and numerous opportunities for solitude and reflection on the wildflower-lined trail, by tranquil ponds, and by Fitzgerald Falls.

DESCRIPTION OF THE GEM HIKE

The gem hike in this section is completing this hike from NY 17A (41.245384, −74.285335) to Elk Pen Parking Lot in Harriman-Bear State Park (41.264698, −74.154283). It begins with spotting a car(s) at the Elk Pen and driving to NY 17A to begin the 12-mile hike (see driving directions below). This hike is great for any spring day. This section features Fitzgerald Falls and numerous wildflowers, including pink lady's slippers and herb Robert, which bloom in late May. The ponds in the spring are diverse shades of green that make them a special treat. This hike also has its own share of vistas, including one from the top of Agony Grind that gives hikers a view of the Hudson Highlands.

SIDENOTES FOR THE GEM HIKE

This hike also allows hikers from outside the area to join you, because they can take the train to Tuxedo, New York, if you don't mind picking them up there once they arrive. It is not recommended to hike this hike on a weekend because the area is just too busy when the New York State Renaissance Fair is going on.

FLORA, FAUNA, AND VEGETATION

Oak, maple, and birch are the most common tree species in this New York section of the Appalachian Trail. The birch part of the forest makes a special treat. The Appalachian Trail in this section also contains a lot of wildflowers that provide wonderful ground cover. The ferns and pink lady's slippers are usually at their peak toward the end of May.

SOLITUDE AND REFLECTION

This trail section of the Appalachian Trail offers ample opportunities for solitude and reflection despite being so close to civilization. The dense forests and challenging terrain create a sense of isolation from the nearby urban areas. Scenic overlooks and quiet woodland areas provide spaces for hikers to pause, reflect, and appreciate the natural beauty of the region.

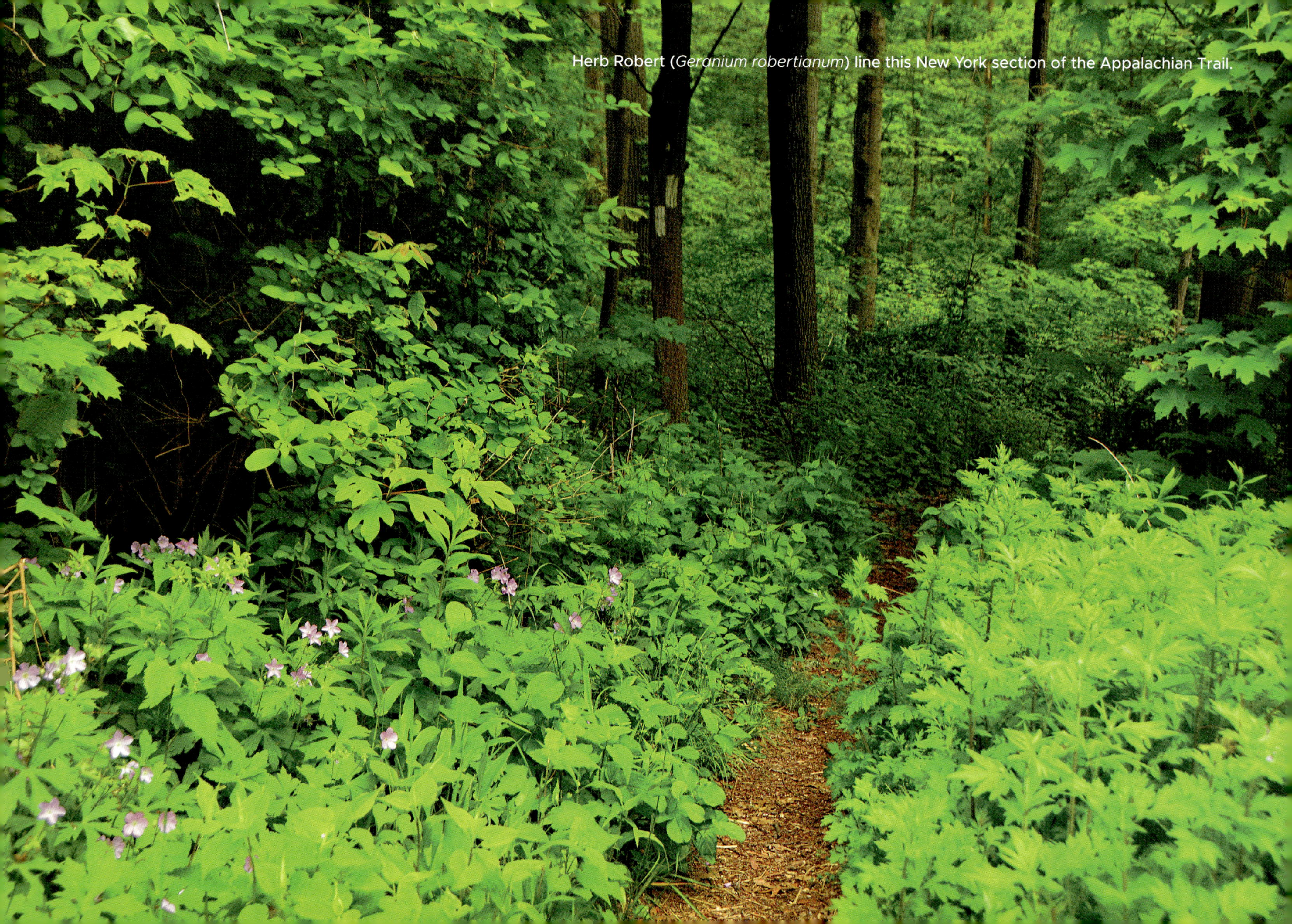

Herb Robert (*Geranium robertianum*) line this New York section of the Appalachian Trail.

Eastern Pinnacles

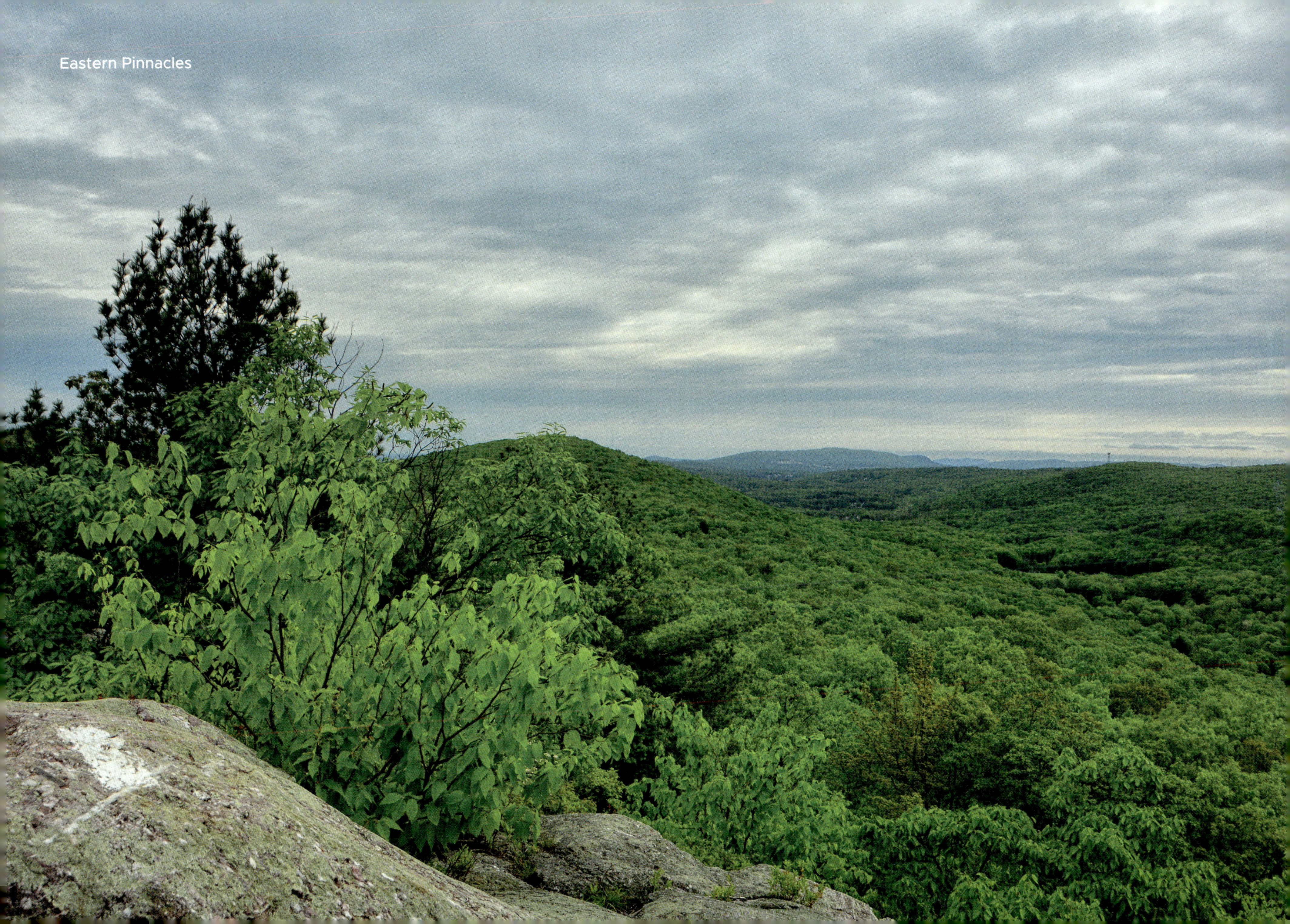

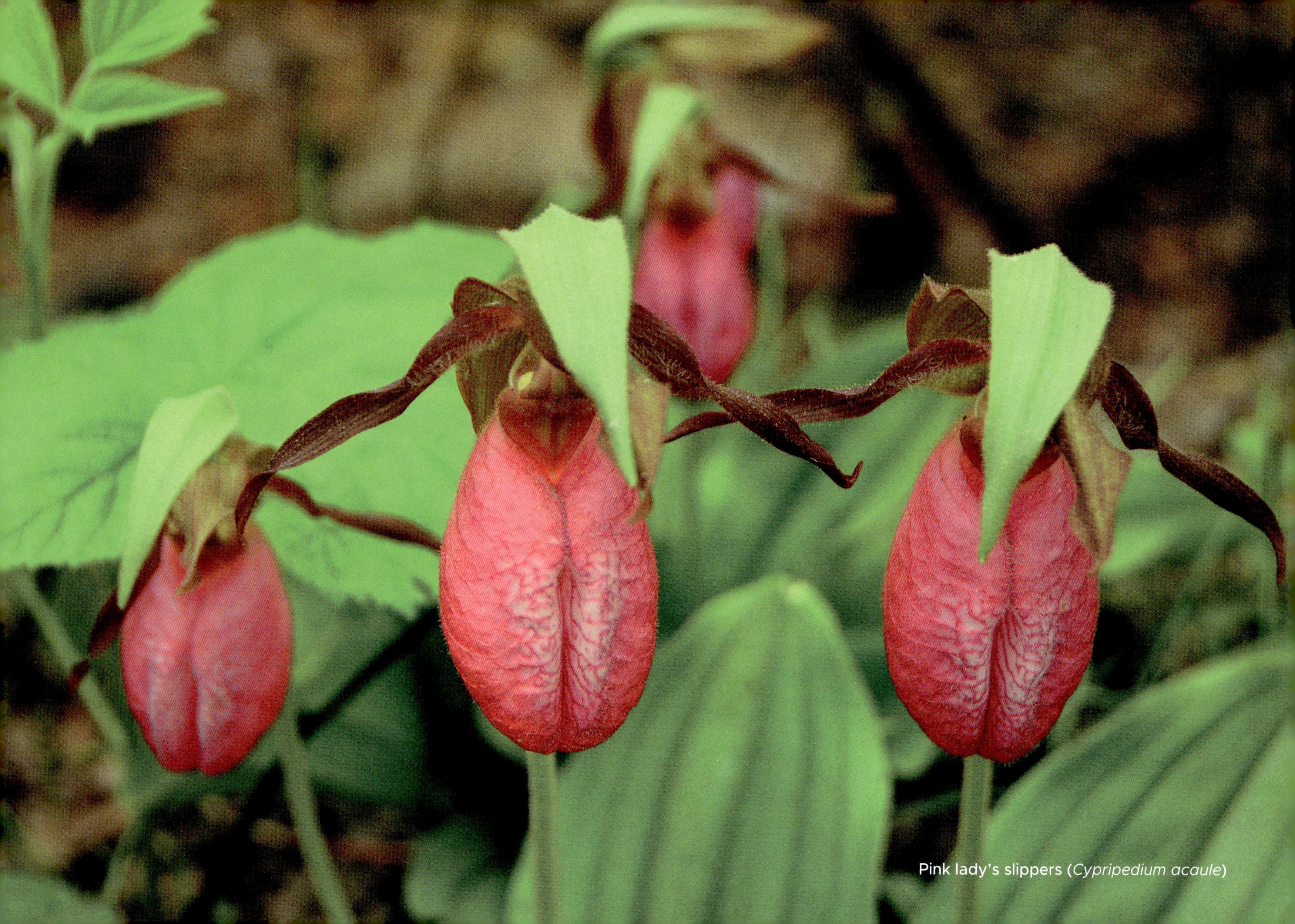

Pink lady's slippers (*Cypripedium acaule*)

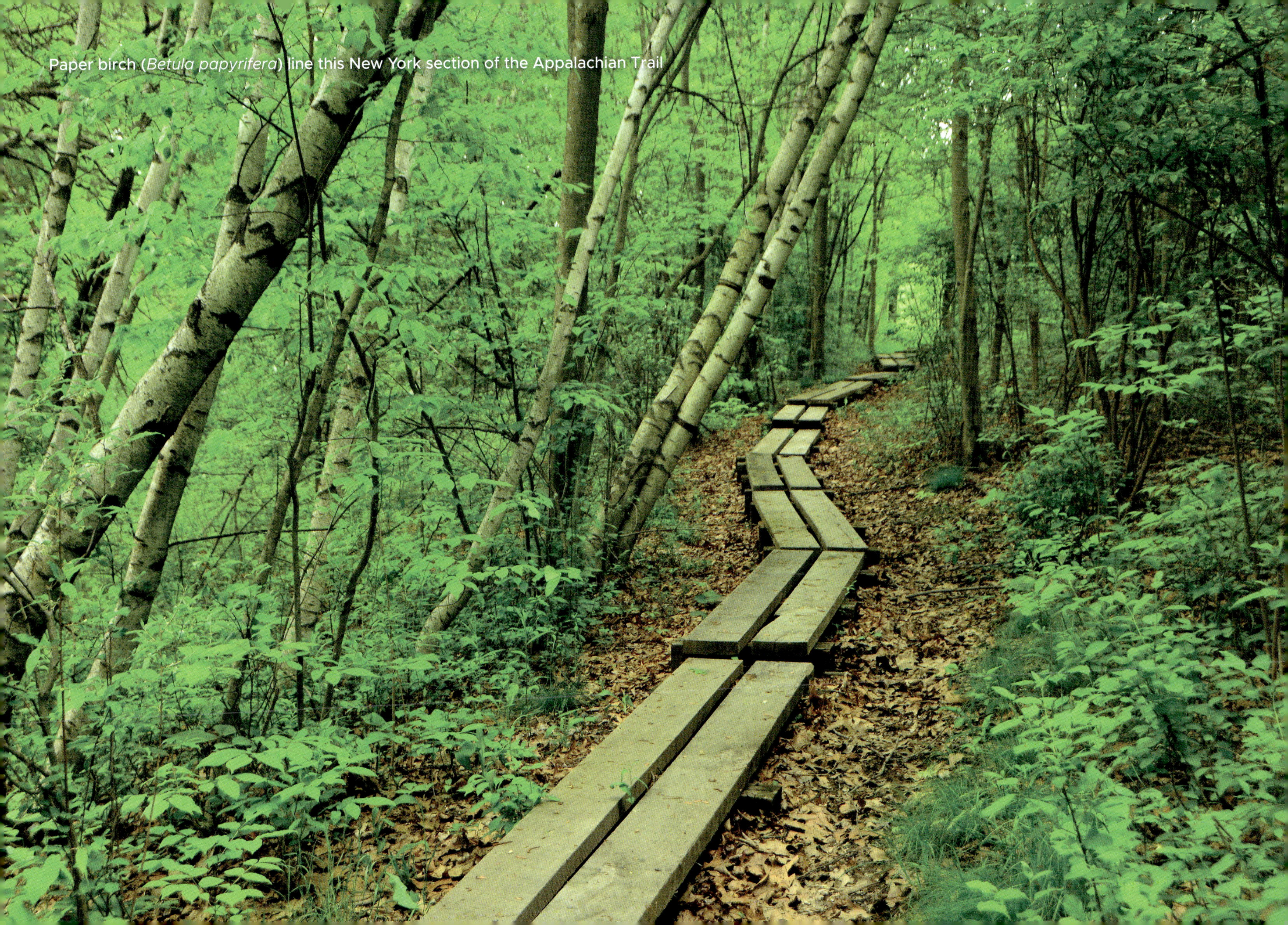

Paper birch (*Betula papyrifera*) line this New York section of the Appalachian Trail

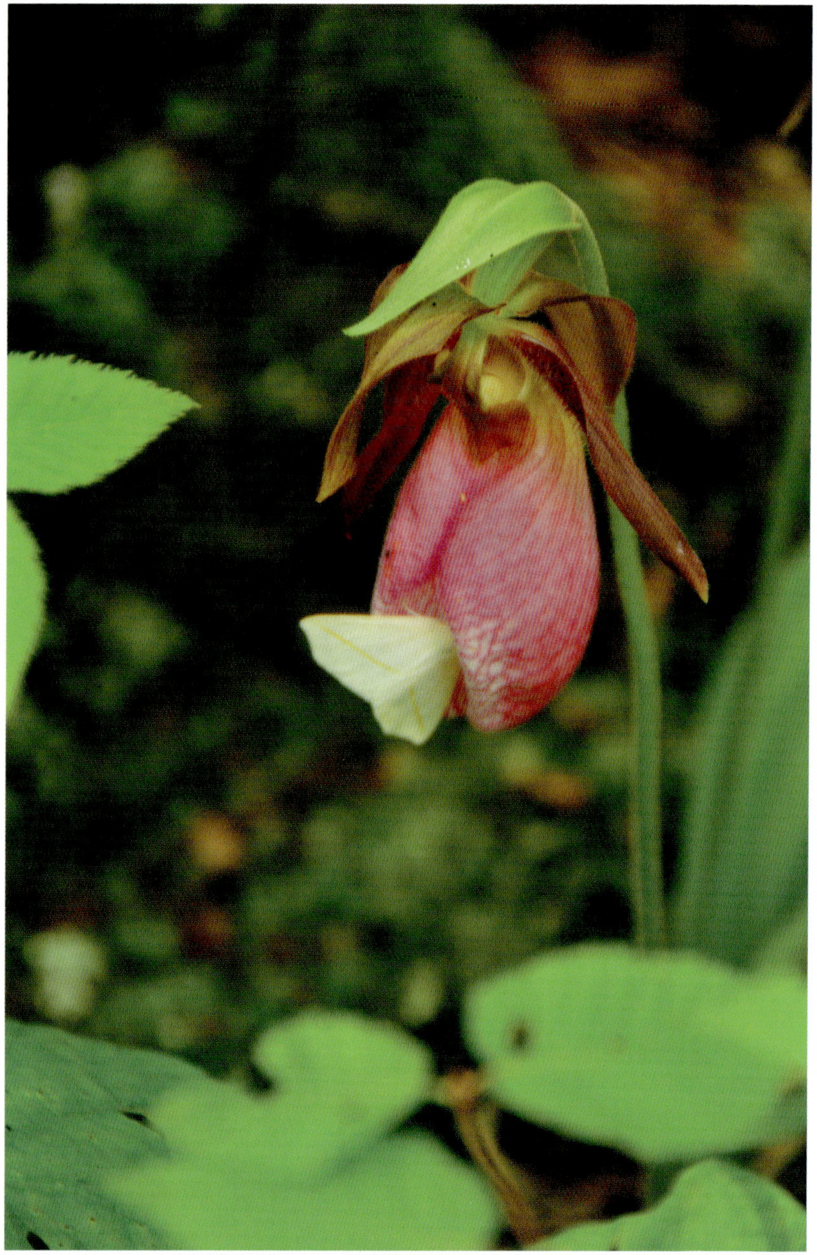

Pink lady's slipper (*Cypripedium acaule*) and white slant-line moth (*Tetracis cachexiata*)

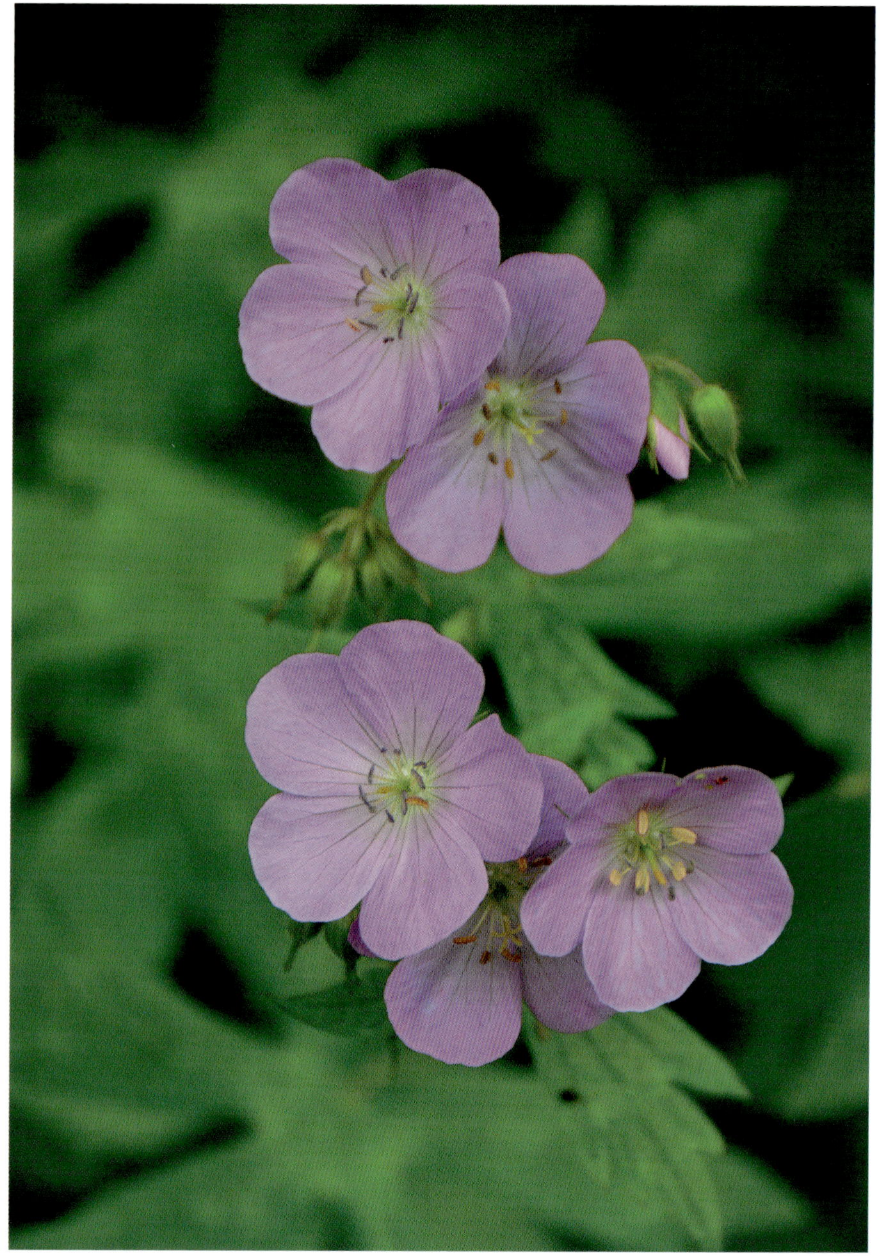

Herb Robert (*Geranium robertianum*)

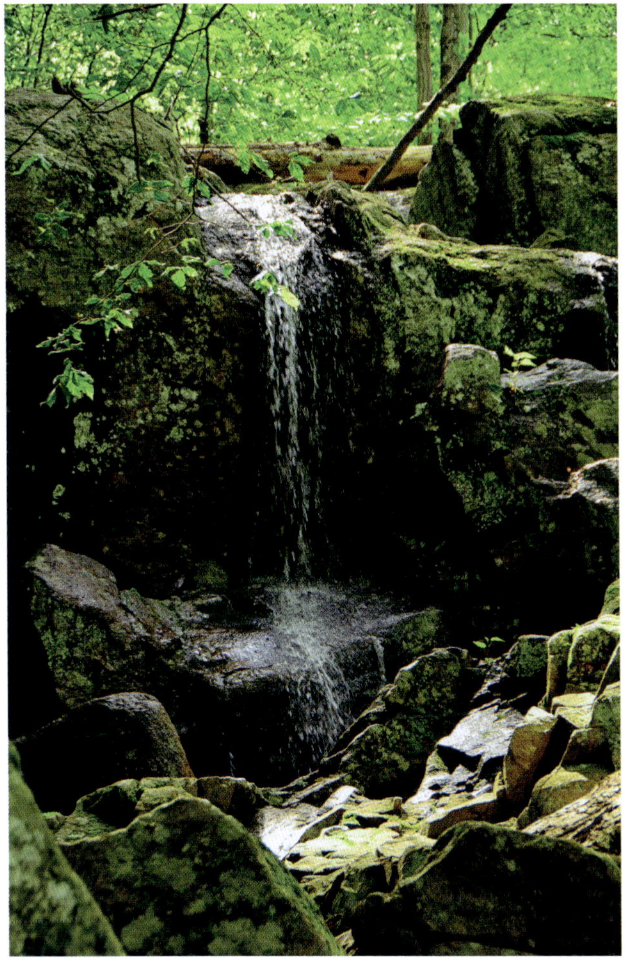

Falls along the New York section of the Appalachian Trail

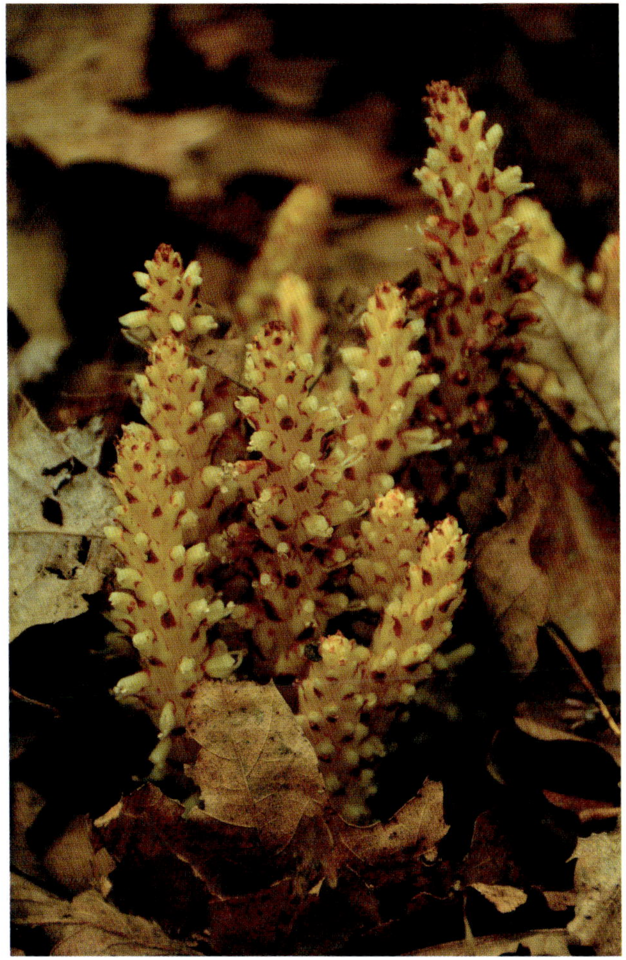

American cancer-root (*Conopholis americana*)

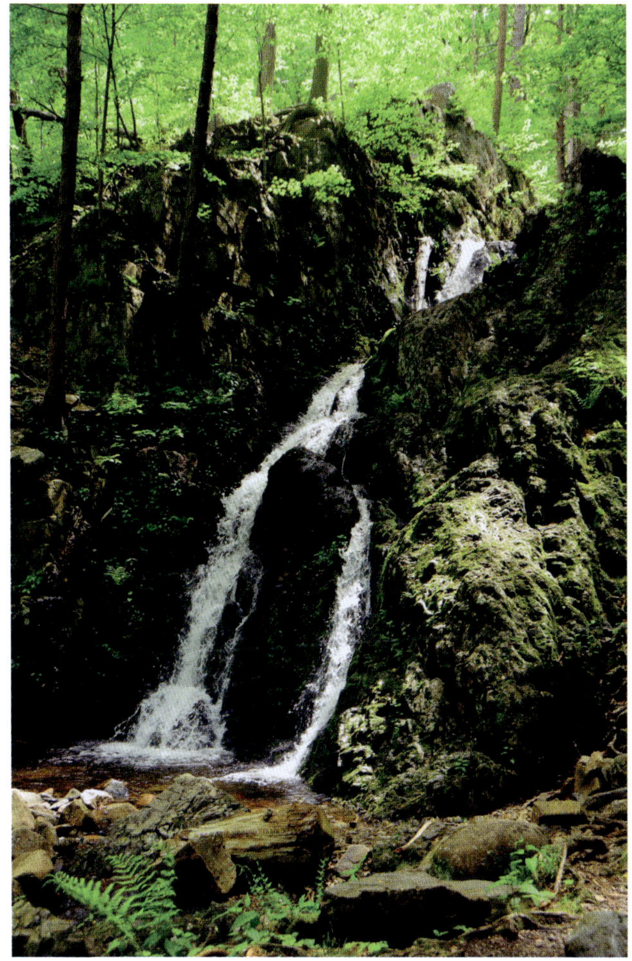

Fitzgerald Falls in New York

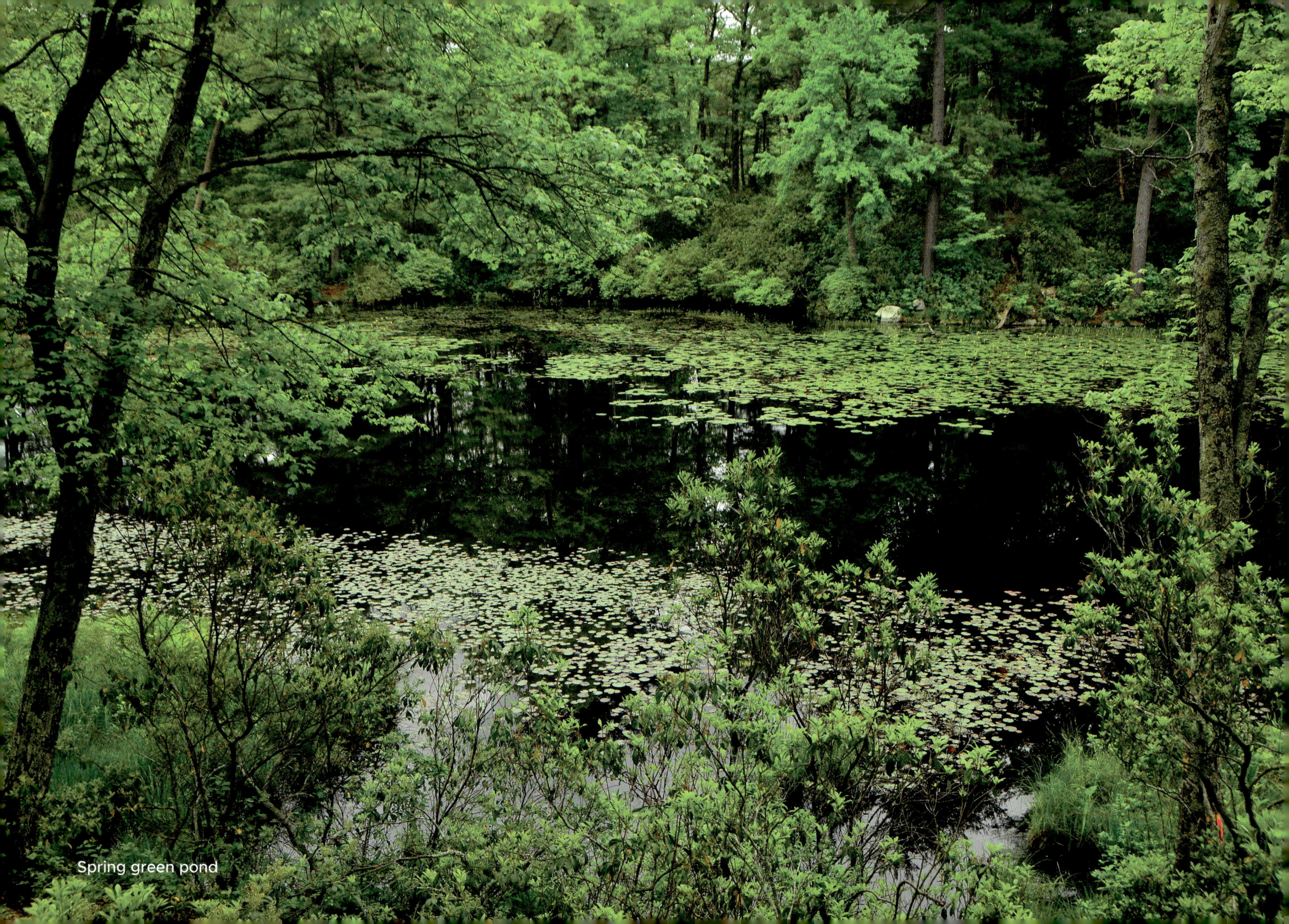

Spring green pond

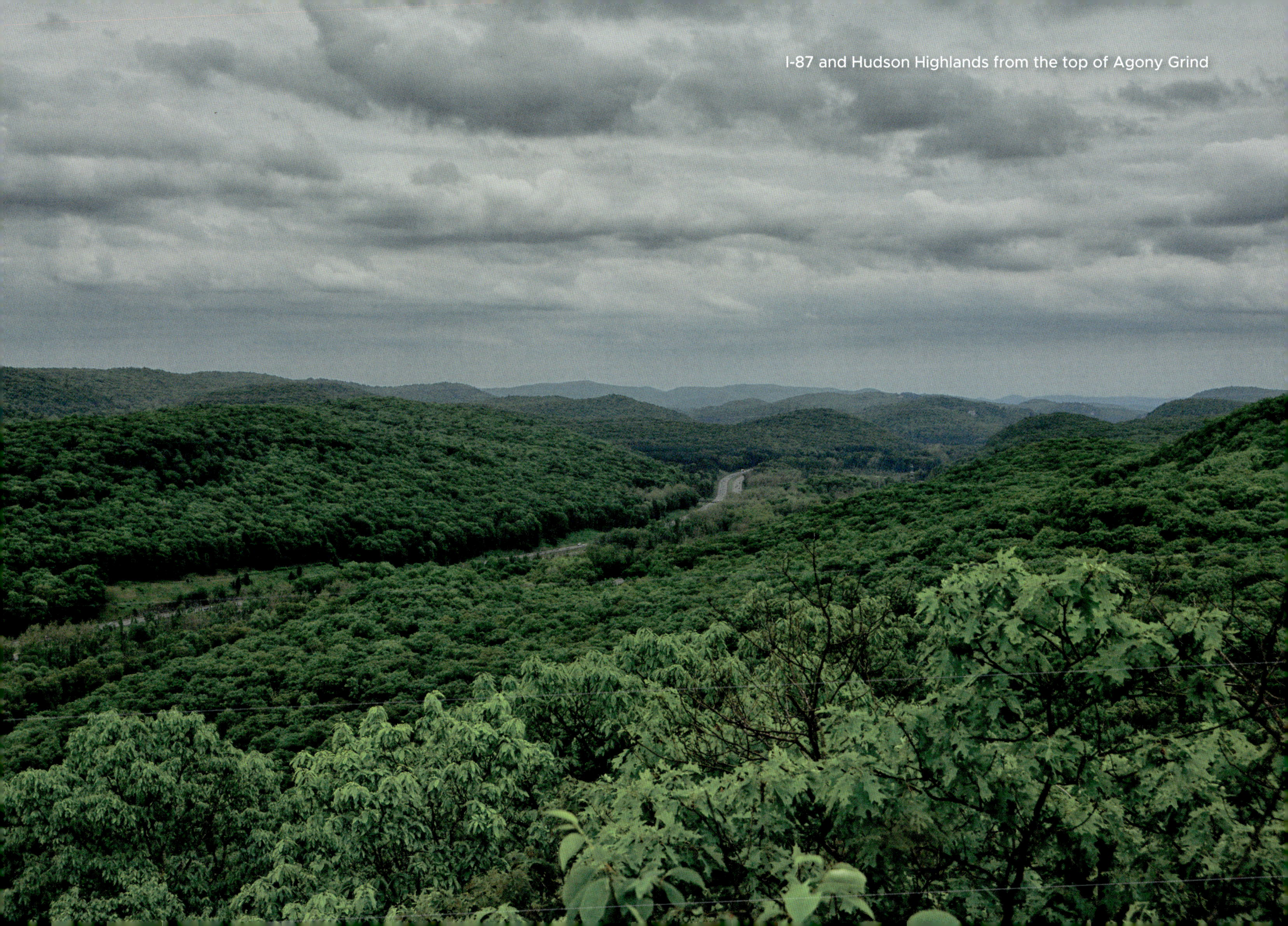

I-87 and Hudson Highlands from the top of Agony Grind

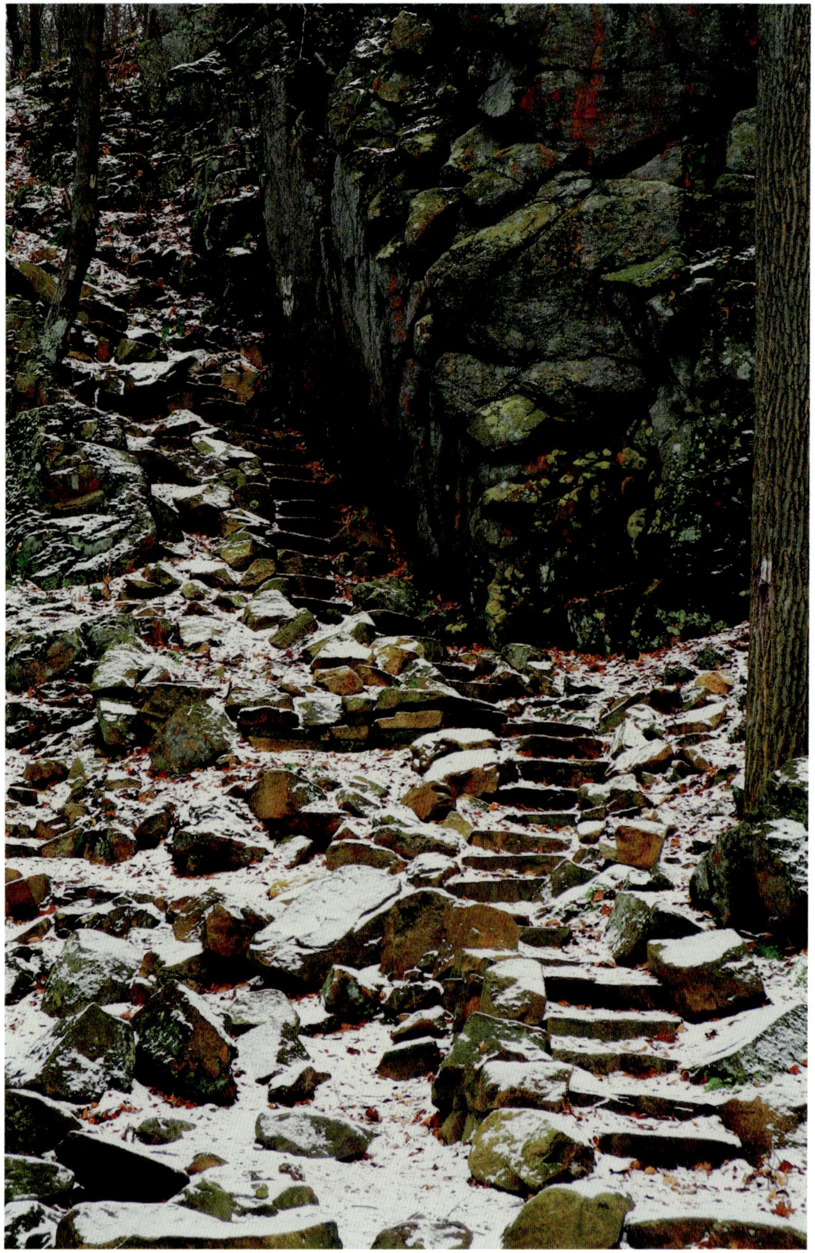

The Appalachian Trail in New York, rock stairs

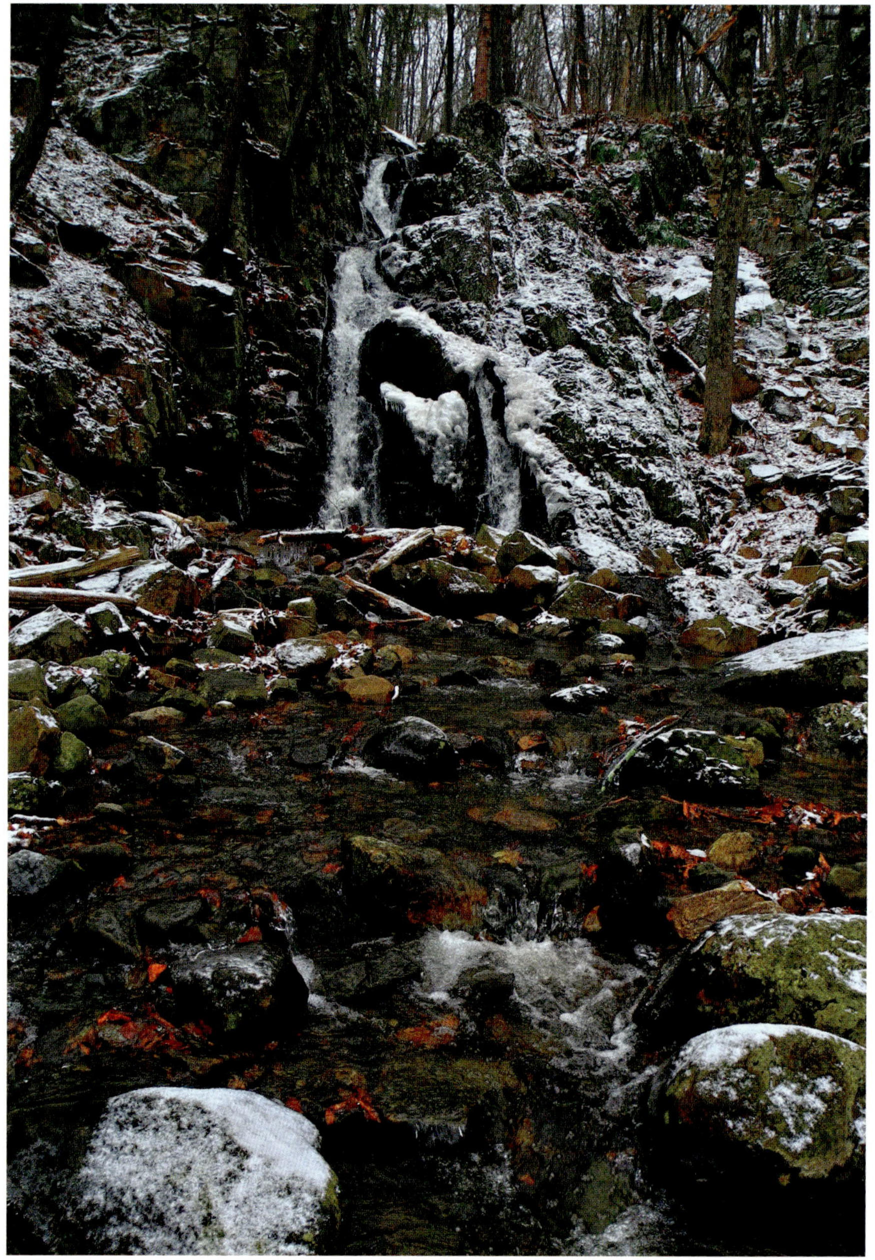

Fitzgerald Falls in New York in winter

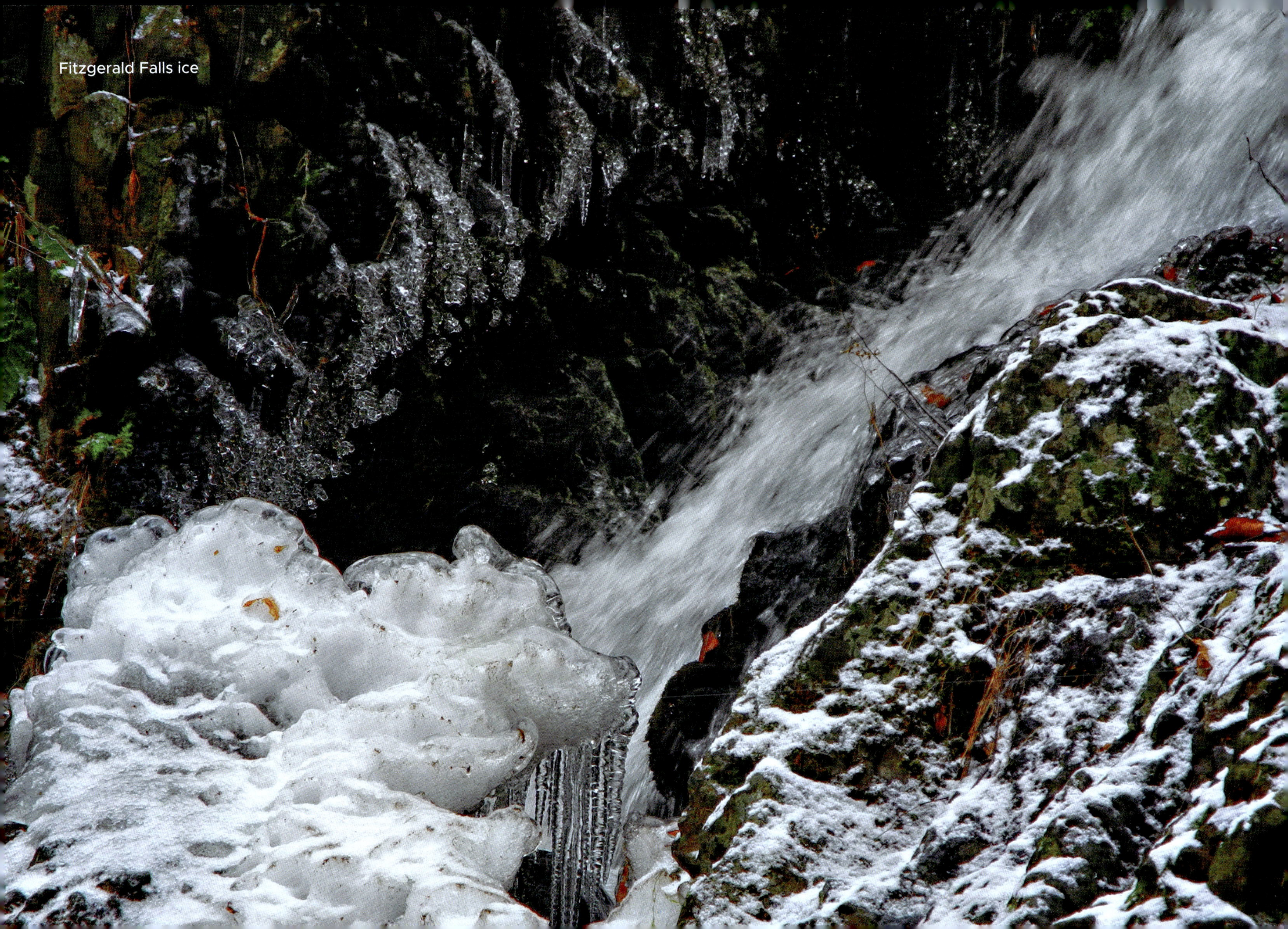

Fitzgerald Falls ice

GEM HIKE MAP

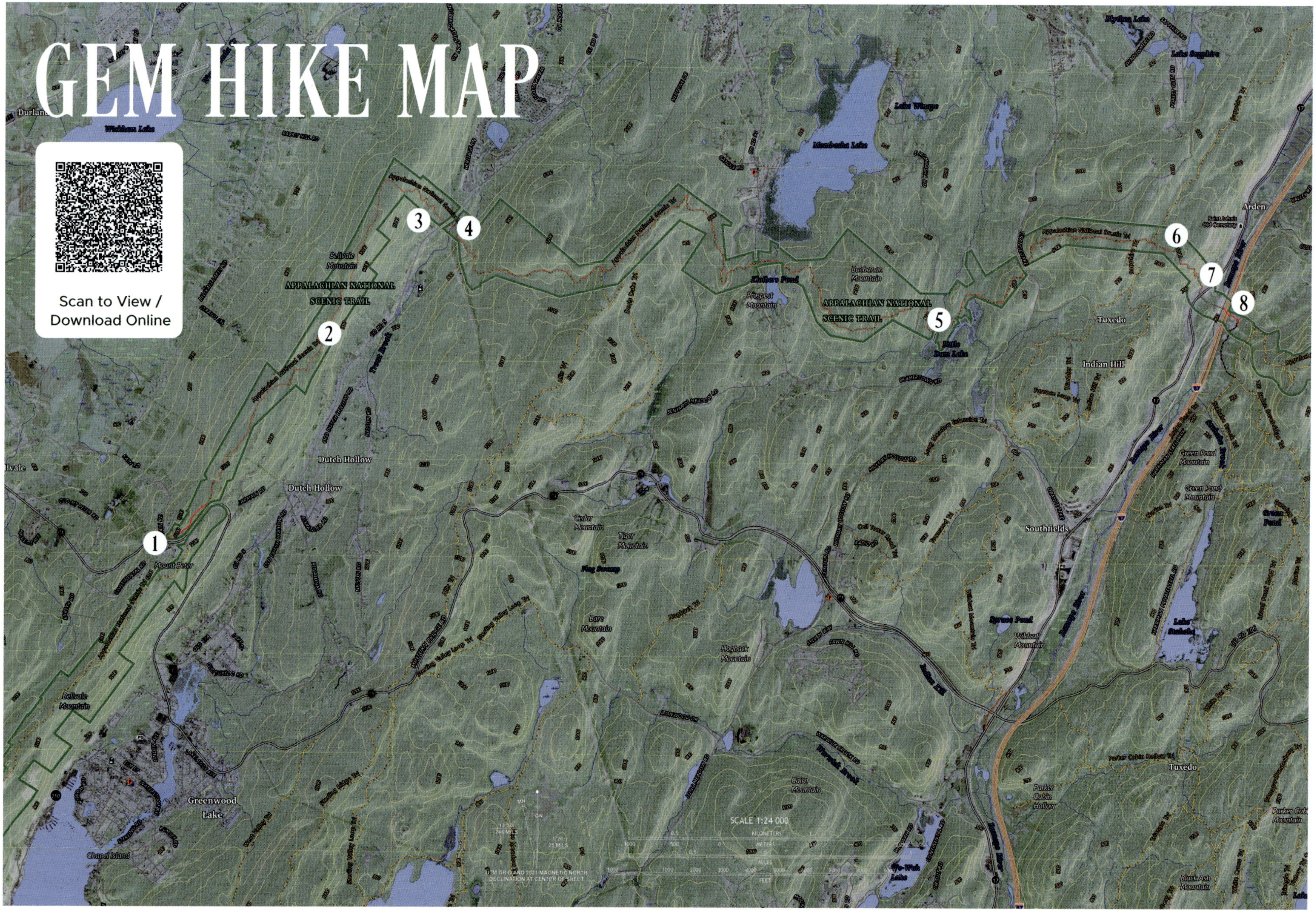
Scan to View /
Download Online
1
2
3
4
5
6
7
8
APPALACHIAN NATIONAL
SCENIC TRAIL
Dutch Hollow
Dutch Hollow
Greenwood
Lake
Tuxedo
Indian Hill
Southfields
Arden
Tuxedo
Durland
SCALE 1:24 000

DIRECTIONS TO THE TRAILHEAD(S)

1. Head south toward NY 17 N for 236 feet
2. Turn right at the first cross street onto NY 17 N, then travel 5.6 miles
3. Turn right onto Arden Valley Rd., then travel for 0.3 mile
4. Turn right, and after 348 feet you have reached the trailhead

Elk Pen Parking Lot (41.264698, −74.154283) to 17-A Warwick, New York, Trailhead (41.245384, −74.285335)

1. Starting at Elk Pen Parking Lot, head northeast toward Arden Valley Rd. for 322 feet
2. Turn left onto Arden Valley Rd. and continue for 0.3 mile
3. Turn left onto NY 17 S and continue for 2.9 miles
4. Take the NY 17A / County Rd. 106 exit for 0.2 mile
5. Turn right onto NY 17A W
6. Stay on for 9.1 miles, and destination will be on the left, ending on the AT trailhead on 17A

GEM HIKE DIRECTIONS

It begins with spotting a car(s) at the Elk Pen and driving to NY 17A to begin the 12-mile hike (see driving directions). [AU Note: In all instances in book, define and clarify spotting a car]

1. Leave 17A trailhead on the Appalachian Trail north
2. Reach Eastern Pinnacles at 1.3 miles
3. At 3.6 miles, reach Lakes Rd.
4. Cross Lakes Rd. and reach Fitzgerald Falls at 3.9 miles
5. You come up on Little Dam Lake at 9.5 miles
6. The top of Agony Grind / Arden Mountain at 10.9 miles
7. At 12 miles, you reach Route 17 and Arden Valley Rd.
8. Continue along this road for 0.4 mile until you reach Elk Pen Parking Area on the right

MORE/LESS AMBITIOUS HIKERS

If you wish to hike some of this hike without the point to point, it can be made easier or harder depending on how many miles you are looking to tackle. Fitzgerald Falls is also an option. There is a small parking area off Lakes Road that gives one a short walk to see Fitzgerald Falls.

From NY 17A: The trailhead at NY 17A provides a relatively gentle start with a more gradual ascent. Hikers begin by traversing through mixed hardwood forests before encountering increasingly more challenging terrain as they approach the Elk Pen parking lot.

From Elk Pen parking lot: Starting from the Elk Pen parking lot, the Appalachian Trail travels a short distance on Arden Valley Road. Then, shortly after crossing over I-87, the Appalachian Trail hits its Agony Grind section.

CHAPTER 10

THE APPALACHIAN TRAIL FROM HESSIAN LAKE TO WEST MOUNTAIN WITH BEAR MOUNTAIN

AREA MAP

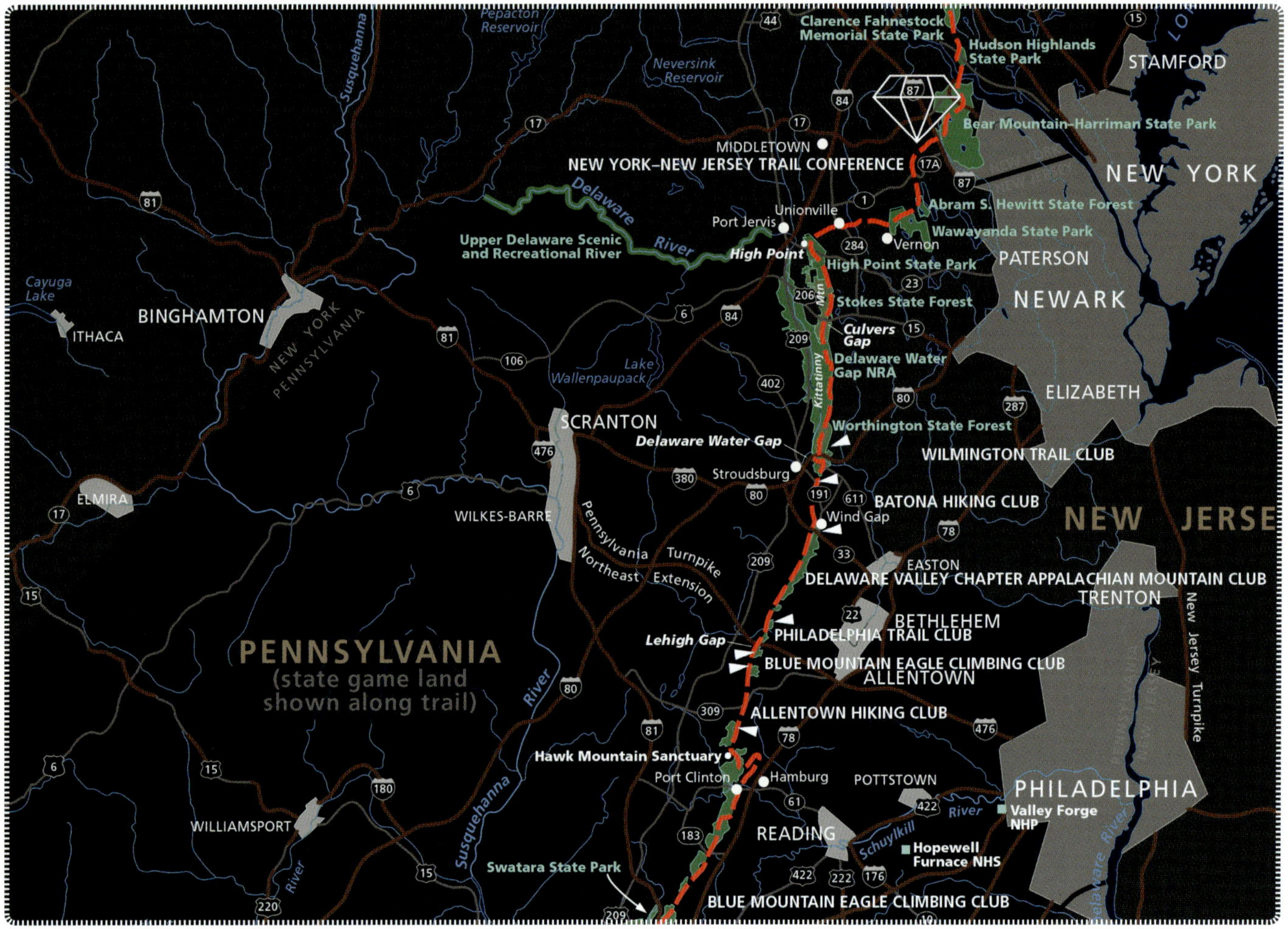

DISTANCE	13.4 miles
ELEVATION GAIN	2,400 feet
ELEVATION LOSS	2,400 feet
LEVEL	Moderate

TYPE: OUT-AND-BACK

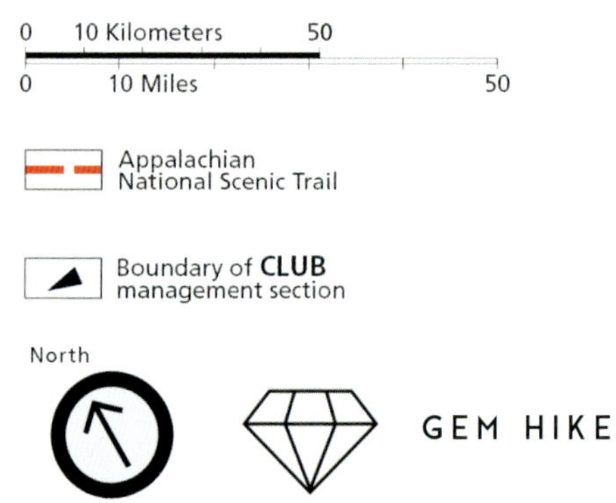

PERSONAL TOUCH

I just love this hike. I have done it at least once in every month of the year, and it is special for me every time I go, because it is always different. The overlook of Bear Mountain from West Mountain is my favorite. The Appalachian Trail feels different every time I go on this hike. One time, I had several different fungi species lining the trail. In the summer months, the mushrooms can look like Oreo-cookie ice cream; others are bright yellows, reds, and oranges; and sometimes they make you feel like you are at a carnival with hot soft pretzels.

Another time, I saw the peak bloom of the mountain laurel flowers. The night before I arrived, it had rained, and it was windy. Since the flowers were still young, the wind moved them around just enough that their pollen was dislodged and had stained the petals of the flowers a rare pink. One winter, I had spikes on my boots for dealing with snow, ice, and eventually sleet and rain, but as the storm recharged, I had a break in the clouds on the summit of Bear to give me the opportunity for some very special photographs.

BRIEF OVERVIEW:

Hiking from Harriman–Bear Mountain State Park's Hessian Lake to the West Mountain summit via the Appalachian Trail is a fantastic way to experience the natural beauty and rugged terrain of the Hudson Highlands. This offers a blend of scenic views, challenging climbs, and serene forested areas with special trail treats.

SPECIAL NOTE

This section is special to the Appalachian Trail and to me. It has so many cool elements that a larger photography chapter was the only way to give it the attention that it deserved. The views are special, and you also have the opportunity for amazing, smaller trail treats to enjoy.

DESCRIPTION OF THE GEM HIKE

This section is truly a gem of the Appalachian Trail. This gem hike was the first blazed section of the Appalachian Trail. The AT connected Bear and Harriman State Parks, with a beautiful hike through forests with several overlooks. Efts, salamanders that are bright orange with red spots, are common. Also, mountain laurels are an amazingly beautiful part of the overlooks.

FLORA, FAUNA, AND VEGETATION

The trail travels through forests and often up to give large panoramic views of Bear Mountain, the Hudson River, and the surrounding landscape. Mountain laurel, which blooms in June, is beautiful and plentiful. Mushrooms are also very common on West Mountain and are colorful as wildflowers.

PERKINS MEMORIAL TOWER

Perkins Memorial Tower stands at the top of Bear Mountain. From the top of Perkins Memorial Tower, visitors can enjoy sweeping views of the Hudson River, the Bear Mountain Bridge, and the rolling hills of the Hudson Highlands. On clear days, views of the New York City skyline and the Catskill Mountains can be had.

HISTORY

Harriman–Bear Mountain State Park is a vast and diverse recreational area located in the Hudson Valley of New York. When the two parks, Harriman State Park and Bear Mountain State Park, were separate, the first blazed section of the Appalachian Trail was the section that connected the two parks. Part of this first blazed section is this featured gem hike. Today, the combined park is over 52,000 acres. It also combines the history of the American Revolutionary War (the special August fog that saved the Americans from the oncoming British army).

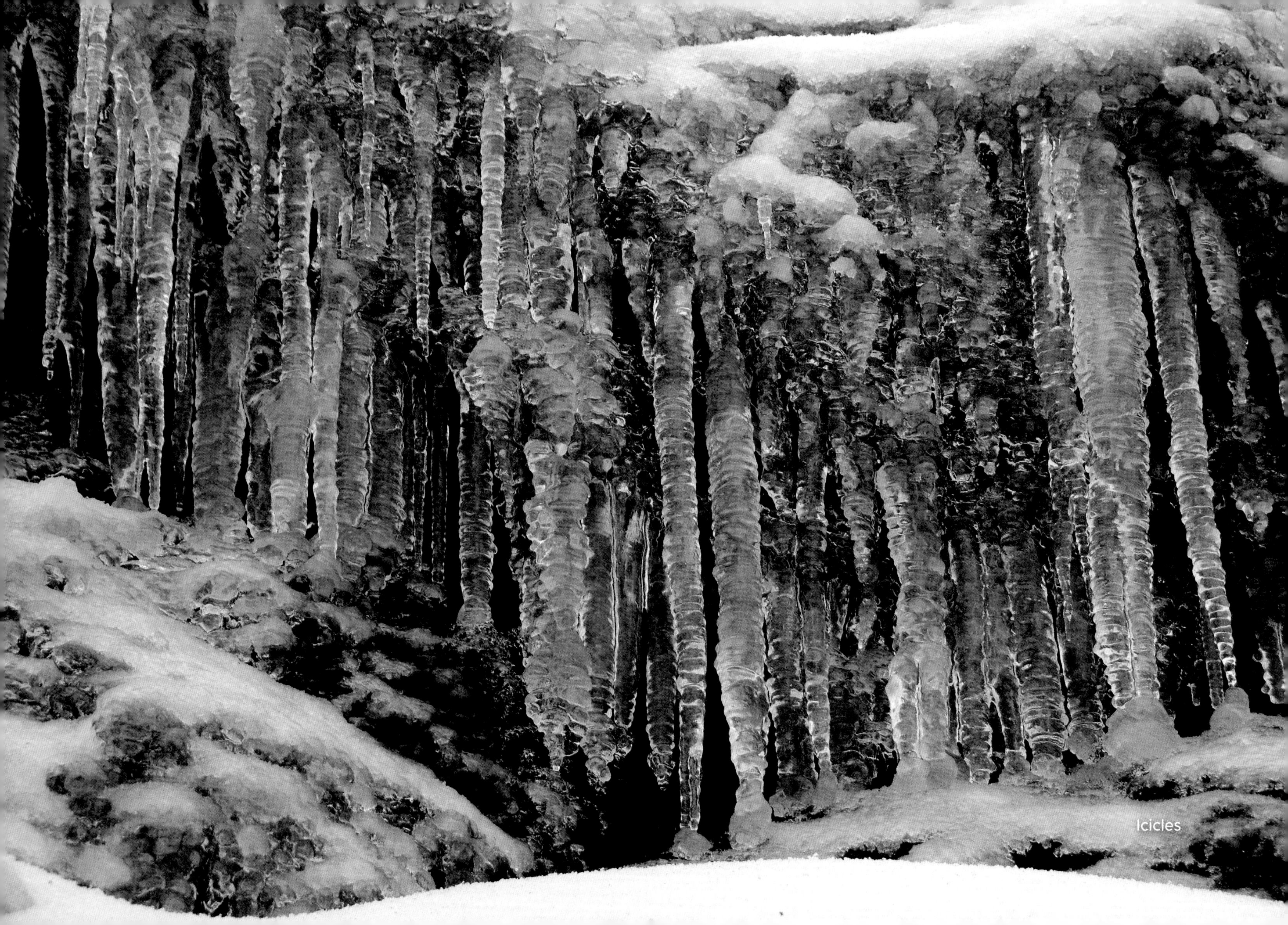

Icicles

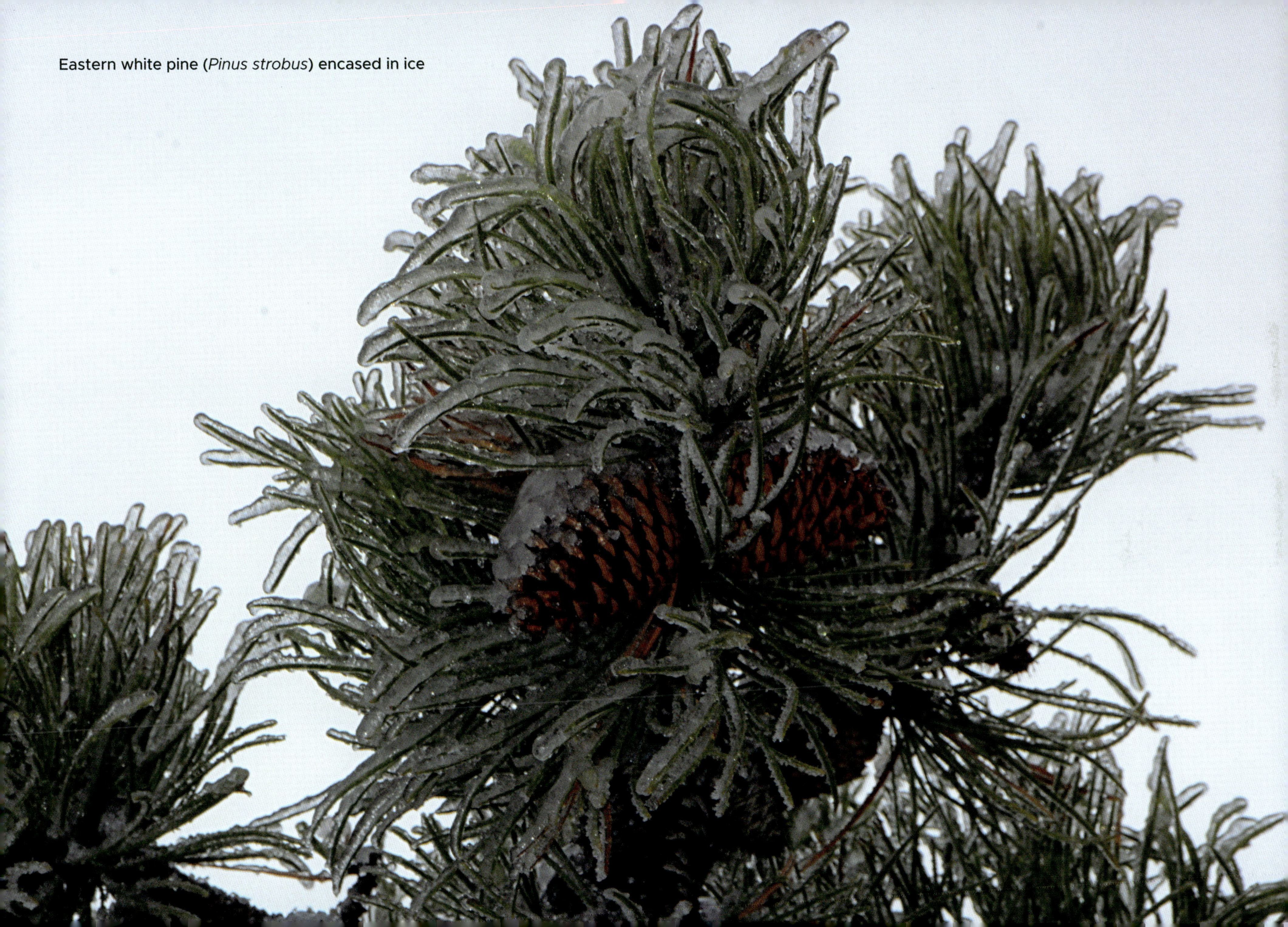

Eastern white pine (*Pinus strobus*) encased in ice

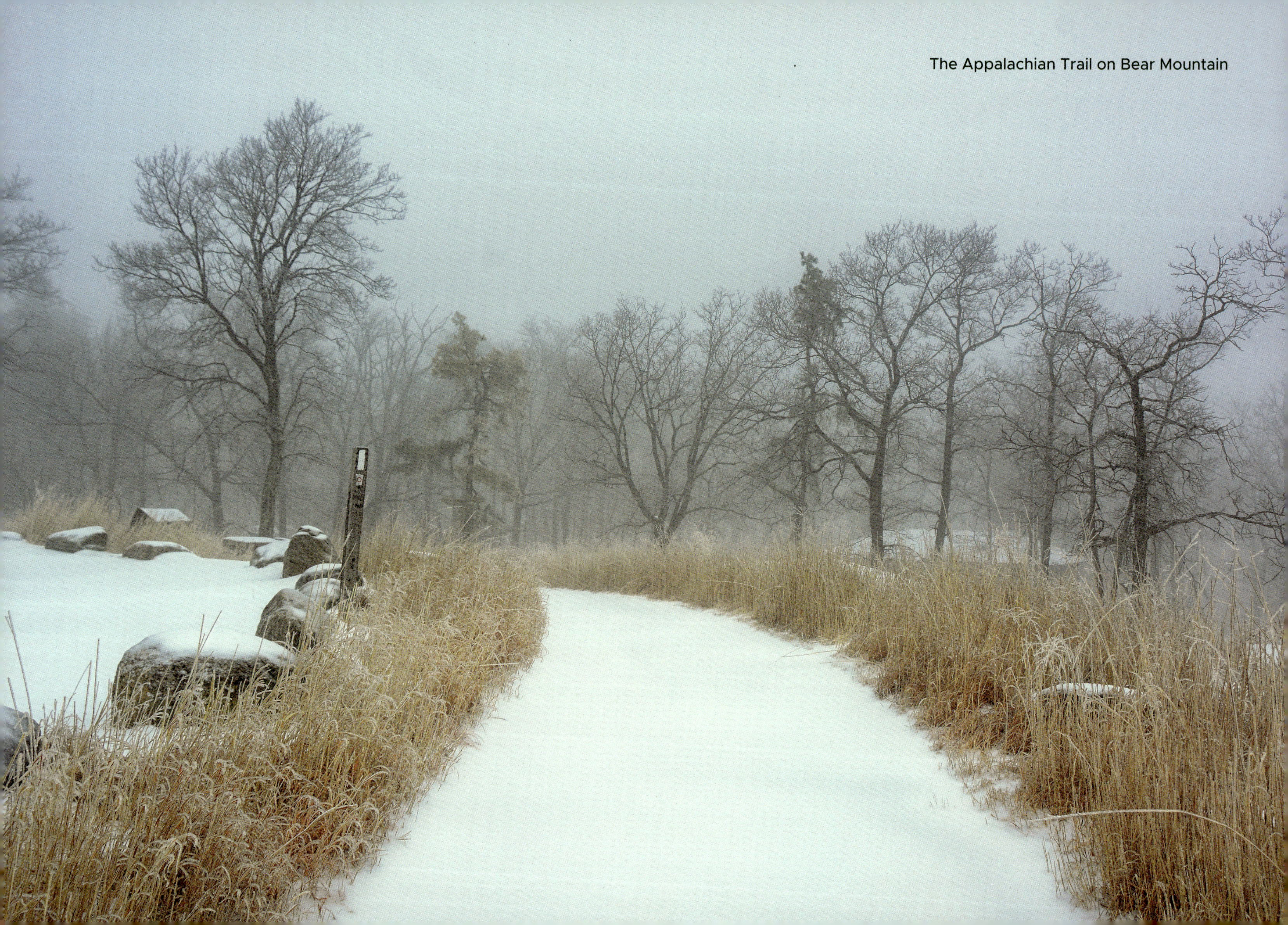

The Appalachian Trail on Bear Mountain

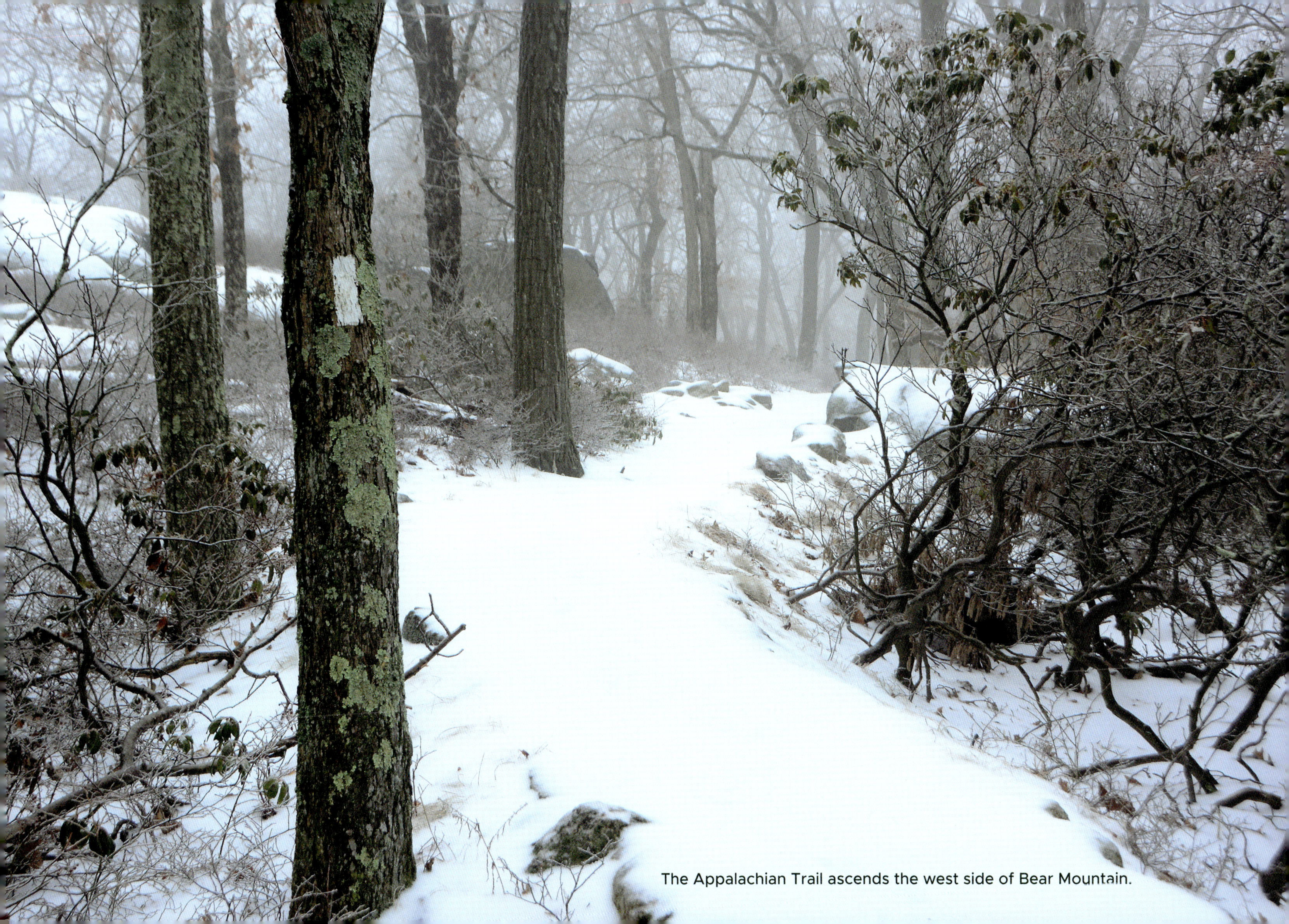

The Appalachian Trail ascends the west side of Bear Mountain.

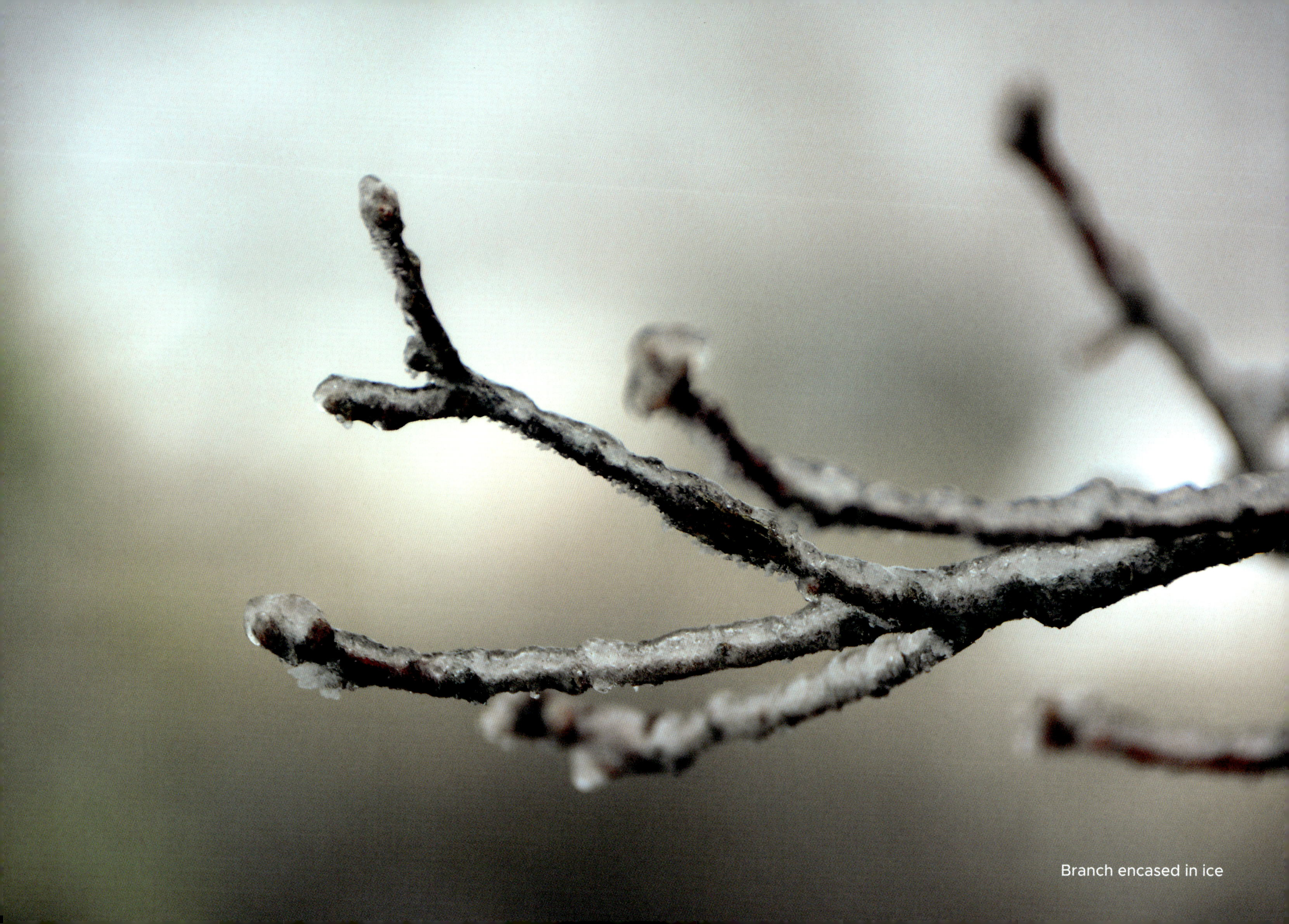

Branch encased in ice

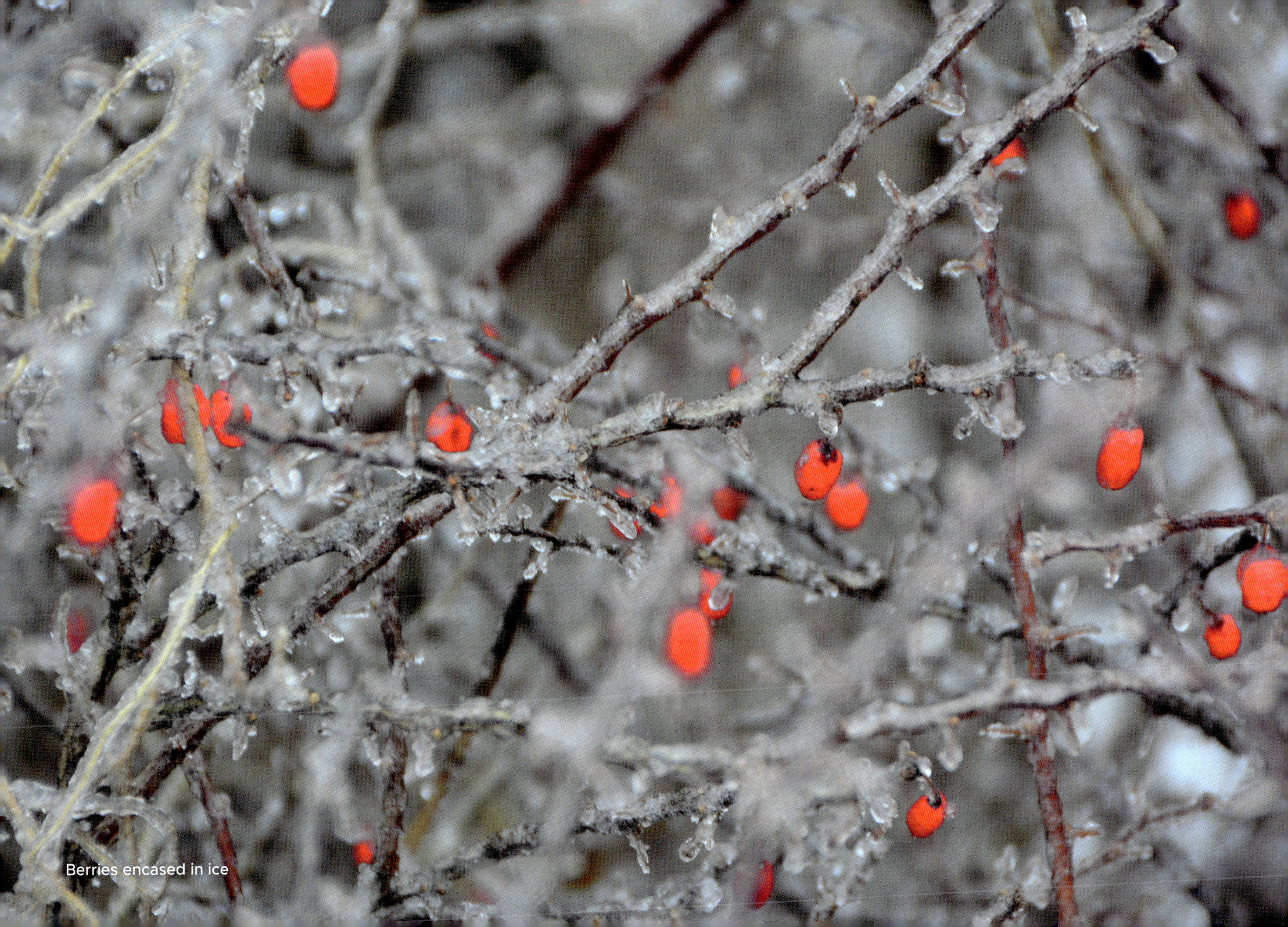

Berries encased in ice

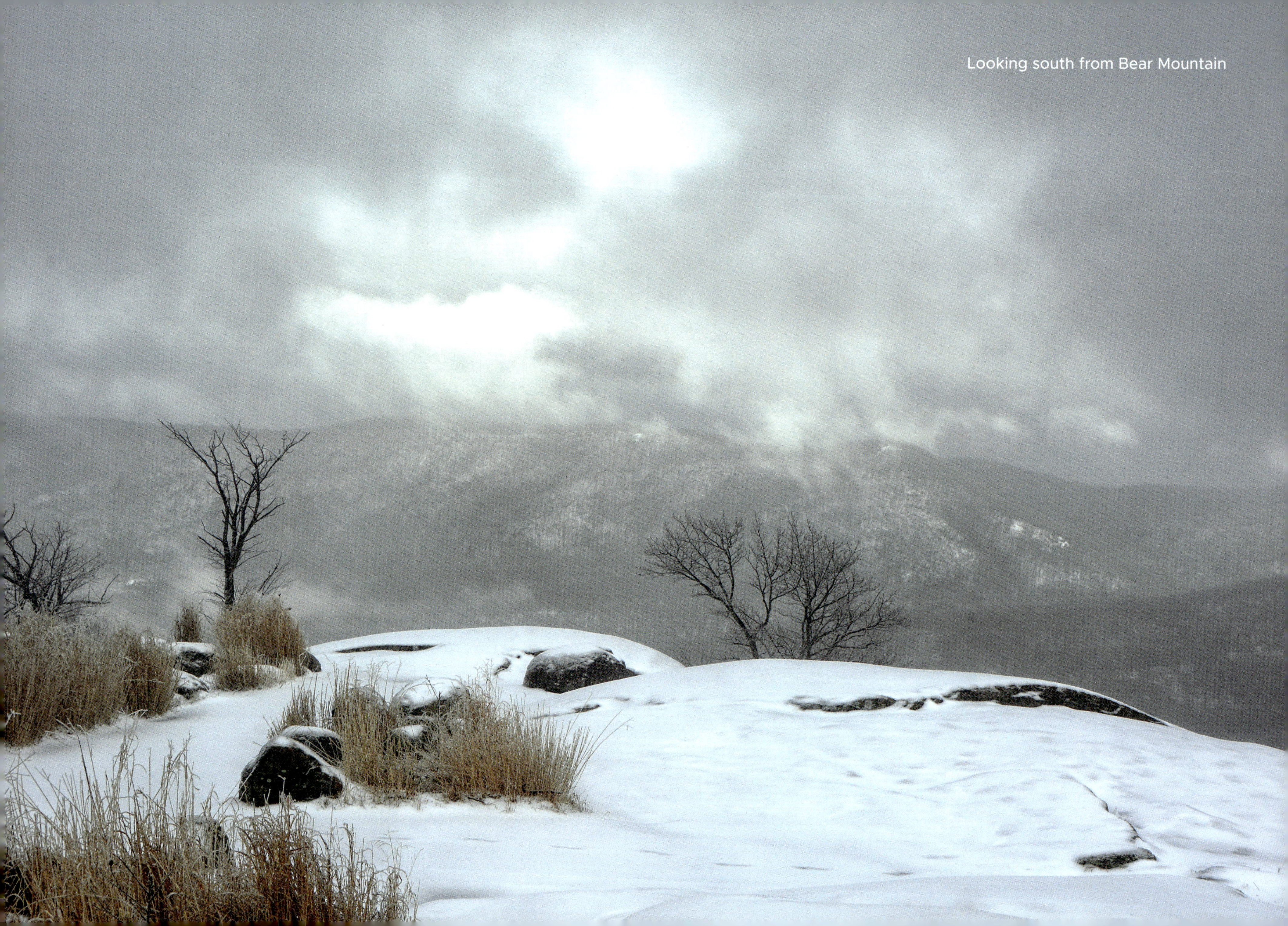

Looking south from Bear Mountain

Looking east from the summit of Bear Mountain

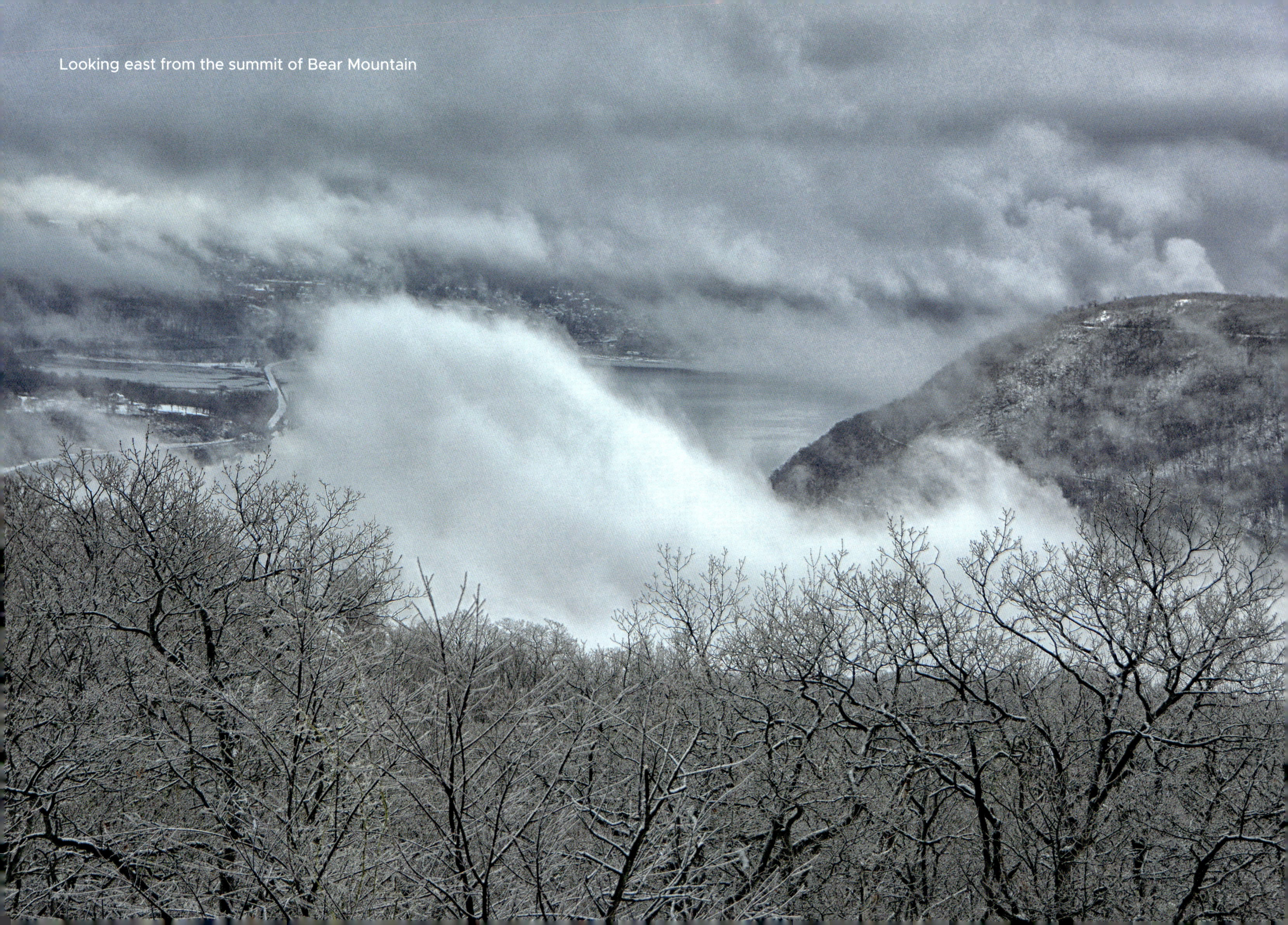

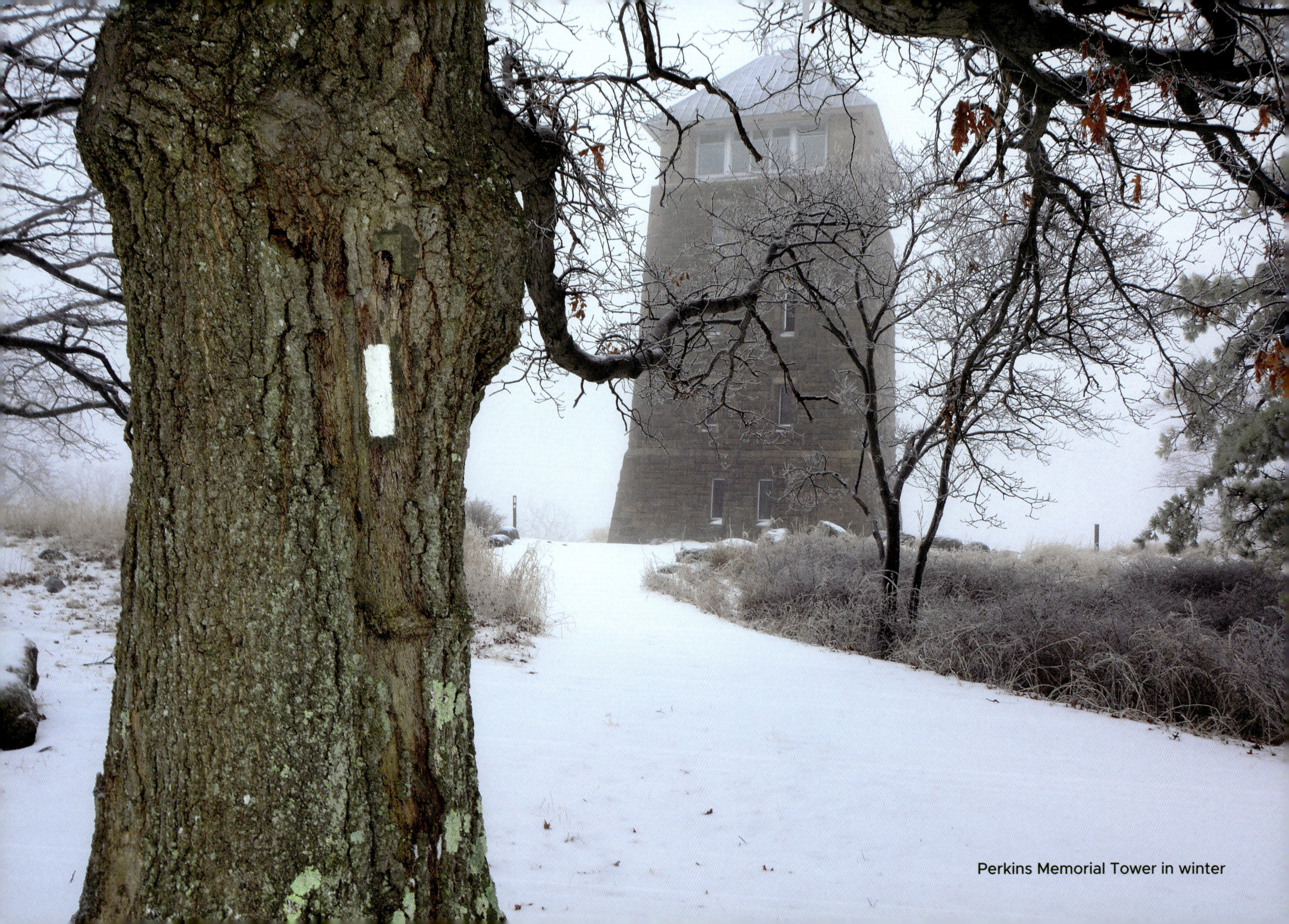

Perkins Memorial Tower in winter

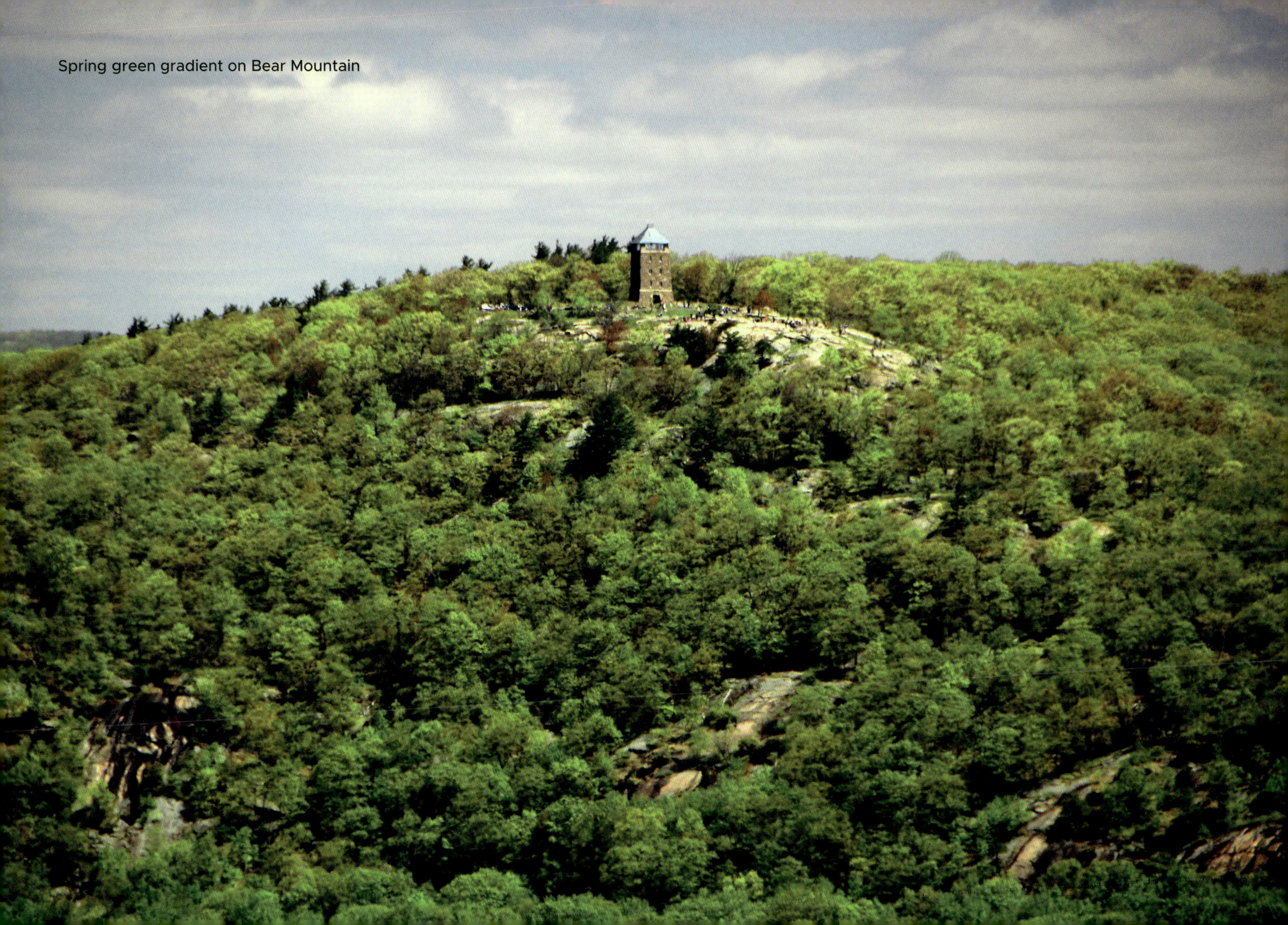

Spring green gradient on Bear Mountain

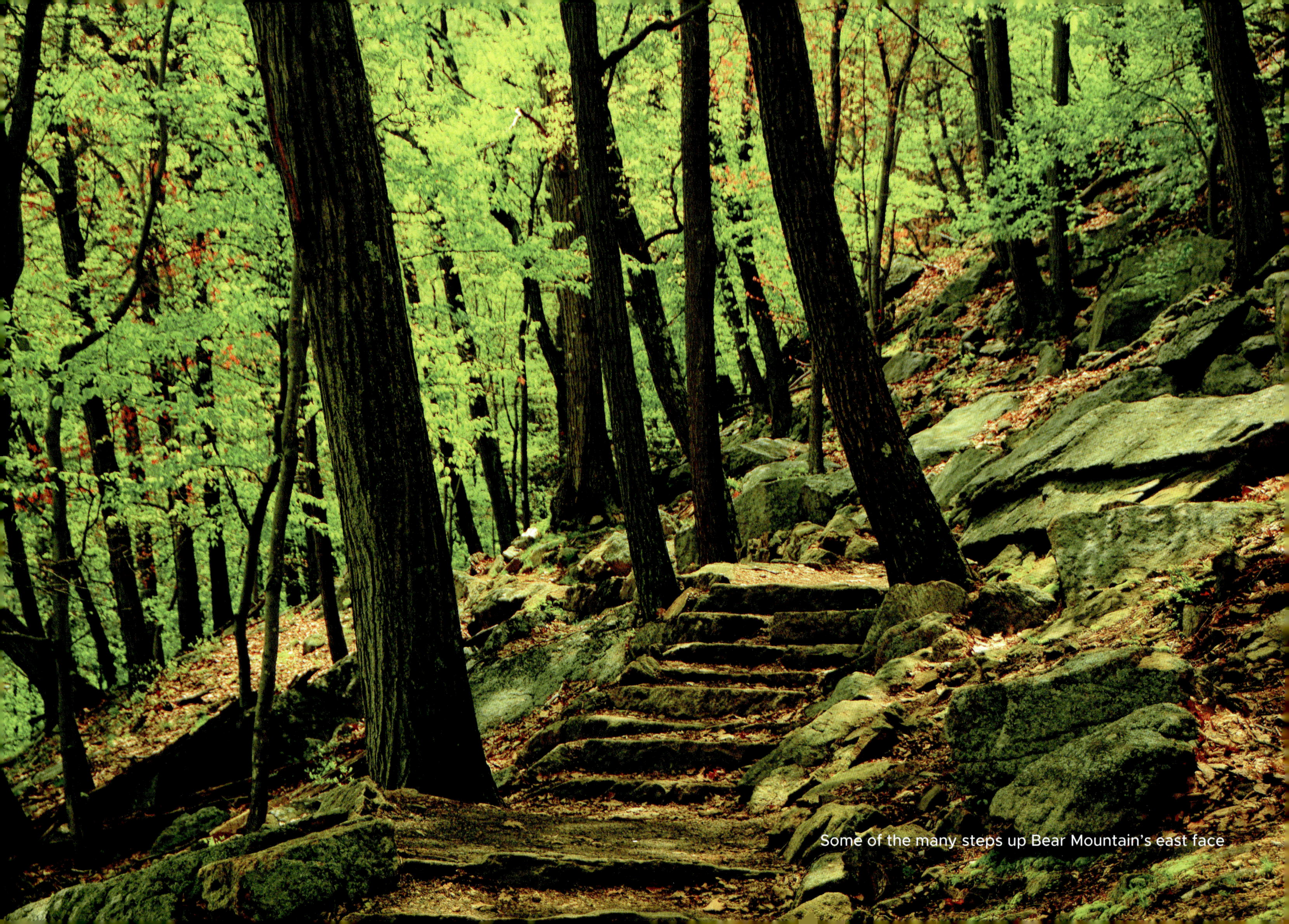

Some of the many steps up Bear Mountain's east face

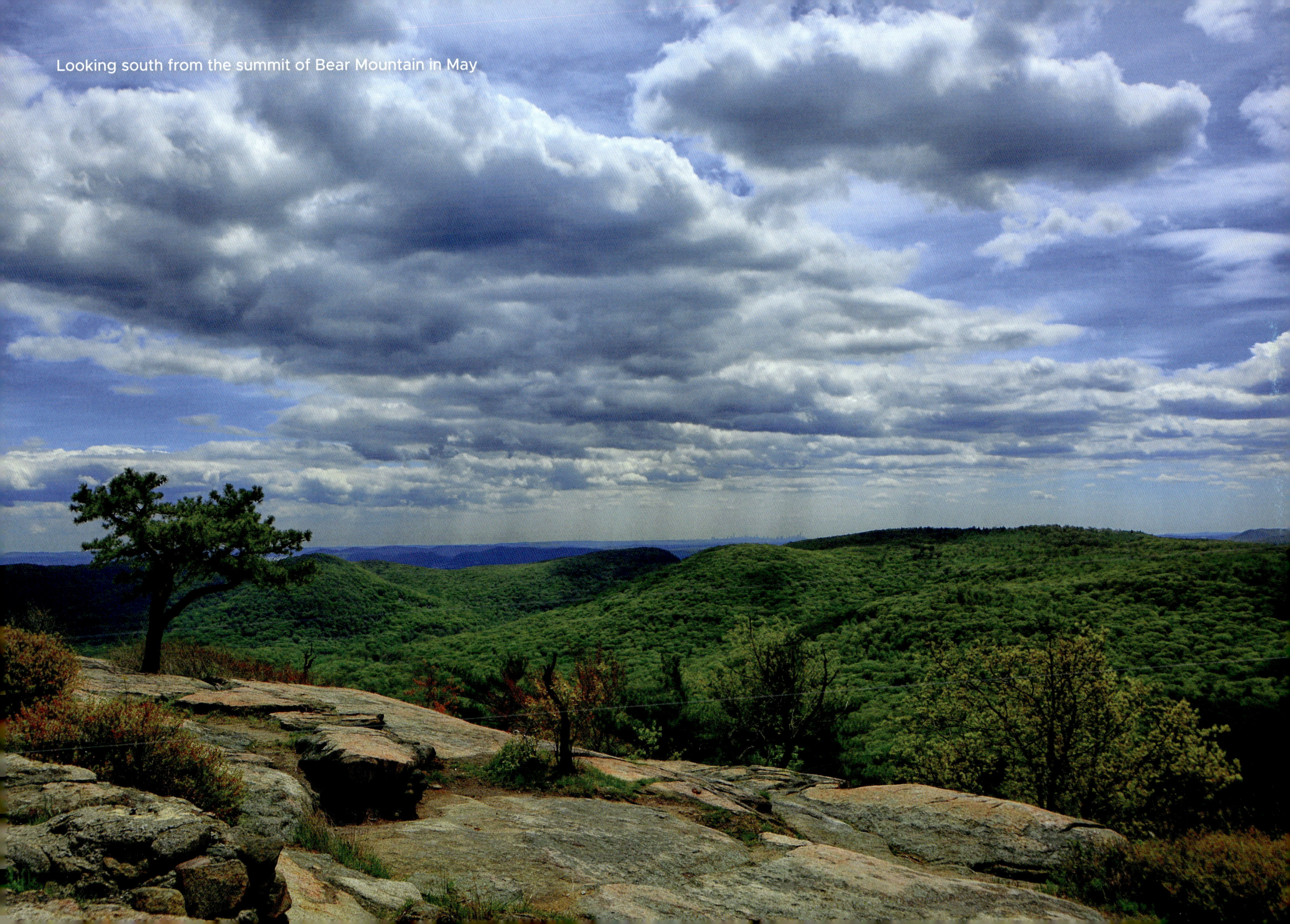

Looking south from the summit of Bear Mountain in May

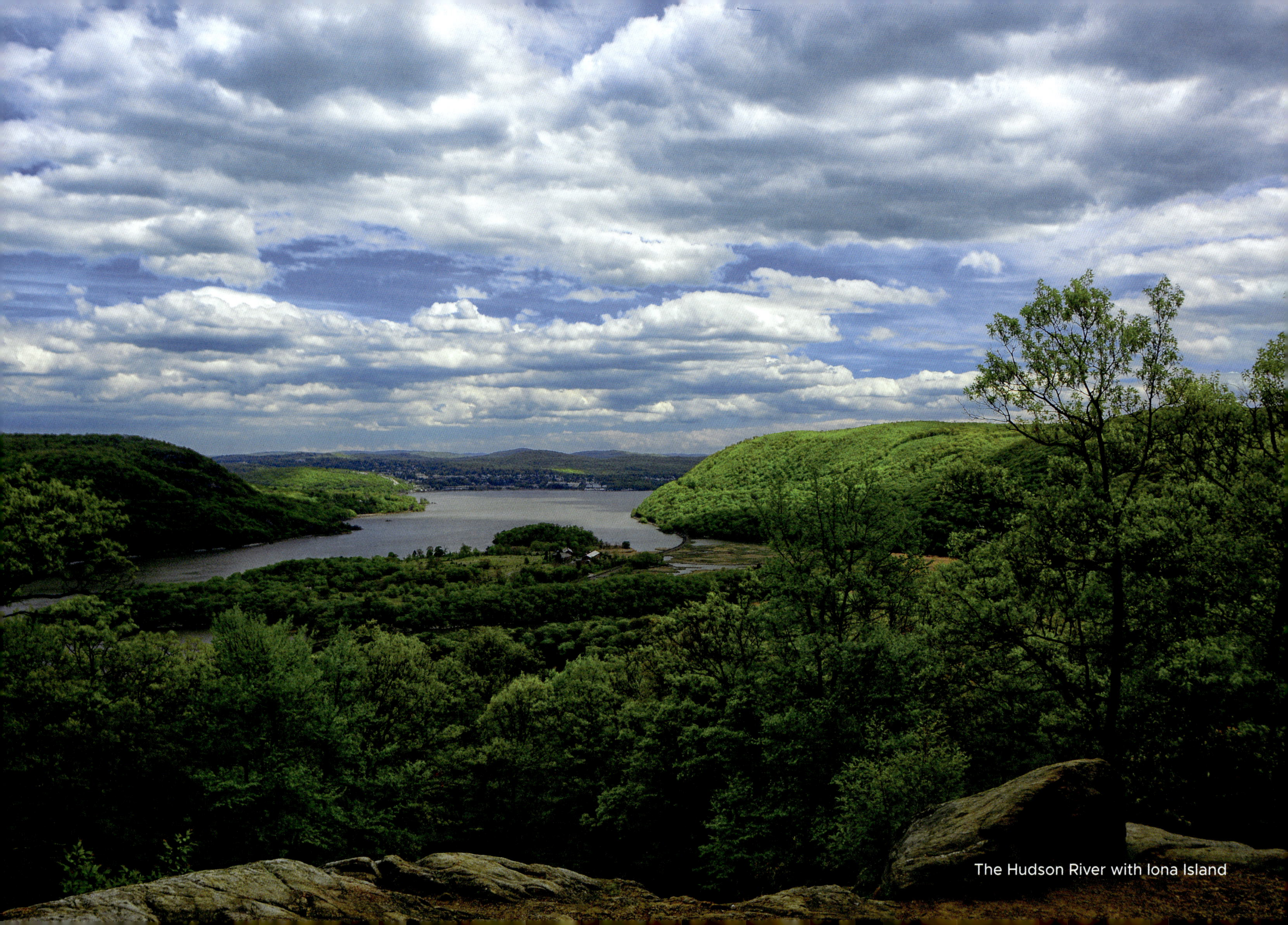

The Hudson River with Iona Island

Looking northeast at Bear Mountain Bridge and Anthony's Nose from the summit of Bear Mountain

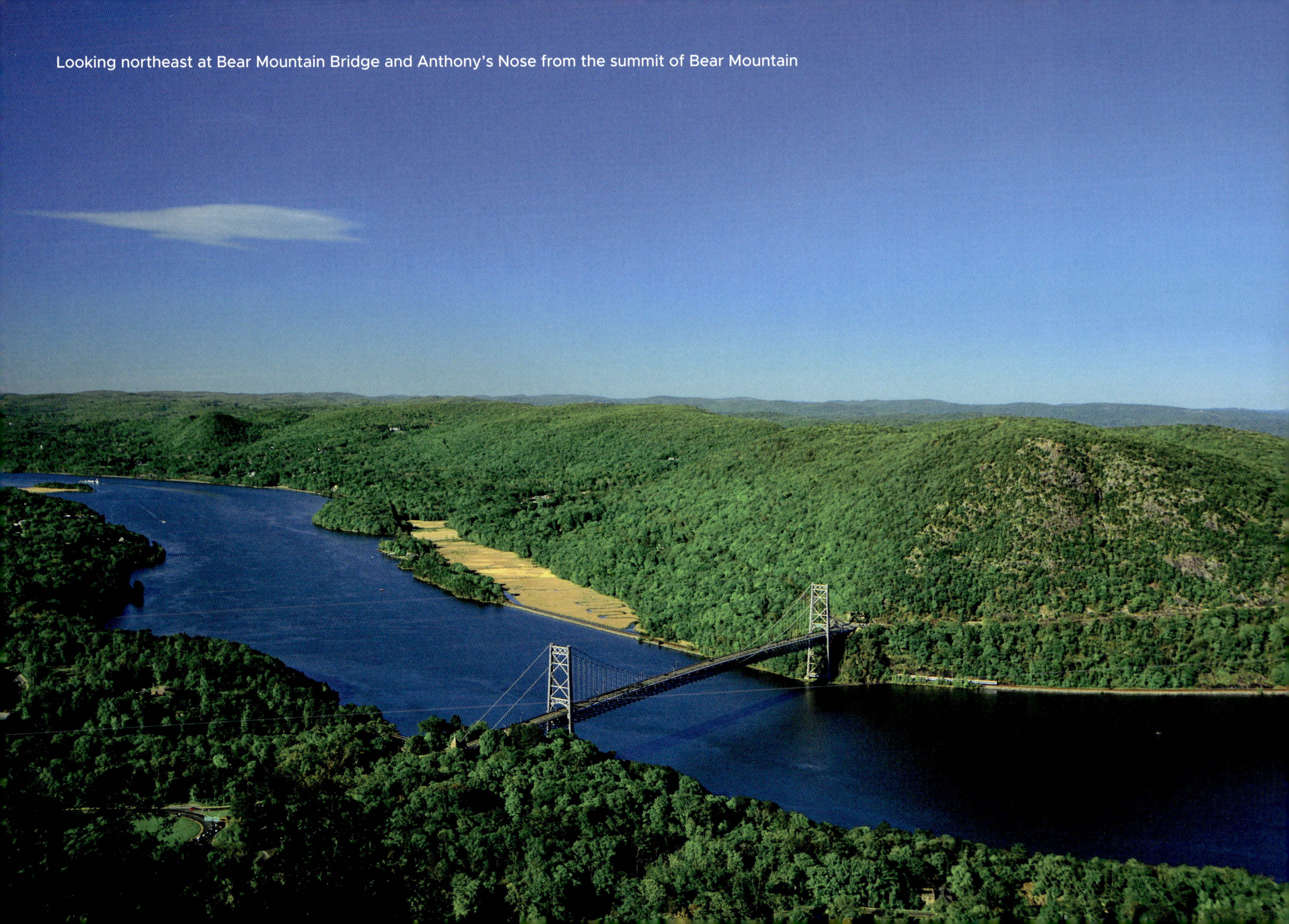

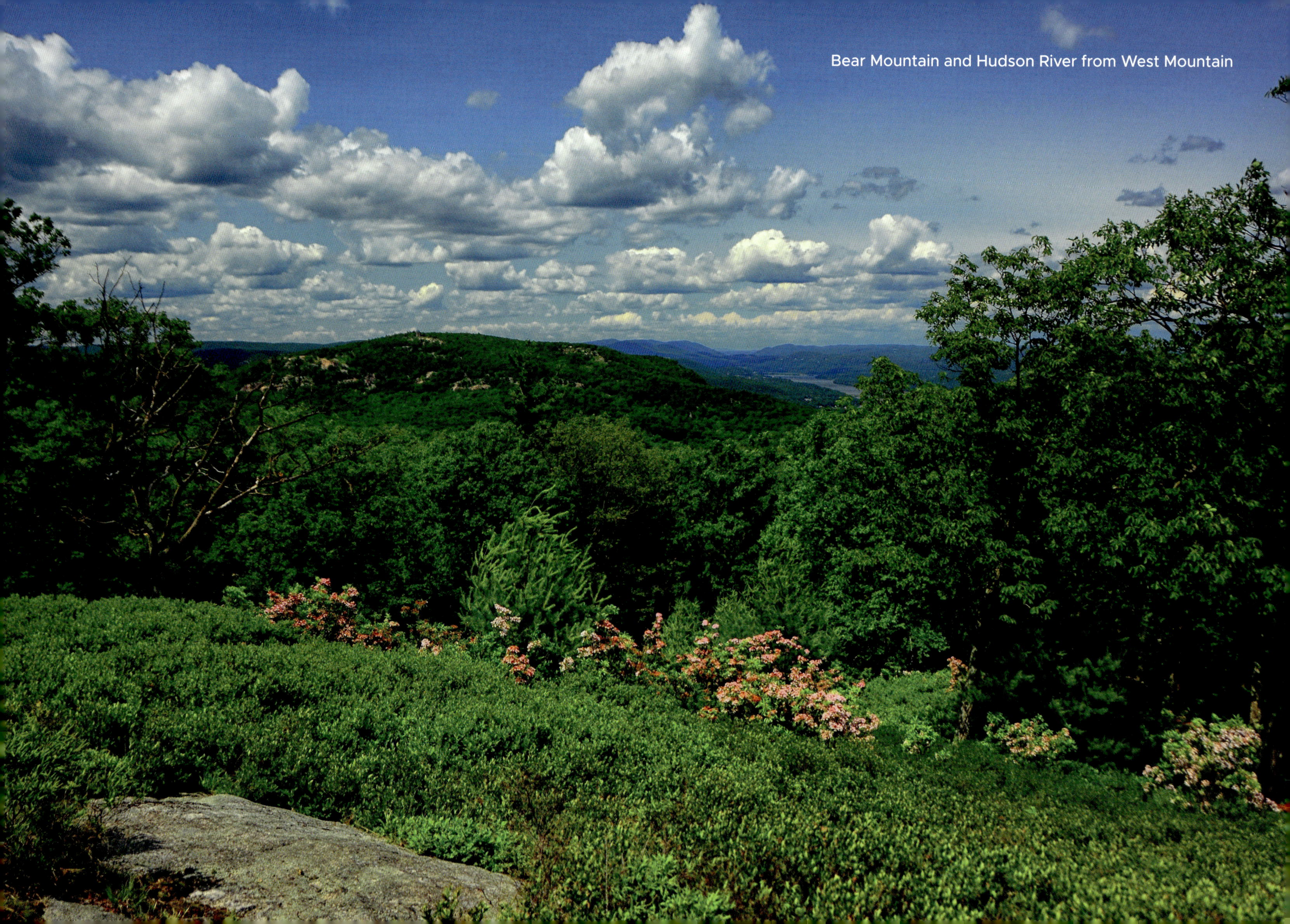

Bear Mountain and Hudson River from West Mountain

Mountain laurel (*Kalmia latifolia*)

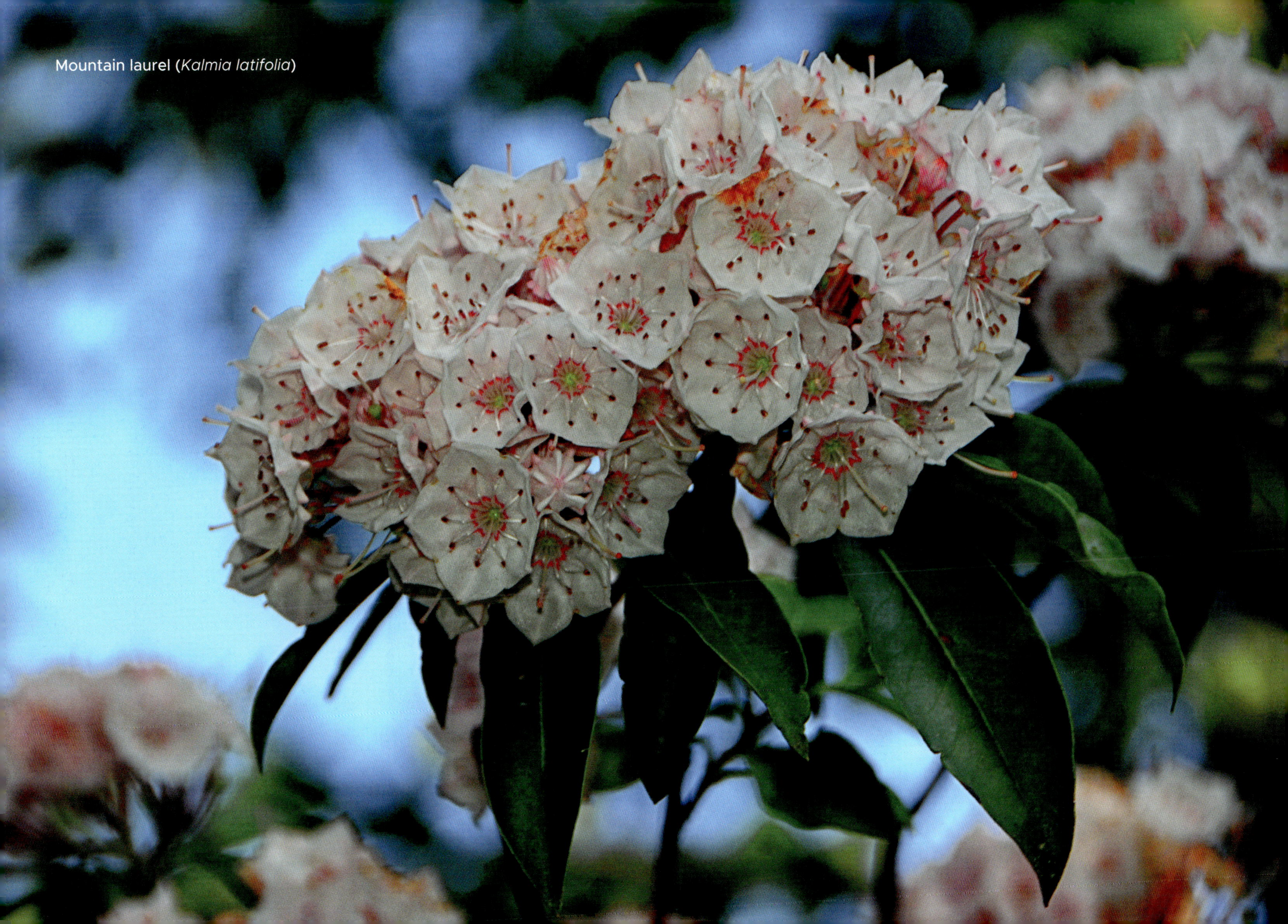

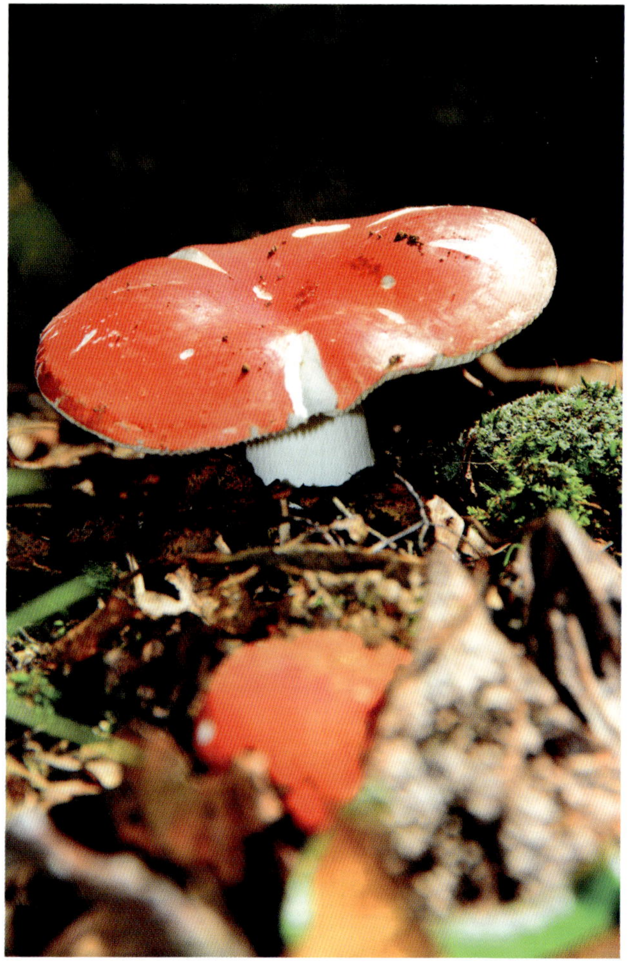

Russula, also known as lactarius-species mushroom (*Hypomyces lactifluorum*)

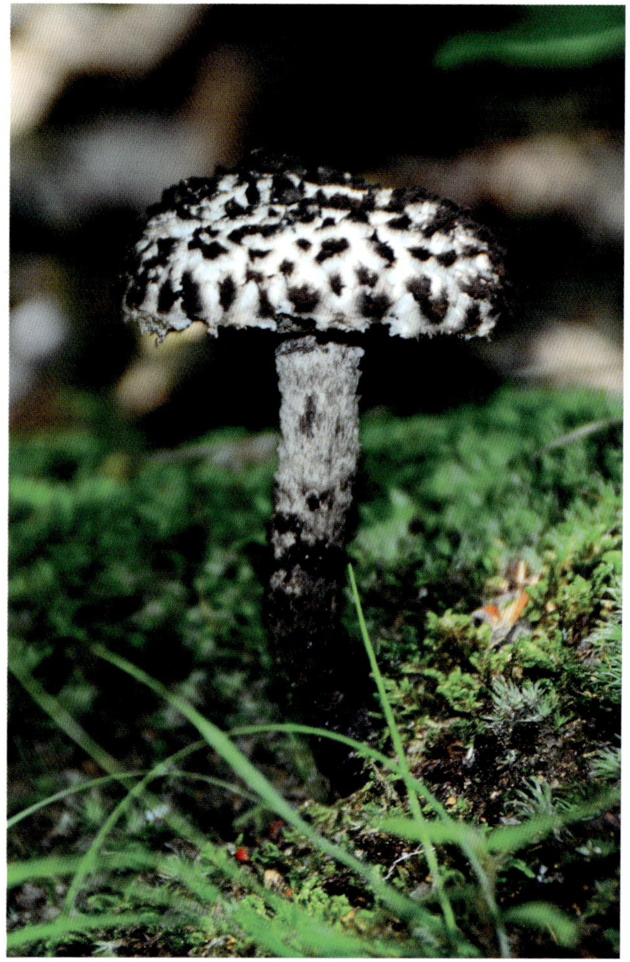

Scaly ink cap, also known as feltscale inky cap mushroom (*Coprinopsis variegata)*

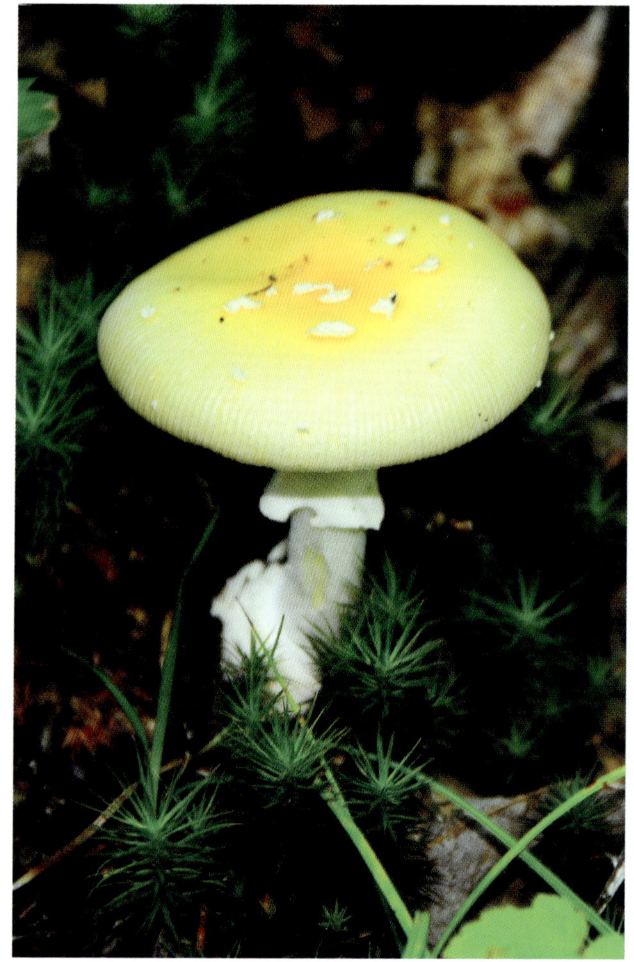

Fly agaric mushroom (*Amanita muscaria*)

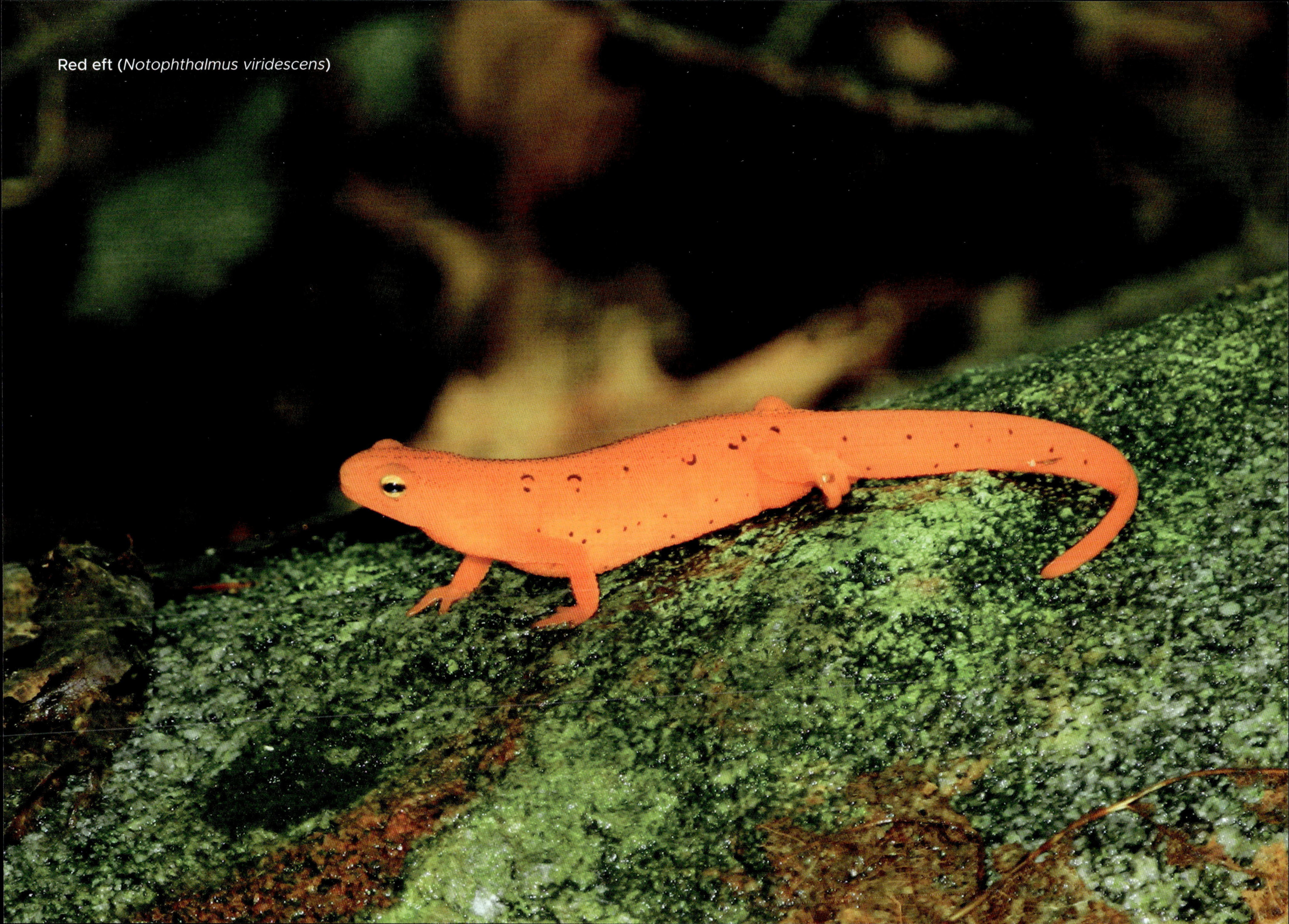

Red eft (*Notophthalmus viridescens*)

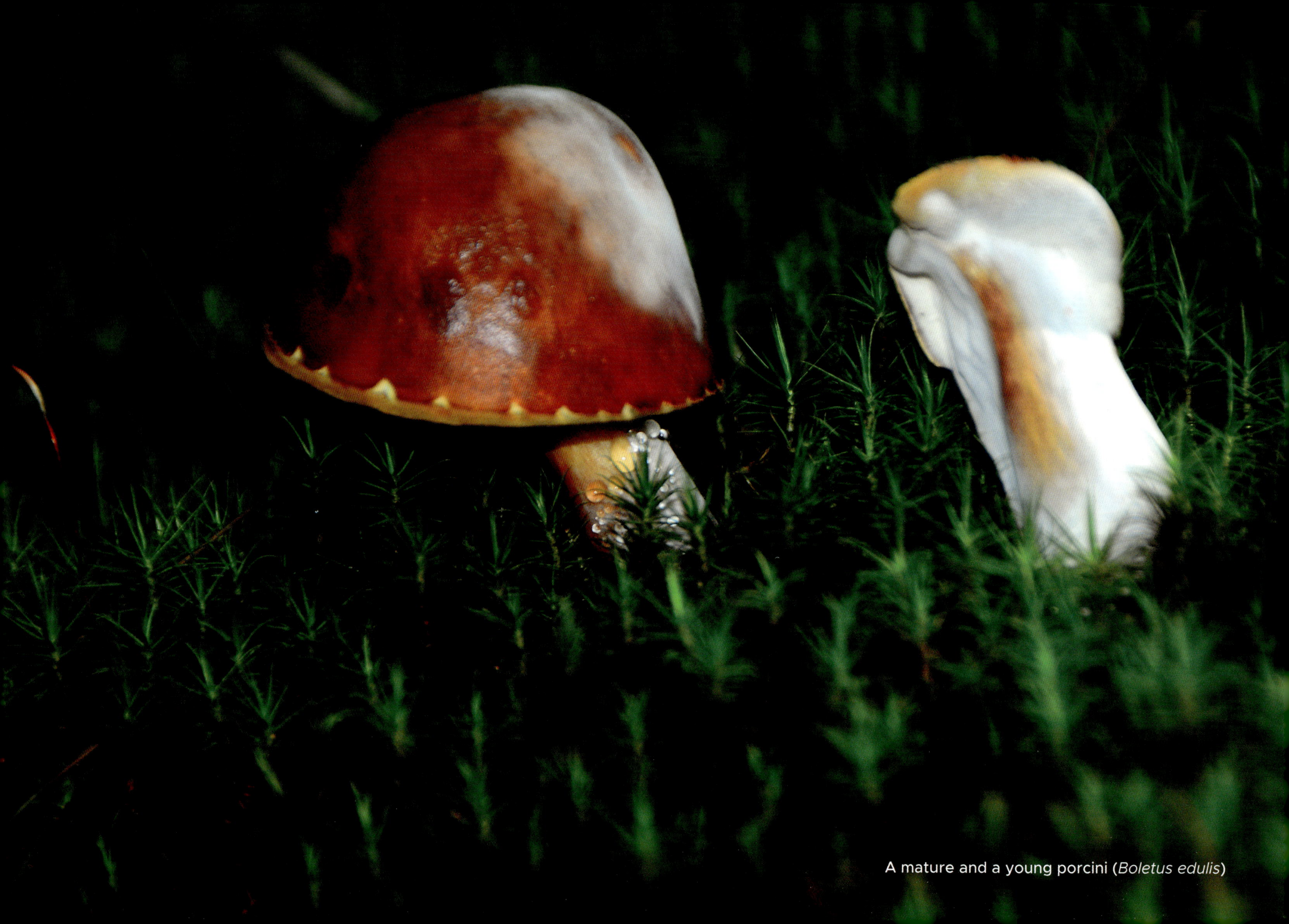

A mature and a young porcini (*Boletus edulis*)

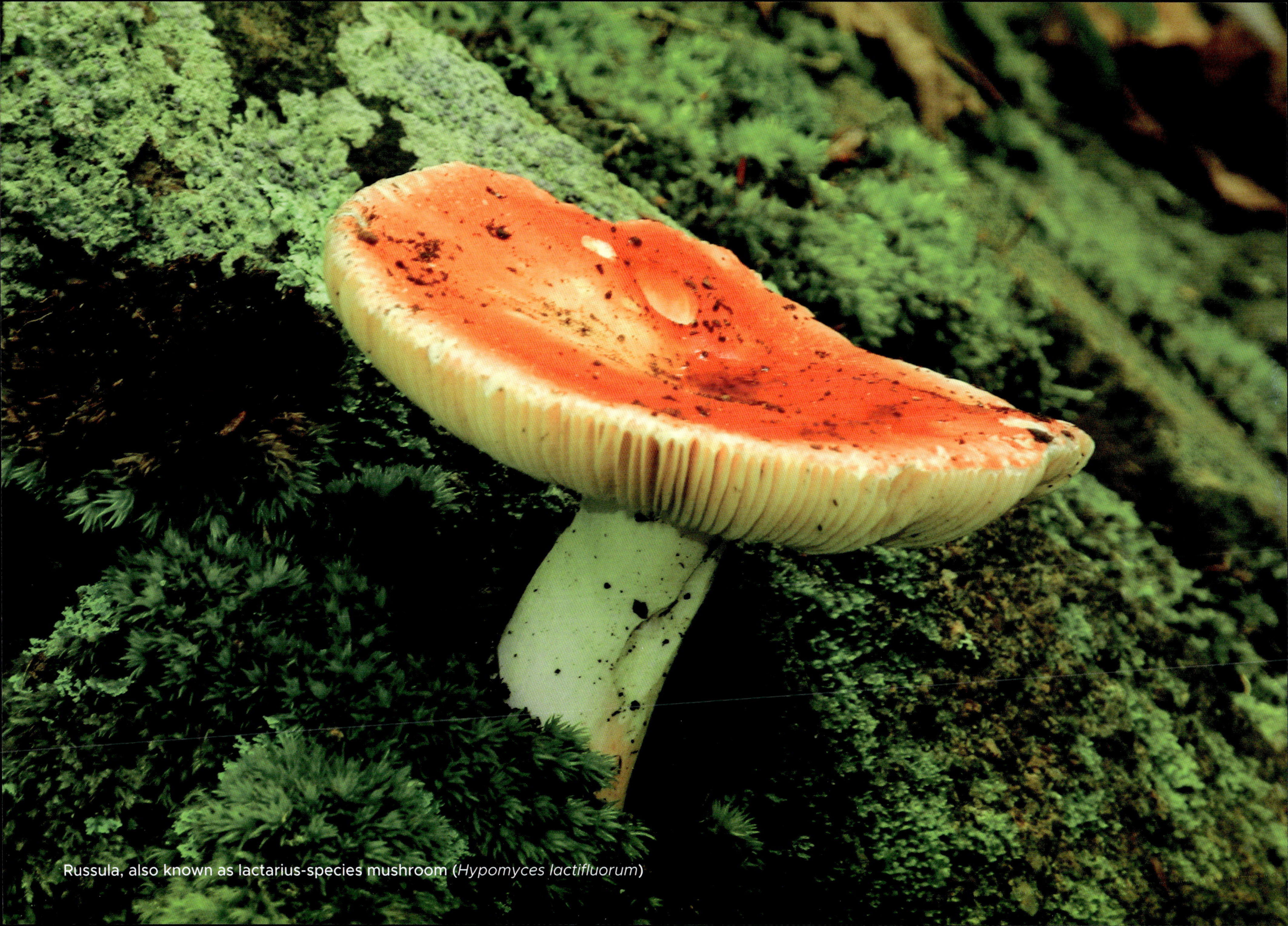

Russula, also known as lactarius-species mushroom (*Hypomyces lactifluorum*)

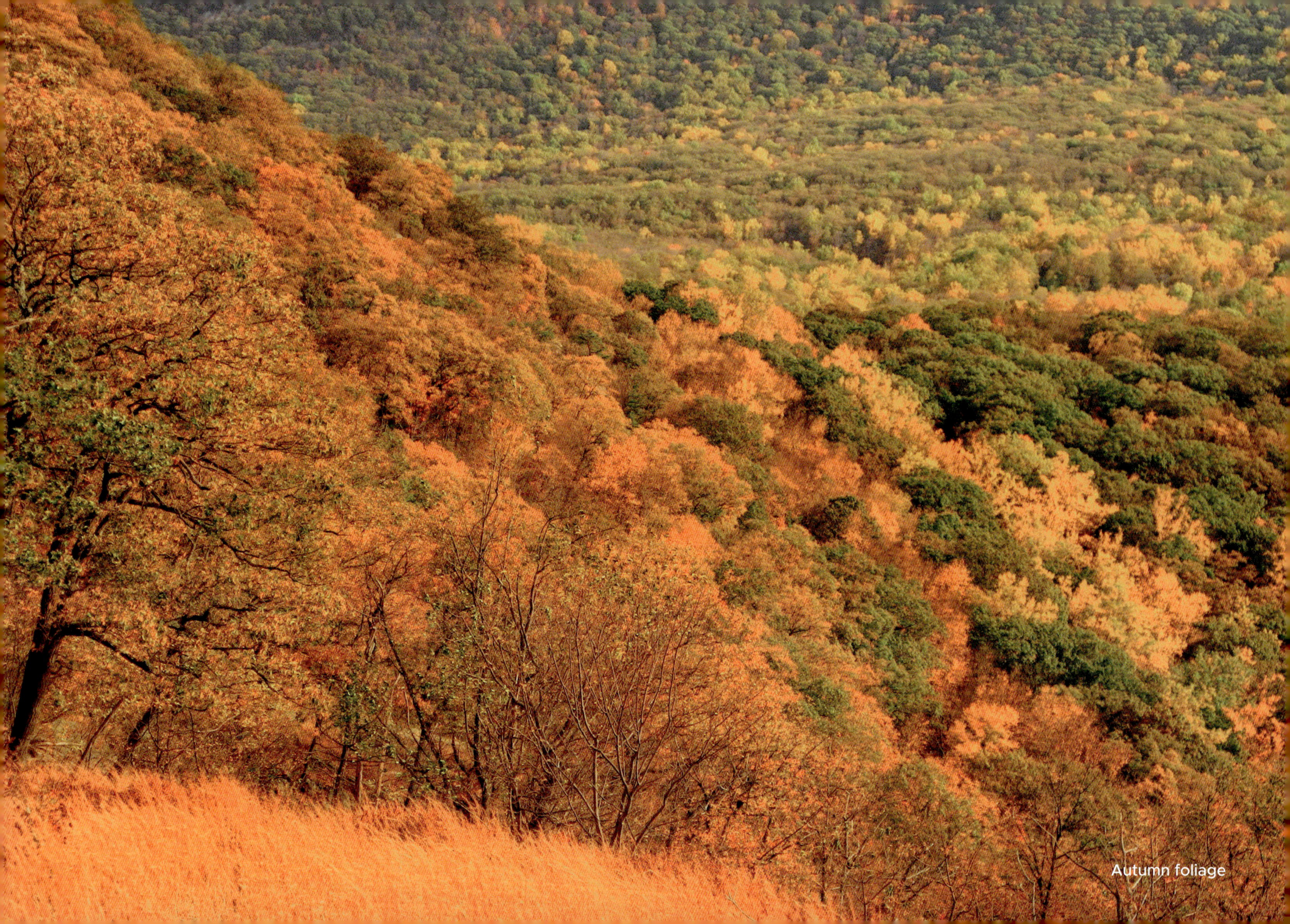

Autumn foliage

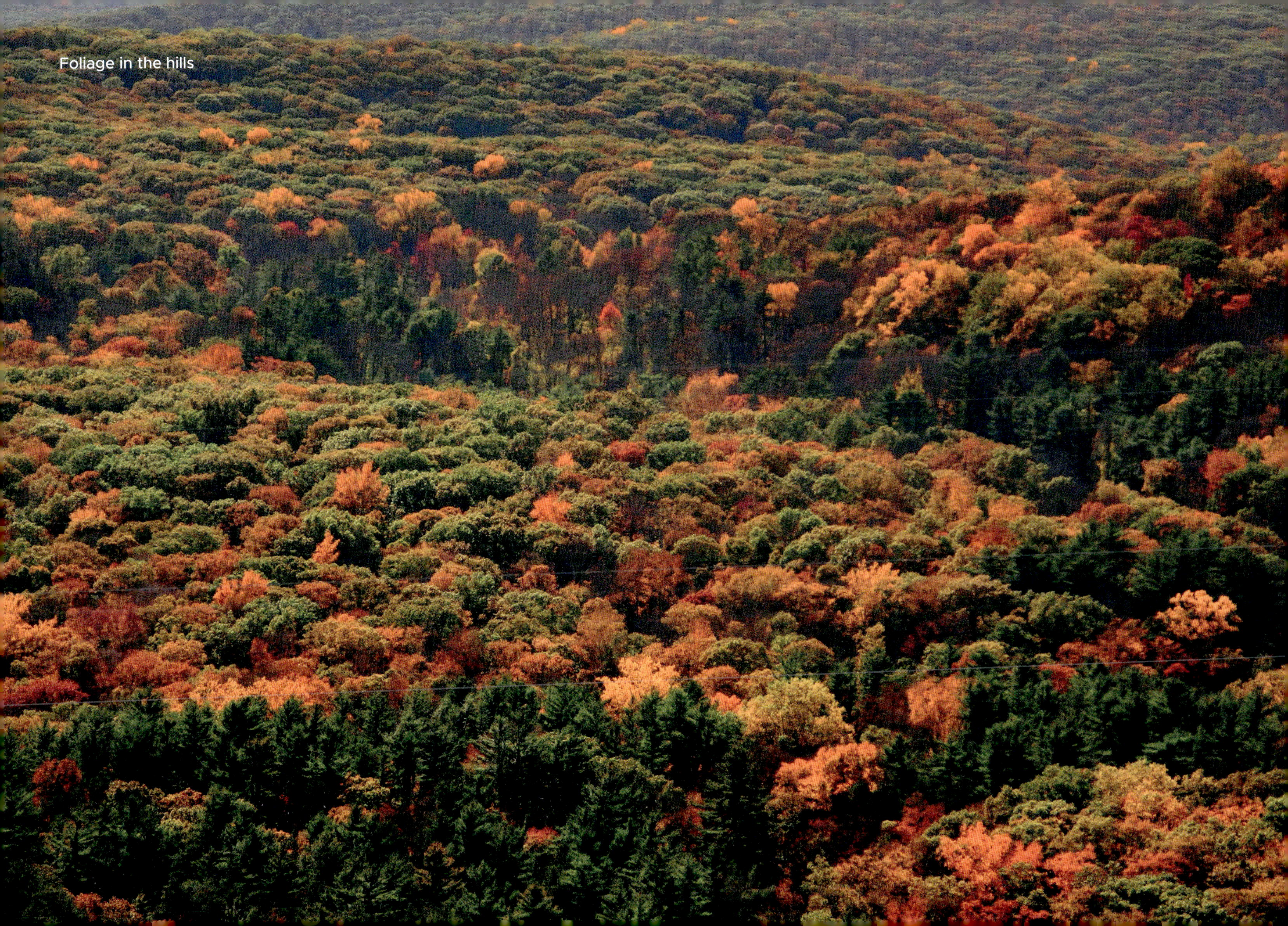

Foliage in the hills

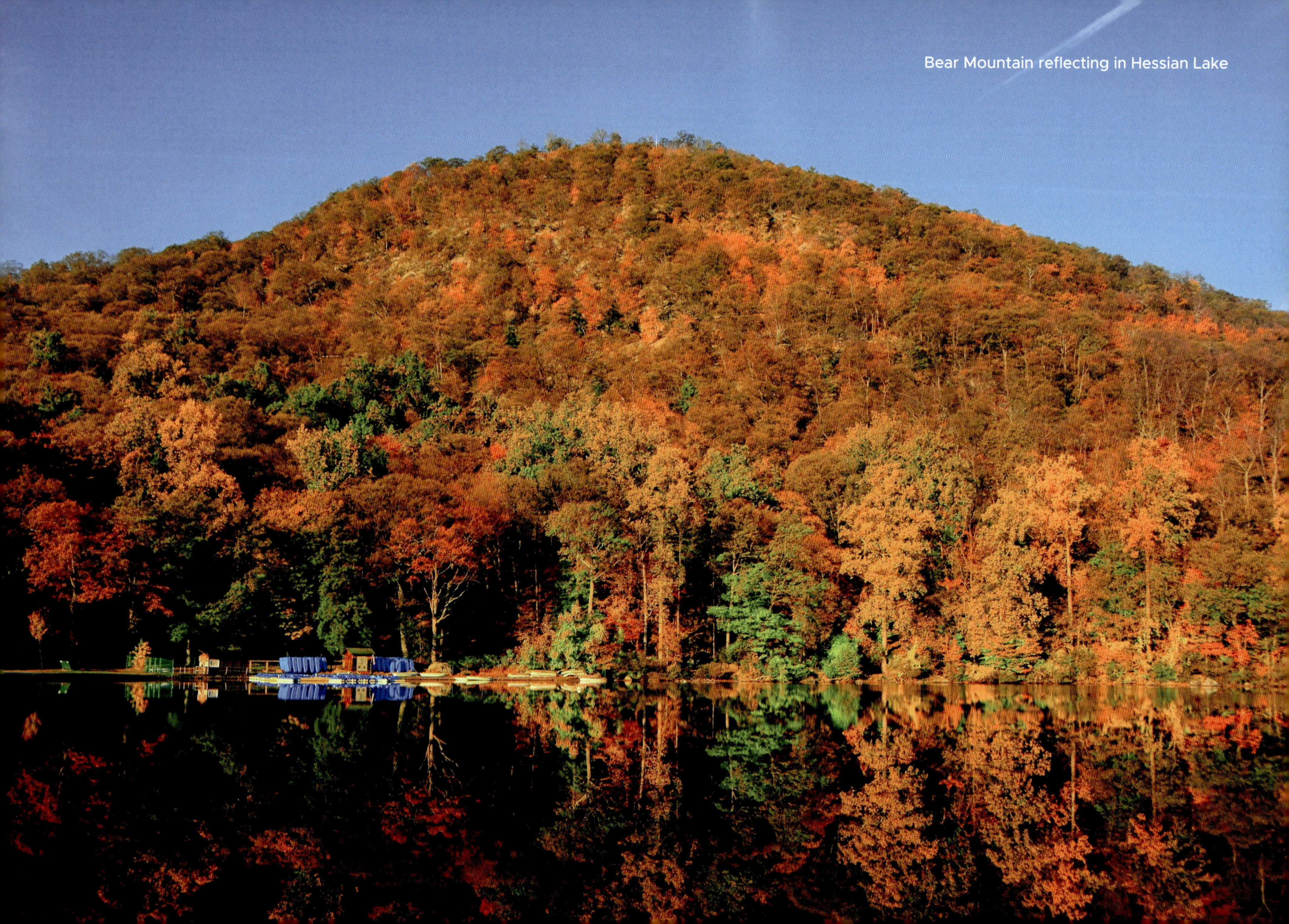

Bear Mountain reflecting in Hessian Lake

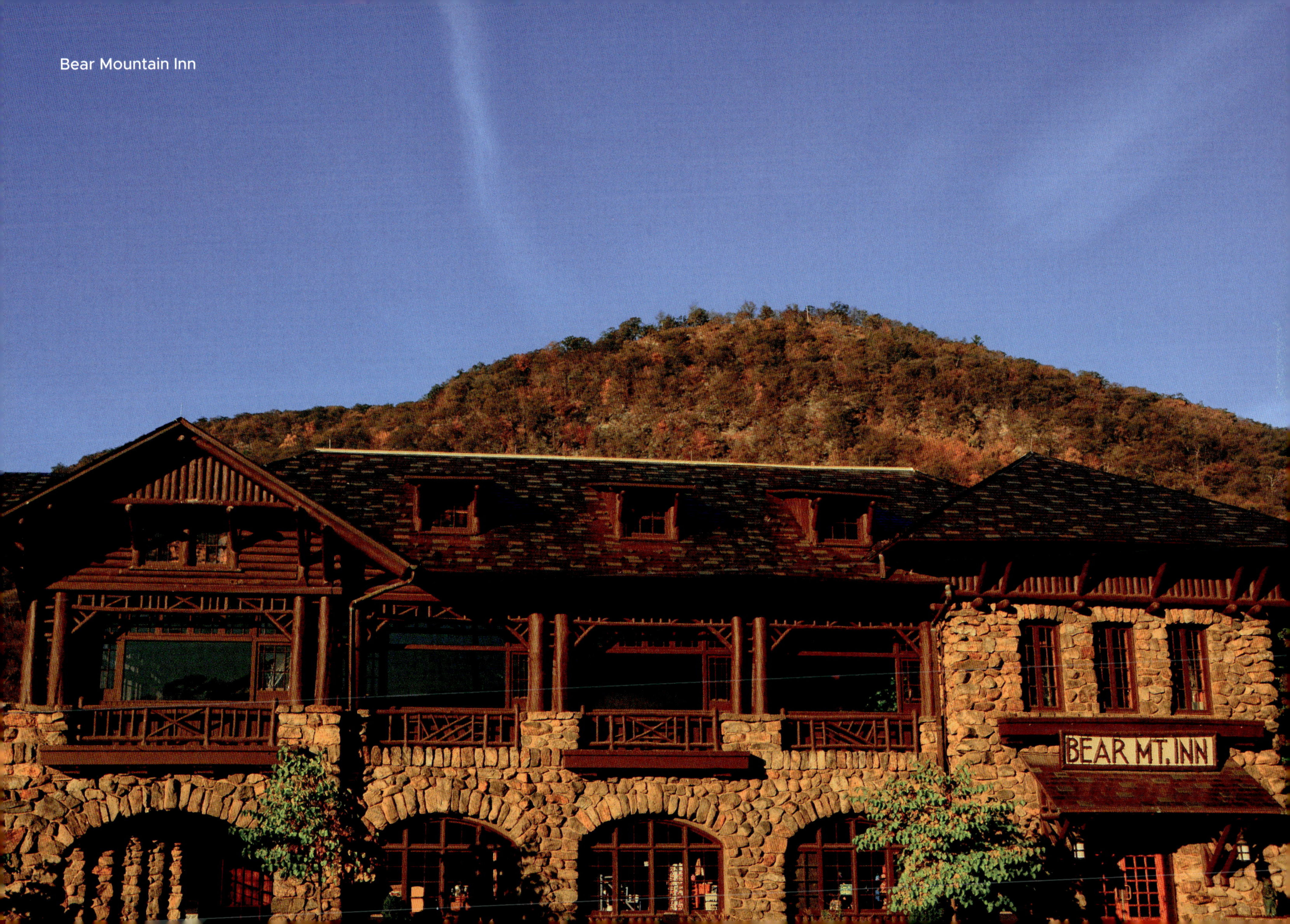

Bear Mountain Inn

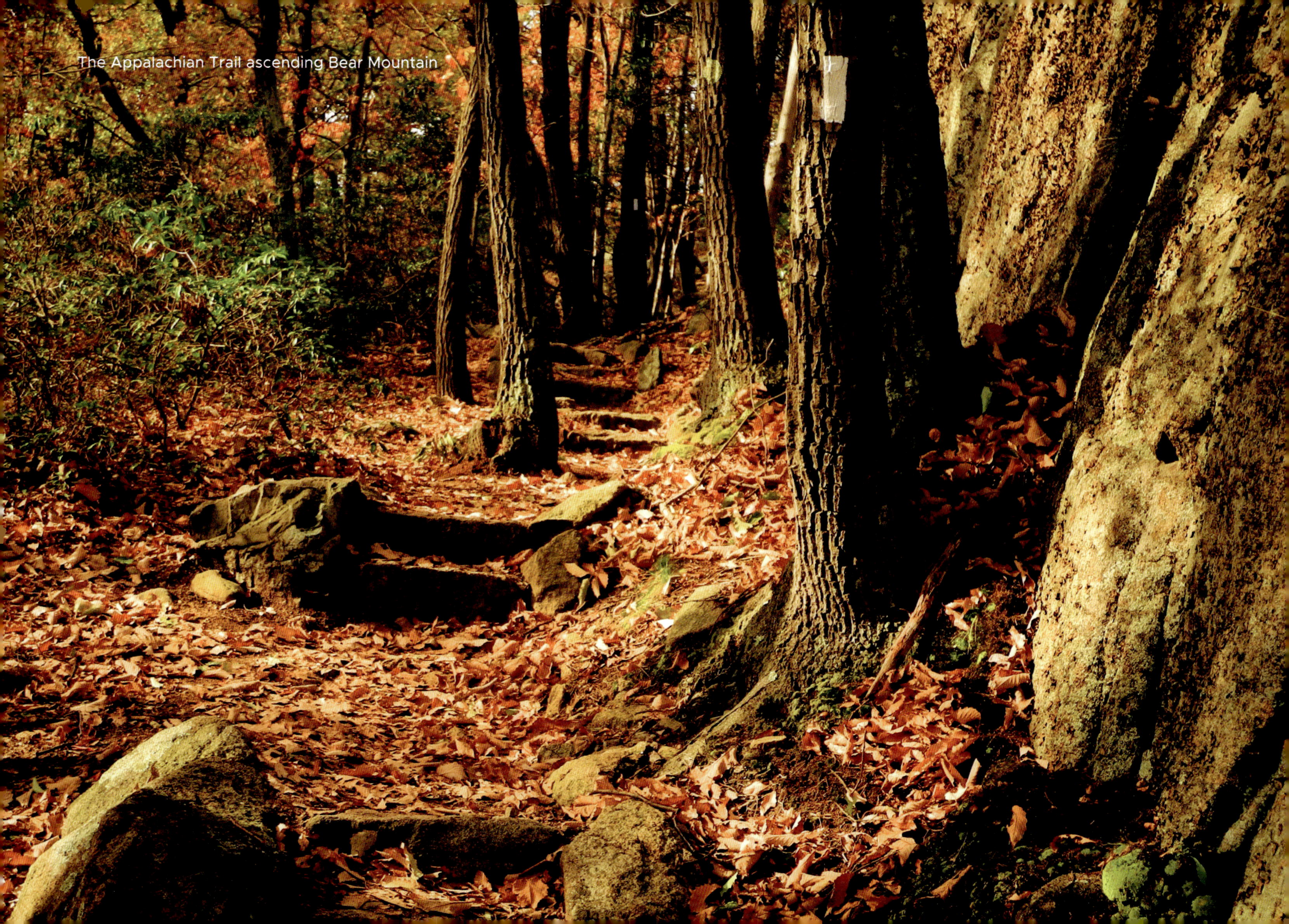
The Appalachian Trail ascending Bear Mountain

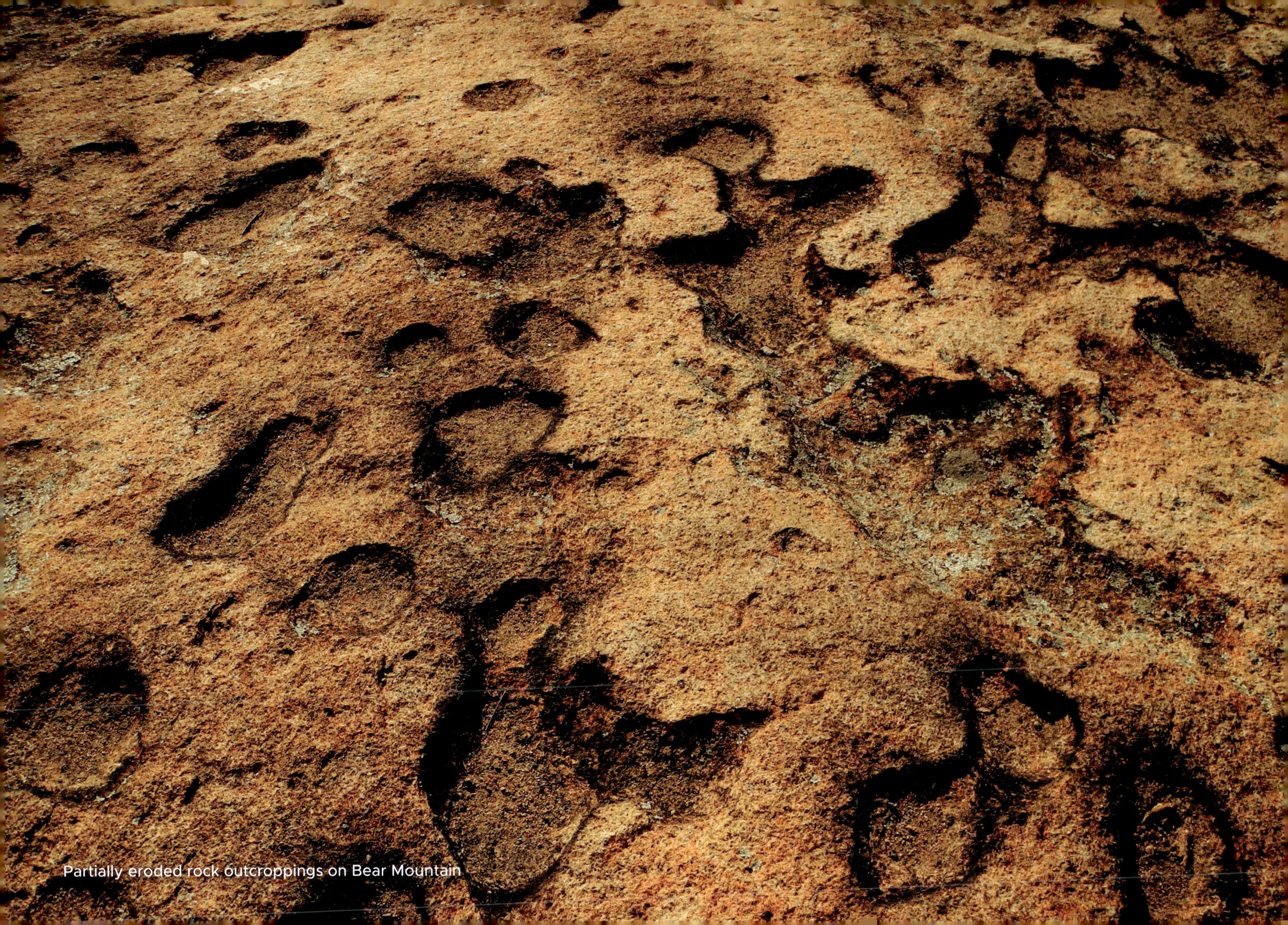

Partially eroded rock outcroppings on Bear Mountain

GEM HIKE MAP

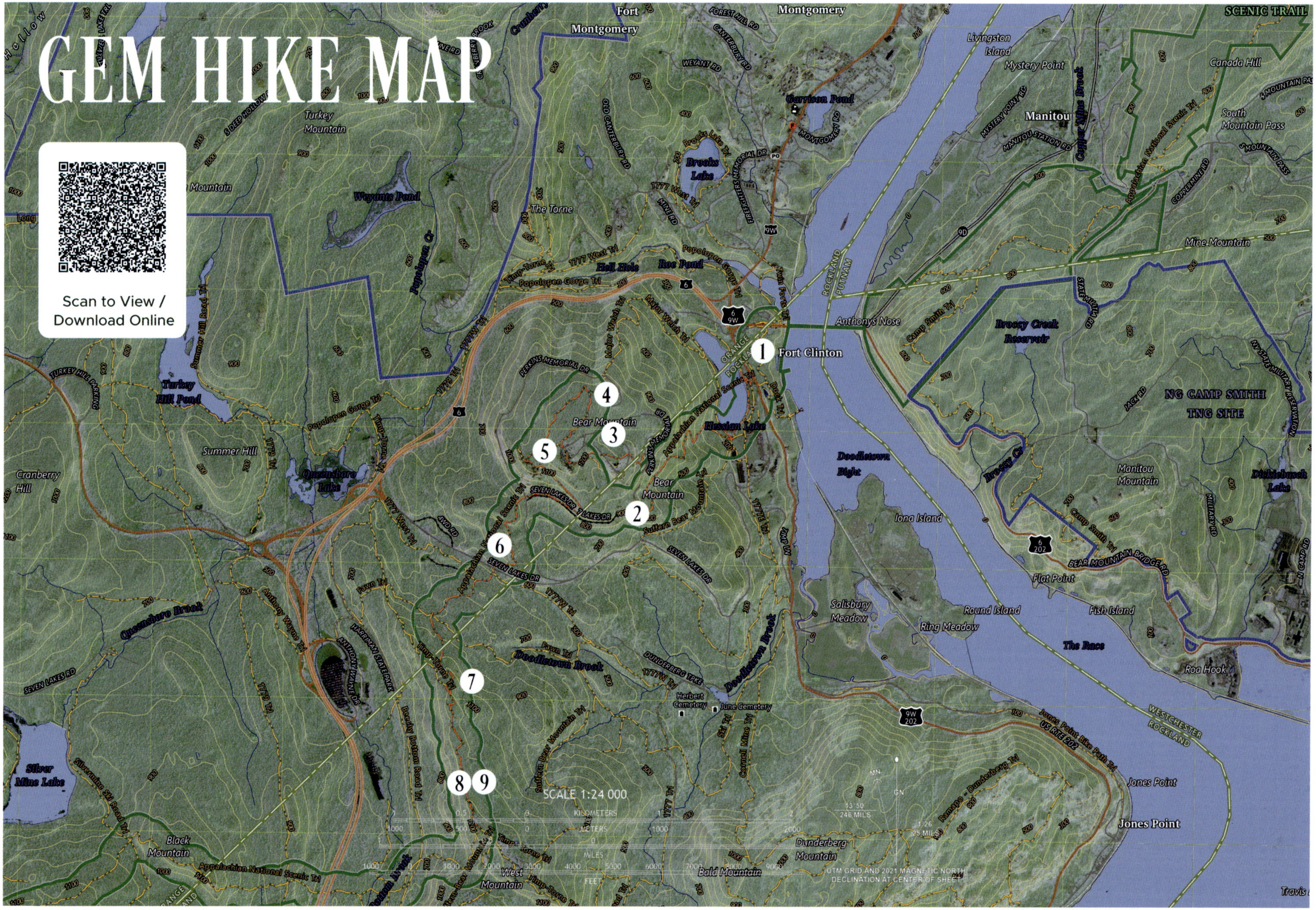
Scan to View /
Download Online
Fort Montgomery
Montgomery
Turkey Mountain
Garrison Pond
Brooks Lake
Manitou
Livingston Island
Mystery Point
Canada Hill
South Mountain Pass
The Torne
Hell Hole
Roe Pond
Mine Mountain
Anthonys Nose
Fort Clinton
Brocey Creek Reservoir
NG CAMP SMITH TNG SITE
Turkey Hill Pond
Summer Hill
Queensboro Lake
Cranberry Hill
Bear Mountain
Hessian Lake
Doodletown Bight
Iona Island
Manitou Mountain
Flat Point
Fish Island
Round Island
Salisbury Meadow
Ring Meadow
The Race
Roa Hook
Doodletown Brook
Queensboro Brook
Silver Mine Lake
Black Mountain
Jones Point
Dunderberg Mountain
Bald Mountain
West Mountain
SCALE 1:24 000
UTM GRID AND 2021 MAGNETIC NORTH DECLINATION AT CENTER OF SHEET
SCENIC TRAIL
1
2
3
4
5
6
7
8
9

DIRECTIONS TO THE TRAILHEAD(S)

From Palisades Information Center to Bear Mountain State Pk Parking Lot 1 (41.312811, −73.988978)

1. Head north toward Palisades Interstate Pkwy N for 27 seconds (0.1 mile)
2. Take US 6 E to US 202 W / Route 9W S in Highlands for 4 minutes (3.7 miles)
3. Merge onto Palisades Interstate Pkwy N and continue for 1.3 miles
4. Continue onto US 6 E / Palisades Interstate Pkwy N for 2.5 miles
5. Continue onto US 202 W / Route 9W S; drive to Service Rd. in Stony Point for 0.6 mile
6. At the traffic circle, take the first exit onto US 202 W / Route 9W S for 0.4 mile
7. Turn right onto Seven Lakes Dr.
8. Turn right on Service Rd.
9. Turn right into the Bear Mountain State Park Parking Lot 1

GEM HIKE DIRECTIONS

For this gem hike, it is best to park in the parking lot closest to Bear Mountain Inn. Google Maps refers it as Bear Mountain State Park Parking Lot 1, and its geographical coordinates are 41.312289, −73.988691. Bear Mountain Inn is located at 41.313067, −73.989886.

1. Begin by leaving Hessian Lake on the Appalachian Trail south
2. After 1.3 miles, you will travel along Perkins Memorial D.
3. After another 0.6 mile, you will reach the summit of Bear Mountain
4. When leaving the summit, make sure you are on the Appalachian Trail south, then descend for 1.8 miles and reach Perkins Memorial Dr. (for the second time, but different location)
5. Cross Perkins Memorial Dr. and hike another 0.6 mile and cross Seven Lakes Dr.
6. After another 1.1 miles, views from the ridge of West Mountain can be had
7. Travel another 1 mile to the junction with the West Mountain Shelter Trail, with views of the Hudson River and New York City
8. Reach West Mountain Shelter Trail
9. Retrace your steps back to Hessian Lake and Bear Mountain Inn

MORE/ LESS AMBITIOUS HIKERS

Less ambitious hikers may wish to turn around at the summit of Bear Mountain and enjoy some of the other amenities of Harriman–Bear Mountain State Park, such as the zoo or the pool (or both).

More-ambitious hikers may wish to arrange a point-to-point hike to increase the amount of new miles on the Appalachian Trail.

CHAPTER 11

THE APPALACHIAN TRAIL: MOUNT RIGA TO BEAR MOUNTAIN TO AND THROUGH SAGES RAVINE

AREA MAP

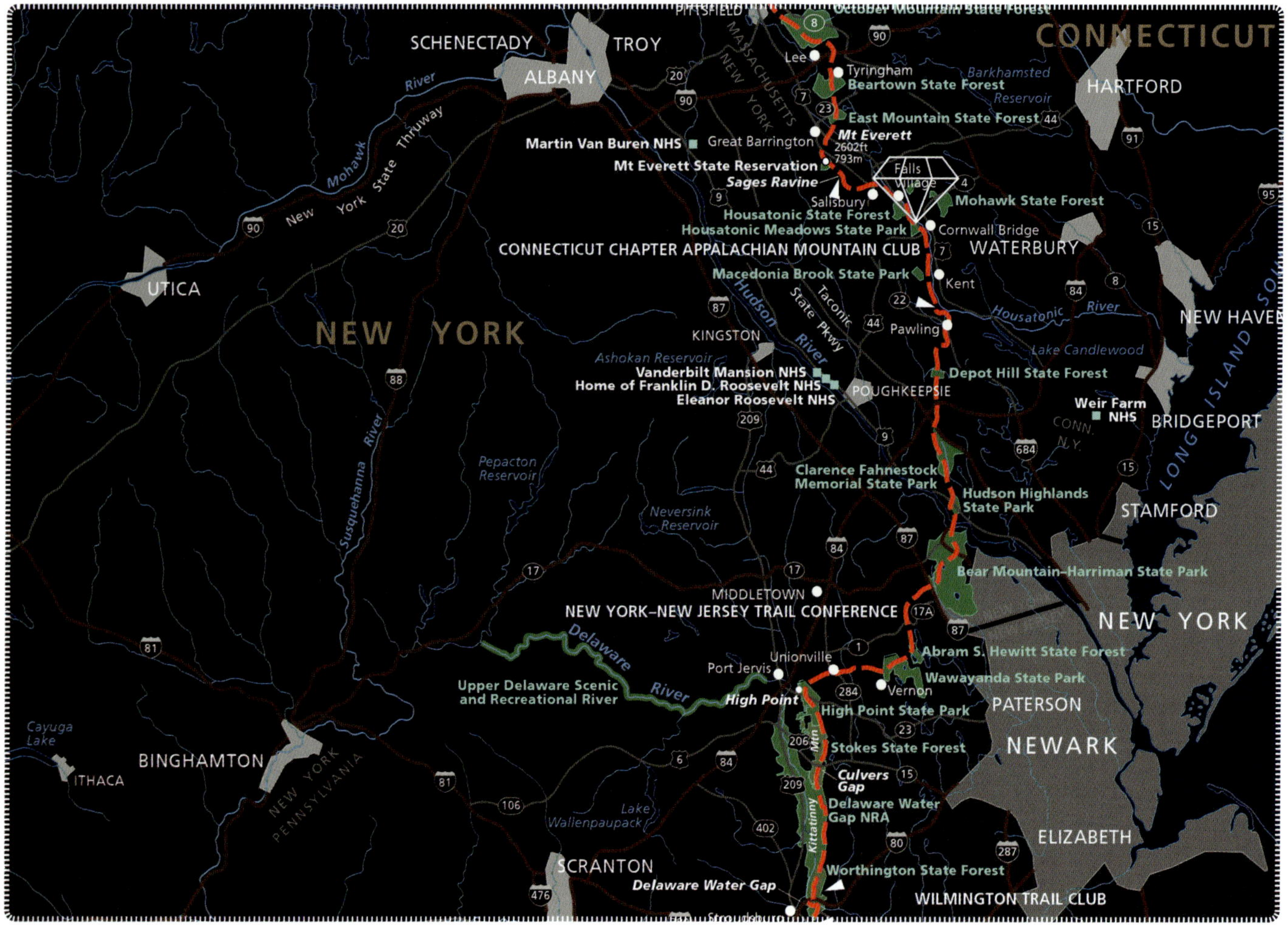

DISTANCE	12.7 miles
ELEVATION GAIN	2,400 feet
ELEVATION LOSS	2,400 feet
LEVEL	Difficult

TYPE: LOOP

0 10 Kilometers 50
0 10 Miles 50

Appalachian National Scenic Trail

Boundary of CLUB management section

North

GEM HIKE

PERSONAL TOUCH

I nicknamed the state of Connecticut section of the Appalachian Trail the General. It contains the feelings of the miles that can been seen throughout the rest of the trail. If you don't have much time to hike the entirety of the Appalachian Trail, Connecticut will welcome you with a perfect summary. Hiking this section is when I had the idea of this book to share the beauty of the Appalachian Trail with all of you. I had mushroom families welcome me into their world. I remember, on several occasions, I dropped down to the ground to photograph them. I had a panoramic vista from the summit of Bear Mountain. I had the rushing water of Sages Ravine.

BRIEF OVERVIEW

This section of the Appalachian Trail in Connecticut provides hikers with a captivating combination of challenging terrain, scenic beauty, and great ecological diversity. This segment covers under 3 miles, but it traverses through diverse landscapes including an ascent, serene forests, and a dramatic ravine. Between Bear Mountain, Sages Ravine, and other sights along the way, this section will simply amaze anyone.

DESCRIPTION OF THE GEM HIKE

Route 41 (Undermountain Rd.)

This trailhead is part of Mount Riga State Park. The geographical coordinate is 42.028701, −73.428941.

If you don't want to hike 17 miles point to point from Connecticut Route 41 to Massachusetts's Jug End Road or want two of the highlights condensed into a short day hike, then this gem hike is for you. This hike is a gem of the Appalachian Trail because it has a taste of what the Appalachian Trail has to offer. It has vistas, a nice climb of Bear Mountain, refreshing streams, and even special, smaller trail treats.

The Appalachian Trail section from Mount Riga through Sages Ravine offers a diverse and inspiring hiking experience. With its challenging terrain, diverse flora and fauna, and significant landmarks such as Bear Mountain and Sages Ravine, this segment provides both physical challenge and natural beauty. Whether seeking solitude, reflection, or a deeper connection with nature, hikers and nature lovers will find this part of the Appalachian Trail a very memorable experience.

FLORA, FAUNA, AND VEGETATION

Vegetation along this section of the Appalachian Trail is mainly hardwood forests. When you get closer to Sages Ravine, plant species that are adapted to cooler temperatures and rocky conditions start showing up, including mosses that grow on the rocks. Fungi serve as very colorful, diverse, and unique trail treats.

BEAR MOUNTAIN

Bear Mountain is a significant peak along this section of the Appalachian Trail in Connecticut, offering special views of the surrounding Berkshire Mountains to the north. The ascent to Bear Mountain is challenging but provides rewarding vistas from the summit. It is Connecticut's highest mountain, but Connecticut's highest land belongs to Mount Frissell. Mount Frissell's summit is in Massachusetts.

SAGES RAVINE

Sages Ravine is one of the highlights of this trail section. It is known for its serene, moss-covered rocks and crystal-clear streams. The ravine a great place for a break, and it provides an excellent opportunity for reflection, relaxation, and enjoyment.

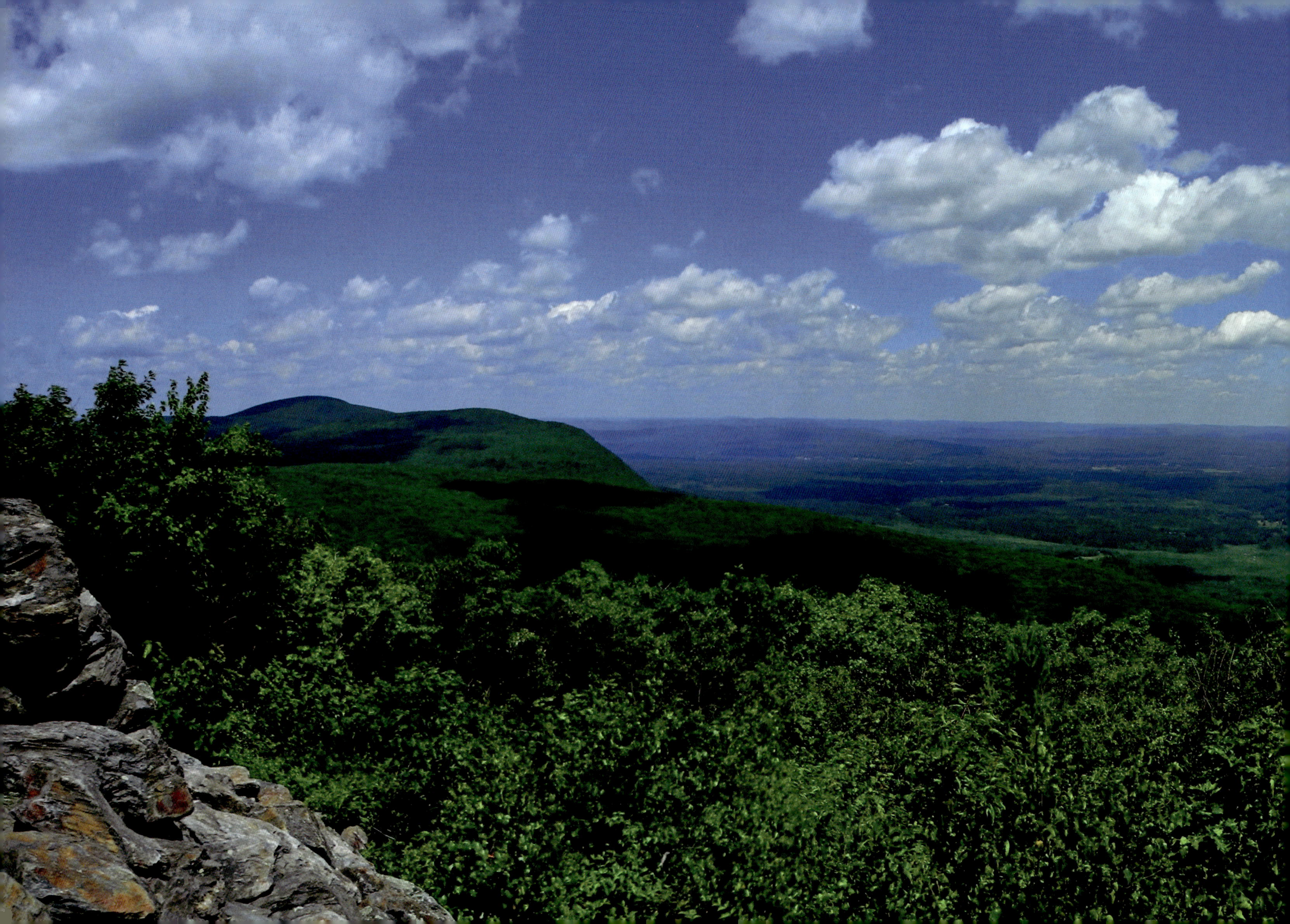

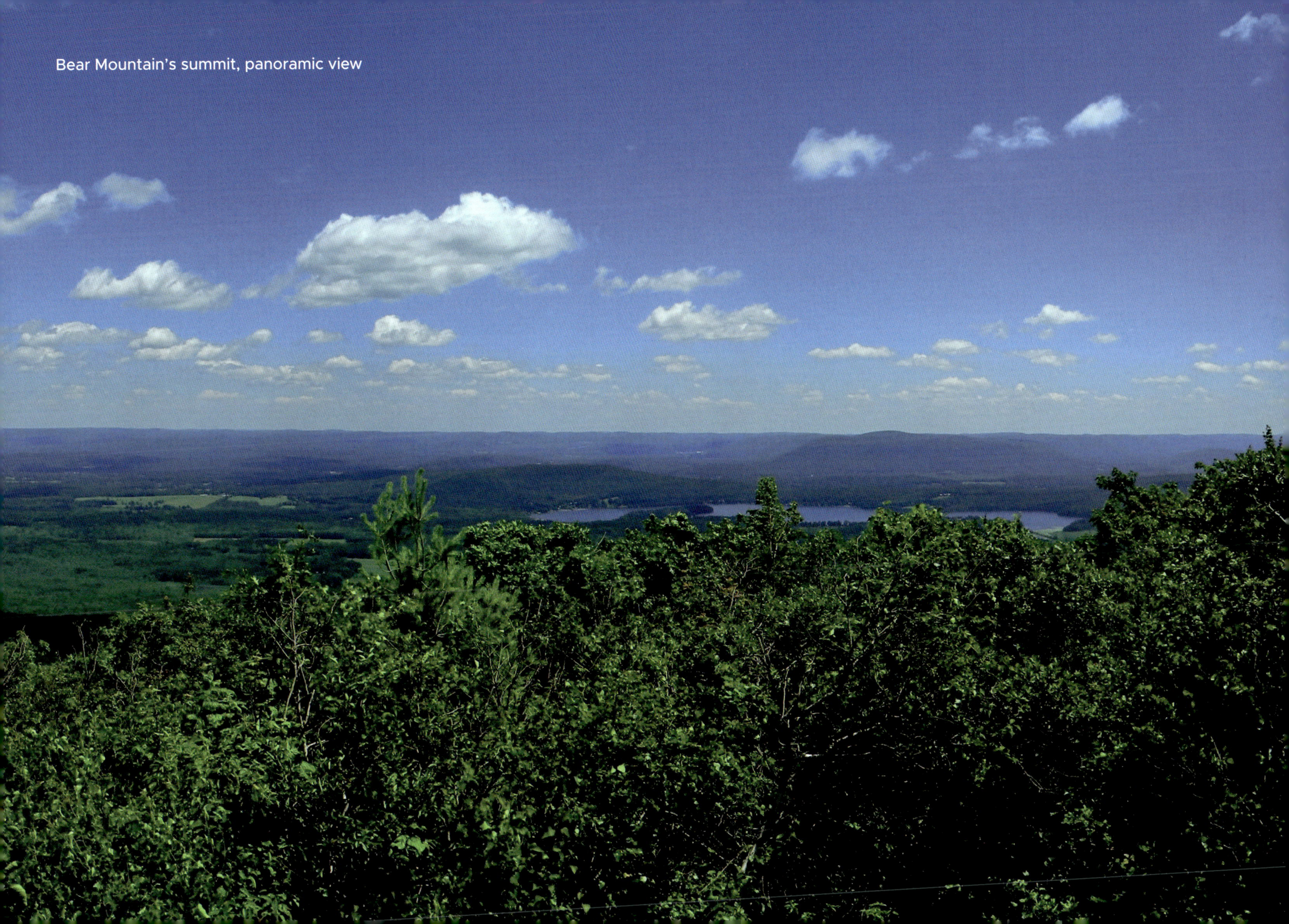

Bear Mountain's summit, panoramic view

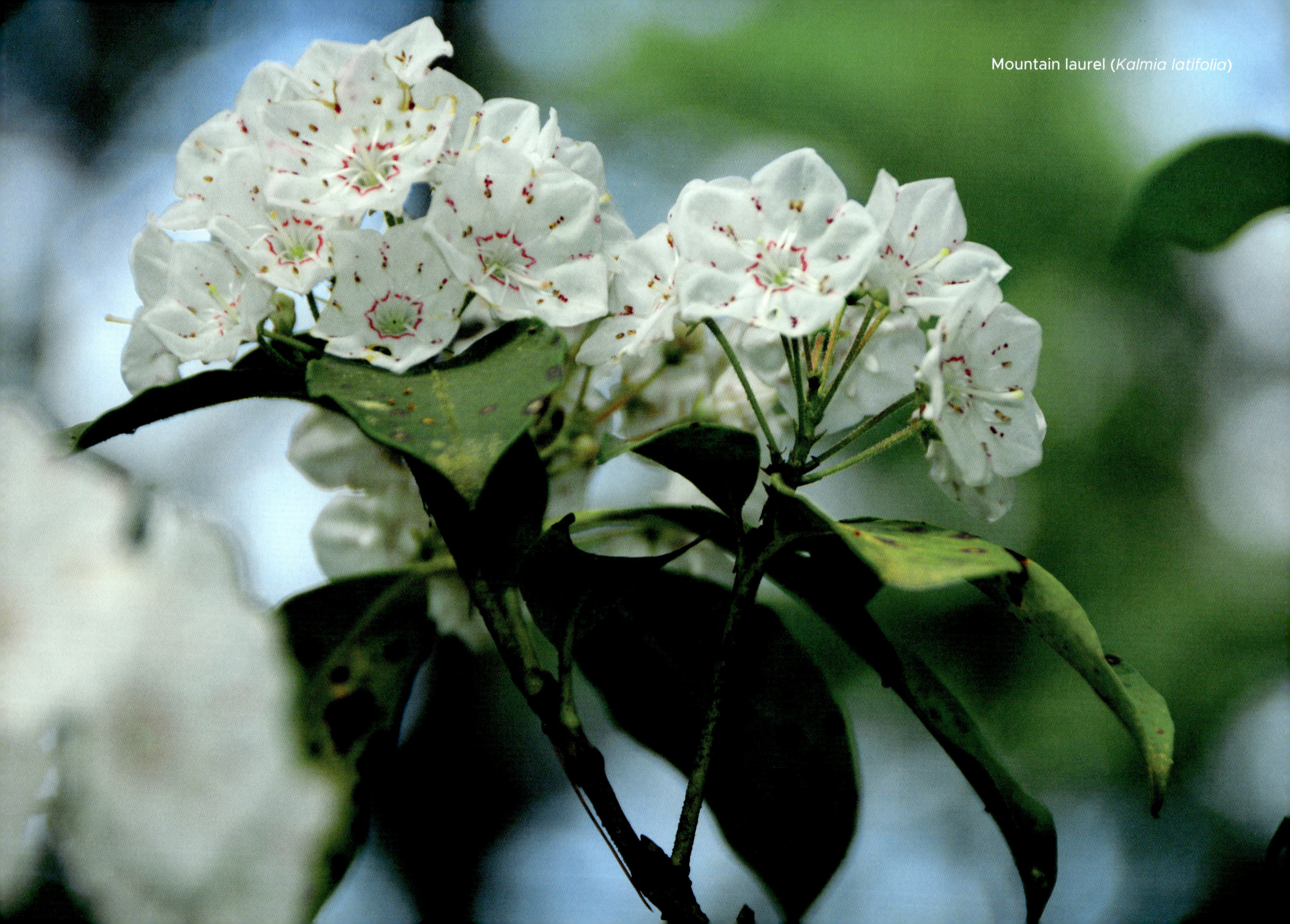

Mountain laurel (*Kalmia latifolia*)

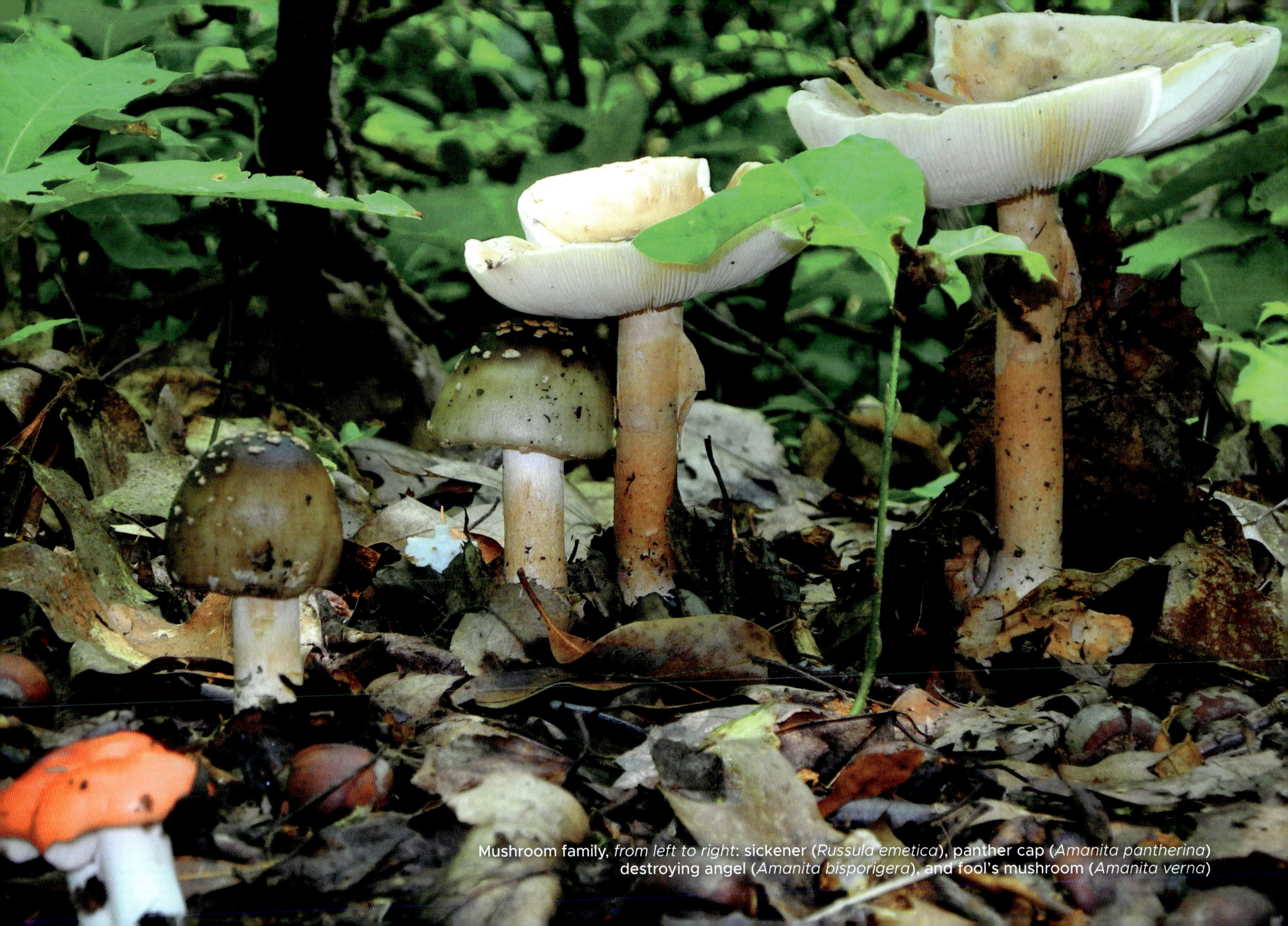

Mushroom family, *from left to right*: sickener (*Russula emetica*), panther cap (*Amanita pantherina*) destroying angel (*Amanita bisporigera*), and fool's mushroom (*Amanita verna*)

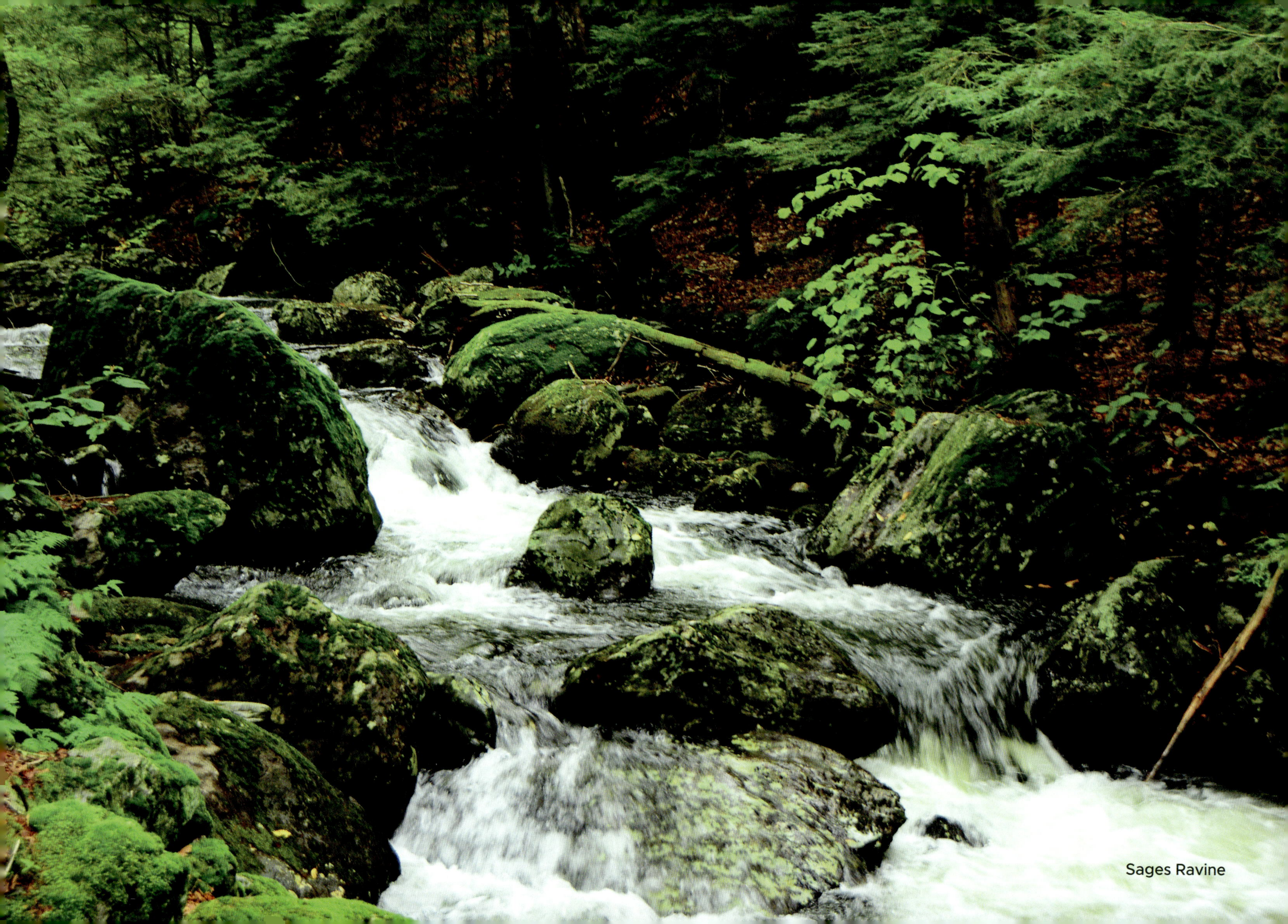

Sages Ravine

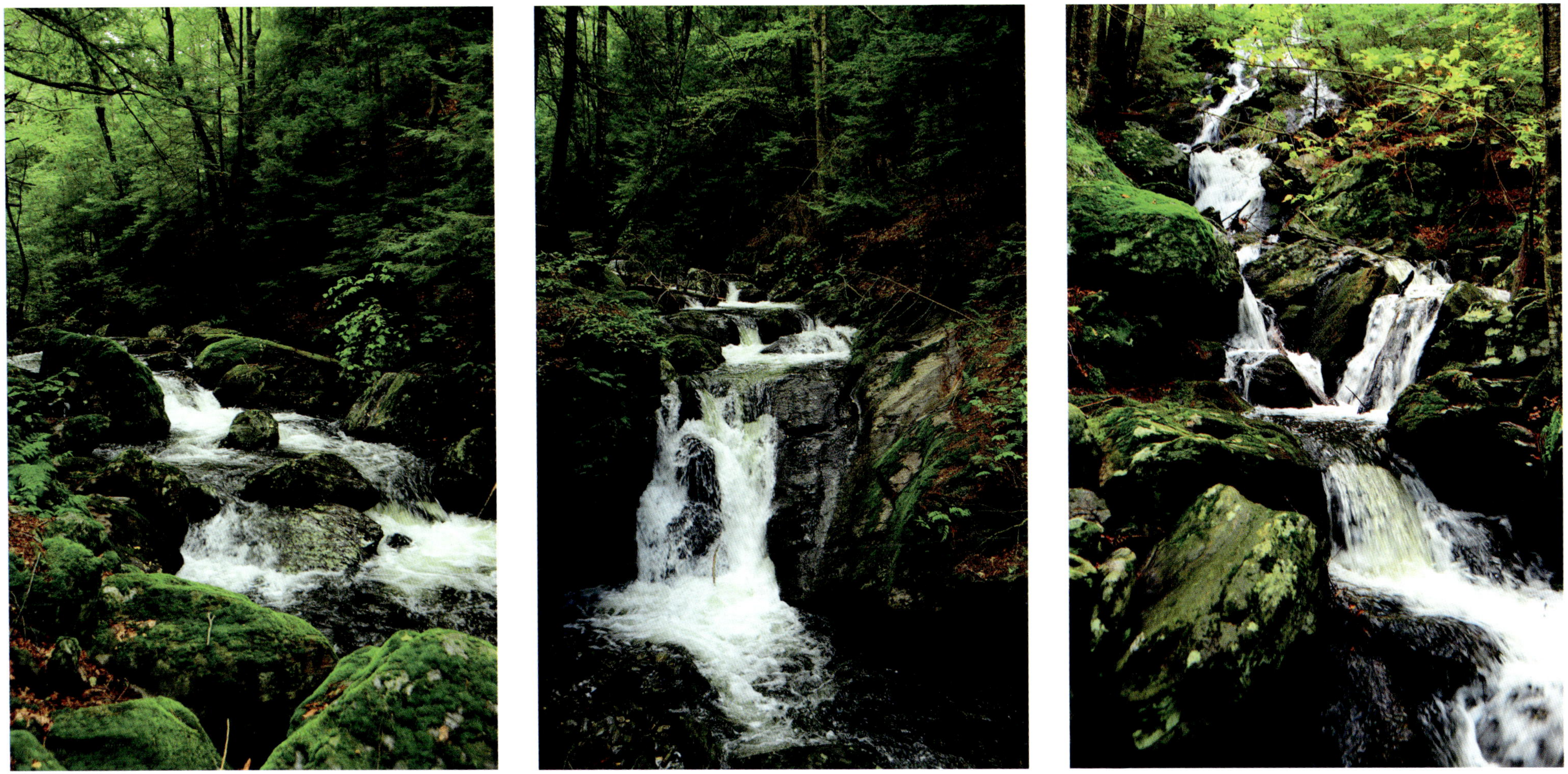

Sages Ravine

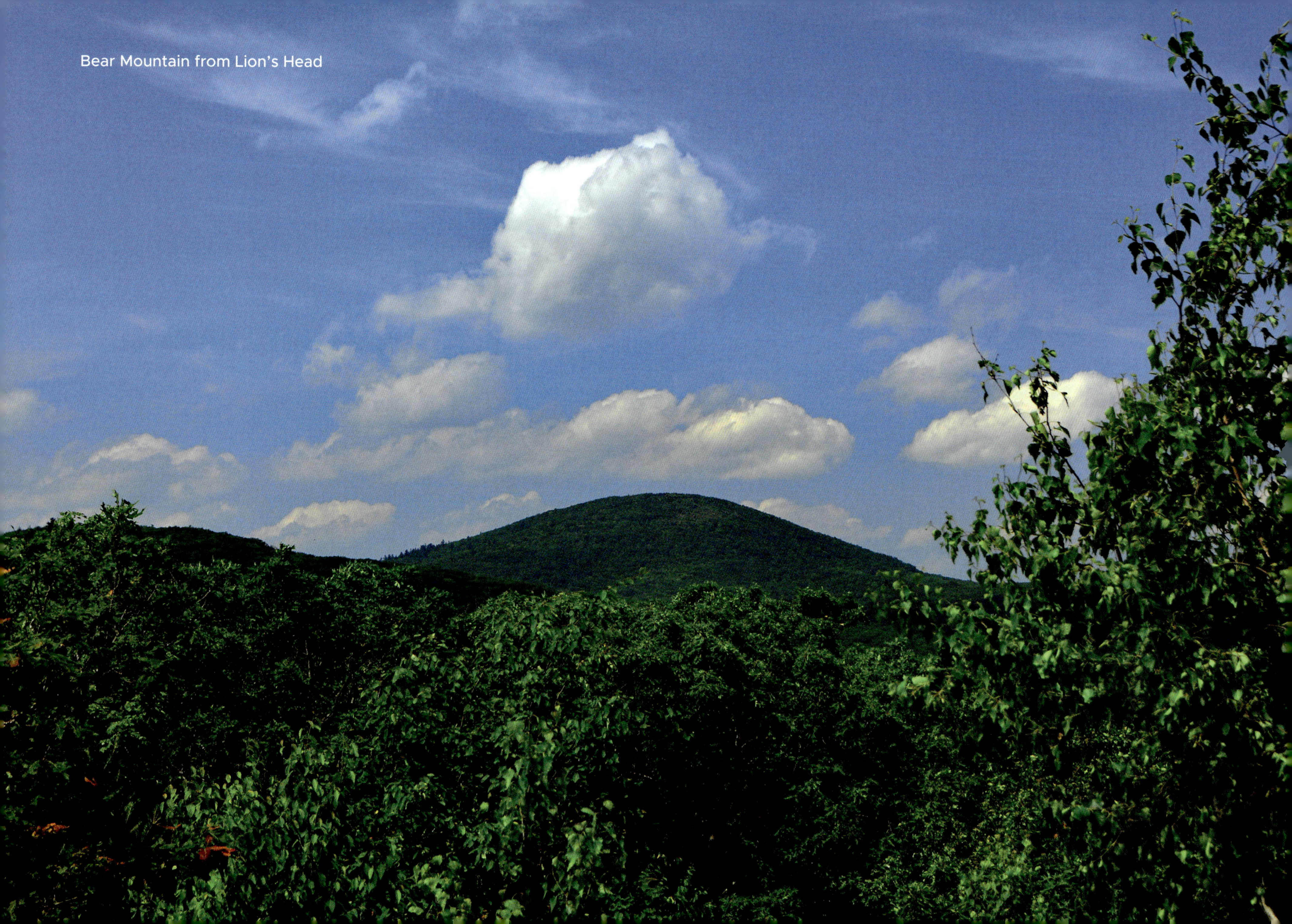

Bear Mountain from Lion's Head

Sages Ravine

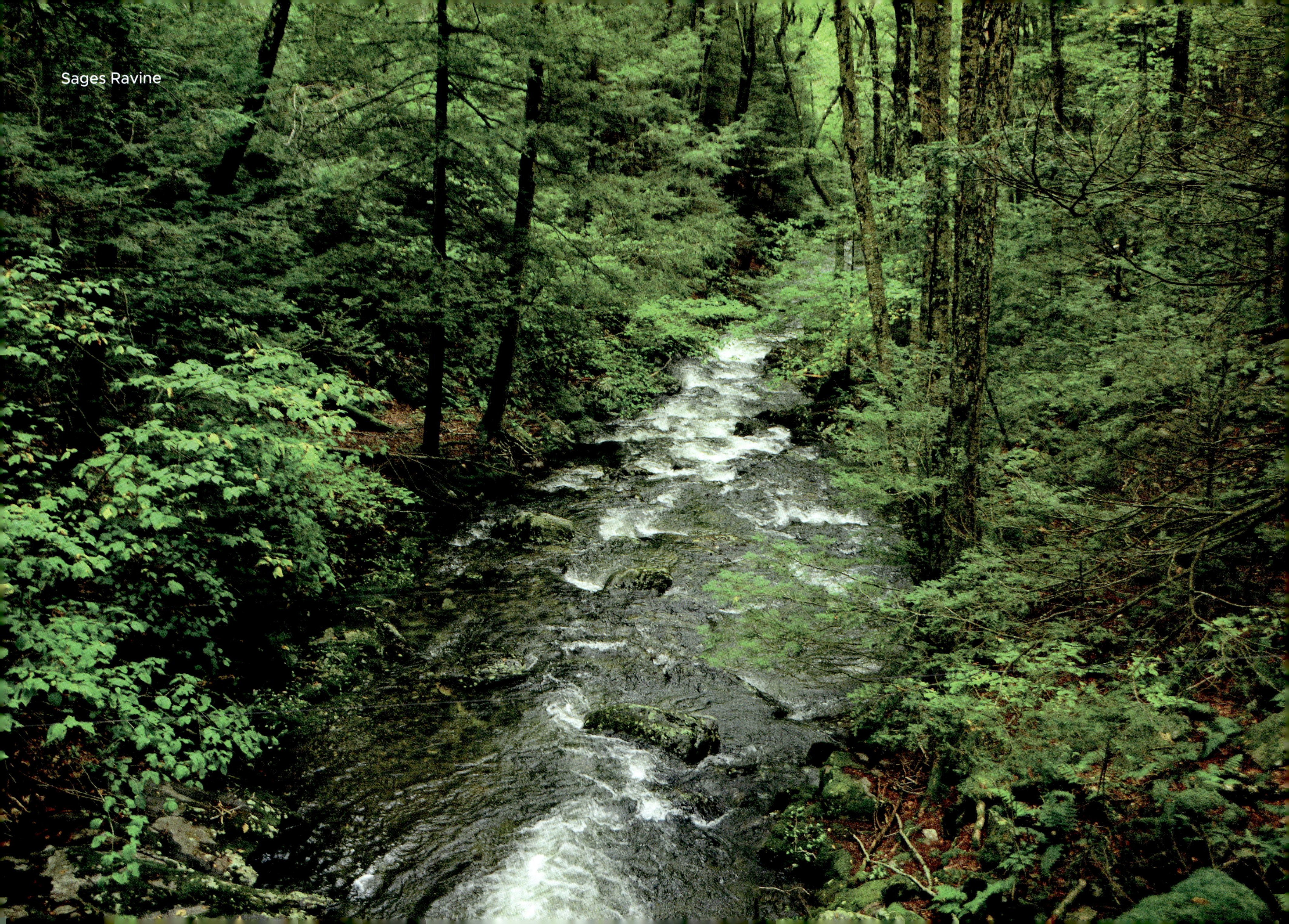

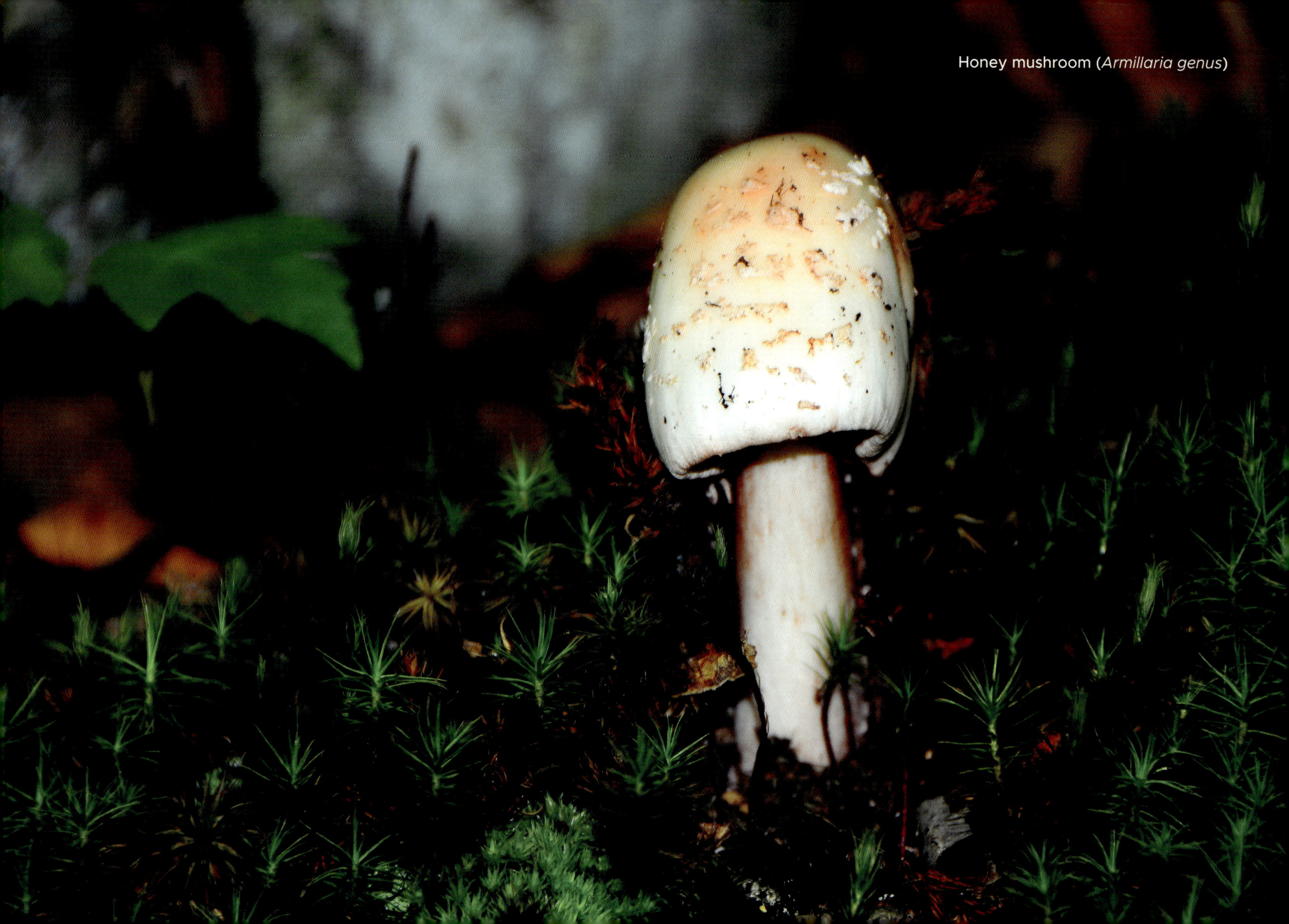

Honey mushroom (*Armillaria genus*)

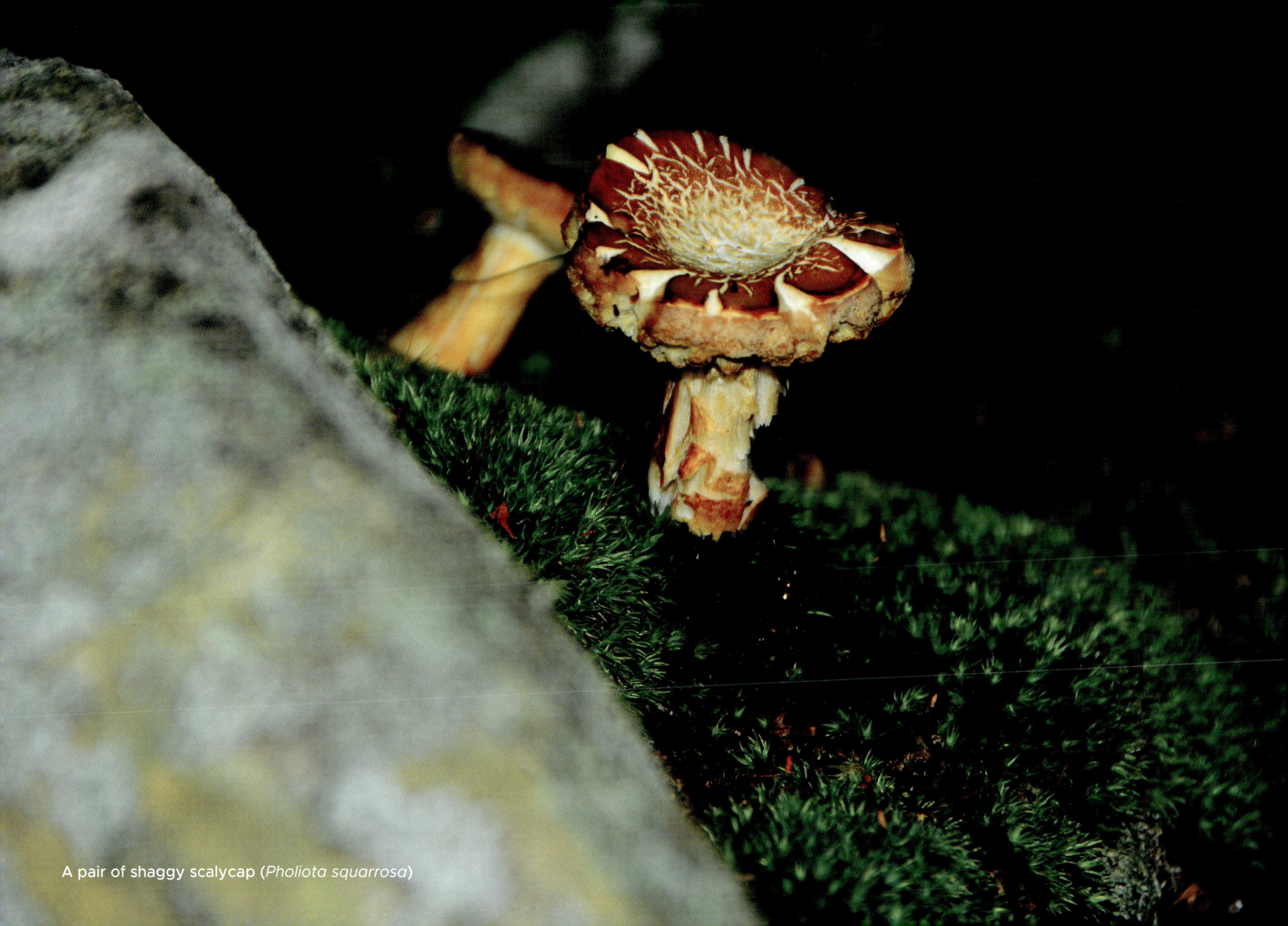

A pair of shaggy scalycap (*Pholiota squarrosa*)

GEM HIKE MAP

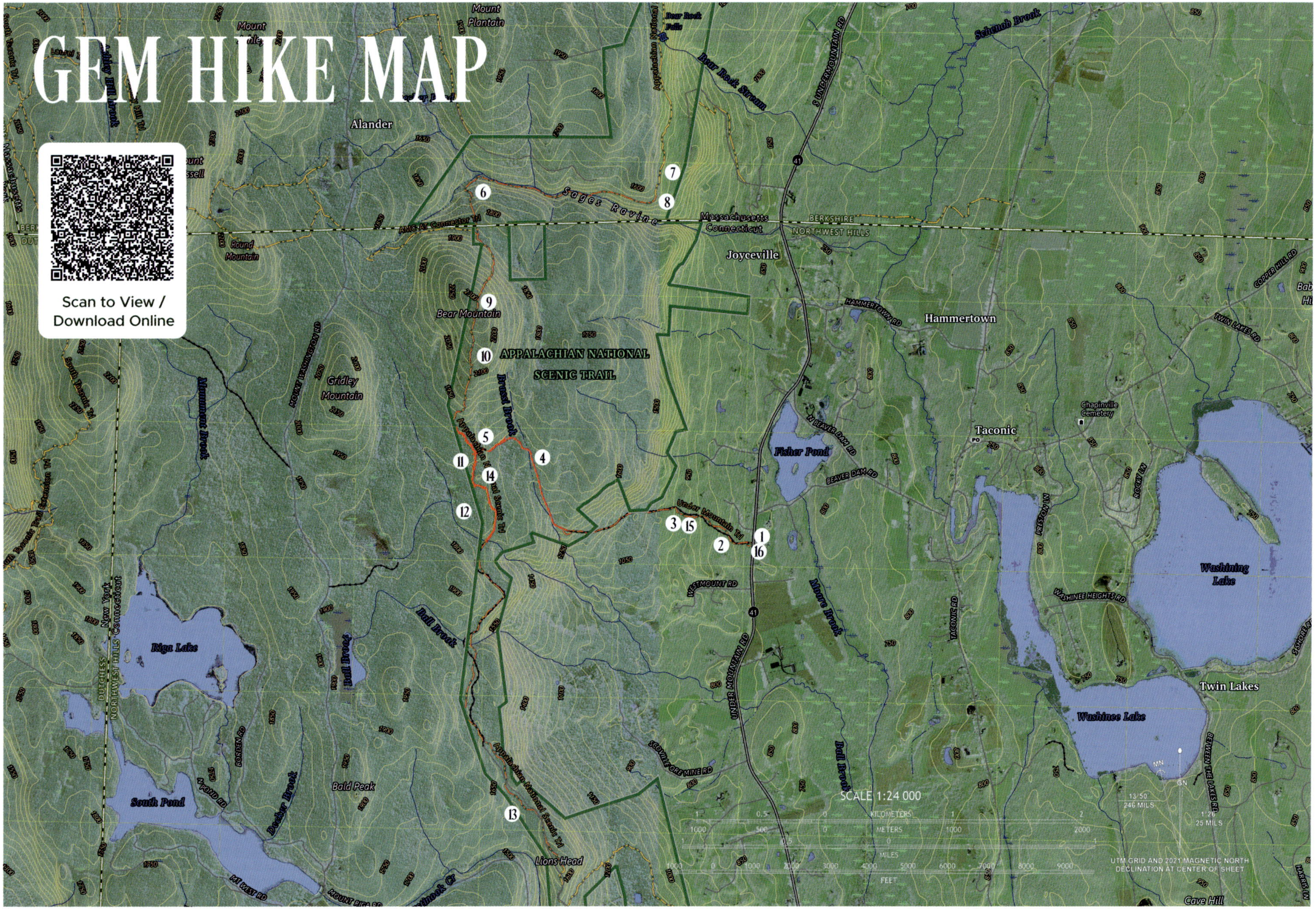
Scan to View /
Download Online
Alander
Mount Plantain
Bear Rock Falls
Bear Rock Stream
Sages Ravine
Massachusetts
Connecticut
BERKSHIRE
NORTHWEST HILLS
Joyceville
Round Mountain
Bear Mountain
APPALACHIAN NATIONAL
SCENIC TRAIL
Gridley Mountain
Monument Brook
Brassie Brook
Ball Brook
Hammertown
Taconic
Chapinville Cemetery
Fisher Pond
Washining Lake
Washinee Lake
Twin Lakes
Riga Lake
South Pond
Bald Peak
Lions Head
Cave Hill
UNDERMOUNTAIN RD
Moore Brook
Bell Brook
Schenob Brook
SCALE 1:24 000
KILOMETERS
METERS
MILES
FEET
UTM GRID AND 2021 MAGNETIC NORTH
DECLINATION AT CENTER OF SHEET
1
2
3
4
5
6
7
8
9
10
11
12
13
14
15
16

DIRECTIONS TO THE TRAILHEAD(S)

West Cornwall, Connecticut, to Undermountain Trailhead, Connecticut (42.028674, −73.428893)

1. Head north on Railroad St. toward CT 128 W
2. Turn left onto CT 128 W / Sharon-Goshen Turnpike and continue to follow Sharon-Goshen Turnpike for 0.2 mile
3. Slight right onto US 7 N and continue for 4.4 miles
4. Slight left onto CT 112 W and continue for 1.8 miles
5. Turn right onto Salmon Kill Rd. and continue for 4.1 miles
6. Turn right onto US 44 E / Main St. and continue for 0.4 mile
7. Turn left onto CT 41 N / Undermountain Rd. and continue for 3.3 miles
8. Undermountain Trailhead Parking Area will be on the left

MORE/LESS AMBITIOUS HIKERS

US 44 / Connecticut Route 41 Trailhead: This trailhead is 7.4 miles on the Appalachian Trail south of Sages Ravine. This would also be a nice challenging day hike.

Race Brook Falls Trailhead: This trailhead is 4 miles and Race Brook Falls Trail away from Sages Ravine. This could also be a nice day hike but doesn't give you the views of Bear Mountain as you climb that you get approaching Bear Mountain's summit from the south.

Jug End Road Trailhead: This trailhead is 9.5 miles on the Appalachian Trail from Sages Ravine.

GEM HIKE DIRECTIONS

To start this gem hike of the Appalachian Trail:

1. Park at the Route 41 (Undermountain Rd.) trailhead
2. Proceed on to the Undermountain Trail heading east for 1.1 miles
3. Turn left on Paradise Lane Trail; in 0.3 mile, keep left at the fork
4. Continue Paradise Lane Trail for 1.2 miles until junction with the Appalachian Trail
5. Turn right on to the Appalachian Trail north and continue 0.3 mile until Sages Ravine
6. Bear right to stay on the Appalachian Trail through Sages Ravine for 0.7 mile, until another trail junction
7. At the trail junction (the end of Sages Ravine), turn around and take the Appalachian Trail 0.7 mile back to the campsite junction
8. At the campsite junction, bear left to stay on the Appalachian Trail south for 0.3 mile to the Massachusetts/Connecticut state line
9. Continue 0.7 mile on the Appalachian Trail south to the summit of Bear Mountain
10. Continue 0.7 mile beyond the summit of Bear Mountain, and Bear Mountain Rd. meets the Appalachian Trail on the right
11. Continue the Appalachian Trail 0.2 mile you reach Riga Junction
12. Continue 2.4 miles to the summit of Lions Head
13. At the summit of Lions Head, turn around and proceed on to the Appalachian Trail, 2.4 miles back to Riga Junction
14. At Riga Junction, take a right on Paradise Lane Trail and continue 0.6 mile
15. Take a hard right on Undermountain Trail and continue until you reach the trailhead after 1.1 miles
16. Arrive back at the Undermountain Trailhead

CHAPTER 12

MOUNT GREYLOCK, MASSACHUSETTS

AREA MAP

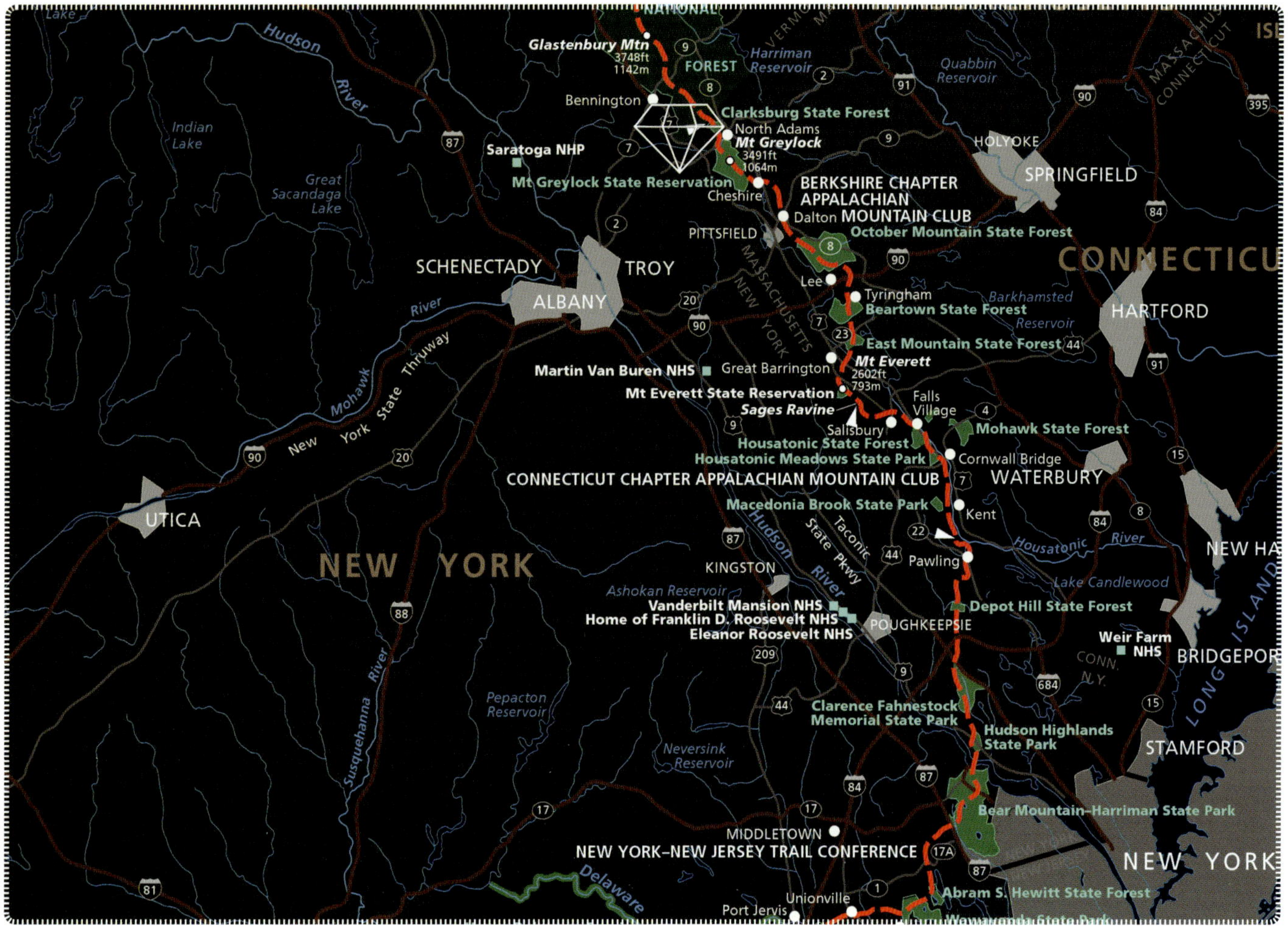

DISTANCE	13 miles
ELEVATION GAIN	3,077 feet
ELEVATION LOSS	2,400 feet
LEVEL	Moderate Difficult

TYPE: POINT TO POINT

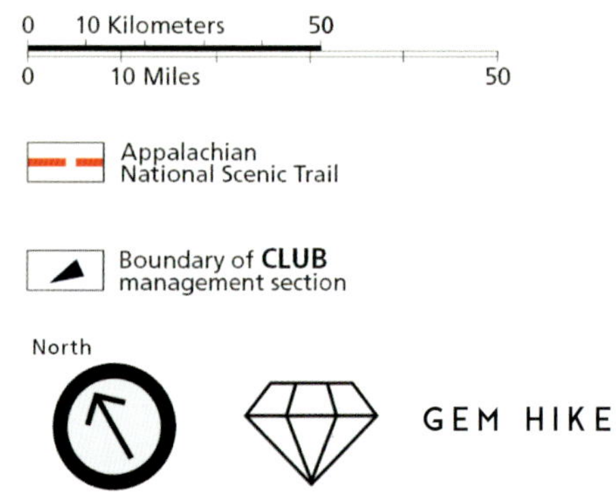

PERSONAL TOUCH

For me, the man-made structures on this hike added to the flavor. The World War I tower was like a decorative king chess piece that needed to be fully explored with the evergreen trees around it, like an army defending their king.

The cabin beside the pond was just perfectly placed to bring out the tranquil nature of the pond. I felt like I was in a time warp to the past. The reflection remained despite breezes above, because the trees protected it long enough for me to have a special moment to share.

BRIEF OVERVIEW

The 13-mile section of the Appalachian Trail on Mount Greylock offers a full hiking experience, blending natural beauty with historical significance. It offers a challenging ascent, stunning vistas, and unique structures, including its historical World War I tower and Bascom Lodge.

DESCRIPTION OF THE GEM HIKE

The section of Mount Greylock is a gem for history buffs, hikers, and vista seekers alike. Mount Greylock, standing at 3,491 feet, is Massachusetts's highest peak. This peak is known to have inspired several artists and authors over the years.

FLORA, FAUNA, VEGETATION

Lower elevations: The lower slopes are characterized by a mix of deciduous forests, including oaks, maples, and birches. The blend of these creates a special treat for leaf peepers as well as hikers.

Higher elevations: As the trail ascends, it transitions to coniferous forests with species such as balsam fir, spruce, and white pine.

WORLD WAR I TOWER

The War Memorial Tower on Mount Greylock is a prominent feature and a historical landmark. It was built in 1932 and is a 93-foot-tall stone tower that was erected as a memorial to veterans of World War I. From the top of the tower, 360-degree views of the Berkshires, New York, and Vermont can be had. The tower has the following inscription: "Erected by Massachusetts in grateful recognition of the loyalty and sacrifice of her sons and daughters in war. They were faithful even unto death." Evergreen trees are perfectly spaced around the tower by Mother Nature.

BASCOM LODGE

Bascom Lodge, located near the summit of Mount Greylock, is an iconic structure that has served visitors since being built by the Civilian Conservation Corps (CCC) in 1937. The lodge provides accommodations and a place to rest for those exploring the Appalachian Trail and Mount Greylock.

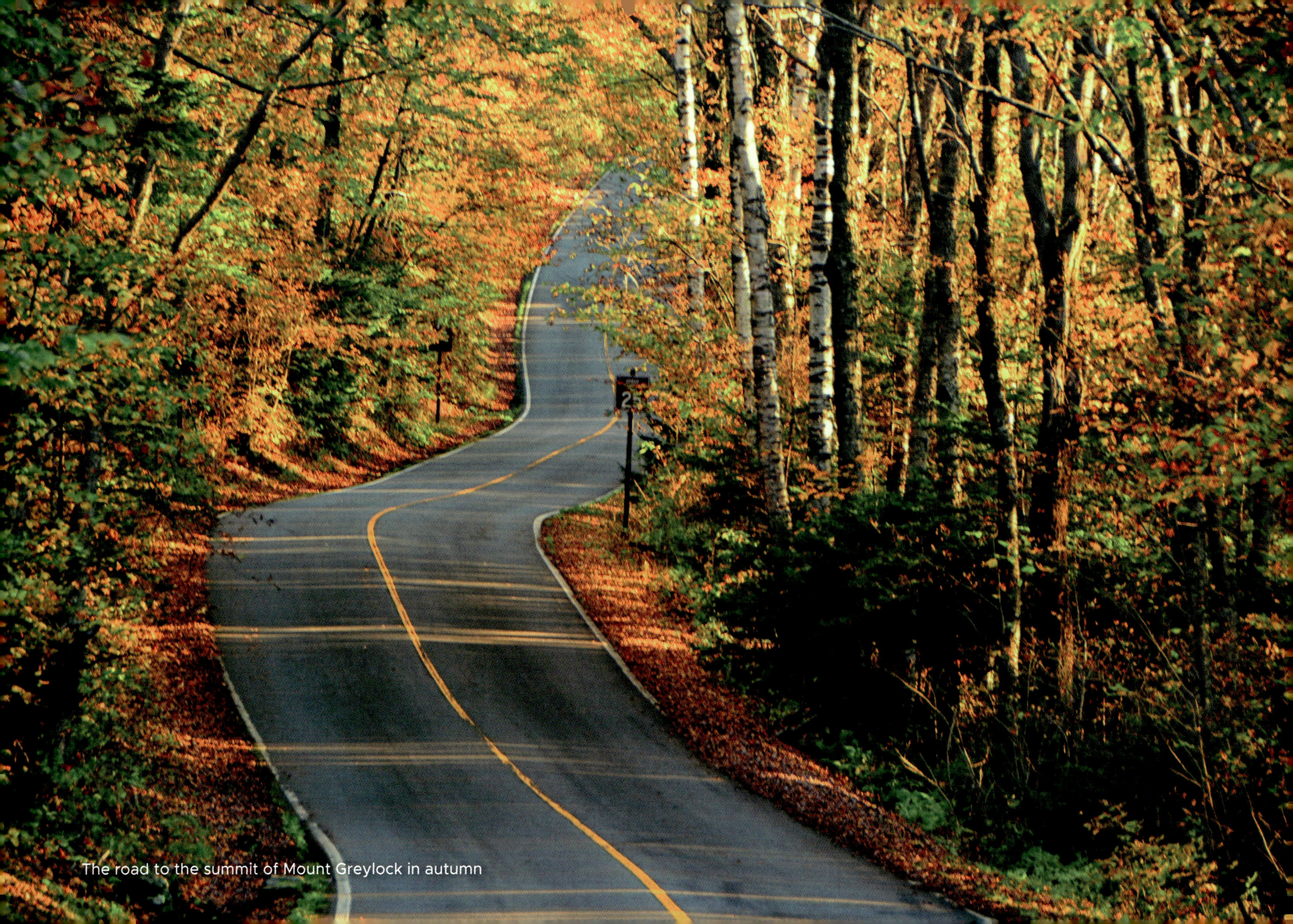

The road to the summit of Mount Greylock in autumn

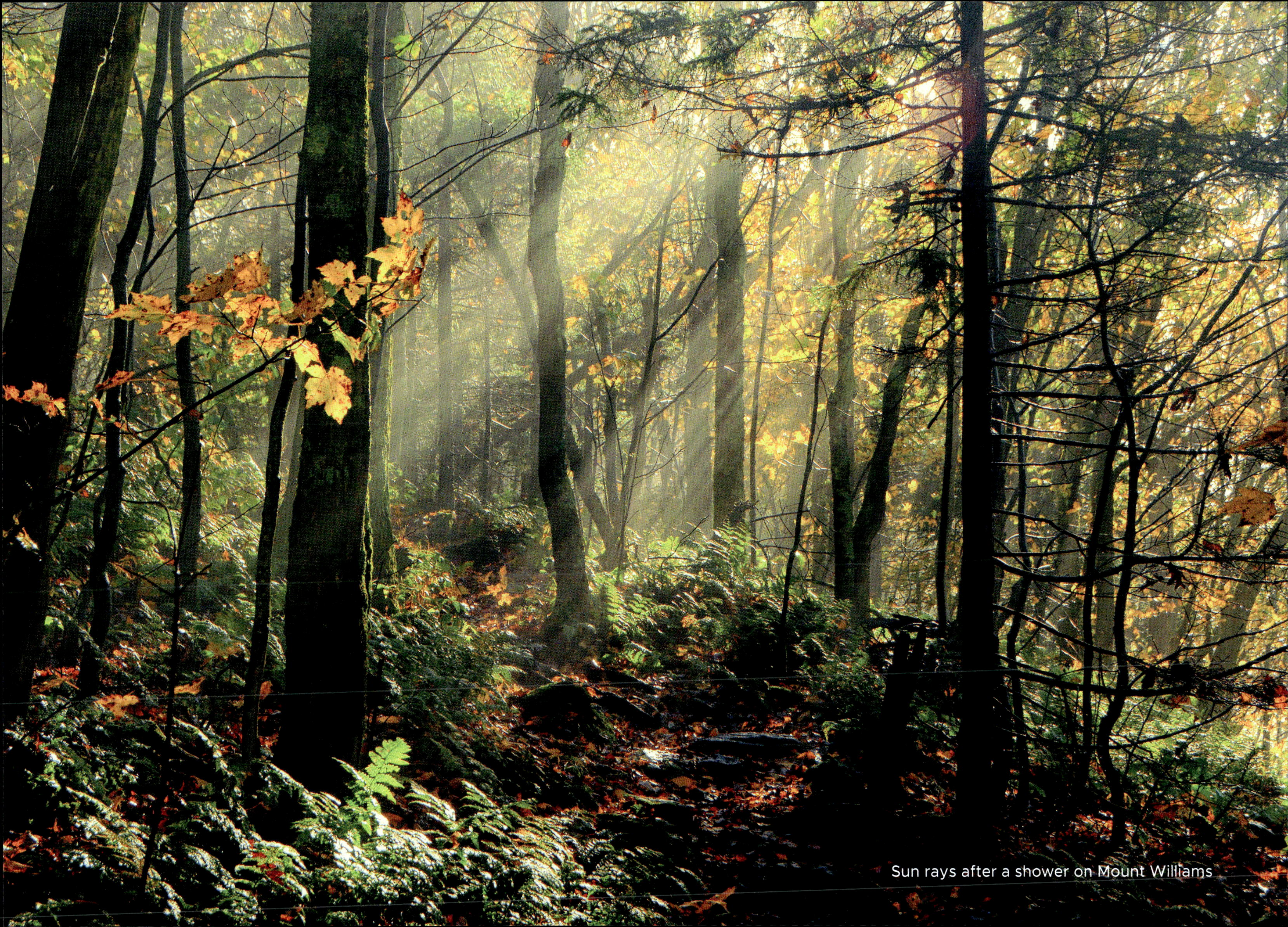

Sun rays after a shower on Mount Williams

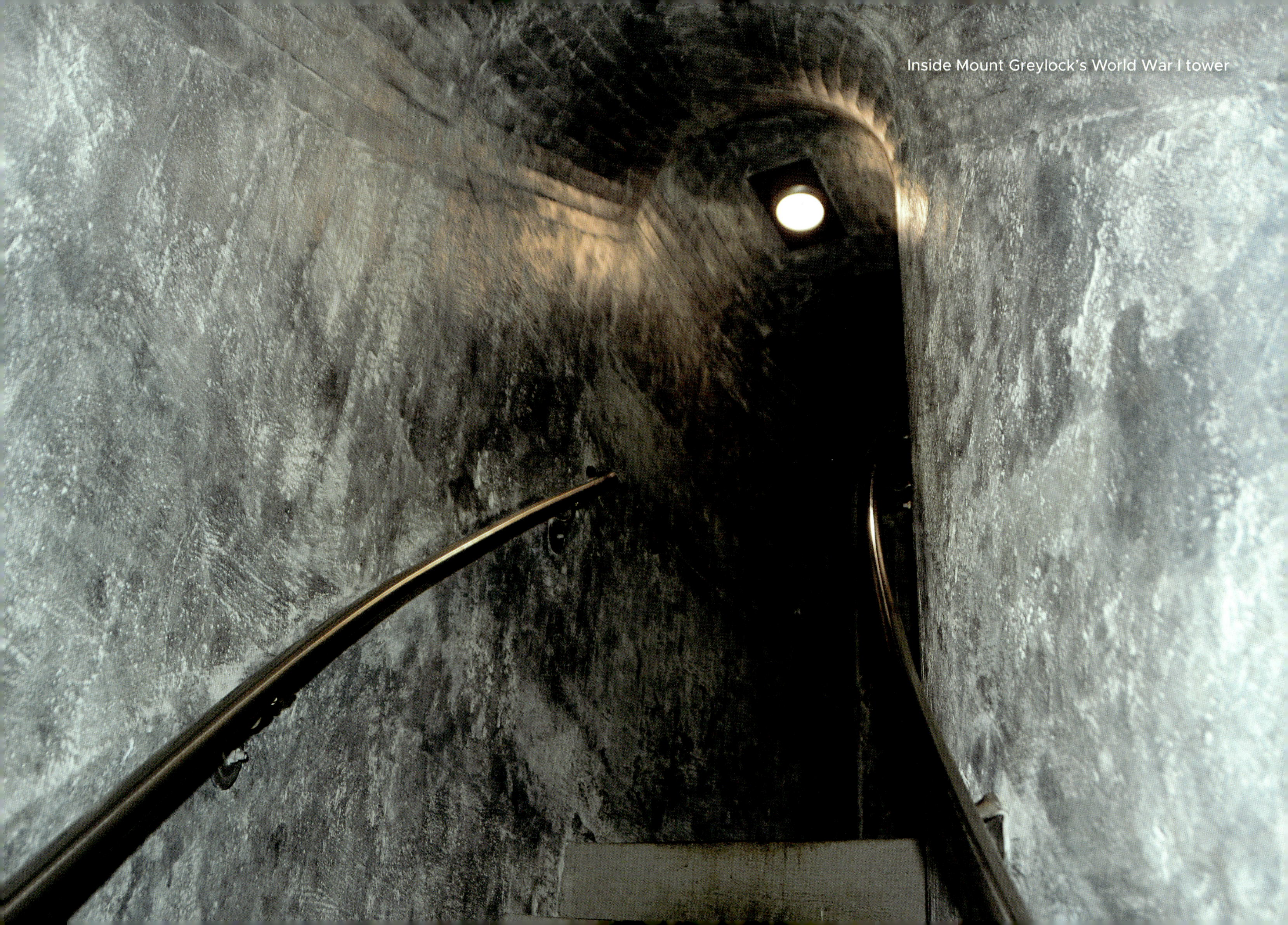

Inside Mount Greylock's World War I tower

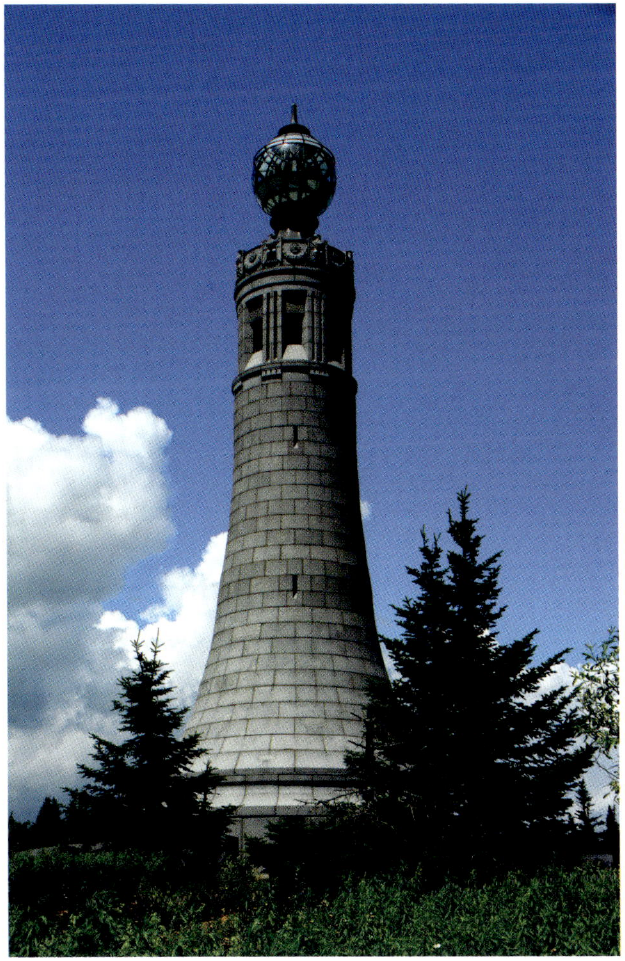

Mount Greylock's World War I tower

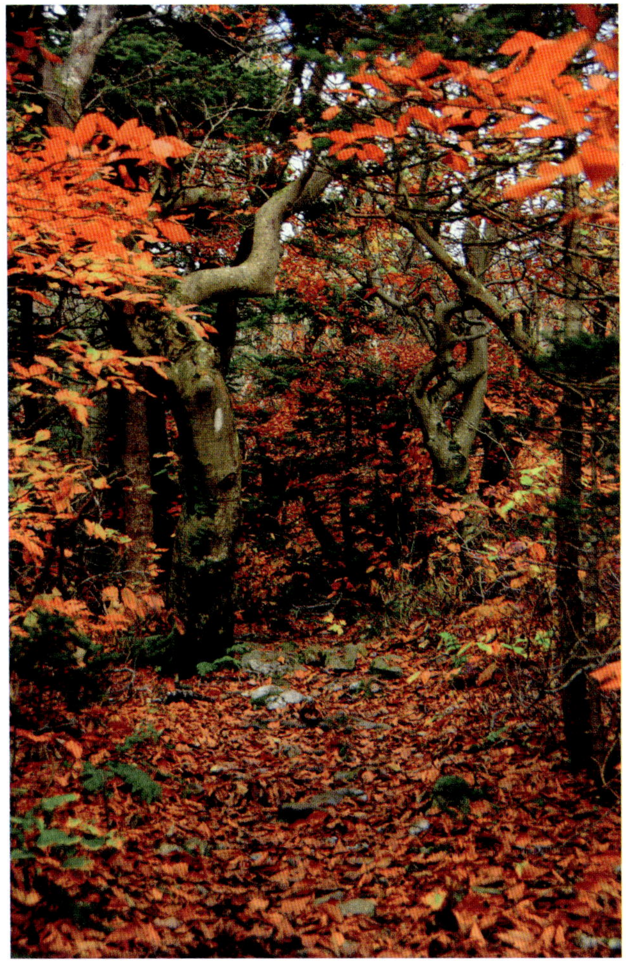

Red oaks line the Appalachian Trail

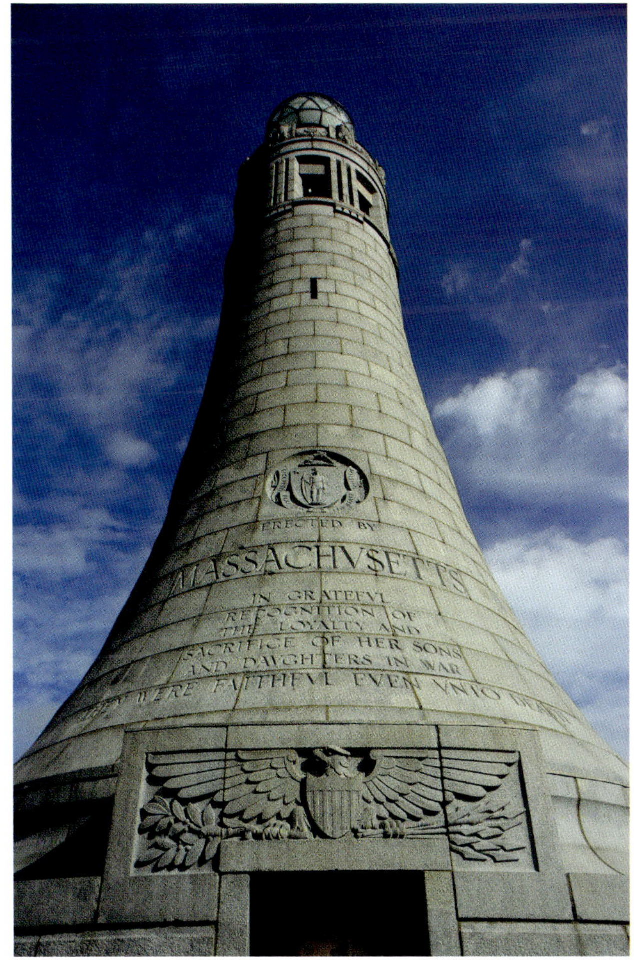

"They were faithful even unto death."

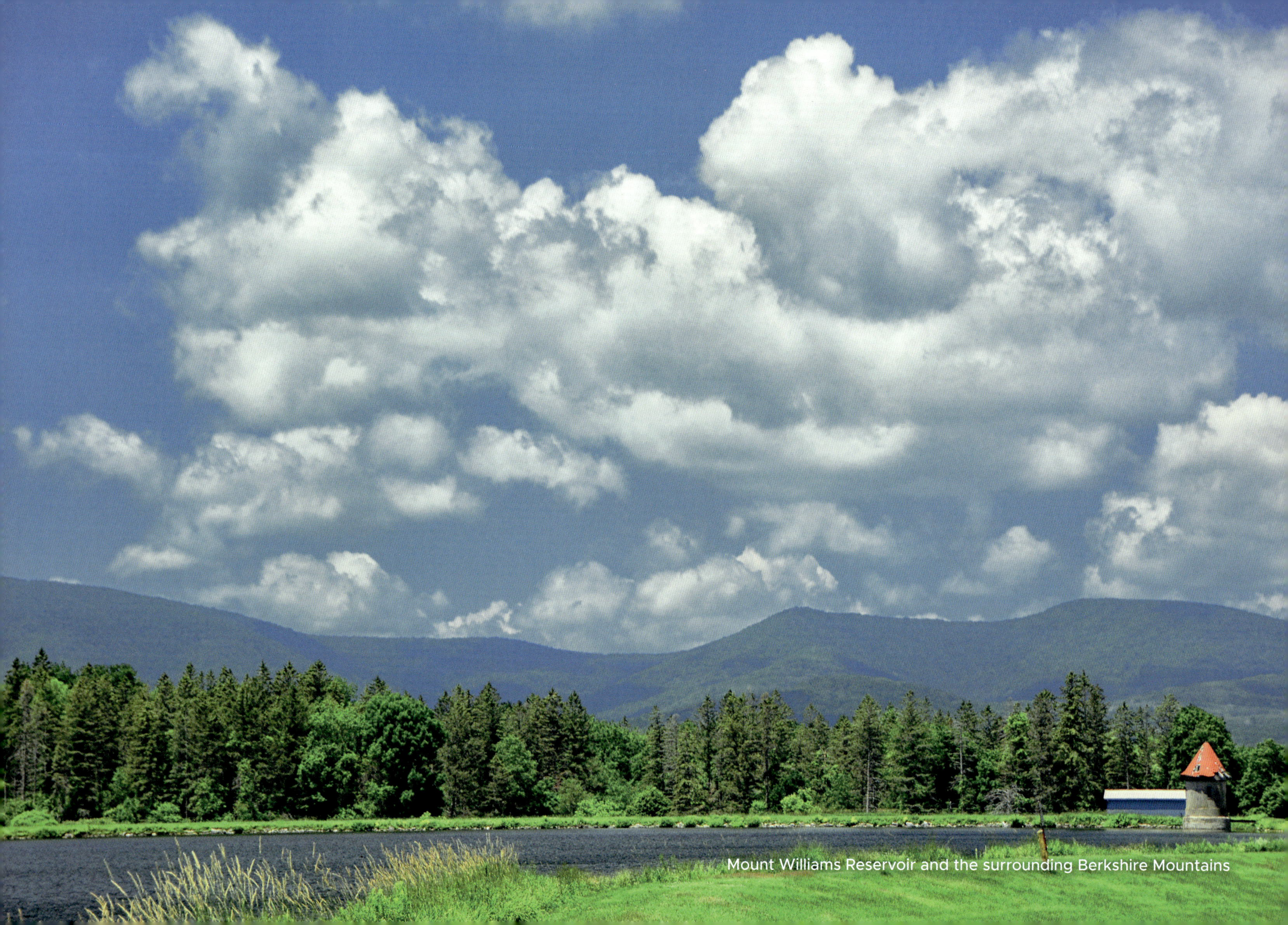

Mount Williams Reservoir and the surrounding Berkshire Mountains

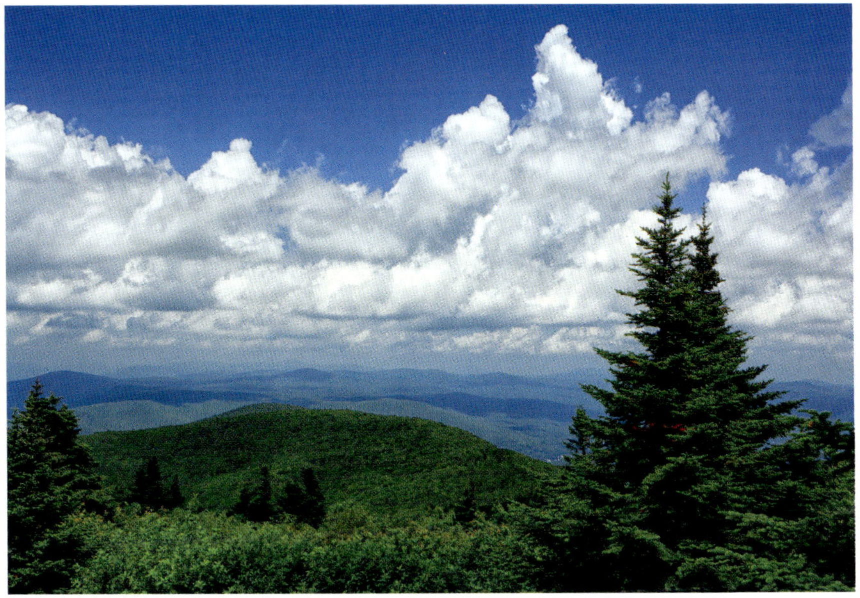

Looking North from the Summit of Mount Greylock

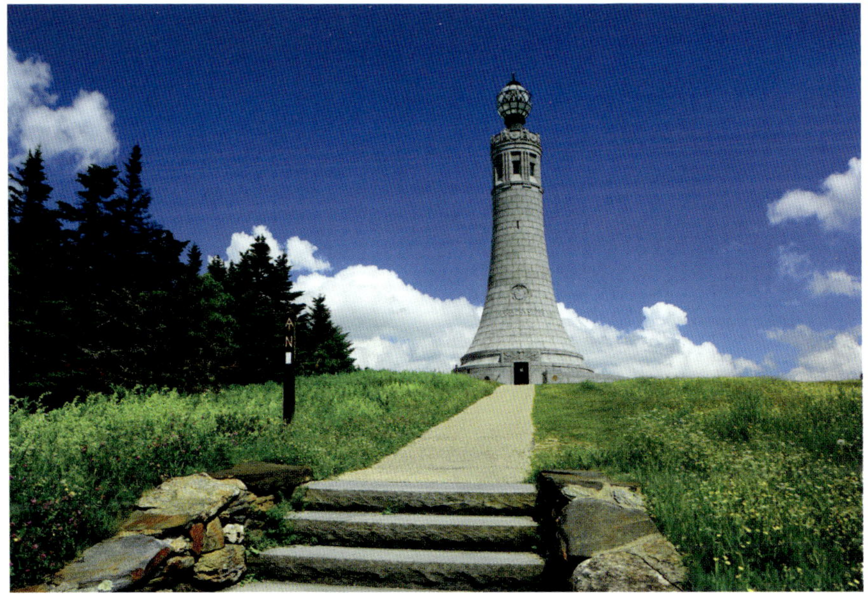

The Massachusetts section of the Appalachian Trail and Mount Greylock's Summit Tower

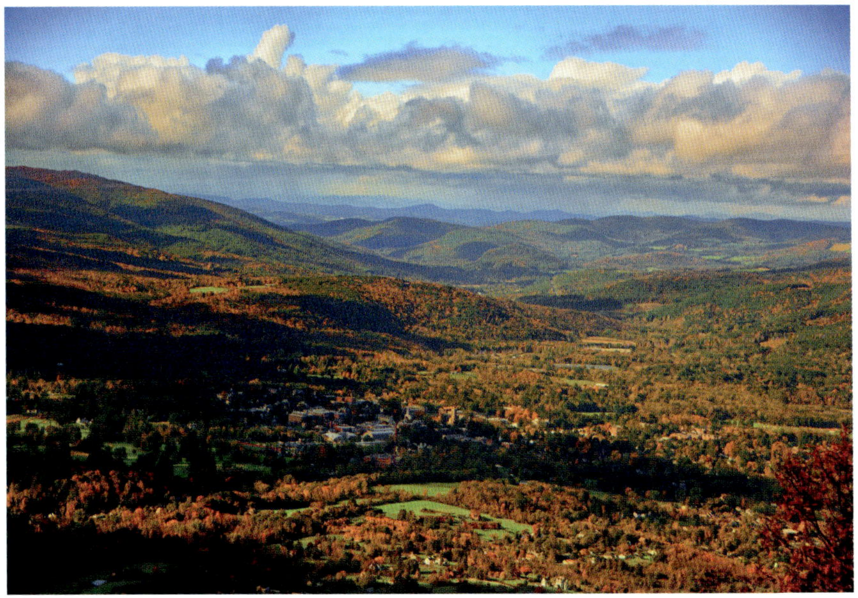

Williamstown, Massachusetts and the New York Adirondacks Mountains from the Appalachian Trail in Massachusetts

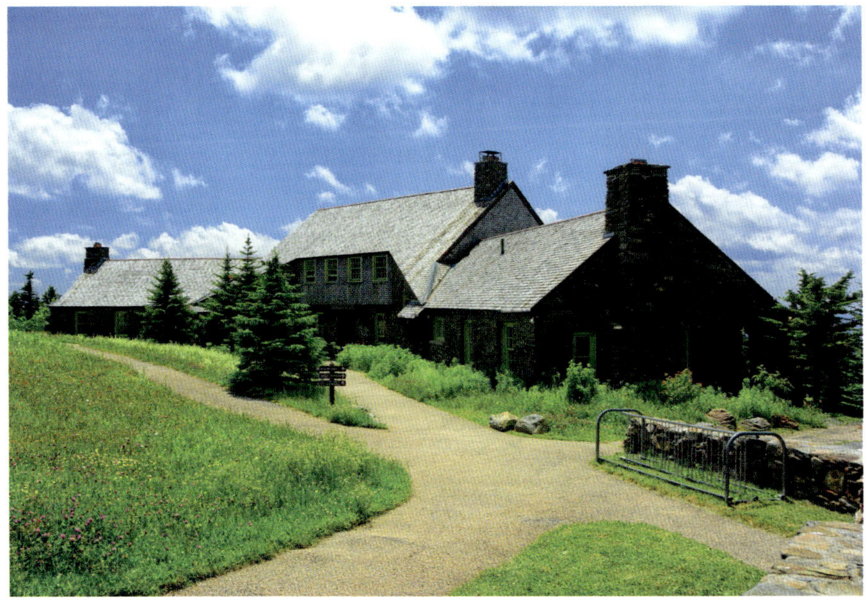

Bascom Lodge

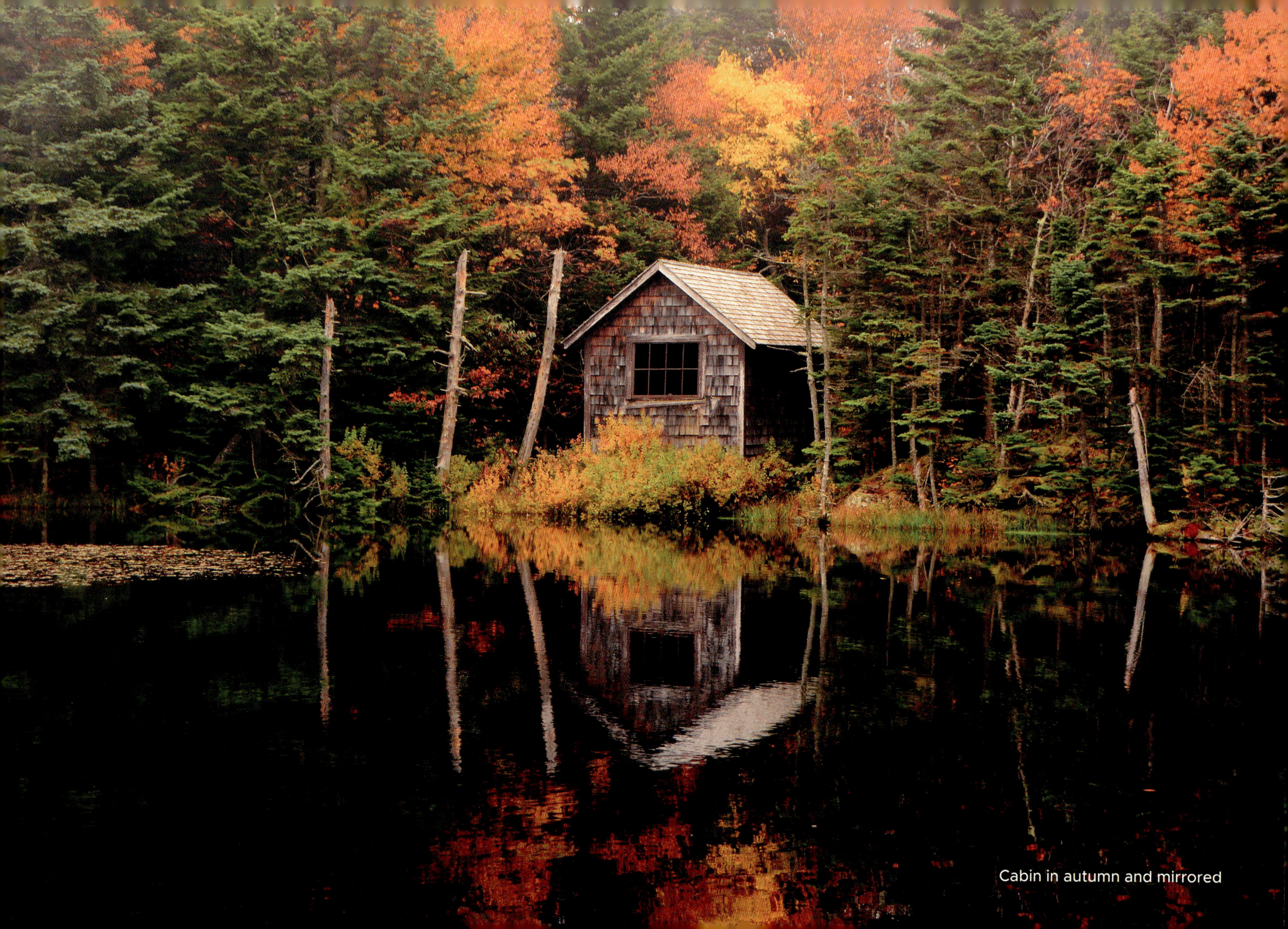

Cabin in autumn and mirrored

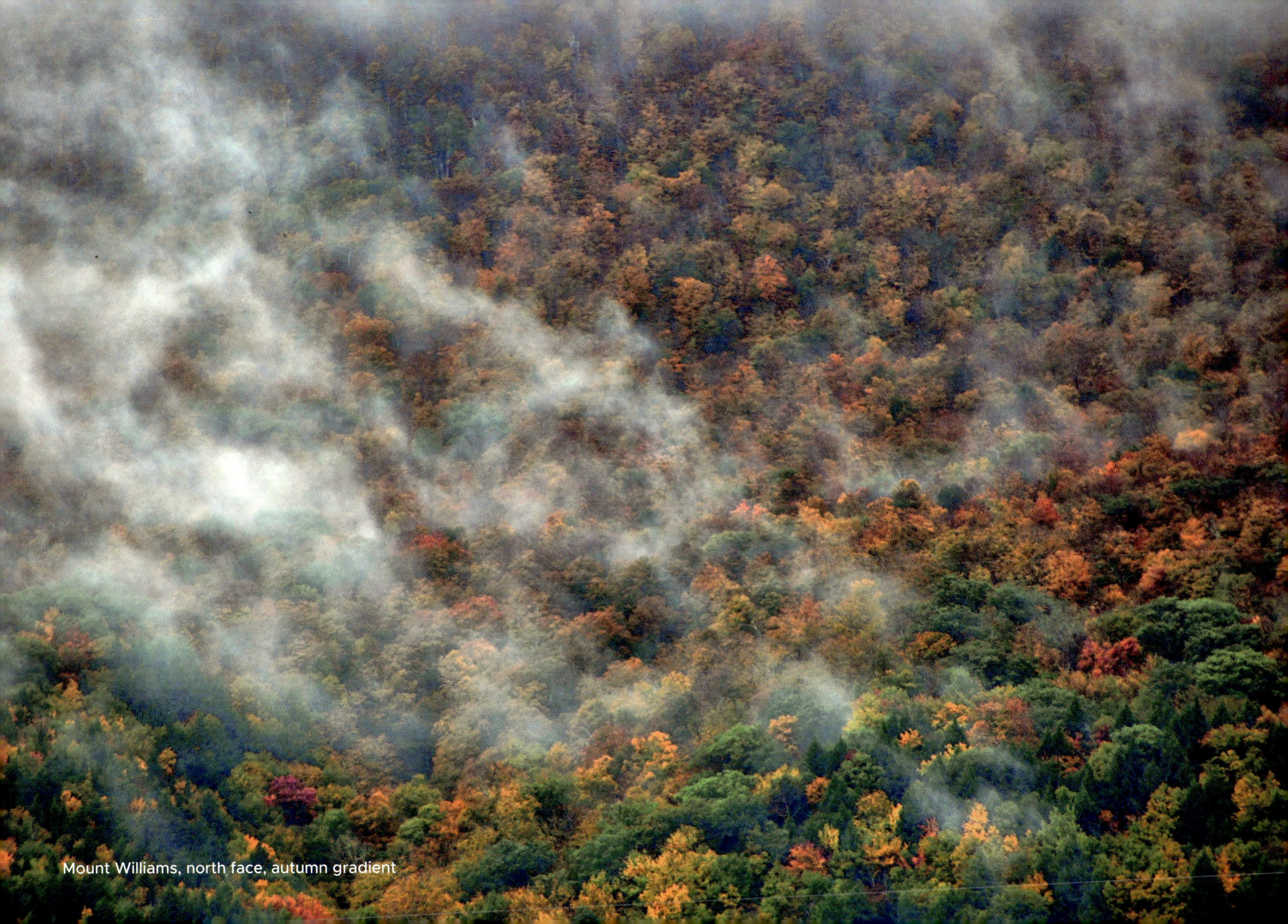

Mount Williams, north face, autumn gradient

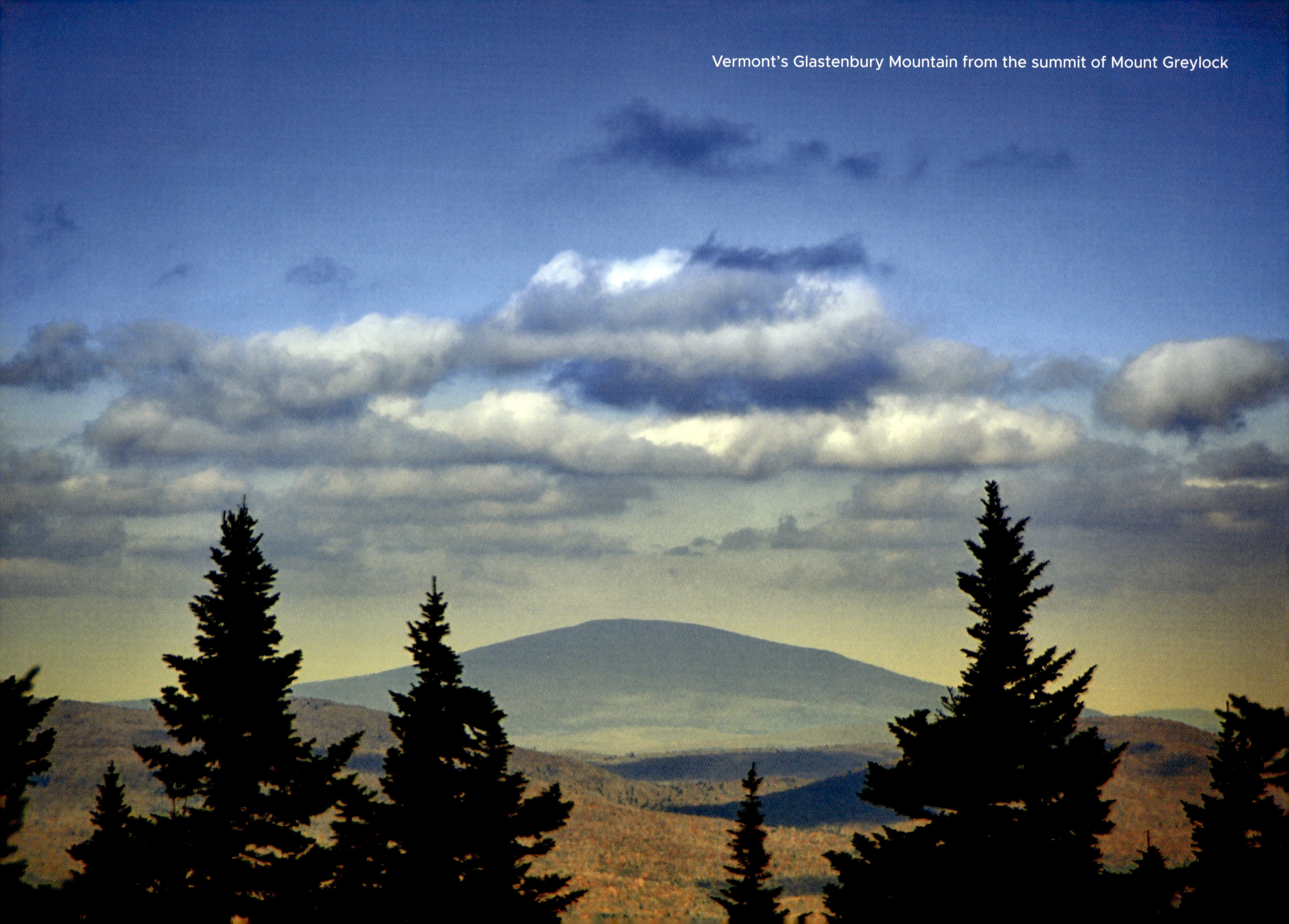

Vermont's Glastenbury Mountain from the summit of Mount Greylock

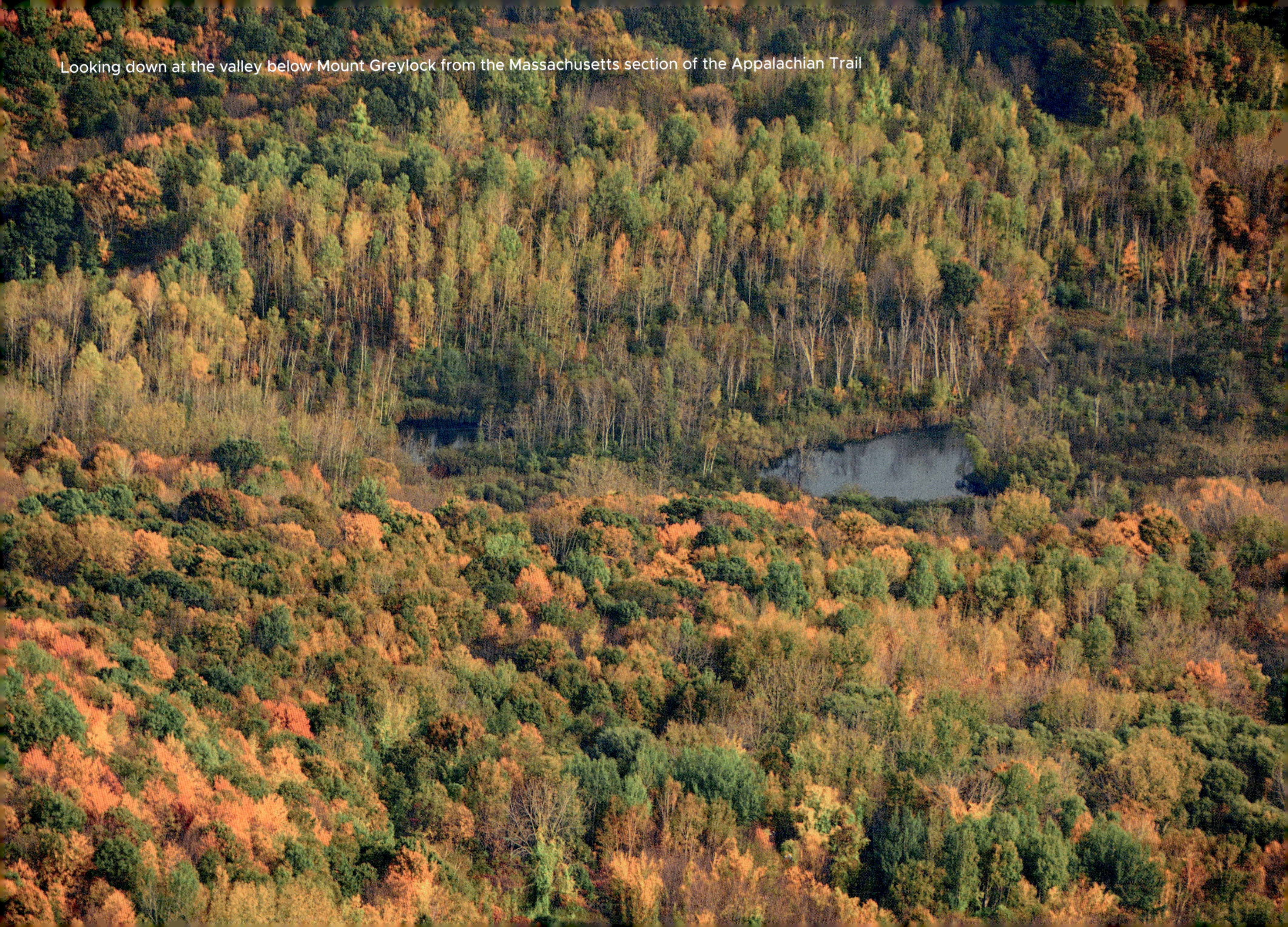

Looking down at the valley below Mount Greylock from the Massachusetts section of the Appalachian Trail

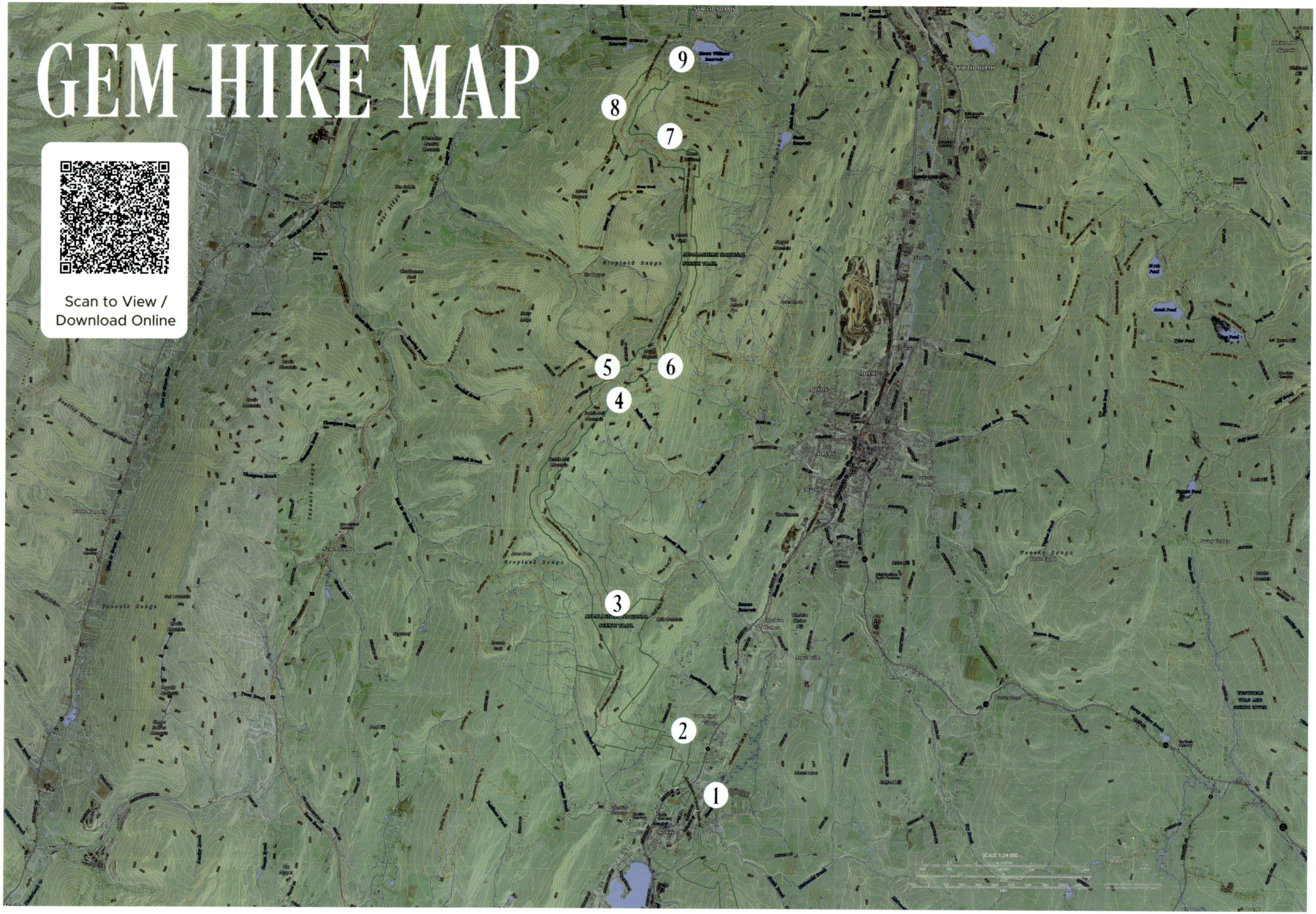
GEM HIKE MAP
Scan to View /
Download Online
9
8
7
5
6
4
3
2
1

DIRECTIONS TO THE TRAILHEAD(S)

Ashuwillticook Rail Trail parking area on Railroad St., Cheshire, MA 01225 (42.561392, −73.157866), to Appalachian Trail Pattison Road parking at 381 Pattison Rd., North Adams, MA 01247 (42.687729, −73.159769)

1. Take School St. to MA 8 N for 0.7 mile
2. Continue MA 8 N to North Adams for 11.3 miles
3. Continue Notch Rd. and drive to Pattison Rd. for 1.8 miles
4. Turn left onto Notch Rd. and continue for 1.2 miles
5. Continue straight onto Pattison Rd., and after 0.6 mile the Pattison Rd. parking will be on your right (42.687729, −73.159769)

GEM HIKE DIRECTIONS

For this gem hike, it is recommended to hike from MA RT 8 to Pattison Rd. / Mount Williams Reservoir (hike north on the Appalachian Trail for 13 miles).

1. Start on the Appalachian Trail north from MA RT 8 parking area and continue for 0.8 mile
2. Cross Outlook Ave. and continue for 2.7 miles of the Appalachian Trail, until Old Adams Rd.
3. At Old Adams Rd., cross the road and continue 0.9 mile, until Mark Noepel Shelter side trail
4. Continue of the Appalachian Trail north for 2.8 miles, until Notch Rd., Rockwell Rd.
5. Cross the road and continue on the Appalachian Trail for 1.5 miles
6. Reach the Bascom Lodge on the summit of Mount Greylock; continue for 2.2 miles
7. You Notch Rd. (different location than before): cross and continue for 0.1 mile
8. Reach and go past Wilbur Clearing Shelter side trail and continue 2.1 miles
9. Reach Pattison Rd.

MORE/LESS AMBITIOUS HIKERS

If hikers do not want to hike 13 miles, then Mount Greylock Reservation has a few parking areas along the road and even has a road to the summit so you can enjoy at least some of the hike. History buffs would like to enjoy structures that include Bascom Lodge, the World War I tower, the cabin along the way that overlooks a pond, and Mount Williams Reservoir. Vista seekers will love the scenic views: the meadows leading up to the foot of Mount Greylock, tranquil ponds, views from the summit, and drop-dead-gorgeous views of the Berkshire Mountains from Mount Williams Reservoir. Hikers will enjoy the combined worlds of the vista seekers and history buffs.

The northern approach to the summit of Mount Greylock is from Pattison Road. This route provides access to the AT via the Mount Greylock State Reservation, allowing hikers to enjoy a gradual climb through scenic woodlands.

CHAPTER 13

THE 22.6-MILE GLASTENBURY MOUNTAIN AND WILDERNESS

AREA MAP

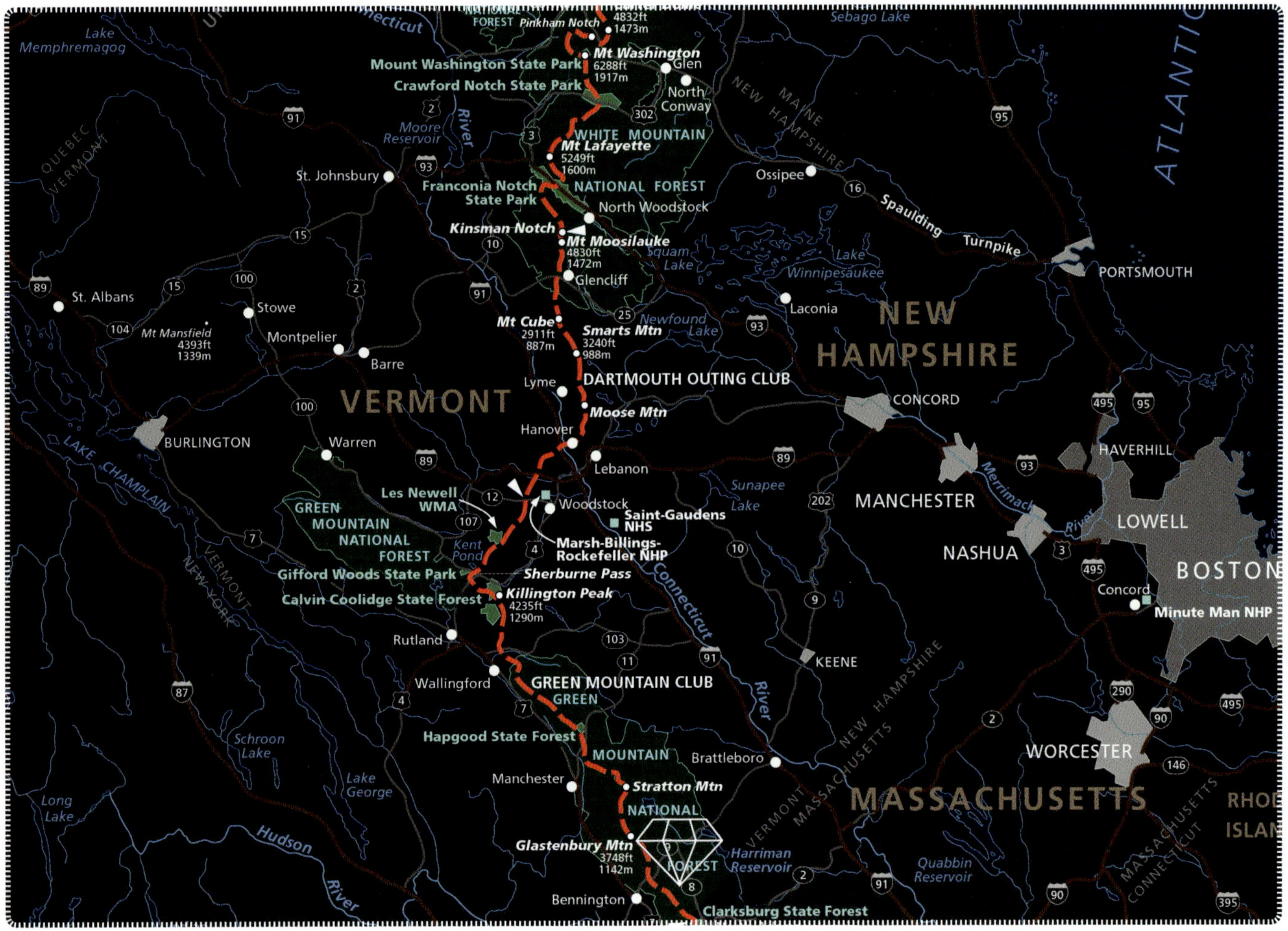

DISTANCE	22.6 miles
ELEVATION GAIN	3,730 feet
ELEVATION LOSS	4,600 feet
LEVEL	Difficult

TYPE: POINT TO POINT

0 10 Kilometers 50
0 10 Miles 50

Appalachian National Scenic Trail

Boundary of CLUB management section

North

GEM HIKE

PERSONAL TOUCH

This hike was both extraordinarily challenging and rewarding. I loved the athleticism that surrounded this hike, 22.6 miles without a road to cross, except for the US Forest Service road in the first 2 miles.

This forest was mystical and magical. I felt like I was in a different world. The trees were larger than their counterparts in other parts of the trail, just like the distances required to reach the next road intersections were longer. The views from the summit of Glastenbury Mountain were special because nearly everything in view had no hint of human activity. The Glastenbury section of the Appalachian Trail is truly a wilderness experience I will never forget.

BRIEF OVERVIEW

The 22.6-mile Glastenbury section of the Appalachian Trail (AT) and Long Trail (LT) represents one of the most demanding and rewarding stretches in Vermont's Green Mountains because of miles between roads. This segment combines challenging hiking conditions with striking natural beauty, diverse ecosystems, and intriguing historical lore. It offers a unique opportunity to explore a super-remote and rugged landscape. It is recommended to travel this hike as a point-to-point hike, but if one wants a shorter hike, it is advised to hike from the south as an out-and-back for your desired hike's length.

Northern trailhead: The northern trailhead to the summit of Mount Glastenbury begins at the trailhead of Stratton-Arlington Road. Hikers enter a dense forest, where the trail initially offers a gentle ascent. As the trail continues, beaver dens can be seen in ponds, and the terrain becomes more challenging, with steeper inclines and more-rocky conditions. It reaches the summit fire tower about 12 miles into the hike.

Southern trailhead: From the south, the trailhead, outside Bennington on VT Route 9, provides a rougher of a start with a mix of hardwood forests. This approach nears the summit Mount Glastenbury's fire tower after 10.5 miles of hiking.

GLASTENBURY MOUNTAIN

Mount Glastenbury is the highlight of this section, standing at 3,748 feet. The summit's fire tower offers expansive views of the surrounding Green Mountains, the Berkshire Mountains, and the distant valleys. The fire tower offers panoramic views that are amazing.

DESCRIPTION OF THE GEM HIKE

This hike takes outdoor enthusiasts through the Glastenbury wilderness in the heart of the Green Mountain National Forest. It spans over twenty hiking miles without any road access.

FLORA, FAUNA, VEGETATION

The vegetation along the Glastenbury section reflects the diverse elevations and microclimates of the Green Mountains. At lower elevations, hikers encounter hardwood forests featuring sugar maples and yellow birches. As the trail ascends, the flora shifts to coniferous species such as red spruce and balsam fir, adapted to the cooler temperatures and harsher conditions found at higher altitudes. These mixes of trees create a special treat for autumn foliage seekers in early to mid-October. Mid-June can offer the enjoyment of different greens and lush forest.

GLASTENBURY MOUNTAIN FOR VIEWS AND SOLITUDE AND REFLECTION

The Glastenbury section offers ample opportunities for solitude and reflection. Due to its challenging nature and very remote location, this section tends to see fewer hikers compared to other parts of the Appalachian Trail or the Long Trail. The tranquil forest environment and amazing views, with very few fellow hikers, make this a gem because you are within 22.6 miles of basically nothing man-made, except for the trail itself.

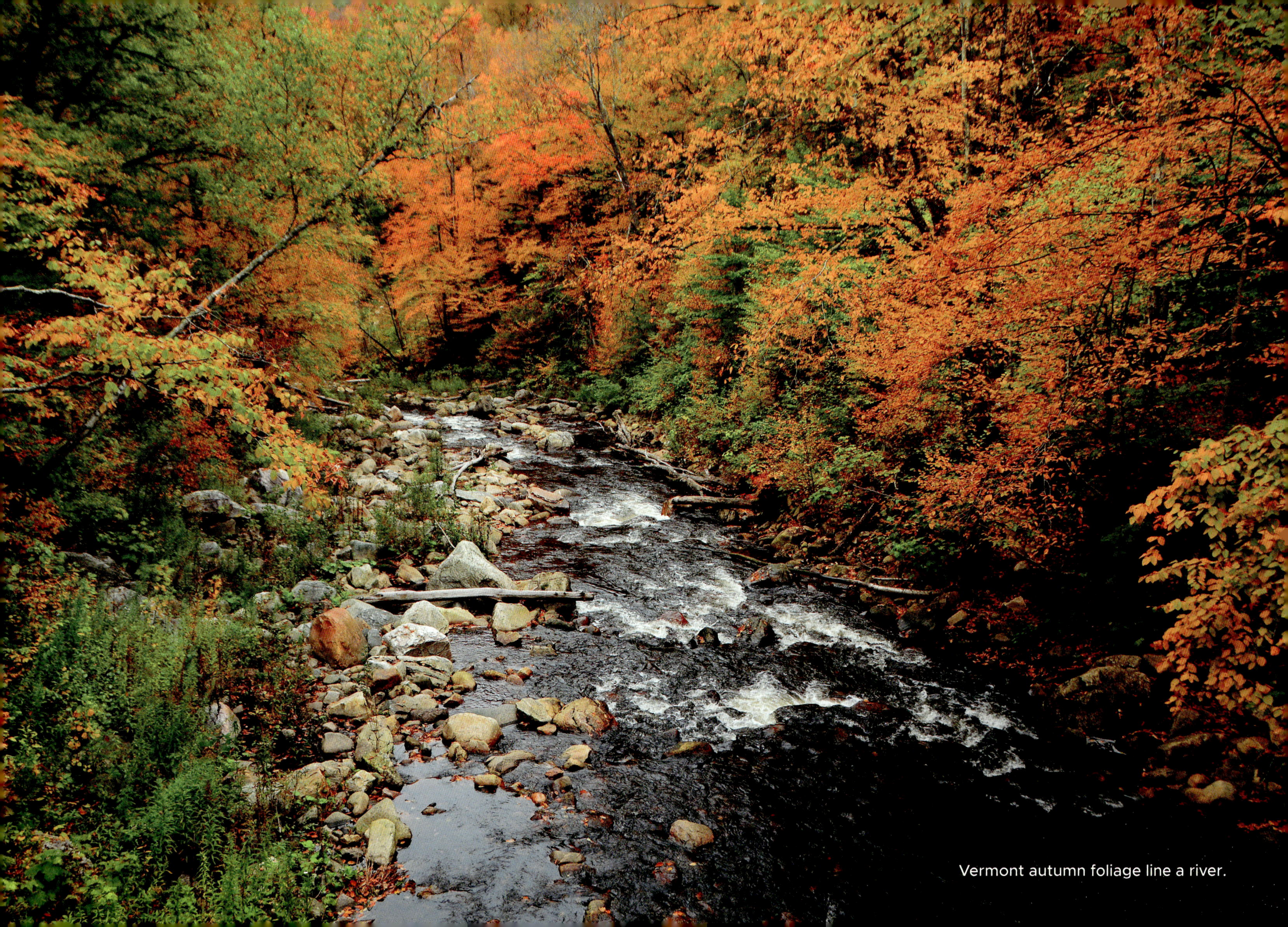

Vermont autumn foliage line a river.

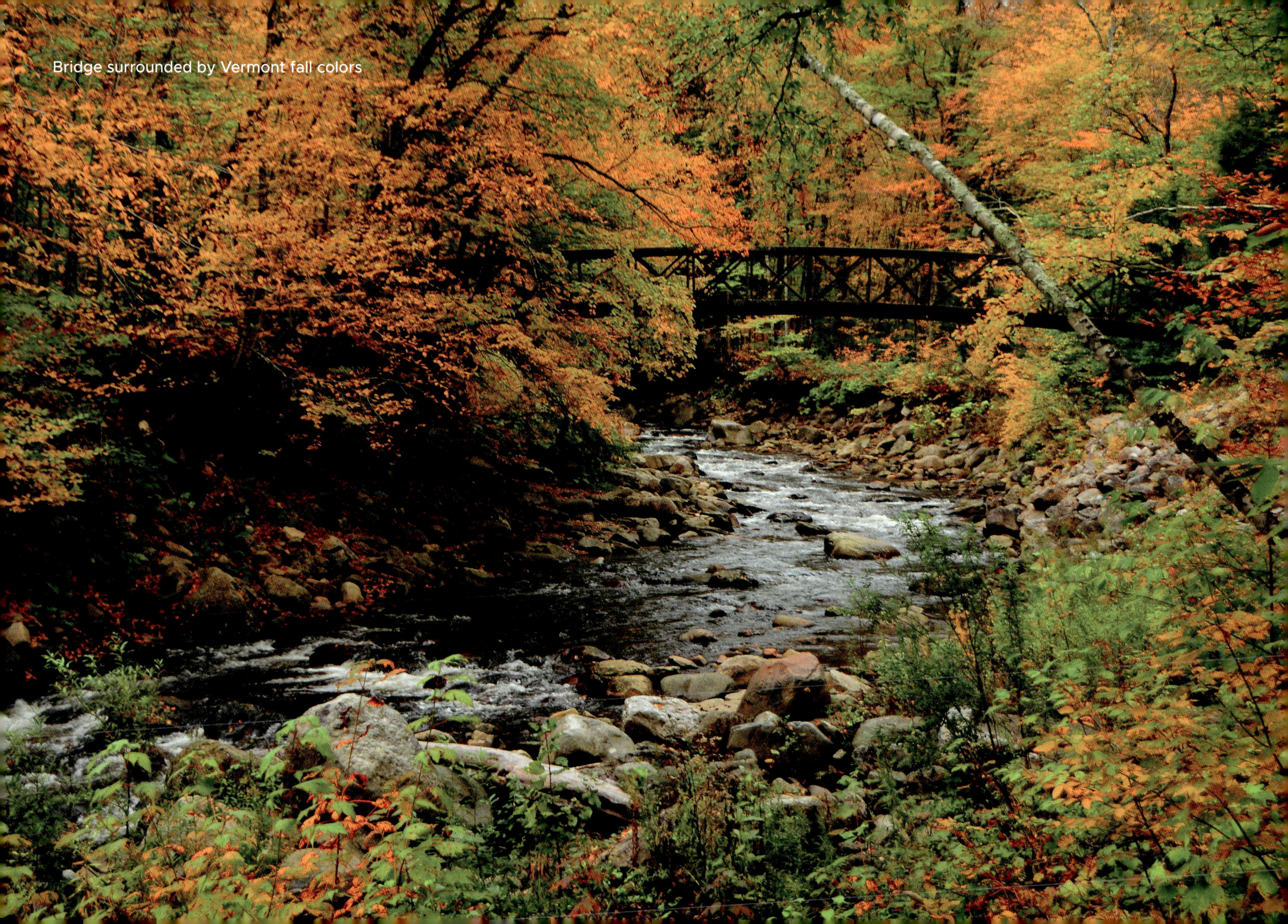
Bridge surrounded by Vermont fall colors

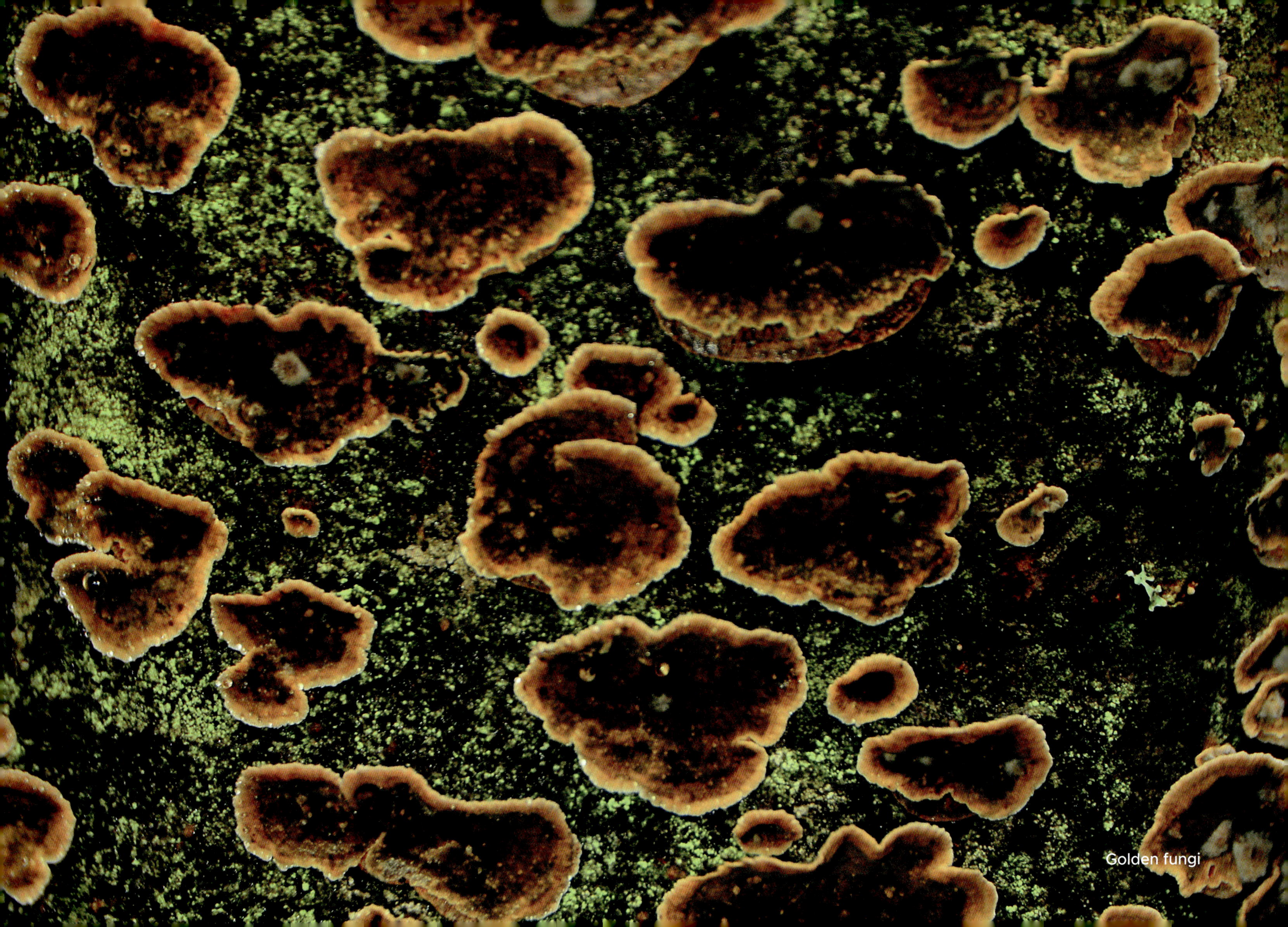

Golden fungi

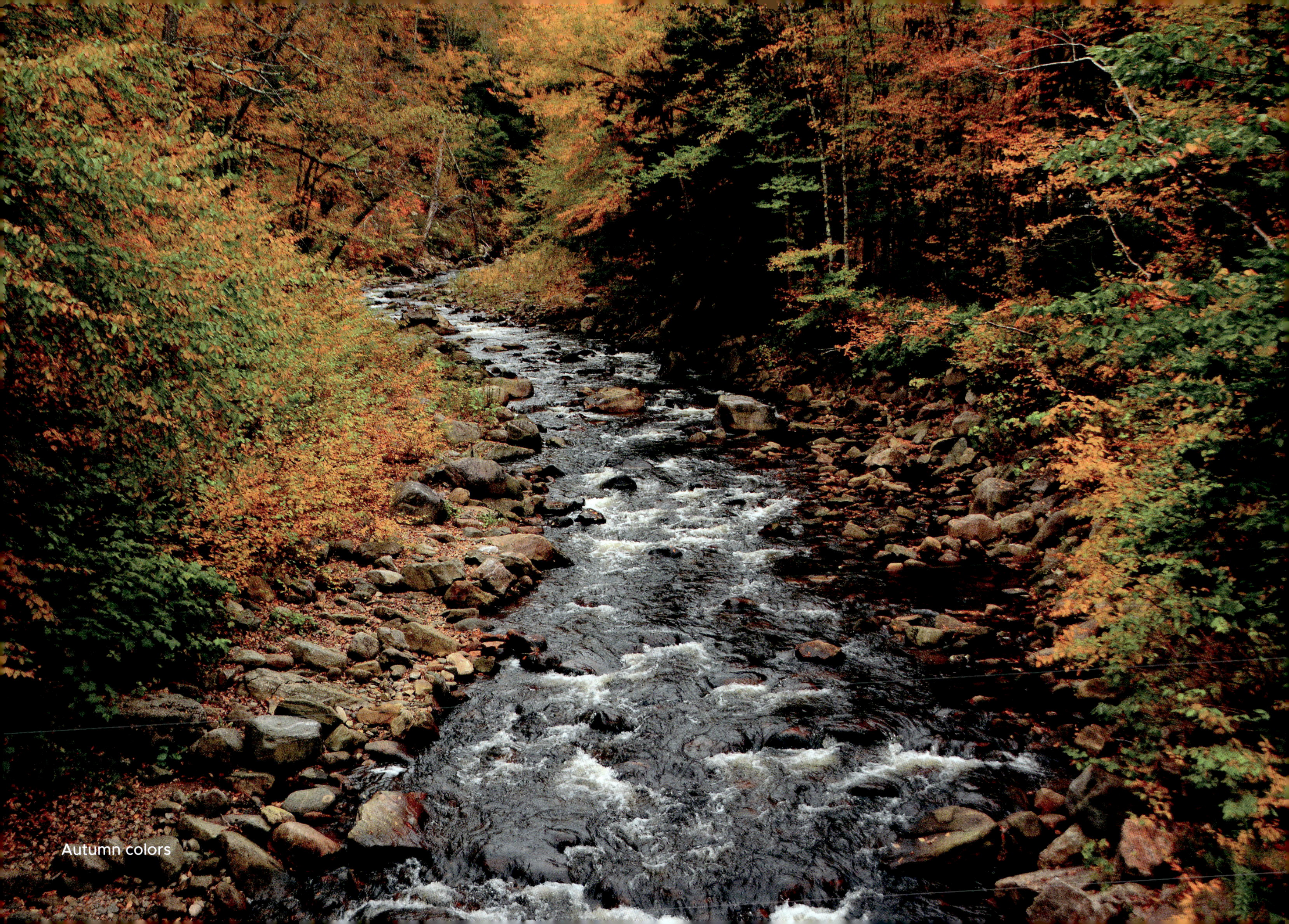

Autumn colors

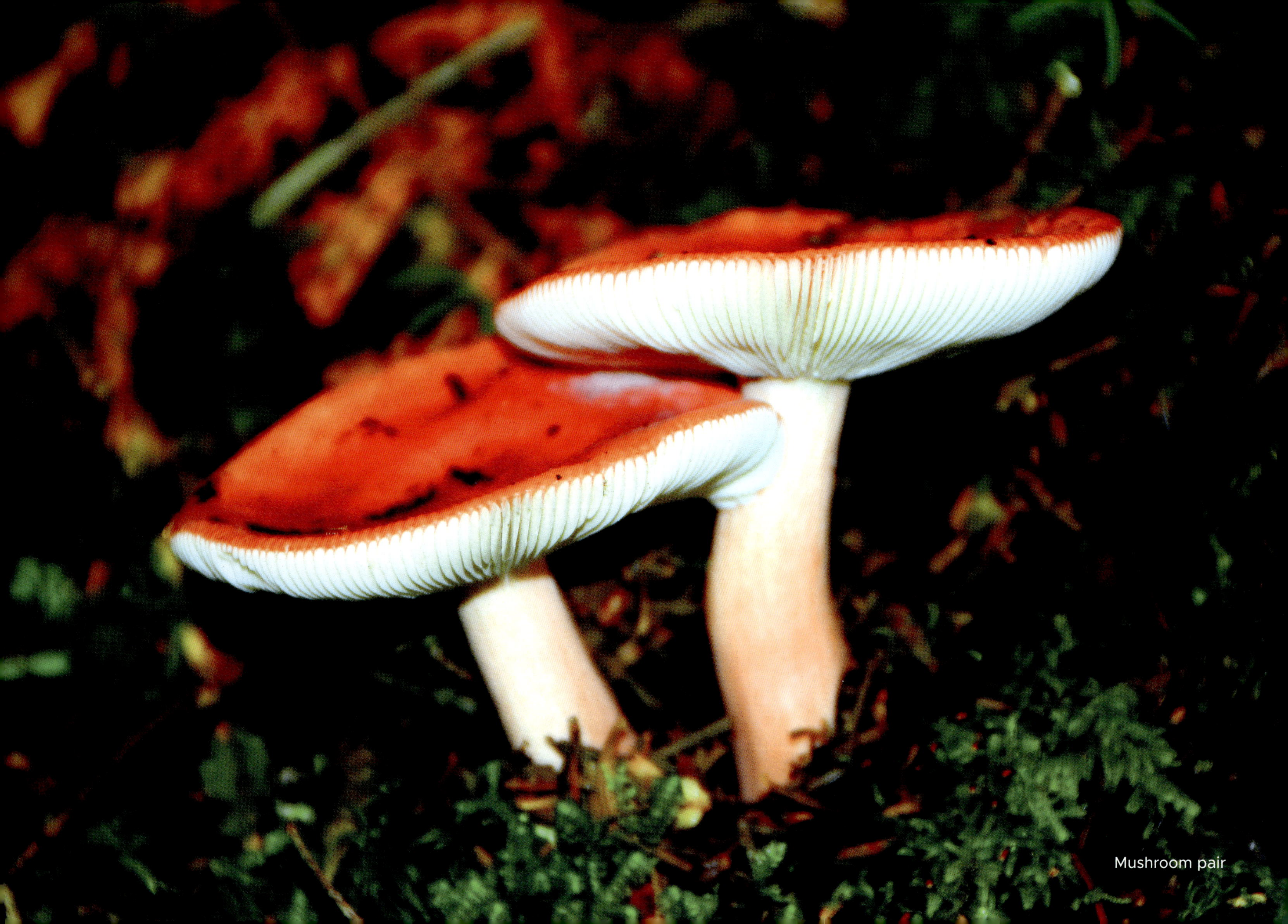

Mushroom pair

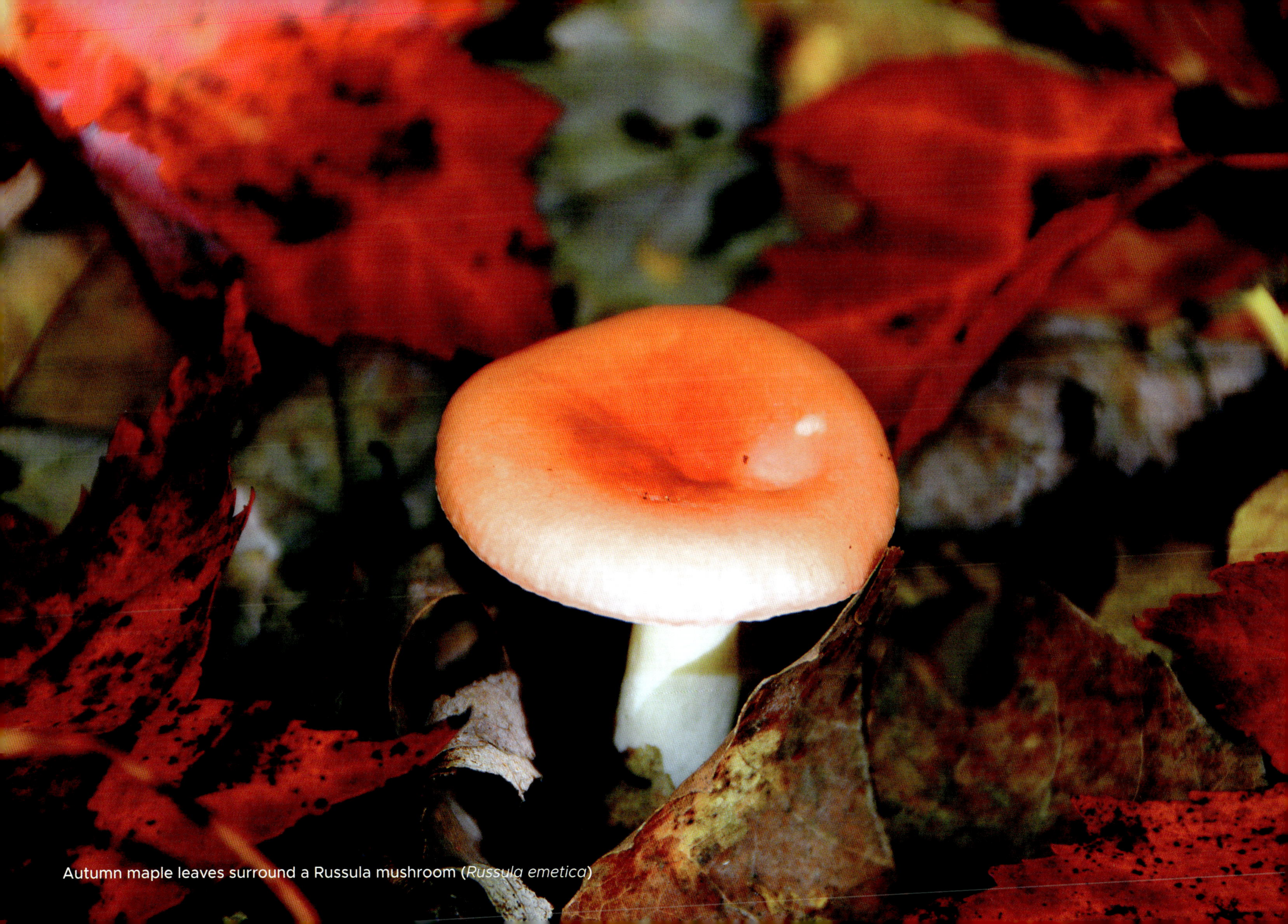

Autumn maple leaves surround a Russula mushroom (*Russula emetica*)

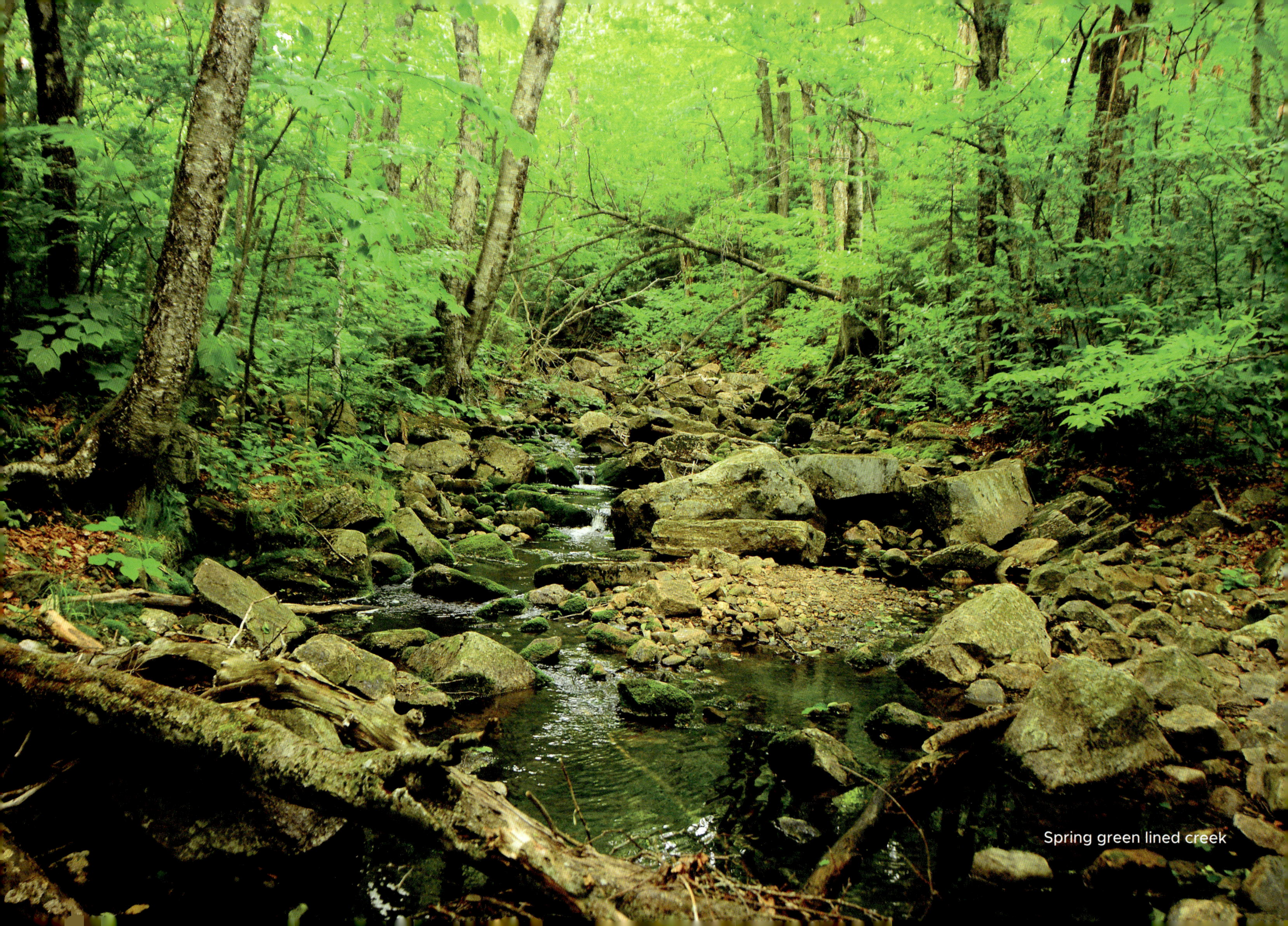

Spring green lined creek

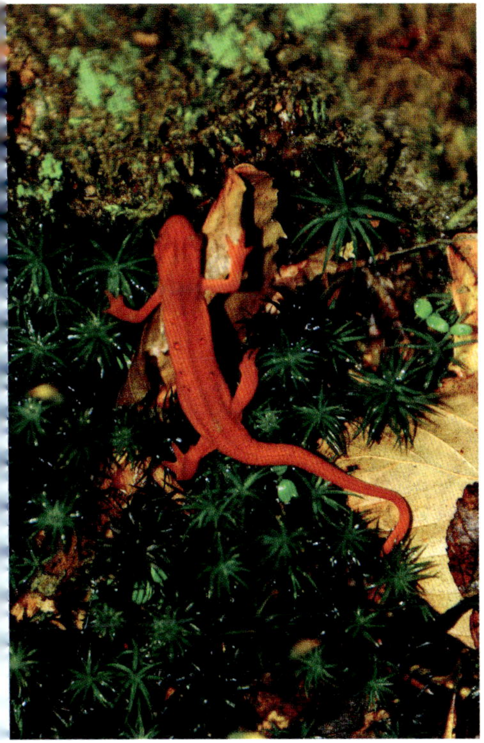

Red eft (*Notophthalmus viridescens*)

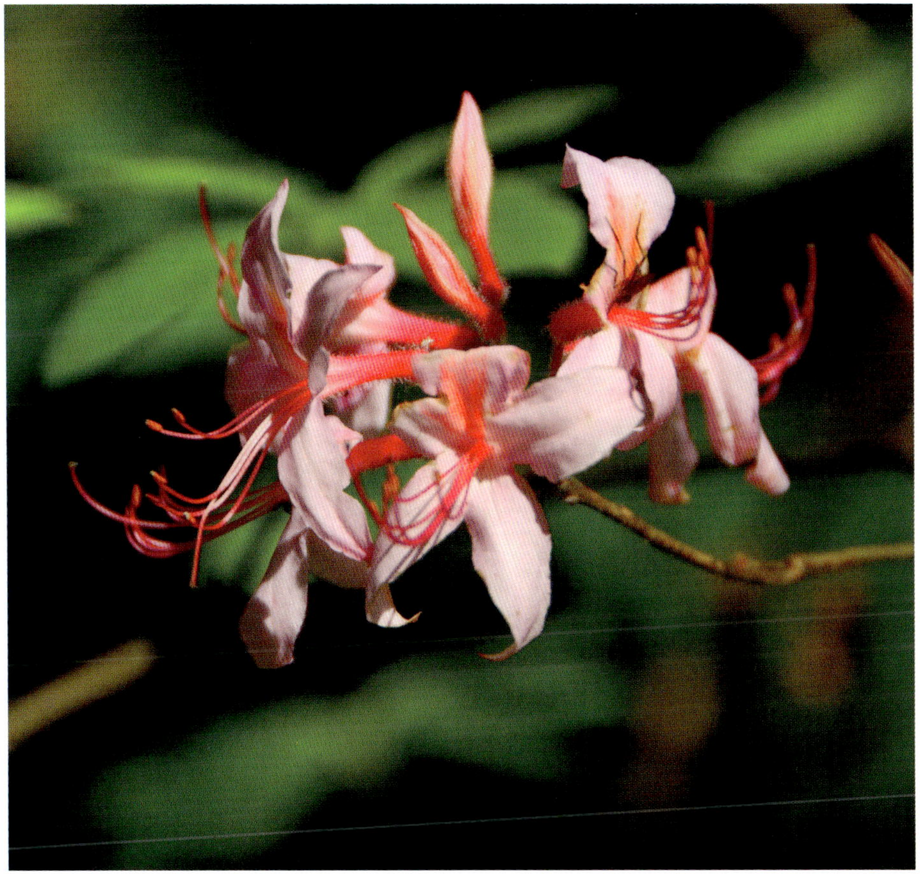

Pink Azalea (*Rhododendron periclymenoides*)

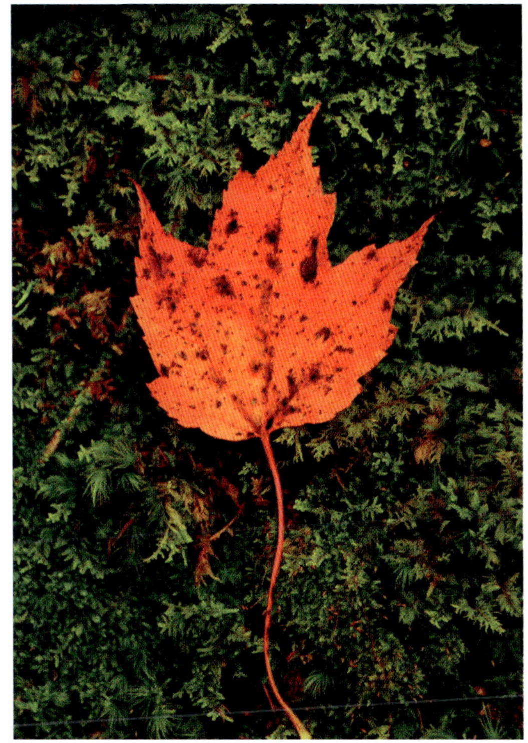

Maple (*Acer rubrum*) leaf on moss

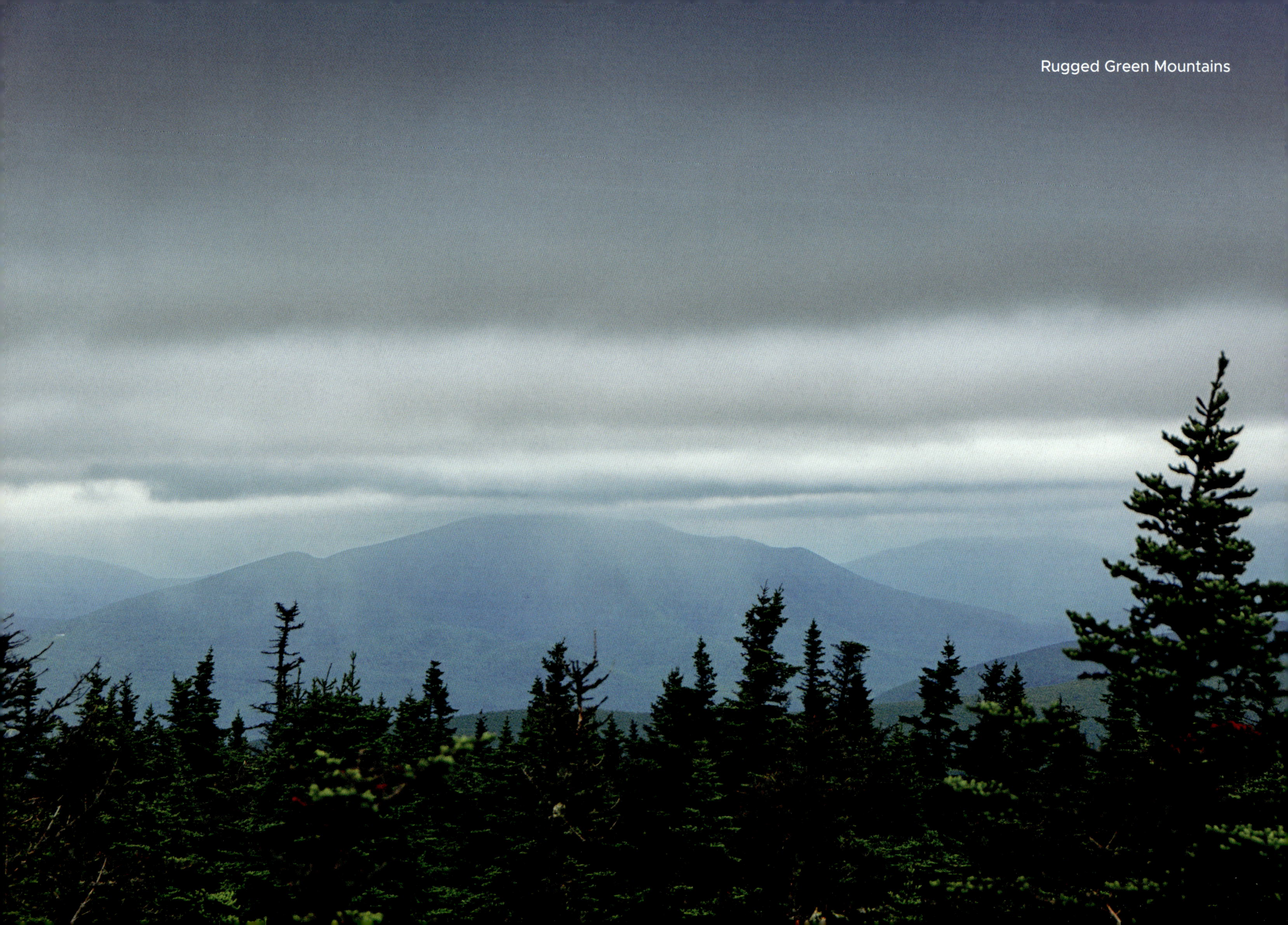

Rugged Green Mountains

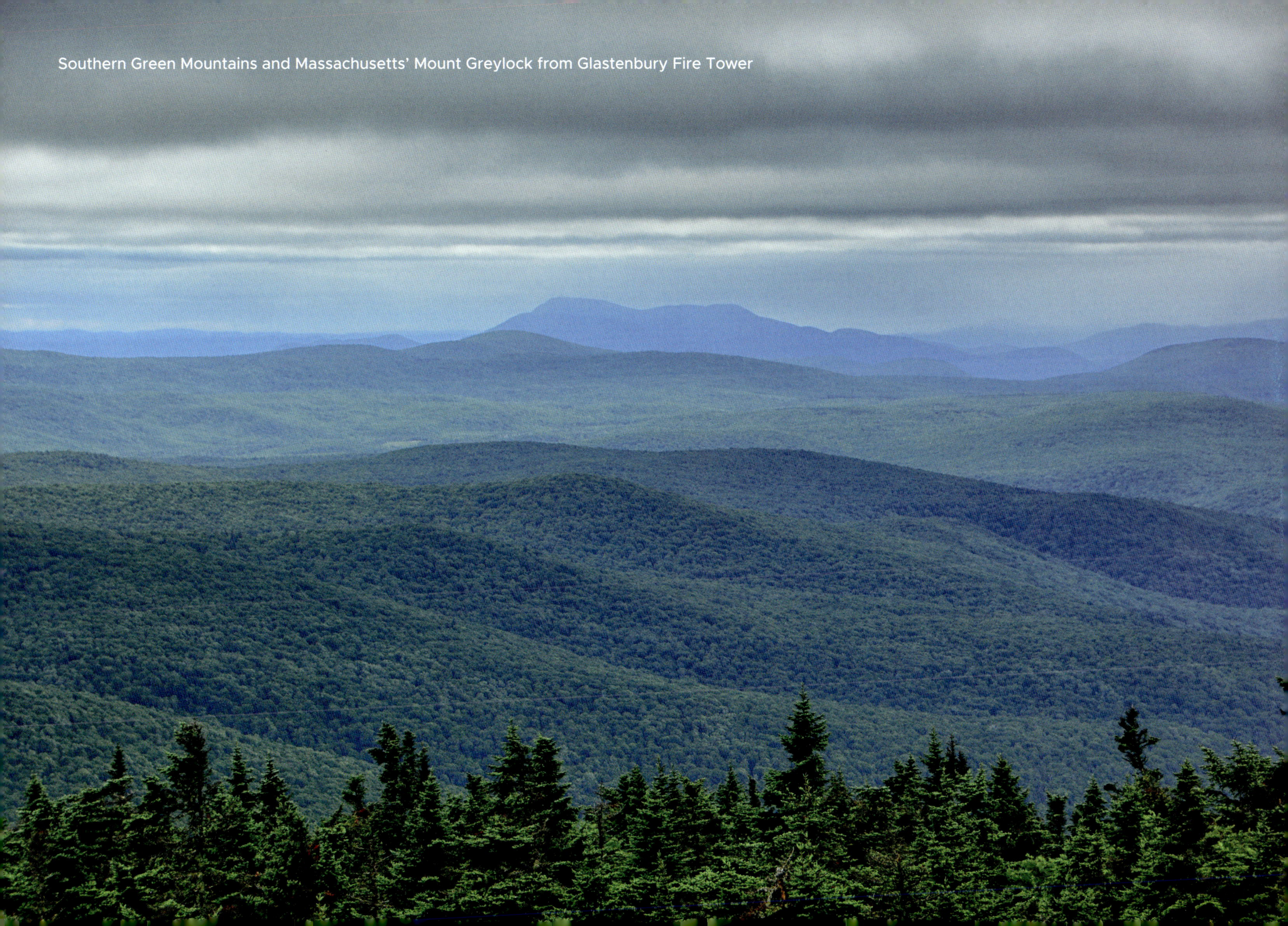

Southern Green Mountains and Massachusetts' Mount Greylock from Glastenbury Fire Tower

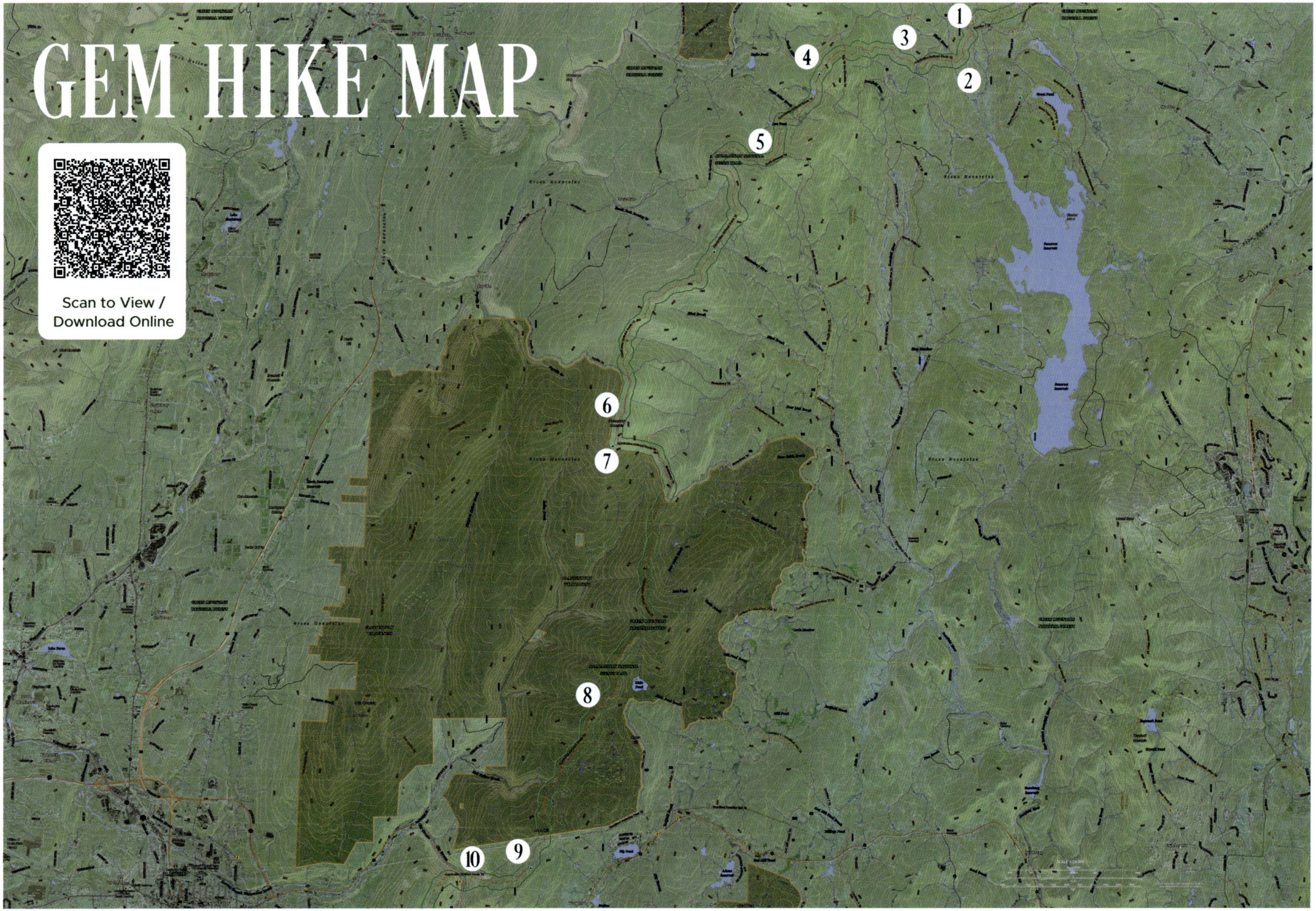
GEM HIKE MAP
Scan to View /
Download Online
1
2
3
4
5
6
7
8
9
10

DIRECTIONS TO THE TRAILHEAD(S)

Bennington, Vermont (42.885200, −73.115399) to Stratton Mountain Trailhead (43.0611506, −72.967844)

1. Head east on Main St. toward School St. and travel 1.5 miles
2. Continue onto VT 9 E / Molly Stark Trail / Woodford Rd. and travel 3.4 miles
3. Reach Appalachian National Scenic Trail / Long Trail AT/LT Route 9; trailhead in Woodford, VT 05201 will be on your left; drop a car here.
4. Turn left out of the trailhead parking lot onto VT 9 E and continue for 15.5 miles
5. Turn left onto N. Main St. / Vermont Route 100 N and continue to follow Vermont Route 100 N for 11.4 miles
6. Turn left onto Penny Ave. and continue for 1.1 miles
7. Turn right onto Pike Hollow Rd. and continue for 0.5 mile
8. Turn left onto Stratton Arlington Rd. and travel for 5.5 miles, until Stratton Mountain Trailhead is on the right

GEM HIKE DIRECTIONS

The hike from Stratton Mountain Trailhead to Vermont Route 9 goes as follows:

1. Leave on the Appalachian Trail south from Stratton Arlington Rd.
2. Continue on the Appalachian Trail for 2 miles
3. Cross USFS 71 and continue on the Appalachian Trail for 1.6 miles and reach Story Spring Shelter
4. Continue for another 4.6 miles on the Appalachian Trail and reach Kid Gore Shelter
5. Continue on the Appalachian Trail south for 4 miles and reach the Glastenbury Mountain fire tower.
6. Continue on the Appalachian Trail for 0.3 mile and reach Goddard Shelter
7. Continue on the Appalachian Trail for 3.3 miles to Little Pond Lookout
8. Continue for 4.2 miles and cross Melville Nauheim Shelter side trail
9. Continue for 1.6 miles
10. Reach VT Route 9 trailhead

MORE/LESS AMBITIOUS HIKERS

Less ambitious hikers may wish to break this hike into a two- or three-day backpack. If one does not want to backpack, it is recommended that you do just one of either of the out-and-backs from the trailhead for your desired distance.

CHAPTER 14

STRATTON MOUNTAIN AND POND

AREA MAP

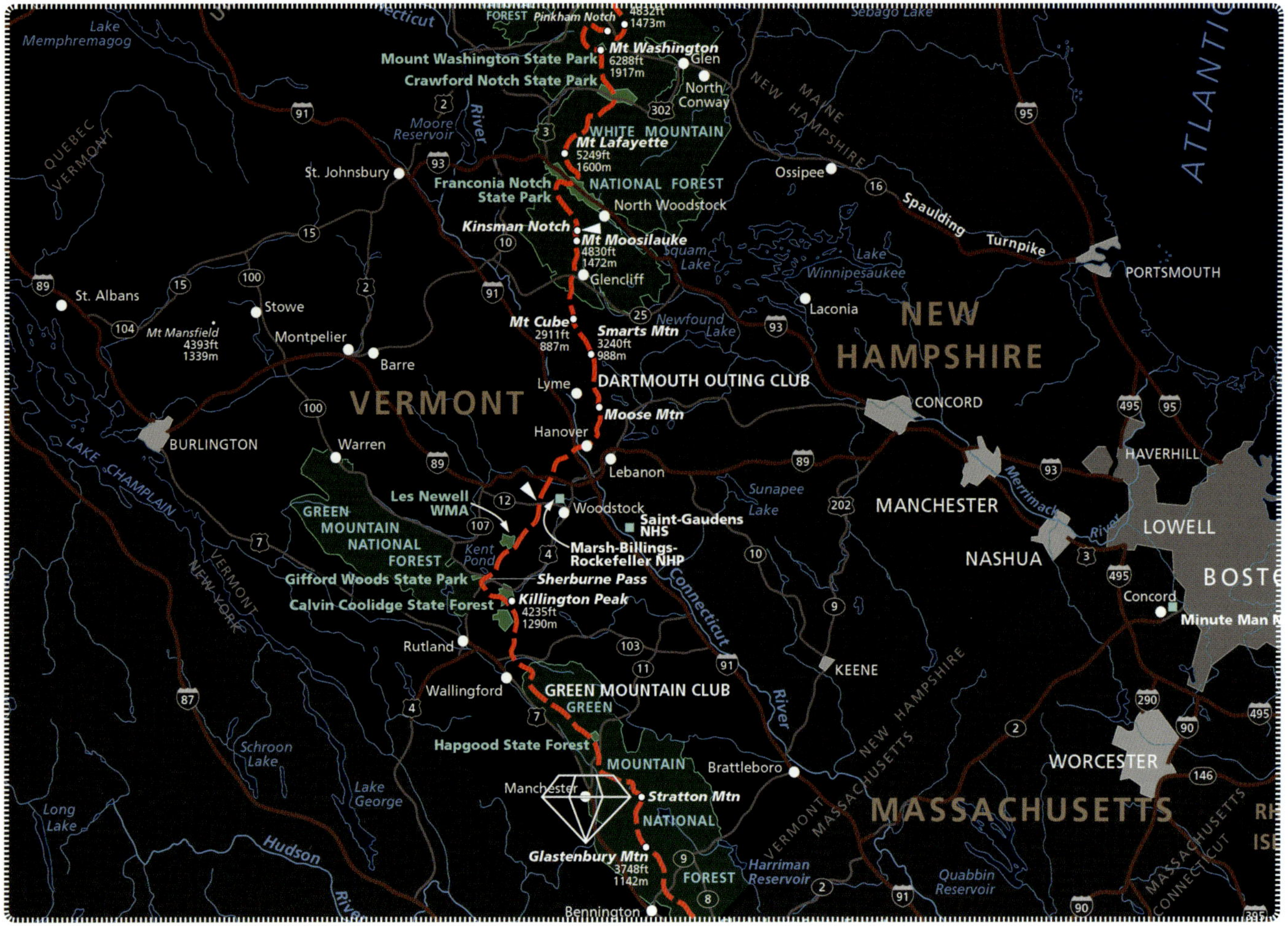

DISTANCE	12 miles
ELEVATION GAIN	2,050 feet
ELEVATION LOSS	2,050 feet
LEVEL	Moderate

TYPE: LOOP

0 10 Kilometers 50

0 10 Miles 50

Appalachian National Scenic Trail

Boundary of CLUB management section

North

GEM HIKE

PERSONAL TOUCH

I really enjoyed the sweeping views of Vermont's Green Mountains looking to the south from the Stratton Mountain fire tower. Mount Greylock (Massachusetts' highest peak) helped put the sense of scale to this beautiful scene. I really enjoyed viewing the Taconics, the mountain range to the west, and the Appalachian Trail to the south and north.

I also enjoyed hiking these miles again in the winter. I would recommend experiencing this hike with snow on the trees and ground, because this was a magical experience for me. Imagine walking in your favorite snow globe with the snow in the trees on your favorite trail.

BRIEF OVERVIEW

The Stratton Mountain and Pond offers views that are absolutely stunning. This section of the Appalachian Trail offers a diverse and very captivating stretch of this iconic trail. It is located in Stratton, Vermont, in the in the Green Mountains of Vermont. It offers a combination of challenging terrain, stunning vistas, and historical significance.

DESCRIPTION OF THE GEM HIKE

The Appalachian Trail and Vermont's Long Trail share the same trail on this hike. To start this hike, you park at Stratton-Arlington Road Trailhead. This is a moderate hike with an elevation of 2,051 feet gained and lost during a travel of 12 miles to the summit of Stratton Mountain and to Stratton Pond.

FLORA, FAUNA, AND VEGETATION

The vegetation along this section of the AT and LT varies with elevation: The lower elevations have maples, birches, and oaks, and the higher elevations have spruces, firs, and pines. Plants include pink lady's slippers, a type of orchid that grows in the late spring in this region.

HISTORY OF BENTON MACKAYE, THE LONG TRAIL, AND THE APPALACHIAN TRAIL

Stratton Mountain is significant to the Appalachian Trail. It was here, while working on the Long Trail, that Benton MacKaye envisioned the idea of the Appalachian Trail in 1921. He envisioned a footpath connecting the entire range of the Appalachian Mountains while looking out from near the summit.

FIRE TOWER

Stratton Mountain features a historic fire tower, constructed in the 1930s. This structure provides hikers with breathtaking 360-degree views of the Green Mountains and surrounding landscapes. The tower stands as a monument to the early-twentieth-century efforts in forest fire management and remains a popular destination for panoramic views. If you have the time, it is a great place to just watch the changing clouds and weather, but please be mindful not to do so during a lightning storm.

STRATTON POND

Stratton Pond, situated 6 miles from the southern end of this trail section, is the largest body of water on the Long Trail. This tranquil pond provides a serene environment for hikers to relax and enjoy the natural beauty of Vermont. The surrounding area offers gentler terrain compared to the steep climbs of Stratton Mountain, making it an ideal location for reflection and relaxation before continuing your hike.

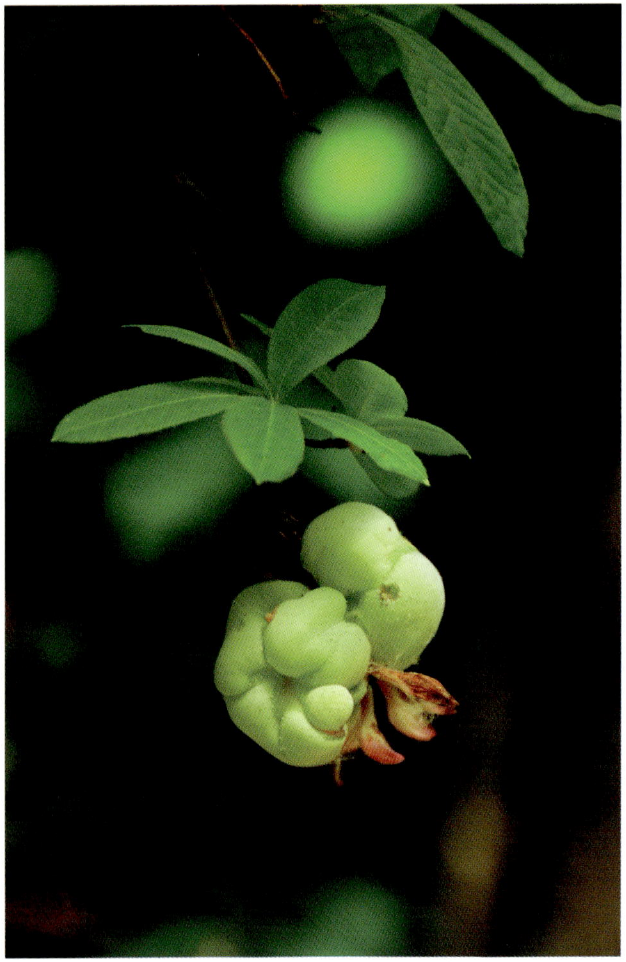

Spring tree gail, caused by insects

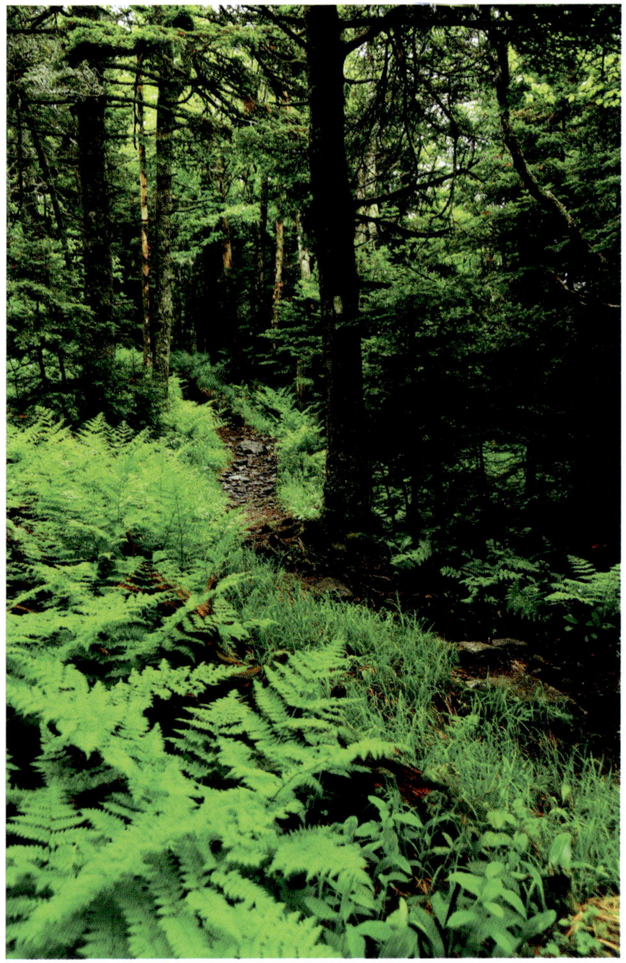

Stratton Mountain, Vermont, ferns and fir trees line the Appalachian Trail

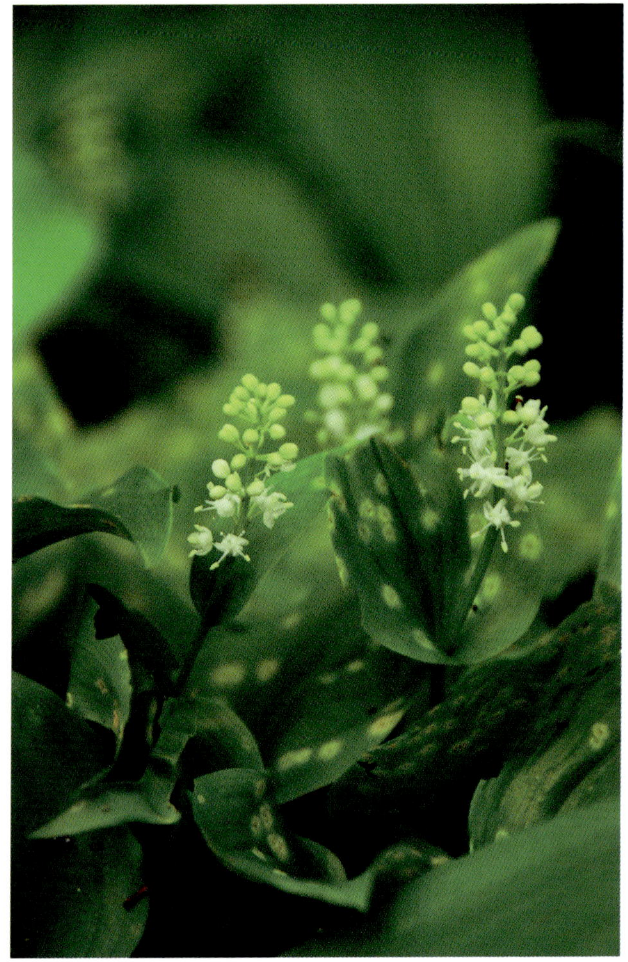

White flowers on Stratton Mountain

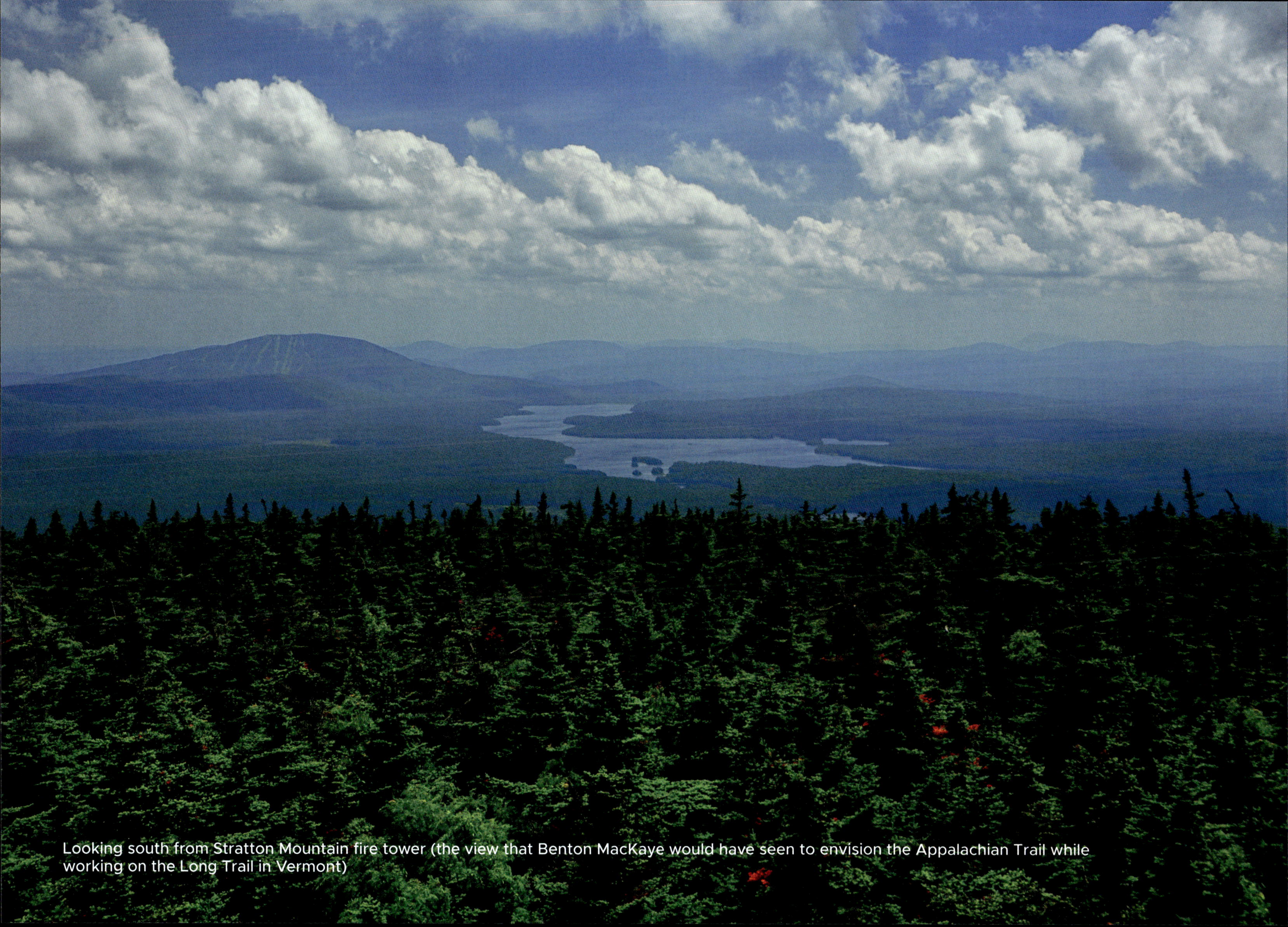

Looking south from Stratton Mountain fire tower (the view that Benton MacKaye would have seen to envision the Appalachian Trail while working on the Long Trail in Vermont)

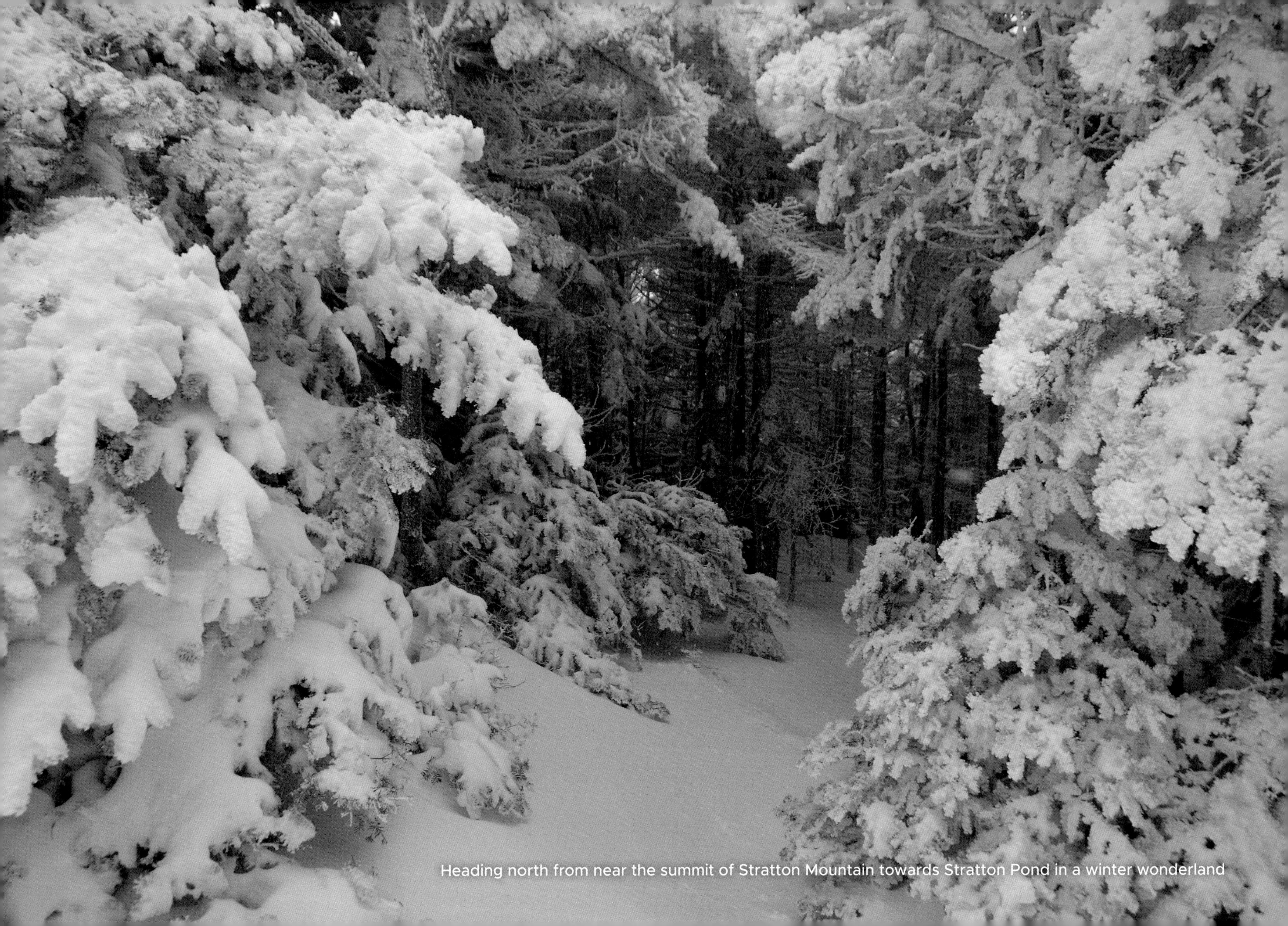

Heading north from near the summit of Stratton Mountain towards Stratton Pond in a winter wonderland

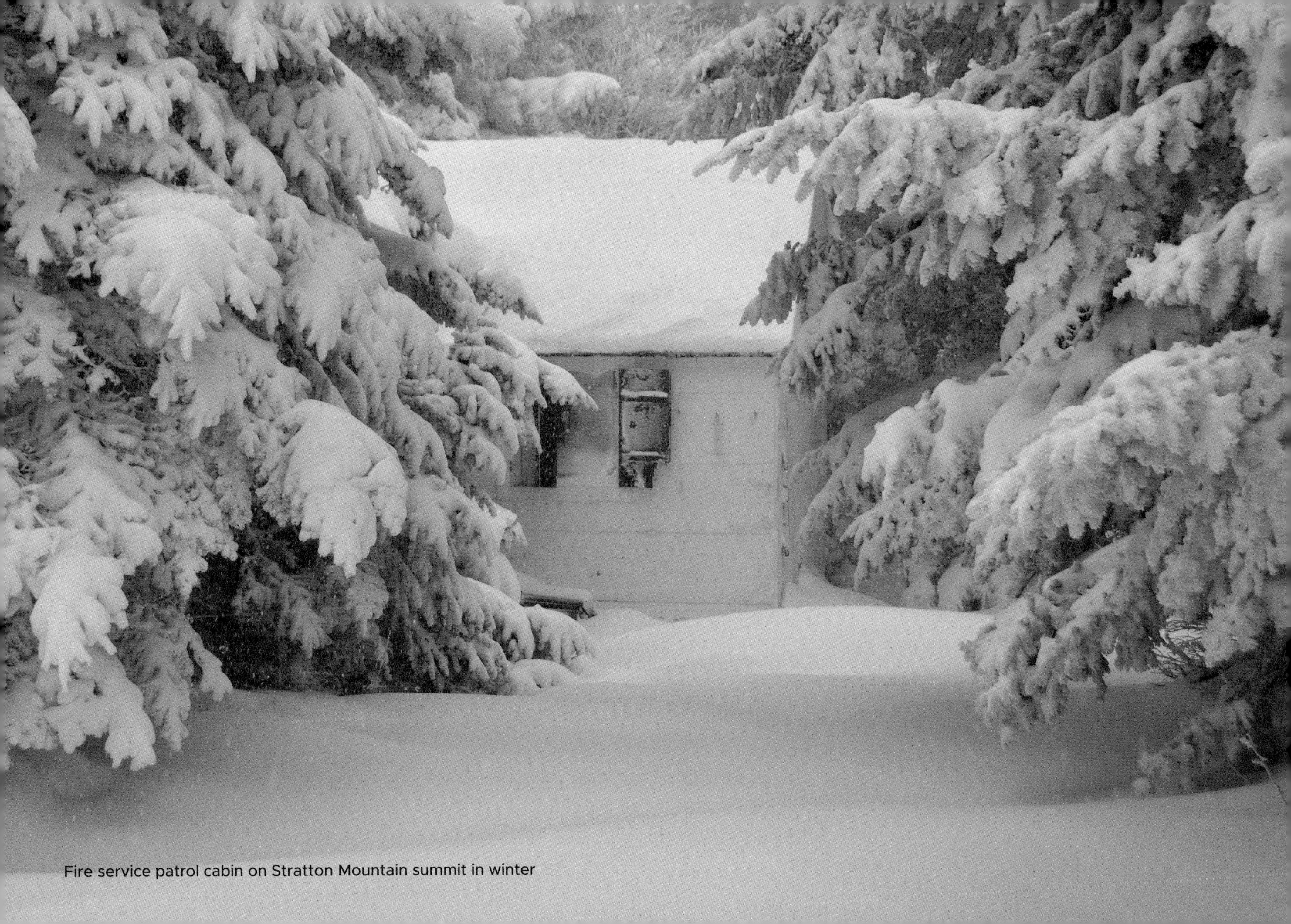

Fire service patrol cabin on Stratton Mountain summit in winter

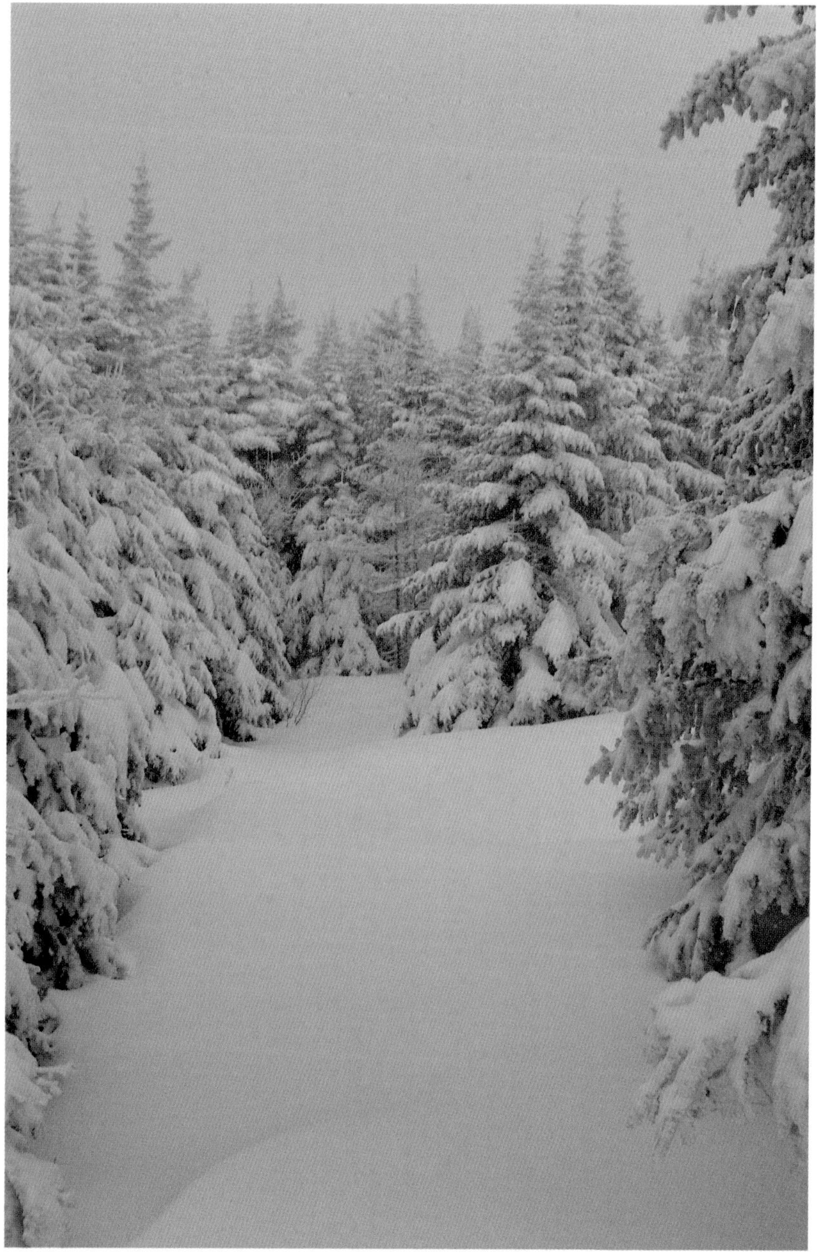

Stratton Mountain fir trees

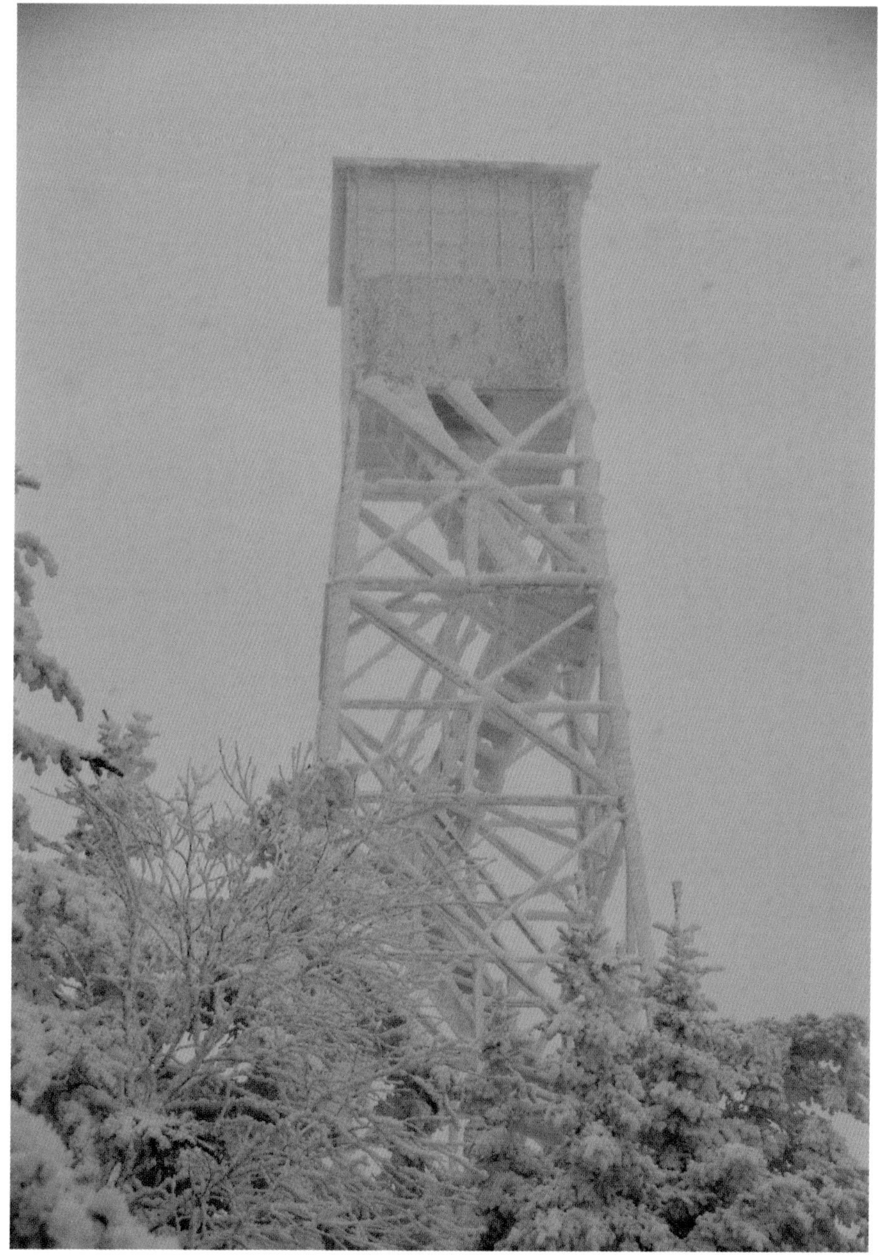

Stratton Mountain fire tower in winter

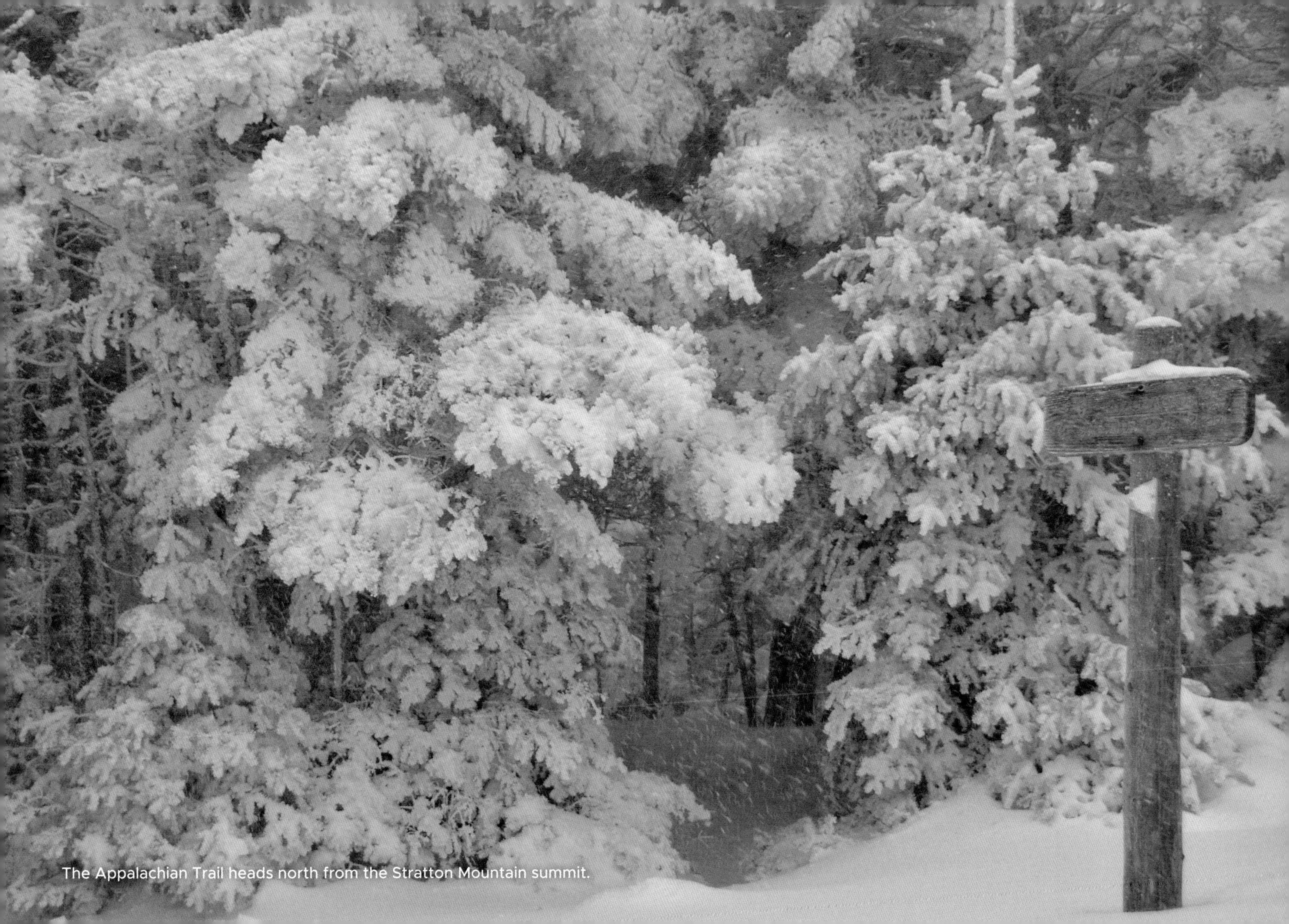

The Appalachian Trail heads north from the Stratton Mountain summit.

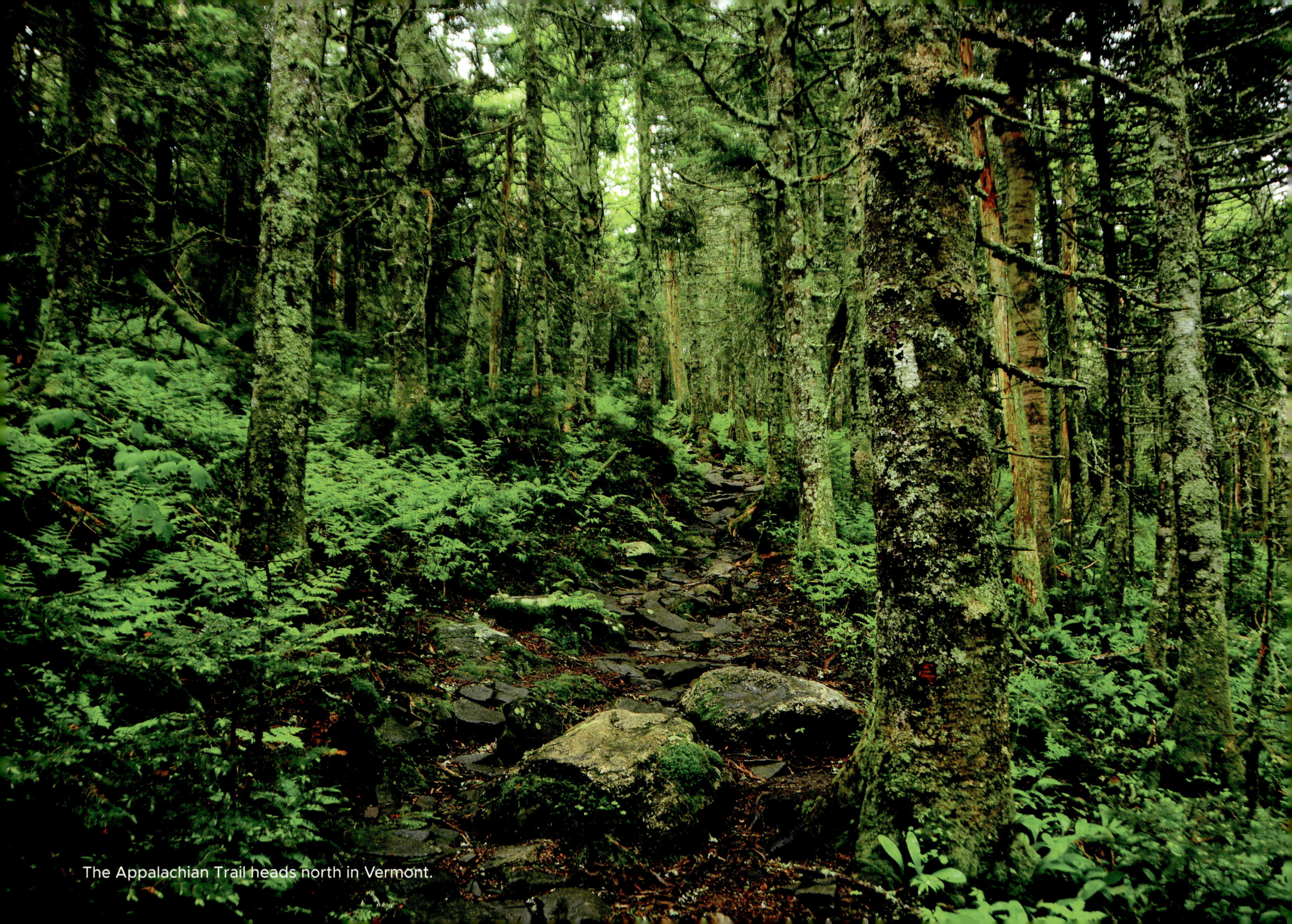

The Appalachian Trail heads north in Vermont.

Ferns line the Appalachian Trail on Stratton Mountain.

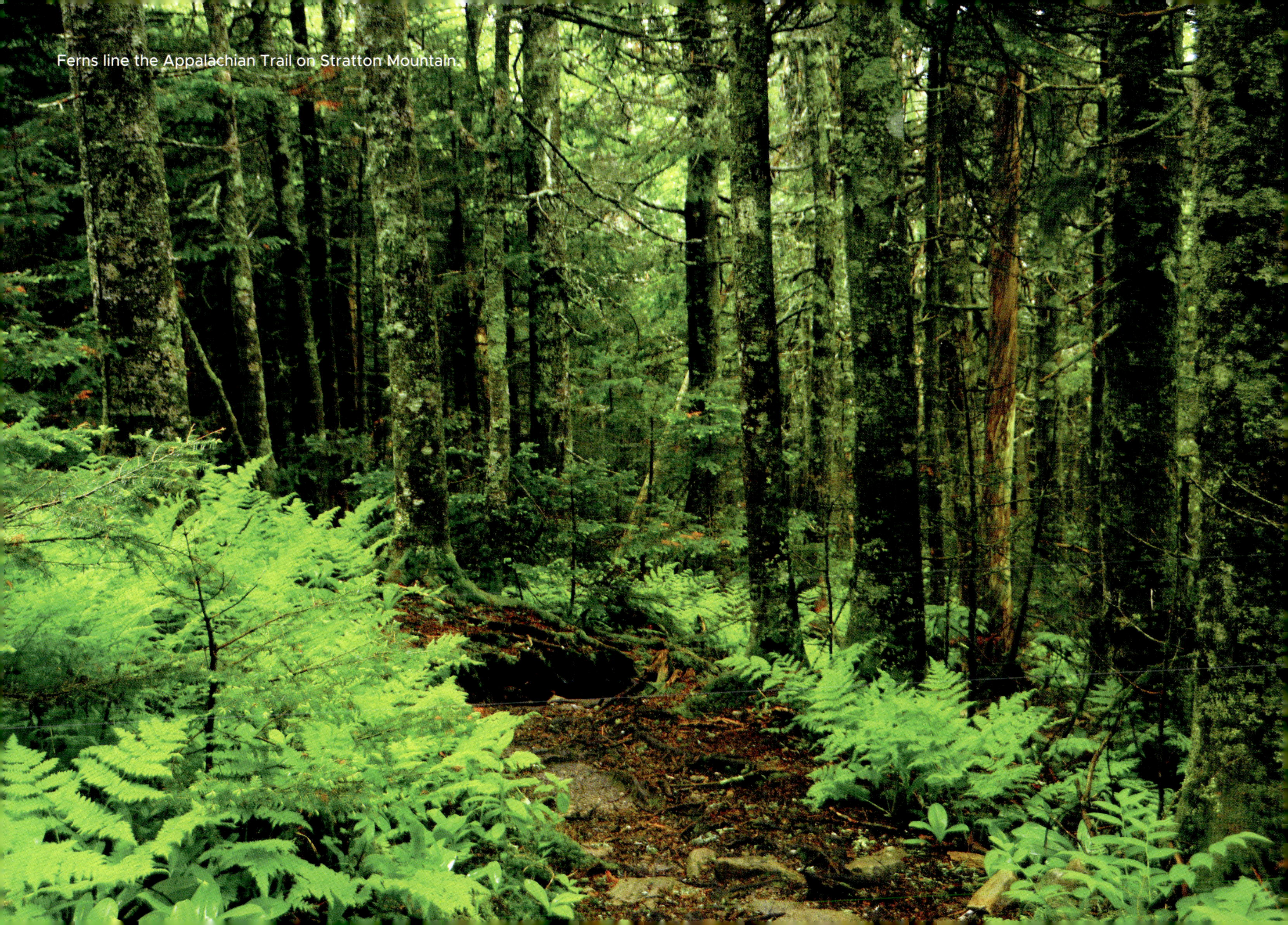

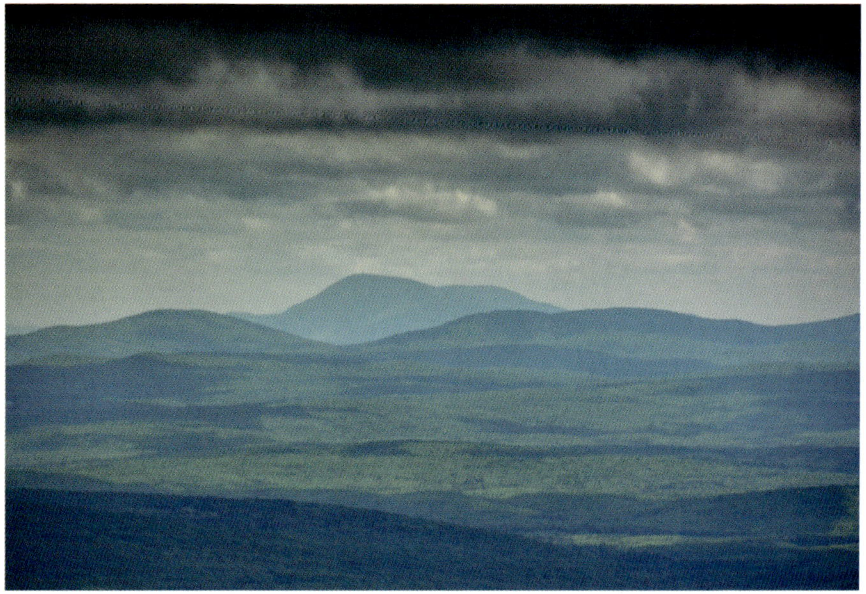

Mount Greylock from Stratton Mountain

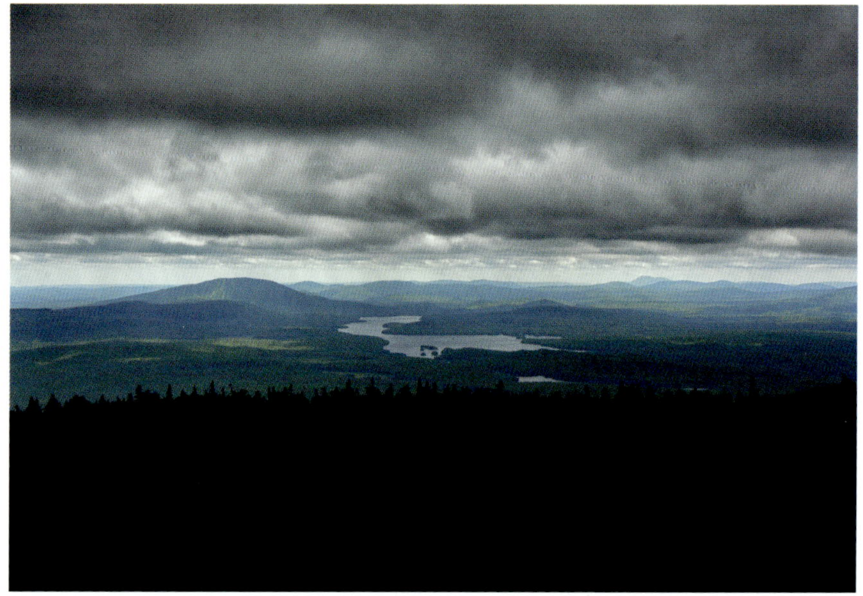

Looking south from Stratton Mountain

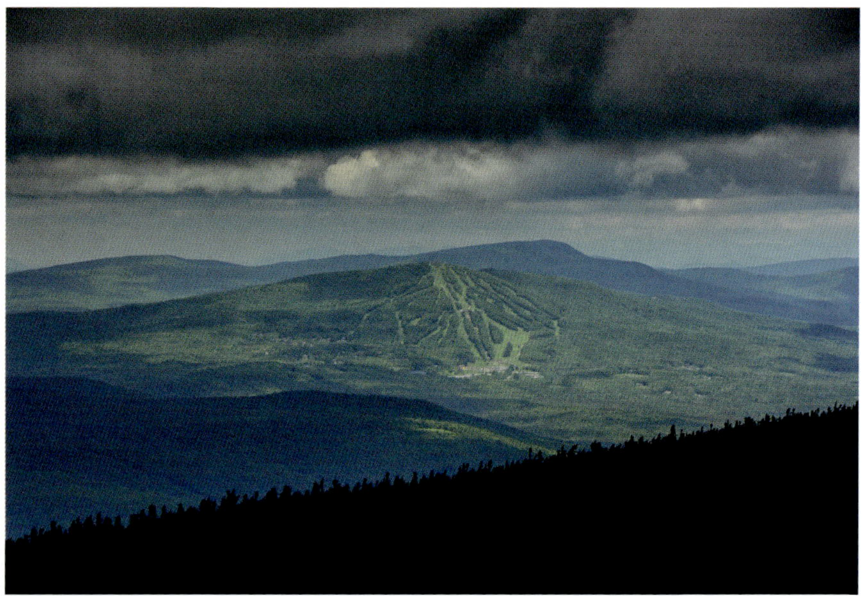

Bromley Mountain from Stratton Mountain

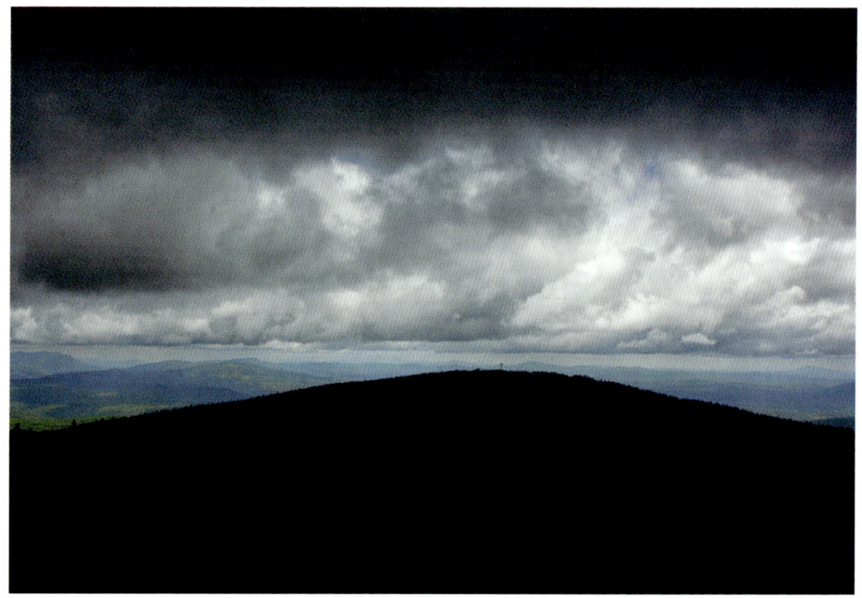

Looking north from Stratton Mountain

Green Mountains from Stratton Mountain

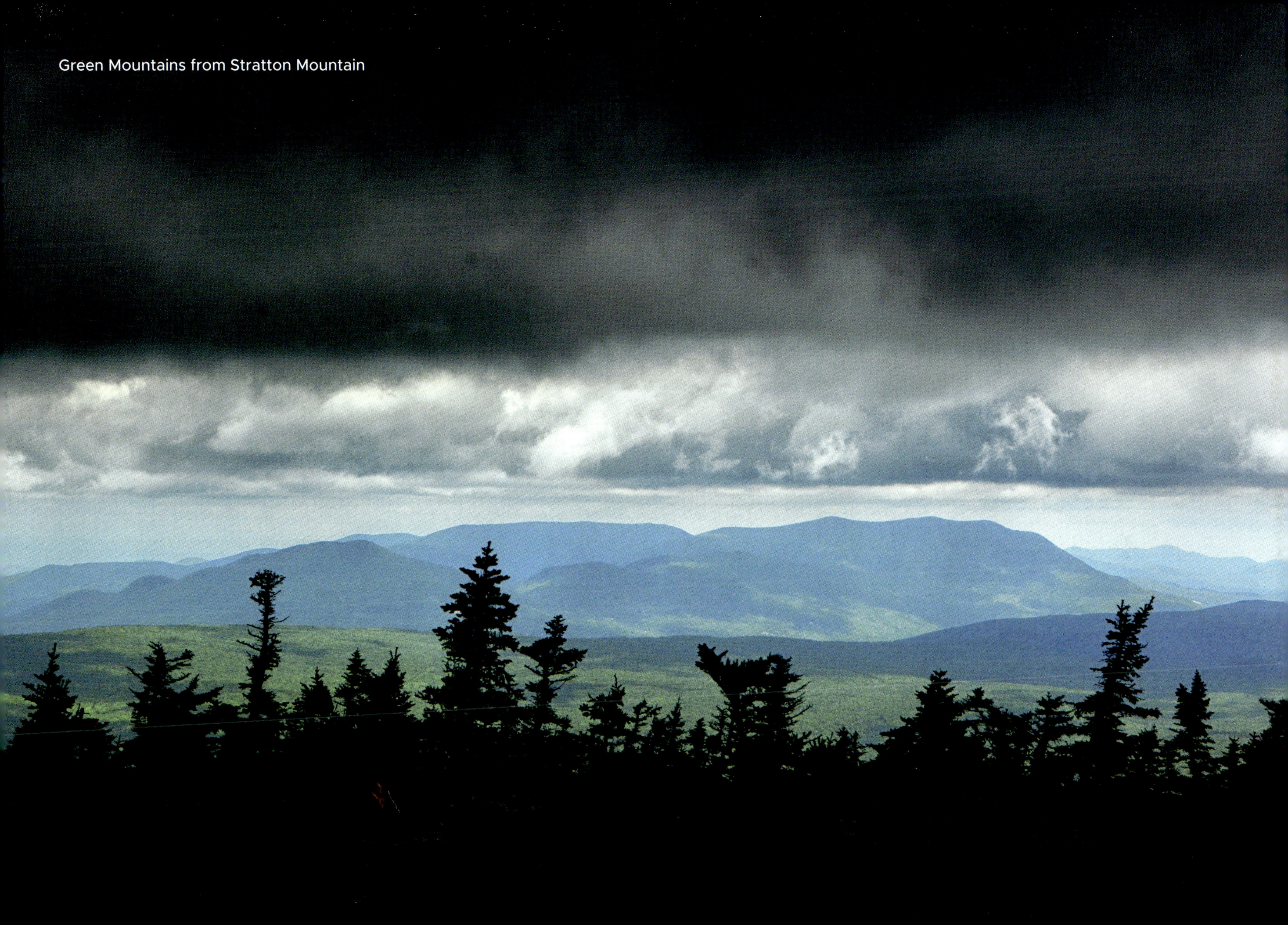

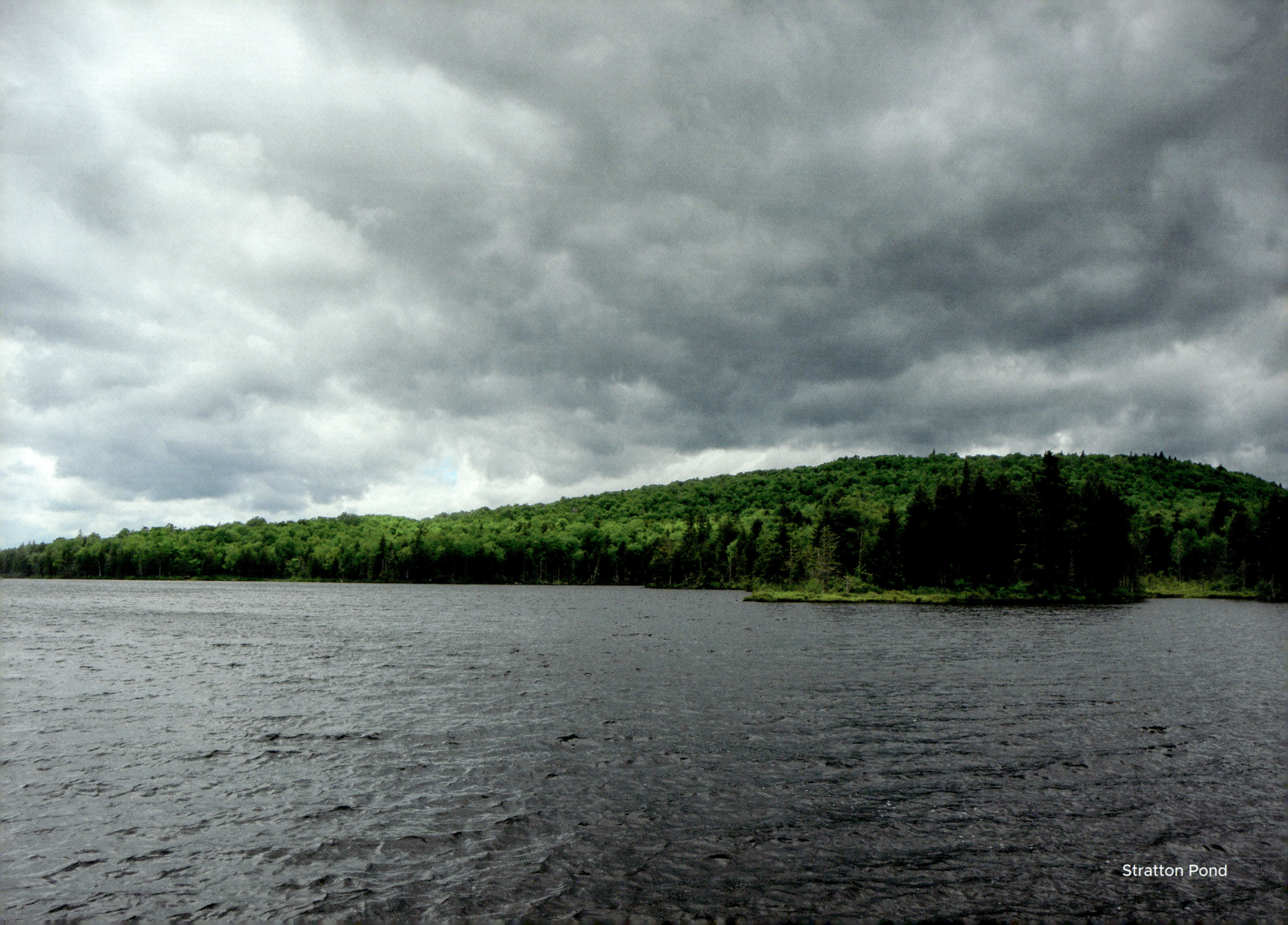

Stratton Pond

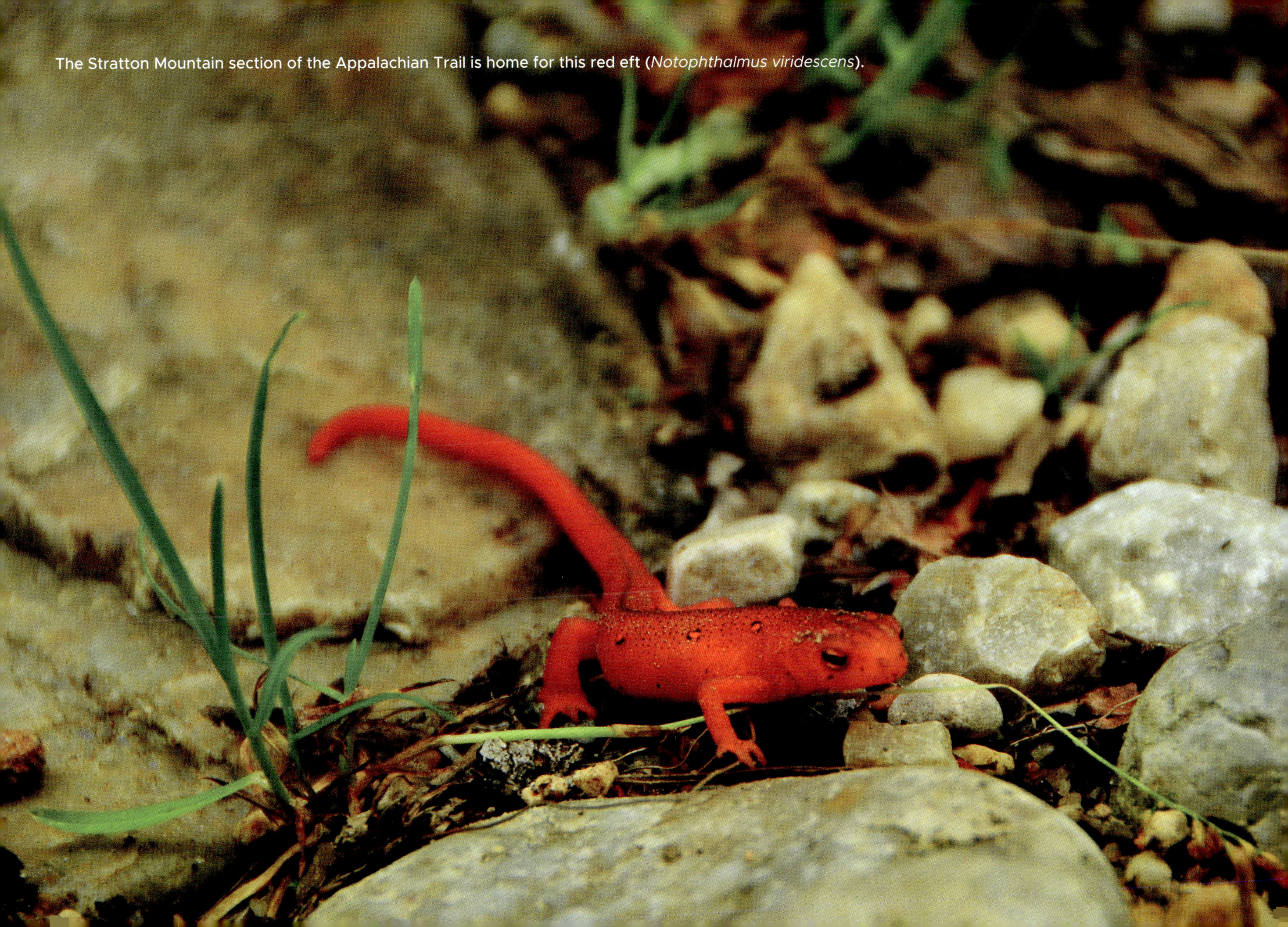
The Stratton Mountain section of the Appalachian Trail is home for this red eft (*Notophthalmus viridescens*).

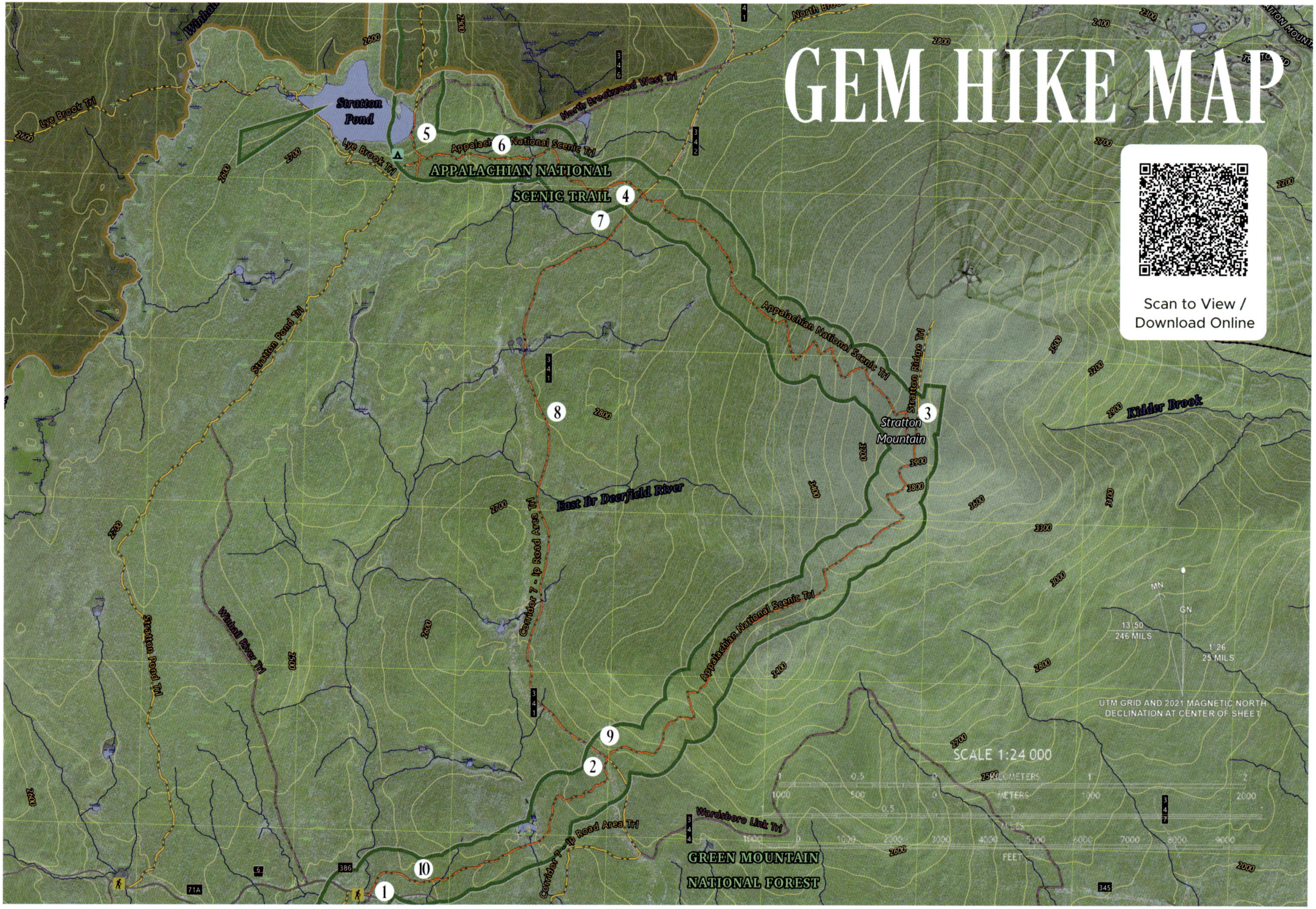

GEM HIKE MAP
Scan to View / Download Online
Stratton Pond
Lye Brook Trl
APPALACHIAN NATIONAL SCENIC TRAIL
North Brockwood West Trl
Appalachian National Scenic Trl
Stratton Ridge Trl
Stratton Mountain
Kidder Brook
East Br Deerfield River
Corridor 7 - Ip Road Area Trl
Stratton Pond Trl
Winhall River Trl
Wardsboro Link Trl
GREEN MOUNTAIN NATIONAL FOREST
UTM GRID AND 2021 MAGNETIC NORTH DECLINATION AT CENTER OF SHEET
SCALE 1:24 000
KILOMETERS
METERS
FEET

DIRECTIONS TO THE TRAILHEAD(S)

For this the Appalachian Trail Gem hike, you will park at the trail access on Stratton Arlington Rd. in Stratton, Vermont. The geographic location is 43.06108394778582, –72.96792084763779, and Google Maps calls it "Stratton Mountain Trailhead." This hike will allow hikers to immediately access the Appalachian Trail and the Long Trail from the parking lot on Stratton-Arlington Rd. and to enjoy a moderate start for the first mile. From Manchester, Vermont, you may follow the following directions for 44 minutes (29.3 miles):

1. Head east on Seminary Ave. toward W Rd. for 2 seconds (69 feet)
2. Turn right onto Main St., 42 seconds (0.1 mile)
3. Take E. Manchester Rd. to VT 11 E / VT 30 S, 6 minutes (3.2 miles)
4. Follow VT 30 S to Stratton Mountain Rd. in Winhall, 14 minutes (11.7 miles)
5. Take Mountain Rd. and W. Jamaica Rd. to Stratton Arlington Rd. in Stratton, 24 minutes (14.3 miles)
6. Arrive at Stratton Mountain Trailhead, Stratton Arlington Rd., Stratton, VT 05360

GEM HIKE DIRECTIONS

1. Head north on the Appalachian Trail toward Forest Rd. 341; at 1.4 miles, cross International Paper Rd. (FS 341)
2. Travel another 2.4 miles, and you will reach the summit of Stratton Mountain
3. Travel another 2.1 miles, and your will reach International Paper Rd. (FS 341)
4. Cross International Paper Rd. (FS 341) and continue 1.1 miles on the Appalachian Trail, and you will reach Stratton Pond
5. You will return on the Appalachian Trail south for 1.1 miles
6. Turn right onto International Paper Rd. (FS 341)
7. Stay on International Paper Rd. (FS 341) for 2.6 miles
8. Turn right onto the Appalachian Trail south
9. Travel on the Appalachian Trail south for 1.4 miles, until you reach the Stratton Mountain Trailhead on Stratton-Arlington Rd.
10. Reach Stratton-Arlington Road and Trailhead

MORE/LESS AMBITIOUS HIKERS

More-ambitious hikers might want to consider doing a point-to-point hike connecting Stratton-Arlington Road and the parking lot off VT RT 11/30 for an 18-mile adventure.

Less ambitious hikers may wish to start a hike from Stratton Resort. When they run their gondola, it can be used on your hike for a fee. Hikers can hike a short trail from the lift to the fire tower. Hikers can also hike an out-and-back from Stratton-Arlington Road to the summit of Stratton Mountain, using the Appalachian Trail / Long Trail.

CHAPTER 15

BROMLEY MOUNTAIN ON THE APPALACHIAN TRAIL

AREA MAP

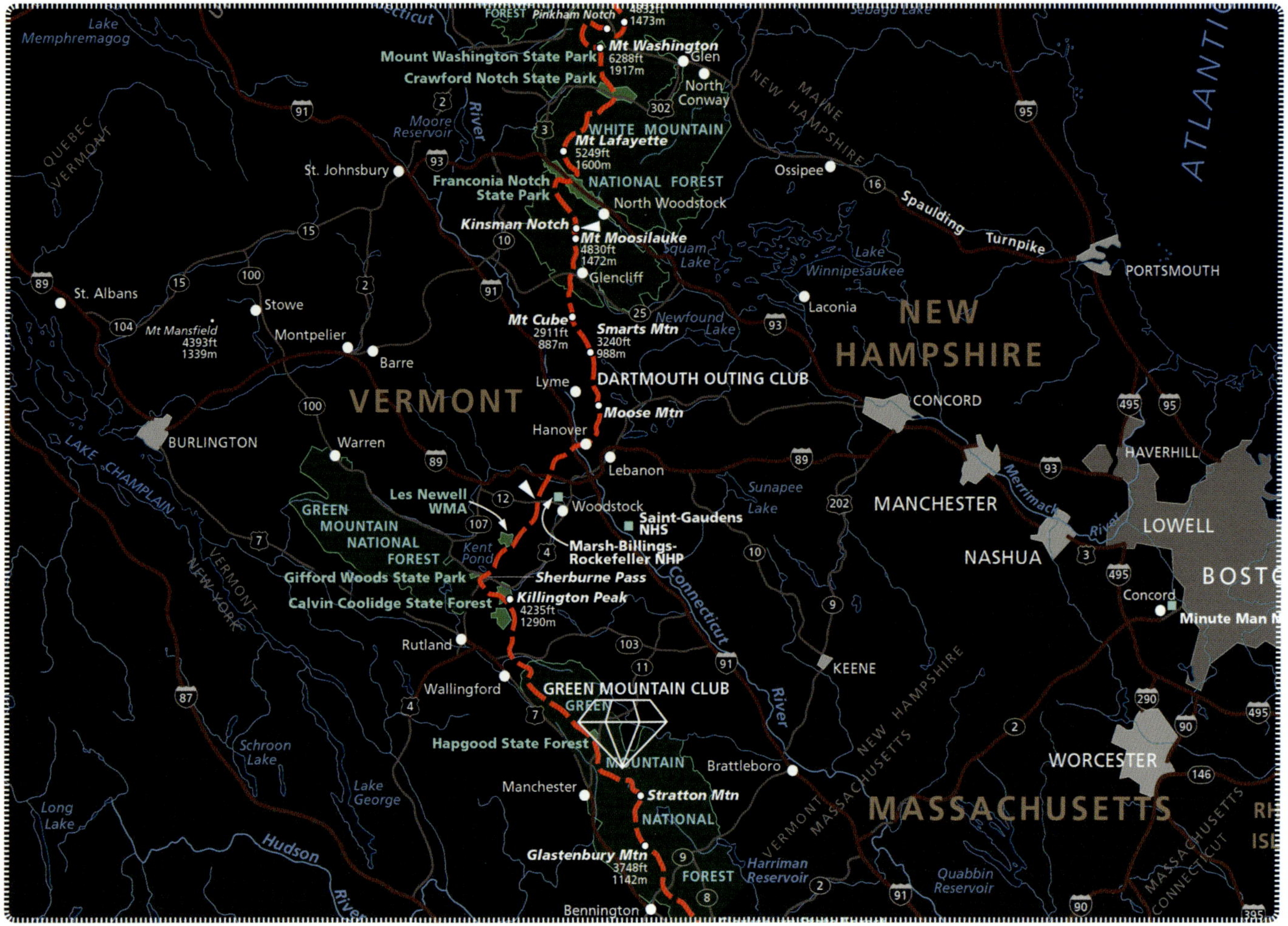

DISTANCE	6 miles
ELEVATION GAIN	1,410 feet
ELEVATION LOSS	1,410 feet
LEVEL	Easy

TYPE: OUT-AND-BACK

0 10 Kilometers 50

0 10 Miles 50

Appalachian National Scenic Trail

Boundary of CLUB management section

North

GEM HIKE

PERSONAL TOUCH

I was lucky to hike the Bromley section of the Appalachian Trail in late spring. The trail came alive with vibrant greenery and blooming wildflowers. Wildflowers were white, orange, yellow, and purple.

The views from Bromley Mountain's summit were especially wonderful in the spring. I was able to see the surrounding valley as it began to bloom, and the different green hues created by the leaves of the different trees as their leaves matured.

One time, I hiked this Vermont section of the Appalachian Trail after a heavy snowstorm. The trees were perfect shapes to hold the snow in their limbs, and the rocks in the creeks held the snow perfectly too. The winter scenes were truly winter wonderland scenes for the ages.

BRIEF OVERVIEW

Hikers encounter a mix of dense forests, a challenging ascent, stunning views, and wildflowers galore. This section includes several notable points of interest. This section is a gem of the Appalachian Trail in early summer, when the wildflowers are everywhere and the young leaves create different hues of green. The final ascent of Mount Bromley on Bromley's ski trail and Bromley Creek contributes to make this section special.

DESCRIPTION OF THE GEM HIKE

This hike begins at the parking area of VT 11/30, on the outskirts of Manchester and on the way to Stratton Mountain Resort. The hike takes the Appalachian Trail / Long Trail north 3 miles along the Appalachian Trail, to the summit of Bromley Mountain, and returns the way you came up.

FLORA, FAUNA, AND VEGETATION

The lower elevations of the hike are characterized by mixed hardwood forests, including species such as sugar maple and beech. As the trail ascends, coniferous trees such as spruce and fir can be found at the higher elevations. The undergrowth includes a variety of shrubs, ferns, wildflowers, and various types of mosses.

BROMLEY CREEK

Bromley Creek is a very beautiful spot to enjoy. Bromley Creek is especially memorable in the winter, after heavy snows, because the tree limbs and rocks collect the snow to make a wonderful winter wonderland.

BROMLEY MOUNTAIN

Bromley Mountain offers sweeping views of surrounding peaks and the valley below. The wildflowers and the vibrate greens in the early summer make the stunning vistas even more special.

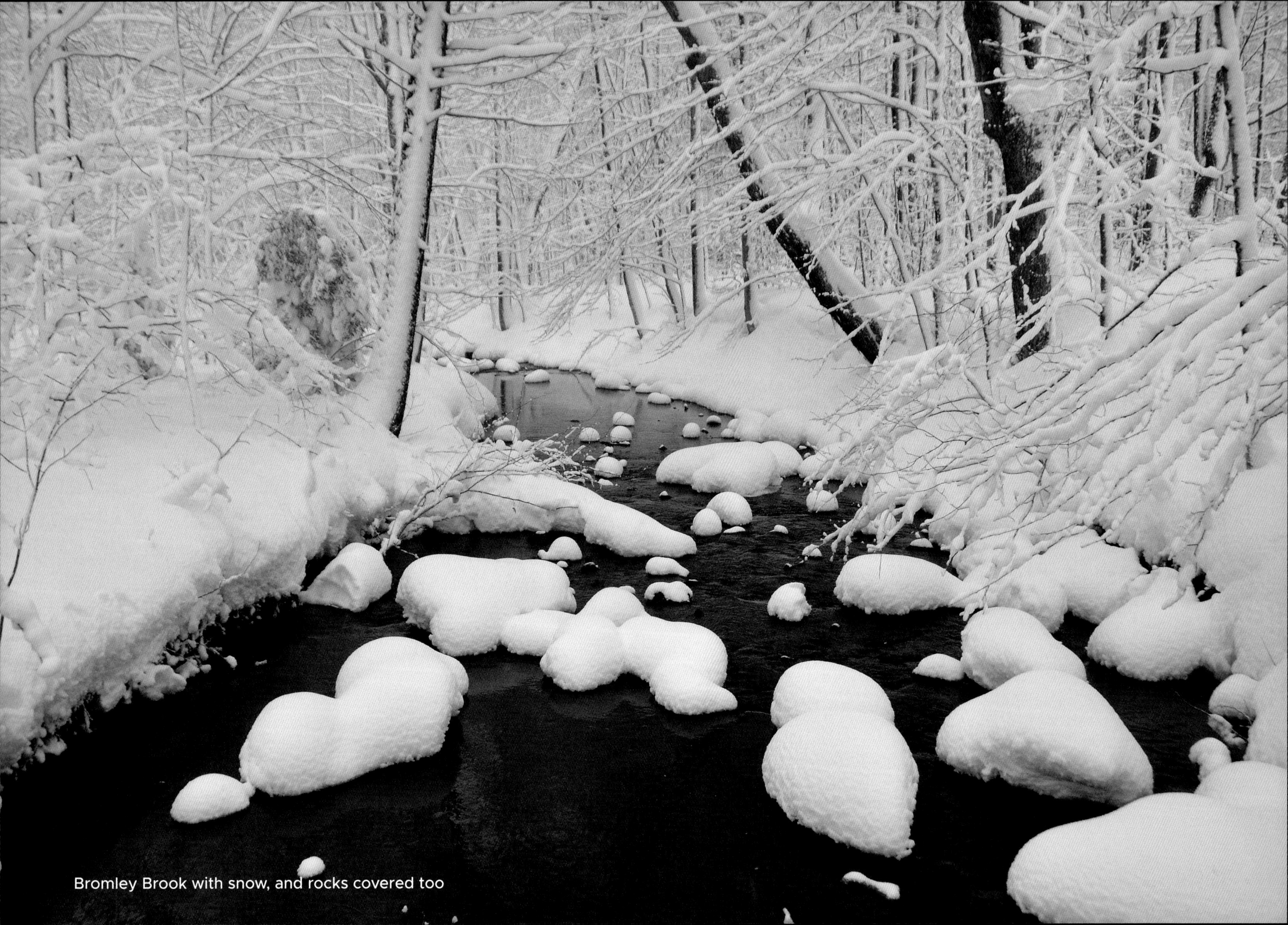

Bromley Brook with snow, and rocks covered too

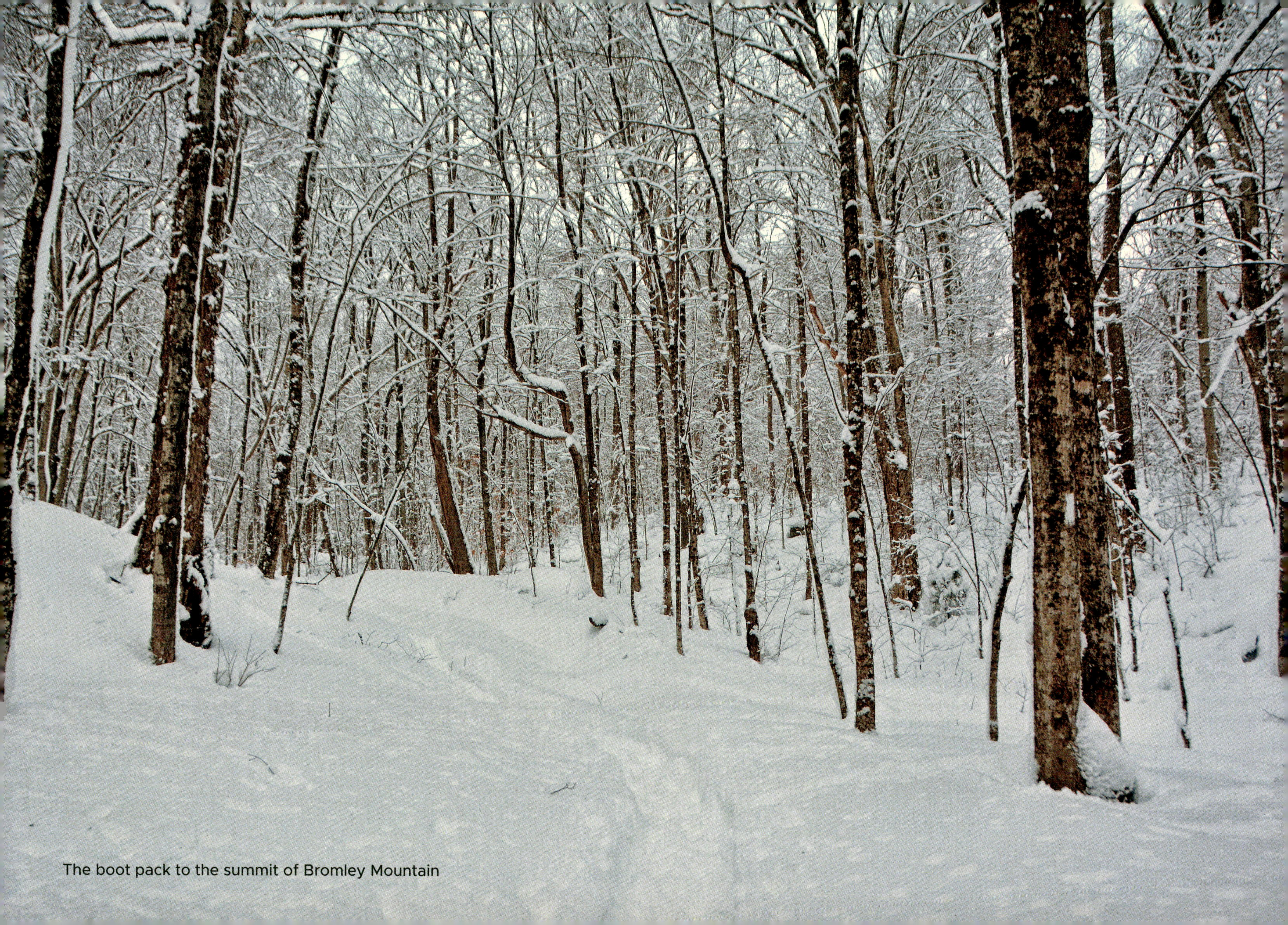

The boot pack to the summit of Bromley Mountain

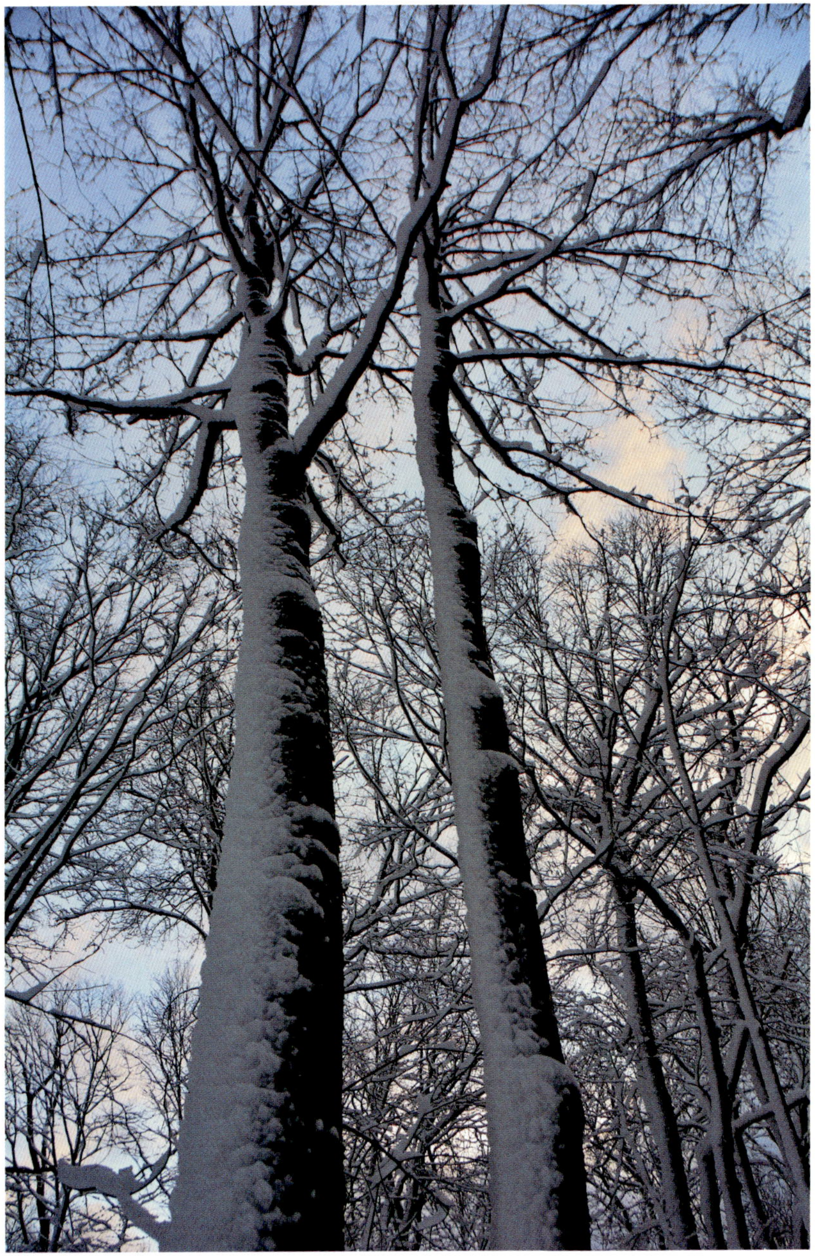

Towering snow-covered giants

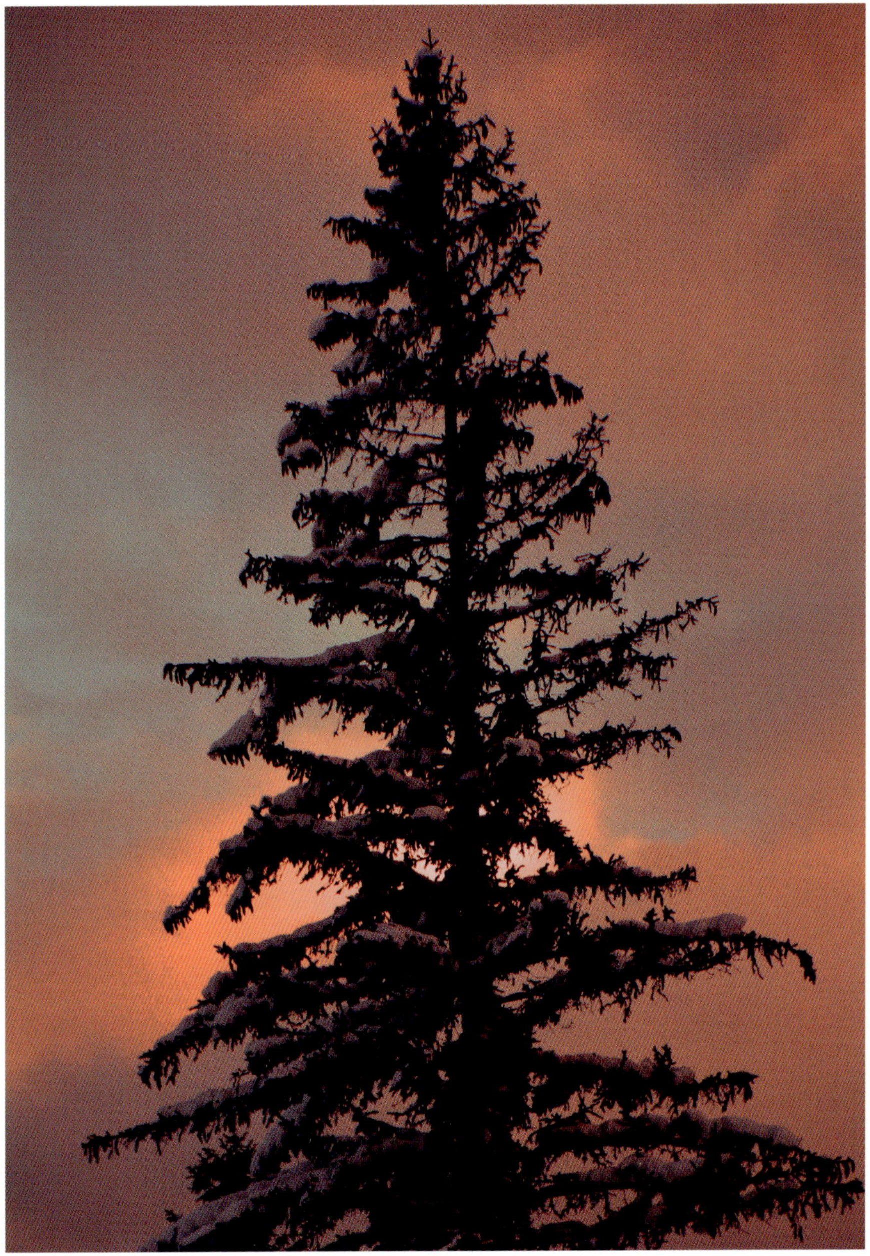

Tall spruce at sunset

Orange hawkweed (*Hieracium aurantiacum*)

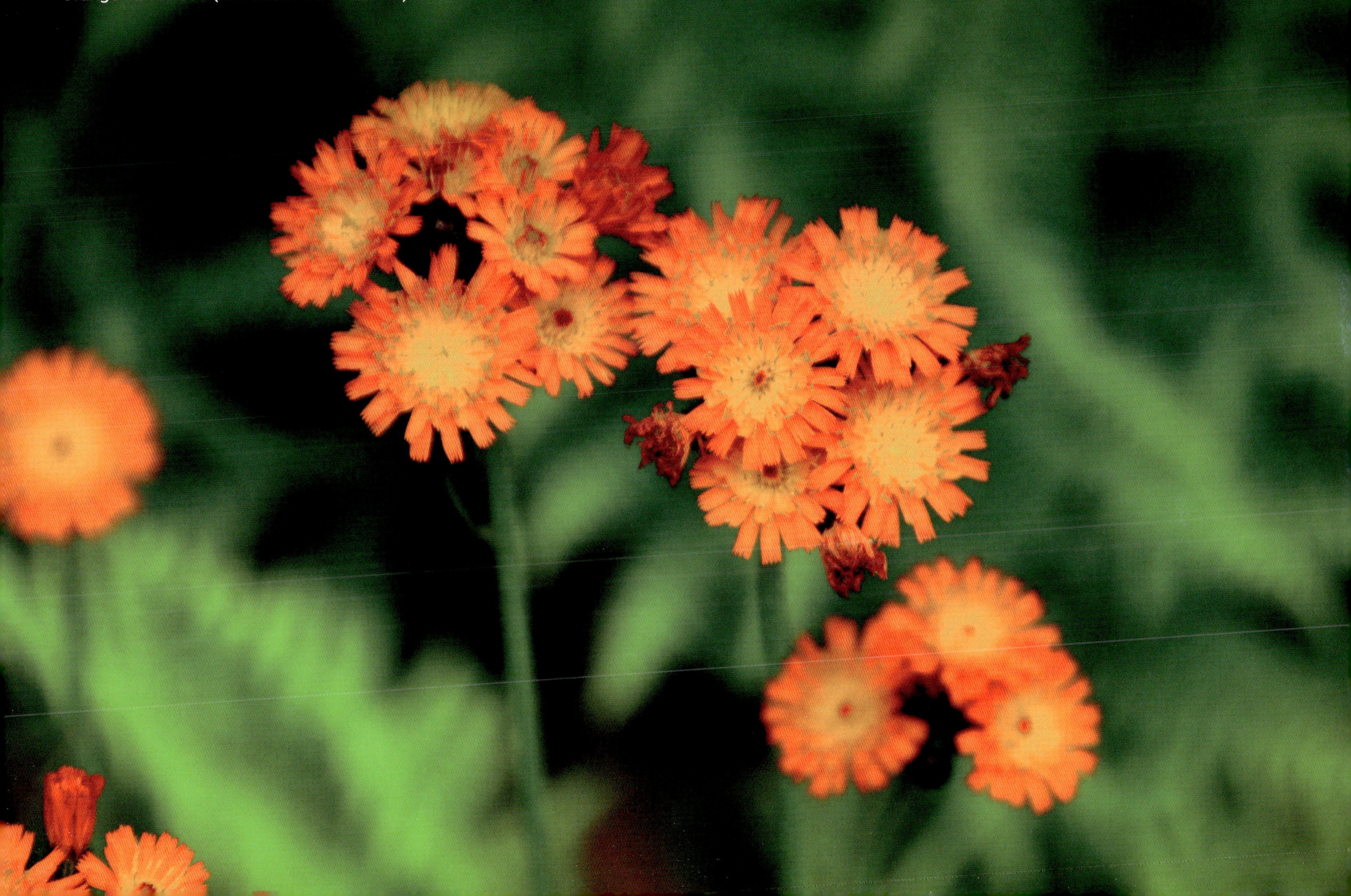

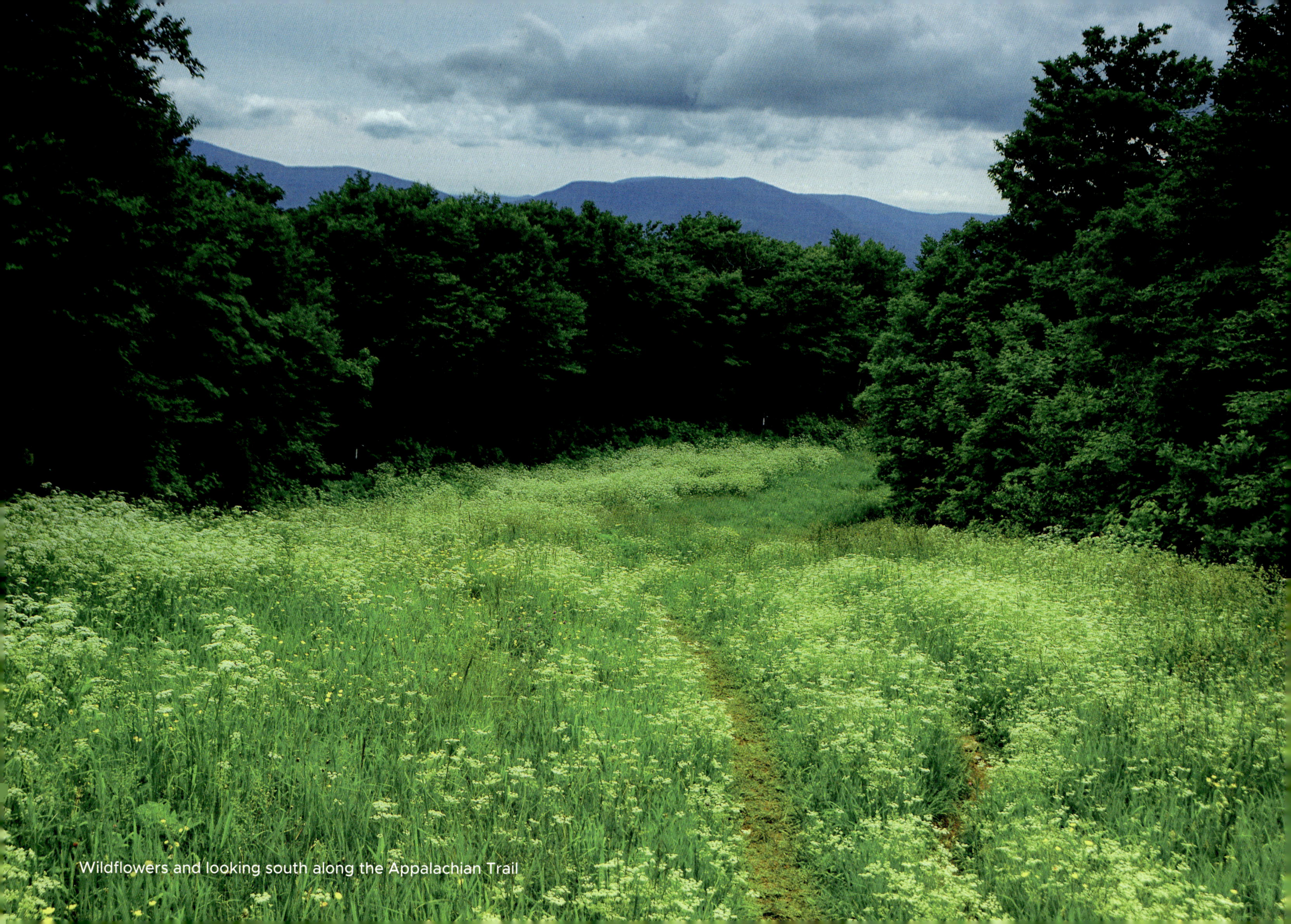

Wildflowers and looking south along the Appalachian Trail

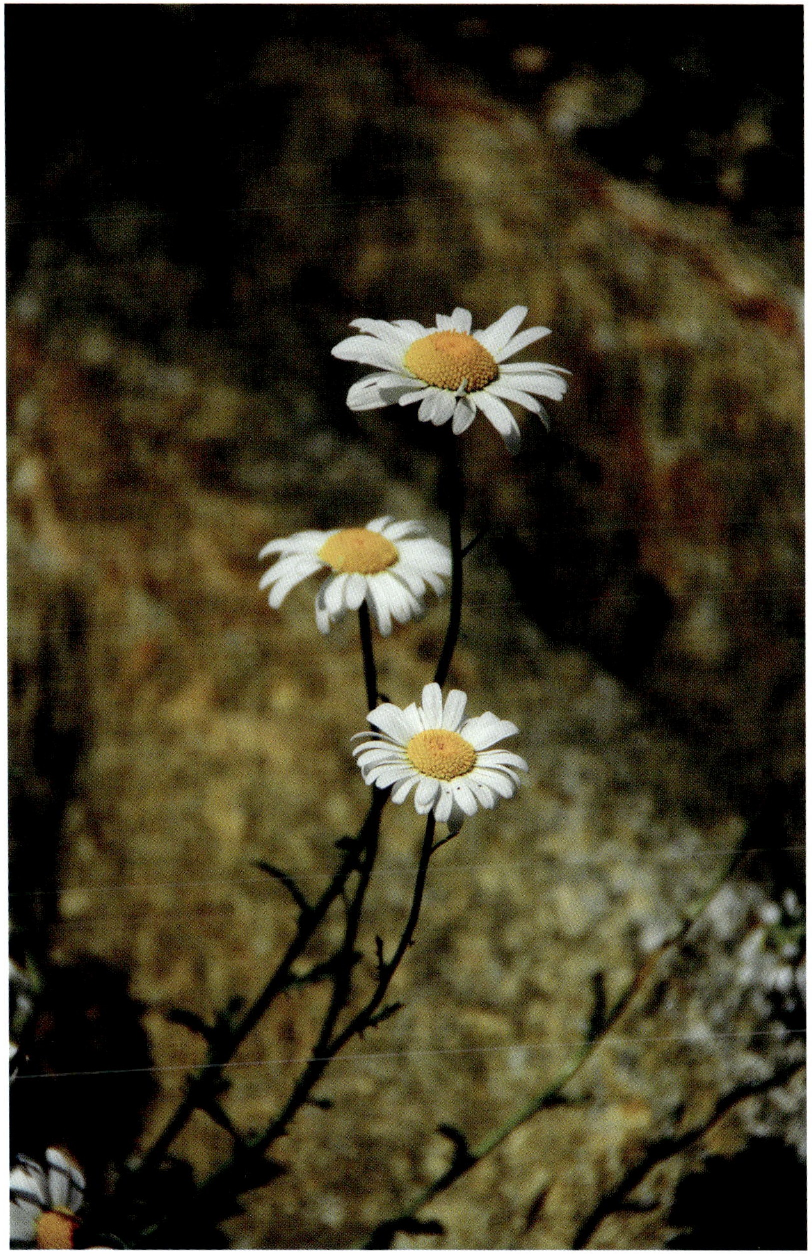

Oxeye daisy (*Leucanthemum vulgare*)

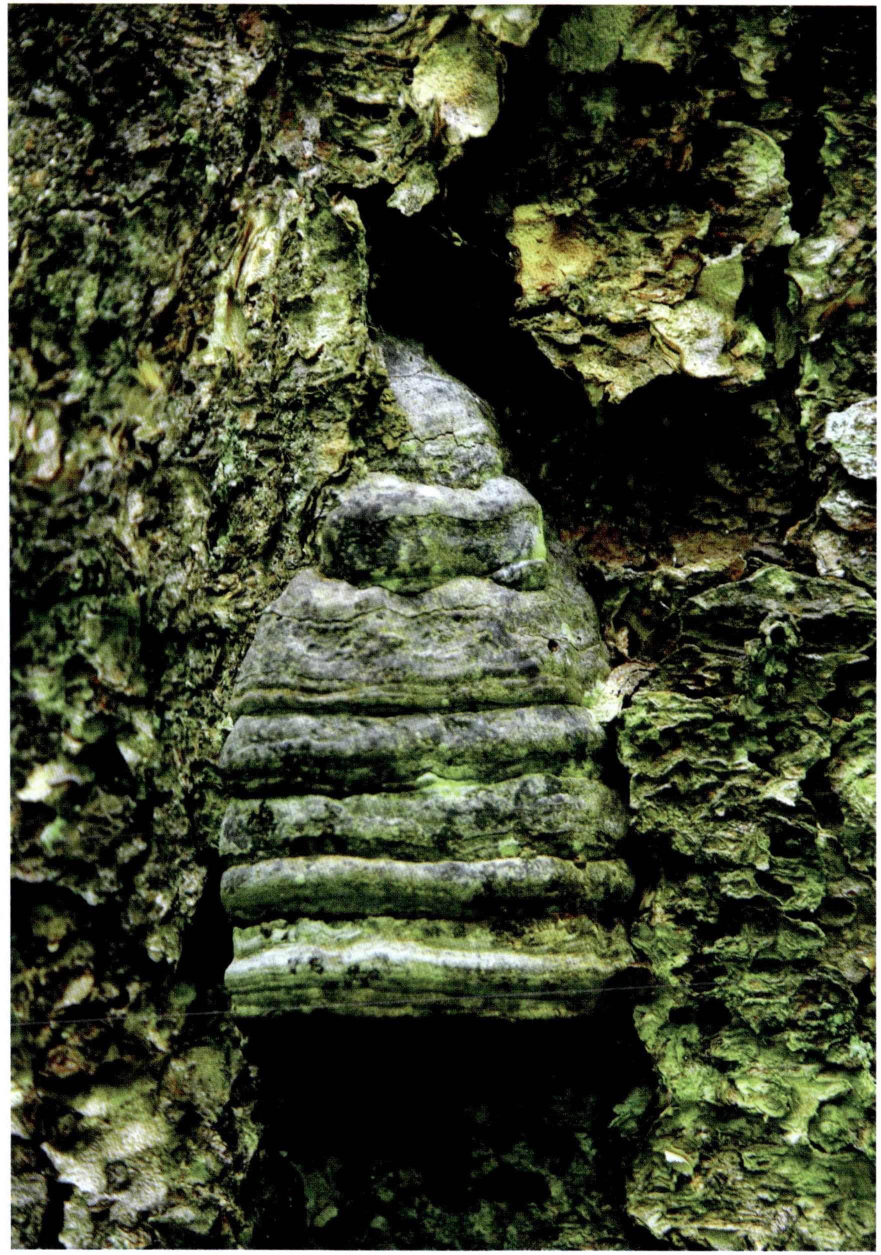

Last year's mushroom

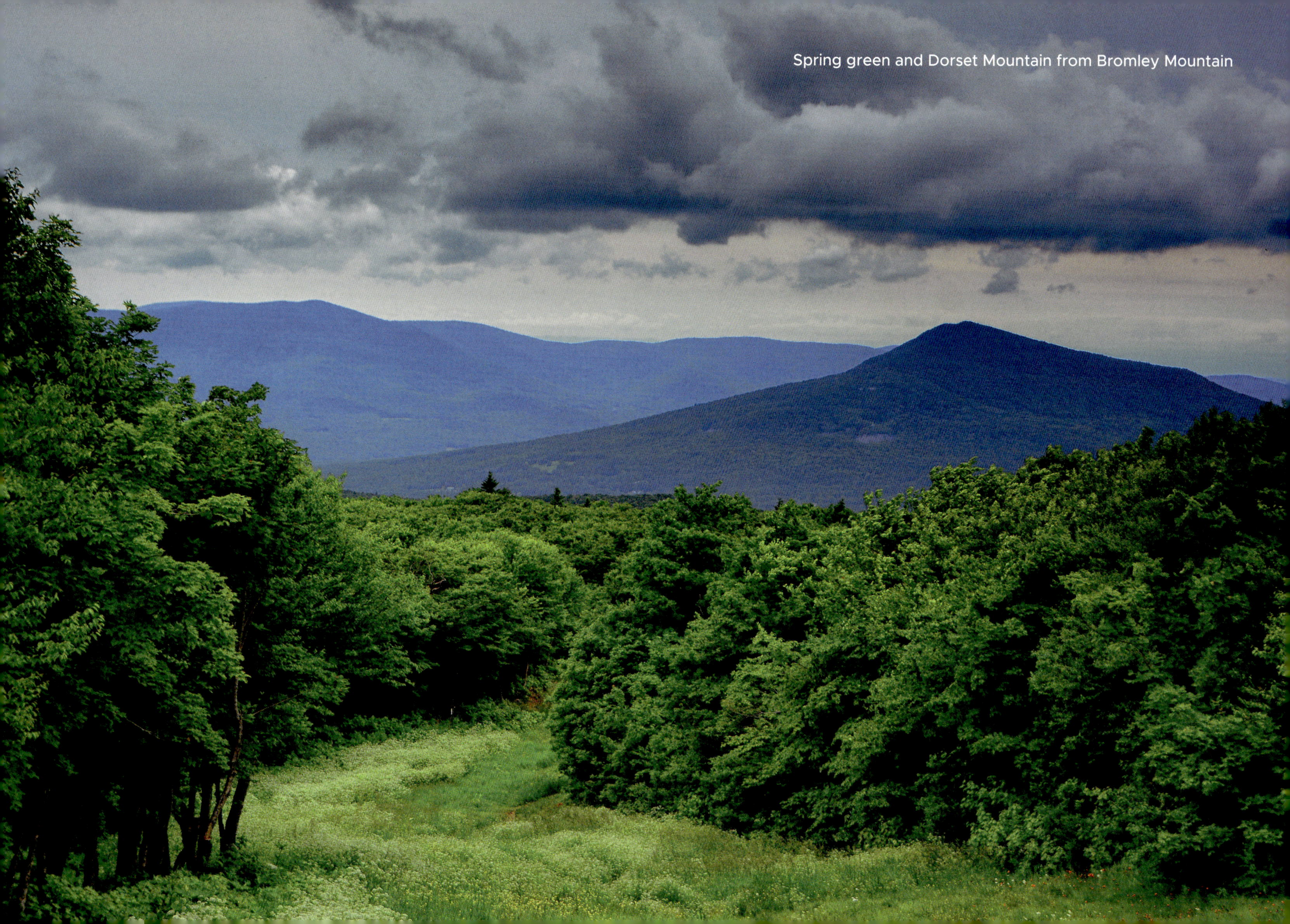

Spring green and Dorset Mountain from Bromley Mountain

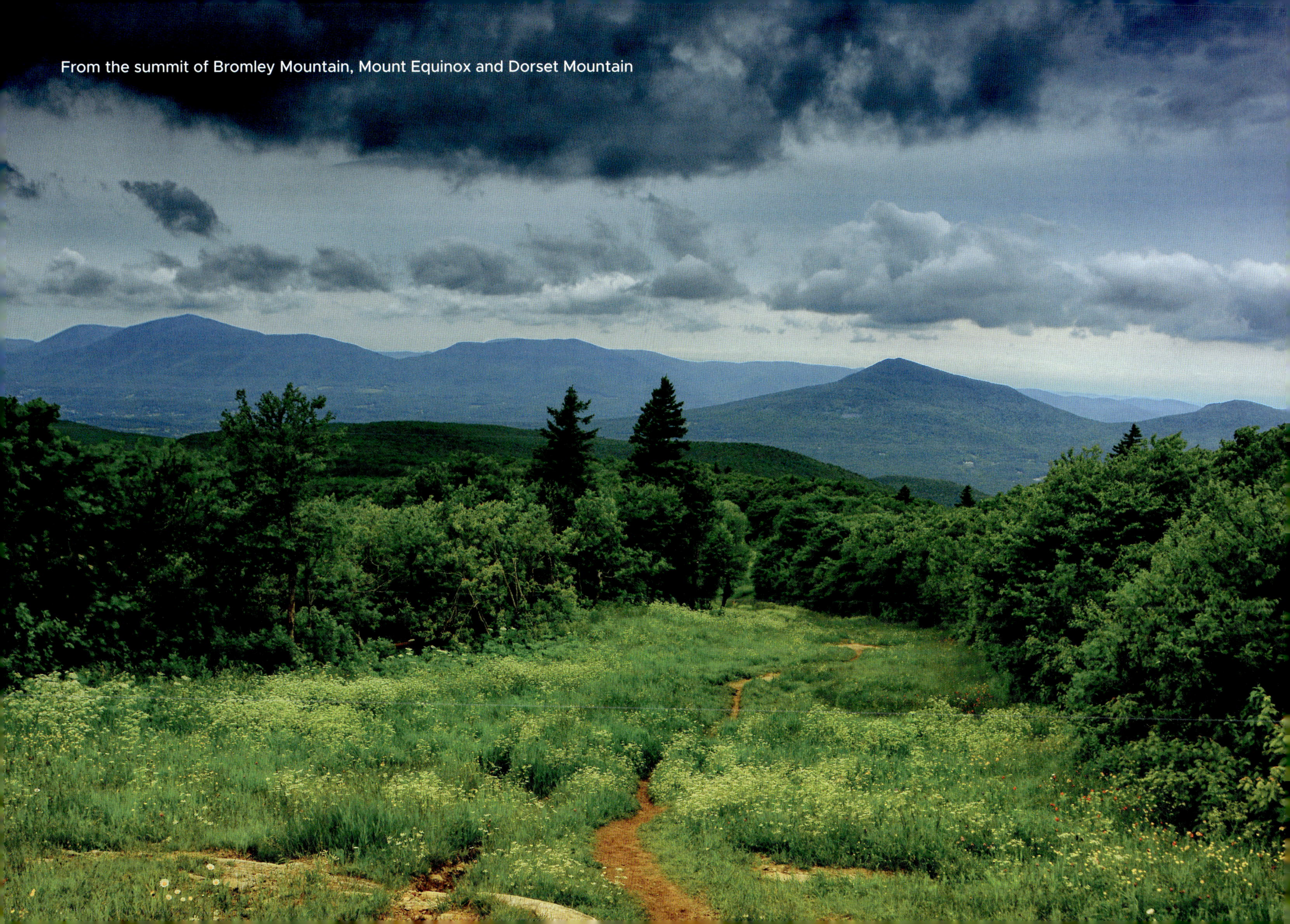

From the summit of Bromley Mountain, Mount Equinox and Dorset Mountain

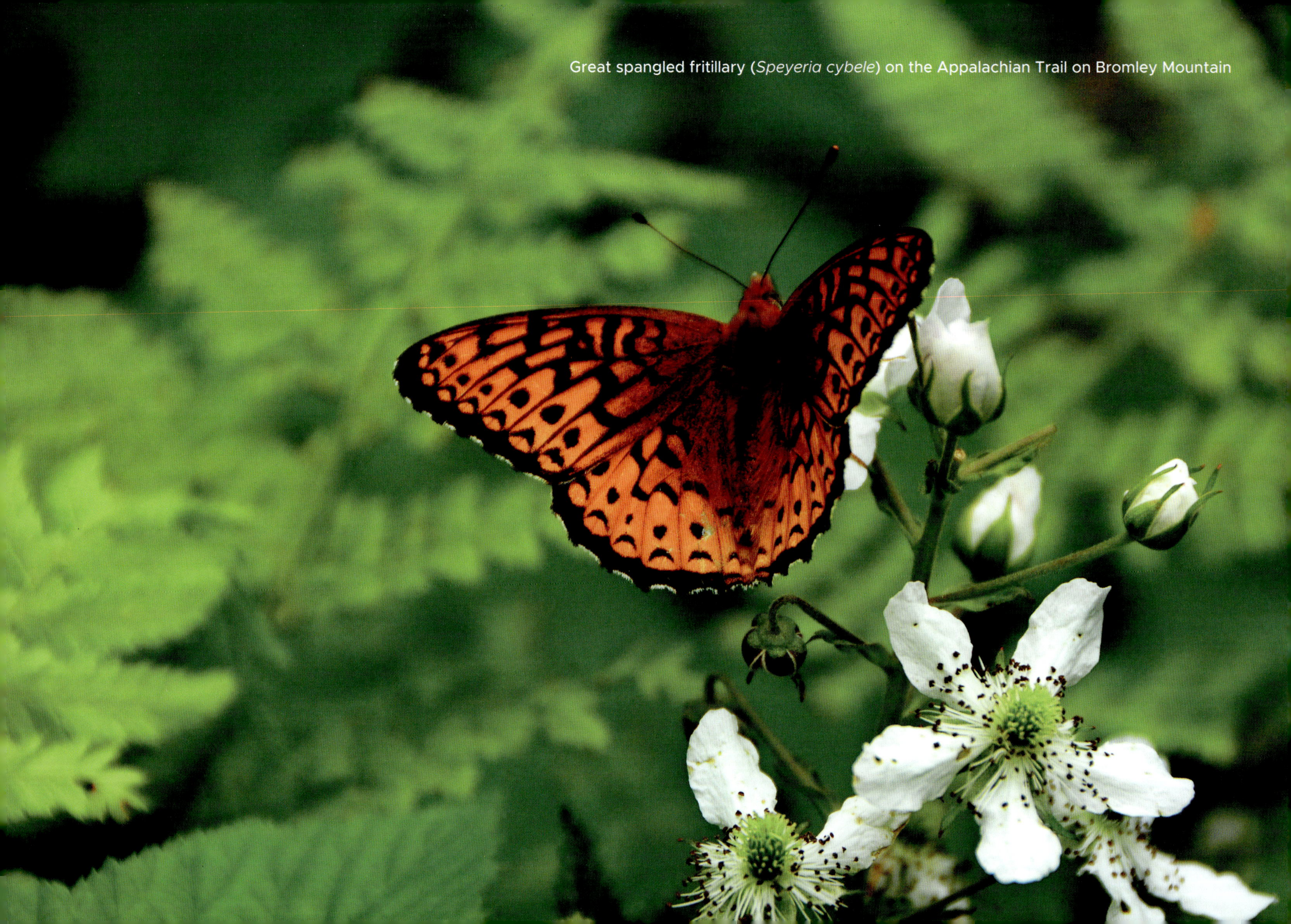

Great spangled fritillary (*Speyeria cybele*) on the Appalachian Trail on Bromley Mountain

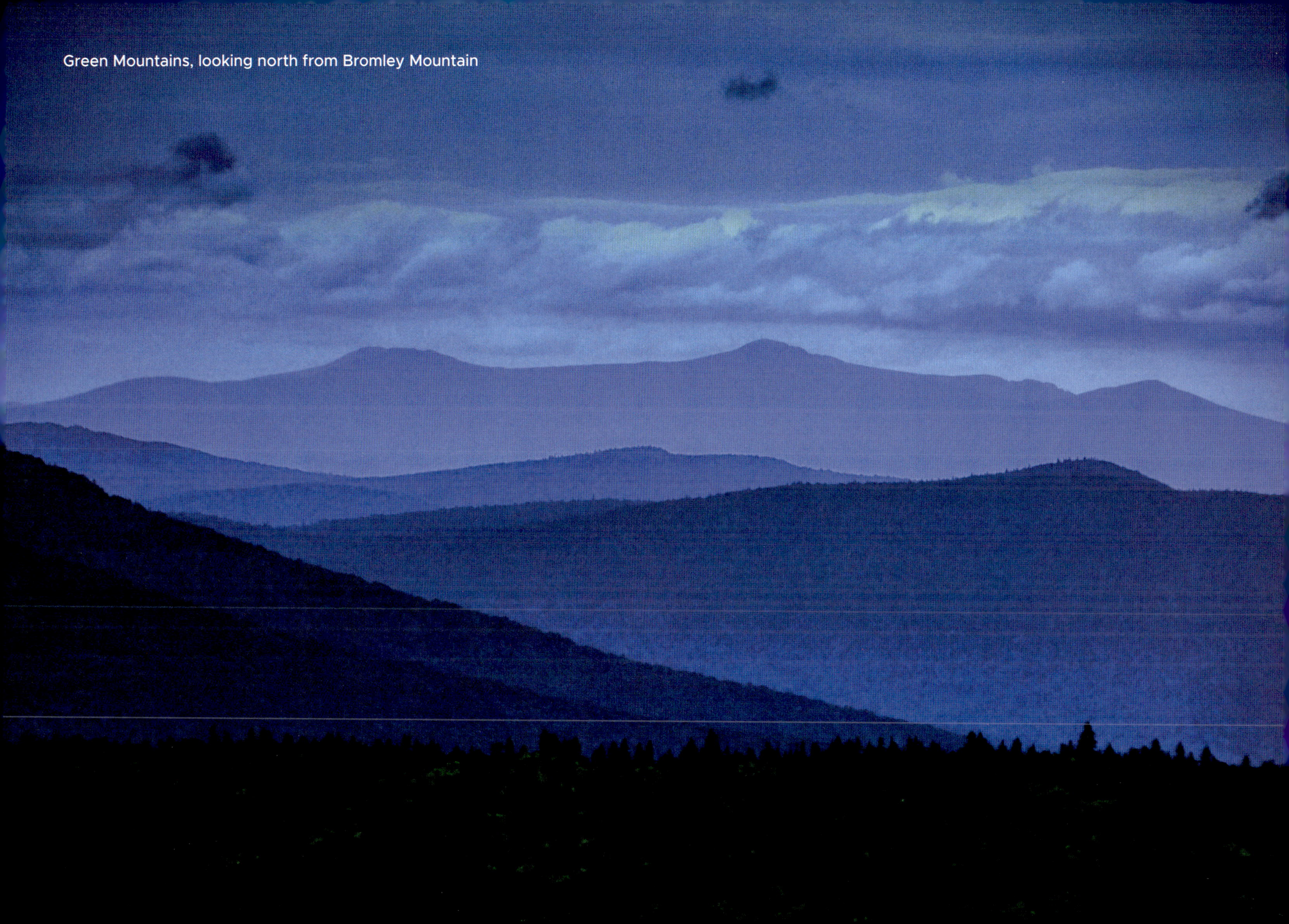

Green Mountains, looking north from Bromley Mountain

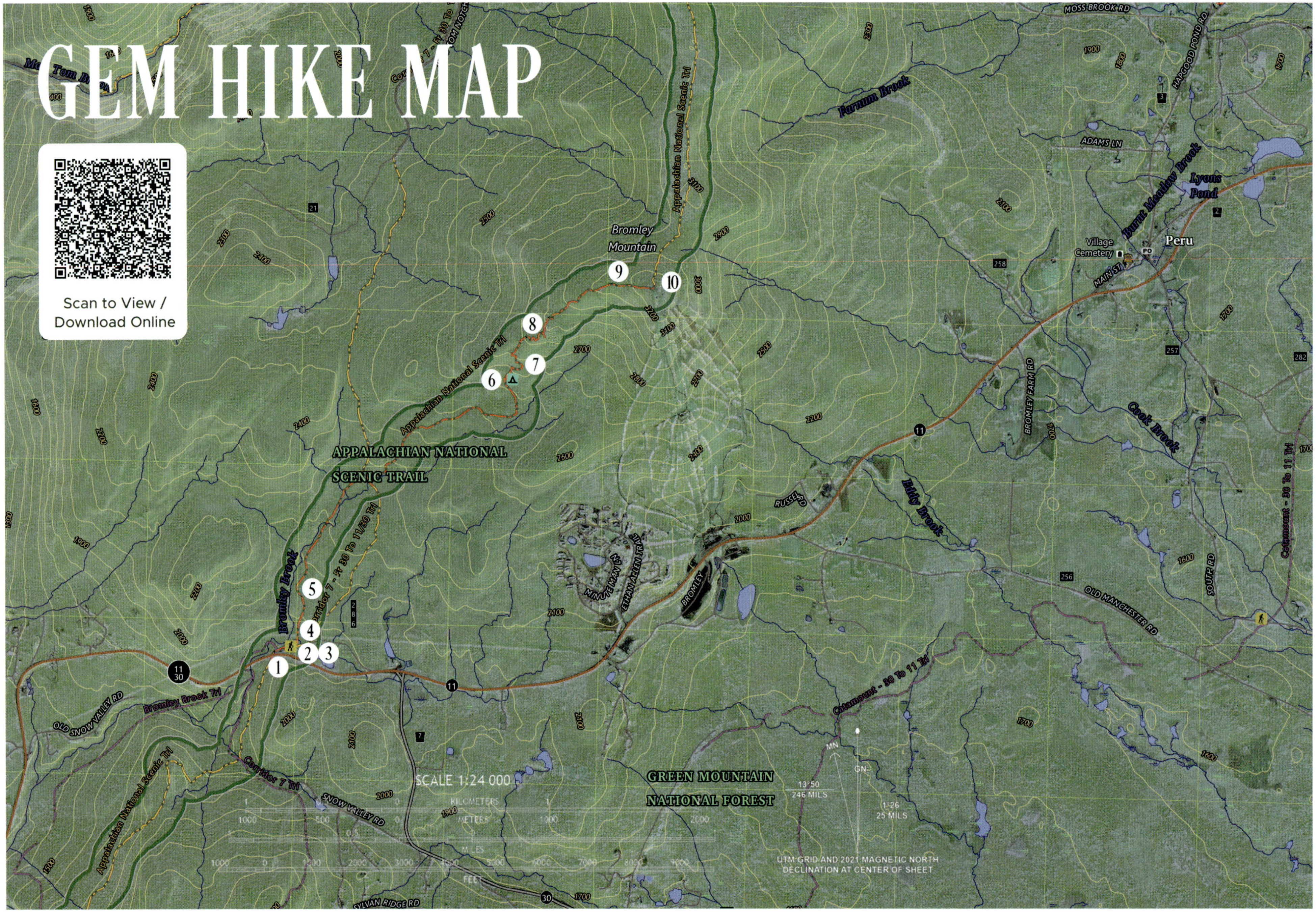
GEM HIKE MAP
Scan to View / Download Online
Bromley Mountain
Appalachian National Scenic Trl
APPALACHIAN NATIONAL SCENIC TRAIL
Farnum Brook
MOSS BROOK RD
HAPGOOD POND RD
ADAMS LN
Burnt Meadow Brook
Lyons Pond
Village Cemetery
Peru
MAIN ST
BROMLEY FARM RD
Cook Brook
Bully Brook
RUSSELL RD
OLD MANCHESTER RD
SOUTH RD
Catamount - 30 To 11 Trl
Bromley Brook
Bromley Brook Trl
OLD SNOW VALLEY RD
SNOW VALLEY RD
Corridor 7 Trl
SYLVAN RIDGE RD
MINUTEMAN
ETHAN ALLEN
BROMLEY
SCALE 1:24 000
GREEN MOUNTAIN NATIONAL FOREST
UTM GRID AND 2021 MAGNETIC NORTH DECLINATION AT CENTER OF SHEET

DIRECTIONS TO THE TRAILHEAD(S)

From Manchester, Vermont, to Bromley Mountain Trailhead on VT 11/30 at geographic coordinate 43.207086, −72.970278

1. Head east on Seminary Ave. toward West Rd. and travel for 69 feet
2. Slight left onto Main St. and travel for 0.8 mile
3. At the traffic circle, continue straight to stay on Main St. and travel for 0.3 mile
4. At the traffic circle, take the first exit onto VT 11 E / VT 30 S / Depot St.; continue to follow VT 11 E / VT 30 S for 5.8 miles
5. Turn left onto Old Turnpike Rd.; the trailhead parking is immediately on the right

GEM HIKE DIRECTIONS

1. Leave the VT 11/30 trailhead on the Appalachian Trail, going north
2. Continue on the Appalachian Trail for 0.1 mile
3. Reach and cross a gravel road and continue on the Appalachian Trail for 0.1 mile
4. Cross brook on the bridge and continue on the Appalachian Trail for 0.1 mile and pass under a power line
5. Continue on the Appalachian Trail for 0.4 mile and cross bridge to cross Bromley Brook
6. Continue for 1.3 miles on the Appalachian Trail to spur trail to Bromley Shelter
7. Continue for 0.1 mile on the Appalachian Trail and pass Bromley Shelter tent platforms
8. Continue for 0.7 mile on the Appalachian Trail, and the trail turns left onto a ski trail; head up the hill
9. Continue on the Appalachian Trail for 0.2 mile, to the summit of Bromley Mountain and its fire tower
10. Retrace your steps back to the trailhead the way you came up

MORE/LESS AMBITIOUS HIKERS

More-ambitious hikers may wish to continue hiking the remaining miles of this section to include Griffith Lake and Baker Peak.

Less ambitious hikers may wish to ride the ski lift on Bromley Mountain, but please note that the chair lift does not go back to the trailhead on Vermont 11/30.

CHAPTER 16

THE APPALACHIAN TRAIL FROM KEIFFER ROAD OR COLD RIVER ROAD (LOWER) TO US 4, WITH THE ADD-ON OF KILLINGTON PEAK

AREA MAP

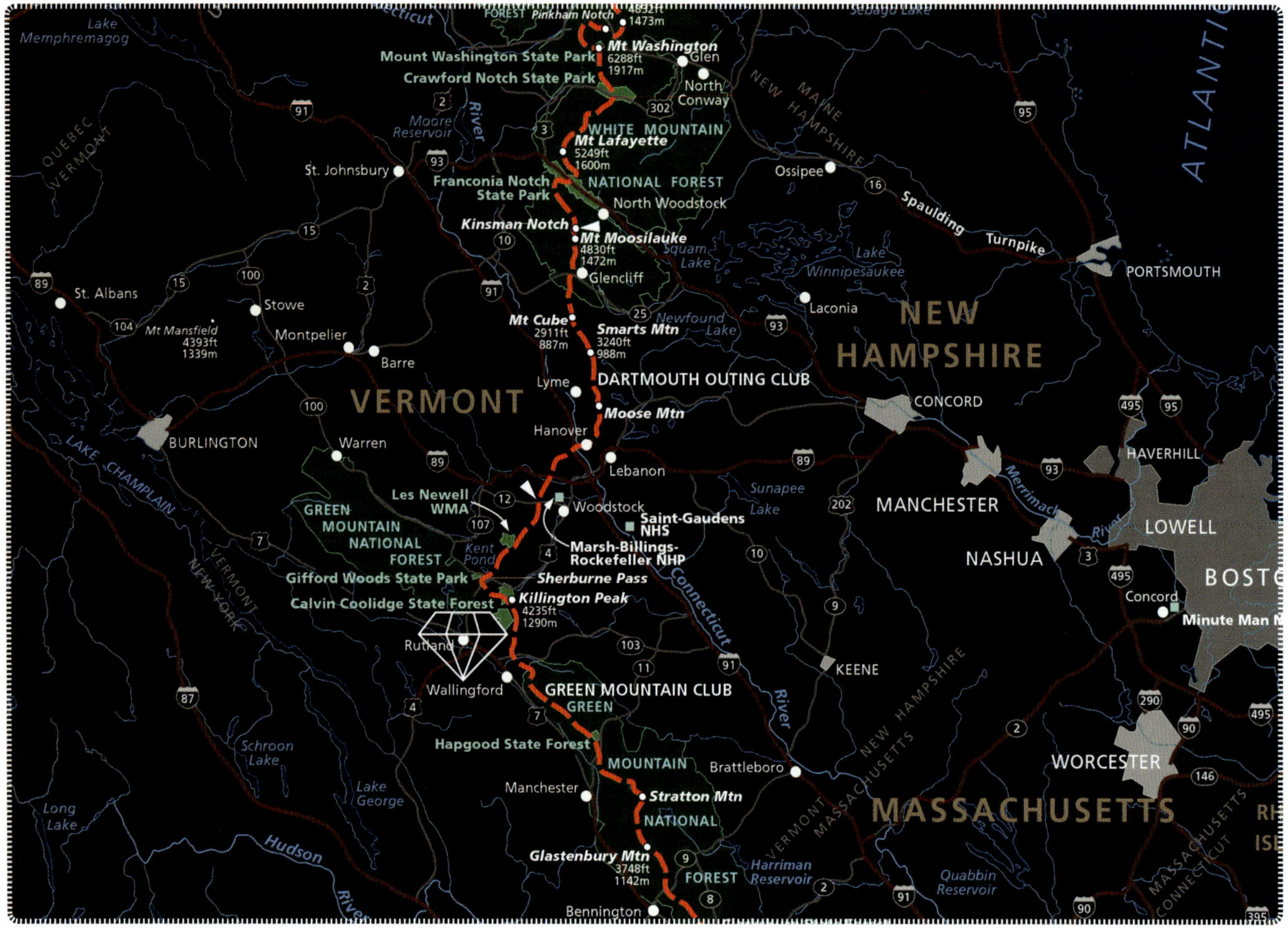

DISTANCE	14.1 miles
ELEVATION GAIN	3,025 feet
ELEVATION LOSS	2,400 feet
LEVEL	Difficult

TYPE: POINT TO POINT

0 10 Kilometers 50

0 10 Miles 50

Appalachian National Scenic Trail

Boundary of CLUB management section

North

GEM HIKE

PERSONAL TOUCH

This is what I trained for. In 2019, I hiked the northern Virginia rollercoaster, two Shenandoah National Park trips, a northern Vermont trip on the Appalachian Trail, and a southern New Hampshire trip, to train for this trip's section. It was a perfect way to peak. It was fitting that the highest point of the Appalachian Trail since Virginia, Killington Peak, was there for the challenge.

The views were outstanding. In one direction, to the east, you could see the White Mountains, and if that was not good enough, you had the Vermont section of the Appalachian Trail as far as Mount Greylock in Massachusetts to the south. If that still wasn't good enough, there were more Green Mountains where the Vermont Long Trail continues to the Canada border to the north, and last, to the west, you had the New York Adirondacks and Lake Champlain. These ridgelines were like waves and ripples of a surf when a hurricane is rapidly approaching the coast, but in all directions.

BRIEF OVERVIEW

Killington Peak, standing at 4,241 feet, is one of Vermont's five 4,000-footers, a group of high peaks that also include Mount Mansfield, Camel's Hump, Mount Abraham, and Mount Ellen. These summits are celebrated for their elevation, their views, and the fact that they are a challenge to climb. The views are spectacular, so it is a gem not to miss along the Vermont section of the Appalachian Trail. The Appalachian Trail shares its miles with Vermont's Long Trail. The Appalachian Trail / Long Trail runs 14 miles end to end to the nearest roads. To obtain the summit, a hiker must hike an extra 0.4-mile round trip, using a blue-blaze trail.

DESCRIPTION OF THE GEM HIKE

The Appalachian Trail from Keiffer Road or Cold River Road (lower) to US 4, with the add-on of Killington Peak. Killington Peak is one of Vermont's highest mountains. A blue-blazed trail will take you from the Appalachian Trail to the summit. This 0.2-mile out-and-back from the Appalachian Trail to the summit of Killington Peak is not for individuals afraid of heights.

FLORA, FAUNA, AND VEGETATION

Since Killington Peak is so tall, the Appalachian Trail / Long Trail in this section contains all the ecosystems found in Vermont's Green Mountains. In the lower elevations, Killington starts out as mainly a hardwoods forest, consisting of maple, oak, and birch. As the trail changes direction and ascends, conifers such as spruce and fir appear, with moss as the undergrowth. The alpine zone near the summit supports the lichen on the rocks.

SUMMIT OF KILLINGTON PEAK

The Appalachian Trail / Long Trail does not summit the Appalachian Trail, so this gem can be easily missed. To reach the gem, you will have to hike from the north or south to the blue-blaze trail. The blue-blaze trail is 0.2 mile from the summit of Killington Peak. This trail is extremely rugged and not meant for someone who fears heights.

EXPANSIVE VIEWS

The summit of Killington Peak is a gem of the Appalachian Trail for its unbelievable views. The views are expansive, showing the Green Mountains and beyond. If it is a partly cloudy day, the clouds add an extra dimension to the landscape as they float by and often collide with the surrounding Green Mountains.

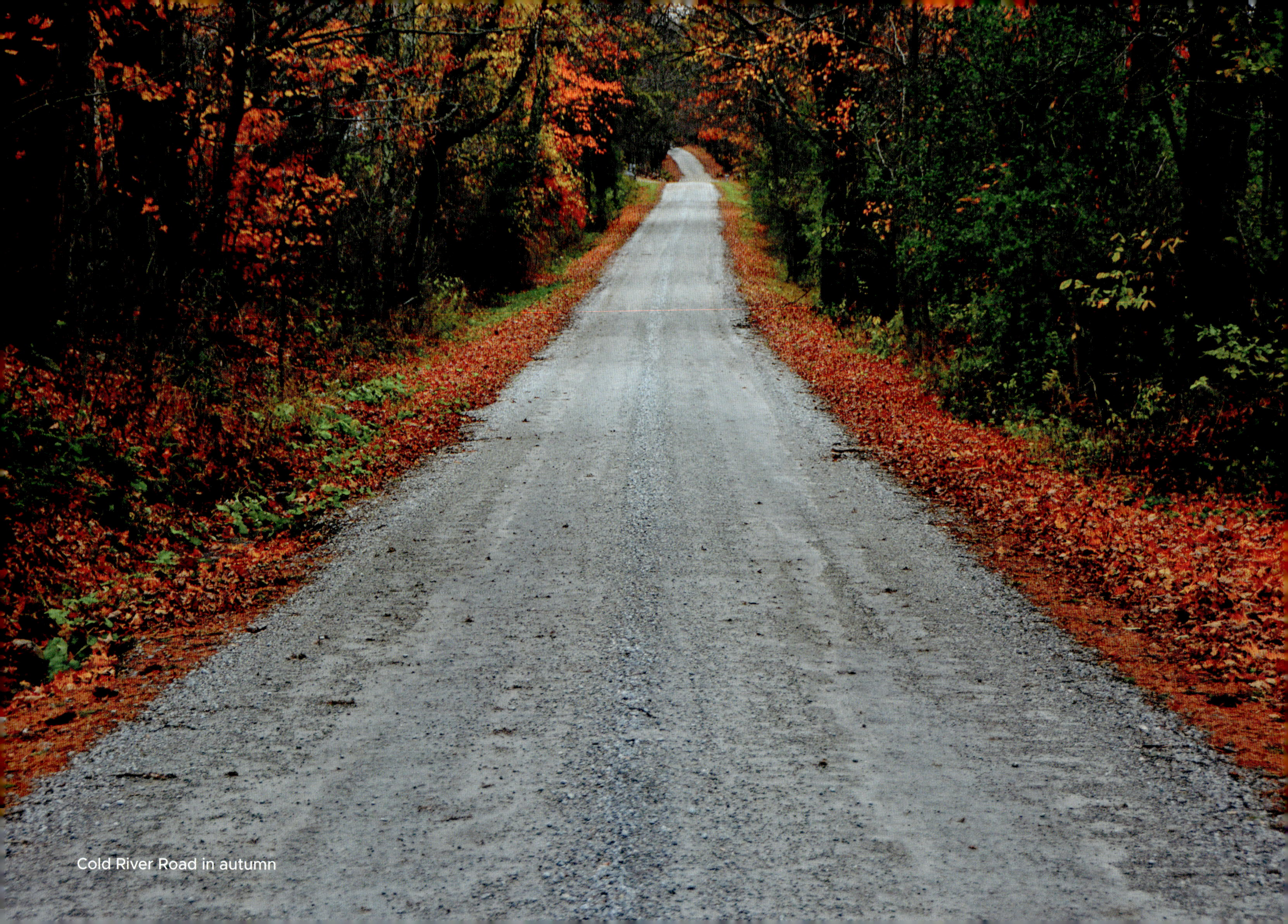

Cold River Road in autumn

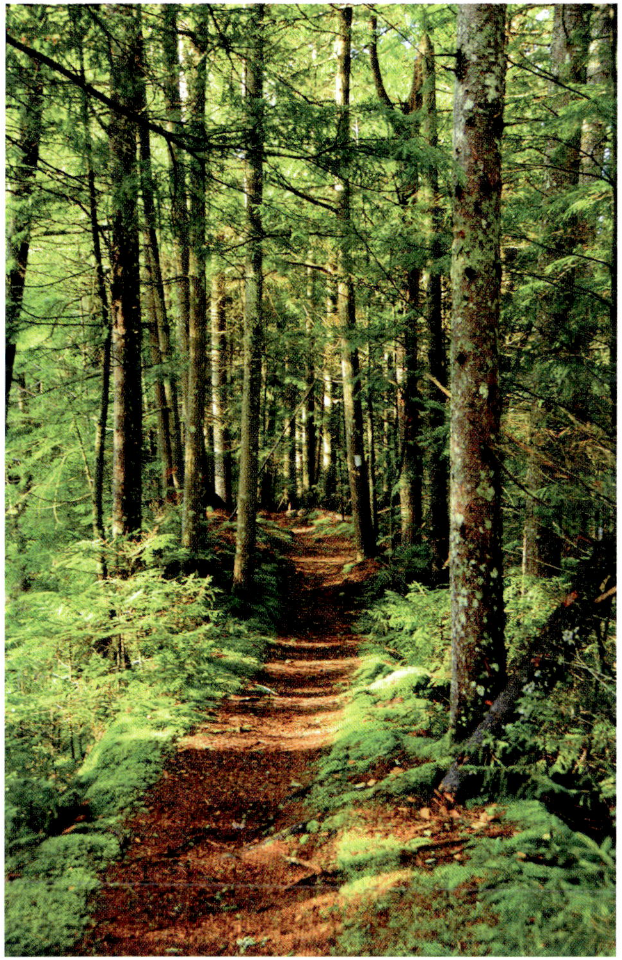

The Appalachian Trail in Vermont

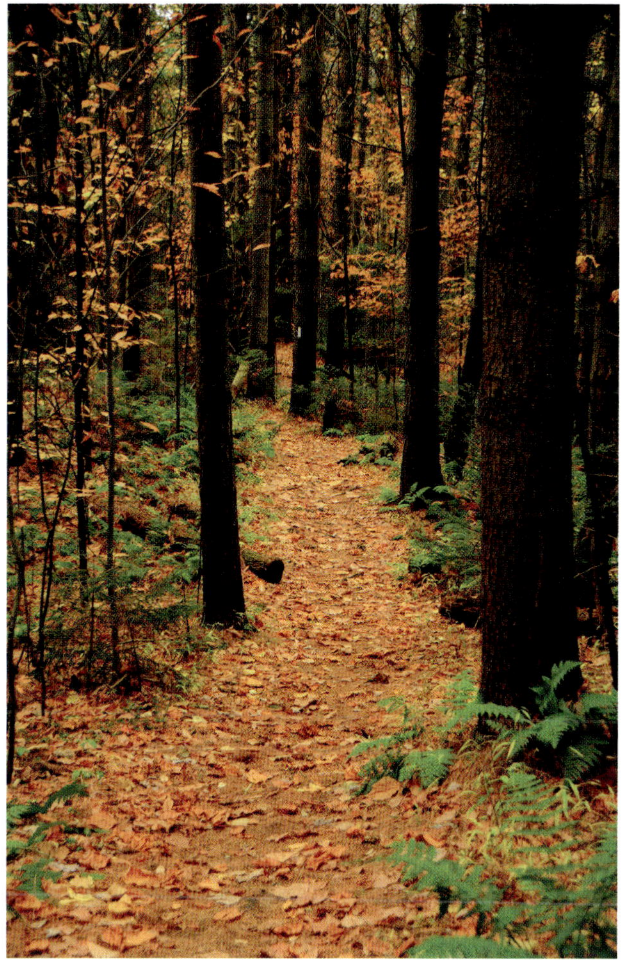

The Appalachian Trail in Vermont in autumn

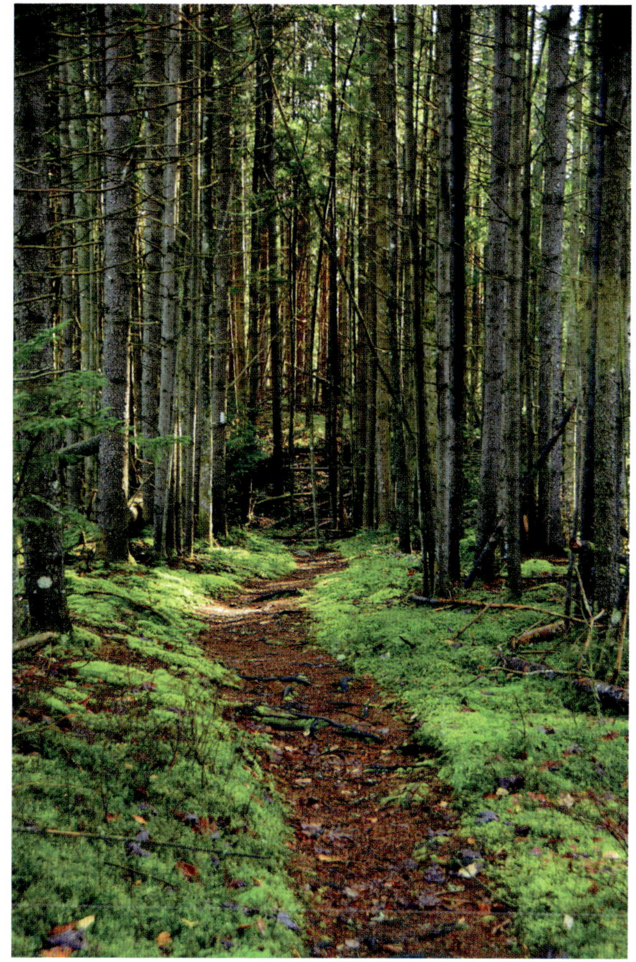

Coniferous trees line the Appalachian Trail on Killington Peak

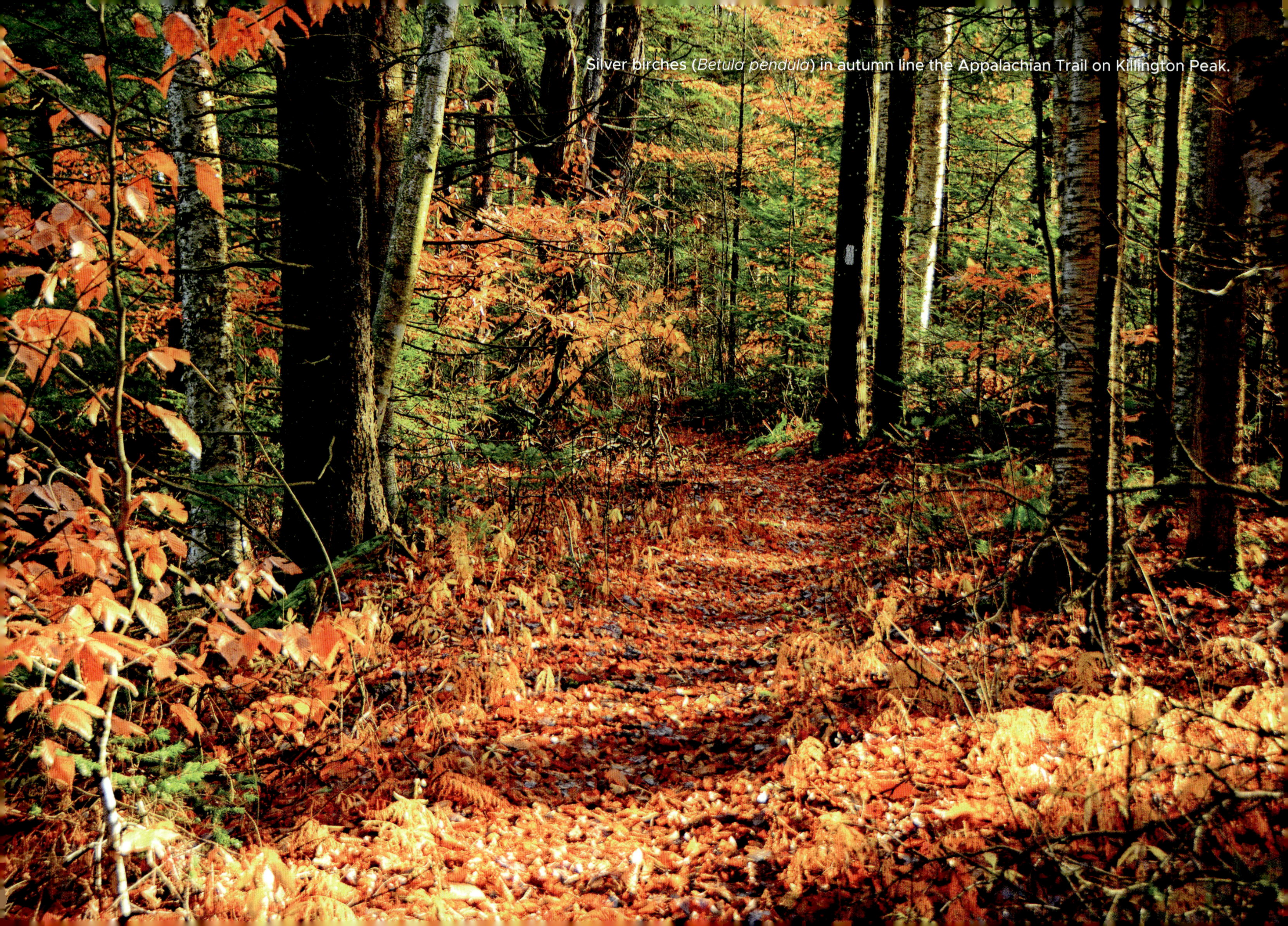

Silver birches (*Betula pendula*) in autumn line the Appalachian Trail on Killington Peak.

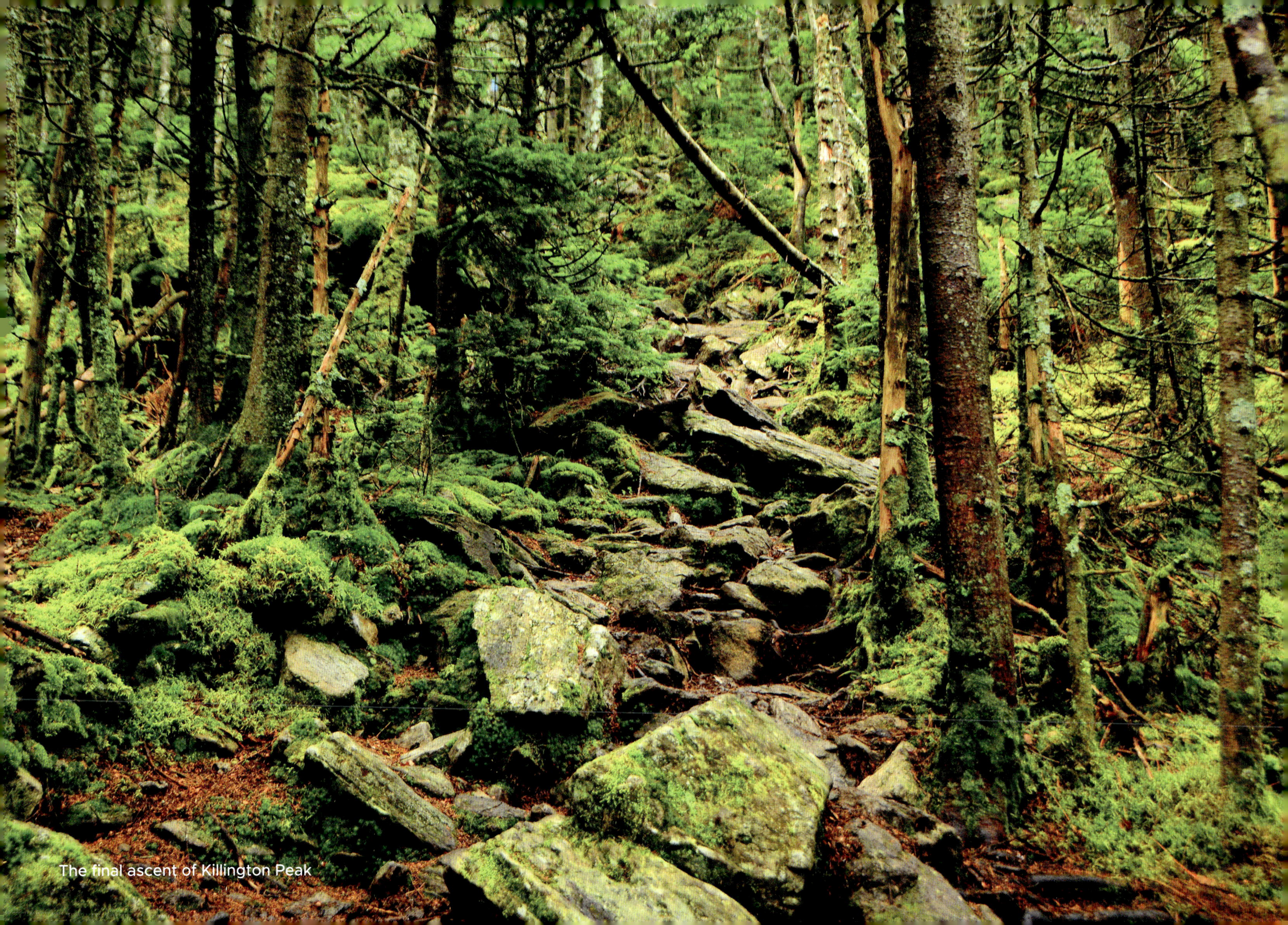

The final ascent of Killington Peak

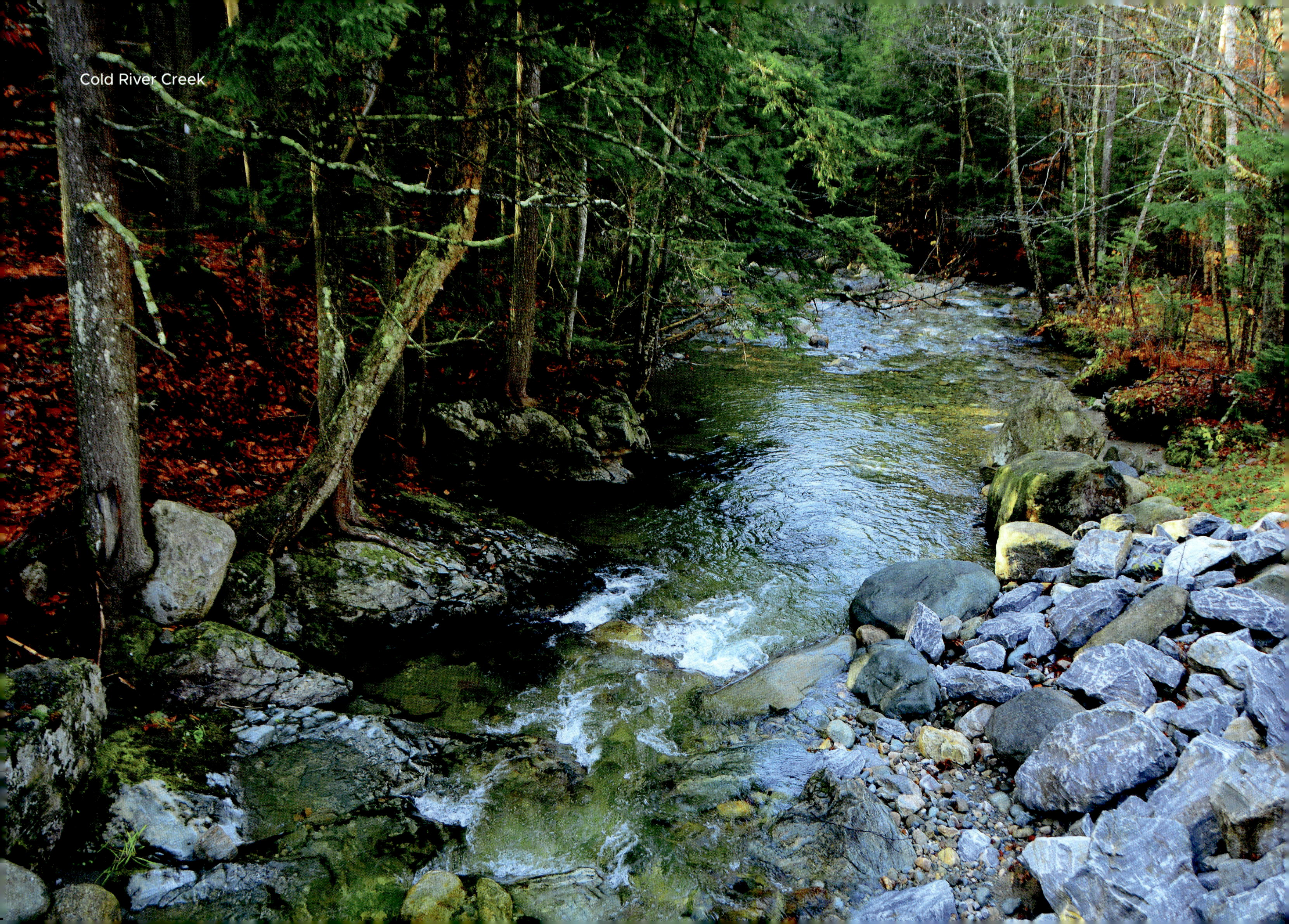

Cold River Creek

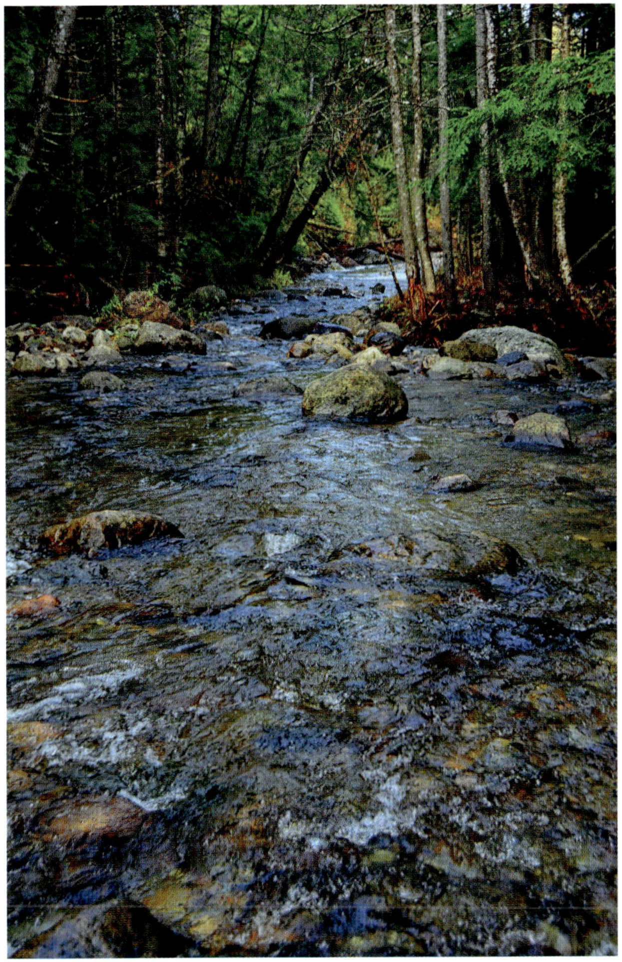

A creek in Vermont along the Appalachian Trail

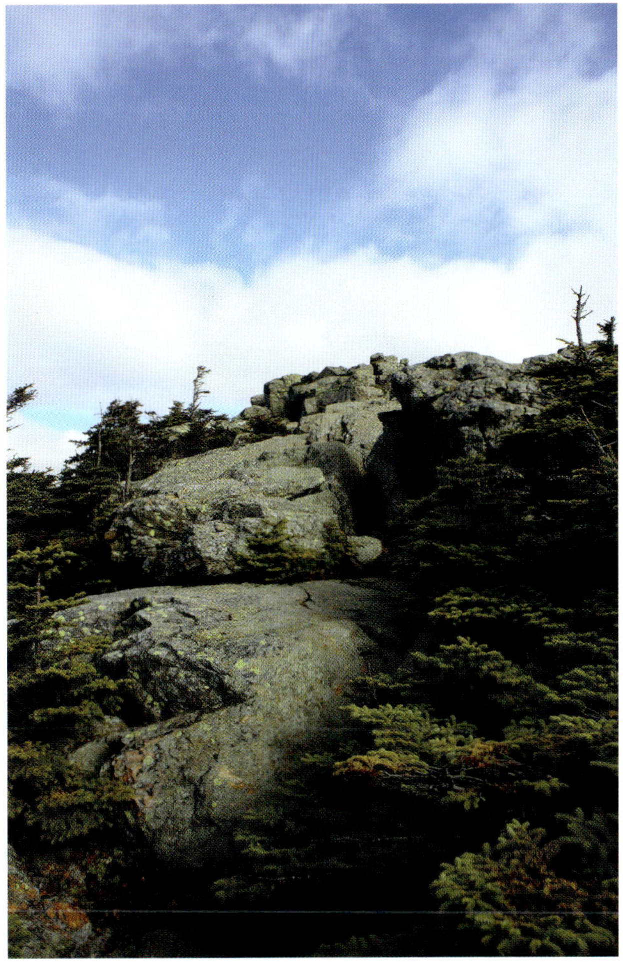

Killington Peak final climb

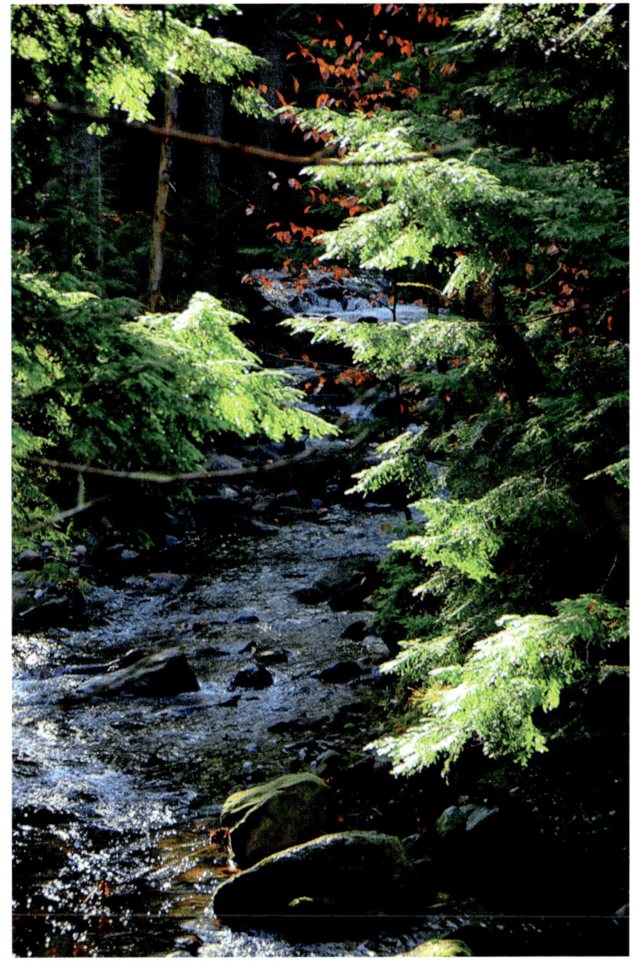

Coniferous trees line a creek in Vermont.

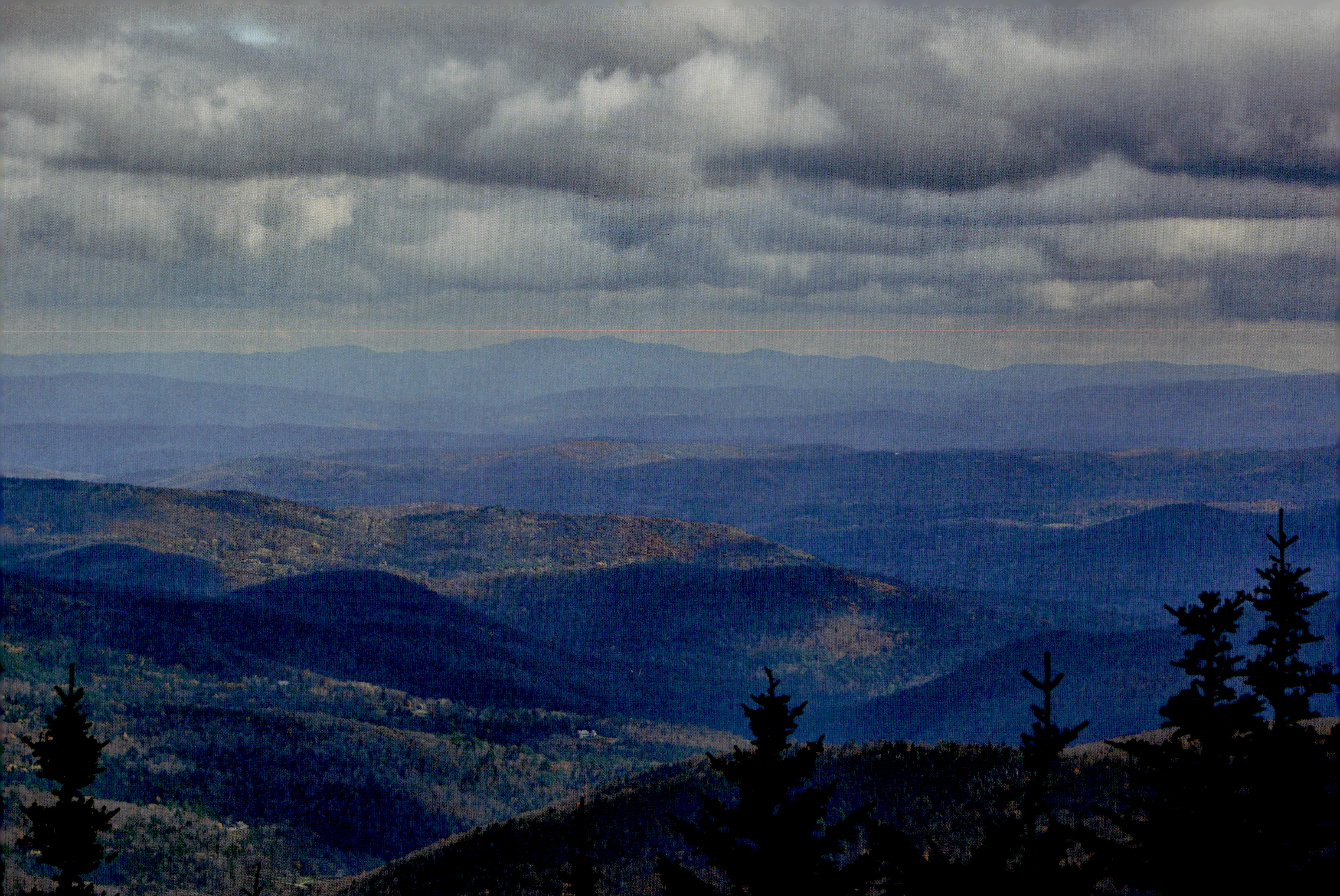

Surrounding Green Mountains in Autumn

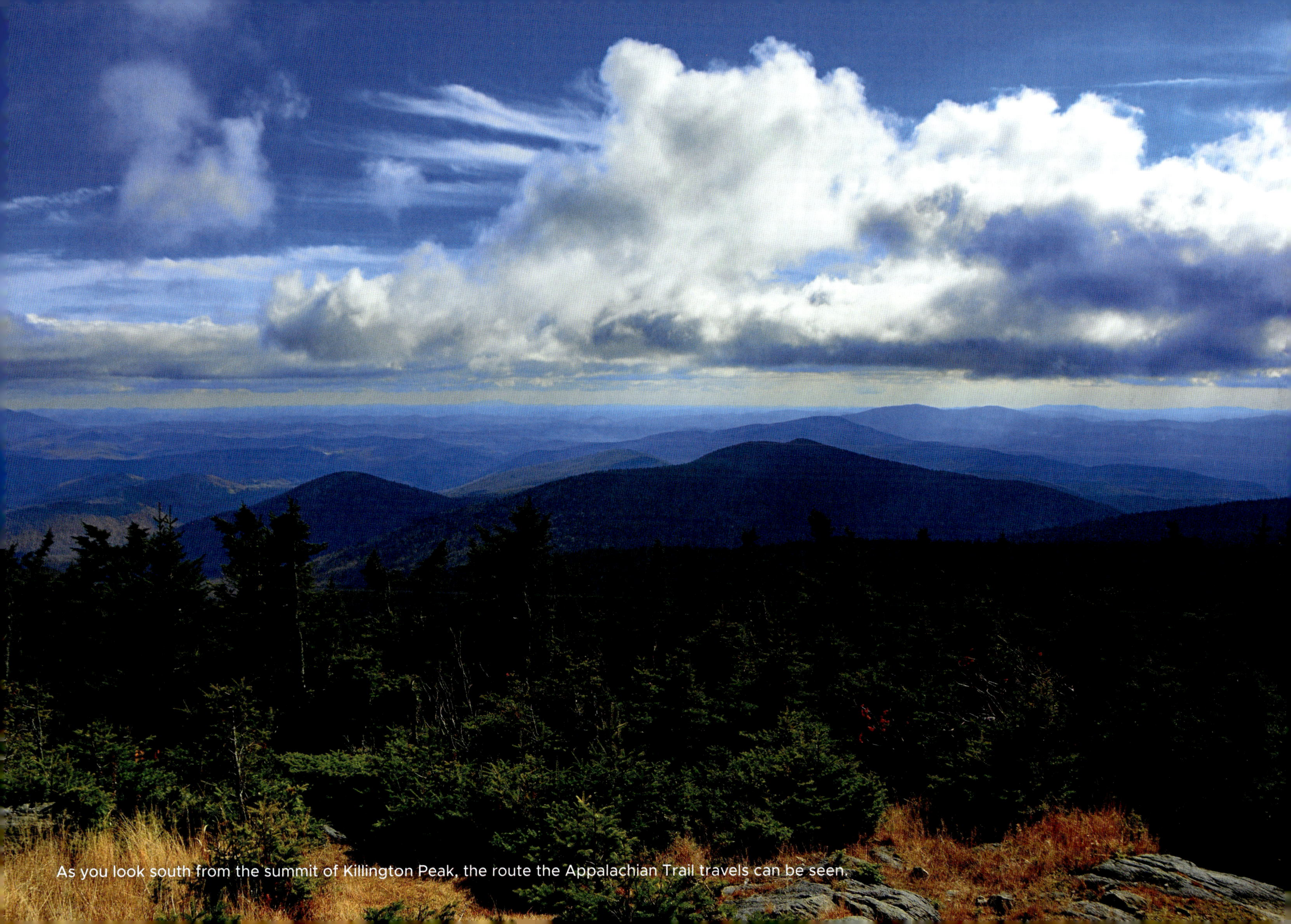

As you look south from the summit of Killington Peak, the route the Appalachian Trail travels can be seen.

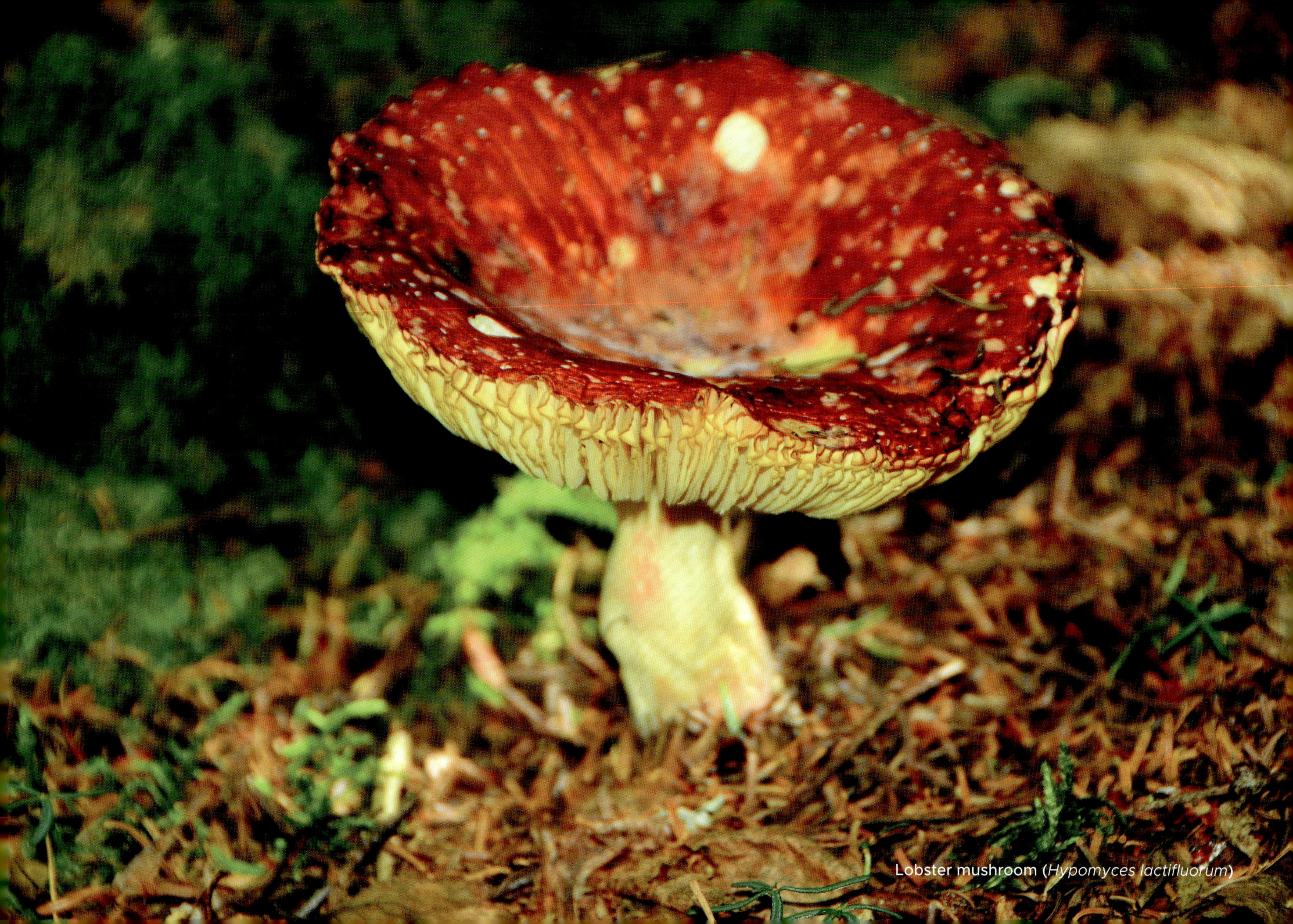

Lobster mushroom (*Hypomyces lactifluorum*)

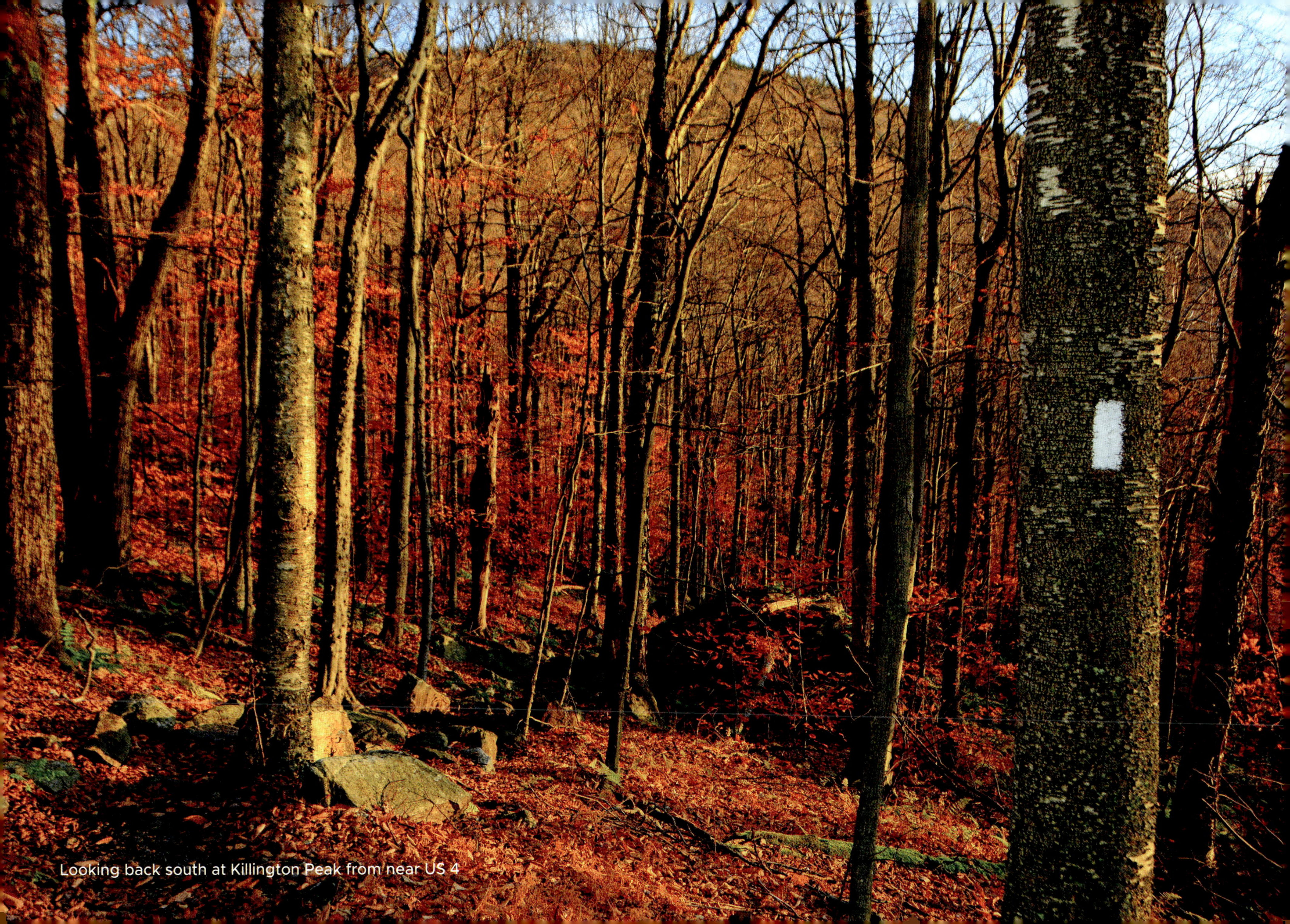

Looking back south at Killington Peak from near US 4

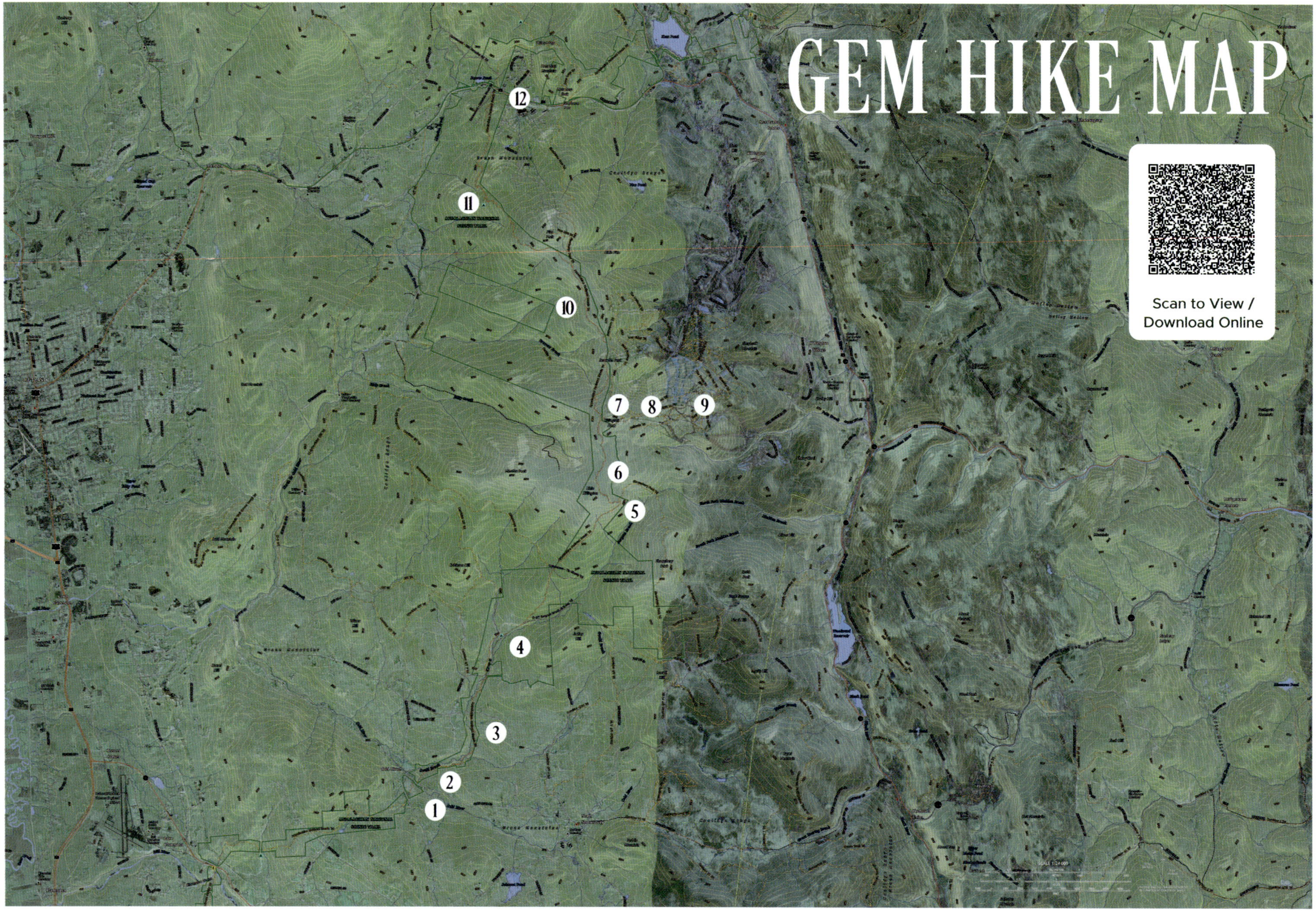
GEM HIKE MAP
Scan to View /
Download Online
12
11
10
7
8
9
6
5
4
3
2
1

DIRECTIONS TO THE TRAILHEAD(S):

From the Appalachian Trail / Long Trail– US Route 4 Trailhead (43.666163, −72.849016) to Keiffer Road Trailhead of the Appalachian Trail (43.533952, −72.873510)

1. Head northwest on US 4 W toward Appalachian National Scenic Trail / Appalachian Trail for 7.3 miles
2. Turn left onto Stratton Rd. and continue for 2.3 miles
3. Continue onto Cold River Rd. for 6.4 miles
4. Turn right onto Keiffer Rd. and continue for 0.4 mile
5. Appalachian National Scenic Trailhead parking on Keiffer Rd. will be on your left

GEM HIKE DIRECTIONS

1. Leave the trailhead on the Appalachian Trail, traveling northbound
2. Continue on the Appalachian Trail for 1 mile and reach Gould Brook
3. Continue on the Appalachian Trail for 0.7 mile to Upper Cold River Rd.
4. Continue on the Appalachian Trail for 1.4 miles to Governor Clement Shelter
5. Continue for 2.5 miles on the Appalachian Trail; arrive at Shrewsbury Peak Trail on the right
6. Continue on the Appalachian Trail for 1.3 miles to a blue-blaze trail on the right
7. Take a right on the blue-blaze trail; 0.2 mile to the summit of Killington Peak
8. After summiting the peak, return to the Appalachian Trail via the 0.2-mile blue-blaze trail
9. Take a left on the Appalachian Trail north and continue for 0.6 mile to Cooper Lodge
10. Continue on the Appalachian Trail for 2.4 miles to Sherburne Pass Trail to Pico Camp
11. Continue on the Appalachian Trail for 1.8 miles to Mendon Lookout and Churchill Scott Shelter Side Trail
12. Continue for 2 miles to US Route 4, Sherburne Pass

MORE/LESS AMBITIOUS HIKERS

More-ambitious hikers may wish to add more miles to the north or the south ends of this hike; after all, 150 miles of the Appalachian Trail are in Vermont.

Less ambitious hikers may wish to make a different hike to Killington's summit by using Killington Ski Area's gondola to shorten their hike.

If you don't wish to shuttle cars, you may approach Killington Peak from the north. If you park in the parking area off US 4, you can hike to the summit of Killington Peak. It is just under a 7-mile hike along the Appalachian Trail / Long Trail southbound to the blue-blaze junction and then an extremely rugged 0.2 mile to the summit of Killington Peak.

CHAPTER 17

VERMONT ROUTE 12 TO CLOUDLAND ROAD AND BACK

AREA MAP

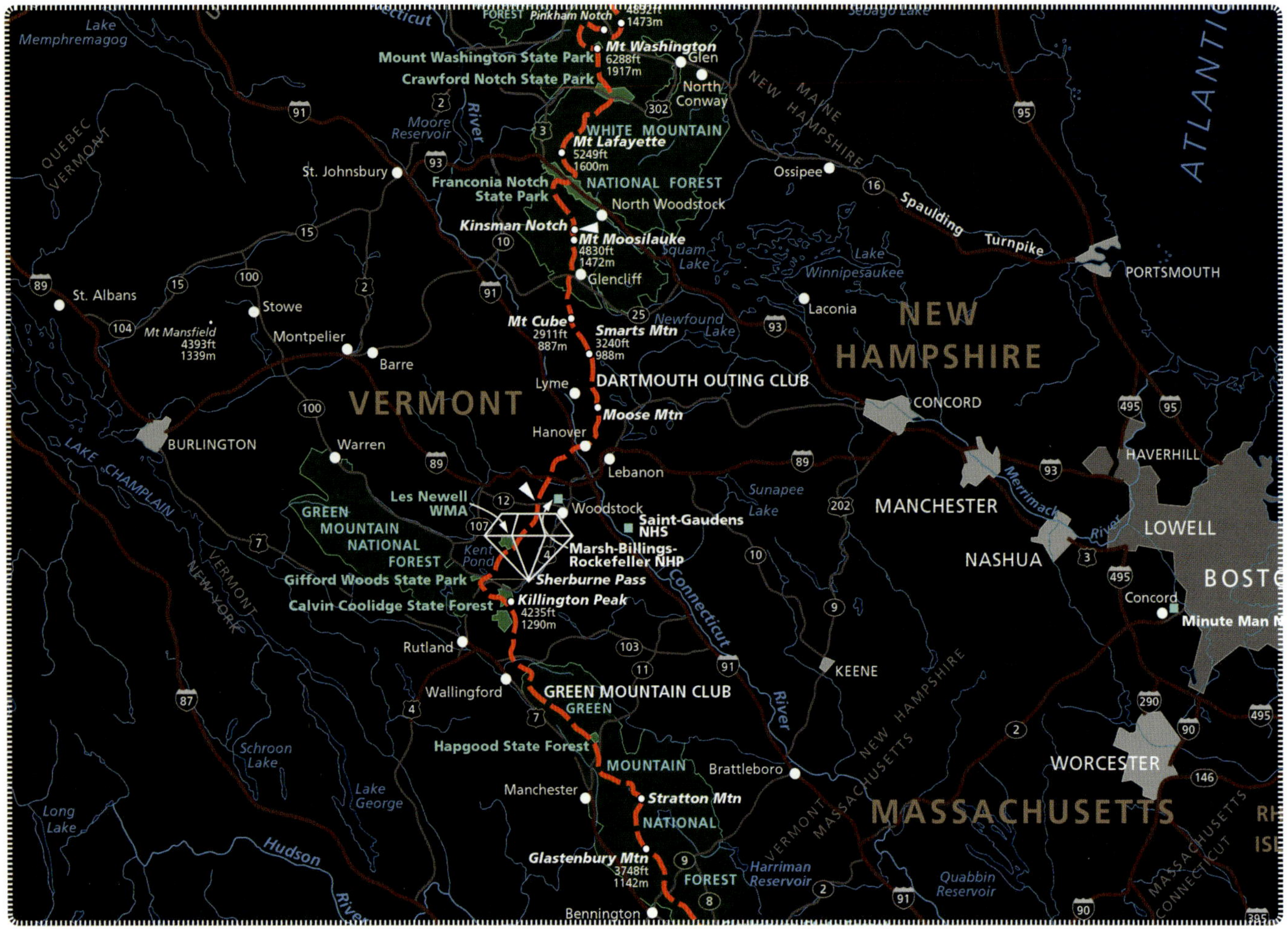

DISTANCE	11 miles
ELEVATION GAIN	2,100 feet
ELEVATION LOSS	2,100 feet
LEVEL	Moderate

TYPE: OUT-AND-BACK

0 10 Kilometers 50

0 10 Miles 50

Appalachian National Scenic Trail

Boundary of CLUB management section

North

GEM HIKE

PERSONAL TOUCH

What do the Roan Highlands, grassy balds in North Carolina / Tennessee, other select hikes in the southern half of Virginia's section of the Appalachian Trail, and this Vermont Cloudland have in common? Open summits. This hike takes the cake from the rest of this list though. Since the Appalachian Trail in the section traverses mainly mostly west to east, it allows hikers and outdoor enthusiasts to witness the moonrise over the Appalachian Trail on their hike instead of just seeing it off to the left or the right without any trail in the foreground.

I planned my hike of this section with a start late in the day, so I could bring the moonrise to life with my photographs. When out after dark, the moon gives the landscape a silvery glow, and I heard the coyotes howling to each other in the distance. It was an exceptionally gorgeous and special treat for me, and I hope you will get to enjoy it too. The views from the open summits of Vermont life below were also stellar on this Vermont section of the Appalachian Trail.

BRIEF OVERVIEW

The hike from Cloudland Road to Vermont Route 12 and back on the Appalachian Trail showcases the natural beauty and ecological diversity of Vermont. With its lush forests, vibrant plant life, and stunning vistas from open summits, this section is an unforgettable experience for hikers seeking both adventure and tranquility. If timed correctly, you can also enjoy views of the moonrise over the Appalachian Trail. This hike also has stellar spring greens like no other because the trees are very diverse. The yellows, greens, and buds put on a show that is like a second fall.

DESCRIPTION OF THE GEM HIKE

Hiking the Appalachian Trail section from Vermont Route 12 to Cloudland Road is a special treat for hikers and outdoor enthusiasts alike. It passes through several mixes of trees with open vistas that, if timed correctly in the spring, can be like a second fall, such are the colors of the buds and new leaves. The vistas give great views of the Appalachian Trail, and the surrounding landscape with full moon rising is an added treat.

FLORA, FAUNA, AND VEGETATION

This Vermont section of the Appalachian Trail contains mixed hardwood forests and coniferous trees. The mixed hardwood parts of the forest include species such as sugar maple and beech trees. The coniferous species include spruce and fir trees. The hike is part of the Appalachian Trail after Maine junction, where the trail heads in an east–west, versus a north-east–southeast, trajectory. This makes a sunlight shift that brings the trees to an earlier and extended growing season along the Appalachian Trail. This allows hikers to enjoy more-pleasing hiking conditions.

SCENIC VIEWS

Vermont offers arguably the best autumn foliage in North America. This Vermont section of the Appalachian Trail in autumn is breathtaking because of vistas that show the surrounding valleys and mountains, and it offers vibrant fall foliage that transforms the scenery into a dazzling display of reds, oranges, and yellows; this draws many visitors to the area, but few know that springtime is like a second fall but without the crowds. The buds and the new leaves of the different species of trees are different hues that offer autumn-like color.

MOON

For those who choose to hike later in the day, witnessing a moonrise can be a truly magical experience. The Appalachian Trail in Vermont provides opportunities to see the moon rising over the surrounding peaks. The tranquility of the forest at dusk/dawn, combined with the sounds of nature, will create a serene atmosphere perfect for reflection and appreciation of nature's beauty. The moon will also appear bigger when it is closer to each of the horizons. If you hike this hike in the dark, the moon will illuminate the landscape with a soft, silvery light.

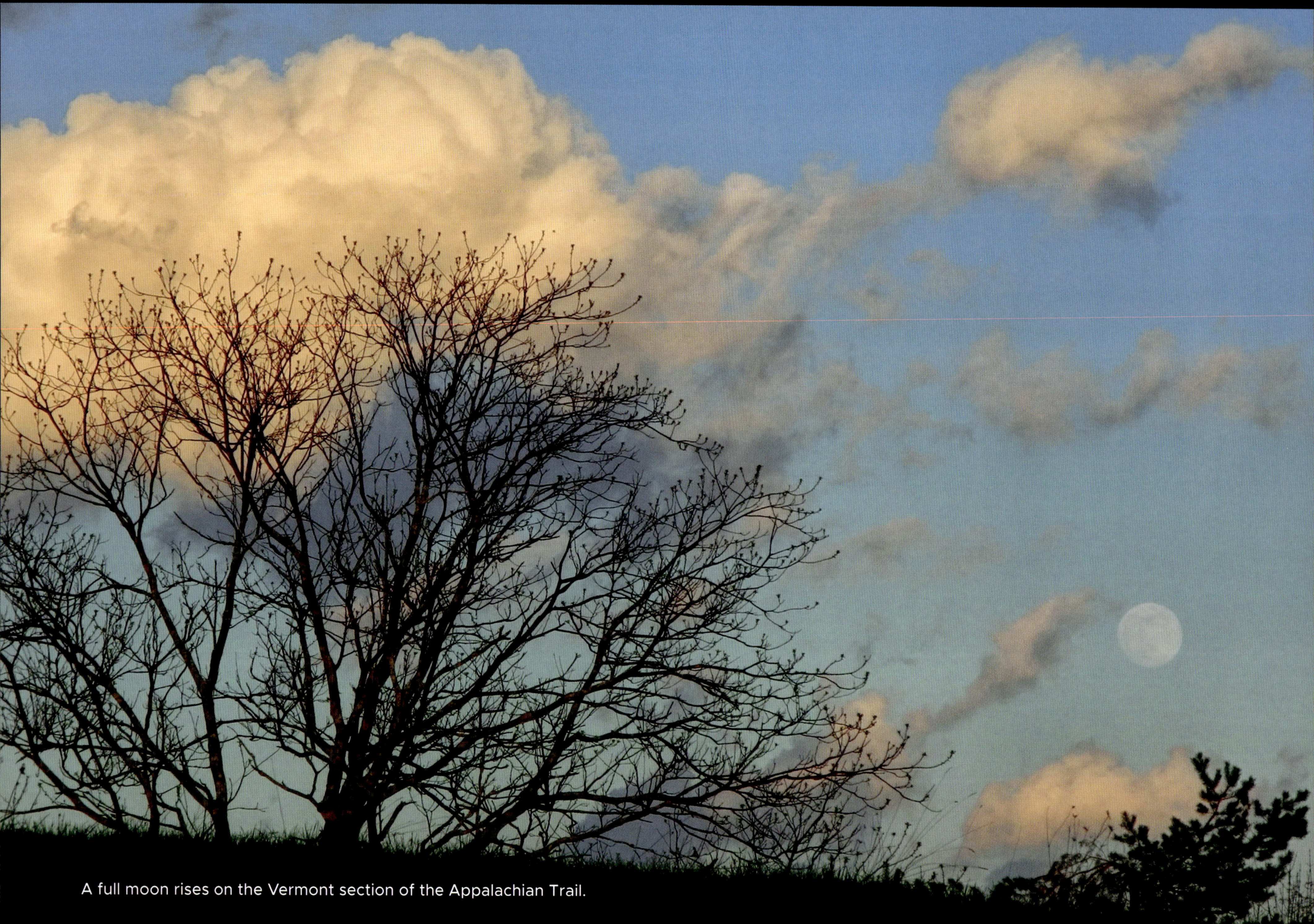

A full moon rises on the Vermont section of the Appalachian Trail.

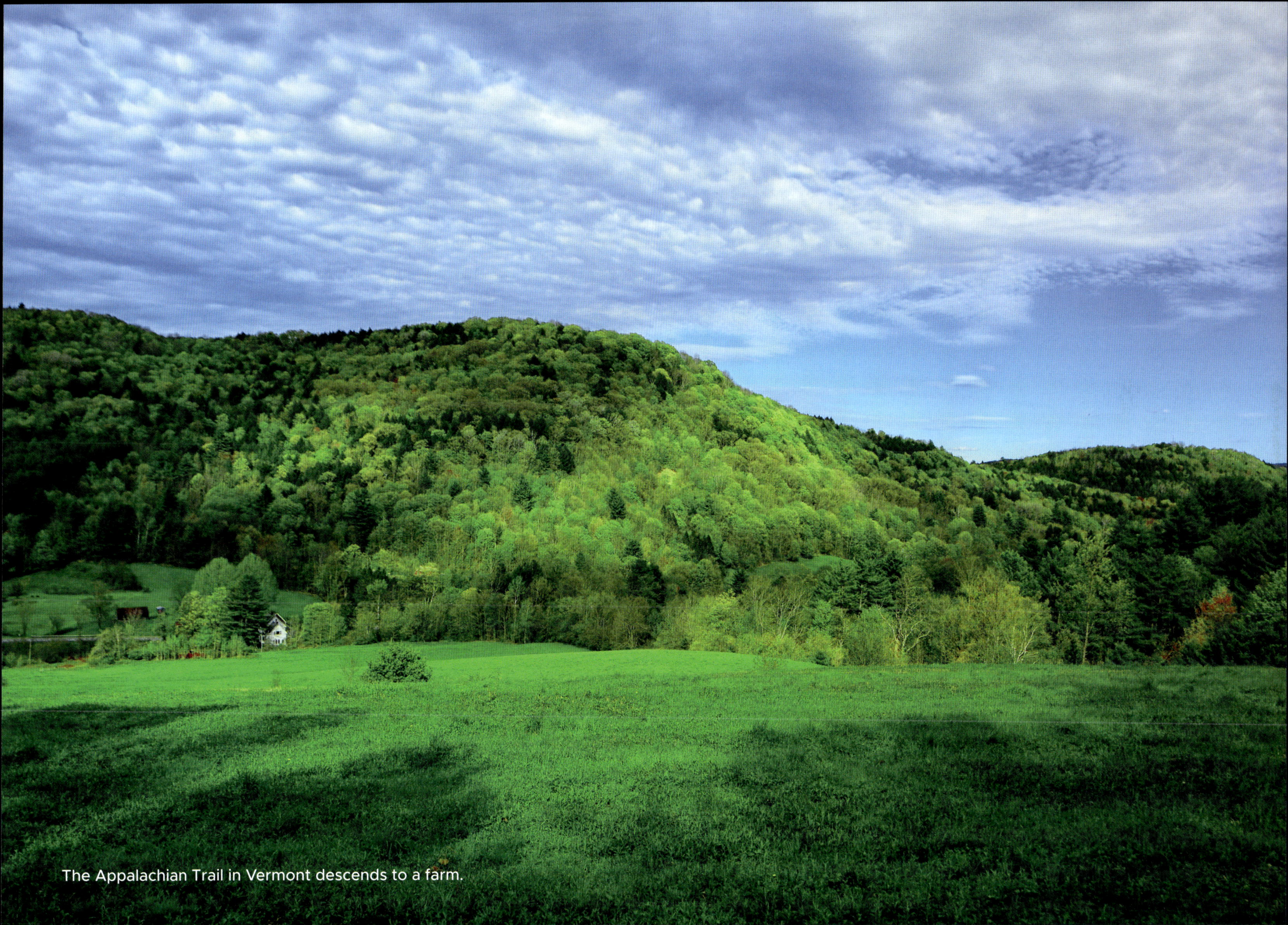
The Appalachian Trail in Vermont descends to a farm.

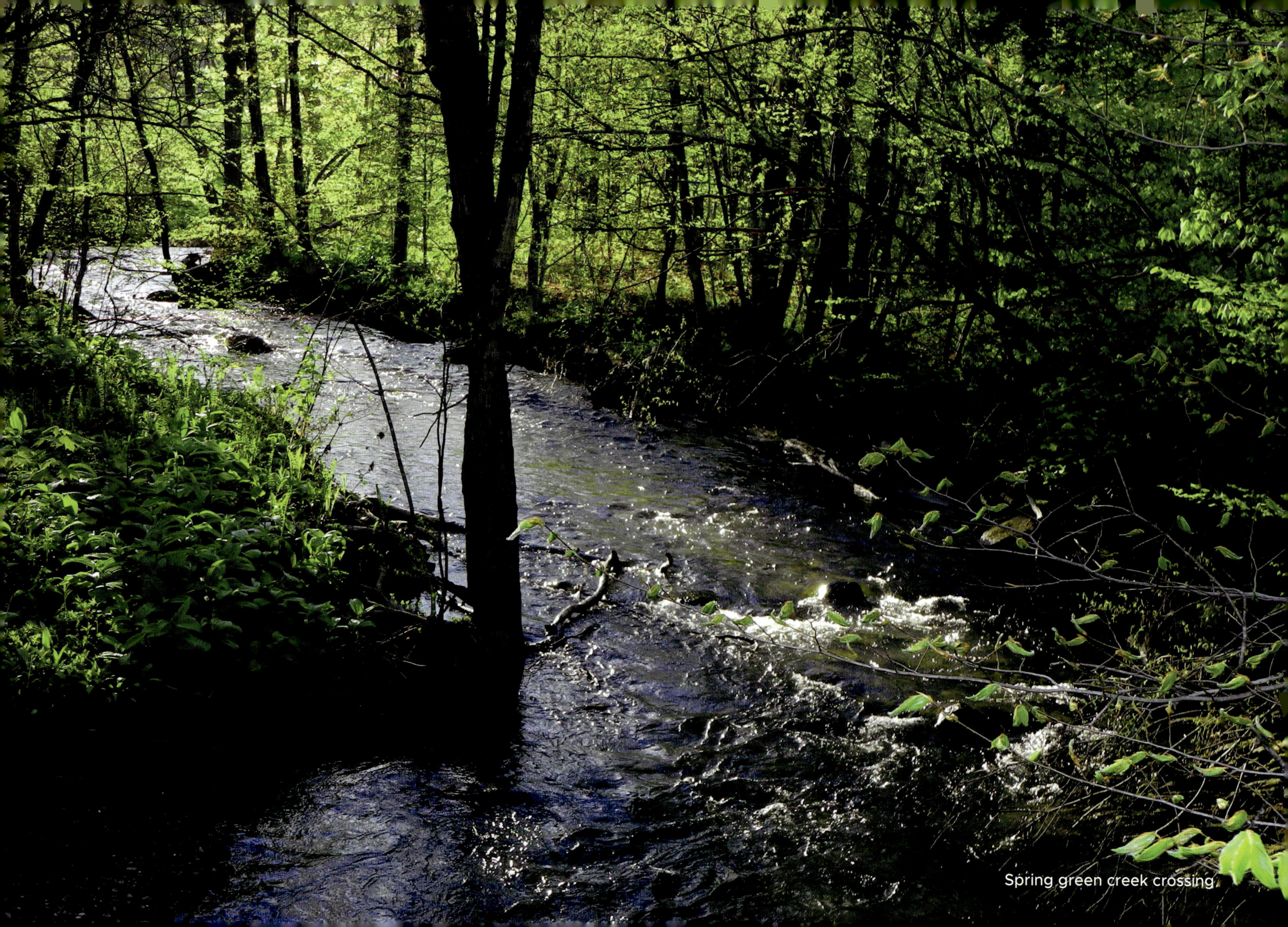

Spring green creek crossing

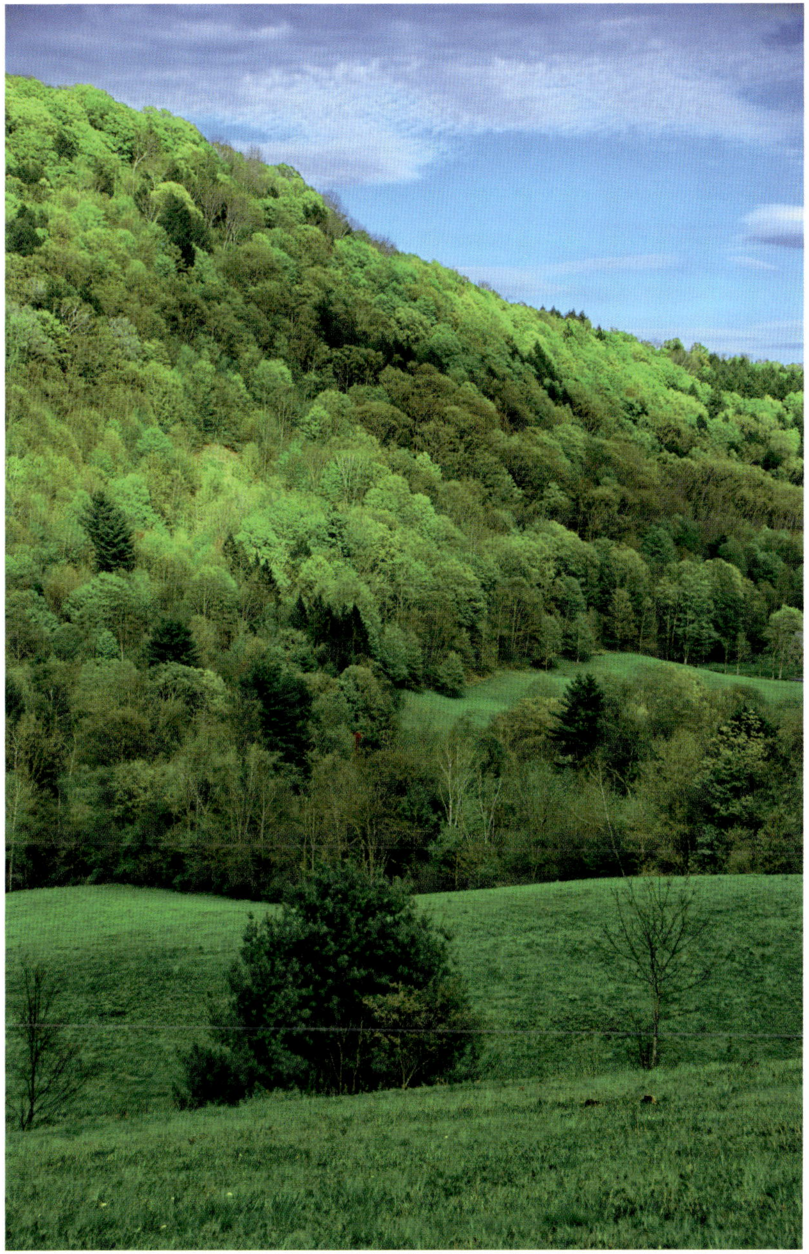

Vermont spring green

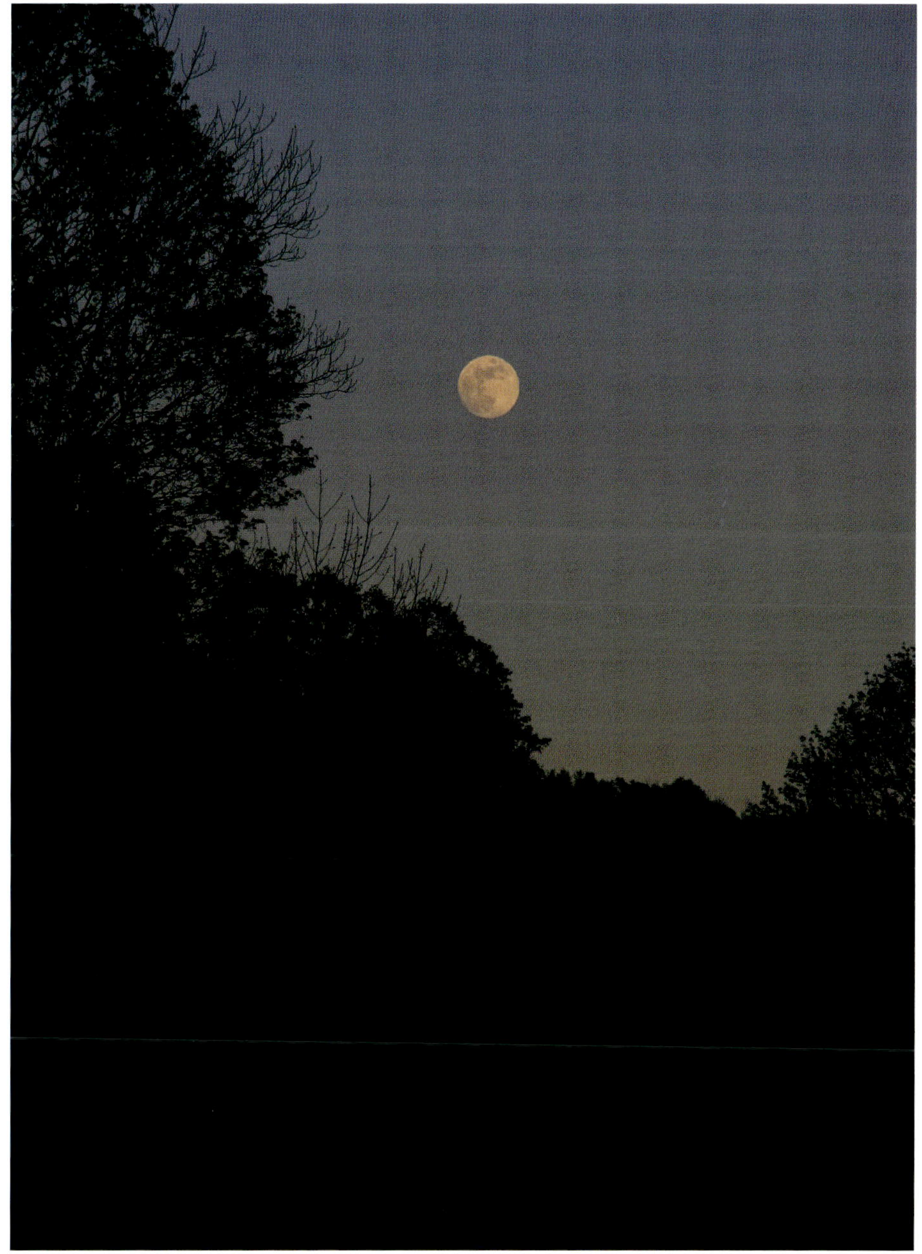

Full moon at blue hour

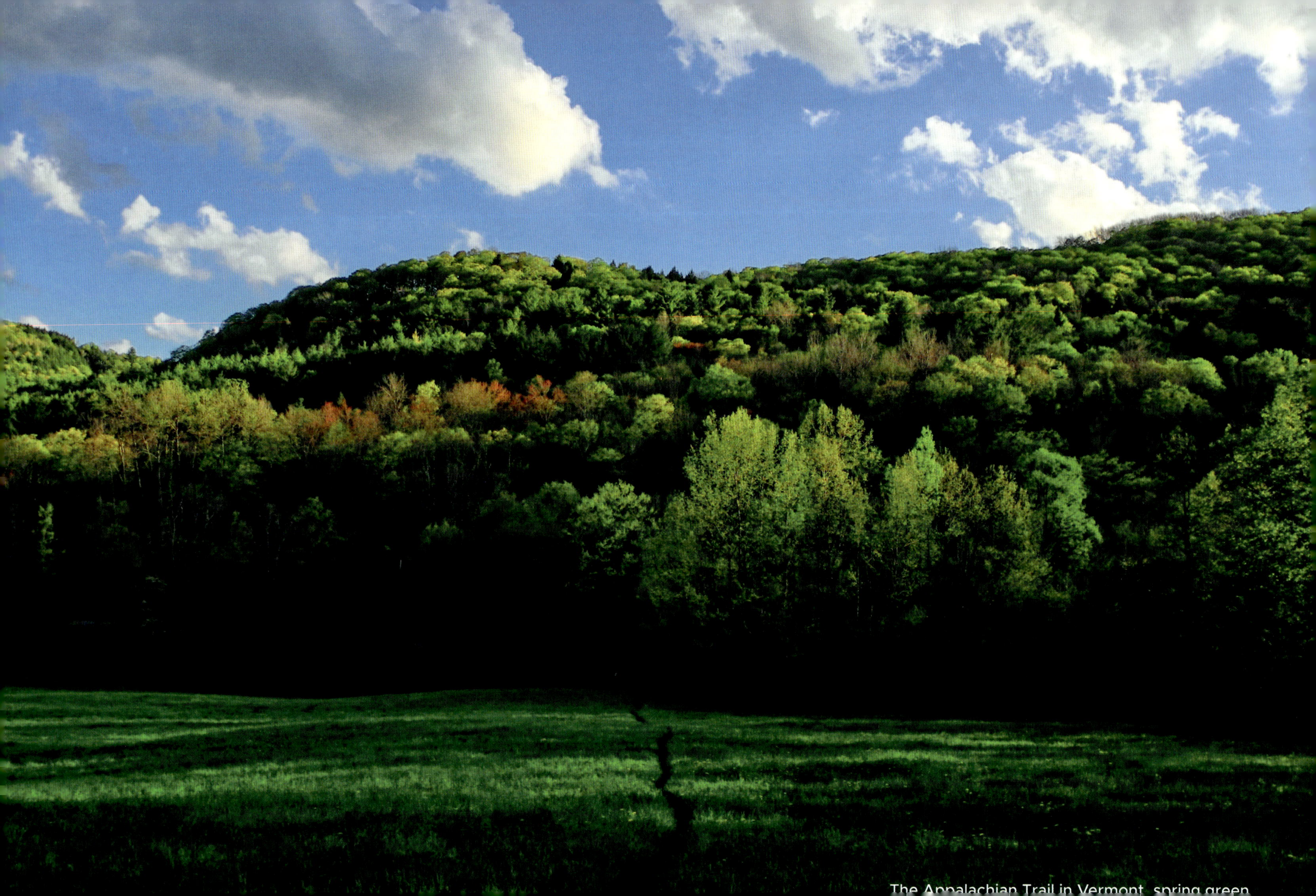

The Appalachian Trail in Vermont, spring green

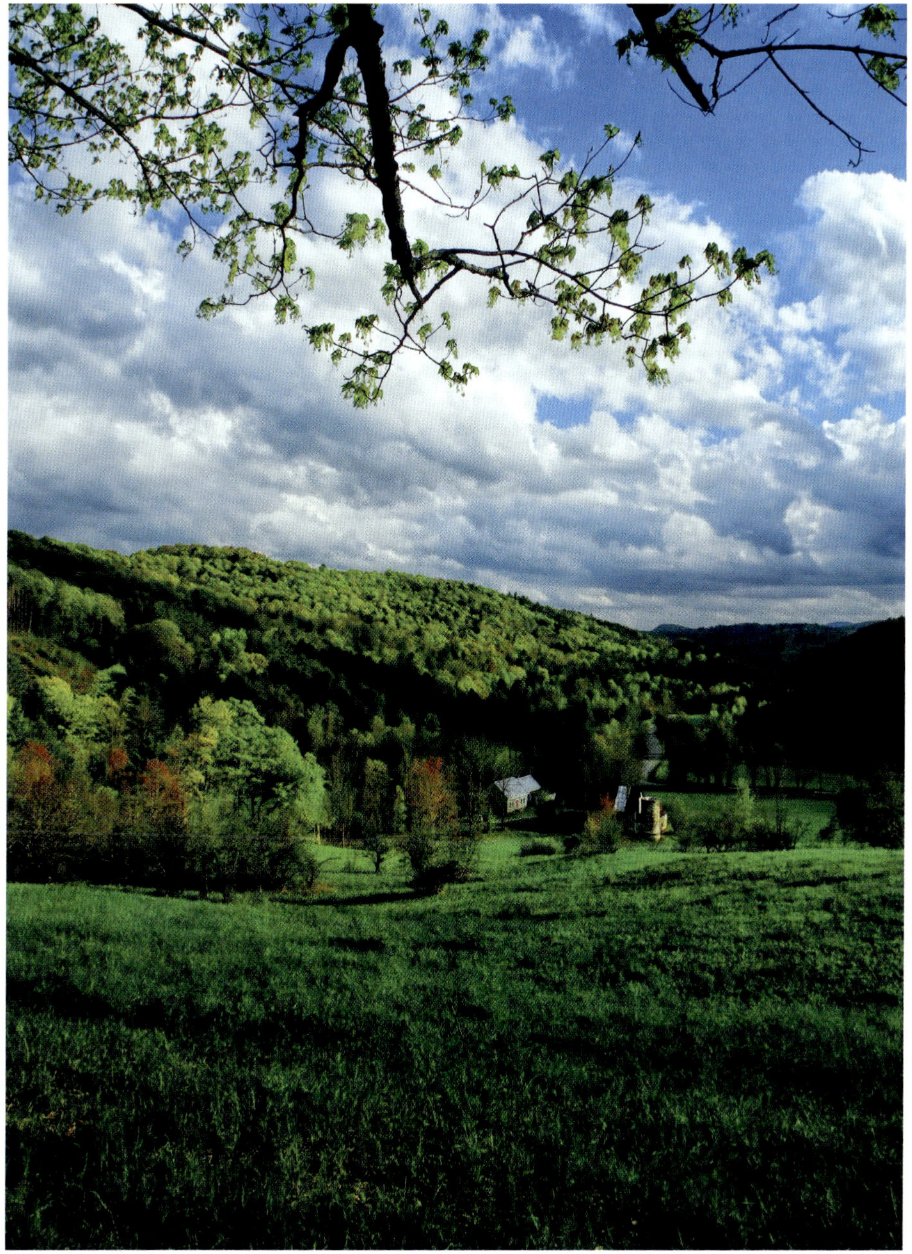

Farm below the Appalachian Trail in Vermont

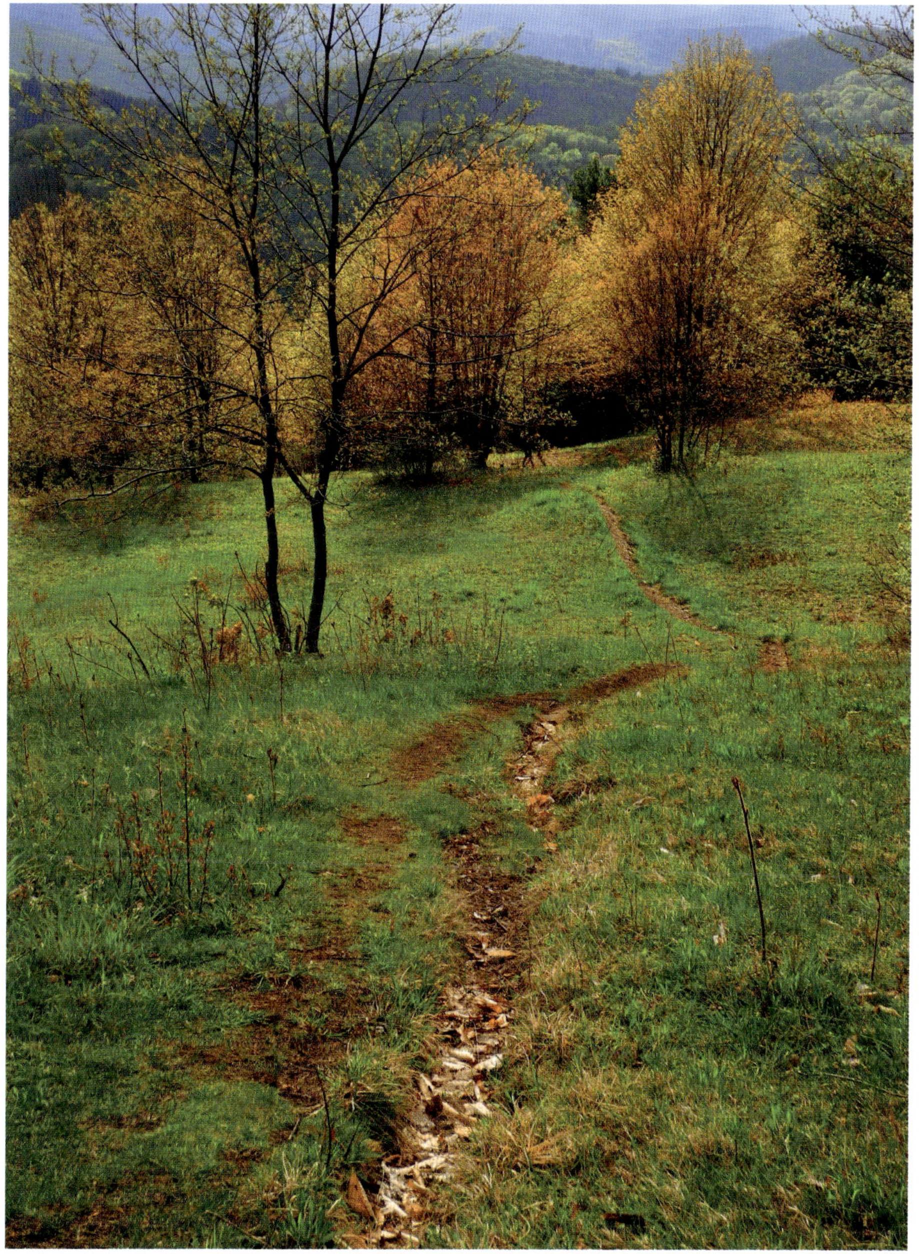

Golden aspens in the spring

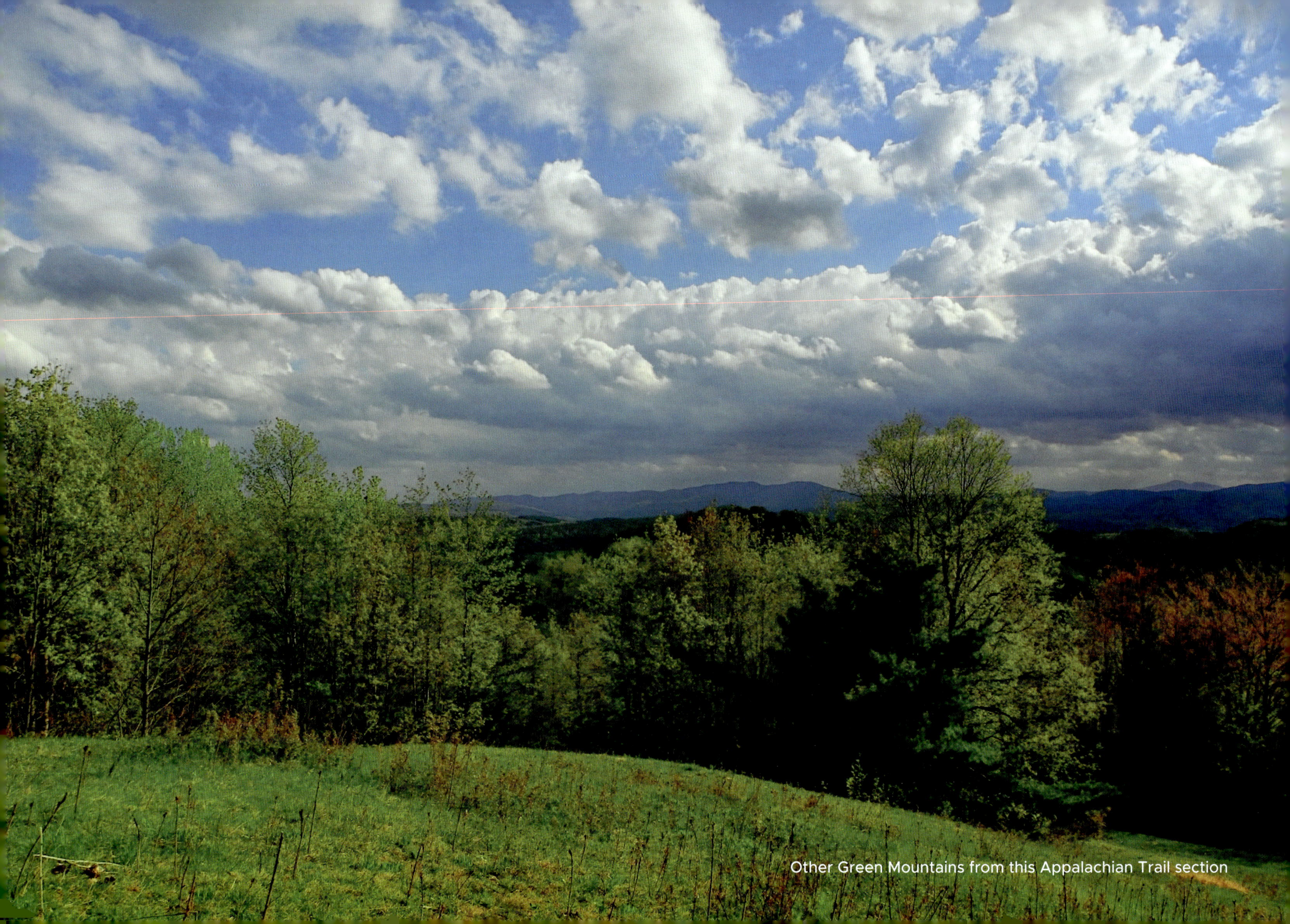

Other Green Mountains from this Appalachian Trail section

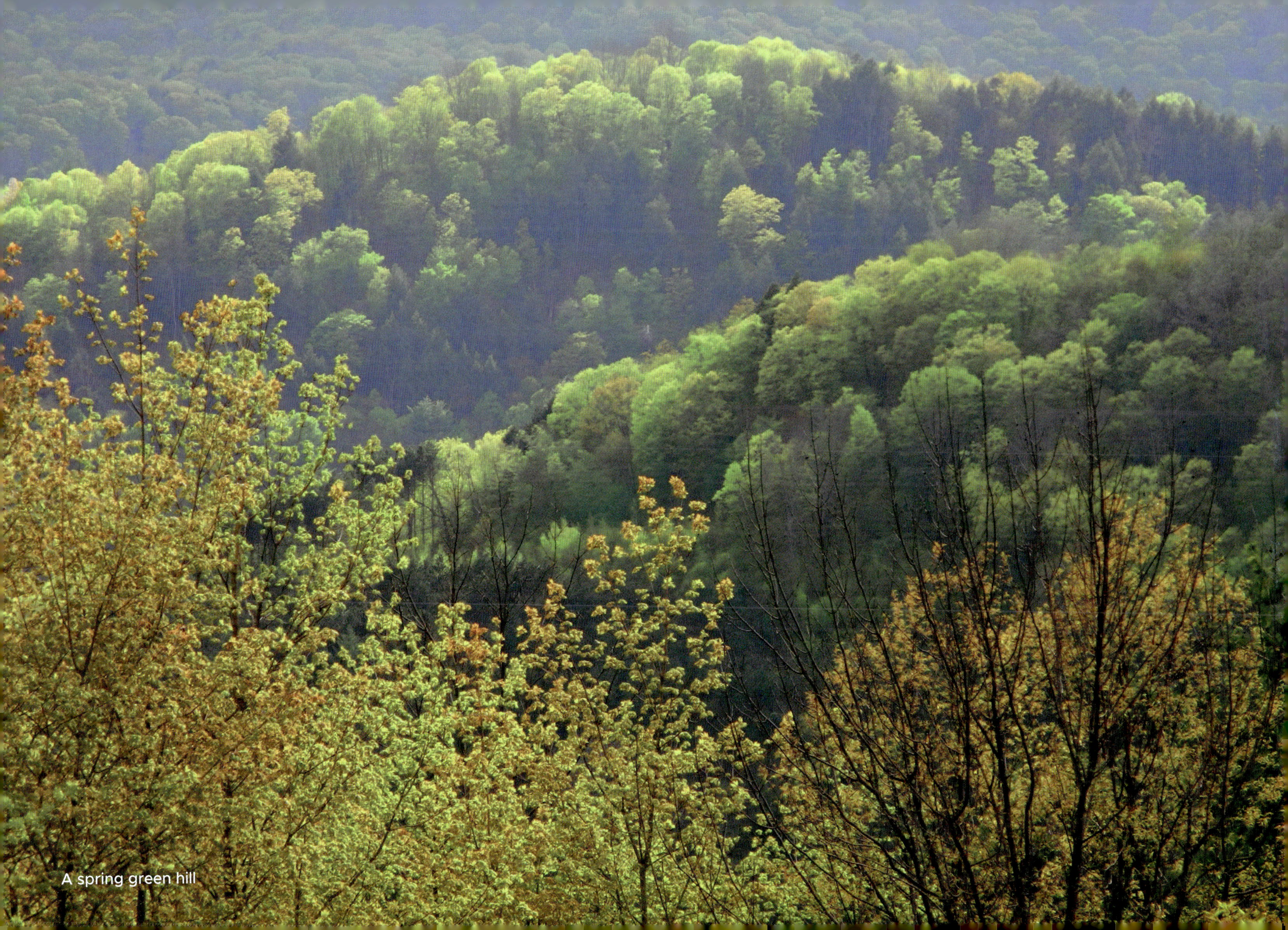

A spring green hill

GEM HIKE MAP

Scan to View / Download Online

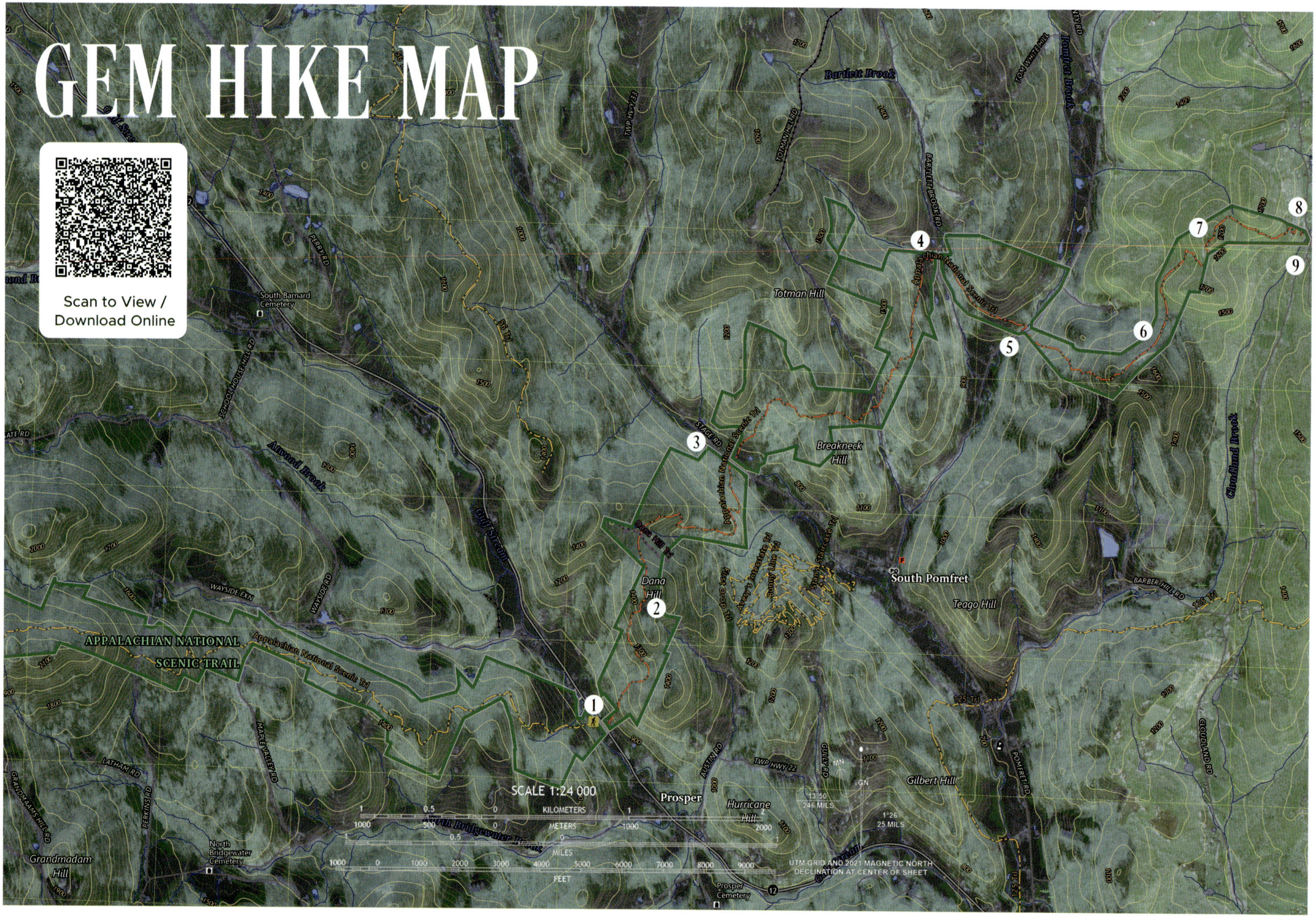

DIRECTIONS TO THE TRAILHEAD(S)

Vermont Route 12 / Barnard Gulf Rd. in Woodstock, Vermont, at geographic coordinate 43.654996, −72.565965

1. Within the town of Woodstock, Vermont, head southwest toward Court St. for 157 feet
2. Turn right onto Court St.
3. Continue 253 feet
4. Turn right onto S. Park St. / the Green
5. Continue 440 feet
6. Turn left onto Elm St.
7. Continue on Elm St. for 1.0 mile
8. Continue onto Vermont Route 12 N
9. Travel on Vermont Route 12 N for 2.8 miles
10. The trailhead off Vermont Route 12 / Barnard Gulf Rd. will be on the left

GEM HIKE DIRECTIONS

1. Leave the Route 12 Trailhead on the Appalachian Trail north
2. Continue on the Appalachian Trail for 0.7 mile, to the summit of Dana Hill
3. Continue on the Appalachian Trail for 0.8 mile to Woodstock Stage Rd.
4. Cross Woodstock Stage Rd. and continue on the Appalachian Trail for 1.5 miles to Bartlett Brook
5. Cross Bartlett Brook and continue on the Appalachian Trail for 0.6 mile to Pomfret–S. Pomfret Rd.
6. Cross Pomfret–S. Pomfret Rd. and continue on the Appalachian Trail for 1.4 miles to the top of DuPuis Hill
7. Reach the summit of DuPuis Hill and continue on the Appalachian Trail for 0.5 mile
8. Arrive at Cloudland Rd.
9. Turn around and retrace your steps back to the trailhead on Vermont Route 12

MORE/LESS AMBITIOUS HIKERS

More-ambitious hikers may wish to add miles to the north or south termini of this hike; after all, 150 miles of the Appalachian Trail are in Vermont.

Less ambitious hikers may wish to hire a shuttle or have a friend drop them off on Cloudland Road and hike back to their cars on Vermont Route 12.

CHAPTER 18

THE APPALACHIAN TRAIL FROM FRANCONIA NOTCH TO SOUTH KINSMAN, NEW HAMPSHIRE

AREA MAP

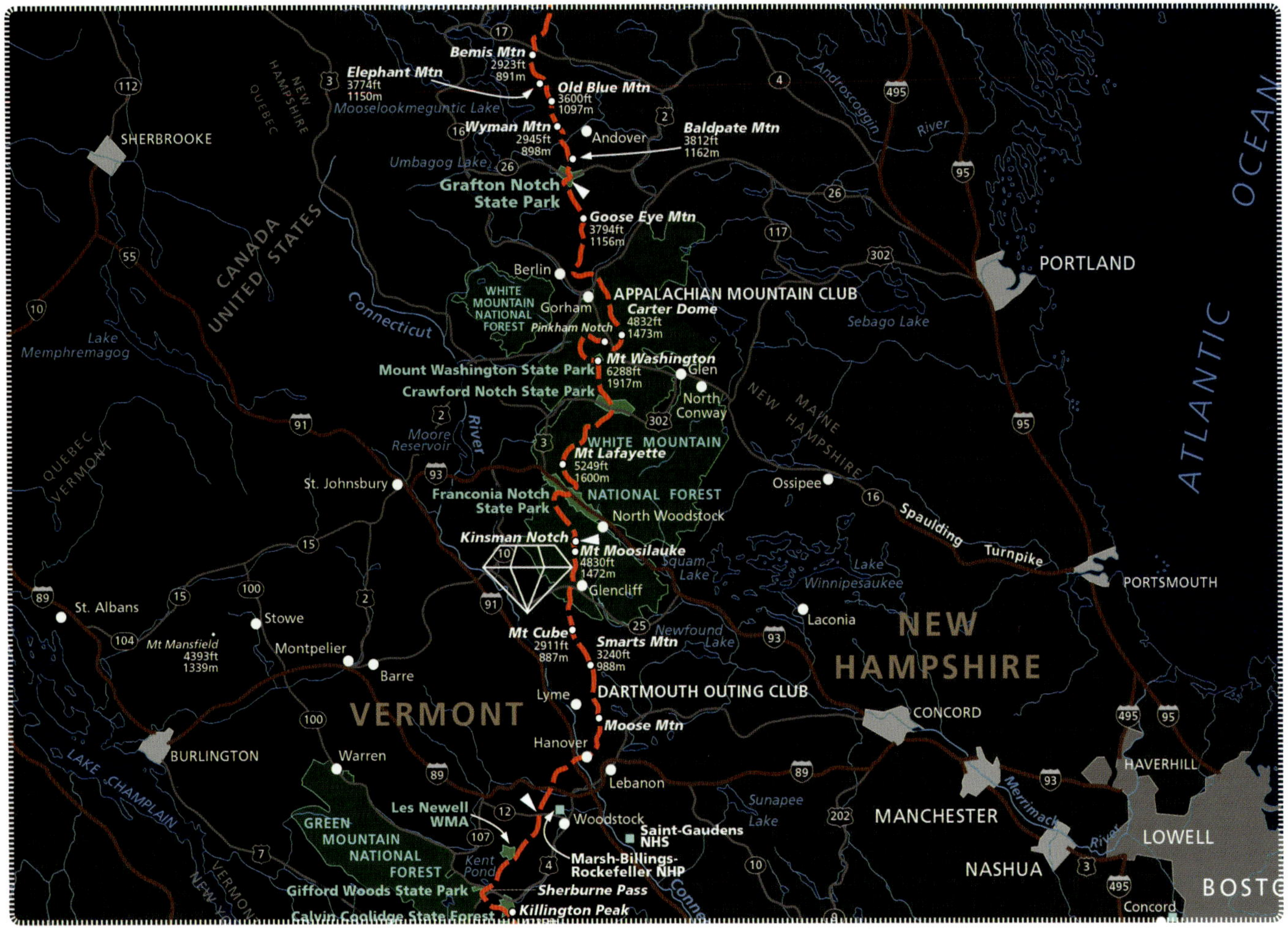

DISTANCE	14 miles
ELEVATION GAIN	3,900 feet
ELEVATION LOSS	3,900 feet
LEVEL	Difficult

TYPE: OUT-AND-BACK

0 10 Kilometers 50

0 10 Miles 50

Appalachian National Scenic Trail

Boundary of **CLUB** management section

North

GEM HIKE

PERSONAL TOUCH

The White Mountains are the White Mountains for a reason. The views and the athleticism requirements work hand in hand. I enjoyed using trees that grew out of the trail on the Fishin' Jimmy Trail to climb and descend from North Kinsman.

The views are mainly of evergreen-tree-covered peaks with their summits above the treeline. The air smelled of evergreens and earth. It was piercing and invigorating. The only sound was the wind passing through the trees.

BRIEF OVERVIEW

The Appalachian Trail from Franconia Notch to the summit of South Kinsman is located near Lincoln, New Hampshire, in the White Mountain Range, within the White Mountain National Forest. The hike to South Kinsman Mountain from Franconia Notch is a challenging yet picturesque hike that spans 7 miles in one direction. The trail leads hikers through dense forests, rocky trails, an alpine meadow, and breathtaking views. The next section to the south on the Appalachian Trail is Mount Moosilauke. The next section to the north on the Appalachian Trail is the famed Franconia Ridge Traverse.

DESCRIPTION OF THE GEM HIKE

For this amazing 14-mile round trip, the Appalachian Trail in New Hampshire's White Mountains, start by parking in the Flume Gorge Visitor Center parking lot, where the Pemi Trail Bike Path leaves to the north. It then follows the Appalachian Trail in both directions, but, in the White Mountains, the Appalachian Trail takes the names of the historical given route names, so please take care to make sure you know your route.

FLORA, FAUNA, AND VEGETATION

Most of the vegetation in this New Hampshire section of the Appalachian Trail is subalpine vegetation: The most-common trees are balsam fir and red spruce. The lower elevations are various birches.

SCENIC VIEWS

This hike is a gem for the scenic views from Lonesome Lake, South Kinsman, North Kinsman, and even from just the trail itself. This may be listed as a challenging hike but can be scaled back by simply turning around after enjoying Lonesome Lake.

LONESOME LAKE

Lonesome Lake, located near Franconia Notch, is a beautiful alpine lake. It offers a picturesque setting with clear waters reflecting the surrounding peaks, including the famed Franconia Notch and Cannon Mountain. The Appalachian Mountain Club's Lonesome Lake hut is located just off the lake.

NORTH KINSMAN AND SOUTH KINSMAN

North Kinsman and South Kinsman are at elevations of 4,293 feet and 4,358 feet, respectively. They both provide a hiker a sense of accomplishment because the views are truly amazing.

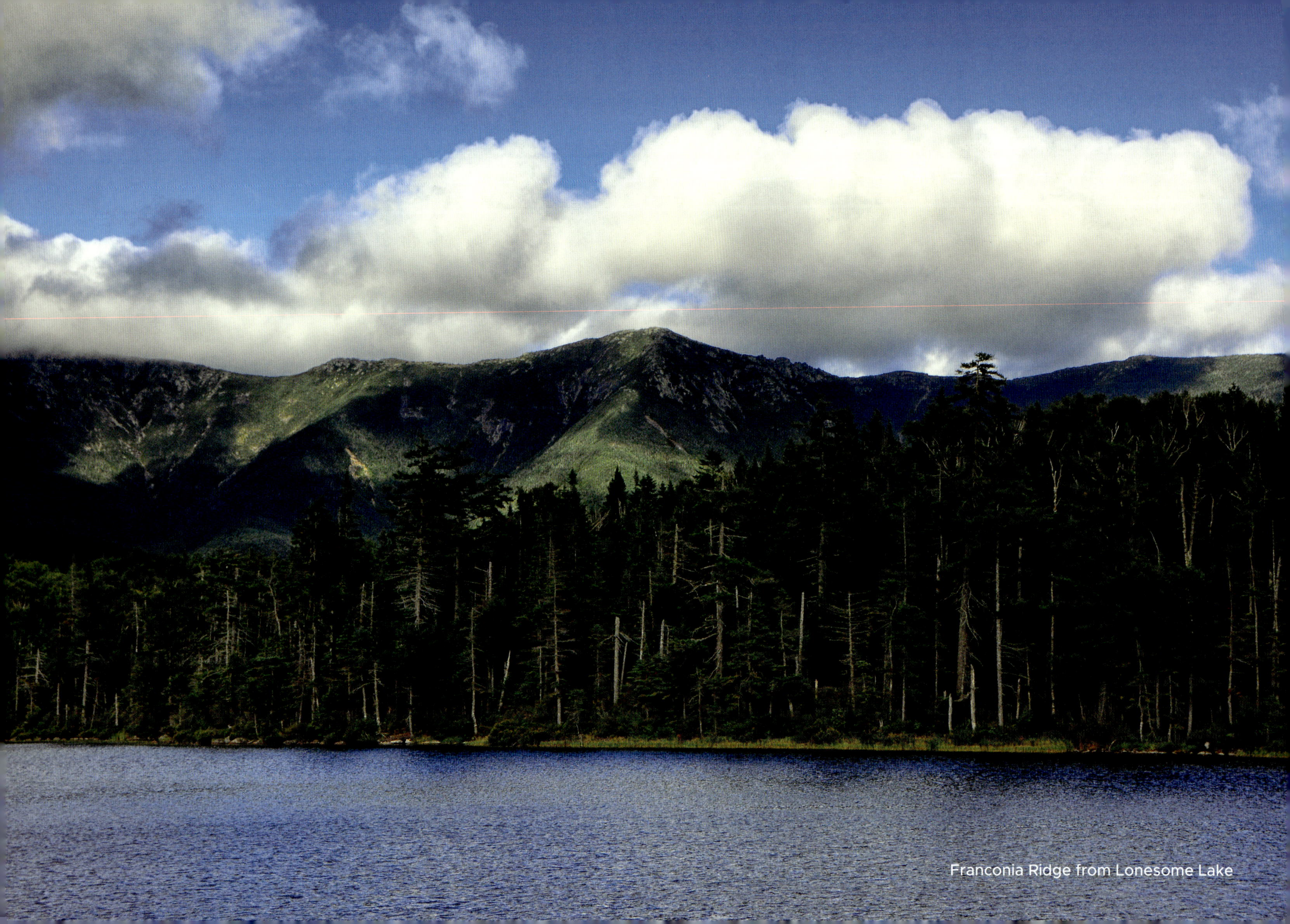

Franconia Ridge from Lonesome Lake

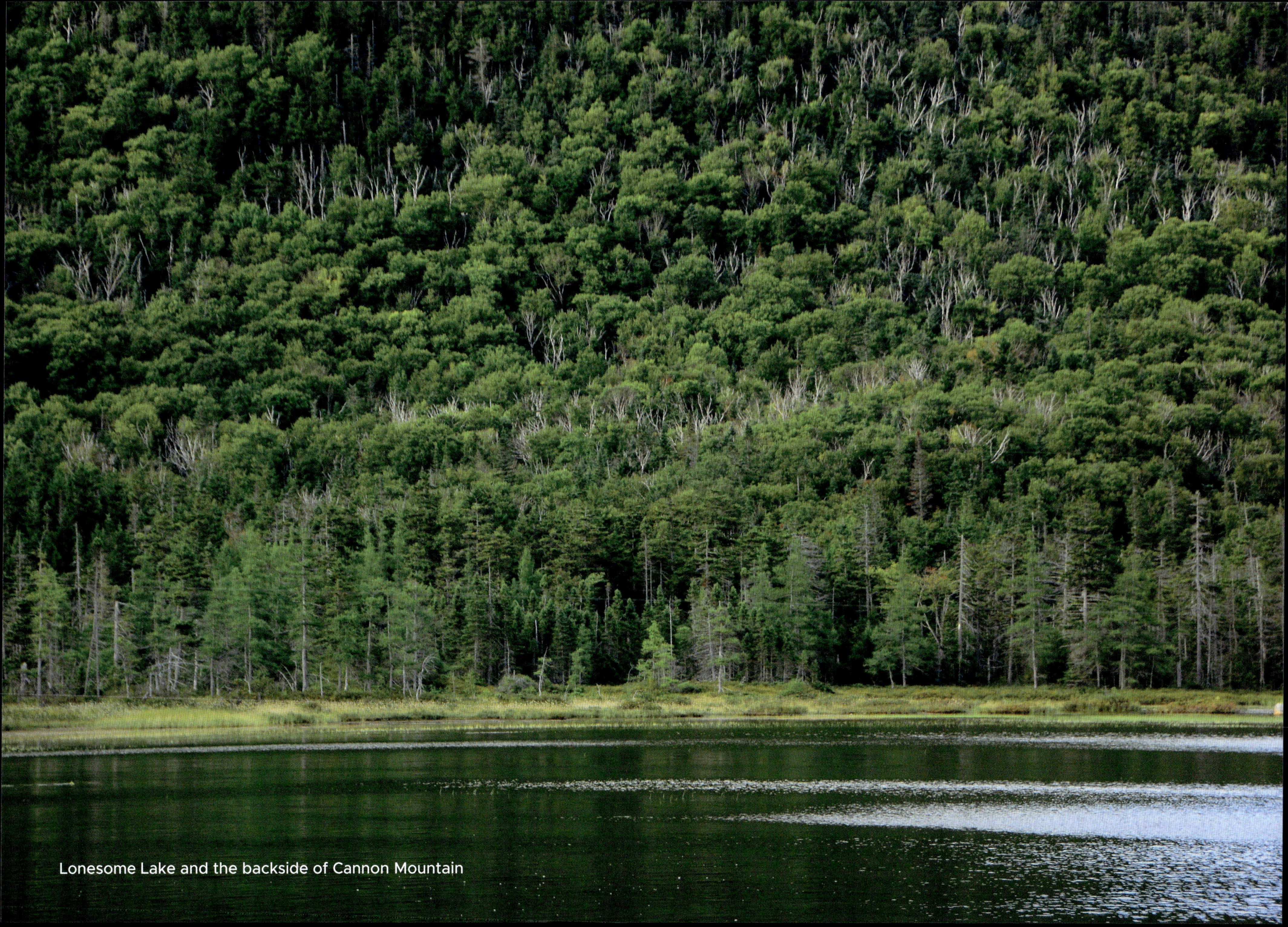

Lonesome Lake and the backside of Cannon Mountain

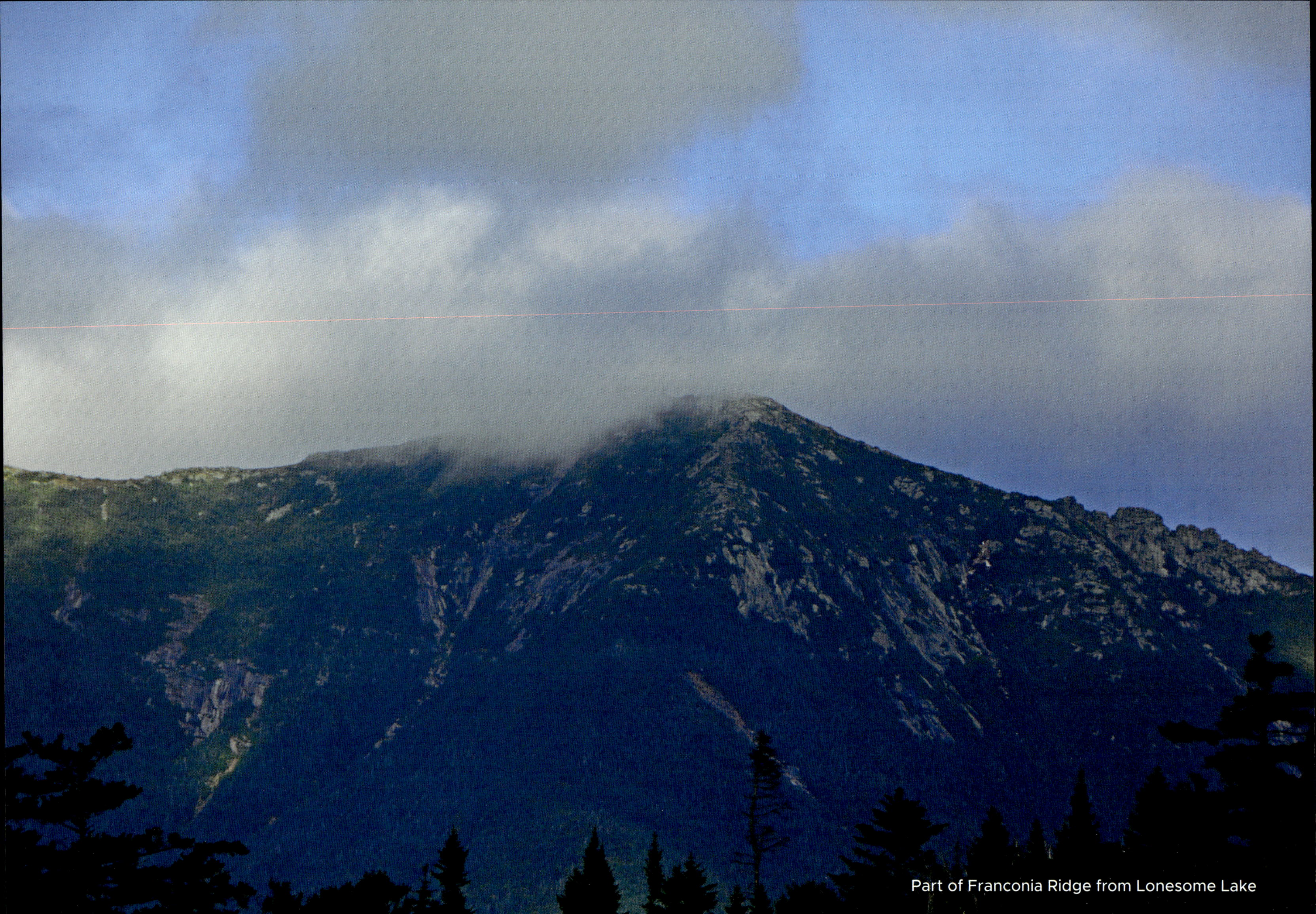
Part of Franconia Ridge from Lonesome Lake

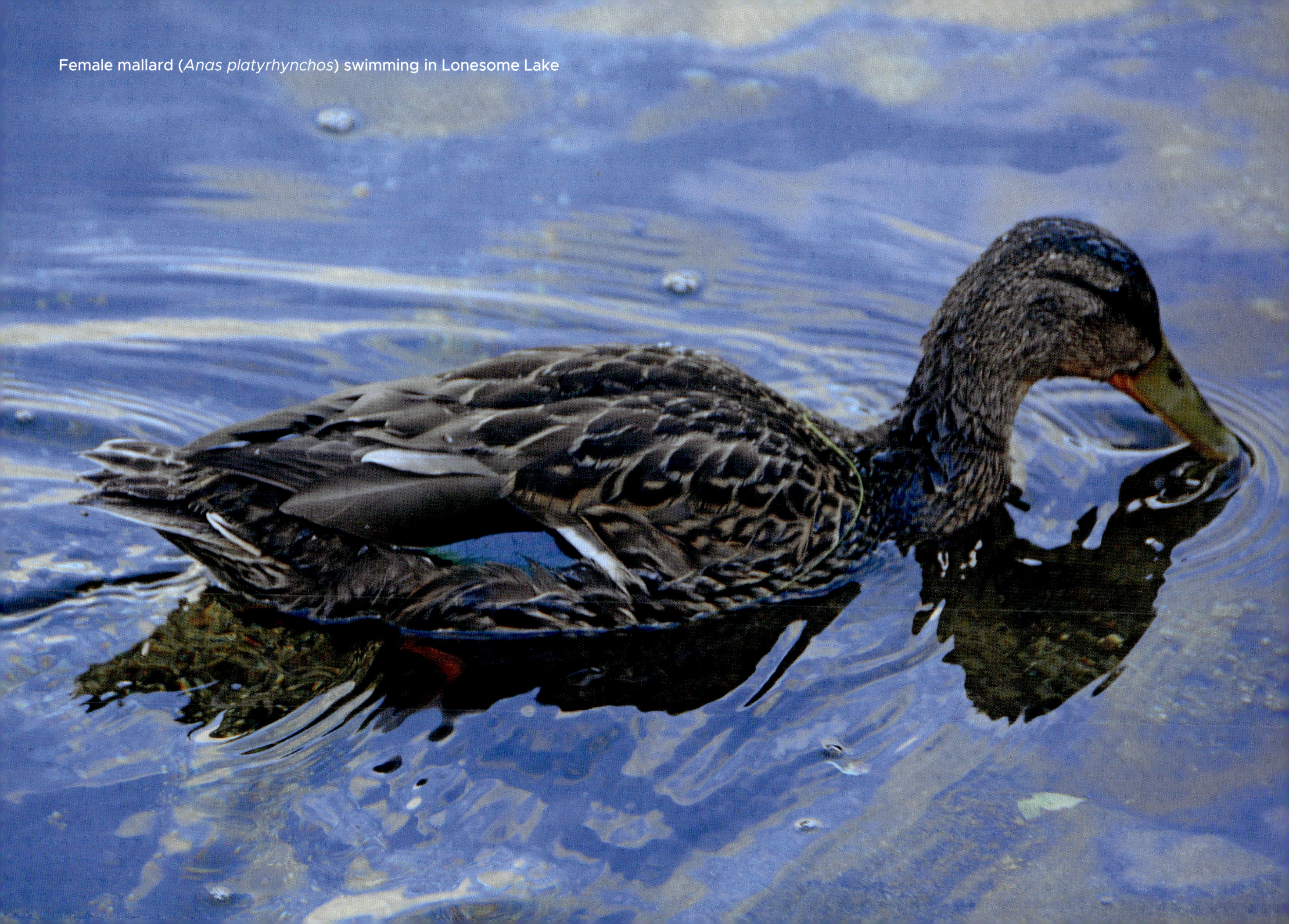

Female mallard (*Anas platyrhynchos*) swimming in Lonesome Lake

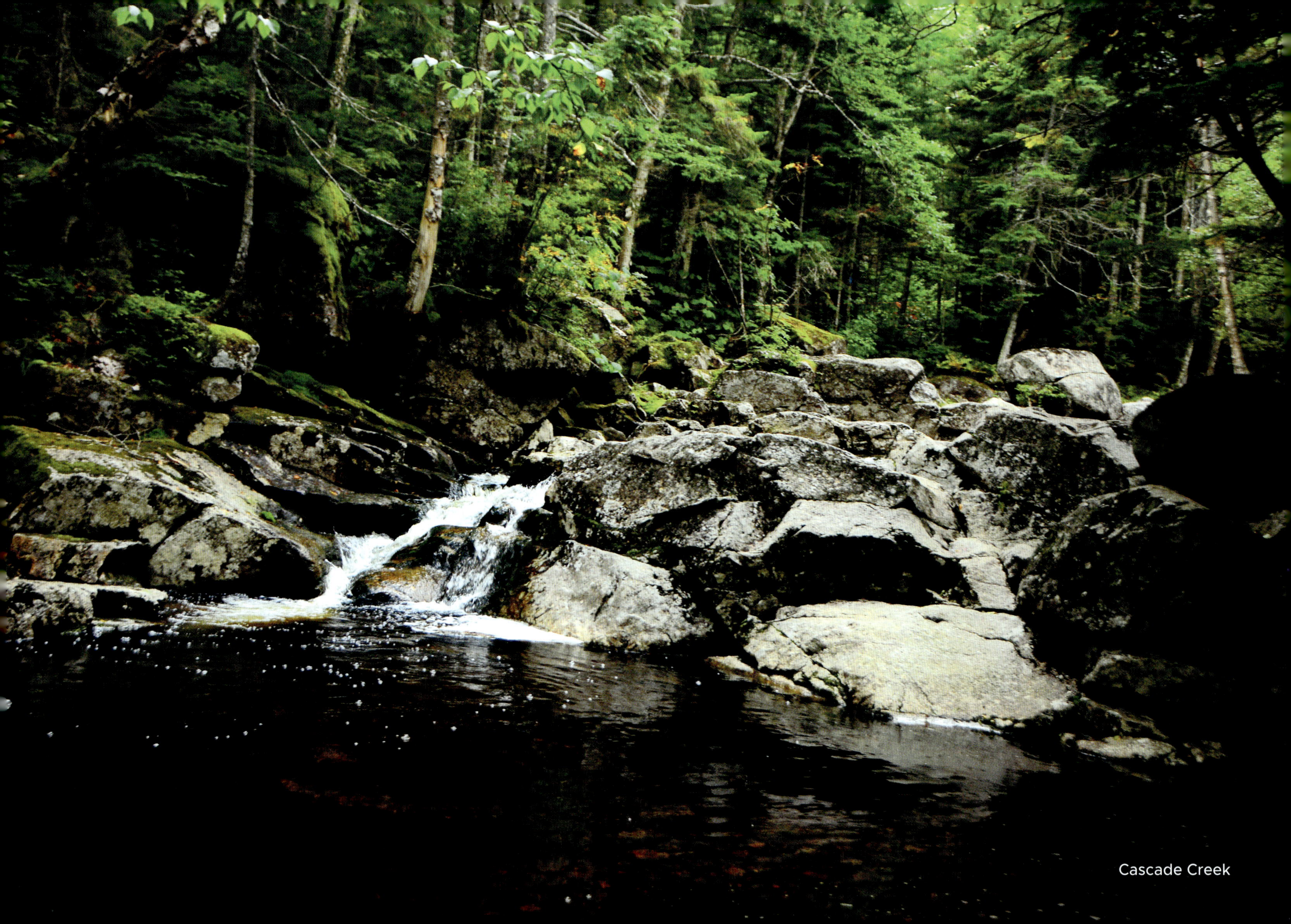

Cascade Creek

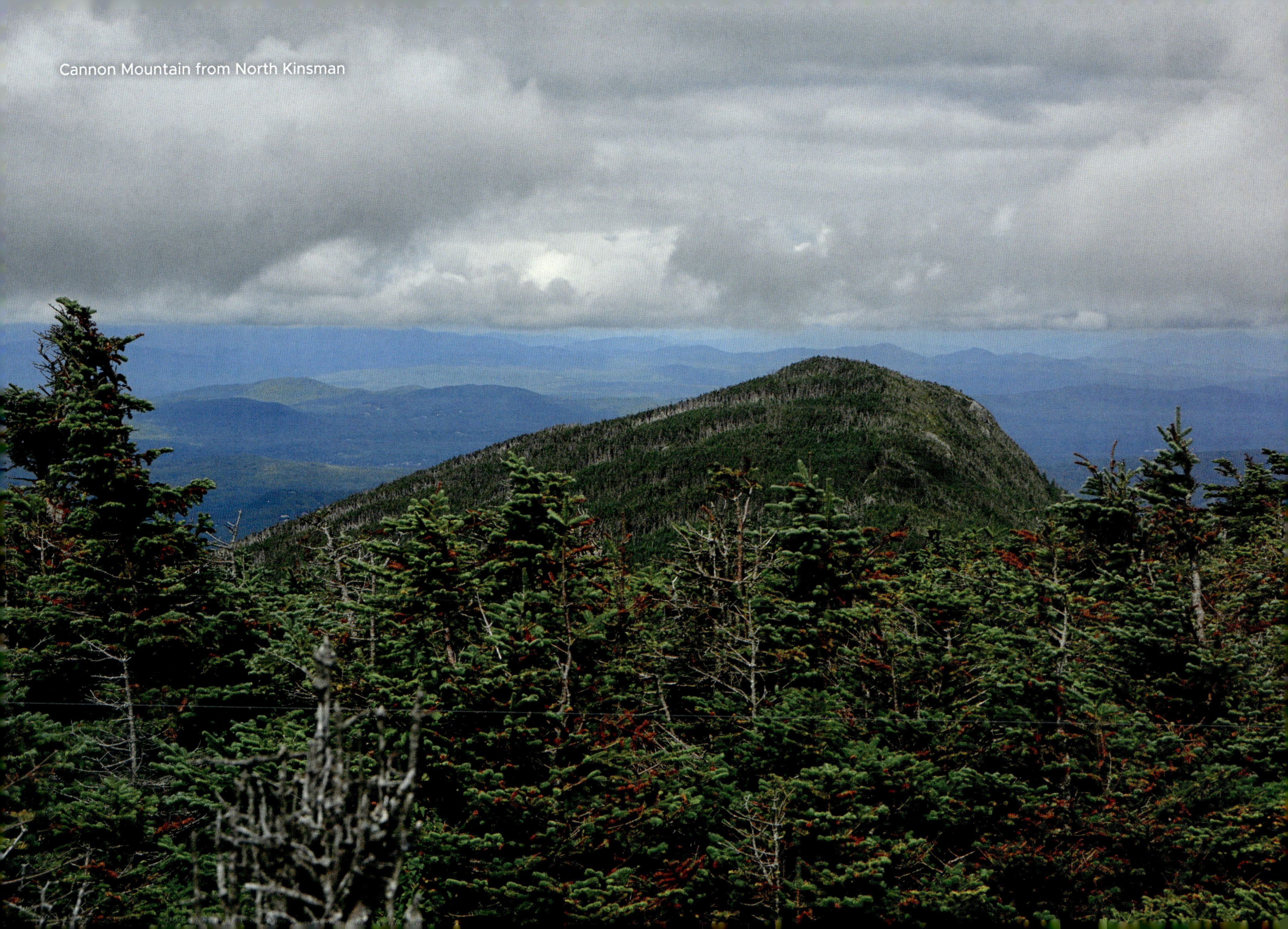

Cannon Mountain from North Kinsman

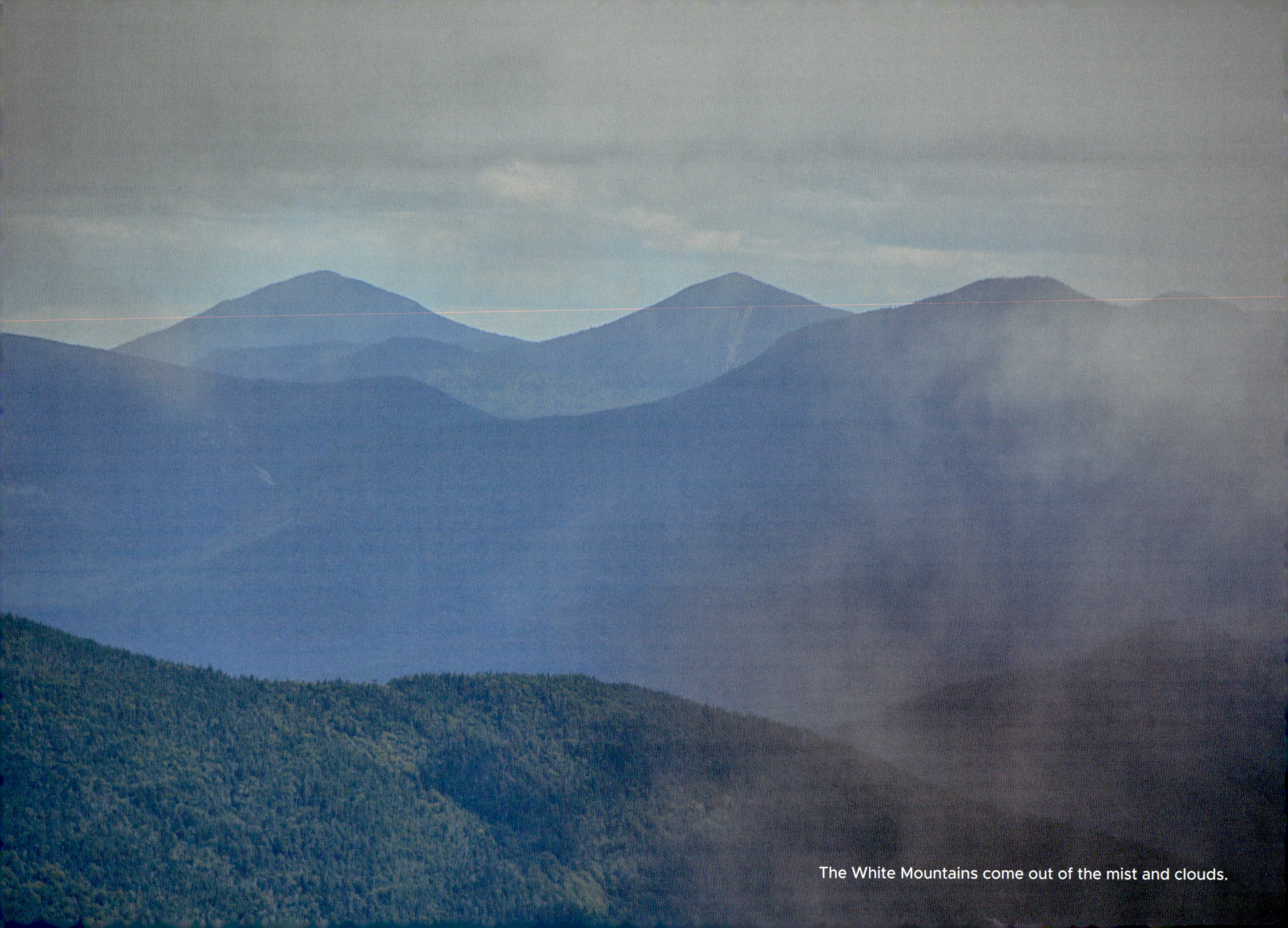
The White Mountains come out of the mist and clouds.

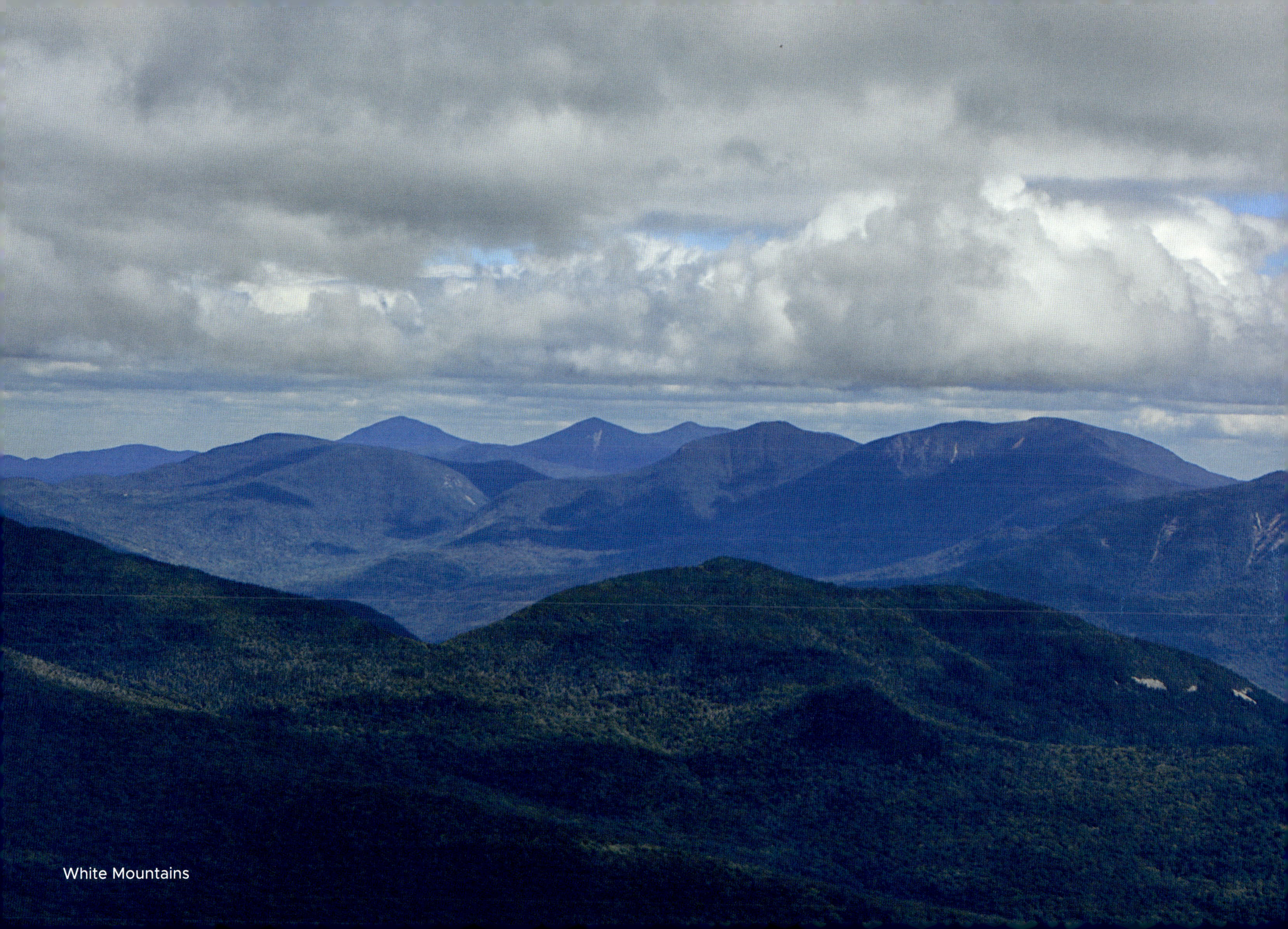

White Mountains

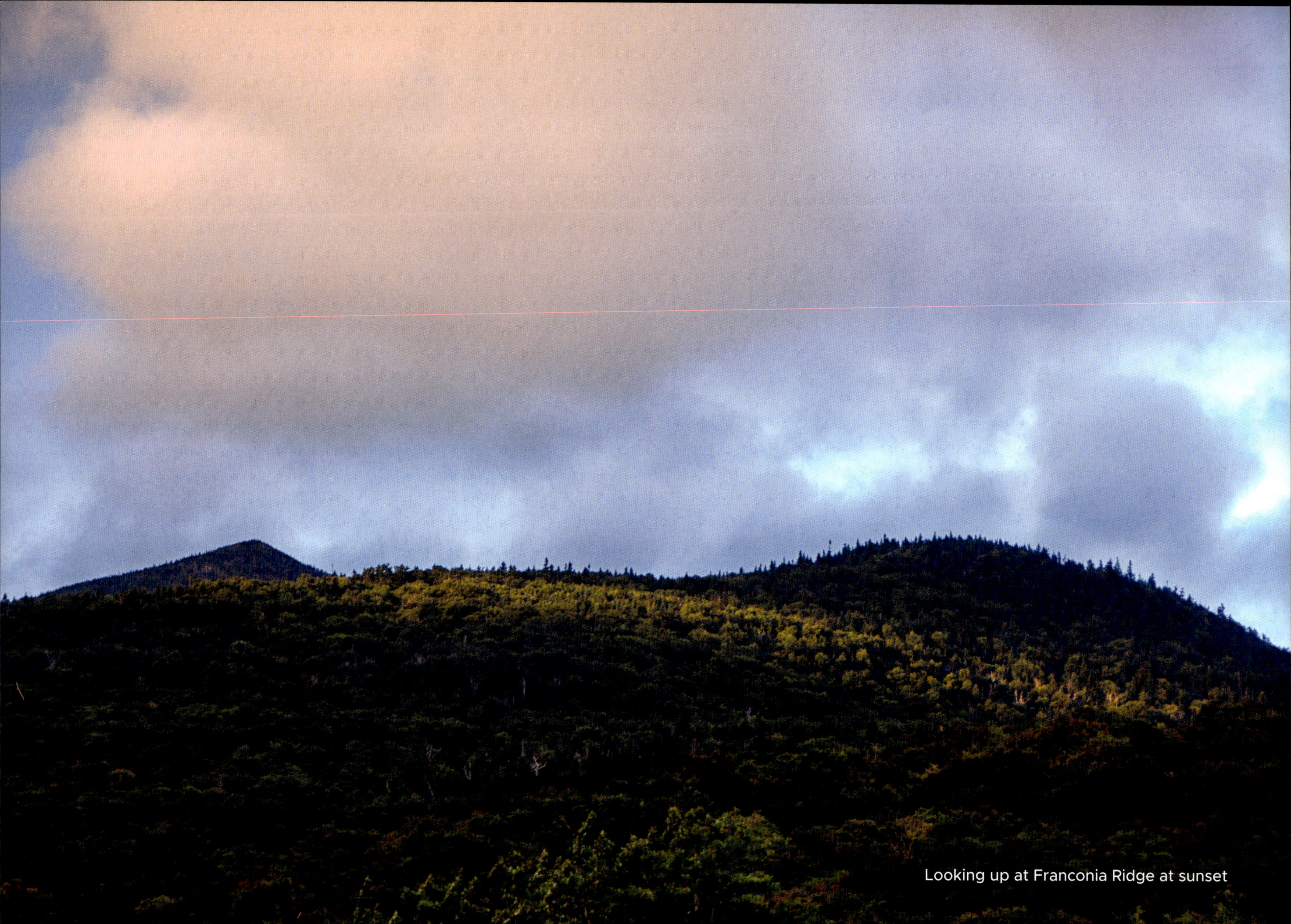

Looking up at Franconia Ridge at sunset

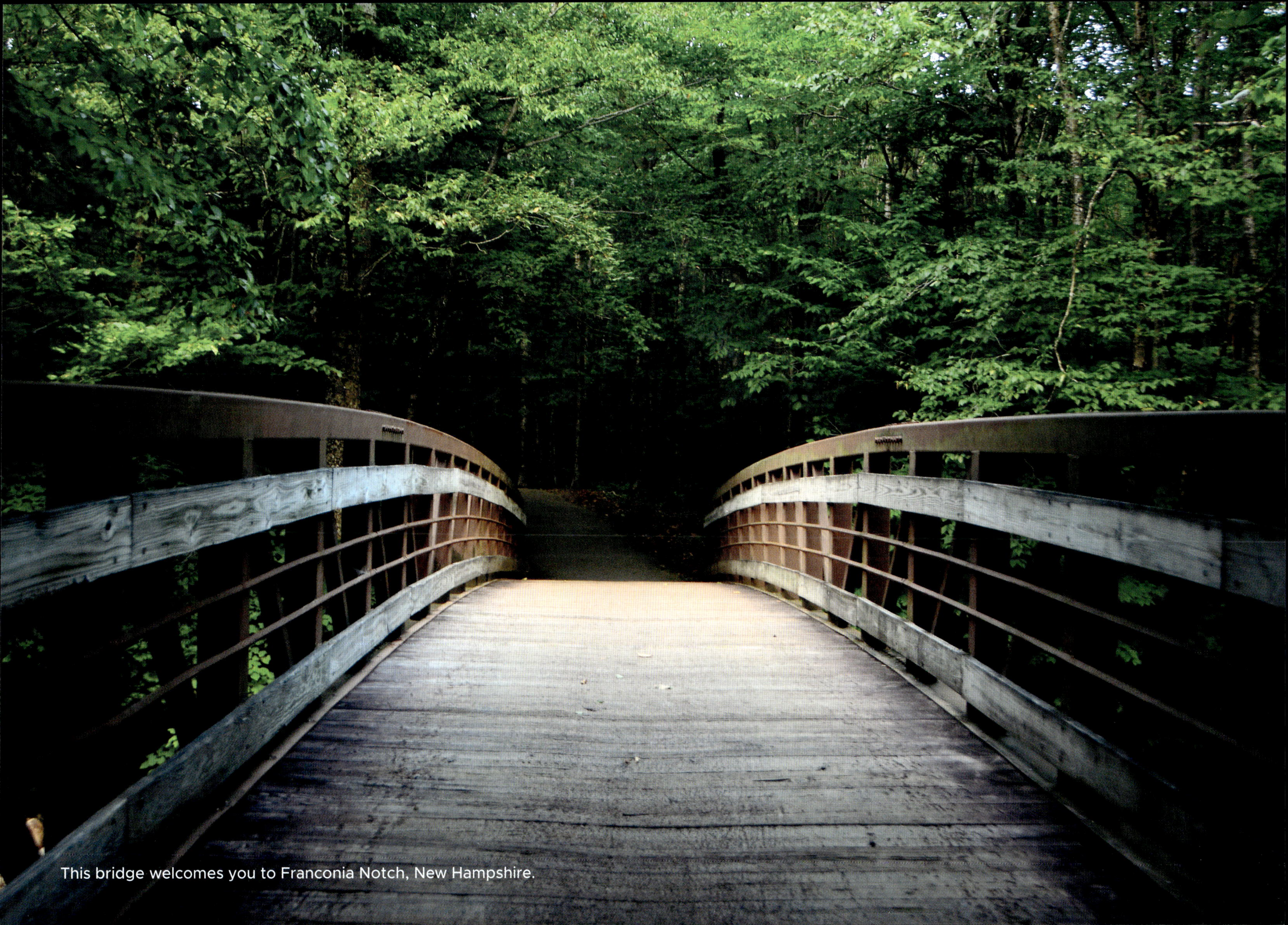

This bridge welcomes you to Franconia Notch, New Hampshire.

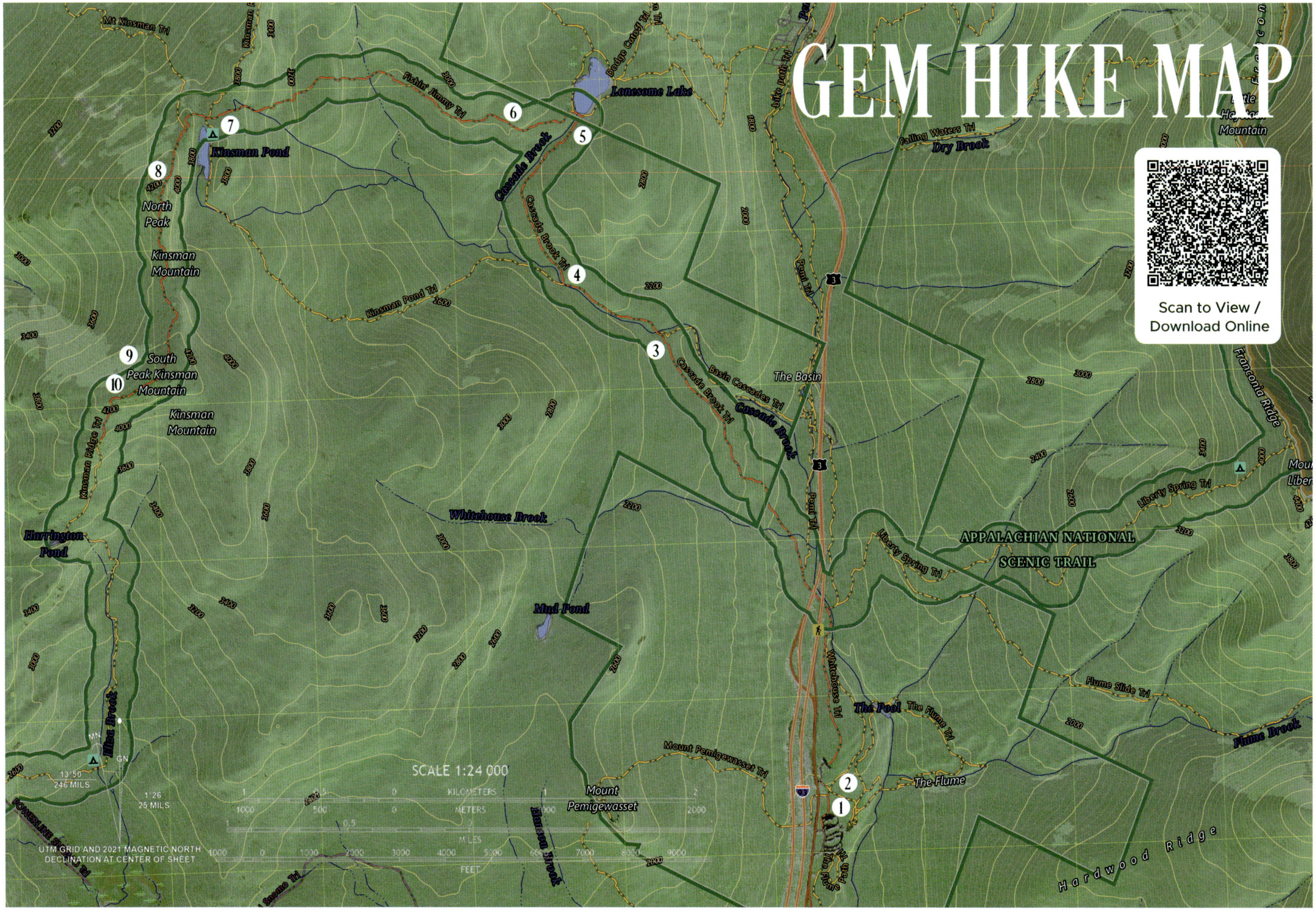
GEM HIKE MAP
Scan to View / Download Online
Lonesome Lake
Kinsman Pond
North Peak
Kinsman Mountain
South Peak Kinsman Mountain
Harrington Pond
Whitehouse Brook
Mud Pond
The Basin
Cascade Brook
Dry Brook
APPALACHIAN NATIONAL SCENIC TRAIL
The Pool
The Flume
Mount Pemigewasset
Hardwood Ridge
Franconia Ridge
Fishin' Jimmy Trl
Kinsman Pond Trl
Cascade Brook Trl
Basin Cascades Trl
Liberty Spring Trl
Flume Slide Trl
Mount Pemigewasset Trl
Falling Waters Trl
Kinsman Ridge Trl
Whitehouse Trl
Pemi Trl
The Flume Trl
Flume Brook
SCALE 1:24 000

DIRECTIONS TO THE TRAILHEAD(S)

Lincoln, New Hampshire, to Flume Gorge Trailhead Lincoln, New Hampshire, at Flume Gorge Visitor Center, 852 Daniel Webster Hwy, Lincoln, NH 03251 (44.097783, −71.681463)

1. Head southwest on Main St. toward Innseasons Dr. for 0.3 mile
2. Turn right onto Connector Rd. and continue for 1.0 mile
3. Connector Rd. turns slightly right and becomes US 3 N;, continue for 3.4 miles
4. Turn right and continue for 433 feet
5. Turn right and continue for 390 feet
6. Turn left, and Flume Gorge Visitor Center will be on the right after 62 feet

GEM HIKE DIRECTIONS

1. Leave the Flume Gorge Visitor Center on the Pemi Trail Bike Path and continue for 0.9 mile
2. Take a left on the Liberty Spring Trail and Cascade Basin Brook Trail for 0.2 mile
3. In 1.3 miles, it passes Basin-Cascades Trail on the right
4. In 0.5 mile, it passes by Kinsman Pond Trail off to the left
5. Continue for 0.8 mile to Lonesome Lake
6. After Lonesome Lake, the Appalachian Trail takes on the name Fishin' Jimmy Trail and turns into a more difficult hike
7. After 2.0 miles, the Appalachian Trail / Fishin' Jimmy Trail meets with Kinsman Pond trail on left and Kinsman Ridge on right
8. The Appalachian Trail at this junction becomes Kinsman Ridge Trail and then travels for 0.2 mile to the summit of North Kinsman, at 4,293 feet
9. The Appalachian Trail / Kinsman Ridge Trail travels 1.3 miles to the summit of South Kinsman, at 4,358 feet
10. This Appalachian Trail gem hike returns the way you came up

MORE/LESS AMBITIOUS HIKERS

More-ambitious hikers may wish to hike point to point from the Reel Brook Trail or the base of Mount Moosilauke.

Less ambitious hikers may wish to turn around at Lonesome Lake. This will eliminate the scramble to the summit of North Kinsman from Lonesome Lake.

CHAPTER 19

THE APPALACHIAN TRAIL: TWINWAY TRAIL AND NORTH TWIN SPUR ADD-ON, WHITE MOUNTAINS, NEW HAMPSHIRE

AREA MAP

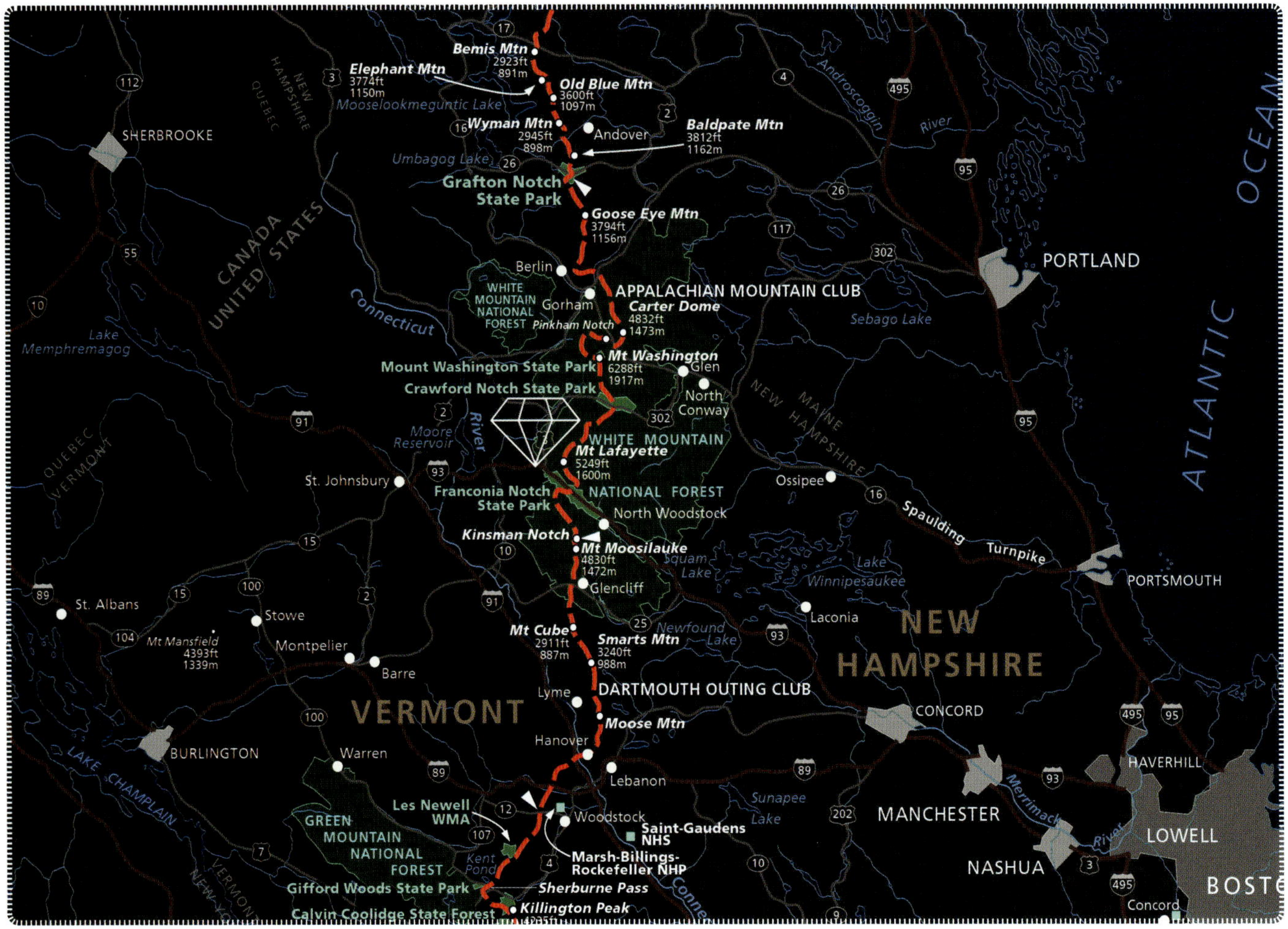

DISTANCE	12 miles
ELEVATION GAIN	4,450 feet
ELEVATION LOSS	4,200 feet
LEVEL	Difficult

TYPE: POINT TO POINT

0 10 Kilometers 50
0 10 Miles 50

Appalachian National Scenic Trail

Boundary of CLUB management section

North

GEM HIKE

PERSONAL TOUCH

I drove up to Vermont's Green Mountains two days before my hike there, which was in the heat and humidity. After I got in the car, the sky opened up and rained buckets with crazy lightning for the length of my drive from the Manchester, Vermont, area.

The hike was the next day. This was epic not just in comparison, but epic as epic goes. I had perfect thermal clouds and felt like I was walking in heaven. Once I reached the Twinway Trail, I had clouds for hiking partners as I traveled from Galehead Hut to South Twin and then on to North Twin Mountain. The clouds made for perfect views from South Twin Mountain of the surrounding area, including the Presidential Range. The views of the Presidential Range were amazingly beautiful, as though they were views of heaven.

BRIEF OVERVIEW

The Pemigewasset Wilderness Traverse of the Appalachian Trail in New Hampshire offers a rugged and spectacular hiking experience through the White Mountains. This section is known for its challenging terrain and breathtaking vistas. In New Hampshire, the Appalachian Trail keeps its localized names, so hikers have to have some extra awareness in order to know where to go. Hikers on the Appalachian Trail must exercise caution here to make sure they are on the proper trail. Twinway Trail is the name the Appalachian Trail has from South Twin to Zealand Trail on the Pemigewasset Traverse.

DESCRIPTION OF THE GEM HIKE

If you wish to experience the Pemigewasset Traverse, then this gem hike that includes part of the Twinway Trail section of the Appalachian Trail in New Hampshire is for you. It provides potential river crossings, epic views, and even a taste of being above the treeline.

The gem hike is Twinway Trail, adding the North Twin Spur. This spur trail adds another of the New Hampshire 4,800-footer peaks called North Twin. It adds a 2.6-mile round trip to the Pemigewasset Traverse. Please note that because of this crossing, this hike can be challenging and is not recommended in wet times of the year. This hike adds beautiful vistas and views of the Appalachian Trail that are not visible otherwise.

FLORA, FAUNA, AND VEGETATION

The Twinway section of the Appalachian Trail in New Hampshire has a lot of ups and downs and is very rugged, so the plants that grow here must have to deal with a lot: short growing season, very cold winters, and very rocky ground. In the middle elevations, coniferous species include spruce and fir. When the new growth's buds open, this hike is at its coolest. The ground cover quite often includes various mosses and ferns, and some select wildflowers. At the upper elevations, above the treeline, vegetation consists of alpine shrubs, grasses, lichens, and mosses.

THE TWINWAY SECTION IS A GEM

The Twinway, New Hampshire, section of the Appalachian Trail is truly a gem of the Appalachian Trail. It is particularly beautiful in the early parts of the summer, when thermal clouds surround the rugged and beautiful landscape. The scenic views often include vibrant greens and select wildflowers. The vistas have views of the Presidential Traverse, Franconia Ridge, and other peaks of the White Mountains that are home to other sections of the Appalachian Trail.

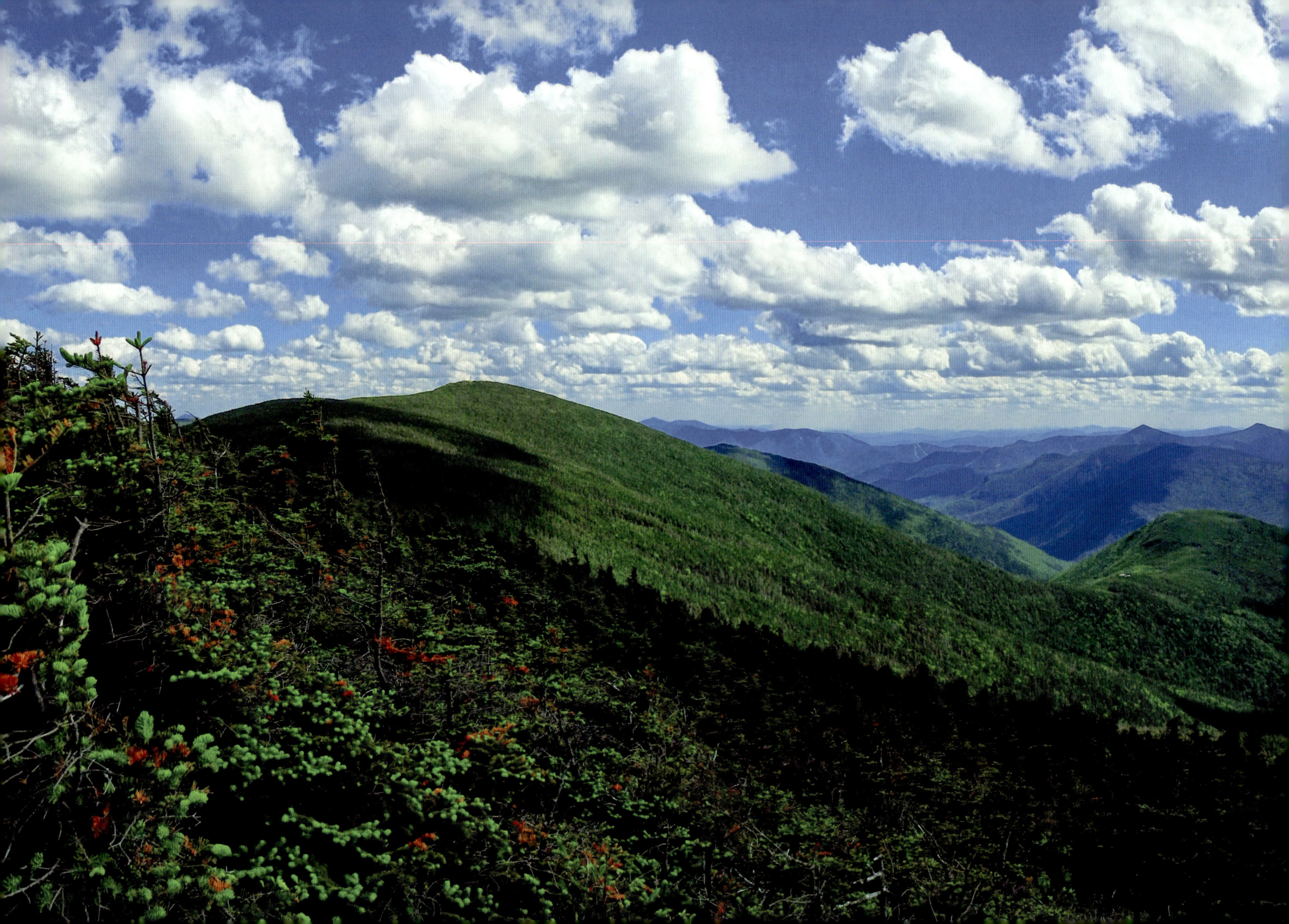

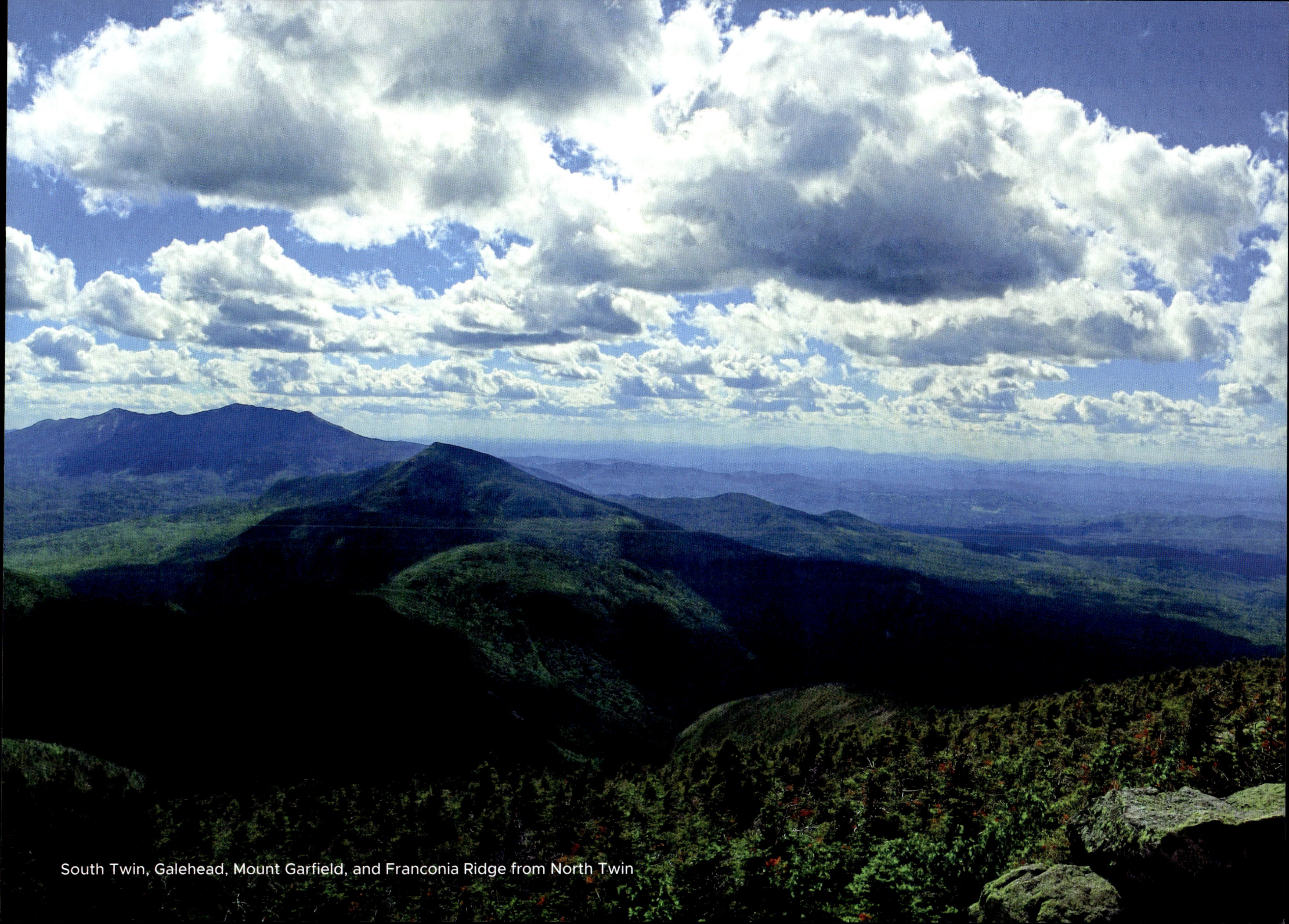

South Twin, Galehead, Mount Garfield, and Franconia Ridge from North Twin

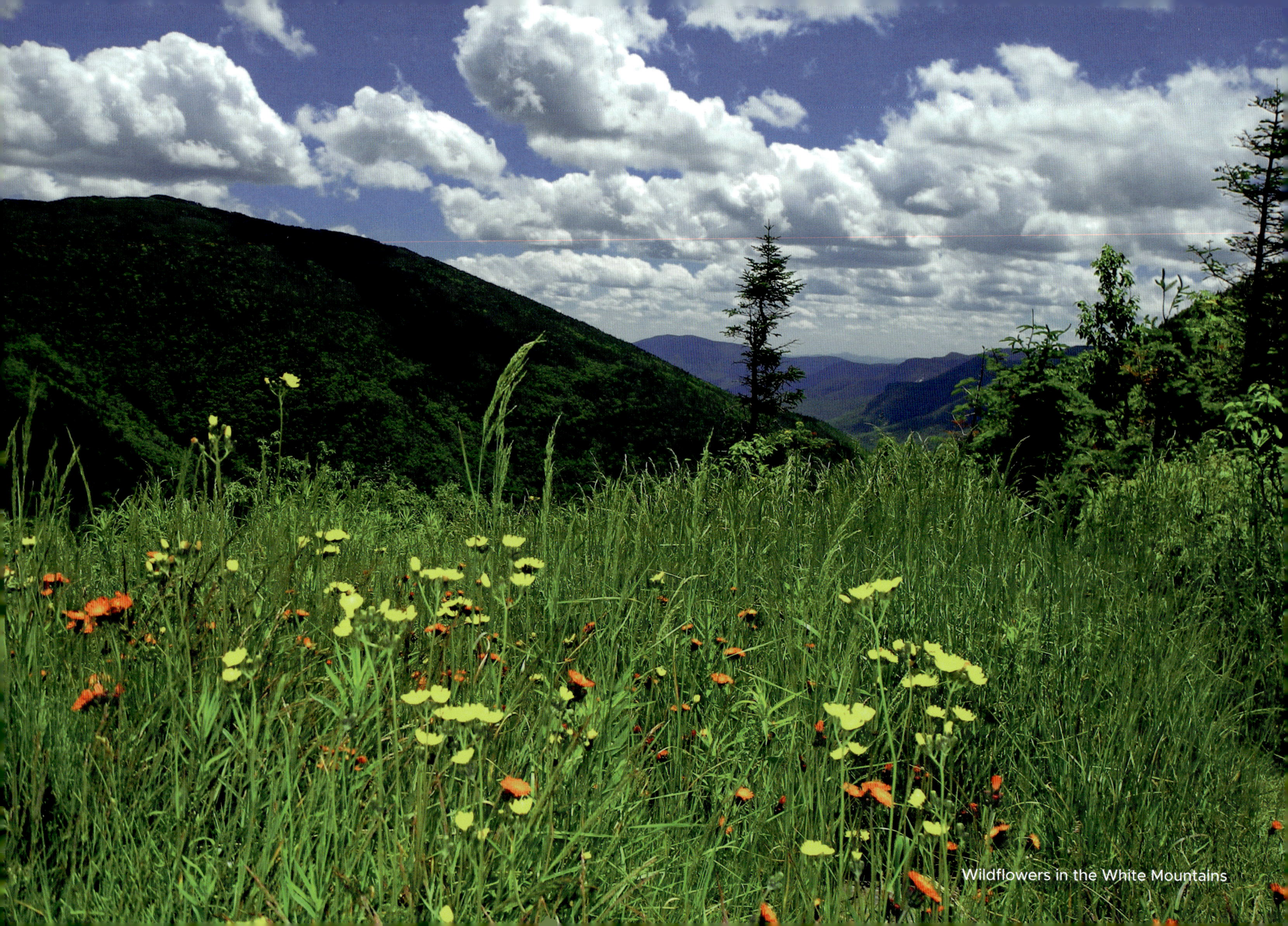

Wildflowers in the White Mountains

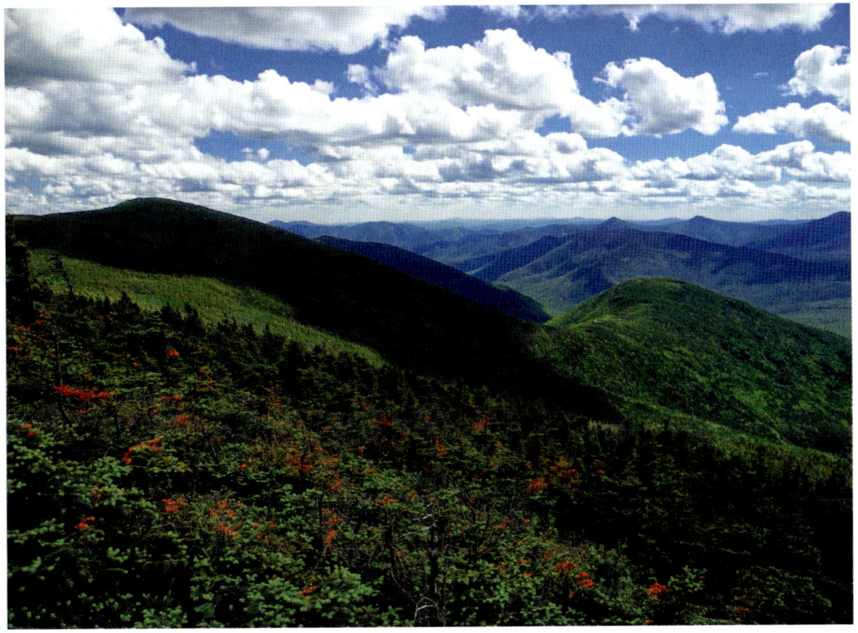

New Hampshire spring green

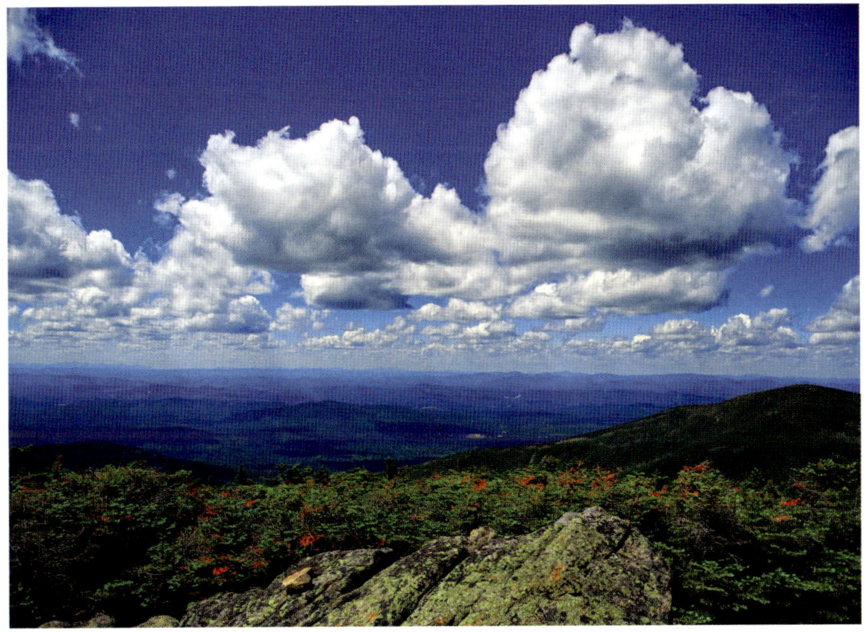

Thermal Clouds from ascending South Twin Mountain

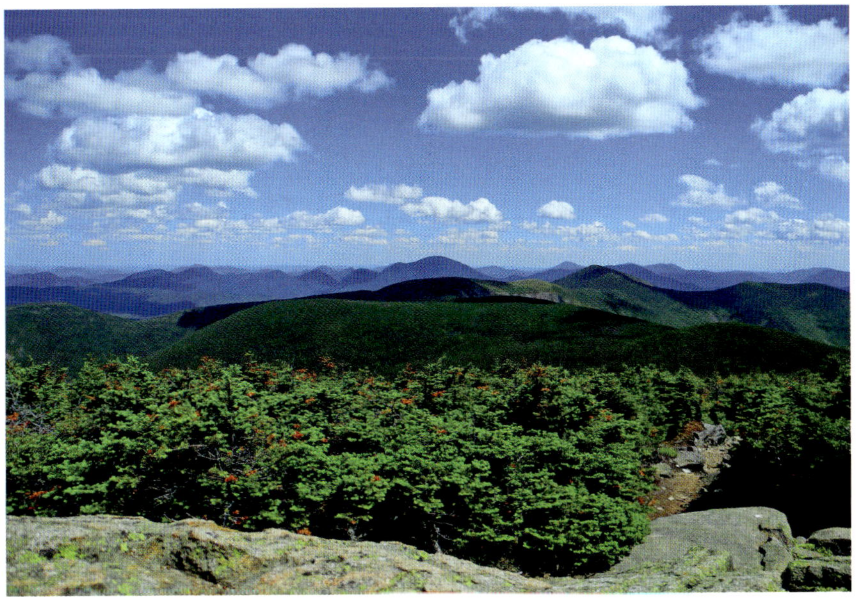

Surrounding White Mountains

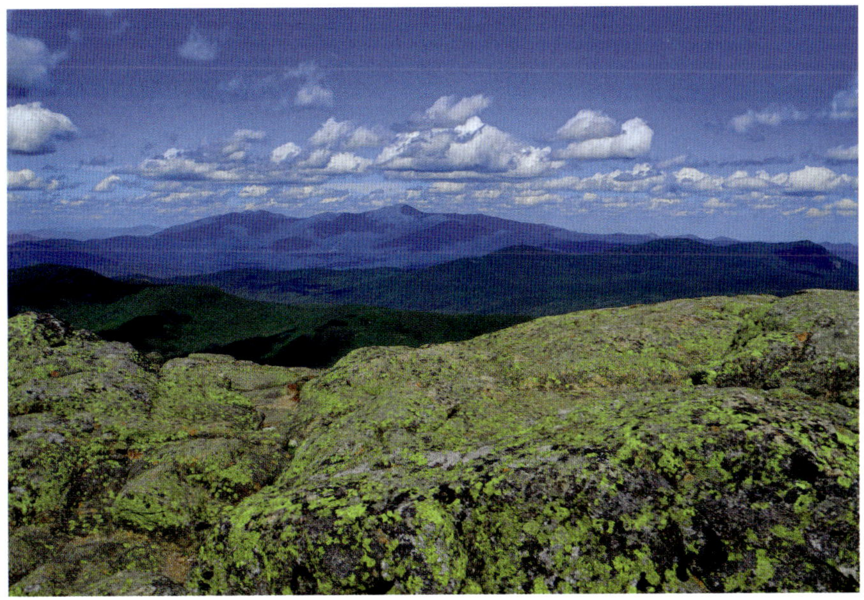

Presidential Range from South Twin

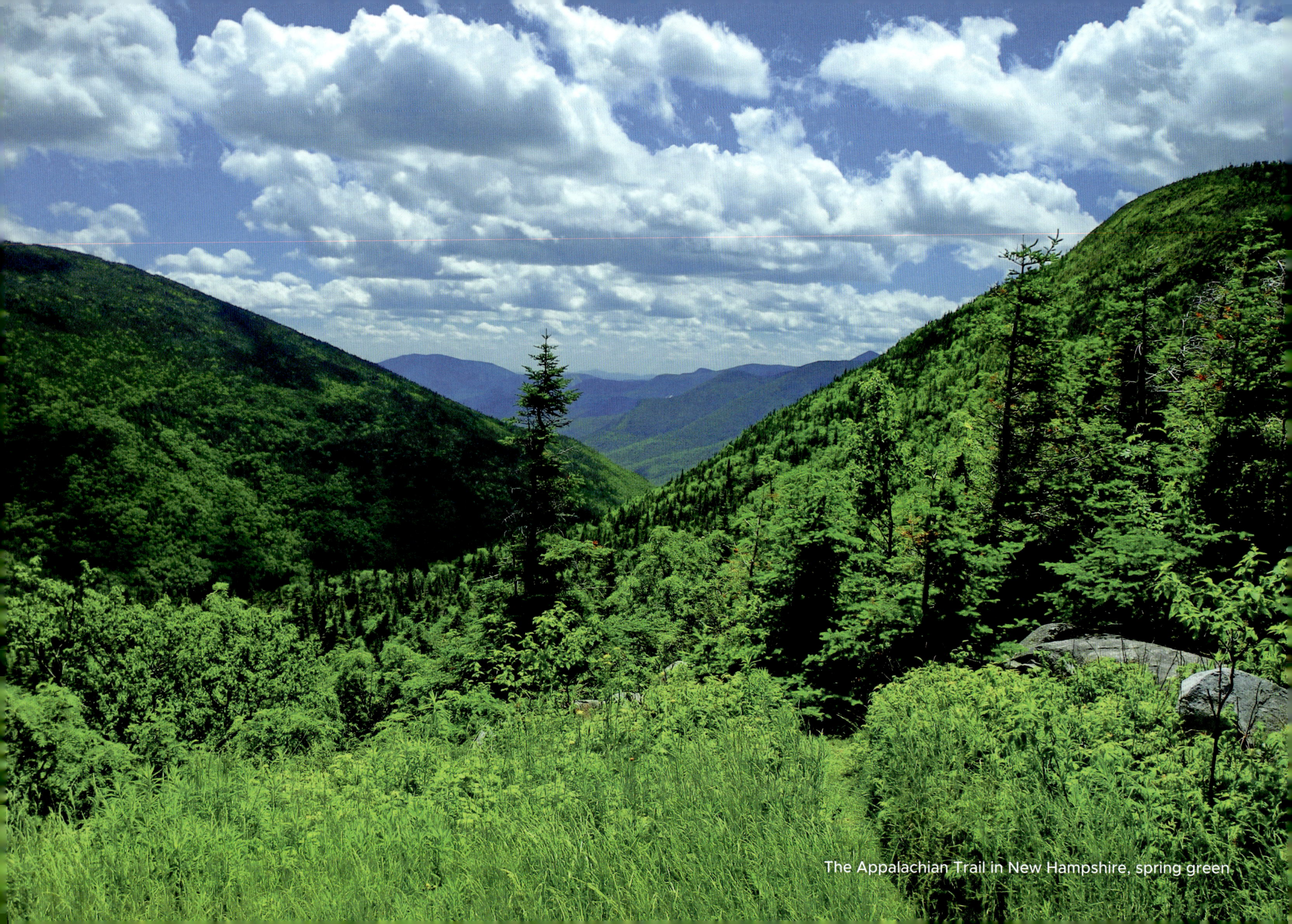

The Appalachian Trail in New Hampshire, spring green

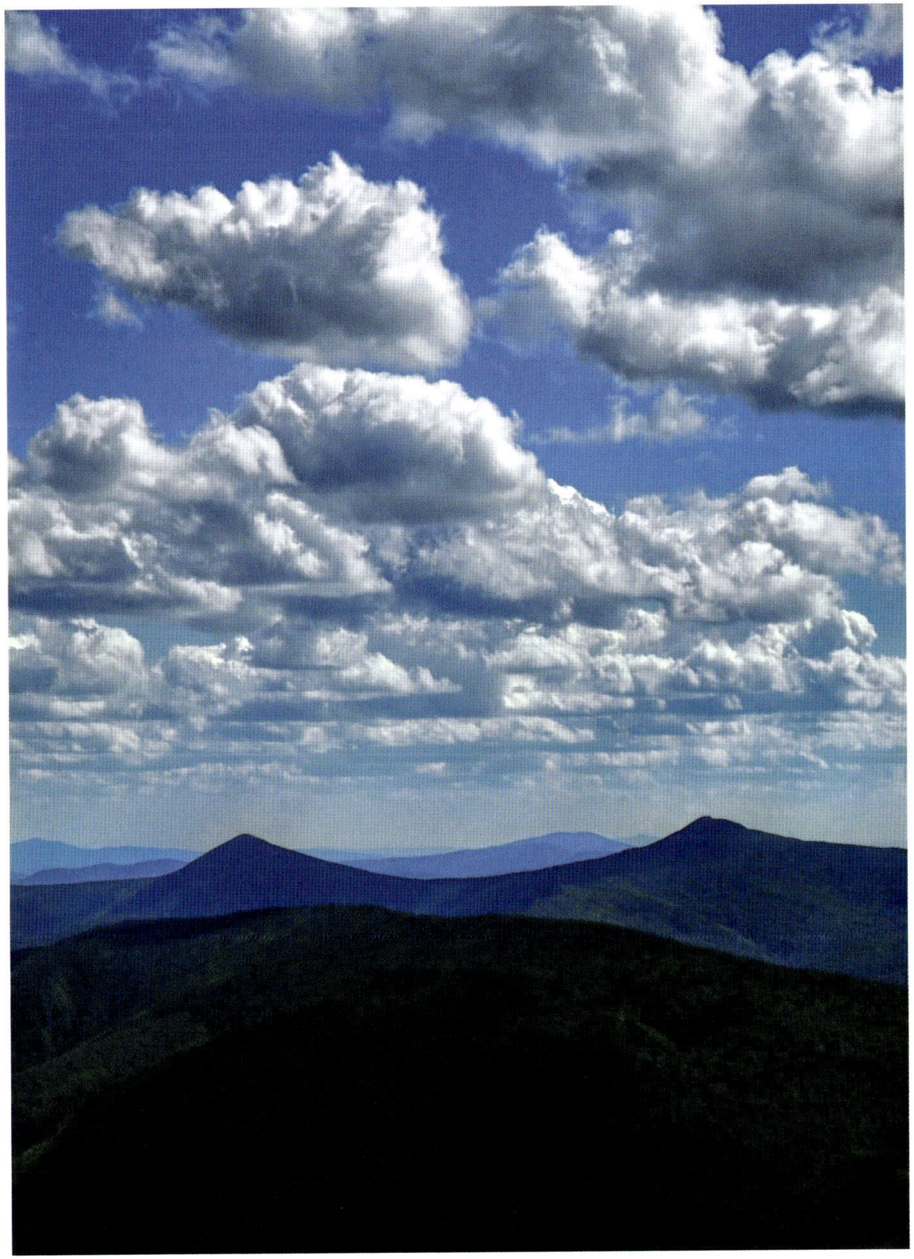

White Mountains from this New Hampshire section of the Appalachian Trail

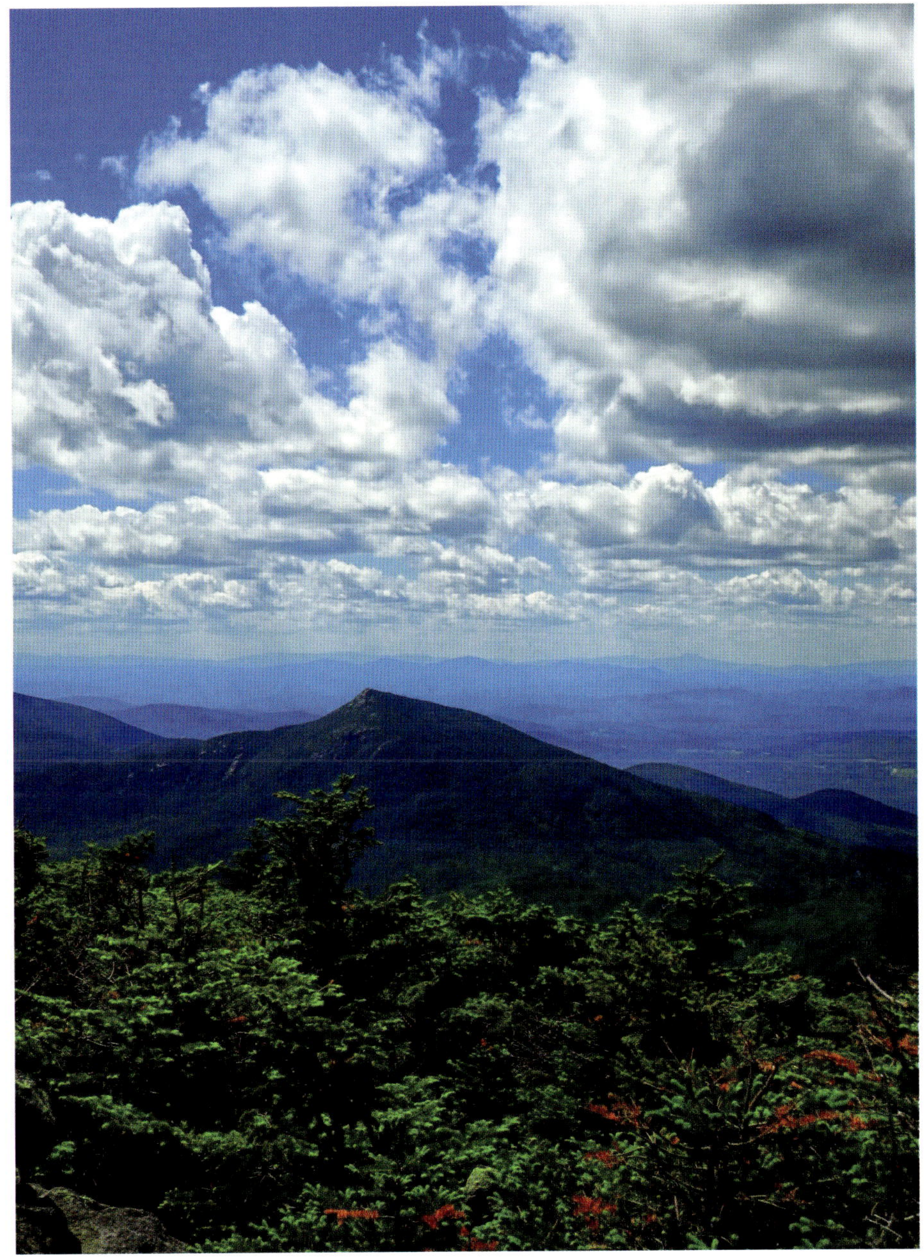

Mount Garfield from South Twin Mountain

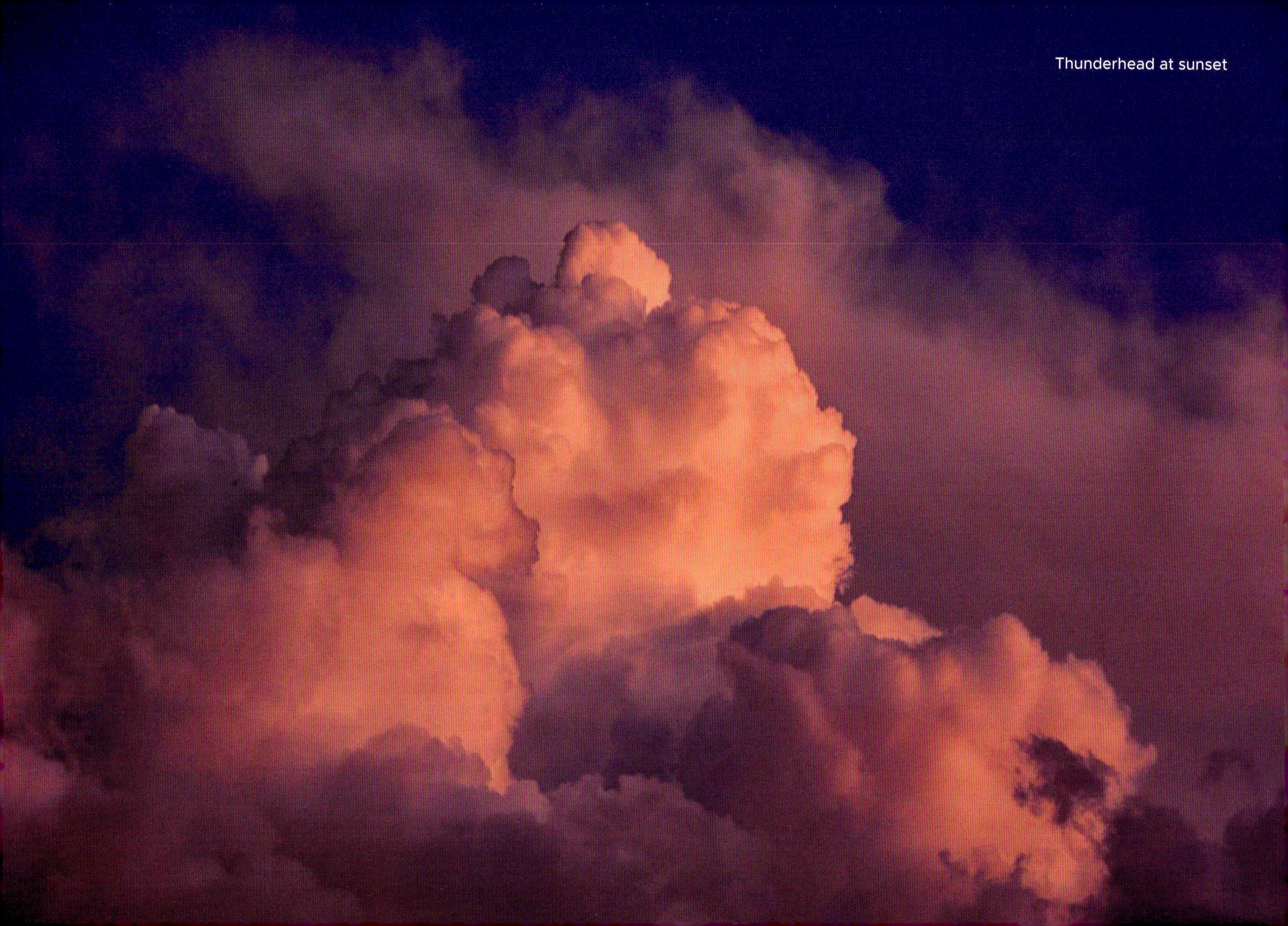

Thunderhead at sunset

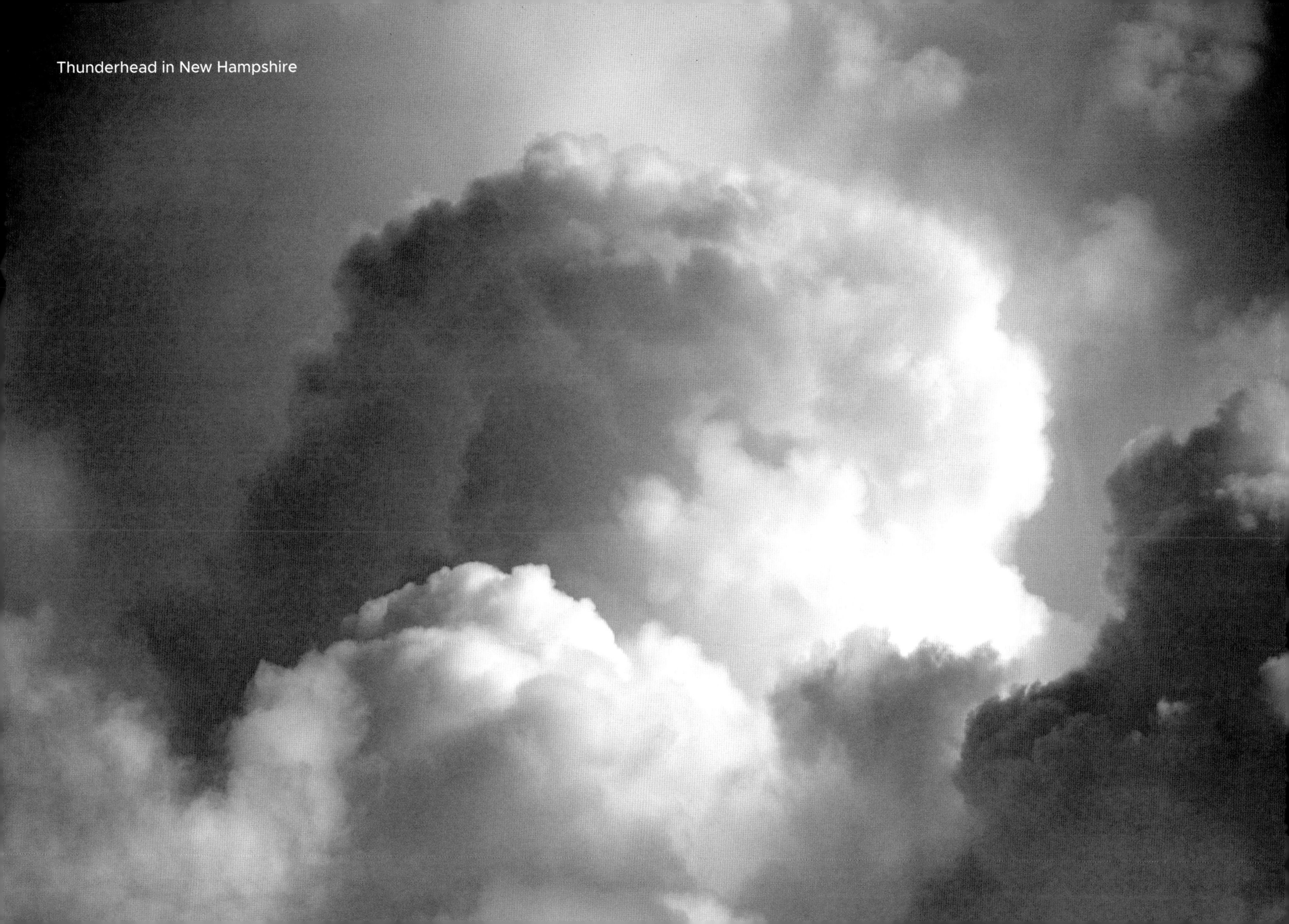

Thunderhead in New Hampshire

GEM HIKE MAP

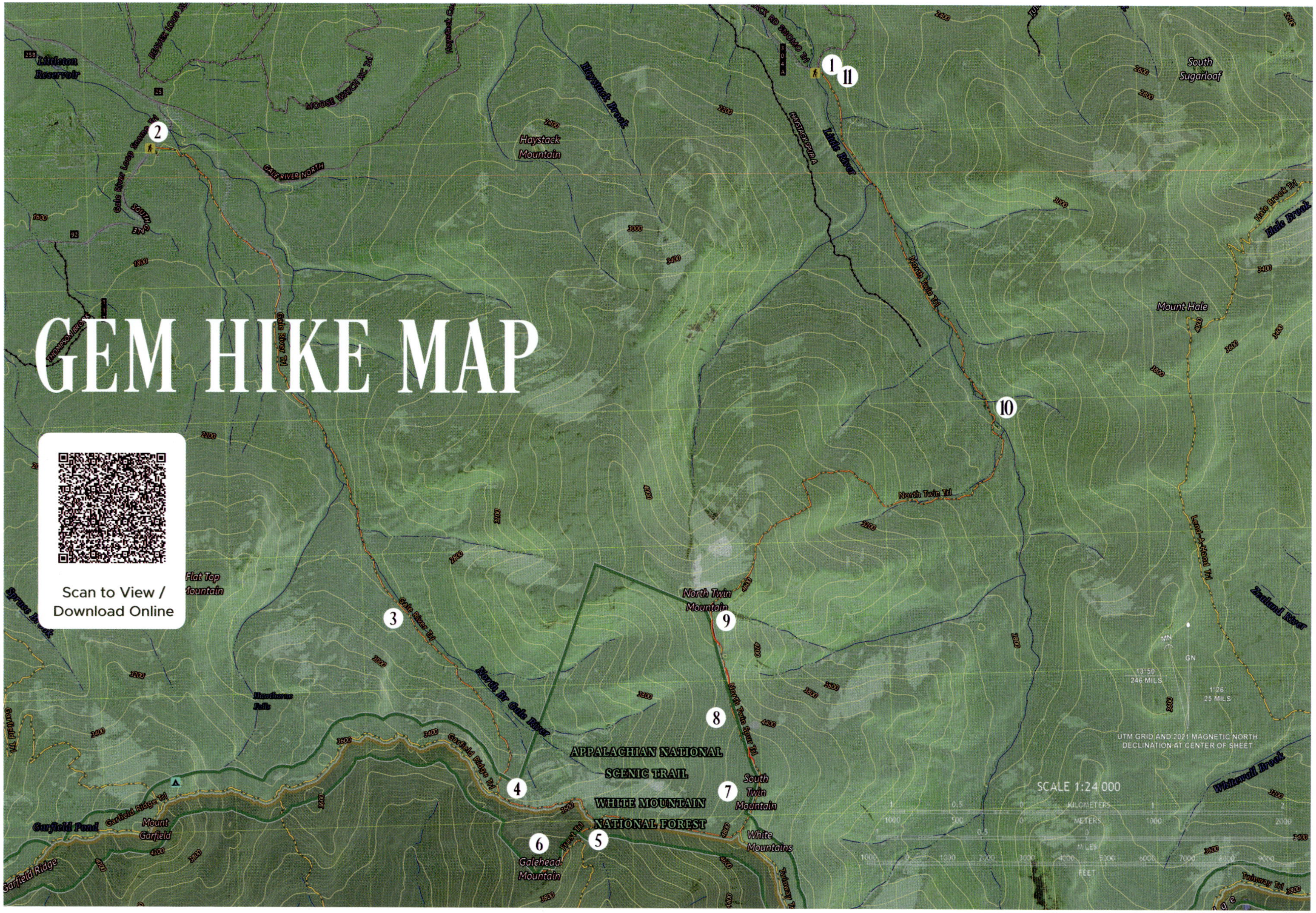

Scan to View / Download Online
Littleton Reservoir
Haystack Mountain
Haystack Brook
Gale River North
Gale River Trl
Little River
North Twin Trl
South Sugarloaf
Mount Hale
Hale Brook Trl
Flat Top Mountain
Hawthorne Falls
North Br Gale River
North Twin Mountain
North Twin Spur Trl
APPALACHIAN NATIONAL SCENIC TRAIL
WHITE MOUNTAIN NATIONAL FOREST
South Twin Mountain
Galehead Mountain
Garfield Ridge Trl
Mount Garfield
Garfield Pond
Garfield Ridge
Zealand River
Whitewall Brook
Twinway Trl
UTM GRID AND 2021 MAGNETIC NORTH DECLINATION AT CENTER OF SHEET
SCALE 1:24 000
KILOMETERS
METERS
MILES
FEET

DIRECTIONS TO THE TRAILHEAD(S)

North Twin Trailhead and Gale River Trailhead

Omni Mount Washington Resort, 310 Mt. Washington Hotel Rd., Bretton Woods, NH 03575
(44.257381, –71.439671)
To North Twin Trailhead, Bethlehem, NH 03583 (44.238038, –71.547514)
To Gale River Trailhead Gale River Trail, Bethlehem, NH 03574 (44.232638, –71.610636)

From Omni Mount Washington Resort:

1. Take Base Station Rd. to US 302 W for 1.1 miles
2. Turn right on US 302 W and continue for 4.4 miles until US 3 S
3. Turn left onto US 3 S and continue for 2.5 miles
4. Turn left onto Haystack Rd. and continue for 2.5 miles to North Twin Trailhead (drop a car here)
5. After dropping a car, take a U-turn and continue for 2.5 miles on Haystack Rd.
6. Turn left on US 3 S and continue 2.7 miles until N. Gale Rd. / Gale River Trail
7. Turn left on N. Gale Rd. / Gale River Trail and continue for 0.3 mile
8. Slight right on Gale River Loop Rd. / Gale River Trail (the hike's start point)

GEM HIKE DIRECTIONS

1. Start by leaving a car(s) at parking area off Haystack Rd. (parking lot for North Twin) and driving to the Gale River Loop Rd. / Gale River Trail Trailhead to start the hike
2. Hike 4 miles up the Gale River Trail, until the Appalachian Trail / Twinway Trail junction
3. At the Appalachian Trail / Twinway Trail, turn left on the Appalachian Trail / Twinway Trail and follow it for 0.6 mile to the Appalachian Mountain Club's Galehead Hut
4. At Galehead Hut, you have the option to add an additional 1-mile round trip to summit Mount Galehead
5. Once back from Mount Galahad's summit, proceed north on the Appalachian Trail / Twinway Trail
6. You reach the summit of South Twin Mountain after 0.8 mile
7. From the summit of South Twin, take North Twin Spur Trail for 1.3 miles
8. Reach the summit of North Twin
9. Take North Twin Trail for 2.4 miles to Little River crossing
10. Cross Little River and continue 1.9 miles
11. Reach your dropped car

MORE/LESS AMBITIOUS HIKERS

More-ambitious hikers may wish to complete the entire Pemigewasset Traverse. This traverse is the corridor the Appalachian Trail runs from Franconia Notch, New Hampshire (US 3), through Crawford Notch (US 302). US 3 is the southern end, and US 302 is the northern end. This full traverse runs 27.7 miles. If you are a backpacker, this would be a wonderful hike; if you are less backpacker-minded, the Appalachian Mountain Club huts can be an option.

Less ambitious hikers may want to make this hike from the start to Galehead Hut and decide if they want to continue Twinway to South Twin and return the way they came up. Please note that the descent of Twinway back to Galehead Hut can be very dangerous when wet or when bad weather moves in.

CHAPTER 20

THE APPALACHIAN TRAIL: MOUNT WASHINGTON, NEW HAMPSHIRE

AREA MAP

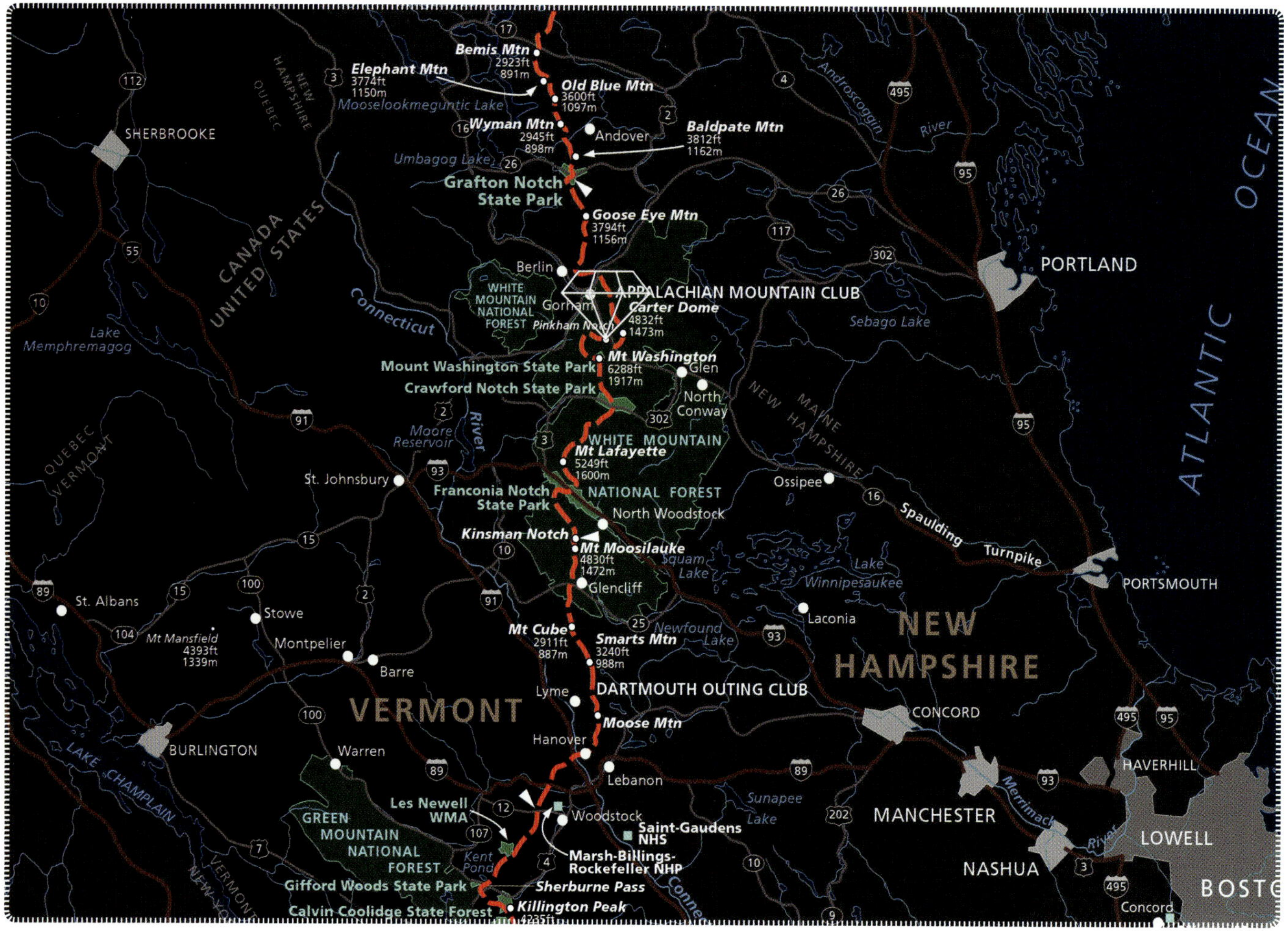

DISTANCE	4 miles
ELEVATION GAIN	1,440 feet
ELEVATION LOSS	1,440 feet
LEVEL	Difficult

TYPE: LOOP

0 10 Kilometers 50
0 10 Miles 50

Appalachian National Scenic Trail

Boundary of CLUB management section

North

GEM HIKE

PERSONAL TOUCH

Mount Washington is the highest peak in the Northeast of the United States of America. It also controls the Northeast's weather. It is extremely rare to have a perfect blue-sky day on Mount Washington; it happens only two or three times a year. I was lucky to have one of those days. Normally, photographers don't get excited on blue-sky days, but, for Mount Washington, they were ideal and unique conditions. I enjoyed seeing and photographing the trail and its surrounds for miles upon miles. The rugged mountain views were enhanced by the sapphire-blue skies above. Since the time I went skiing in Colorado when I was in sixth grade, I have aways enjoyed above-treeline experiences. This blue-sky day on Mount Washington will never be forgotten.

BRIEF OVERVIEW

This section of the Appalachian Trail that includes Mount Washington is known for its alpine environment, challenging conditions, and panoramic vistas. It is known as the Presidential Range. It spans approximately 26 miles from the southern end at Crawford Notch (US 302) to the northern end at the base of Mount Washington at Pinkham Notch (NH Route 16). Hikers can hike hut to hut to the Appalachian Mountain Club huts. Mitzvah, Lake of the Clouds, and Madison Huts are the huts encountered as the Appalachian Trail heads north.

DESCRIPTION OF THE GEM HIKE

Mount Washington Summit is a gem that no one wants to miss. If you want the chance to experience the above-treeline vistas without having to hike 26 miles, then this hike could be for you. This hike uses the Appalachian Trail and other trails on Mount Washington to create a nice short-distance but very challenging hike.

FLORA, FAUNA, AND VEGETATION

The trees in this section of the Appalachian Trail vary with the elevation. In the lower elevations, hardwood forests are composed of mainly maple, oak, and birch. As the Appalachian Trail ascends, the vegetation shifts to coniferous trees such as spruce and fir. Above the treeline (where trees no longer can grow because of the environment being too harsh), the vegetation transitions to alpine meadows with low-growing plants and lichen. This hike features the higher two of the three ecosystems.

SCENIC VIEWS

The section of the AT that includes Mount Washington offers some of the most stunning views along the Appalachian Trail. If one is lucky enough for a clear day (extremely rare) from the summit of Mount Washington, hikers can see panoramic vistas of the Presidential Range and beyond, extending into Vermont, New Hampshire, and Maine. Views can also be enjoyed when on the above-treeline ridges along the way to and from the summit.

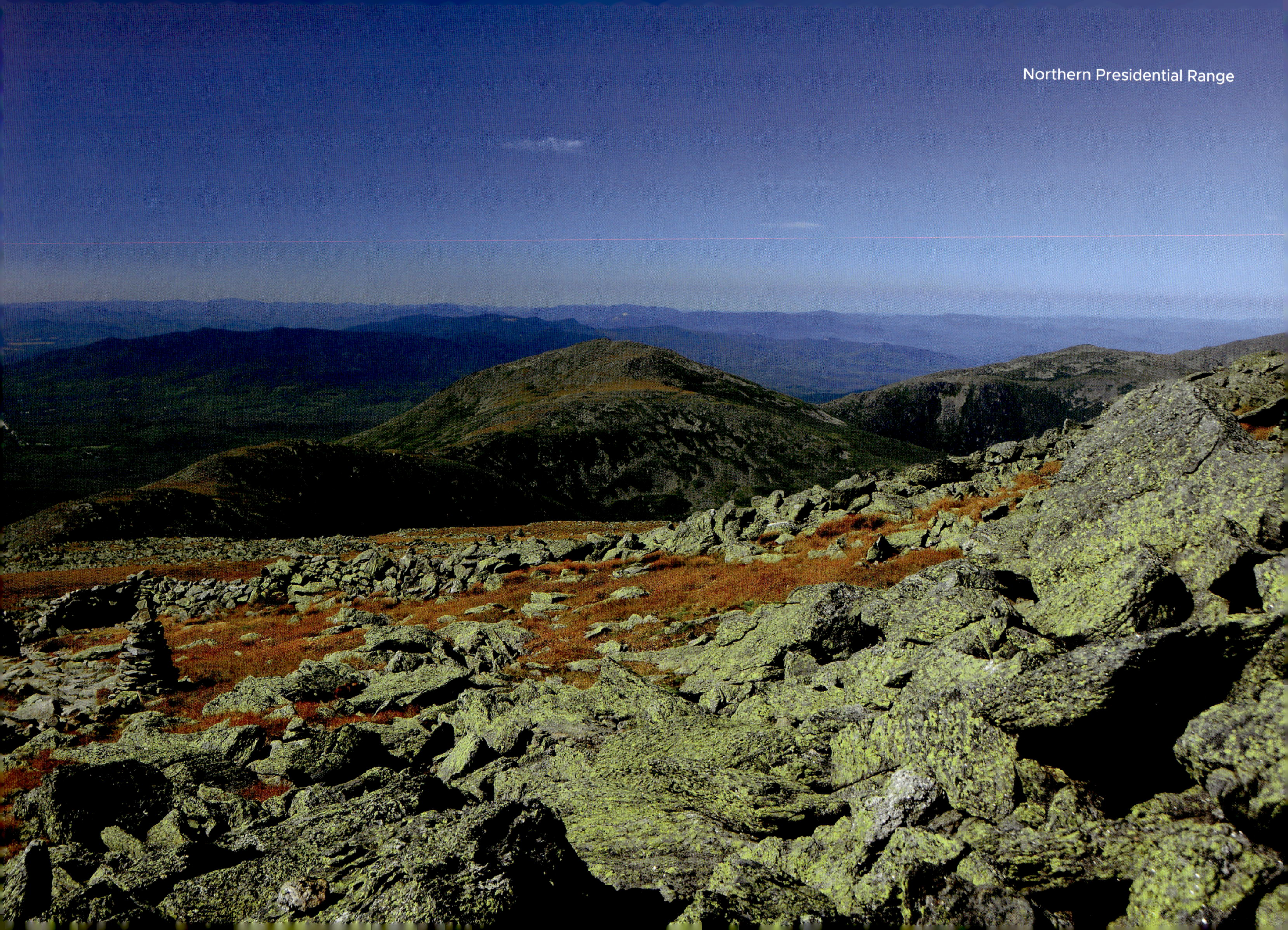

Northern Presidential Range

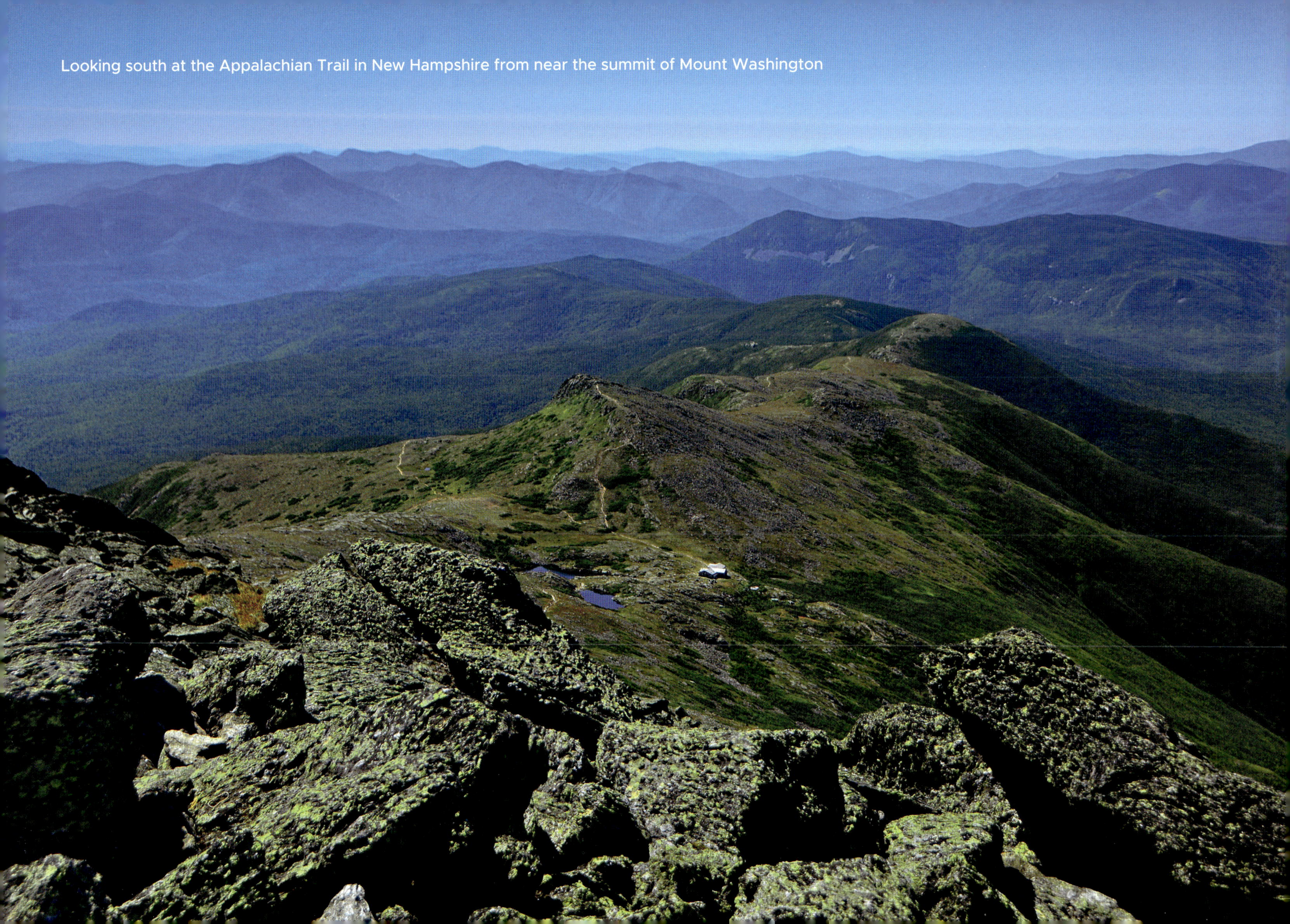

Looking south at the Appalachian Trail in New Hampshire from near the summit of Mount Washington

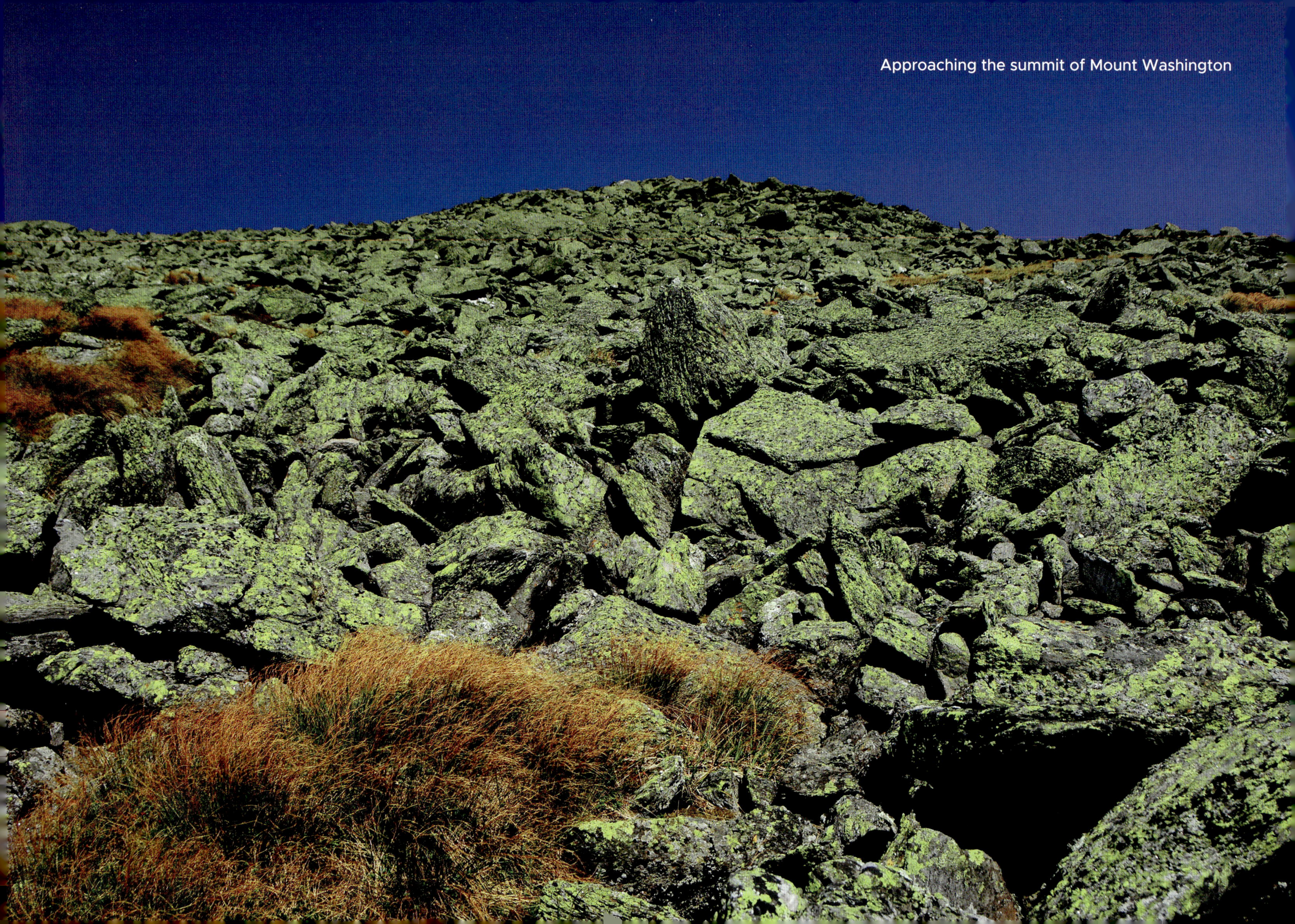

Approaching the summit of Mount Washington

Lakes of the Clouds and the summit of Mount Washington

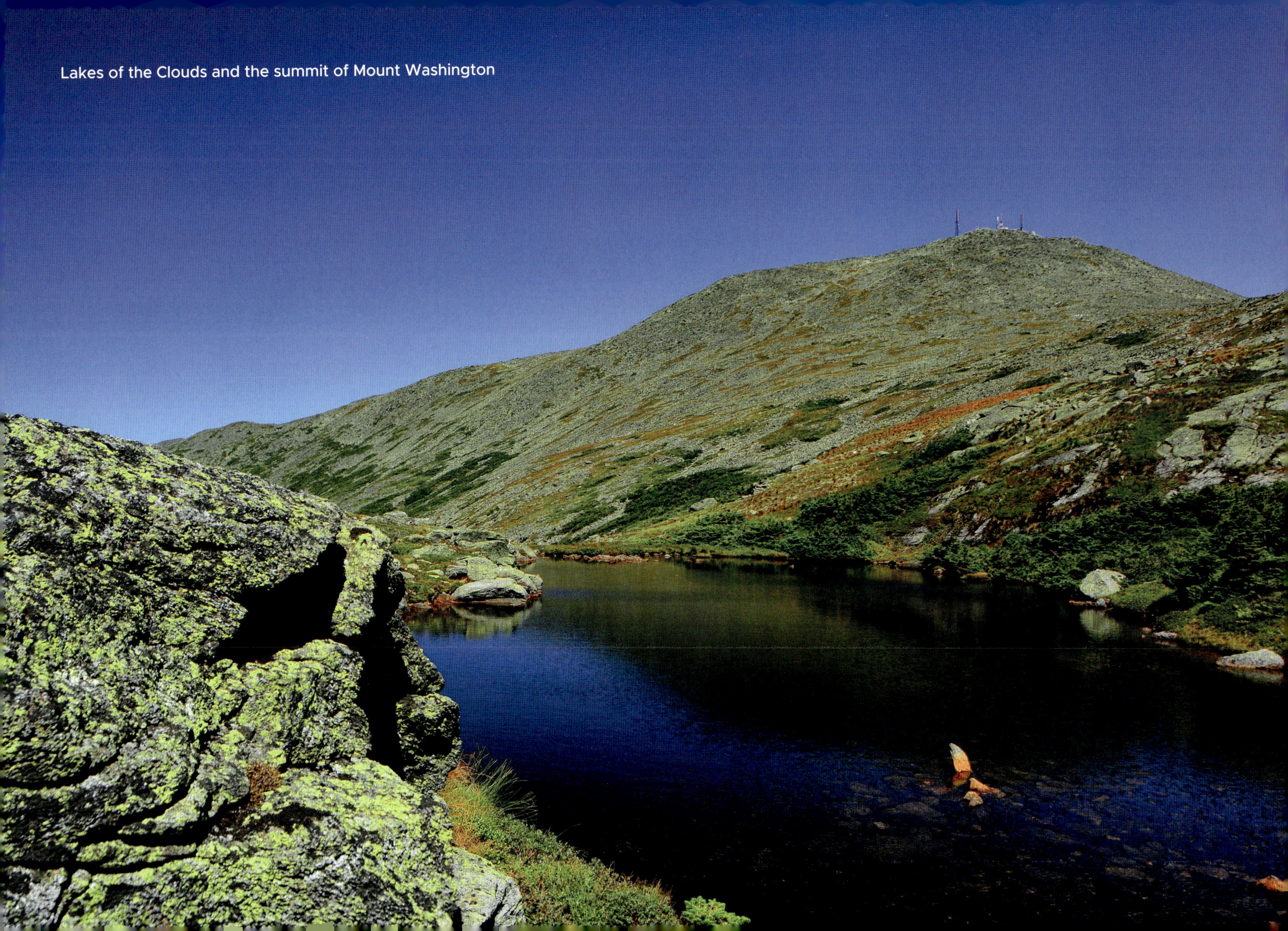

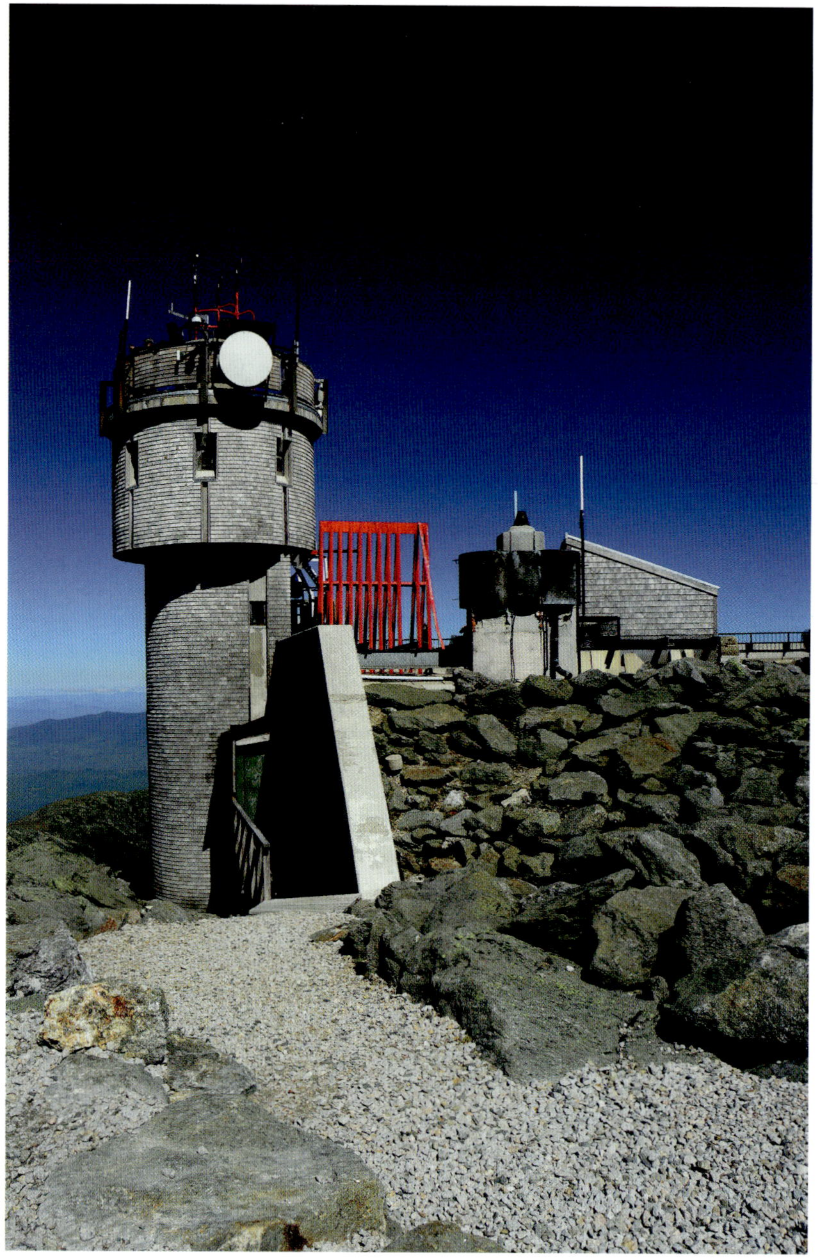

Mount Washington Observatory

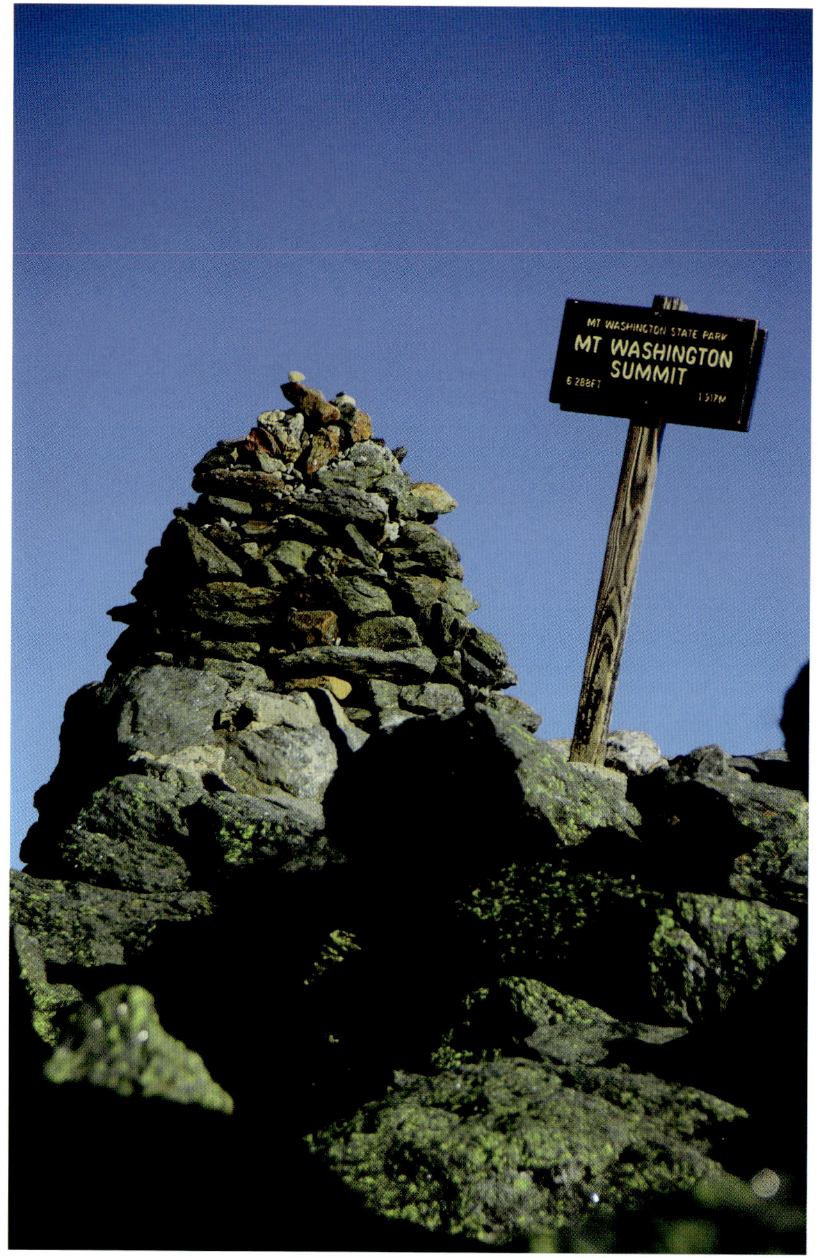

Mount Washington's summit cairn

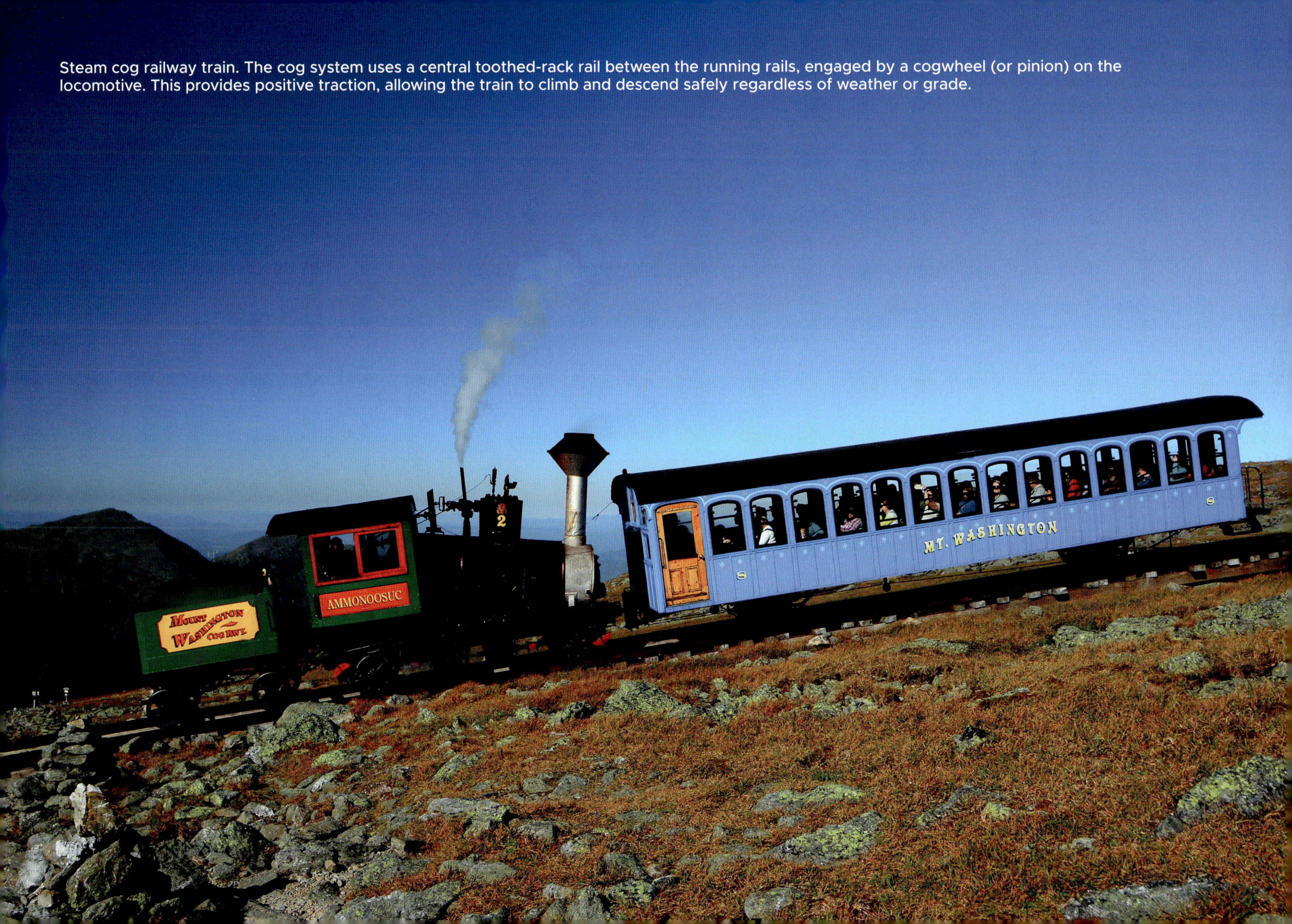

Steam cog railway train. The cog system uses a central toothed-rack rail between the running rails, engaged by a cogwheel (or pinion) on the locomotive. This provides positive traction, allowing the train to climb and descend safely regardless of weather or grade.

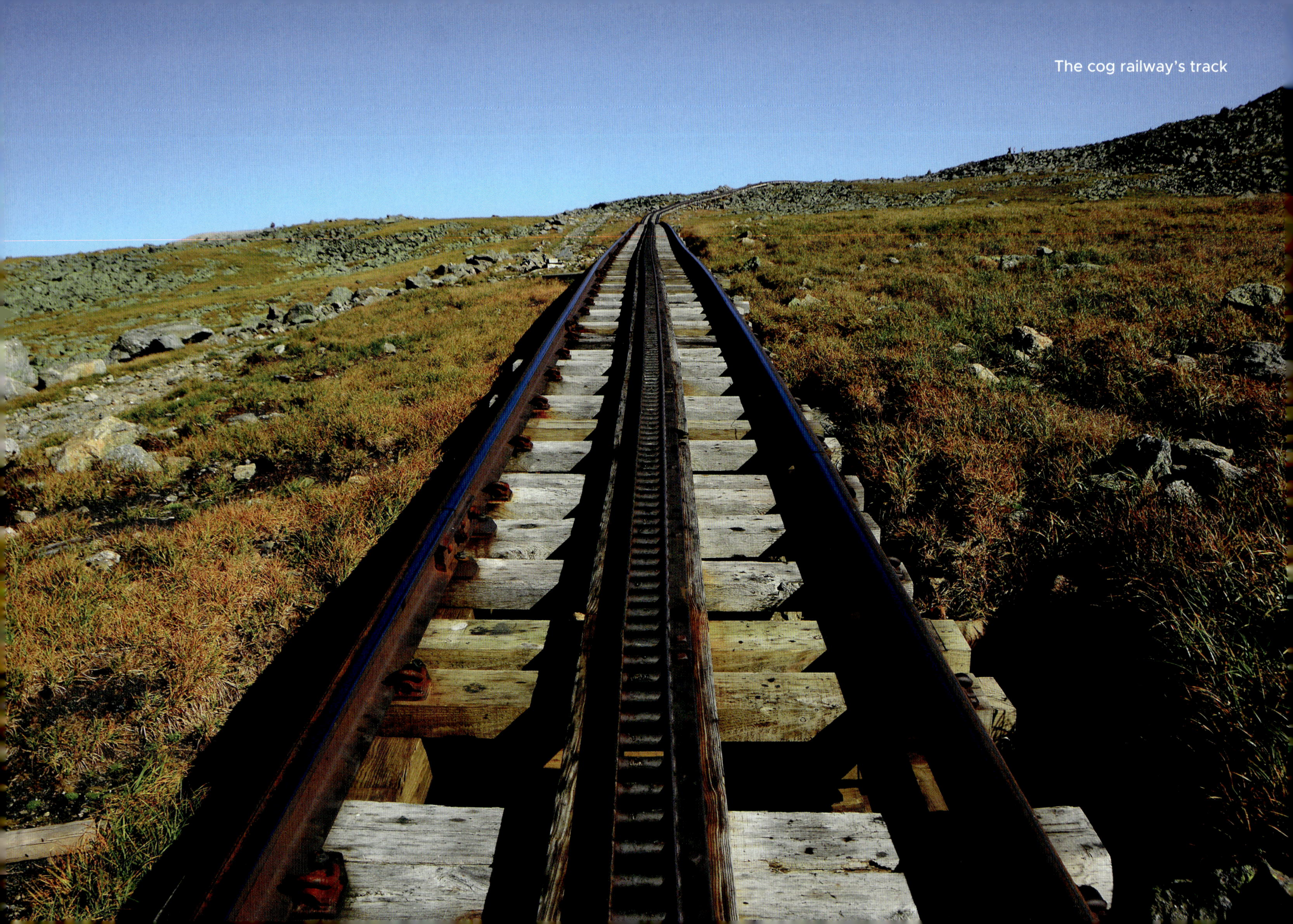

The cog railway's track

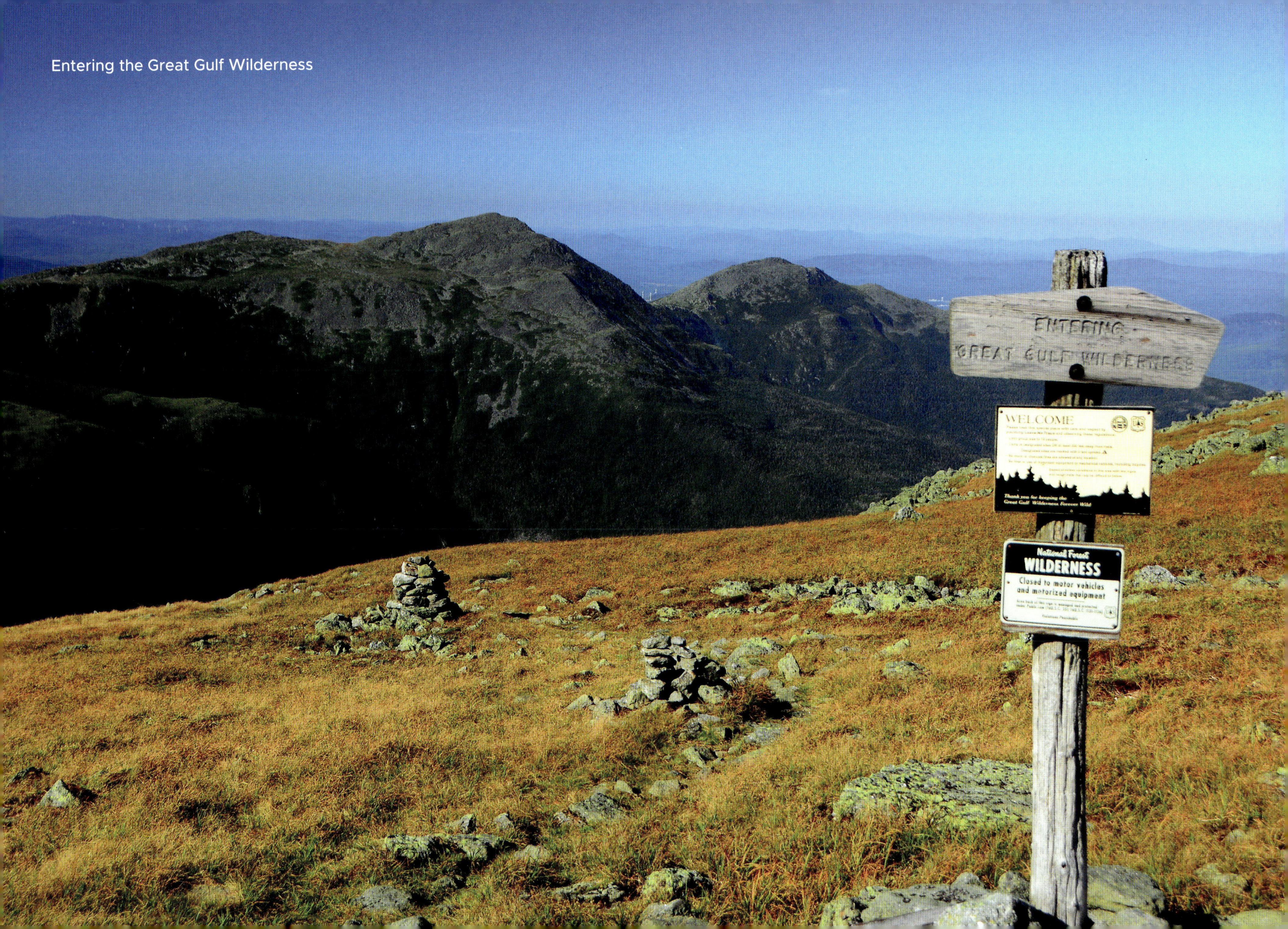

Entering the Great Gulf Wilderness

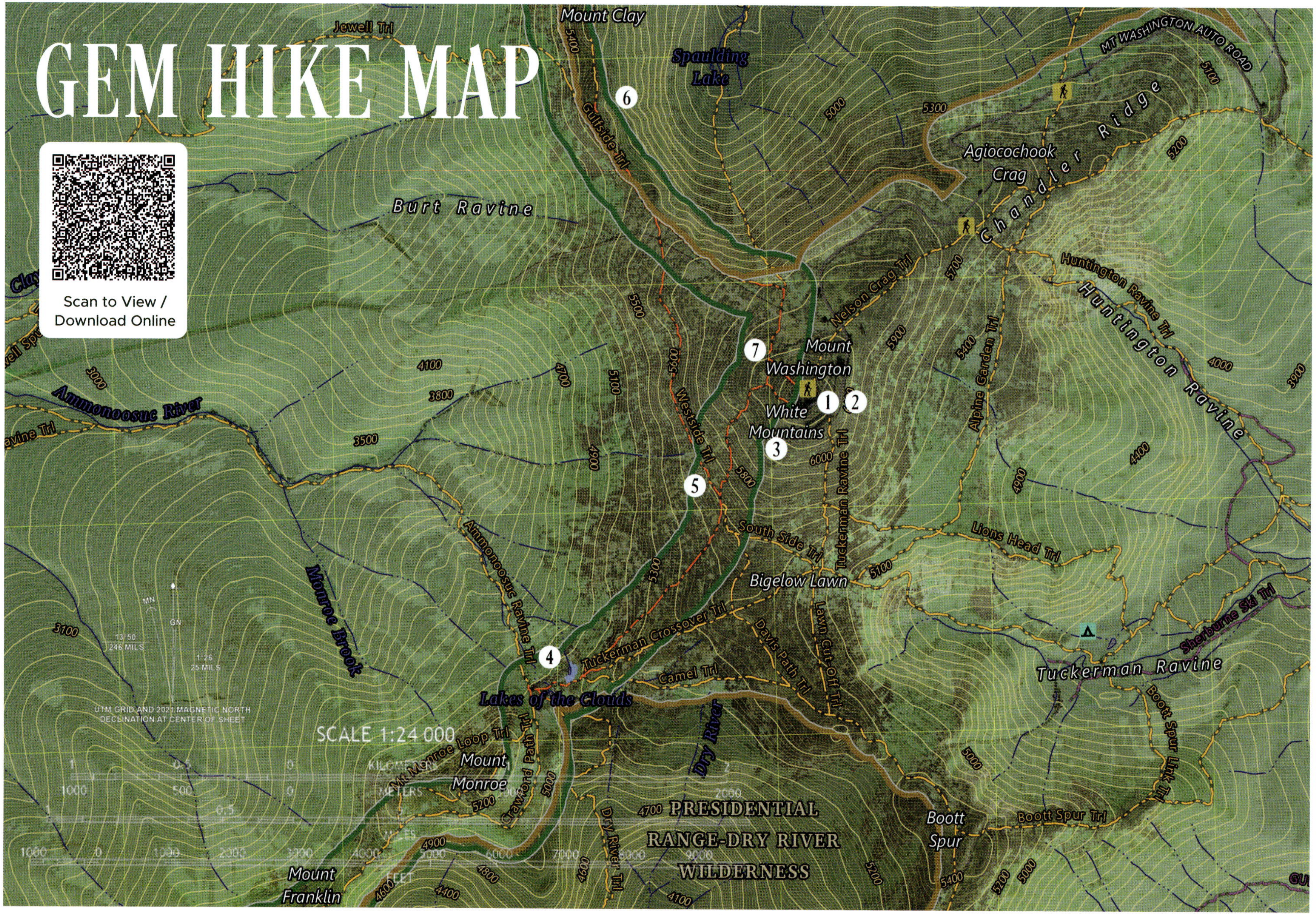
GEM HIKE MAP
Scan to View / Download Online
Mount Clay
Jewell Trl
Spaulding Lake
Gulfside Trl
MT WASHINGTON AUTO ROAD
Agiocochook Crag
Chandler Ridge
Burt Ravine
Nelson Crag Trl
Huntington Ravine Trl
Huntington Ravine
Alpine Garden Trl
Mount Washington
White Mountains
Westside Trl
Tuckerman Ravine Trl
Ammonoosuc River
Ammonoosuc Ravine Trl
South Side Trl
Lions Head Trl
Bigelow Lawn
Monroe Brook
Tuckerman Crossover Trl
Davis Path Trl
Lawn Cut-Off Trl
Sherburne Ski Trl
Tuckerman Ravine
Camel Trl
Lakes of the Clouds
Boott Spur Link Trl
Dry River
Mt Monroe Loop Trl
Mount Monroe
Crawford Path Trl
Dry River Trl
PRESIDENTIAL RANGE-DRY RIVER WILDERNESS
Boott Spur
Boott Spur Trl
Mount Franklin
SCALE 1:24 000
UTM GRID AND 2021 MAGNETIC NORTH DECLINATION AT CENTER OF SHEET
KILOMETERS
METERS
MILES
FEET
1
2
3
4
5
6
7

DIRECTIONS TO THE TRAILHEAD(S)

Mount Washington Summit

AMC Pinkham Notch Visitor Center, 361 NH 16, Gorham, NH 03581 (44.257502, −71.252991), to Mt. Washington State Park, 1598 Mt. Washington Auto Rd., Mount Washington, NH 03589 (44.269723, −71.302519)

1. Proceed 404 feet to NH 16 N
2. Turn left onto NH 16 N and continue for 2.8 miles
3. Turn left onto Mt. Washington Auto Rd. and continue for 7.6 miles
4. Arrive at the parking lot at the top of Mount Washington (Mount Washington State Park, 1598 Mt. Washington Auto Rd., Mount Washington, NH 03589)

GEM HIKE DIRECTIONS

1. Start by driving to the summit of Mt. Washington Auto Rd. to the start point of this hike
2. Continue through the parking lot for 0.1 mile, until the Appalachian Trail / Crawford Path junction
3. Turn left on the Appalachian Trail south / Crawford Path and continue for 1.4 miles
4. Reach the Appalachian Mountain Club's Lakes of the Clouds Hut and turn around and continue 0.8 mile until Westside Trail
5. Turn left on Westside Trail and continue for 0.8 mile until the Appalachian Trail / Gulfside Trail
6. Turn right on the Appalachian Trail / Gulfside Trail and continue 0.65 mile until Trinity Heights Connector Trail
7. Turn left on Trinity Heights Connector Trail and continue 0.25 mile until you reach the parking lot

MORE/LESS AMBITIOUS HIKERS:

More-ambitious hikers can extend this hike by going farther beyond the Lake of Clouds Hut or Jewell Trail (or both), but be careful, because the terrain is rugged and the weather can change at a moment's notice. The summit of Mount Washington can also be approached from Crawford Notch. This is the southern approach, and it begins at Crawford Notch, where hikers can access the AT via the Webster Cliff Trail and Crawford Path. The summit of Mount Washington can also be approached from Pinkham Notch. From Pinkham Notch, hikers use Old Jackson Road Trail, Madison Gulf Trail, Osgood Trail, and Gulfside Trail to summit Mount Washington. More-ambitious hikers may wish to hike the famous Presidential Traverse.

Less ambitious hikers can drive up or take the cog railway to the summit and enjoy the views.

WORKS CITED

"Appalachian Trail Distance Calculator," Appalachian Trail Distance Calculator

Apple Maps. "Lehigh Gap." Accessed September 17, 2024.

Apple Maps. "The Priest and Crabtree Falls." Accessed September 17, 2024.

AT Dist. "Appalachian Trail Distances." Accessed September 4, 2024. https://www.atdist.com/at/atdist.

AT Dist. "Appalachian Trail Distances." Accessed October 26, 2024. https://www.atdist.com/at/atdist.

Chazin, Daniel D, and Appalachian Trail Conference. 2011.Appalachian Trail Guide to New York-New Jersey.

Google Maps. "Directions from 38.767824, -78.233559 to Range View Overlook, Washington, VA." Accessed October 26, 2024. https://www.google.com/maps/dir/38.767824,+-78.233559/Virginia+22835/Range+View+Overlook,+Washington,+VA/@38.7138306,-78.3215857,17366m/am=t/data=!3m2!1e3!4b1!4m18!4m17!1m3!2m2!1d-78.233559!2d38.767824!1m5!1m1!1s0x89b44a2482580a8f:0xbf6b4cac688d9164!2m2!1d-78.3215885!2d38.6598424!1m5!1m1!1s0x89b5cb0af129bed3:0xa330707e8d1411b4!2m2!1d-78.2273652!2d38.7642602!3e0?entry=ttu&g_ep=EgoyMDI0MTAyMy4wIKXMDSoASAFQAw%3D%3D.

Google Maps. "Directions from Allentown, PA to Lehigh Gap Nature Center, Slatington, PA." Accessed October 27, 2024. https://www.google.com/maps/dir/Allentown,+PA/Lehigh+Gap+Nature+Center,+8844+Paint+Mill+Rd,+Slatington,+PA+18080.

Google Maps. "Directions from Allentown, PA to Lehigh Gap Nature Center, Slatington, PA." Accessed October 27, 2024. https://www.google.com/maps/dir/Allentown,+PA/Lehigh+Gap+Nature+Center,+8844+Paint+Mill+Rd,+Slatington,+PA+18080/@40.7825114,-75.6057991,559m/am=t/data=!3m2!1e3!4b1!4m14!4m13!1m5!1m1!1s0x89c439929f4adce1:0xeaf9df4b246824a1!2m2!1d-75.4714098!2d40.6022939!1m5!1m1!1s0x89c44eb98d00b2e5:0x5080d93fe98ca7a3!2m2!1d-75.6090171!2d40.784195!3e0?entry=ttu&g_ep=EgoyMDI0MTAyMy4wIKXMDSoASAFQAw%3D%3D.

Google Maps. "Directions from Appalachian National Scenic Trail / Long Trail Route 9 Trailhead, Woodford, VT to Stratton Mountain Trailhead, Stratton, VT." Accessed September 25, 2024. https://www.google.com/maps/dir/Appalachian+National+Scenic+Trail+%2F+Long+Trail+AT%2FLT+Route+9+Trailhead,+Unnamed+Road,+Woodford,+VT+05201/Stratton+Mountain+Trailhead,+Stratton+Arlington+Road,+Stratton,+VT.

Google Maps. "Directions from Bromley Mountain, Long Trail, Peru, VT to 44°05'51.7"N 71°40'53.2"W." Accessed September 28, 2024. https://www.google.com/maps/dir/43.2278349,-72.9396243/Bromley+Mountain,+Long+Trail,+Unnamed+Road,+Peru,+VT+05152.

Google Maps. "Directions from Cold River Rd & Keiffer Rd, Shrewsbury, VT to AT/LT Trailhead Parking, Mendon, VT." Accessed September 27, 2024. https://www.google.com/maps/dir/Cold+River+Rd+%26+Keiffer+Rd,+Shrewsbury,+VT+05738/AT%2FLT+Trailhead+Parking,+141+Fox+Hollow+Village(pvt,+Mendon,+VT+05701.

Google Maps. "Directions from East Lexington, VA to Crabtree Falls Parking Lot." Accessed September 30, 2024. https://www.google.com/maps/dir/East+Lexington,+VA/Crabtree+Falls+Parking+Lot/The+Priest+Wilderness+Parking+Area,+Unnamed+Road,+Tyro,+VA+22976.

Google Maps. "Directions from East Stroudsburg, PA to Fox Gap, Stroud Township, PA." Accessed September 17, 2024. https://www.google.com/maps/dir/East+Stroudsburg,+PA/Fox+Gap,+Stroud+Township,+PA.

Google Maps. "Directions from Kittatinny Point Visitor Center, Hardwick Township, NJ to Fox Gap, Stroud Township, PA." Accessed September 17, 2024. https://www.google.com/maps/dir/Kittatinny+Point+Visitor+Center,+Kittatinny+Point+Visitor+Center,+Interstate+80,+Hardwick+Township,+NJ/Fox+Gap,+Stroud+Township,+PA.

Google Maps. "Directions from Luray, VA to Mary's Rock Summit Trailhead parking, Luray, VA." Accessed September 29, 2024. https://www.google.com/maps/dir/Luray,+VA/Marys+Rock+Summit+Trailhead+parking,+Luray,+VA+22835.

Google Maps. "Directions from Pinkham Notch Visitor Center to Summit of Mount Washington." Accessed September 26, 2024. https://www.google.com/maps/dir/44.257502,-71.252991/44.269723,+-71.302519.

Google Maps. "Directions from The Priest Wilderness Parking Area to Overlook." Accessed September 30, 2024. https://www.google.com/maps/dir/The+Priest+Wilderness+Parking+Area/Overlook/The+Priest/37.8253051,-79.0820546/Meadows+Lane+Crabtree+Falls+Parking.

Google Maps. "Directions from Woodstock, VT to 43.654996, -72.565965." Accessed November 4, 2024. https://www.google.com/maps/dir/Woodstock,+VT/43.654996,-72.565965/@43.6358828,-72.5621227,8054m/am=t/data=!3m2!1e3!4b1!4m9!4m8!1m5!1m1!1s0x89e1d71659f33f81:0x43d2d7256dade364!2m2!1d-72.5185112!2d43.6242442!1m0!3e0?entry=ttu&g_ep=EgoyMDI0MTAyOS4wIKXMDSoASAFQAw%3D%3D.

Google Maps. "Directions from Woodstock, VT to 43.6549961, -72.5659649." Accessed November 3, 2024. https://www.google.com/maps/dir/Woodstock,+VT/43.6549961,-72.5659649/@43.6359789,-72.5628586,8118m/am=t/data=!3m1!1e3!4m14!4m13!1m10!1m1!1s0x89e1d71659f33f81:0x43d2d7256dade364!2m2!1d-72.5185112!2d43.6242442!3m4!1m2!1d-72.5489617!2d43.6249039!3s0x89e1d7bc94df3649:0x962c-86661d7549eb!1m0!3e0?entry=ttu&g_ep=EgoyMDI0MTAyOS4wIKXMDSoASAFQA-w%3D%3D.

Google Maps. "Directions from Woodstock, VT to Bromley Mountain, Long Trail, Peru, VT." Accessed October 27, 2024. https://www.google.com/maps/dir/Woodstock,+VT/Brom-ley+Mountain,+Long+Trail,+Peru,+VT.

Google. "Directions from [AMC Pinkham Notch Visitors Center] to Mount Washington Summit Parking Lot." Google Maps. Accessed September 12, 2024. https://www.google.com/maps/dir/AMC+Pinkham+Notch+Visitor+Center,+New+Hampshire+16,+Gor-ham,+NH/Mt.+Washington+State+Park/@44.2766045,-71.2848104,14z/data=!4m24!4m23!1m5!1m1!1s0x89e5d4475e413bbf:0x342925312e3e99a7!2m2!1d-71.2746936!2d44.2743518!1m5!1m1!1s0x89e5d38269731f9f:0x24f6022680c59a2c!2m2!1d-71.3039912!2d44.2761162!3e0!5m1!1e4?entry=ttu&g_ep=EgoyMDI0MDgyOC4wIKXMDSoASAFQAw%3D%3D

Google. "Directions from [Elk Pen Parking Lot, Tuxedo, NY] to Appalachian National Scenic Trail Trailhead Parking." Google Maps. Accessed September 12, 2024. https://www.google.com/maps/dir/Elk+Pen+Parking+lot,+Tuxedo,+NY/Appalachian+Nat%27l+Sce-nic+Trail+Trailhead+Parking/@41.2619009,-74.2630413,13z/data=!3m1!1e3!4m13!4m12!1m5!1m1!1s0x89e0e407381d53ad:0x2a6c7f6d07f732a7!2m2!1d-74.2870752!2d41.2617545!1m5!1m1!1s0x89e0e407381d53ad:0x-2a6c7f6d07f732a7!2m2!1d-74.2830282!2d41.2648903!3e0!5m1!1e4?entry=ttu&g_ep=E-goyMDI0MDgyOC4wIKXMDSoASAFQAw%3D%3D

Google. "Directions from [Gale River Trailhead] to North Twin Trailhead." Goo-gle Maps. Accessed September 15, 2024. https://www.google.com/maps/dir/Gale+River+Trailhead/North+Twin+Trailhead/@44.2627726,-71.7363652,12.08z/data=!4m10!4m9!1m5!1m1!1s0x89e5d36d4a80e7ad:0x8e717e233dc72b0e!2m2!1d-71.7341307!2d44.2635819!1m5!1m1!1s0x89e5d5dbde478f43:0x35cf8e8fdfdc4ae3!2m2!1d-71.7305979!2d44.2742767!3e0!5m1!1e4?entry=ttu&g_ep=EgoyMDI0MDgyOC4wIKXMD-SoASAFQAw%3D%3D

Google. "Directions from [Lincoln, NH] to Flume Gorge Visitor Center." Google Maps. Ac-cessed September 15, 2024. https://www.google.com/maps/place/Flume+Gorge+Visi-tor+Center/@44.0668625,-71.7202561,13z/data=!3m1!4b1!4m13!4m12!1m5!1m1!1s0x89e5d41738f9775f:0xd4c229b3b643a01e!2m2!1d-71.7211333!2d44.0700042!1m5!1m1!1s0x89e5d41738f9775f:0xd4c229b3b643a01e!2m2!1d-71.7211333!2d44.0700042!3e0!5m1!1e4?entry=ttu&g_ep=EgoyMDI0MDgyOC4wIKXMDSoASAFQAw%3D%3D

Google. "Directions from [Manchester, VT] to [Stratton Mountain Trailhead]." Google Maps. Accessed September 3, 2024. https://www.google.com/maps/dir/Manchester,+VT/Stratton+Mountain+Trailhead,+Stratton+Arlington+Rd,+Stratton,+VT+05360/@43.1635521,-73.0746512,17z/am=t/data=!4m18!4m17!1m5!1m1!1s0x89e05e5afaeb0cc5:0x9feb9b-066b1e15ba!2m2!1d-73.0723268!2d43.1636875!1m5!1m1!1s0x89e0f6eae6f85dfd:0x-4fa399bd793d62ef!2m

ABOUT THE AUTHOR

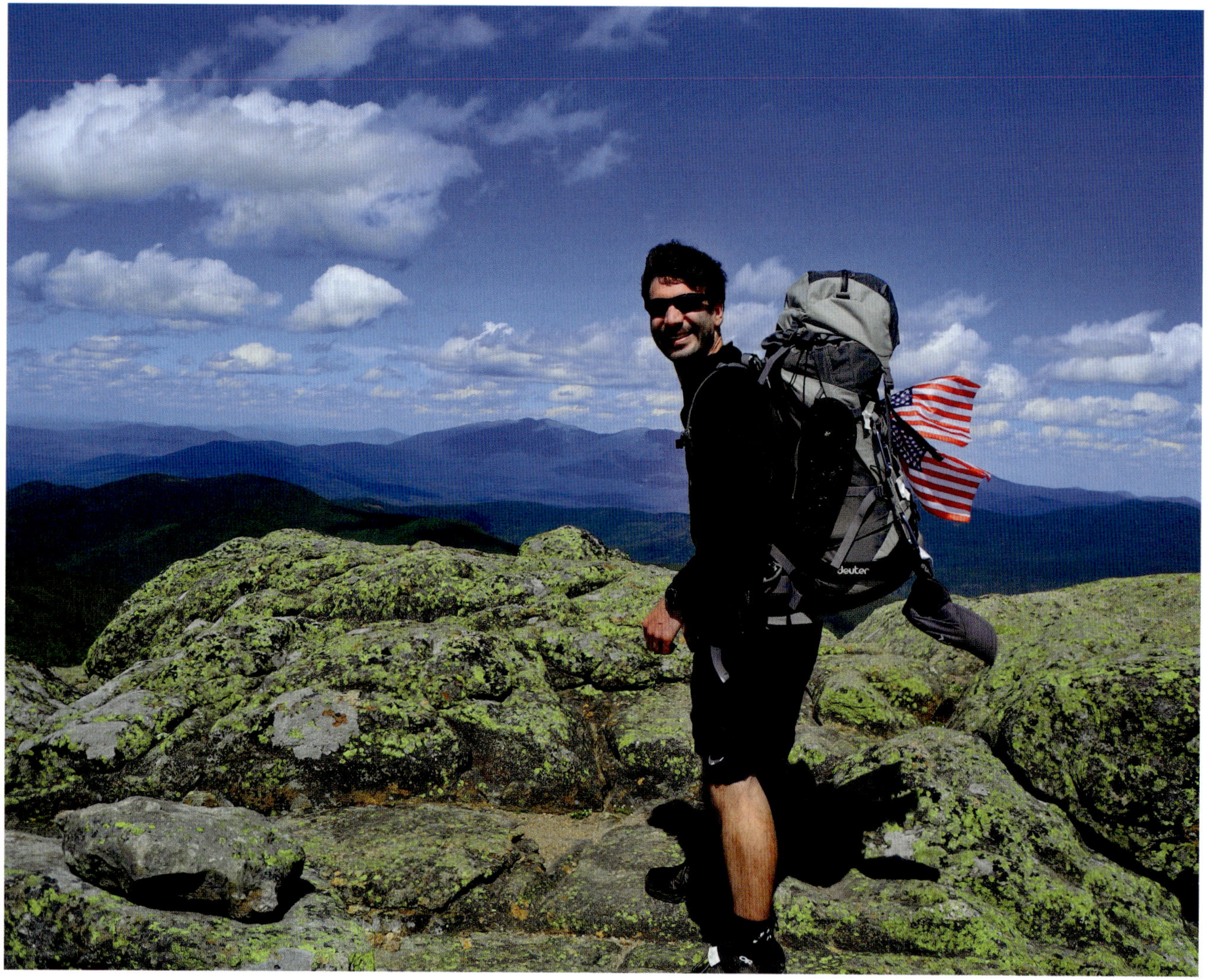

Raymond Salani III is an outdoor photographer known for his dedication, often hiking over 20 miles in a day with full camera gear to capture distinctive images. While his portfolio features vibrant color photography, he also has internationally recognized black-and-white works. His passion for photography stems from his father and the inspiration of Ansel Adams, allowing him to connect with nature in profound ways. As of now, he has over 30 photographs published and awarded at *One Exposure* (1X.com), a prestigious gallery with a stringent acceptance rate of less than 1%. Following his photo book of the Appalachian Trail and subsequent photographic guidebook of 10 gem hikes, he is excited to begin a coffee-table project focused on the Tetons, showcasing both iconic and hidden gems of the area. His work has appeared in National Geographic's *Great Mountains Calendar 2021* and various other calendars, including four covers. He also received an honorable mention award in the 2023 Monochrome Awards. He lives in Tinton Falls, New Jersey.

His limited-edition artwork is available at www.BeautifulandScenicPhotography.com

His printed clothing and lifestyle items are available at www.SalaniPhotography.com

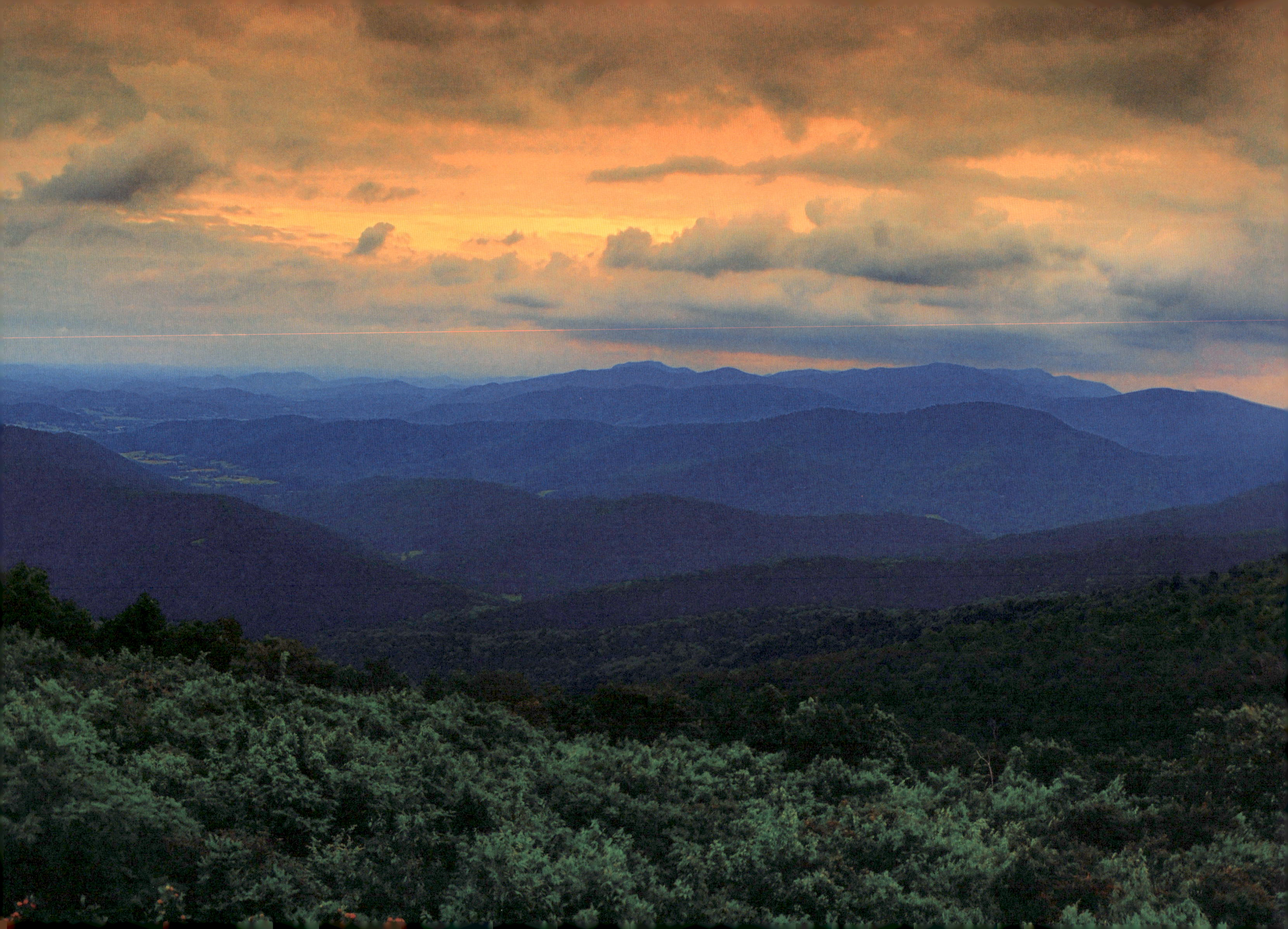